ANGLO-IRISH LITERATURE
A Review of Research

ANGLO-IRISH LITERATURE

A Review of Research

Edited by

RICHARD J. FINNERAN

The Modern Language Association of America

NEW YORK
1976

Library of Congress Catalog Card No. 74-31959
ISBN 0-87352-252-4

Published by The Modern Language Association of America
62 Fifth Avenue, New York, New York 10011

Contents

Preface

The primary purpose of this volume is to provide essays on writers of
Anglo-Irish background whose careers have been completed and who
have been the subject of a substantial body of published research. A
liberal definition of "background" accounts for the inclusion of Wilde
and Shaw, whose credentials are otherwise open to some debate. The
other criteria explain the lack of any detailed discussion of writers
such as Beckett, Clarke, Colum, O'Faolain, and many others.

Considerations such as the allotment of space and the amount of
published research have necessarily produced a diversity among the
chapters as to the organizational scheme, the degree of selectivity in
coverage, the citing of reprints, and so forth. Place of publication is
generally given for books only if not within England, Ireland, Canada, or the United States. Coverage of important work is complete
through 1974, with numerous items from 1975 added.

Each chapter has been read by another contributor and by one or
more outside scholars. We are most grateful to the following for their
comments on chapters or sections of chapters: Russell K. Alspach,
Ronald Ayling, Karl Beckson, Bernard Benstock, Zack Bowen, Robert
Boyle, S.J., David R. Clark, Alan M. Cohn, Louis Crompton, Kathleen
Dell' Orto, Janet Dunleavy, Michael Durkan, Richard Ellmann,
Thomas Flanagan, James J. Ford, Edwin Gilcher, George Mills Harper,
Clive Hart, Sir Rupert Hart-Davis, K. P. S. Jochum, Dan H. Laurence,
A. Walton Litz, Phillip L. Marcus, Frederick P. W. McDowell, Edward
B. Partridge, Ann Saddlemyer, Hugh B. Staples, Donald T. Torchiana,
Keith Owen Tribble, John Van Voorhis, and Jack Wayne Weaver.
Finally, we should like to thank the staff of the Modern Language
Association, particularly Walter S. Achtert, for their assistance and
encouragement.

R. J. F.

Table of Acronyms

The following acronyms are used throughout the volume. In addition, the chapters on Synge and on Irish Drama have some special forms, cited at the beginning of those chapters.

ABC	American Book Collector
AL	American Literature
ALM	Archives des Lettres Modernes
AN&Q	American Notes and Queries (New Haven, Conn.)
AntigR	Antigonish Review
AQ	Antioch Review
AR	Ariel: A Review of International English Literature
ArielE	American Quarterly
ArQ	Arizona Quarterly
AWR	Anglo-Welsh Review (Pembroke Dock, Wales)
BB	Bulletin of Bibliography
BC	Book Collector
BJA	British Journal of Aesthetics (London)
BMQ	British Museum Quarterly
BNYPL	Bulletin of the New York Public Library
BuR	Bucknell Review
BUSE	Boston University Studies in English
CathW	Catholic World [now *New Catholic World*]
CE	College English
CEA	CEA Critic
CentR	Centennial Review (Mich. State U.)
CL	Comparative Literature
CLAJ	College Language Association Journal (Morgan State Coll., Baltimore)
CLQ	Colby Library Quarterly
CLS	Comparative Literature Studies (U. of Ill.)
CompD	Comparative Drama
ContempR	Contemporary Review (London)
CQ	Cambridge Quarterly
Criticism	(Wayne State)
CritQ	Critical Quarterly
Daedalus	(Proc. Amer. Acad. of Arts & Sciences)
DAI	Dissertation Abstracts International [supersedes *DA*]

DM	Dublin Magazine [as *The Dubliner*, 1961–64]
DNB	Dictionary of National Biography
DR	Dalhousie Review
DramasS	Drama Survey
DUJ	Durham University Journal
EA	Études Anglaises
E&S	Essays and Studies by Members of the English Association
EFT	English Fiction in Transition
EIC	Essays in Criticism (Oxford)
Éire	Éire-Ireland: A Journal of Irish Studies (St. Paul)
EJ	English Journal
ELH	Journal of English Literary History
ELN	English Language Notes (U. of Colo.)
ELT	English Literature in Transition (1880–1920)
EM	English Miscellany
EngS	Englische Studien
ES	English Studies
ESA	English Studies in Africa (Johannesburg)
ETJ	Educational Theatre Journal
EUQ	Emory University Quarterly
FortR	Fortnightly Review
FR	French Review
FS	French Studies
GaR	Georgia Review
GL&L	German Life and Letters
HAR	Humanities Association Review
HLQ	Huntington Library Quarterly
HudR	Hudson Review
IB	Irish Book
IM	Irish Monthly
IrishR	Irish Review
IUR	Irish University Review
IW	Irish Writing
JAAC	Journal of Aesthetics and Art Criticism
JAF	Journal of American Folklore
JEGP	Journal of English and Germanic Philology
JGE	Journal of General Education
JIL	Journal of Irish Literature
JJQ	James Joyce Quarterly (U. of Tulsa, Okla.)
JJR	James Joyce Review
JML	Journal of Modern Literature
KM	Kilkenny Magazine
KR	Kenyon Review
Lang&S	Language and Style
LCUT	Library Chronicle of the U. of Texas
LHY	Literary Half-Yearly
LonM	London Magazine

LWU	Literatur in Wissenschaft und Unterricht (Kiel)
MD	Modern Drama
MFS	Modern Fiction Studies
MHRev	Malahat Review
MissQ	Mississippi Quarterly
MLN	Modern Language Notes
MLQ	Modern Language Quarterly
MLR	Modern Language Review
MP	Modern Philology
MR	Massachusetts Review (U. of Mass.)
MTJ	Mark Twain Journal
N&Q	Notes and Queries
NCBEL	New Cambridge Bibliography of English Literature
NCF	Nineteenth-Century Fiction
NEQ	New England Quarterly
NewS	New Statesman
NL	Nouvelles Littéraires
NLH	New Literary History (U. of Va.)
NM	Neuphilologische Mitteilungen
NRF	Nouvelle Revue Française
NVT	Nieuw Vlaams Tijdschrift
NY	New Yorker
OCR	Oxford and Cambridge Review
OL	Orbis Litterarum
PBA	Proceedings of the British Academy
PBSA	Papers of the Bibliographical Society of America
PCP	Pacific Coast Philology
PEGS	Publications of the English Goethe Society
PLL	Papers on Language and Literature
PMLA	Publications of the Mod. Lang. Assn. of America
PoetryR	Poetry Review (London)
PP	Philologica Pragensia
PQ	Philological Quarterly (Iowa City)
PR	Partisan Review
PrS	Prairie Schooner
PsyR	Psychoanalytic Review
PULC	Princeton University Library Chronicle
QJS	Quarterly Journal of Speech
QQ	Queen's Quarterly
QR	Quarterly Review
RAA	Revue Anglo-Américaine
RDM	Revue des Deux Mondes [now *Nouvelle Revue des Deux Mondes*]
REL	Review of English Literature
RES	Review of English Studies
RLC	Revue de Littérature Comparée
RLM	La Revue des Lettres Modernes
RLR	Revue des Langues Romanes (Montpellier)

RLV	Revue des Langues Vivantes (Bruxelles)
RR	Romanic Review
RUS	Rice University Studies
SAB	South Atlantic Bulletin
SAQ	South Atlantic Quarterly
SatR	Saturday Review
SB	Studies in Bibliography: Papers of the Bibliographical Society of the U. of Va.
SEL	Studies in English Literature, 1500–1900
SF	Sinn Féin
SFQ	Southern Folklore Quarterly
SH	Studia Hibernica (Dublin)
ShawR	Shaw Review
SHR	Southern Humanities Review
SJW	Shakespeare-Jahrbuch (Weimar)
SLitI	Studies in the Literary Imagination (Ga. State Coll.)
SNNTS	Studies in the Novel (North Texas State U.)
SoQ	Southern Quarterly (U. of So. Miss.)
SoR	Southern Review (Louisiana State U.)
SoRA	Southern Review: An Australian Journal of Literary Studies (U. of Adelaide)
SQ	Shakespeare Quarterly
SR	Sewanee Review
SSF	Studies in Short Fiction (Newberry Coll., S.C.)
Studies	(Dublin)
TA	Theatre Annual
TC	Twentieth Century
TCL	Twentieth-Century Literature
TDR	The Drama Review [formerly *Tulane Drama Review*]
TFSB	Tennessee Folklore Society Bulletin
ThS	Theatre Survey (Amer. Soc. for Theatre Research)
TLS	[London] Times Literary Supplement
TQ	Texas Quarterly (U. of Texas)
TriQ	Tri-Quarterly
TSE	Tulane Studies in English
TSL	Tennessee Studies in Literature
TSLL	Texas Studies in Literature and Language
UI	United Irishman
UKCR	University of Kansas City Review
UNCSCL	U. of N.C. Studies in Comparative Literature
UnivR	University Review (Dublin)
UTQ	University of Toronto Quarterly
UWR	University of Windsor Review (Windsor, Ontario)
VN	Victorian Newsletter
VQ	Visvabharati Quarterly
VQR	Virginia Quarterly Review
VS	Victorian Studies (Ind. U.)
WascanaR	Wascana Review

WHR	Western Humanities Review
WN	A Wake Newslitter (Newcastle U. Coll., N.S.W.)
WSCL	Wisconsin Studies in Contemporary Literature
YCGL	Yearbook of Comparative and General Literature
YeatsS	Yeats Studies
YES	Yearbook of English Studies
YR	Yale Review
YULG	Yale University Library Gazette

ANGLO-IRISH LITERATURE
A Review of Research

GENERAL WORKS

Richard M. Kain

Anglo-Irish creative energies (Maria Edgeworth, Mangan, and others) had already appeared before the Irish Revival got under way about 1890. Its momentum was obvious, its direction unclear. Constantly debated were such topics as the use of English and the appropriateness of Irish legend, as well as religious and political attitudes. Thirty years later Yeats reassessed the high hopes once voiced and recalled the instant publicity they received. His wry amusement does not hide his disillusion. His suggestion of a London literary society had been almost instantly put into action and "In a few months somebody had written its history, and published that history, illustrated by our portraits"—then the mocking anticlimax—"at a shilling." Yeats's account is found in the section "Ireland after Parnell" of *The Trembling of the Veil* (1922). The shilling volume has a portentous title. *The Irish Literary Revival: Its History, Pioneers, and Possibilities, with Portraits*, by W. P. Ryan (1894). Amid the alliterative array of the title, the portraits are perhaps the most interesting today. There are halftones of O'Leary, Hyde, Yeats, and several almost forgotten figures. The author expresses concern about the future of Yeats as a writer, questioning whether he "has not really done his best work, or if there is, or will be much in his poetry of the enduring kind." One prophecy deserves quotation:

> As the Irish Revival expands in new directions, will not some one take heart and attempt something for Irish dramatic literature? The real Irish drama is a thing unknown. Why it is so is to me something of a marvel; for in our tastes, ideas, and lives we are essentially dramatic. . . . We may see in our day in Dublin genuine Irish plays, of truth and talent, written for the people, prized by the people, moving and moulding the people.

In defining the movement, Ryan holds that "its aim is to teach Ireland to see herself . . . realising her nature and her mission," and if Irish writers "tend, as they promise, to keener interpretation than hitherto of Ireland's life, to bring brighter developments of Ireland's genius, the gain will be not only hers but humanity's." The work is of interest both as a somewhat unknown landmark and as a reflection of the idealism that permeated the movement, despite Yeats's gibes at the Southwark society, with shopgirls giggling and every member saying "all he had to say many times over."

Only recently has critical attention been widened from Yeats, Joyce, and the Abbey Theatre. The result is that a fertile and largely uncharted area remains to be explored. Though the student may at times feel frustrated by difficulties such as obscurity of reference, lack of competent and accurate guides, and dispersal of material, he will be rewarded by the discovery of works of literary merit and by an understanding of the complex social, political, and philosophical forces which both aided and impeded the movement.

I. Bibliographies and Library Holdings

GENERAL BIBLIOGRAPHIES

Two truly monumental bibliographies have been edited by the former director of the National Library of Ireland, Richard J. Hayes. The eleven-volume *Manuscript Sources for the History of Irish Civilisation* (1965) is based on holdings of 678 libraries and of more than 600 private collections. Entries are arranged by persons (4 vols.); subjects, places, and dates (2 vols. each); and material in Irish (1 vol.). A sample of places conveys some idea of the extensive coverage and also the wide dispersal of material: "Naumur, Nancy, Naples, Nashville, New Brunswick." Manuscripts from 1900 to 1961 fill pages 804 to 874 of Volume x, beginning with "Letters to W. G. Fay and his wife . . . including a few from W. B. Yeats, G. B. Shaw and others. Also miscellaneous accounts and contracts, 1908–1944." So general an entry indicates that a good deal of sifting still awaits the diligent scholar.

Sources for the History of Irish Civilisation: Articles in Irish Periodicals (1970), in nine volumes, lists materials from about 150 journals, itself a valuable bibliography. Here are *The Arrow* (1906–07, 1909), *The Bell* (1940–54), the *Dublin Magazine* (1923–58), *Envoy* (1949–51), and many others so central to the Revival. As an example of content, Padraic Colum has about 200 entries. Unfortunately omitted were the weekly journals, such as the important ones edited by Griffith and by A. E. The value of this material can scarcely be overemphasized, though it is just now being studied (see Richard M. Kain, "Irish Periodical Literature, An Untilled Field," *Éire*, 1972, esp. the note on work in progress).

A basic bibliography is Alan R. Eager's *A Guide to Irish Bibliographical Material* (1964). An exhaustive survey (about 330 pages) of topics arranged under the Dewey decimal system, it includes entries from general works to history. One of the richest sections is that of biography. Yeats is represented by eighteen items, including bibliographies in book or article form and exhibition catalogs (Kansas,

Manchester, Trinity, Yale), as well as studies containing lists of Yeatsiana.

The diffusion of Irish talent indicated in the Eager *Guide* suggests the primary need for a dictionary of Irish biography comparable to the *Dictionary of National Biography*. The Irish figures in the *DNB* are usually those least needing identification, for the topicality of Irish literature makes imperative a knowledge of lesser-known persons. Bernard Share's *Irish Lives* (1970) extends the field to include fifty names from other areas such as politics, learning, art, music, and science. Writers are outnumbered four to one. Brian Cleeve's three paperback volumes—*Dictionary of Irish Writers*—contain more than a thousand names in compilations on imaginative literature (1966), nonfiction (1969), and writers in Irish (1971). Of necessity the entries are brief, as is the case with Thom's *Irish Who's Who* (1923) and John S. Crone's *A Concise Dictionary of Irish Biography* (1928). Three of the five volumes of Thomas W. H. Fitzgerald's *Ireland and Her People* (1909–11) consist of biographies, though few are of literary figures. With each of these biographical dictionaries caution is advised, because of errors and omissions.

The first and still the most comprehensive work is that of a librarian of University College, Dublin, D. J. O'Donoghue, *The Poets of Ireland* (1912). The compiler mentions the problem of biography in his introduction:

> A close and persistent following of clues in Irish literary journals, a patient tracking . . . afforded for the first time a true insight. . . . I spared no pains in attempting to unravel any doubtful matter, and the elucidation of the smallest point often entailed real and prolonged trouble.

Any student of the Irish cultural scene can attest the truth of this statement.

O'Donoghue's net was spread wide, his 504 pages containing some three thousand names. Entries are brief: A. E. is accorded approximately 250 words, Yeats twice as many. The compiler avoids a major pitfall of the Celtic enthusiast, that of including everyone even remotely Irish. The Brontë family, a test case, is dealt with circumspectly. Father and son are each entered, but of the sisters it is observed that "Ireland has only a partial claim on them. Therefore," O'Donoghue concludes, "I merely set down their names here."

O'Donoghue was fortunate in the time of his compilation, for the major figures are included, even Joyce, who had only *Chamber Music* (1907) to his credit, and Gogarty, who had published only in periodicals. Though it may at times seem a graveyard of talent, O'Donoghue's book preserves many a name that might be overlooked.

Comparable but less extensive are Stephen J. Brown's *A Readers' Guide to Irish Fiction* (1910), *A Guide to Books on Ireland* (1912), and a revision of the first, *Ireland in Fiction* (1916), in which the topical checklist is replaced by an alphabetical series of biographies. The *Guide to Books on Ireland* comes closer to a true bibliography, with long sections on music and theater, the latter by Joseph Holloway, giving information on premieres. More recent, but still not exhaustive, are *A List of Books on Modern Ireland in the Public Library of the City of Boston* (1921) and the short *Books on Ireland* (1953) issued by the National Library of Ireland.

For current scholarship, James J. Ford of the Boston Public Library (to whom I am especially indebted for suggestions in this account) has annually compiled an extensive list, "Current Books of Irish Interest," published in the *Newsletter* of the American Committee for Irish Studies (Jan. 1969 ff.). Ford has mentioned to this author the *Essay and General Literature Index; The Year's Work in English Studies*; the *MLA International Bibliography*; T. H. Howard-Hill, *British Literary Bibliographies* (1969); and Lucien Leclaire, *A General Analytical Bibliography of the Regional Novelists of the British Isles, 1800–1950* (1954). The preface to E. H. Mikhail's *A Bibliography of Modern Irish Drama 1899–1970* (1972) contains a helpful listing.

Ford also suggests inclusion of three regional bibliographies, with many writers of merely local interest but also with some otherwise unnoticed information. Sara Cullen's *Books and Authors of County Cavan* (1959) and Mary Kavanagh's *Bibliography of the County Galway* (1965) are arranged topically, while Marian Keaney's *Westmeath Authors* (1969) is alphabetical. The extent of Irish miscellaneous writing can be estimated by the 1,421 items collected by the first compiler and the 1,669 by the second. As for the distribution of Irish talent: to County Cavan belong Father Finlay of U.C.D., Percy French, Francis Sheehy-Skeffington, and Thomas Sheridan. County Galway claims Sir William Gregory and Edward Martyn. County Westmeath offers John D'Alton, the historian; "Brinsley MacNamara" (John Weldon); the Pakenhams: the Sixth Earl of Longford, of the Gate Theatre; the Seventh Earl, author of *Peace by Ordeal* (1935), the basic study of the 1921 Treaty negotiations between England and Ireland; and Thomas, whose *The Year of Liberty* (1969) has been highly acclaimed.

The *New Cambridge Bibliography of English Literature* (Vol. III, ed. George Watson, 1969; Vol. IV, ed. I. R. Willison, 1972) mirrors current neglect of secondary writers, with only twenty-seven Anglo-Irish writers in the first volume and twenty-two in the second. Yeats, Synge, Joyce, O'Casey, and Beckett are well covered, but Lady Gregory is accorded only thirteen critical items, Douglas Hyde seven. Elgin W. Mellown's *A Descriptive Catalogue of the Bibliographies of 20th Century British Writers* (1972) is amazingly comprehensive.

A recent general list is Maurice Harmon's *Modern Irish Literature 1800–1967: A Reader's Guide* (1967). Harmon divides his book into four units, three chronological—1800–90, 1890–1920, and "Post-Revolutionary Irish Literature"—and the fourth entitled "Irish History and Culture." The divisions are prefaced by brief but perceptive surveys. The book does suffer from what seems excessive subdivision. To take one example, recent literature is listed under eight headings: Novel, Short Story, Drama, Poetry, Autobiography and Biography, The Revolution, Scholars and Editors, and The New Writers. Within these groups there are still further divisions, thirty-seven altogether. The book lacks an index, and there is no single listing of books by author. It is thus more a reading guide than a research tool. Despite some errors, it contains more than six hundred titles and constitutes a useful survey of modern Irish culture and its background.

Probably the most extraordinary collection of Irish literature ever assembled was that of the New York lawyer John Quinn, a quarter of whose 12,100 items were Irish. Quinn was the collector quintessential (if a pun be permitted). He first visited Ireland in 1902, an energetic and successful young man of thirty-two. He brought to his collecting personal warmth, a shrewd business sense, and considerable generosity. As B. L. Reid recounts in his fine biography, *The Man From New York: John Quinn and His Friends* (1968), the American visitor in 1902 and 1903 was as quick to spot important works as he was to aid worthy cultural developments, and, in the early years at least, made warm friendships. Discovering in London that Sir Charles Dilke was not interested in the "new poetry," Quinn presented him with five volumes of Yeats. He bought paintings from Jack Yeats, commissioned portraits by the elder J. B. Yeats, suggested a lecture tour for W. B. Yeats, made a donation to the Irish Theatre before seeing a performance, and became a patron of the Dun Emer (later Cuala) publications. Lady Gregory, years later, recalled that entertaining him at Coole was like having "an angel unawares."

Quinn's library was auctioned on sixteen days between 12 November 1923 and 20 March 1924. The five-volume catalog is a virtual bibliography of Irish literature in English. Practically every writer, minor as well as major, is represented, and many are accorded brief biographical sketches. Portraits by the elder Yeats of Colum, Dowden, Eglinton, Moore, Russell, and Synge and reproductions of manuscripts are of unique value. Among the most important manuscripts were those of Joyce's *Ulysses* and *Exiles*, and his unpublished translation of Hauptmann's "Before Sunrise," dated "Summer 1901," the vacation before Joyce's final year at University College, Dublin. Synge is represented by manuscripts of *The Playboy of the Western World* and *Deirdre*, Yeats by *The Land of Heart's Desire*, *The Hour Glass*, *A Reverie over Childhood and Youth* (the first title), and *The Wild Swans at Coole*. The extent of the library may be suggested by the approximate number of items for major figures: Yeats, 286; Moore, 148; Shaw, 97; Lady Gregory, 83; Russell, 74; Hyde, 50; Synge, 47; Joyce, 20. *The Library of John Quinn* (1923–24) has fortunately been reprinted (1971).

THE NATIONAL LIBRARY, DUBLIN

No attempt can be made to survey the holdings of libraries here and abroad. One may note that P. S. O'Hegarty's extensive collection is now at the University of Kansas; the Berg Collection of the New York Public Library may be mentioned; most major universities have large holdings of Irish material, greatly in need of inventory. A collection meriting more than this cursory glance is the National Library of Ireland, basic to Irish studies.

Irish writing is so thoroughly rooted in the diurnal, whether historic or contemporary, that full understanding demands acquaintance with a mass of what might otherwise seem irrelevant knowledge. Annotation of Yeats or Joyce provides ample illustration. The allusions in *Ulysses* alone would fill several volumes, since the large collection by Weldon Thornton contains only historical and literary references, and supplementary books on personages and places would be equally extensive—witness the necessarily short entries in Don Gifford and Robert J. Seidman, *Notes on Joyce: An Annotation of James Joyce's* Ulysses (1974). The subject catalog in the National Library, Dublin, under "Dublin," has subheadings that could almost provide a sourcebook for the Joyce reader. Practically all of these topics are relevant to *Ulysses*, such as "Bridges," "Cemeteries," "Charitable Institutions," "Directories," "Hospitals," "Maps," "Monuments," "Police," "Public Buildings," "Railways," "Streets," "Theatres," even "Water Supply." Equally extensive is the Yeatsiana, from the legendary and occult to the personalities he celebrates and the modern political, social, and artistic events he reflects.

Thus no bibliography can supply what may be learned from the bound paste-in alphabetical and subject catalogs in the National Library. Six large volumes are required for the general headings "Ireland" and "Irish." An entire floor of closed stacks, adjacent to the Main Reading Room, contains the general collection of books on Ireland, under the Dewey classification with an "Ir" prefix. In addition to the manuscripts, rare books, and periodicals, this "Ir" collection must number about 80,000 items, many of which are bound miscellanies of news cuttings, broadsides, and other documents. The controversial Dublin Municipal Gallery, so often invoked by Yeats in poems and prose, is represented by five large books of cuttings, covering the years from 1904, when Hugh Lane first initiated the project, to 1915, when he lost his life on the torpedoed *Lusitania*, leaving his disputed bequest of paintings, a legacy claimed by the Tate Gallery in London and the Municipal Gallery of Dublin.

Among the major groups of historical works in the main collection may be mentioned Geography and Travel ("Ir 910"), with a subsection on Leinster and Dublin ("Ir 91413"), Biography ("Ir 920"), and General History ("Ir 940"). Under Dublin ("Ir 914133") are several hundred guides and historical works, as well as a file of the Dublin Corporation Reports and Sir John Gilbert's *Calendar of Ancient Records of Dublin*, in nineteen volumes, containing transcripts of municipal documents. The annual Thom's Dublin directories date from 1844.

An excellent bibliography of Dublin histories is given in Maurice Craig's *Dublin: 1660–1860: A Social and Architectural History* (1952), which merits attention not only for its authoritative text and lively style, but also for its prints, photographs, and appendix of selected streets and buildings of historic and esthetic value—a list that, incidentally, serves a second purpose as an index to the text. John Harvey's *Dublin* (1949) is a less detailed but more wide-ranging account, also enriched by many plates and maps.

Some sense of the wealth of the National Library was given by an exhibit of Joyceana on the occasion of the Fourth International James Joyce Symposium in June 1973. Mounted displays of photographs of Dublin in 1904 were selected from the extensive collection of some

40,000 glassplate negatives, acquired in 1942 from the photographic firm of William Lawrence. Most of these were made by Robert French (1841–1917) to be used as picture postcards. They constitute an irreplaceable record of social life from about 1880 to 1914. In addition to the photographs, and, of course, Joyce's own works, which include *A Portrait of the Artist as a Young Man* in manuscript, and copy number one of the first edition of *Ulysses*, the library found in its files the program of the bazaar *Araby, Grand Oriental Fête, 1894,* which plays a central role in one of Joyce's finest stories. A pictorial account of this bazaar from *The Illustrograph* was also displayed. Early appearances of Joyce's work were the rare *Two Essays* of 1901; "James Clarence Mangan" in the college magazine, *St. Stephen's,* May 1902; and an interview with the motor-racer Fournier in 1903, relevant to another story in *Dubliners.* Finally, there was a firsthand account of Joyce in 1909 by the inveterate diarist Joseph Holloway, whose 221-volume manuscript *Impressions of a Dublin Playgoer,* though often tedious and wrongheaded, is an exhaustive account of Irish theatrical history from the late nineties to the early forties. Four volumes of selections, edited by Robert Hogan and Michael J. O'Neill, have been published (1967–70).

It may not be amiss to record the unfailing generosity, helpfulness, and cordiality of the entire library staff which the present writer has enjoyed during many visits. The present Director, Patrick Henchy, has published a brief description of the library holdings in *An Leabharlann* (June 1968).

II. Journals and Newsletters

Indicative of revived interest in Irish studies is the recent formation of literary societies, often with journals or newsletters. No attempt will be made to cover the numerous seminars and summer schools, with the exception of the Yeats International Summer School in Sligo, which began in 1960 and has continued a high level of lectures and seminars for a fortnight each August. In recent years other Irish writers have been included.

The earliest of groups is the James Joyce Society of New York, established in 1948. Its programs for the first twenty years have been compiled by Richard M. Kain (*JJQ,* 1968); it has sponsored several studies of Joyce. The American Committee for Irish Studies (ACIS), formed in 1963, holds annual conferences and publishes a quarterly *Newsletter* (since April 1965) with reports of Irish events, book reviews, and the annual list already mentioned. A distinctive feature of the ACIS is that the arts, social sciences, folklore, language, and history as well as literature are represented.

The Irish American Cultural Institute began publication of the quarterly *Éire-Ireland* in the spring of 1966. It too includes historical and current cultural activities, such as art exhibitions, concerts, and recordings. The *James Joyce Quarterly* (from 1963) may be mentioned here for its special issues on Yeats (1966), O'Casey (1970), and Beckett (1971).

The International Association for the Study of Anglo-Irish Literature (IASAIL), formed in Ireland in 1969, issues a semiannual *News-letter*, with supplements on research in progress and related items. The first mimeographed issue was that of Spring-Summer 1971. Members receive subscriptions to the *Irish University Review: A Journal of Irish Studies* (Autumn 1970 ff.). Thus far the review has attracted some of the best talent in Ireland and elsewhere: poetry by John Montague and Seamus Deane, a short play by Austin Clarke, Conor Cruise O'Brien's farewell to the United States, and many articles of historical and literary interest. The "Bibliography Bulletin" is comprehensive, an indicator of worldwide research. Austin Clarke died while the special Clarke issue was in press (Spring 1974). It contains a chronology and a bibliography.

Though rather specifically Joycean in content, the *Newsletter* of the James Joyce Foundation may be mentioned for its occasional entries on things Irish. It has appeared three times a year since October 1969. *The Carleton Newsletter*, a specialized quarterly, was issued from July 1970 to April 1975. Both newsletters have a breezy informality which sometimes belies their scholarly value: an example is the short essay in the first issue of the Carleton journal devoted to Irish curses as delineated by Carleton and used, or buried, in *Finnegans Wake*. A comparable tidbit is found in the second Joyce Foundation letter, wherein it is reported that the Nobel Prize physicist Murray Cell-Mann adopted a word (?) from the *Wake*, "quark," to refer to subunits of neutrons and protons. Thus does life, or science, borrow from literature.

The year 1971—more properly "Bealtaine 1971"—saw the first issue of a joint Canadian-Irish publication, *Yeats Studies*. The opening statement in the first number, describing it as "the first periodical to be devoted exclusively to the work of W. B. Yeats," was contradicted in the second issue a year later which covered Jack Yeats and Synge exclusively. (No scholar of Anglo-Irish literature can remain a narrow specialist.) *Yeats Studies* is almost unique among literary journals in its profuse illustrations. The journal has now been superseded by the hardcover Yeats Studies series.

The Journal of Irish Literature, beginning in January 1972, has adopted the policy of devoting each issue to a specific subject. In sequence these have been Paul Vincent Carroll, Listowel Writers, Juanita Casey, Padraic Colum, A Drama Portfolio, Flann O'Brien, Conor Cruise O'Brien, Thomas Murphy, and Frank O'Connor. This journal reveals that diligence can find valuable and readable material, unpublished, from or about writers who are too often overlooked. Of especial interest are the transcripts of recorded interviews with Carroll and Colum, unpublished plays by the same writers, and the reminiscences of Colum. The Listowel number (May 1972) contains useful checklists of George Fitzmaurice, Maurice Walsh, Bryan MacMahon, and John B. Keane.

For the varied aspects of Irish civilization *Studies* (1912–   ) and the *Dublin Historical Record* (1938–   ) are preeminent. *Studies* gives in its subtitle the areas of "Letters, Philosophy, and Science." To these must be added, from the *General Index of Volumes 1–50, 1912–1961*, such topics as Agriculture, Economics, Education, Industry, Religion, and Social Problems. A comparable range of antiquarian subjects is found in the *Dublin Historical Record*. To cite one example, Denis Johnston contributed an elegy on "The Dublin Trams" (1951). The system (1871–1949) pioneered in many technical advances and was considered a model. It is surprising to find that one horse driver was still alive in 1951. John Ryan had joined the company in 1881, and the horse trams died in the same month as did Queen Victoria, January 1901. Johnston mentions the despatcher in *Ulysses*, a Captain Delayney, who called the trams by route name, as Joyce remembered.

Bibliographical in nature are *The Irish Booklover* (1909–57) and its successor, *The Irish Book* (1959–   ). The Belfast publication *Irish Booklore* (1971–   ) resembles the *Dublin Historical Record*.

III. General Studies

One of the challenges in the field of modern Irish literature in English is that there is no satisfactory general introduction. The cross-currents of this literature are often obscure to a non-Irish reader and emerge only after long saturation in the works themselves and in a multiplicity of background materials. This section will discuss, first, histories of modern Irish literature, with the exception of the theater, and surveys of modern English literature. Next will come the rich field of reminiscence, prompted in part by quarrels and animosities. Anthologies present unusual opportunities to become aware of minor figures, and they often furnish valuable annotation. The recent resurgence of interest in things Irish is beginning to bear fruit in reprints of hitherto scarce works. Finally, such subjects as guides and dialect studies will be mentioned.

SURVEYS: ANGLO-IRISH LITERATURE

Ernest A. Boyd's *Ireland's Literary Renaissance* (1916; enlarged ed., 1922) remains the standard work. Conceived as "an account of the literature produced in Ireland during the last thirty years, under the Celtic Renaissance," it does not deal with writing in Irish or with authors such as Wilde and Shaw. In Boyd's words, again, "the term Irish (or Anglo-Irish) can be most properly reserved for that literature which, although not written in Gaelic, is none the less informed by the spirit of the race." After some fifty years the text holds up remarkably well. It conveys much of the enthusiasm that permeated the Revival, and its literary judgments are sound, with a refreshing absence of the idolatry now accorded Yeats and Joyce. The plan of the volume is as follows: four chapters on precursors, one on the 1888 *Poems and Ballads of Young Ireland*, then three on Yeats—poems, plays, and prose—two on other poets, a most interesting chapter on theosophy and its influence, three on the drama, and, finally, one on fiction, described by Boyd as the weakest part of the movement.

Collation of the 1916 edition with the revision six years later reveals interesting shifts in emphasis. The updating of the history required some insertions, but clever omissions allowed most of the earlier text to be reprinted verbatim. The change in evaluation of Yeats is significant. In 1916 his best poetry was considered to be that collected in the 1895 *Poems* (an opinion still heard occasionally in Dublin). Since that time, "the enigmatic has grown more obscure without any corresponding profundity" and "criticism has been quick to notice the presence of mannerisms where felicities were at first admired." While gaining craftsmanship, he has tended "to lose something of himself" and to indulge in "too deliberate evocations of superficial mysticism." What Boyd calls "the wrappings of mystical symbolism" are deemed "often ornamental but seldom useful." By 1922 Boyd was able to recognize "a note of cold, austere beauty, which fittingly replaces, with the advancing years, the magical glamour, the prodigal loveliness of his early poetry." In regard to the Noh plays Boyd is honest enough to state his opinion that "the drama cannot be restored to dignity by a negation of the material framework of its existence."

Room is found in 1922 for the later work of A. E. and of Lennox Robinson and for "that prodigal wealth of colour and imagery, that enchanting magic of evocation" in the young Austin Clarke. Boyd had pulled a gaffe in his early comment on *Dubliners*, finding it "impossible to base any hope upon these isolated works, which are rarely the beginning of a continuous effort." In contrast, Padraic Colum was considered "obviously qualified to undertake the novel for which the Revival has been waiting," a book to surpass the high standard set by George Moore's *The Lake*, which until then "will be without an equal." By 1922 Boyd could make amends; in Joyce he found "that Moore's only successor has enriched Irish fiction with all that the older novelist might have given to it." Ten pages are devoted to Joyce. *Ulysses* is hailed as "a daring and valuable experiment, breaking new ground" in moving beyond realism to expressionism. Other fiction writers introduced in the 1922 edition are Seumas O'Kelly, Daniel Corkery, and Brinsley MacNamara. In fact, the chapter on fiction constitutes the major expansion, with the addition of twenty-seven pages. The bibliographies, especially the later, enlarged one, are still useful (William Buckley and James H. Cousins were eliminated in 1922, but seven authors were added).

Two general studies of Boyd's generation deserve mention. Simone Téry's *L'Ile des bardes* (Paris, 1925) contains chapters on the legends, on Yeats, A. E., Synge, Stephens, Moore, and Joyce. Unfortunately never translated, and even more unfortunately rather rare, this volume gives perceptive accounts of the writers from firsthand observation (with the exception of Synge, of course). John Eglinton's *Irish Literary Portraits* (1935) reflects an earlier time, for the author had left Dublin and thus goes back in memory to the early years of the century. For this reason, perhaps, his treatment of Joyce, whom he knew least well of his subjects, is, oddly, the most vivid. George Moore regarded Eglinton as a close friend, but there is little of distinction in the two essays devoted to Moore. In his essay on A. E., Eglinton may have felt hampered by his more extensive book-length memoir.

Stephen Gwynn's *Irish Literature and Drama* (1936) disappoints by its impersonality, for the author was one of the early witnesses of the movement. He is surprisingly fair to Joyce, giving a full and sympathetic account of *Ulysses*. He does not consider Joyce's last work or the late, mature Yeats, and the volume was a decade out of date on its appearance. Hugh A. Law's *Anglo-Irish Literature* (1926) and Aodh de Blacham's *A First Book of Irish Literature* (ca. 1930) are rather sketchy. *The Modern Irish Writers* (1954) by Estella Ruth Taylor is most valuable for its citations regarding such topics as Exile, Irish Character, and Literary Theories.

In sharp contrast to the academic surveyors of literature, Frank O'Connor is his own man. *A Short History of Irish Literature: A Backward Look* (1967) opens with a discussion of early Irish literature, seen with the eyes of an experienced scholar-translator. His account of the present age vibrates with life, sturdy common sense rendering judgments sometimes cantankerous but always provocative. No one has succeeded so well in evoking the magical quality of Irish writing at its best. Yeats is depicted as an "old sorcerer" who was able to conjure up "a decade of cultural achievement," virtually creating Lady Gregory and Synge, imposing upon his generation subject matter, dialect style, and theater method. Joyce's exile, like a saint's retreat, resulted in another kind of magic, a sacramental rhetoric. James Stephens had natural genius but, when that deserted him, little talent. Unawed by predecessors or contemporaries, O'Connor provides what might seem a critical counterpart of the tale of the Emperor's clothes, but in the end he does come through with an evaluation which deserves serious consideration. Personal encounters illuminate the study, but they are always pertinent, as O'Connor eschews anecdote for its own sake, the constant temptation for a witness and participant, especially if he be Irish.

Although early Irish literature falls outside the scope of this volume (as well as outside the competence of this writer), Frank O'Connor's work in this field must be mentioned. It enables the reader to understand the significance of the ancient Irish tradition. So too does Vivian Mercier's *The Irish Comic Tradition* (1962), which traces modern humor to its roots in the past. Lively chapters on fantasy, the grotesque, satire, and parody reveal touches of Irish wit in the most profound modern writers. Even those with the least Gaelic (Yeats, Joyce, Beckett) were somehow infected with traditional temptations toward word-play, mockery, and absurdity. Mercier's wide acquaintance with the Irish past should humble the American scholar. Most of us could be indicted with Joseph Campbell and Henry Morton Robinson in this genial ridicule of the *Skeleton Key to* Finnegans Wake: "they show so much knowledge of Sanskrit and so little of 'stage Irish,' so much of the Egyptian *Book of the Dead* and so little of the Irish book of the living."

Herbert Howarth's *The Irish Writers 1880–1940* (1958) in a brilliant series of studies relates the major figures to the political myth and the social reality of modern Ireland. The subtitle (in the British edition), "Literature under Parnell's Star," stresses the Messianism of the Revival. No short account can do justice to this penetrating, humane book which opens new perspectives on the Irish question and new insights into the authors. The stature of Moore, Lady Gregory, and A. E. is elevated but not exaggerated. Each essay stands alone as a model of interpretation yet illuminates the central theme.

For the preceding period Thomas Flanagan's *The Irish Novelists, 1800–1850* (1959) is basic. More specifically political in orientation are Malcolm Brown's *The Politics of Irish Literature from Thomas Davis to W. B. Yeats* (1972) and *Nationalism in Modern Anglo-Irish Poetry* (1964) by Richard J. Loftus. Brown describes the tangled forces that entrapped and enervated cultural energies, the paralysis that Joyce found endemic and with which he refused to sympathize or compromise. The tragic ironies of Irish history and the paradoxes Brown uncovers provide correctives to usual views of Yeats and Joyce and thus run counter to the common American adulation of the masters. Extensive documentation makes it a bibliographical tool, as is the Howarth volume. Loftus does not probe twentieth-century political history in such detail, his aim being literary evaluation. His study is the most thorough to date of the 1916 poets and is of interest for Colum, Stephens, Higgins, and Clarke. Sixty pages of notes and bibliography are provided. See also William Irwin Thompson, *The Imagination of an Insurrection* (1967).

A convenient chronology of Irish events, literary and political, from 1885 to 1941 and an informal history can be found in Richard M. Kain's *Dublin in the Age of William Butler Yeats and James Joyce* (1962). Herbert A. Kenny's *Literary Dublin* (1974) is similar, though it ranges through the entire span of Irish culture. The treatment of oratory and journalism is deserving of special mention. Two chapters are devoted to current writers, and the problem of censorship is well treated. An earlier study by Benedict Kiely, *Modern Irish Fiction—A Critique* (1950), discusses more than fifty recent figures under topics such as Rebels, Peasants, Townsmen, Heroes.

SURVEYS: ENGLISH LITERATURE

Among the more valuable studies of modern literature are Frank Swinnerton's *The Georgian Scene* (1934), R. A. Scott-James, *Fifty Years of English Literature* (1951), William York Tindall's *Forces in Modern British Literature* (1956), and *The Pelican Guide to English Literature: The Modern Age* (ed. Boris Ford, 1961; 3rd ed., 1973). Characteristic of modern neglect is the treatment of writers other than Yeats and Joyce by W. W. Robson in his otherwise adequate *Modern English Literature* (1970). Synge gets one paragraph, O'Casey two sentences, A. E. three words: "the Irish mystic." Lady Gregory is identified only as a hostess to Yeats, and George Moore is referred to in discussions of Arnold Bennett and James Joyce.

Frank Swinnerton offers more generous treatment and invaluable personal touches. He shares with us his discovery of James Stephens, and affords a picture of Shaw's platform manner:

> a tall, bony, energetic man with a brogue and a brain sprang to his feet. . . . With his hands on his hips, his head back, his words full of subtle aitches and lovely variations of emphasis, he put everybody right. . . . The audience was appeased; everybody clapped and glowed; my friends said, "Well that was Shaw."

Such glimpses make up for an idiosyncratic proportion of emphasis: George Moore's six pages are double the space allotted to either Yeats or Joyce. And when Swinnerton asserts that the Irish "in general have no sense of humour," one's eyebrows are raised.

Scott-James devotes a chapter to "The Irish Literary Movement," with brief but appreciative comment on a number of the participants. He describes the Revival as "a breath of wind" which brought "something new, strange and alluring," comparable to the Romantic movement a century before.

If one discounts Tindall's odd placement of the Irish writers under the heading "Right" (which they share with Kipling, Conrad, and the conservative Lawrence, Hulme, and Eliot), the reader will find a high-speed, *Time*style coverage that touches upon at least thirty writers and well over a hundred titles in less than twenty pages. The author's awareness of historical background and of literary achievement commands respect, but he often falls victim to a sophomoric humor better suited to the classroom than to literary history.

Grattan Freyer's chapter on "The Irish Contribution" in *The Pelican Guide* is more sensitive to problems. He raises questions he admits he cannot answer and brings the mystery of creativity to our attention. He characterizes Irish society as fluid, with the result that the people are easygoing but almost devoid of moral earnestness. There is no tradition of artistic or musical taste. He is puzzled at the cause for "the surge of creative writing" and replies simply, "It is neither easy nor necessary to give a precise answer." Perhaps it might be that "nationalistic fervour was seeking an outlet outside politics," yet oddly enough once the political struggle ceased, "life in a predominantly lower-middle-class republic seemed to provide no stimulus to creative development." Freyer rejects the simplistic view that "a priest-led mob" was the only antagonist to "an enlightened band of artists and patriots." The situation is far more complicated than that.

REMINISCENCES

"The greatest talkers since the Greeks," Wilde said of the Irish, according to Yeats. Wilde's own epigrams and paradoxes are proof, and his fables preserve something of his extempore ability at monologue. But perhaps the finest native art is storytelling, where aptness of phrase, appreciation of individuality, dramatic sense, and the spice of malice are presented with well-timed and melodious delivery. Autobiography and reminiscence, too, provide a rich source of enjoyment, if not always of accurate information.

George Moore's *Hail and Farewell* (1911–14) holds precedence. Despite the author's eccentricities, it captures the excitement of the Dublin literary world at the turn of the century. Yeats's *Autobiography* can be placed on the same level, though it could be that here, for once, Moore has the edge on his old rival. More personal than social, impressionistic rather than historically accurate, Yeats's autobiography is important for the poet's theories of image, mask, personality, and historical development.

In comparison with these masters, all the rest, even O'Casey, fall behind. O'Casey's *Mirror in My House* (1956; as *Autobiographies*, 1963; as *Autobiography*, 1971–73), originally published in six volumes

(1939–54), is marred by excessive verbiage, but it presents what Yeats might call the anti-self of the Revival. Oliver St. John Gogarty is perhaps the best raconteur of all, with unpredictable leaps of imagination, casual gibes, classical allusions, and constant awareness of audience. *As I Was Going down Sackville Street* (1937) is the best known, but his other prose pieces deserve to be recalled.

Earliest in the time covered is Katharine Tynan's *Twenty-Five Years* (1913), which deals with the period up to Parnell's death in 1891. It is refreshing to read of the "Dutch feeling" of Dublin canals before the days of the trams and to hear William Butler Yeats referred to as "Willie," as he was by most Dubliners in those early days. The Invincibles, the Land League, and Parnell, whose funeral closes the book; Wilde, the O'Learys, Douglas Hyde, and A. E.—all are here. Some of the character sketches in this volume and its successors—*The Middle Years* (1916), *The Years of the Shadow* (1919), *The Wandering Years* (1922)—are found in *Memories* (1924), which includes Parnell, Redmond, the O'Learys, Tyrrell, and many others, especially the women poets of Tynan's generation.

Those who knew Joyce—J. F. Bryne, Padraic Colum, Constantine Curran, Eugene Sheehy, as well as Gogarty—tell enlivening anecdotes about that undergraduate "rebell," as he was jokingly labeled in the college magazine, *St. Stephen's.* The story of the Abbey Theatre has often been recounted—by Lady Gregory, the Fays, and by Mary Colum, whose *Life and the Dream* (1947; rev. ed., 1966) describes the thrill of coming up from the country into Dublin: "I was stepping right into the Irish Revival." Her book is full of Joyce too, for Padraic and Mary Colum were among his friends.

Continuing chronologically, Page L. Dickinson's *The Dublin of Yesterday* (1929) covers developments in art, literature, theater, and politics from 1904 to 1914. An observer's account of the Easter Rising is given by James Stephens (*The Insurrection in Dublin*, 1916). A valuable assessment shortly afterward is *Dublin Explorations and Reflections by an Englishman* (1917), that is, Douglas Goldring, a sympathetic but not uncritical outsider. To these may be added Lennox Robinson's *Dark Days* (1918).

The story is carried past 1916 by Terence de Vere White (*A Fretful Midge*, 1957), Austin Clarke (*Twice round the Black Church*, 1962, and *A Penny in the Clouds*, 1968), Frank O'Connor (*An Only Child*, 1961, and *My Father's Son*, 1968), and Sean O'Faolain (*Vive Moi!*, 1965). There is also a vast literature of the "Troubles" and later revolutionary events, of which two classics may be mentioned: Ernie O'Malley's *On Another Man's Wound* (1936; U.S. title, *Army without Banners*, 1937), and Brendan Behan's record of his imprisonment, *Borstal Boy* (1958). This vigorous and earthy narrative, poetic, humorous, bawdy, and blasphemous, reveals the author as much as do his plays and sketches.

A few others may be listed: Dominic Behan, *Teems of Times and Happy Returns* (1961); Elizabeth Bowen, *Seven Winters* (1942), early childhood in Dublin; Padraic Colum, *The Road round Ireland* (1926), sketches and biographical essays; C. P. Curran, *Under the Receding Wave* (1970), on the 1880's and the 1890's; Elizabeth, Countess of Fingall, *Seventy Years Young* (1939), Ascendancy life;

Monk Gibbon, *Mount Ida* (1948); Beatrice, Lady Glenavy, *'Today We Will Only Gossip'* (1964); Stephen Gwynn, *Experiences of a Literary Man* (1926); Brian Inglis, *West Briton* (1962); Denis Johnston, *Nine Rivers from Jordan* (1955); Shane Leslie, *Long Shadows* (1966); Maire Nic Shiubhlaigh (Marie Walker) with Edward Kenny, *The Splendid Years* (1955), the Irish theater; Maud Gonne MacBride, *A Servant of the Queen* (1938), of obvious importance; Micheál MacLiammóir, *All for Hecuba* (1946); Seumas MacManus, *The Rocky Road to Dublin* (1938); Peadar O'Donnell, *The Gates Flew Open* (1932); Francis Stuart, *Things to Live For* (1934).

ANTHOLOGIES

Anthologies constitute an index of taste and thus are of historical interest in themselves. They also include facts and judgments unobtainable elsewhere, especially for minor figures. If one accepts the early poetry of Yeats as a starting point, the first important anthology in the Irish Revival is H. Halliday Sparling's *Irish Minstrelsy* (1887; enl. ed., 1888). Few contemporaries are found in the first edition; among them are Rose Kavanagh, Rosa Mulholland, George Sigerson, and Katharine Tynan. Included in the enlarged edition are A. P. Graves and Yeats, whose "The Priest of Coloony" appears. This poem was later given the title, "The Ballad of Father O'Hart." The editor states that Yeats has not yet published a book "but has contributed many poems of striking beauty to sundry magazines." Slightly earlier, but seldom noticed, is *The Poets and Poetry of Ireland* (1881), by Alfred M. Williams, who claims, with some justice, that he has no predecessor in collecting "all forms of expression, from the bardic ode to the drawing-room song and street ballad." He provides introductory essays for each section, that on "The Hedge Poets" of the eighteenth century being of great value. Mangan, Ferguson, and George Sigerson are the principal translators. The most recent poet is A. P. Graves.

In *Ireland's Literary Renaissance* (1916) Ernest Boyd hailed *Poems and Ballads of Young Ireland* (1888) as a harbinger: "This slim little book, in white buckram covers, will always be regarded with special affection by lovers of Irish literature, for it was the first offering of the Literary Revival." It is a beautiful book, with title and date stamped in gold on the upper corner of the cover and a small harp below (to which Yeats objected: *Letters*, ed. Wade, p. 71). The unsigned dedicatory verses are to John O'Leary, with the four opening stanzas beginning "Because you suffered for the cause"; "Because you failed, and grew not slack"; "Because you hated all things base"; and "Because you loved the nobler part." The characterization of the veteran patriot resembles that given by Yeats, though the poem has not been attributed to him. Four Yeats poems are included: "The Stolen Child," "King Goll," "The Meditation of the Old Fisherman," and "Love Song." Rolleston, Todhunter, and Douglas Hyde (under his pseudonym *An Chraoibhin Aoibhinn*, as it is spelled here) are added to Kavanagh and Tynan. Boyd admits to some immaturity and rhetoric, but praises the use of folklore and legend, and "the spiritism of the

Irish countryside," which constitute "the lines upon which contemporary poetry has developed."

In prefacing his *Modern Irish Poets* (1894), W. J. Paul asserts, "At no period in the history of Ireland have we had so great poets, and so many of them." Thirty-three writers are included, each with a brief biographical sketch. The book opens with Louis H. Victory, who later earned the dubious distinction of being mocked by Stephen Dedalus in *Ulysses*. Victory's first line, quoted by Stephen, is unconscious parody, "In quintessential triviality," and the title of that poem even more so: "Self-Perturbating Mimicry." Paul's collection may be the first to include "The Lake Isle of Innisfree," which has seldom been omitted since. "Father Gilligan" is also printed. A continuation (1897) is unimportant.

Yeats complimented his friend Katharine Tynan in writing that "Your poems in *A Book of Irish Verse* seem to me by far the finest things in all the latter part of the book." Yeats's collection, published in 1895, is highly selective; no Louis H. Victory here. Approximately a quarter of the poems are adaptations from the Irish, by Mangan, Ferguson, Rolleston, Hyde, and others. Among contemporaries Katharine Tynan was featured, five of her lyrics being included, compared with four by Lionel Johnson, and two each by A. E. and Charles Weekes. In the same letter Yeats apologized for the tone of his introduction, hoping that Tynan would not consider it "unpleasantly fault-finding." "I felt my criticism would carry no weight unless I separated myself from the old gush and folly." The preface enunciates the familiar quarrel with political rhetoric, but an air of defeat can be discerned in his words regarding educated taste, "which is our greatest need and perhaps our vainest hope." For Yeats's revisions in the second edition of 1900, see Phillip L. Marcus, *Yeats and the Beginnings of the Irish Renaissance* (1970). The Marcus study is also valuable for the treatment of minor Irish writers in the nineties, such as Tynan, Nora Hopper, and John Todhunter. Marcus makes a convincing presentation of the neglected poet William Larminie.

A unique contribution to the short-lived Pan-Celtic movement is *Lyra Celtica* (ed. Elizabeth A. Sharp and William Sharp, 1896), which includes translations from the ancient and modern literatures of Celtic peoples—Irish, Scottish, Cornish, American, Cymric, and Welsh. In his introduction Sharp speaks of the vast output of Celtic studies within the less than thirty years since Matthew Arnold's essay and of the immense amount of manuscript material, which if printed "would fill at least twelve hundred or fourteen hundred octavo volumes." He concludes with a hope that the Celtic spirit in its various manifestations will have an even greater influence.

Some inclusions may be questioned: Byron, Emily Brontë, Meredith. The introduction makes even wider claims, though tentatively, for Milton, Burns, Keats, Swinburne, and Stevenson. It is amusing to see that Sharp includes his alter ego, "Fiona Macleod," who is described as "one of the younger writers most intimately associated with the Celtic Renascence in Scotland." The editor does refrain from praising his own counterfeit efforts. Nonetheless, *Lyra Celtica* indicates the spreading enthusiasm generated by the movement. The introduction contains a listing of Celtic scholars.

Translations from the Irish are not within the present topic, but reference must be made to the work of Douglas Hyde and to what is possibly the largest single collection of translations, Dr. George Sigerson's *Bards of the Gael and Gall* (1897; rev. ed., 1907).

An extensive coverage of nineteenth-century Anglo-Irish poetry is that of Stopford A. Brooke and T. W. Rolleston, *A Treasury of Irish Poetry* (1900). In his long introductory essay Brooke explains the purpose of the work and analyzes the qualities of Irish verse. His original hope was to demand "a relatively high standard of excellence" as a criterion, but this purpose "had already been carried out by Mr. Yeats in his too brief Anthology," and it was felt that a more representative collection should be made. The essay traces the development from the ballads and songs through the patriotic, elegiac and humorous verse of midcentury to the current phase, which had "passed into a quieter land, with wider horizons." Distinctive features of Anglo-Irish poetry are discussed: nationality, religion, rebellion, melancholy, and mysticism; and the lack of nature poetry is remarked. This is a large book, about six hundred pages, with more than a hundred writers, each with a brief biographical account (Yeats introduces Lionel Johnson, Nora Hopper, Althea Gyles, and A. E., and is introduced by Rolleston). The six-part division is never clearly explained. Yeats, A. E., and Katharine Tynan are treated most fully, with nine poems by each. Yeats says of A. E.'s poems that they are "the most delicate and subtle" of the time, an opinion he was soon to qualify. Rolleston's valuation of Yeats remains the prevailing judgment today: "the first of the English writing poets" in his generation.

The ten-volume *Irish Literature* (ed. Justin McCarthy, 1904) is comprehensive. It is not restricted to belles-lettres; oratory, history, and science are also represented. The political leaders Isaac Butt, Michael Davitt, John Mitchel, Parnell, and Wolfe Tone are included, as well as the astronomer Sir Robert Ball, whose popular *The Story of the Heavens* went through many editions and is to be found in Leopold Bloom's library in *Ulysses*. There are about 350 Irish writers in the 4,126 pages of text, over a hundred of whom were active at the time of publication, and many of whom contributed to the work in the form of introductory essays. The topics range from Douglas Hyde's "Early Irish Literature" through such popular subjects as "The Sunniness of Irish Life" and "Irish Wit and Humor" to Stephen Gwynn's account of "The Irish Literary Theatre" and Yeats's "Modern Irish Poetry," in which the poet attempts to bridge the conflicting claims of the Irish and English languages as poetic media:

> I have, indeed, but little doubt that Ireland, communing with herself in Gaelic more and more, but speaking to foreign countries in English, will lead many that are sick with theories and with trivial emotion, to some sweet well-waters of primeval poetry.

Yeats is represented by two portions from *Ideas of Good and Evil* on "The Celtic Element in Literature" (an excerpt) and "Ireland and the Arts," six portions of *The Celtic Twilight*, the play *Cathleen-Ni-Hoolihan*, and thirteen poems. The biographical account, unsigned as are the others, refers to his American tour: "Thousands who heard him in this country in 1903 know him to be a most gifted orator, and not a mere reader." In such ways is *Irish Literature* an important document.

Only passing mention can be made of later anthologies. A. E.'s *New Songs* (1904), mentioned in *Ulysses*, prints eight poets (including Colum, Eva Gore-Booth, and Seumas O'Sullivan) but not Joyce. Thomas Mosher published *A Little Garland of Celtic Verse* (1905; rpt. 1907). *The Dublin Book of Irish Verse 1728–1909* (ed. John Cooke, 1909) includes three lyrics from Joyce's *Chamber Music*, which had been published two years before. The title is misleading, as the book does not relate specifically to Dublin; it is based on the plan of *The Oxford Book of English Verse*, with a minimum of notes but a generous selection from living writers. The text of Katharine Tynan's *The Wild Harp* (1913) is ornately decorated in Irish strapwork, with title and frontispiece in color, a late echo of William Morris design. Again, three of Joyce's poems are included, but the "essential poets" highlighted in the introduction are Yeats, who "established, or at least reestablished, the artistic conscience and the artistic ideal in Irish poetry," and six others: A. E., James Stephens, Seumas O'Sullivan, Padraic Colum, Joseph Campbell, and Alice Milligan.

There is a minimum of duplication in the two anthologies edited by Lennox Robinson: *A Golden Treasury of Irish Verse* (1925); and *The Oxford Book of Irish Verse* (1958), in which Donagh MacDonagh's name takes precedence as coeditor. Both are of high quality, and basic to the understanding of modern Anglo-Irish poetry. Almost half of the poems in the second volume are by the newer generation of poets whose work appeared after 1930. To these two books may be added a fine collection with most useful notes, Kathleen Hoagland's large volume, *1000 Years of Irish Poetry* (1947). With these three volumes a wide representation of Anglo-Irish literature may be attained, and one becomes aware of the extraordinary number of talented writers Ireland produced within three generations.

The one prose anthology which cannot be omitted is *1000 Years of Irish Prose: The Literary Revival* (ed. Vivian Mercier and David H. Greene, 1952). Chronologically the second of a projected two-volume work, it covers only seventy of the thousand years in the title, beginning with Standish O'Grady and coming down to Patrick Kavanagh. The inclusion of some political material is noteworthy: passages from A. E., Pearse, Connolly, and the 1916 Proclamation. Short stories predominate, but there are also short plays and some extracts from novels. It is impossible to list even a selection of the numerous collections of Irish short stories which have appeared during the last half century or so, but perusal of these easily accessible volumes brings to light still more unfamiliar names from the almost inexhaustible reservoir of Irish talent.

Greene's *An Anthology of Irish Literature* (1954) is divided equally between translations from Irish and work in English, one volume to each, the second beginning with "I am of Ireland" from the fourteenth century (familiar, of course, to readers of Yeats) and concluding with poems by Louis MacNeice and W. R. Rodgers. Continued demand for Irish collections is attested by Diarmuid Russell's *Viking Portable Irish Reader* (1947); Devin A. Garrity's Signet edition, *The Irish Genius*

(1959); George Brandon Saul's *The Age of Yeats* (1963); Garrity's *The Mentor Book of Irish Poetry* (1965); Brendan Kennelly's *The Penguin Book of Irish Verse* (1970); and Derek Mahon's *Modern Irish Poetry* (1972). To these may be added *Choice* (ed. D. Egan and M. Hartnett, 1973); and the *Faber Book of Irish Poetry* (ed. John Montague, 1974), notable for the inclusion of about thirty living writers and for fresh translations of early Irish lyrics, many by the editor.

REPRINTS AND STUDIES

A welcome result of the revival of interest in the field is the growing number of reprints, facsimiles, and studies of Irish authors. The Irish University Press has issued facsimiles of the Dun Emer and Cuala Press books. The quality of these reproductions is extraordinary. Periodicals, such as *Dana, The Irish Review*, and the Seamus O'Sullivan *Dublin Magazine*, are available. Twayne's English Authors Series includes studies of many Irish writers, while the Bucknell University Press Irish Writers Series has some thirty or more titles in process or published. De Paul University is reprinting plays in an Irish Drama Series. The Proscenium Press also has a Lost Play Series.

Any listing is sure to be incomplete and out of date, but one can consult files of *Guide to Reprints, Paperbound Books in Print, Paperbacks in Print, Books in Print*, and *British Books in Print*.

IV. *General Topics*

The Encyclopaedia of Ireland (1968) achieves several goals seldom even approximated in books of this type. First of all, it has a rationale of organization, beginning with sections on "The Island" and "Wild Life" and proceeding through archaeology and history, demography and language, to phases of modern politics (defense, education, social welfare), business, culture, science, and sport. Here, in brief compass, is Ireland, past and present. Other notable features are readability and attractiveness of format. More than five hundred black-and-white illustrations picture the landscape, the people, and the places. Twenty double-column pages are devoted to Irish literature, with an additional section on the theater.

Equally attractive is *The Shell Guide to Ireland* (1962; rev. ed., 1967) by Lord Killanin and Michael V. Duignan. A forty-page historical introduction is followed by a gazetteer of the entire island, with black-and-white illustrations on almost every other page and many color plates. Drumcliff is afforded one column as well as a photograph of the High Cross. Comparable to Herbert A. Kenny's *Literary Dublin* is an informal travelogue by Susan and Thomas Cahill, *A Literary Guide to Ireland* (1973).

Two neglected areas of study deserve mention, Irish dialects in English and writers in Northern Ireland, both suggested to this writer by Thomas Staley. Staley mentions Patrick L. Henry's *The Anglo-Irish Dialect of North Roscommon* (1957). A. J. Bliss provides "A Synge Glossary" in *Sunshine and the Moon's Delight* (ed. S. B. Bushrui,

1972). The Henry study is the most thorough to date, though limited to one region. It treats the dialect under such headings as phonology, accidence, and syntax, with numerous examples. Included are a selected bibliography, a useful introductory summary, and a glossary of pronunciations and definitions. James M. Clark's *The Vocabulary of Anglo-Irish* (1917) is slighter, treating more briefly the same features, and expressing the extravagant claims generated by the Revival: "If we wish to know what Shakespeare's speech sounded like, the Irish peasant can do much to enlighten us," a remark not entirely devoid of truth, especially with the author's important proviso, "if we are careful to eliminate everything extraneous." Patrick Weston Joyce's *English as We Speak It in Ireland* (1910) is the most readily accessible, but it has to be taken with caution, for a large number of the expressions listed can be found as well in English speech. Certainly many are common in the United States, but this may be the heritage of immigration. Clark cites P. W. Joyce's characterization of Anglo-Irish as given to hyperbole, fine words, and rhetorical display, delivered with melodious charm.

According to Grattan Freyer in a recent lecture at the University of Louisville, some of the best current writing is that of the Northern Irish. Staley calls attention to a list in *The Bell* (1942), to which, of course, many names can be added. The tragic conflicts of recent years have already brought forth a literature marked by pity and terror.

For years now the Irish have mocked American enterprise in the "Joyce industry" and similar exercises, but all the while they have themselves engaged in discussion of "Irishness." Explaining the Irish to the Irish—and to others—may not yet be an industry; certainly it has not flown to the heights of scholastic abstraction and symbolist extrapolation which mark, and often mar, literary scholarship in the United States.

Two Irish books on the Irish temperament are literate discourses, eminently fair and unhesitantly critical. Sean O'Faolain's *The Irish* (1947; rev. ed., 1969) isolates five branches or aspects—the peasantry, the Anglo-Irish, rebels, priests, and writers. Arland Ussher, in *The Face and Mind of Ireland* (1950), also presents a severely honest appraisal. Both have the imaginative insight and sympathy which aids the reader to a balanced understanding of the eternal Irish paradoxes and problems.

Several recent histories have almost attained the status of classics. Constantia Maxwell's *Dublin under the Georges* (1936) is a thoroughly documented and extremely readable social history of the city's culture under the eighteenth-century aristocracy, the "most Grand, Polite, and Crowded Audience," as it was described at the first public rehearsal of Handel's *Messiah*. Maurice Craig's *Dublin 1660–1860* (1952) is architecturally oriented. Edmund Curtis, *A History of Ireland* (1936) contains only a brief account of twentieth-century events; Dorothy Macardle's *The Irish Republic* (1937) concentrates in great detail on the period of 1913–36. It is clearly Republican in sympathy. For an extensive coverage of political and economic developments see F. S. L. Lyons, *Ireland since the Famine* (1971, rev. ed., 1973). A bibliography of about 700 items is given.

Incisive essays on aspects of modern Irish culture by various authors are included in *Conor Cruise O'Brien Introduces Ireland* (ed. Owen Dudley Edwards, 1969). A constant theme is ambivalence—as Edwards puts it, "the Irish predilection for mixing intense enthusiasm with intense irony, cynicism, and self-mockery." Benedict Kiely's bitter attack on the widespread suspicion of writers among Irishmen suggests that romantic Ireland may indeed be dead and gone, or perhaps have become transformed into sentimentality.

Another volume that indicates the diversity of Irish forces during the Revival is *The Shaping of Modern Ireland* (1960), ed. Conor Cruise O'Brien. Politics, journalism, religion, and business join literature in these well-informed and highly literate essays, originally broadcast by Radio Éireann. A glimpse of Irish periodical opinion is given by Brian Hughes in his account of the *Leader* and the *Irish Peasant*; two of Joyce's brilliant contemporaries, Kettle and Sheehy-Skeffington, are contrasted by Roger McHugh; the master shipbuilder Pirrie, whose firm constructed the White Star liners, including the *Titanic* and the *Olympic*, is included. No single book conveys so well the energies of Ireland at the beginning of this century.

Regarding the sentimentality that Kiely deplored, it is true, as Micheál MacLiammóir says in his introduction to the sumptuous photograph album *Ireland* (1966), "the land itself is rich in the stuff of imagination," a statement borne out by the color and black-and-white plates of Edwin Smith. An equally beautiful book is *Dublin: A Portrait* (1967) by V. S. Pritchett, whose account is enlivened by his reminiscences of his life there from 1923 to 1926. It is richly illustrated with photographs by Evelyn Hofer which capture the warm color of Dublin façades and doorways and the autumnal atmosphere of city vistas. That old Dublin is fast disappearing makes Flora H. Mitchell's *Vanishing Dublin* (1966) something of an elegy. Its hundred color sketches underscore the price of progress, for concrete-and-glass office blocks are now replacing gracious but crumbling houses.

Ludwig Bieler's scholarly *Ireland: Harbinger of the Middle Ages* (German ed., 1961; trans. 1963) is a lavishly illustrated account of Irish culture before the ninth century. With tipped-in color plates of Irish manuscripts and ornaments, and numerous drawings and photographs, the book surveys the golden age of the early Christian art.

Padraic Colum's *A Treasury of Irish Folklore* (1954) and Helen O'Clery's *The Ireland Reader* (1963) provide selections on various phases of Irish culture. In the words of Colum's subtitle, "The Stories, Traditions, Legends, Humor, Wisdom, Ballads and Songs of the Irish People." Both volumes contain interesting items, and there is little duplication. The Colum book is more comprehensive, with perhaps two hundred passages ranging from ancient saga to the words and music of ballads and songs, including "Finnegan's Wake."

Irish Houses and Castles (1971), by Desmond Guinness and William Ryan, is splendidly pictorial, a tribute to the work of Guinness and the Irish Georgian Society he founded in 1958. The society has done much restoration, especially Castletown, its headquarters. Oldest of the houses is Bunratty (ca. 1425), familiar to Americans for its "medieval banquet," a feature of many tours. Most are Palladian, as in Malton's Dublin views, but Regency and other styles appear, including the freak classical-Gothic Castleward in County Down. The mélange was a marital compromise. Swift's friend Mrs. Delany rightly described the couple: "He wants taste, and Lady Anne is so whimsical that I doubt her judgment." The Ascendancy could afford eccentric notions, such as planting trees in Waterloo battle formations (Lyons, County Kildare), or the Earl of Rosse's submerged telescope at Birr. Irish houses are redolent of anecdote, down to the present "kidnapping" of masterpieces from Russborough in 1974. Many are near Dublin, like Malahide, where the Boswell papers were discovered, and Howth, of *Finnegans Wake* fame (but who knew that the Sixth Earl commissioned a portrait of his friend Swift?). Another Joycean association is Belvedere (County Westmeath), built by Robert Rochfort, First Earl of Belvedere, who imprisoned his wife from 1743 to 1774, in a true "Gothic" tale. In *Ulysses*, Father Conmee errs as he visualizes how "A listless lady, no more young, walked alone the shore of lough Ennel," for she was forced to reside several miles away at Gaulstown, while her outraged husband lived near the lake, a baronial spender in baronial splendor. Belvedere College, which Joyce attended and of which Father Conmee was rector, as he had been at Clongowes Wood, was built by the Second Earl in 1786.

Some reference must be made to the recent upsurge in studies of Irish writers other than the perennial Shaw, Yeats, and Joyce. A comparison of the *MLA Bibliography* for 1962 with that of 1972 shows that while the number of items listed under twentieth-century English literature (including Anglo-Irish) tripled in ten years, those of the secondary Irish writers rose from 22 to 129, a gain which may be considered either encouraging or alarming. One cannot deny the fact that modern Anglo-Irish literature has been discovered by scholars. The twenty-one writers who honor Professor Tindall in *Modern Irish Literature* (ed. Raymond J. Porter and James D. Brophy, 1972) treat thirteen figures. In addition to Yeats and Joyce there are J. B. Yeats, Lady Gregory, George Moore, Hyde, Pearse, and Gogarty (no Synge or O'Casey); of the later generation O'Connor and Clarke; while the most recent are Beckett, Montague, and the publisher Liam Miller. As noteworthy as this diversity is the locus of first delivery. Three come from the Yeats Summer School, one from a Joyce Symposium in Trieste, one from a Yeats Centenary at Indiana University, and one from a conference of the American Committee for Irish Studies.

Current activity in Anglo-Irish scholarship, hedged with reservations about the literature itself and the quality of recent work, is evident in the special Winter 1976 issue of *The Sewanee Review*, devoted to "The Literature of Modern Ireland." Denis Donoghue's essay, "Being Irish Together," stresses the lack of an Irish tradition, the domination of Yeats and Joyce, and other limiting factors. He concludes that there is "a rift between experience and meaning, but in reverse: the meaning is premature, already inscribed by a mythology . . . and the experience is too narrow to be entirely natural and representative." These forebodings are somewhat belied by the contents of the issue—a long story by James Plunkett, a few poems, and essays on Shaw, O'Connor, and MacKenna, as well as essay-reviews of books on Wilde, Yeats, Synge, O'Casey, Stephens, Casement, and contemporary poets. Altogether more than fifty studies are mentioned. The aspiring scholar may take warning, however, from the survey of Yeats scholarship by A. Norman Jeffares entitled (after Yeats) "Coughing in Ink." A second echo of the master, "What is there left to say?," is answered by the sobering observation that "The price of a professional approach is that many of these academic studies are unduly expanded, boringly written, and unduly heavy-handed." *Caveat scriptor.*

POSTSCRIPT

A Bibliography of Modern Irish and Anglo-Irish Literature (1976), compiled by Frank L. Kersnowski, C. W. Spinks, and Laird Loomis, contains entries for sixty modern authors. Periodical items are excluded, but the listing of collections, selections, translations, and introductions should make this a brief, basic handbook.

NINETEENTH-CENTURY WRITERS

James F. Kilroy

Anglo-Irish literature begins, paradoxically, at the death of Anglo-Ireland. With the Act of Union in 1800 Dublin died as a center of art and architecture just as its political power was passed to Westminster. Grattan's Parliament, the classic beauty of Dublin revealed in James Malton's drawings of its major buildings, even the excitement of Smock Alley—those were the glories of the age that died; but their loss was not forgotten by the writers to come. The nineteenth century was almost unimaginably harrowing, marked by unsuccessful attempts at revolution, by the rise and fall of O'Connell and Parnell, the two who achieved the greatest popular support, and by the famine which racked the countryside and started in process the pattern of emigration that continued for a century. Yet out of the deprivation and suffering came the first novelists and poets to speak in a voice distinct from the English and the first to write for a popular Irish audience. A sense of identity and even pride in national character grew, and new forms of literary expression rather naturally appeared.

General accounts of literary history of the period are incomplete in their coverage. The three chapters of Frank O'Connor's *A Short History of Irish Literature: A Backward Look* (1967) are unusually perceptive, but regrettably brief. W. L. Renwick's *English Literature 1789–1815* (1963) and Ian Jack's *English Literature 1815–1832* (1963), two volumes of the Oxford History of English Literature, give useful comments on some of the authors of the period. Those historians who concentrate on the Irish alone are less successful; Stephen Gwynn's *Irish Literature and Drama in the English Language* (1936) is so intent on its patriotism that too little attention is given to literary merit. Only one recent study, Patrick Rafroidi's *L'Irlande et le Romantisme* (Paris, 1972), attempts a comprehensive study of Ireland's literature in this period in relation to the major esthetic movement of the time. Rafroidi's comments on the writers of the period from 1789 to 1850, particularly as they relate ancient culture and nationalist sentiments to the romantic and revolutionary theories of the time, deserve the wider recognition that translation into English would bring. Of special use is the second half of the book, a bibliography of major authors, translations, and principal Irish periodicals of the period.

The discussions that follow are grouped by genres and include the major Irish writers in English whose works appeared in the nineteenth century.

I. Fiction

No single work is as valuable, and few are as interesting, as Michael Sadleir's *XIX Century Fiction, A Bibliographical Record* (1951). Not only is it the standard bibliography of the major novelists, but his introductory comments recognize the permanent importance of the Irish novels. Supplementary to it are the standard bibliographies of the period, the *CBEL*, and annual listings.

Of the histories of the novel two need to be mentioned for their full treatment of these writers: Ernest Baker's *History of the English Novel* (10 vols., 1924–39) includes several enduring chapters on Irish novelists. Thomas Flanagan's *The Irish Novelists 1800–1850* (1959) is the most original and thorough study available, a model work of literary criticism. Other works of more limited scope appear in the discussions of individual authors that follow.

MARIA EDGEWORTH: BIBLIOGRAPHIES, EDITIONS, BIOGRAPHIES, CRITICAL STUDIES

Of the Irish writers of the nineteenth century, critics would grant only Maria Edgeworth an indisputable place in literary history. So it follows that her life and certain of her works have been given careful attention. Even bibliographic aids are more complete in her case. The standard works, *CBEL* and Sadleir's *XIX Century Fiction, A Bibliographical Record*, are supplemented by Bertha Coolidge Slade's *Maria Edgeworth 1767–1849: A Bibliographical Tribute* (1937). But most students of Edgeworth will find the bibliography at the end of Marilyn Butler's *Maria Edgeworth: A Literary Biography* (1972) more useful than such longer lists in that it gives the standard first editions but adds what must be a complete list of manuscript sources, including the several collections of letters in the possession of the Butler family as well as collections in Ireland, England, Scotland, Switzerland, and the United States.

There has been no new collected edition of Maria Edgeworth's publications in this century. The ten-volume Longford Edition, *Tales and Novels of Maria Edgeworth* (1893; rpt. 1967), is recognized as the standard edition even though the children's stories, the biographical writings, and the writings on education are missing.

Lengthy as the list of editions of her letters is, there are still more extant only in manuscript. Christina Colvin's edition of Maria Edgeworth's *Letters from England, 1813–1844* (1971) consists of more than six hundred pages of letters, mostly to relatives, written in a lively, appealing style. Of particular interest are the letters exchanged between Maria Edgeworth and Sir Walter Scott, whose widely recalled tribute did much to establish her fame; along with those in editions of Scott's letters should be noted the ones printed by H. J. and H. E. Butler (*MLR*, 1928) and by R. F. Butler (*RES*, 1958). H. E. Butler's edition of *Tour in Connemara, and the Martins of Ballinahinch* (1950) contains some of the most lively accounts, but the breadth of her interests and her keen perception made many of her letters compelling.

Of the novels, *Castle Rackrent* has been most often reprinted; its short length accommodates inclusion in anthologies as well as separate editions. The Oxford English Novels edition (ed. George Watson, 1964) is based on the first edition (1800) with only the author's corrections included but without corrections or revisions of her peculiar punctuation. Recently *Ormond* was reprinted in the Irish University Press Irish Novels Series (1972), a photolithographic facsimile of the 1900 edition, with an excellent introduction by A. Norman Jeffares.

In the series of book-length accounts of Edgeworth's life can be seen a summary of trends in literary biography over the past century. Grace A. Oliver's *A Study of Maria Edgeworth* (1882), for all its limitations in biographical data and outmoded critical approaches, constitutes a sensible and well-documented argument for Edgeworth's continuing claim to a place in literary history. Augustus J. C. Hare's *Life and Letters of Maria Edgeworth* (1895) is one of those familiar nineteenth-century attempts at stringing together a long series (2 volumes' worth) of letters in the hopes of letting the author's own words reveal the whole life; for all Maria Edgeworth's skill in letter-writing the attempt fails to be cohesive. Emily Lawless' *Maria Edgeworth* (1905) was part of the English Men of Letters series, and, as if to underline her defiance of that series title, Lawless insists that previous English critics have misconstrued Edgeworth's writings by failing to note how un-English, how truly Irish, her best works are. Despite the too dominant patriotic bent, the biography is often fresh in its insights and always readable. Publication of *The Black Book of Edgeworthstown and Other Edgeworth Memories* (ed. Harriet J. and H. Edgeworth Butler, 1927) provided new materials from family accounts which sparked reexamination of Maria's relationship to the family, particularly her strong-willed father. Isabel C. Clarke, in *Maria Edgeworth, Her Family and Friends* (1950), makes good use of the information in placing the author in relation to the highly charged family circle and brilliant intellectual set she reached. In a more popular vein Elisabeth Inglis-Jones' *The Great Maria* (1959) is nicely written but lacking in critical analysis or careful documentation. Nevertheless, her easy telling of a life that has seemed to some uneventful reveals its daring and even excitement.

All of the above, however, are superseded by Marilyn Butler's *Maria Edgeworth: A Literary Biography* (1972). Not only is her account of the life exhaustively detailed, based as it is on previously inaccessible family collections of letters and other manuscript material, but it is solid in terms of literary criticism. Butler takes Edgeworth seriously, calling her a "key figure in the development of the novel," and traces the progress of her career from writing novels of upper-class fashion and sentiment to unusually realistic accounts of life in Ireland. She argues that a central theme of her works became the relations between social classes and, related to that theme, man's need to find a viable place in the evolving structure of society. Like Defoe, she says, Edgeworth became a voice for the middle class when it was in the ascendant. Butler's is the most complete and convincing argument for considering Edgeworth a social critic. On matters such as narrative technique she records the author's intentions but elaborates on further possibilities as well. For instance, the function of Thady Quirk, the unreliable narrator of *Castle Rackrent*, was regretted by Edgeworth because his domination overshadowed her moral point. But Butler recognizes his artistry and calls him her best creation. Butler's most important contribution to scholarship comes in establishing that Maria's father was not the destructive influence some previous biographers had made him out to be. He did correct Maria's manuscripts and suggest revisions and new subjects, but so did the rest of the family. She was a self-motivated serious writer from the start, and after the death of her father she continued writing quite as intensely.

The nature and extent of Richard Edgeworth's contribution to his daughter's books has been a point of continuing debate. Patrick Murray's "Maria Edgeworth and Her Father: The Literary Partnership" (*Éire*, 1971) establishes the amount of his share in the writing, but he recognizes that the father's most important contribution was the tremendous and sobering influence he had on her thinking. No one denies she is her father's child in her theories of education and social relations.

Outclassed by the substantial biographies and full length critical studies, James Newcomer's *Maria Edgeworth* (1973), the Bucknell Series book on Edgeworth, serves little function; at best it provides familiar information in a convenient format. Similarly constrained by the too brief format, P. H. Newby's *Maria Edgeworth* (1950) is occasionally original and consistently appreciative. Michael Hurst's *Maria Edgeworth and the Public Scene* (1969) uses a solid historical approach, and attempts "through the life of one highly intelligent and observant woman to pinpoint many of the problems" of the first half of the nineteenth century. As such it is extremely useful to the social historian but of slim use for students of literature. Similarly, Donald Davie's *The Heyday of Sir Walter Scott* (1961) regards Edgeworth's letters as more important than her novels. In attempting to describe life in a country so close in geography but so absolutely foreign to the English, he says, she undertook a task different from that of Jane Austen, a writer she otherwise resembles. Evidence of how difficult that task was can be seen in the Irish response to her efforts; Stephen Gwynn's chapter on Edgeworth in his *Irish Literature and Drama in the English Language* (1936) is severely critical but representative of the Irish critics: she is rejected as a product of the narrow Anglo-Irish Ascendancy, ignorant of Ireland's history and culture, unsympathetic to its native class, and unable to apprehend the reality of her own times. Right as he is in pointing out that she was incapable of fully understanding Thady Quirk, for instance, Gwynn's dogmatism makes him incapable of recognizing her artistic skill, albeit in a circumscribed area.

Treatment of Edgeworth in the standard literary histories is unusually strong. Ernest Baker's *History of the English Novel* volume on Edgeworth, Austen, and Scott (1935) sets the standard for good sense and accuracy. He remarks on similarities between the two women in confining their subjects to their own class and argues that neither is much affected by the Romantic movement. What Baker said in 1935 has only rarely been much expanded by subsequent critics. The Oxford History of English Literature volume on this period, W. L. Renwick's *English Literature 1789–1815* (1963), repeats the standard interpretations but argues that the main targets of her novels were the irresponsibility and extravagance of the upper classes. In answer it could be argued that although her field of vision is restricted, she could not have been expected to know the lower classes or to learn much about Gaelic culture or history.

For Edgeworth, as for each of the novelists he treats, Thomas Flanagan, in *The Irish Novelists 1800–1850* (1959), sets the highest standard. He covers the pertinent aspects: the impact of her father, her relation to both the Ireland of Grattan and the dramatically changing Ireland she lived in during her later years. But best of all, his comments on the individual novels are original and convincing. He considers *Castle Rackrent* "that rare event, an almost perfect work of fiction" and "as damning a judgment as English fiction has ever passed on the abuse of power and the failure of responsibility." Flanagan's interpretation of the theme of control of the land and the destructive power of claiming property is brilliant and checks with what Edgeworth says in other novels. Flanagan also praises *Ormond*, seeing it as a fuller novel and a sympathetic portrayal of a class she hardly knew: the old Catholic gentry. What is finally most admirable about this critic's analysis is his consideration of Edgeworth's works as modern novels, centering on themes of self-deception, eschewing set scenes, and allowing ambiguity as part of a realistic portrayal.

Turning to books and articles on Maria Edgeworth alone or primarily, one finds the same approaches. The best book-length study of her fictional techniques and literary theories is O. Elizabeth McWhorter Harden's *Maria Edgeworth's Art of Prose Fiction* (1971). She recognizes the centrality of moral education in Edgeworth's theories and goes as far as arguing that "the unrelaxed intensity" of that moral and educational drive harmed the novels: the unbending stress on duty, for instance, forced her to awkward plots and wooden characters. It follows, then, that her best characters are those, like Thady, who do not serve as puppets in some morality plot. Harden analyzes each of the major works in full detail and discusses technique in particularly incisive ways. The narrator of *Castle Rackrent*, for instance, is described as incapable of recognizing the full implications of what he relates, but because of that the reader is allowed "to see the truth underneath the external statement and draw his own conclusion."

With that and some other standard views of Edgeworth's fiction James Newcomer disagrees in *Maria Edgeworth the Novelist* (1967). Although he overstates the originality of claiming historical importance for her or pointing out the accuracy of her social observations, the book's last two chapters on *Castle Rackrent* are original if not convincing. He calls Thady Quirk disingenuous, which he is to some limited extent, but to read the whole novel as ironic because it is the Quirks who ultimately win out is unjustified by internal evidence and by Edgeworth's other novels.

Two subjects tend to dominate critical discussion: Edgeworth's historical importance as the originator of the regional novel and the overriding and at times overbearing moralistic and didactic strain of all her writings. On the first subject, Walter Allen in *The English Novel* (1954) credits her with being the first novelist to relate the local habitation to the people who dwell in it, and he considers *Castle Rackrent* the first "saga novel" in which is traced several generations of a single family. But despite Sir Walter Scott's acknowledgment of debt to her, his historical fiction is far different from her works; and in presentation of characters, plot construction, and themes there is no clear ground for claiming influence. Another product of her influence often cited was Ivan Turgenev; it is the sort of claim that once voiced seems to be repeated over the years without regard for accuracy. It is unnecessary to cite all the critics who repeated the claim, but Padraic Colum's essay (*British Review*, 1915) is the fullest statement. Building on a supposed admission of influence, he compares the two dissimilar writers and finds Edgeworth lacking in national sympathy. But Eileen Kennedy's skillful note, "Genesis of a Fiction: The Edgeworth-Turgenev Relationship" (*ELN*, 1969), lays the subject to rest by pointing out that the biographical data do not support claims made; she quotes the noted Turgenev scholar, Avrahm Yarmolinsky, as calling the influence of Edgeworth on Turgenev "more than dubious."

Maria Edgeworth's educational philosophy and her whole intellectual position are made abundantly clear in all her writings—too clear in fact for many readers. But Mark D. Hawthorne's *Doubt and Dogma in Maria Edgeworth* (1967) sets out to trace the development of her thought in hope of defining some coherent philosophy. To do so he has to disregard *Castle Rackrent* and *The Absentee* as atypical, and he even omits *Leonora* on the grounds that Richard Edgeworth had a greater share in its composition. Not only is this method questionable, but the result is disappointing; at the end Maria Edgeworth is seen only as representing "the reconciliation of opposites that we now call Victorianism." More useful is Joanne Altieri's "Style and Purpose in Maria Edgeworth's Fiction" (*NCF*, 1968) which shows how her moral and socially didactic purpose determines her style. The essay is carefully argued and informative, and the fiction is appropriately considered. Edgeworth's distinctive and effective style deserves further study, not without recognition of the author's didactic purpose but in terms of verbal manipulation. The frequency of puns and verbal tricks has been often noted but not yet thoroughly analyzed.

The specifically Irish character of Maria Edgeworth's novels has been debated repeatedly. Roger McHugh (*Studies*, 1938) repeats the accusation that her knowledge of Irish people and traditions was severely limited and that her interest in the dialect was restricted to its peculiarity. But he concludes in admitting her achievement, at least by comparison with her predecessors. Thirty-two years later, Patrick Murray (*Studies*, 1970) makes a similar judgment. Her faults are listed—contrived plots and moralistic tone especially—and her virtues cited—a keen eye for telling details and skill with language—but finally the evaluation is no more generous: they are achievements "of which many a more celebrated novelist might justifiably be proud."

Linking of Edgeworth's novels with those of other women writers has not served their reputations well. Muriel Masefield's *Women Novelists from Fanny Burney to George Eliot* (1934; rpt. 1967) gives only brief coverage of life and works. Vineta Colby's *Yesterday's Woman: Domestic Realism in the English Novel* (1974) provides a much more promising approach, tracing the effects of her "novels of education" in anticipating the Victorian novel of childhood and even the *Bildungsroman*.

Maria Edgeworth's novels were popular in France, as were many of the Irish novels of the time. Special reasons for her fame are personal, sustained by rich friendships with friends on the Continent. Hans Walter Häusermann traces her debt to Geneva in *The Genevese Background* (1952). Through Étienne Dumont and the comments of Madame de Staël her fame in France was long lasting. M. G. Devonshire's *The English Novel in France 1830–1870* (1929; rpt. 1967) traces the reaction to her later works and notes that the French regarded her as an essentially instructional writer. Henri Dominique Paratte's "Maria Edgeworth's *Madame de Fleury*, an Anglo-Irish View of the French Revolution," in *France-Ireland: Literary Relations* (ed. Guy Fehlmann, Maitiu MacConmara, and Patrick Rafroidi, Paris, 1974), claims that her sympathies with aristocrats and her didactic use of history make that novel no more than a political tract.

Several essays on individual novels deserve further attention. *Helen* is not often seriously studied and is usually dismissed as a novel of manners. But an unsigned essay, "Humours and Moralities" (*TLS*, 20 May 1949), points out such strengths in it that we are led to reconsider the theory that deliberate moralizing in her fiction brought a deterioration of artistic effects. *Helen* is Edgeworth's "most mature in moral and social judgment, the strictest in standards, the most inflexible in integrity" yet it is called superior to her other novels. The republication of *Ormond* (1972) includes an introductory essay by A. Norman Jeffares which cogently places the novel in the context of English fiction. He relates it to *Tom Jones*, noting the realism of the hero, the accuracy in portraying Pre-Grattan Ireland, and the fast-paced, entertaining plot. But finally it is "the highly discerning account of a volatile young man's development and the gradual growth of self-discipline in him" which dominates the book and allows it to avoid having the hero becoming merely an Irish blackguard, a Celtic Tom Jones.

As was noted above, *Castle Rackrent* has been the most popular and often reprinted of Edgeworth's novels, so it follows that it has received more attention than any of the other novels. George Watson's introduction to the Oxford English Novels edition (1964), a comprehensive and informative essay, praises the novel as prefiguring the sociology and social history of the century that began at its publication. Then each of the stock approaches to the novel is mentioned and analyzed: her "femininity" is downplayed because her concerns are so often practical management; her handling of a narrator who is observer, not participant, is seen as providing a deeper sense of realism to the tale; Thady's appealing humor is regarded as functional, compensating for the book's episodic design. Watson admits that at times the novel's dialect seems strained but points out that in the Regency period a novel written entirely in dialect would have seemed daring. Finally, if she never questioned the need for class distinctions, she was more compassionate than Jane Austen or the lesser writers with whom she is too often dismissed. W. B. Colby's "An Early 'Irish' Novelist" in *Minor British Novelists* (ed. Charles Alva Hoyt, 1967) treats some of the same concerns in its analysis of *Castle Rackrent* but adds a modern twist that challenges critics to a new view of the novel. Comparing the rise of the Quirk family with that of the Snopes family in Faulkner's *The Hamlet*, Hoyt finds provocative similarities in the accounts: similar uses of humor, a strong sense of place, deliberate exaggerations, and unusual ordering of narrative and plots. His point is not that Faulkner read *Castle Rackrent* but that such a comparison may lead us to a more accurate account of our sense of pleasure at reading the 1800 novel. A deeper moral is implicit, for the essay points to the paucity of approaches used in analyzing this novel and the need for new views of works that have withstood the years. Edgeworth's historical importance cannot be denied, but several of the novels have a life not accounted for by the dry classifications of "regional novelist," "woman author," or "moral teacher" with which she has been too often cataloged and dismissed.

NOVELISTS OF THE NATION: LADY MORGAN, CHARLES LEVER, GERALD GRIFFIN, WILLIAM CARLETON, AND STANDISH O'GRADY

Popular as Maria Edgeworth's novels were in Ireland and England and on the Continent, her influence is not seen in the group of novelists who achieved popularity in the succeeding generations. Ernest A. Baker in his chapter "Irish Novelists" in Volume III of his *History of the English Novel* (1935) says they were more indebted to Scott than to Edgeworth. In many respects they would have done better to learn the craft from her.

Sydney Owenson, Lady Morgan, is the most fascinating of characters, even though her self-advertising and personal eccentricities made her contemporaries and later readers doubt the seriousness of her artistic intentions. Because accounts of Glorvina, clad in Irish cloak and carrying or playing a harp she thought looked Irish, were so widespread the mentions are numerous. But the best biography is Lionel Stevenson's *The Wild Irish Girl* (1936; rpt. 1969). Not only is the account of her life full, but the commentary on the novels is sensible. He recognizes, for instance, that in the novel *The Wild Irish Girl* the hero's falling in love with Glorvina is taken as a matter of course, while his love affair with Ireland becomes the story's main theme. Lady Morgan's flaunted liberalism brought popularity in France, and several recent critics have surveyed French attitudes: M. I. Moraud's *Une Irlandaise libérale en France sous la Restauration* (Paris, 1954) and R. Bolster's "French Romanticism and the Irish Myth" (*Hermathena*, 1964); earlier M. G. Devonshire's *The English Novel in France 1830–1870* (1929; rpt. 1967) had discussed French reaction in that period. The best critical discussion of Lady Morgan's novels is Thomas Flanagan's chapter on her in *The Irish Novelists 1800–1850* (1959). Proceeding from the observation that in her life as in her work there is seen a "quintessentially Irish preoccupation with pedigree," he argues that her most famous novel is really just a "passionately imagined fantasy" with herself as the title character. Of course its immense popularity needs to be accounted for; and Flanagan argues that for all its sentimentality and inaccuracy, it did provide consolation for generations of Irish smarting at the loss of even a fictional glorious past caused by the hated Act of Union. She was the first novelist to express the nationalist fervor of some members of the Ascendancy and the first to present an Irish Catholic as a gentleman rather than a peasant. Not that such achievements redeem the novels as literature; Flanagan admits, for instance, that she "tended to regard plot as a tedious necessity."

Charles Lever tends to be linked and usually dismissed as half of a pair with Samuel Lover. Of the two his achievements are somewhat greater, and his reputation in England was more firmly agreed upon. The collected edition arranged by his daughter runs to thirty-seven volumes (1897–99), but only three of the novels are much read today: *Harry Lorrequer, Charles O'Malley*, and *The Martins of Cro-Martin*. Lionel Stevenson's *Dr. Quicksilver: The Life of Charles Lever* (1939; rpt. 1969) provides the necessary information and goes some way in rescuing Lever from accusations that he travesties the Irish. Roger McHugh's essay in *Studies* (1938) ends a survey of his works with only faint praise, and the estimate seems about right. The only serious critical article on individual novels does even greater harm to his reputation; in "Charles Lever and Rodolphe Toepffer" (*MLR*, 1948), John Henning accuses him of "ruthless plagiarism" after comparing Lever's *Arthur O'Leary* with Toepffer's *Le Lac de Gers*.

Despite his much thinner output, Gerald Griffin is recognized as a more important novelist. The chapter on him in Flanagan's *The Irish Novelists 1800–1850* comments on *The Collegians* in great detail and includes useful criticisms of the other works as well. All the work is characterized by "a strong and attractive parochialism," Flanagan observes, but he finds more serious awareness in Griffin: detection of "the explosive, anarchic power which lay at the center of Irish life, unchecked by social forms." Despite the great contemporary popularity of the novel and further notoriety which followed Boucicault's adaption or distortion of it as *The Colleen Bawn*, there has not been much close analysis of its literary merits. What has been written on Griffin tends to center on his life, particularly the romantic aspect of his long but unfulfilled love for a married woman and his turning from a literary career to become a Christian Brother. The biographical accounts are no more than tributes to him: his brother's biography of Griffin (1843) and W. S. Gill's short life and survey of works, *Gerald Griffin: Poet, Novelist, Christian Brother* (1941).

More interesting and useful is the Griffin half of Ethel Mannin's *Two Studies in Integrity* (1954). Her account is based on previously inaccessible letters and journals and adds important biographical data. Recently one scholar has published several articles on fugitive or neglected works of Griffin. John Cronin's article on *Adventures of an Irish Giant* (*Éire*, 1970) claims importance for that humorous, satiric work published a dozen years after Griffin's death. His discussion of one of the few manuscripts Griffin did not destroy when he entered the religious life, "Gerald Griffin's Common-Place Book A" (*Éire*, 1969), throws some light on the author's intention for his historical novel, *The Invasion*. Cronin's essay on *The Collegians* (*UnivR*, 1968), his essay on parallels between Griffin and Joyce (*Studies*, 1969), and his article on Griffin's years in London (*Irish Booklore*, 1972) are useful additions. Scheduled for publication in the Irish University Press series of Irish novels is a volume containing *The Rivals* and *Tracy's Ambition*, with an introduction by Cronin.

William Carleton, it is generally claimed, is a much more solid writer. In his introduction to his edition of *Stories from Carleton* (1889), W. B. Yeats credits Carleton for being the first of modern Irish writers. But for all the expressions of high regard, his personality and important aspects of his work remain enigmatic. His autobiography and the extensions of it by D. J. O'Donoghue (1896) serve as standard sources for information on his life. Benedict Kiely's *Poor Scholar* (1948) fictionalizes his life and the setting in which he lived; it is probably the most vivid account of Irish country life in the nineteenth century. But finally his treatment of Carleton does not escape the same kind of adulation of him as a peasant that has characterized criticism since Thomas Davis' tribute in *Essays Literary and Historical* (ed. O'Donoghue, 1914), "William Carleton is a peasant's son. His frame and heart are those of a peasant. His intellect and passions are great." In an attempt to support such a claim of Carleton's native genius, Stephen Gwynn in *Irish Literature and Drama in the English Language* (1936) was led to hyperbole: comparison with Burns and even with Synge in his handling of Irish dialect: "Carleton attempted instinctively what Synge, nearly a century later, was to do by study with a finished literary art; he tried to bring from one language into the other the form and colour of the Irish mind." Thirty years later, Frank O'Connor, in his *Short History of Irish Literature: A Backward Look* (1967), reaches just the opposite conclusion: "For Carleton there are not as many languages as there are people. There are only two languages—correct English and peasant English." Gwynn is more convincing than O'Connor when he argues that Carleton was different from his contemporaries in that he conveys a sense of writing for the Irish rather than for the amusement of the English audience. And in admitting that Carleton tends to be so redundant that he is incapable of sustaining a long narrative, Gwynn comes closer to literary criticism than most recent writers on Carleton's work. The question of the authenticity of the dialect in Carleton has become a central issue. Thomas Flanagan, in the Carleton chapter of *The Irish Novelists 1800–1850* (1959), also compares him with Synge and argues that he does quite as well. Flanagan claims that in Carleton are combined the three central figures of Gaelic Ireland: the priest, the scholar, and the hedge poet. Yet neither Flanagan nor the other critics account for Carleton's extreme vacillations in political allegiances; accurate though many of his observations on Irish life are, and engrossing as sections of his works are, there is a recurring problem of inconsistency in his work as in his life. It is, apparently, Carleton's insight into human nature and individual folly which brought Patrick Kavanagh to compare him to the author of *Don Quixote* in the preface to a new edition of Carleton's *Autobiography* (1968).

In recent years there has been a remarkable increase in publication about Carleton primarily due to the efforts of one admirer of his work. Eileen Ibarra Sullivan is the author of an introductory, adulatory essay on that author (*Éire*, 1970) and at least one essay on folktales in one of his stories (*TFSB*, 1970); but her most extensive contribution is the *Carleton Newsletter*, of which she has served as editor since its founding in July 1970. In the quarterly have been published occasionally sound essays on specific stories and tales, news of research in progress and letters to the editor in praise of Carleton or of the newsletter, and most useful of all, checklists of Carleton holdings in all kinds of libraries. The distinct character, positive or negative, of the journal is conveyed by the editor's statement of intention in the first number:

> to illustrate Carleton's appeal to different age levels and educational backgrounds . . . to avoid the contamination of sterile scholarship which exists for the scholar and scholarship rather than for the author and his literature. . . . [Articles] will not attempt to judge his literary output according to twentieth century diction and modern rules for story telling. Quite simply, we are striving for a meaningful dialogue about the voluminous output of an Irish peasant's son.

It is doubtful that such deliberately undiscerning work will lead us far in accounting for Carleton's continued appeal, no matter how well intentioned the effort may be. And it is a shame, because critical commentary has been more unanimous on him than on any of his contemporaries. Ernest Baker, who would have had no reason to praise him for patriotic or sentimental sympathies, agreed in his *History of the English Novel* (1935) that for all Carleton's cited faults—his verbosity, his inadequacy in constructing plots, and his tendency to melodrama—he is "greater than any of his rivals." The precise sources of his artistry, in terms of technique and content, need to be discovered, and the method most likely to be of use is that of the most careful, scholarly criticism. Timothy Webb, in arguing that the fatalistic atmosphere created in *The Black Prophet* is a source of that novel's artistry, is on the right track, but his discussion is too short in the introduction to the 1972 reissue of that work.

In the group of fiction writers on purely Irish subjects Standish O'Grady deserves the final mention. Repeatedly referred to as "the father of Irish literature," he is as accurately the culmination of the school of Carleton. In an essay on O'Grady, Austin Clarke, with a master's eye for language, remarks on O'Grady's difficulties in combining vivid idiomatic speech with stylized but stilted dialogue (*DM*, 1947). He prefers O'Grady's history of Ireland, which he refers to as "a strange eccentric work of imaginative scholarship." Vivian Mercier's essay on O'Grady (*CLQ*, 1958) is well balanced in its comments on his achievements as a historian, politician, storyteller, and journalist. He concludes with two defenses for crediting O'Grady with inspiring the Revival: he used the Irish legends for artistic purposes, thus paving the way for Yeats and others, and he presented the Irish heroes as something other and more vivid than Victorian gentlemen. Phillip Marcus' *Standish O'Grady* (1970) in the Bucknell series provides a succinct overview of his literary works. In describing O'Grady's distortions of the Irish legends and bardic materials, Marcus' descriptions are especially useful. The discussion of O'Grady in Marcus' other recent book, *Yeats and the Beginning of the Irish Renaissance* (1970), is equally perceptive; in establishing Yeats's debt to O'Grady, he reveals much about O'Grady's historical importance as a man if not as a writer. O'Grady's son, Hugh Art O'Grady, wrote a memoir of tribute to his father (1929); it is, of course, laudatory but of some use too. In that volume are tributes by two of his literary offspring, A. E. and Alice Milligan; their expressions of praise confirm claims that he was a hero to the early group of twentieth-century Irish writers.

Two Novelists of Terror: Maturin and LeFanu

When one considers the popularity in the eighteenth and nineteenth centuries first of Gothic tales and then of stories of terror ranging from ghost mysteries to fictionalized accounts of abnormal psychology, it is not surprising that Ireland produced two major writers of terror fiction. But the quality of the works of both Charles Robert Maturin and Joseph Sheridan LeFanu is rare in any country.

Maturin's personality was so eccentric that one would expect him to be a favorite of biographers, but little of merit has been published on his life. Niilo Idman (1923) provides fairly detailed biographical information, but his greater interest is in his survey of the novels. Idman's claims are well documented and remarkably perceptive, and he ranges far in relating Maturin's novels to those of contemporary and later writers. Dale Kramer (1973) concentrates on his relation to Gothicism and analyzes the novels and plays judiciously and clearly. Robert E. Lougy's Bucknell volume (1974) considers Maturin within the framework of the Romantic tradition and analyzes each of the major works as it reveals the strange psychology of the author. Because almost all of Maturin's papers were destroyed, there is little material for the biographer to work on; *The Correspondence of Sir Walter Scott and Charles Robert Maturin* (1937) is therefore a misleading title; it contains only one letter by Maturin and twenty-seven by Scott. But the subject of the correspondence is primarily Maturin, and the reactions to Coleridge's scathing attack on Maturin's *Bertram* in *Biographia Literaria* are particularly interesting. Even from one side a strong impression of Maturin's pathetic later life is conveyed.

In addition to *Bertram* Maturin wrote two other tragedies; but as a dramatist he has only historical interest. In *English Literature 1815–1832* Ian Jack accurately notes the extent to which the plays rely on Gothic trappings, bombastic dialogue, and stock characters, particularly the outlaw hero. Bertrand Evans' *Gothic Drama from Walpole to Shelley* (1947) is the standard study of that peculiar genre.

The main impact of Maturin and the reason for his continued fame is one novel, *Melmoth the Wanderer*. It was this novel which brought him fame on the Continent; G. T. Clapton's "Balzac, Baudelaire and Maturin" (*French Quarterly*, 1930) and Pierre Reboul's "Villiers de l'Isle-Adam et le *Melmoth* de Maturin" (*RLC*, 1951) describe particular influences on later French writers. Claude Fierobe's "France in the Novels of Charles Robert Maturin" in *France-Ireland: Literary Relations* (ed. Fehlmann, MacConmara, and Rafroidi, Paris, 1974) attributes his antagonism to France to Maturin's position as an Anglican curate, to his British conservative sympathies, and to his Huguenot ancestry. One of the masters of the fiction of terror, H. P. Lovecraft, expresses high praise for the novel in his critical work, *Supernatural Horror in Literature* (1945). A single-page article, "Maturin and the Novel of Terror" (*TLS*, 26 Aug. 1920) proceeds from a statement of that influence to a short but perceptive critique of the novel. Noting the novel's defects in construction and its chilling achievement in slowly building to sheer terror, the article, brief as it is, succeeds in defining the central issues of criticism. Subsequent critical essays on the novel have expanded on various themes or techniques: Muriel E. Hammond (*English*, 1956) calls him the first psychological novelist; Leven M. Dawson (*SEL*, 1968) calls paradox the central technique of Gothic fiction; and Veronica M. S. Kennedy (*PCP*, 1969) attempts to list the main myths that underlie the novel: Faust, Prometheus, the Wandering Jew, and others. A recent edition of *Melmoth* (1968) in the Oxford English Novels series includes a sensible introduction by Douglas Grant which interprets the book as essentially romantic. The elements cited as characteristic are its obsession with violent emotion, its interest in the occult and in damned souls, its sometimes ostentatious display of antiquarian and learned details, and its strong sense of local color. A much fuller analysis appears in the chapter on *Melmoth* in Robert Kiely's *The Romantic Novel in England* (1972); characteristic of that genre, Kiely argues, are the novel's concern for the dark side of the human mind, its republican spirit, and its curious structure: it "defies chronological sequence and replaces it with obsessive variations on the single theme of human misery." But Kiely is best in his description of the strong and deep religious attitudes that pervade the novel: a combination of the Christian hope of redemption with the perverse obsession with man's fallen state. He treats the book with respect—as an important statement rather than a series of shocks—and he argues that even the most extreme attitudes it expresses are consistent within the novel. Some of the elements noted by Kiely and others derive from Eino Railo's important but broad survey of Gothic fiction and its relation to English romanticism, *The Haunted Castle* (1927; rpt. 1964). Robert D. Hume's "Gothic versus Romantic: A Revaluation of the Gothic Novel" (*PMLA*, 1969) considers sadism of various sorts to be the center of the novel, and even claims that in evoking in readers such an ambiguous response—both repulsion and awe-filled sympathy for one so immensely tortured—Melmoth resembles Frankenstein and his monster as well as Captain Ahab and Marlowe's Faustus. Hume's essay prompts attention to readers' responses and, by convincingly calling attention to the centrality of self-destructive impulses in the novel, relates it to the literature of terror of that time.

In attempting such serious analysis of fictional techniques only one essay that ranges beyond *Melmoth* to Maturin's other works is worth mentioning: H. W. Piper and A. Norman Jeffares' "Maturin the Innovator" (*HLQ*, 1958). Maturin's blend of nationalism and romanticism are considered historically influential. Comments on the minor fiction of Maturin receive more attention than *Melmoth*, on which comments are rather standard. But the approach is most promising, and if Maturin's own comments on his intentions are to be trusted, some combination of the approaches of Kiely, Hume, and Piper and Jeffares deserves even further application to Maturin's novels. In his preface to *The Wild Irish Boy* Maturin described his own talent as "darkening the gloomy, deepening the sad . . . painting life in the extremes" and admitted that he chose Ireland as the place where "extremes of refinement and barbarism" and other wild and incredible contradictions are "hourly passing before modern eyes." A closer study of his artistic use of such extremes would be helpful.

Although Joseph Sheridan LeFanu followed Maturin by less than thirty years, critics note an important development in fiction of terror as revealed in his works. In *The Supernatural in Fiction* (1952), Peter Penzoldt claims that LeFanu's fiction represents a clear break from the Gothic novel and a turn to accurate analysis of nervous and mental disease and aberrant psychology. Two essays by a master novelist, Elizabeth Bowen, are the best short pieces on LeFanu. In her introduction to the reissue of *The House by the Churchyard* (1968), Bowen praises his "depth-charging perceptions into feeling and motive, his sympathy with the off-beat, with deviation, his nonetheless uncompromising sense of what *is* ethical, and, most of all, the acute, sometimes almost unbearable emotion" of key scenes. She finds three attitudes of the novel peculiar to Irish culture: the acceptance of the supernatural, the portrayal of the relationships between servant and master, and the strong sense of the illimitable majesty of death. Her essay on *Uncle Silas* (rpt. in *Collected Impressions*, 1950) likewise calls attention to its Irish atmosphere and certain attitudes she associates with Irish fiction: a sense of a time lag, the sexlessness of the characters, and even a kind of sublimated infantilism. But even more informative are her comments on the novel's narrative techniques: the use of an uninformed narrator forces the reader to share in the terror even when it is imagined. *Uncle Silas* was more recently republished (1966), with a brief introduction by F. Shroyer. Michael Begnal's Bucknell volume (1971) agrees in noting manifestations of psychological disturbances in the novels, and he analyzes several of the best-known short tales in accurate detail. At times his claims are more ambitious than convincing: his claim that *In a Glass Darkly* constitutes a complete study of aberrant sexuality and a consistent critique of society is not fully convincing. However, in providing accurate biographical data and fresh critical views on the whole range of writings the volume is eminently useful. In the same class is Nelson Browne's *Sheridan LeFanu* (1951). His survey of the life and works is candid and his estimates convincing; in every way it is a reliable if not startling guide. Two short essays by familiar critics of the novel should be mentioned: E. F. Benson (*Spectator*, 1931) remarks on his careful, cumulative method of building an atmosphere of terror; and V. S. Pritchett's "An Irish Ghost" (*The Living Novel and Later Appreciations*, 1964) calls him a master of suspense, paradoxically in the short tale. LeFanu's life does not attract much curiosity; it is little wonder that few have written biographies. W. R. LeFanu's *Seventy Years of Irish Life* (1893) is merely a series of reminiscences by his brother, and Stewart Marsh Ellis' *Wilkie Collins, LeFanu and Others* (1931; rpt. 1968) is useful only for the checklist it contains. Tangential subjects have been treated in Kevin Sullivan's "*The House by the Churchyard*: James Joyce and Sheridan LeFanu" in *Modern Irish Literature: Essays in Honor of William York Tindall* (1972); Enid Madoc-Jones' "Sheridan LeFanu and North Wales" (*AWR*, 1969); and Austin Clarke's letter to *TLS* (12 Dec. 1968) ascribing Yeats's line "a terrible beauty is born" to a poem by LeFanu.

SOMERVILLE AND ROSS

If a survey of nineteenth-century fiction must start with Maria Edgeworth, it must end with that pair of master novelists, Edith Somerville and Martin Ross (Violet Martin). Just as the proper spinster of Edgeworthstown seemed unsuited to be the author of *Castle Rackrent*, this pair of Ascendancy ladies seem the least likely collaborators on what must be the best Irish novel of that century, *The Real Charlotte*. Not only were their lives uneventful, even their personalities are less than fascinating.

It is not entirely the fault of the authors, then, that the several attempts at biography fall short of success. Geraldine Cummin's *Dr. E. OE. Somerville: A Biography* (1952) is especially detailed in describing the last years of the elder of the two women. But the fact that she was a fellow spiritualist—in fact, she served as medium for a time—sets a definite tone to it all. The introductory essay by Lennox Robinson is at least closer to being criticism; he praises Somerville as a tragic novelist, and says that even if she never understood the peasant mentality, she was never condescending. Violet Powell's biography *The Irish Cousins* (1970) gives Violet Martin a fuller share of credit for the writing, but it is marred by giving too many plot summaries and concentrating too much on the early works. Of the biographies, Maurice Collis' *Somerville and Ross* (1968) is the fullest in details. Collis had access to seventy-five volumes of Somerville's diaries and thirty volumes of Martin's, as well as scores of letters. But little analysis or evaluation of the novels is attempted. Somerville's nephew Patrick Coghill provides further reminiscences and very brief appraisal of the novels in his "Somerville and Ross"

(*Hermathena*, 1952). John Cronin's *Somerville and Ross* (1972) in the Bucknell Irish Writers Series fills a particular need, combining a brief biographical account with sane, perceptive analysis of the novels. Like most critics, he calls *The Real Charlotte* their masterpiece, but differs from most in treating the "Irish R. M." stories with equal seriousness as "the comic obverse" of the serious novels: "only the angle of vision is different." Cronin does not underrate Somerville and Ross's gift for comedy, but ends by stressing their skill as keen but sympathetic social critics. F. S. L. Lyon's "The Twilight of the Big House" (*ArielE*, 1970) does little more than amplify that last point by considering them as prisoners of their class but "the truest and most compassionate interpreters" of those isolated gentry.

It seems difficult for critics to account for the comic achievements of Somerville and Ross. C. L. Graves's "The Lighter Side of Irish Life" (*QR*, 1913), Sir Arthur Quiller-Couch's "Tribute to Ireland" in his *The Poet as Citizen and Other Papers* (1935), and Orlo Williams' "A Little Classic" in his *Some Great English Novels* (1926) are all sensible but short appreciative essays on that aspect of their work. V. S. Pritchett's "The Irish R. M." in *The Living Novel and Later Appreciations* (1964) extends somewhat further, but his piece is finally an appreciative sketch. In essays on the serious novels, and especially on *The Real Charlotte*, the analysis is more precise. Sean McMahon's "John Bull's Other Island: A Consideration of *The Real Charlotte*" (*Éire*, 1968) interprets the novel as an accurate presentation of the "big house" at that most poignant time: "in full heavy bloom before the winds of nationalism and the late awakened English liberal conscience scattered the petals." McMahon observes that the women characters, and Charlotte especially, are more convincing than the men, and he notes how cleverly the title character is revealed through the keen observations of her servants and tenants. Thomas Flanagan, in "The Big House of Ross-Drishane" (*KR*, 1966), also gives high praise to *The Real Charlotte* ("a long, perfectly proportioned novel which presents an entire society"), and he goes on to claim a unity of theme in the works, in which both the comic and serious novels record the life and death of the class symbolized by the "big house." In his contribution to *Somerville and Ross: A Symposium* (1969), John Cronin finds a similar unity in their works in realistic portrayal of the Irish. Even though they were not personally involved, he claims, they were serious students of Irish dialect and folk life: as a result he claims for them an early place in the Irish Literary Revival. Hilary Mitchell's essay in that symposium traces their literary careers. Their class, it is argued, "made a virtue of amateurism" which, combined with pressures to turn out popular comic novels, undermined their genuine talent. After noting how their visits and knowledge of France provided details for the novels, Guy Fehlmann's "Somerville and Ross in France," in *France-Ireland: Literary Relations* (ed. Fehlmann, MacConmara, and Rafroidi, Paris, 1974), points out similarities between *The Real Charlotte* and Balzac's novels, especially *Eugénie Grandet*.

Conor Cruise O'Brien's radio talk on Somerville and Ross, published in his *Writers and Politics* essay collection (1965), tackles the question of whether they can be classified, and perhaps disregarded, as Ascendancy writers. His analysis is clear: they are alienated from the native Irish world, but they do not mock it; nor are they unsympathetic to the people. The exaggerations of the comic novels are not exploitative. And *The Real Charlotte*, although it presents a narrowly defined and closed world, is not un-Irish: "There is nothing un-Irish about aristocratic pride; a great part of our Gaelic literature throbs with a full and blue-blooded contempt for the lowborn." He has particular praise for *The Real Charlotte* as a rare presentation of evil, exhibited in everyday life but with terrible cumulative force.

Ann Power's "The Big House of Somerville and Ross" (*DM*, 1964) points to the kind of detailed original analysis still needed on these works. Beginning with the usual praise for Somerville and Ross's skill in observing a highly stratified society, she goes on to argue that the comic novels are essentially satiric, with the nouveau riche middle class as the target. She notes serious strains in the recurring pattern of a child of the Big House befriended by someone from the peasant class and admits that some condescension does creep in. But she is strongest in her high praise for *The Real Charlotte*. She even compares it with *Middlemarch* and concludes that the Irish novel is "a considerably more intelligent book, perhaps because Somerville and Ross have a sense of humour." Her praise of *The Big House at Inver* is nearly as full, and she concludes by proposing possible reasons for the comparative failure of the other, later books. Their isolation from other writers and the distracting effects of the success of the R. M. novels are likely causes. Power's essay is original in the serious manner in which she treats the most central issues of the novels. Much more of this careful analysis needs to be done, especially on the novels other than *The Real Charlotte*.

II. Poetry

In his brief introduction to his edition *Irish Poets of the Nineteenth Century* (1951), Geoffrey Taylor calls the poetry of that period "inevitably and not dishonourably Provincial: but not at its best parochial." But after one surveys the criticism, one finds it hard to maintain such a distinction between those two. Praise seems to be showered on the most sentimental, nationalist, or self-congratulatory verse, while poetic technique and realism, or the use of mythology and folklore in poetry, the unique features of the literature, too often go without comment. Patrick G. Power's *The Story of Anglo-Irish Poetry: 1800–1922* (1967) is an exception in that he closely examines poems of the period to determine the exact influence of Gaelic literature and folklore. Admittedly it is only an introductory survey, but even pointing out the precise influence of the meters of Gaelic literature, for instance, serves as a fruitful approach for subsequent studies. Power's comments on Mangan, Moore, and the other major figures are too short, but they are uniformly sensible.

THOMAS MOORE

Of the Irish poets before Yeats, Thomas Moore has attracted by far the most criticism. No doubt his appealing personality has drawn one kind of critic; in fact sheer hero worship characterizes some of the biographical pieces, and works like *Moore in Bermuda* (1909) by J. C. L. Clark serve only the converted. It is not surprising, then, that the two best biographies read like novels, with the poet as hero. Howard Mumford Jones's *The Harp That Once* (1937) is the best of those, and it remains the single best work relating Moore to his time. Jones considers Moore the quintessential Romantic. Jones does not shy away from the vastly popular verse, noting "one of the most peccant humors of literary judgments is to be afraid of popularity," but neither does he deny faults. In dismissing *Lalla Rookh*, for instance, his language is stronger than the subject: "The book lies stranded in the Dead Sea of literature like a lavishly decorated Oriental galley. . . . If the poem was too extravagantly praised in Moore's lifetime, history has extravagantly avenged the indiscretion." Throughout, Jones's judgment is firm; he considers the biography of Byron "one of the four or five great literary biographies in the English language." He traces the historical setting, including political history, so accurately that he achieves a rounded picture of Moore and his milieu. Second to Jones's biography is L. A. G. Strong's *The Minstrel Boy* (1937). It makes no pretense at being scholarly, and it makes no high claim for Moore as a writer. But it is nicely written and enjoyable. Not as much can be said about Seamus MacCall's *Thomas Moore* (1935), a purely adulatory, short biography, although the bibliography appended is still useful. Of recent books, Miriam Allen DeFord's *Thomas Moore* (1967) in the Twayne series is sensible and comprehensive. Her appraisal of the works matches that of earlier critics but is more complimentary of his satiric verse, ranking him as "of almost Swiftian stature." On the biographies of Byron, Sheridan, and Lord Edward Fitzgerald, she is more temperate in her praise than Jones; she considers the biographies to be little more than compilations of the subjects' own statements. Her final estimate is cautious in its praise, but on the whole convincing in its temperance.

There has been no complete edition of Moore in this century, but recently Wilfred Dowden edited a two-volume edition of his *Letters* (1964). Moore was not a great letter writer, but his descriptions of regency life, his comments on Byron and the major Romantic poets, and his account of his own life are of considerable interest. For similar reasons Peter Quennell's short selection of the *Journal* (1964) is useful. In preparation is a full edition of Moore's journal, edited by Wilfred Dowden and Joy Wilson.

Moore's relations with Byron and the famous destruction of the Byron papers are described in many works on Byron. Doris Langley Moore's *The Late Lord Byron* (1961) reconstructs the events surrounding the publication of Moore's book on his friend. In tracing possible influences between the two, Hoover H. Jordan (*MLQ*, 1948) is rather vague and ends with only a claim that they have a "harmony of mind." Ernest Lovell (*SR*, 1967) gives high praise to Moore as the author of a work "magnificently alive."

It is not necessary to list the numerous short articles on disputed attributions to Moore. Most interesting, because it would be the most important historically, is the series of articles on the question of whether Moore was the author of the 1816 review of Coleridge's "Christabel." First proposed by Elisabeth Schneider in articles in *MLN* (1946) and *PMLA* (1955), it is further debated by Kathleen Coburn (letter in *TLS*, 20 May 1965), by Wilfred Dowden (*MP*, 1962), and by Hoover H. Jordan (*MP*, 1956). All three build their cases on manuscript material, and in the final analysis attribution to Moore seems extremely doubtful. Two other articles of special interest are Sylva Norman's "Leigh Hunt, Moore and Byron" (*TLS* 2 Jan. 1953) and Elisabeth Schneider's "Thomas Moore and the *Edinburgh Review*" (*MLN*, 1946); the latter attributes an 1826 review of Irish novels to Moore.

Moore's reputation outside the British Isles is treated in Allen B. Thomas' *Moore en France . . . 1819–1830* (1911) and Herbert G. Eldridge, "Anacreon Moore and America" (*PMLA*, 1968). Because of his contemporary popularity, influences are widespread if not deep.

The best criticism of Moore is in the form of essays on limited aspects of his work. Hoover H. Jordan's "Thomas Moore: Artistry in the Song Lyric" (*SEL*, 1962) takes on a subject recognized as important since Moore's first publications, but previously treated only superficially. Jordan analyzes tempo, the relation of words to melody and other musical devices, thus positing the artistry of the lyrics in the inseparability of words from music. His analysis is detailed and its method appropriate, for it supports claims that have earlier seemed hollow or at least were unproven. Howard O. Brogan's "Thomas Moore, Irish Satirist and Keeper of the English Conscience" (*PQ*, 1945) surveys the satiric writings and concludes by terming Moore's position "enlightened moderation." That seeming virtue made him "too aristocratic for liberals, too heterodox for Catholics, and too lukewarm a patriot for the Irish." A special but important subject, "*Lalla Rookh* and the Romantic Tradition of Islamic Literature in English" is discussed by G. M. Wickens (*YCGL*, 1971). Although Moore's vastly popular poem was not the last romantic epic on an oriental subject, Wickens claims it was the peak, and after it general taste for such compositions was surfeited. He confirms suspicion that it is inexact in its attempt to imitate Islamic themes and literature and calls the major themes "grotesquely Romantic and European." But compared with Fitzgerald's *Rubaiyat*, which was close to the originals in spirit, Moore's influence on subsequent writers, even on leading scholars of Islamic literature, has been greater. Wickens' article is built on firm knowledge of Eastern literature, and it places Moore in literary history, at least in part. The origins of Romantic interests in orientalism deserve much fuller study, with Moore, and Mangan as well, included with the whole series of European nineteenth-century poets, novelists, and painters who attempted Oriental subjects.

On the subject of Moore's particularly Irish qualities no critic is wholly satisfactory. Praise for his handling of the *Irish Melodies* alternates with admissions of the disaster he called a *History of Ireland*.

Of the lot, Stephen Gwynn's book (1905) is most balanced. Further study is due, for despite their excesses and occasional inflation, the *Irish Melodies* were among the most influential works of the century, and the authenticity of the songs is germane to literary history.

JAMES CLARENCE MANGAN

After Thomas Moore, James Clarence Mangan has received the most careful attention, although in number of pages his literary production is slim. Rudi Holzapfel's *James Clarence Mangan: A Check List of Printed and Other Sources* (1969) is a thorough and reliable guide to criticism of Mangan; it includes and briefly annotates all studies, and even includes brief mentions, no matter how trivial. The devotion which went into completing this work is evident in Holzapfel's brief introduction, where he calls Mangan "the absolute front-runner of the poets of Ireland in the 19th Century." To Holzapfel's volume of secondary sources should be added his definitive bibliography of Mangan's contributions to the *Dublin University Magazine* (*Hermathena*, 1968) and P. S. O'Hegarty's bibliography (*DM*, 1941).

The last full editions of Mangan's works were those edited by D. J. O'Donoghue early in this century, *Poems* (1903) and *Prose Writings* (1904). A complete edition with full annotations is clearly needed; there has been continued interest in Mangan's poems and by now most editions are unavailable. The only other Mangan item recently published was the *Autobiography* (ed. James Kilroy, 1968).

The only full-length biography is D. J. O'Donoghue's *Life and Writings of James Clarence Mangan* (1897). Mangan's life was short but tortured, and it is surprising that recent biographers have not reexamined it.

Essays on Mangan by James Joyce and W. B. Yeats have been reprinted, but they reveal more of their authors than of Mangan's works. Joyce's essay, originally published in *St. Stephen's* in 1902 and included in his *Critical Writings* (1959), praises Mangan as superior to Poe in creating unusual effects. Excerpts from Yeats's essay from *Irish Fireside* (1888) appear in *Davis, Mangan, Ferguson* by W. B. Yeats and Thomas Kinsella (1970); Yeats praises Mangan as a strange, exotic, but uniquely powerful personality. Marvin Magalaner claims such similarities and sympathies between Joyce and Mangan as to call them "spiritual brothers" (*PQ*, 1952). Several Irish writers of succeeding generations have also dealt with Mangan. Padraic Colum's essay on Mangan (*Commonweal*, 1932) is short but closely analytical, noting the poet's basic pessimism—for Ireland as well as himself. Of the poets discussed in Thomas Kinsella's essay "Irish Poets of the Nineteenth Century" in *Davis, Mangan, Ferguson* (1970), Mangan received at least comparative praise for a small number of "indispensable poems."

But of the large number of praising articles there are few which are truly critical. A. Norman Jeffares (*Envoy*, 1951) nearly discards Mangan as a self-indulgent romantic. Roibeard O Faracháin's essay in *Thomas Davis and Young Ireland* (ed. M. J. MacManus, 1945) is short but useful in its recognition of Mangan's technical proficiency. Rudi Holzapfel's "Dangerous Hero" (*Hibernia*, 1 Nov. 1968) is assertive and convincing in its praise of Mangan as Ireland's strongest voice. Most recently, James Kilroy's *James Clarence Mangan* (1970) in the Bucknell Irish Writers Series gives the essential information and analyzes the verse primarily in terms of poetic techniques, of which Mangan was an undoubted master. Patrick Power's *The Story of Anglo-Irish Poetry: 1800–1922* (1967) also has detailed comments on techniques.

Criticism is fuller on Mangan's influence outside of Ireland. A long-debated argument over the influences of Edgar Allan Poe on Mangan, or vice versa, is treated by Henry E. Cain (Diss. Catholic Univ. 1929) and more recently by Francis J. Thompson (*DM*, 1950); the parallels are intriguing but solid evidence is lacking, so that specific influence remains doubtful. The latter critic's article "Mangan in America, 1850–1860" (*DM*, 1952) does little more than cite similarities to Mangan in the verse of a wide group of writers. Much more solid is Eoin McKiernan's "James Clarence Mangan: Ireland's 'German Poet'" in *Anglo-German and American-German Cross Currents*, 1 (ed. Shelley, Lewis, and Betts, UNCSCL, 1957); McKiernan praises Mangan's translations from the German as better than most of his competitors', including recent translators'. The careful method employed in this essay is rare but absolutely appropriate. What remains to be undertaken is a full-scale analysis of Mangan's wild experimentation with poetic meter relating it to Gaelic, Continental, and Oriental sources, and to similar experiments by his contemporaries.

FOUR RESOUNDING VOICES: DAVIS, MAHONY, ALLINGHAM, AND FERGUSON

Of the other Irish poets of the nineteenth century, four are often mentioned as influences on Yeats or other later poets, and claims are repeated on the historical importance of any or all of them. But for the most part the four suffer from neglect of their poetry on its own terms.

Thomas Davis is the most colorful of the four; his tragically short life and his vocal patriotism have made nationalists regard him as inspirational. Of the biographies, J. M. Hone's short book (1934) is sane and useful; he describes Davis' split with Daniel O'Connell in clear, unemotional terms so that Davis' historical significance is established. More pertinent yet, he assesses the literary efforts with equal care; although he recognizes the persistent nationalist bias of all that Davis wrote, Hone praises the dramatic intensity of some of the poems and the fairness of the best of the reviews. Arguments that Davis' revolutionary mission excuses faults of inflated rhetoric and inordinate appeals to sentiment have been repeated often. Padraic Fallon's essay on Davis' poetry in *Thomas Davis and Young Ireland* (ed. M. J. MacManus, 1945), is the fullest but not most original of those. W. B. Yeats mentioned Davis in several places, but he seems to hedge when it comes to evaluating his skill. In a 1915 essay reprinted in *Davis, Mangan, Ferguson,* he argues that Davis could have been a great poet if he had lived in Elizabethan times—before the language was "worn down to mere abstraction by perpetual mechanical use." John Eglinton (W. K. Magee) was less generous in "The De-Davisation of Irish Literature" in *Bards and Saints* (1906); he faults Davis and his imitators for their self-congratulatory inclinations. He argues, convincingly, that John Mitchel's *Jail Journal* surpasses Davis' work as pure literature. There have been precious few attempts to reconsider Davis' work in recent years. Sean McMahon's "Eagle of the Empty Eyrie" (*Éire,* 1969) surveys Davis' range of subjects and makes some evaluative comments, but he says little that would make us want to look more closely at the verse or essays.

Francis Mahony (Father Prout) fares even less well in criticism, usually rating only a contemptuous note on the one poem by which he is known, "The Bells of Shandon." But his eccentric personality and his undeniable but perverse genius should attract biographers if not critics. By far the most valuable work on his life is in Ethel Mannin's *Two Studies in Integrity* (1954). Hers is the only full-scale biography, and it provides the necessary information about his career as a priest, his fierce antagonism to O'Connell, and his literary pranks, especially in *Fraser's.* But the literary merits of his poems and essays have hardly been touched upon. "Father Prout" himself was not the least of Mahony's creations; he was claimed to be the son of Swift and Stella, now a parish priest in a village near Cork. Mahony's name turns up in works on Moore and Byron for his hoaxes; he translated pieces into Greek, French, and other languages and then accused the literary idols of his time of plagiarism. But a few critics have claimed there is more to the author than to the vindictive but often hilarious expatriate. Cyril Clemens (*CathW,* 1933) and L. A. G. Strong (*IW,* 1950) at least call for serious consideration. And Edward McAleer's brief note on "The Bells of Shandon" (*MLN,* 1951) answers the severe criticism of that poem in Brooks and Warren's *Understanding Poetry* (1939) by pointing out what should have been recognized all along: the poem is designed to be humorous and mock-pathetic.

Because of his relations with the best Victorian poets, Tennyson and Browning, William Allingham's name is more familiar to most readers. His *Diary* (ed. H. Allingham and D. Radford, 1907) and his letters to Robert and E. B. Browning (1914) are important source books. Of critical examinations of his poetry, the unsigned review in *The Critic* (15 Oct. 1850) attributed to Dante Gabriel Rossetti is one of the best. The piece ends with praise for his "poetical comprehension of nature," but is sanely temperate in ranking him with his leading competition, Tennyson and Browning. True to form, the question of how Irish he was—at least how sympathetic to the cause of nationalism—became a dominant issue early in this century. Alfred Perceval Graves's fairly thorough survey of Allingham (*Trans. of the Royal Soc. of Lit.,* 1913) comes to focus on his sympathy for Ireland. Some of the same tendency underlies Sean McMahon's "The Boy from His Bedroom Window" (*Éire,* 1970). After defending Allingham's Irishness, the essay goes on to comment on the major works; it ends giving highest marks to the *Diary.* John Hewitt's introduction to a recent selection of the poems (1967) is much more judicious. He places Allingham's political analysis squarely in the radical tradition of Ruskin and Morris and concludes, "compared with him, all but a very few of the eminent literary men of the period must appear politically naive and blandly unaware of the nature and dynamics of their society." The only noteworthy essay on an individual work of Allingham's is Patrick MacDonogh's "Lawrence Bloomfield in Ireland" (*DM*, 1950), which treats that poem with the seriousness and care the author would have expected. Alan Warner's *William Allingham: An Introduction* (1971) provides a short selection of poems and a perceptive critical essay on the poetry. His Bucknell book (1975) eschews inflated claims for Allingham's place either as an Irish spokesman or as a poet, but his estimates of the poetry, and the letters and diaries as well, are judicious and detailed.

Sir Samuel Ferguson is mentioned most often for his serious experiments at putting Irish legends in verse. For his attempts at bardic and epic poems, and for inspiring a revival of interest in the Irish literary heritage, W. B. Yeats praised him as "the greatest poet Ireland has produced, because the most central and most Celtic"; Yeats's 1886 essays are reprinted in *Davis, Mangan, Ferguson* (1970). But Yeats's critical comments are not always models of informed judgment, and he tended to promote the authors he found useful in justifying his own work. Nevertheless, Yeats was right in so far as Ferguson is important historically. Robert O'Driscoll in "Ferguson and the Idea of an Irish National Literature" (*Éire*, 1971) argues that he deserves credit for originating and fostering a distinctive and authentic revival of literature. Two essays by Herbert V. Fackler, "Nineteenth Century Sources for the Deirdre Legend" (*Éire*, 1969) and "Sir Samuel Ferguson: 'The Death of the Children of Usnach' and Deirdre" (*Éire*, 1972), carefully examine Ferguson's handling of that most popular of the Irish legends and the sources on which his poetic versions were based. The only full biography of Ferguson is his wife's two-volume *Sir Samuel Ferguson and the Ireland of His Day* (1896); it is adulatory but on the whole reliable; the checklist included is essential for critics of his work. Padraic Colum's introduction to the 1963 selection of the poems is complimentary but not sufficiently specific. Malcolm Brown's book on Ferguson in the Bucknell Irish Writers Series (1973), therefore, fills a particular need. Not only does he give new information placing Ferguson in the political scene, but he traces the growth of the poet's interest in Irish culture with precision and wisdom. In the final estimate Ferguson does not seem a major poet, and his handling of the legends is seen as flawed by idiosyncrasies, but the evaluation is well documented and scholarly.

III. Drama

DION BOUCICAULT

The rich days of Smock Alley that made Dublin a center of dramatic activity in the eighteenth century ended with the Act of Union. For a whole complex of reasons, including the general dearth of playwriting in the nineteenth century, the story of Irish drama in that century can be written in the career of only one man: Dion Boucicault. Until the last years of the century with the efforts of Yeats, Synge, Martyn, and Lady Gregory in creating a new national drama, only Boucicault can claim either historic importance or artistic merit. On his life and works one book is clearly indispensable: Robert Hogan's entry in the Twayne series (1969). Not only are the biography and survey of his works informative and perceptive, but in the section on Boucicault's influence on subsequent writers Hogan presents a thorough, convincing case for recognition. The bibliography, although entitled "Selected," would seem to be the definitive list of primary and secondary sources. The entire book is a model of scholarship, yet also a strong, convincing analysis of a masterful and vastly popular dramatist. Recent successful productions of several of Boucicault's plays have revived popular interest, and the Irish plays have been republished in a handsome edition (1964). In David Krause's introduction to that edition Boucicault is placed in theatrical history as a literary ancestor of Synge and O'Casey. Krause's comments on individual plays are intelligent and interesting, and his evaluations are sound.

Although superseded by Hogan's book, Walsh Townsend's *The Career of Dion Boucicault* (1915) deserves mention for its surprisingly full comments on the plays and important information on the life. It and Albert E. Johnson's "The Birth of Dion Boucicault" (*MD*, 1968) treat the question of his paternity; whether Dionysius Lardner was his real father, as Townsend suggested, is now apparently impossible to answer with certainty. The remaining articles listed and annotated in Hogan's bibliography are more useful on theater history than on literary matters. Other than those, three articles by A. Cleveland Harrison (*QJS*, 1970; *ETJ*, 1969; and *Players*, 1970) are short defenses of various aspects of Boucicault's theories or stage practices; and Sean McMahon's "The Wearing of the Green: The Irish Plays of Dion Boucicault" (*Eire*, 1967) is a review and amplification of Krause's edition, which adds little original to the estimate.

The revival of drama at the beginning of the twentieth century is all the more remarkable considering the lack of playwrights in the years preceding 1900. Except for a handful of folk dramas and imitations of popular English plays, there were no works that elicited critical attention other than those of Boucicault.

OSCAR WILDE

Ian Fletcher and John Stokes

In the absence of essential instruments, such as a proper edition of the collected works, a proper bibliography, a proper life, a proper iconography; and in the presence of so many improper studies, what is offered here belongs to the modest category of a prolegomenon to the study of Wilde.

That Wilde should have been treated so shabbily is at once puzzling and readily explicable. He is more than a figure in the dense literary history of Britain; he is a figure in world culture, as both hero and victim. Wilde is public, international. There have been biographies in many languages, translations into many languages; criticism and comparative criticism in many languages. Wilde has been too eminently appropriable. This, it is to be hoped, will justify what may seem our suspicious generalizations about *national* types of response. The life and writings have been too dramatic for many dramatists and too much like fiction for many novelists. Wilde entered pop culture long ago with the collections of epigrams, the calendars, the coffee-table biographies full of the same illustrations and the same anecdotes. Most important of all, there have been continuous revivals, on the stage, in the movies and on television. The life, the plays, the fiction all seem one. The absence of Wilde's Boswell is frequently lamented, but too much perhaps would have been explained away, had such existed; Wilde perhaps would have suffered the eclipse of Dr. Johnson's darkly witty masterpiece; didn't Macaulay go some way toward suggesting that Doctor Major was no more than a vivid character in Boswell's fiction?

The journalists and the populace have been perpetually fascinated, although the English pieces from before the fall are too many, too well known and too well documented to require listing here (typical are *Biograph and Review*, 1880, and *The Ludgate Monthly*, 1892). But fascination implies vulgarization, collusion, mutual and profitable hostility, till the game could be played no further. As early as 1889

Alice Meynell was heterogeneously yoking Wilde's name to her empty pomps in "The Unit of the World" (*Scots Observer*, 2 Feb. 1889). A New York paper in 1895 remarked that when the British press was unmuzzled, free of the laws of libel, it was the nastiest in the world; and the blow-by-blow accounts of the trial bore the judgment out. If ever a man was tried by the newspapers, it was Wilde.

One feature of his vivid *Nachwirkung*, of his "afterlife," has been till very lately marked: Anglo-Saxon academics have been hostile or indifferent, too busy, it may be, with that standard Anglo-Saxon article: "*Middlemarch*: re-Revisited." The entry for Wilde, for example, in the recent revise of the *Cambridge Bibliography of English Literature* is notable for the brilliance of its lacunae and, where it could bring itself to cite, the insecurity of its citations. It was an English scholar, unassisted by public funds, Christopher Millard (also known as Stuart Mason), who made the first and still usable attempt at a bibliography. It was an English scholar, unassisted by public funds, Sir Rupert Hart-Davis, who gave us an edition of the letters which is the best biography we have, whose publication in 1962 dramatically altered Wilde's fortunes. Work on Wilde has indeed been done by British academics, but rarely from Departments of English. Reactions to Wilde have been influenced by propaganda for an autonomous "modern movement" springing from the head of Ezra Pound and for a "new" criticism. It has been left to a still newer criticism to define a Wilde who played some considerable part in both that movement and that criticism.

As a figure not in English literature only, but in English social history, Wilde has been an embarrassment. Lady Singleton in "Concerning Some of the Enfants Trouvés of Literature" (*Nineteenth Century*, 1904) discussed both Wilde's poetry and that of some of his circle, but her apologetics could not involve mentioning the dangerous name. R. H. Gretton in his *The Modern History of the English People* (3 vols., 1913) observed.

> The case against Mr Wilde was, of course, no real indictment of aestheticism, but it was the end of the aesthete as he had been felt for fifteen years in social life. . . . In his assertion of the function of criticism, and in his richly varied vocabulary, lay his chief artistic claim. In his social gifts of wit and swiftness lay his most lasting effects. The widespread modern capacity for "taking things with a light hand," the distaste for solemn attitudes and obvious statements, the easy carrying of personal attainments, which formerly had taken some generations of high breeding to produce, may be largely traced to Oscar Wilde's influence. The particular form of wit for which he was most famous, the paradoxical epigram, was not exclusively his. . . . He bore a large part in a readjustment of values in life which survived his own fall. The crash of the fall certainly affected the whole spirit of this year. There were few great houses in London where he was not known; fewer still where there was not among the younger generation an aggressive, irresponsible intolerance which had some relation, however vague, to his brilliant figure.

Besides making even athletic types Aesthetic, Wilde is credited with having involuntarily assisted the triumph of Lord Salisbury's Conservatives in the Election of 1895. The notion of Wilde as a general cultural precedent was certainly well established. The Conservative Party was a party of Union and Empire and Wilde's vice was one with peculiar historical resonances; one of the popular theories for the collapse of earlier Empires was decline in moral standards and particularly the prevalence of homosexuality. In the desperate months of the last German offensive on the Western Front in 1918, the English could once more respond to Wilde and his works as threat to Empire: Pemberton Billing and the Maud Allan affair. These connections are also made in a letter of Robert Ross to Charles Ricketts. (Given in a truncated form in *Self-Portrait*, 1939. The letter is preserved among the Ricketts papers at the British Museum.) Ross quotes from a Danish newspaper: "but the English could do with a little German degeneracy, if that includes admiration for Wilde as they might then gain at least one victory in the field." Safe British ground was still well trodden after the end of the First World War, as can be established from another witness, E. T. Raymond in the *Outlook* of 4 Dec. 1920:

> those who would pass by this ill-starred man of genius because of the event which interrupted his career as a writer would be acting almost as foolishly as the absurd people (mostly Germans) who on the same account yield him a perverse and irrational homage. Wilde was not only important in himself; he was still more important as the representative of a mood still to some extent with us, but extraordinarily prevalent in the latter years of the nineteenth century. Of this mood he was in letters the only able English representative.

The perspective was still distorting: Raymond proceeds to argue that Wilde should have learned a trade. And in *The Old Drama and the New* (1923) William Archer decided that the continued popularity of Wilde in Germany must "be taken largely as a political demonstration —a wilful glorification of a man whom England cast out."

But the German homage had begun in Wilde's lifetime, is not altogether perverse or irrational, and demands attention at some length. Arnold Weiss (*Beilage zur Allgemeinen Zeitung*, 8 Feb. 1893) prefaced his remarks on Wilde's work up to that date with anecdotes. Nonetheless, though Weiss considered Wilde to be talented enough, he considered Wilde's work to be dominated and flawed by acute sensationalism and "aesthetomania," to say nothing of the questionable moral stance that Wilde exhibited as a person. Johannes Gaulke (*Die Gegenwart*, 1896) admitted that the work had been made famous by scandal, but claimed that some of it achieved a major status. The "red thread" that ran through all that Wilde had written was contempt for women and for the hypocrisies of British society. Much of Gaulke's piece paraphrased "The Soul of Man under Socialism." That essay proved Wilde to be the "fanatic high priest of the cult of personality" who should be credited with always searching for individual freedom and with compassion for proletarian suffering. Gaulke takes a similar stance in *Die Neue Zeit* (Stuttgart, 1897), and in yet another article (*Die Gegenwart*, 1901), he notes that the work no less than the man has been persecuted and that only *Salome* and various essays have appeared in German. This article concludes with an interpretative summary of *Dorian Gray*. Gaulke's own translations, like those of Greve, were to be as free as his criticism. Gaulke is an impressionist critic and not altogether typical of the German response. It is with the emergence of Max Meyerfeld as translator and apologist, and Franz Blei as critic, that the Wilde renaissance in Germany may be said to be truly formalized. The seminal article is Meyerfeld's "Oscar Wilde in Deutschland" (*Das Literarische Echo*, 1903; also, see his "Erinnerungen an Oscar Wilde," *Neue Deutsche Rundschau*, 1903). This provides a model for the more elaborate later bibliographies of Wilde in Germany such as Anselm Schlösser's *Die Englische Literatur in Deutschland von 1895 bis 1934* (Jena, 1937) and Rudolf Defeiber's *Oscar Wilde: Der Mann und sein Werk im Spiegel der Deutschen Kritik und sein Einfluss auf die Deutsche Literatur* (Heidelberg, 1934). Defeiber gives paraphrases of the many articles on Wilde which appeared in newspapers and periodicals in the earlier years of this century. According to Meyerfeld, Wilde's name was first introduced into Germany by Hermann Bahr, but the general public paid little attention until that famous spring of 1895. Commenting on the success of *Salome* and *The Importance of Being Earnest*, Meyerfeld doubted, wrongly as it happened, whether as representative of art for art's sake Wilde would ever become more popular in Germany. This article concludes by asking for better translations of Wilde into German than those of Gaulke, Greve, Teschenberg, and Pavia, and those furnished by the Spohr publishing house in Leipzig which specialized ostensibly in homosexual literature. Two years later Meyerfeld translated *De Profundis* as part of a series. In Germany as in other countries from its appearance as a public document, then as a private letter, that work controlled the image of Wilde and much of the discussion about him. Meyerfeld's translations were matched in excellence by those of Hedwig Lachmann, or Landauer, to use her married name.

One aspect of German scholarship was its concern with criminal pathology which was sometimes distinctly progressive but could also serve narrower purposes. H. Hauck in *Monatsschrift für Kriminalpsychologie und Strafrechtsreform* of 1910 uses Wilde to attack the apparently enlightened British penal system. The interest in Wilde over those years from 1903 coincided with the rise of German Expressionism; and from several sources we gather that Wedekind, Dehmel, Bierbaum, and other writers of that period found in Wilde a precursor. But Wilde was available to the Germans more widely as a culture counter. While a critic such as Adolf Danneger admires and censures with moderation (*Deutschland Monatsschrift für die Gesamte Kultur*, 1905), for others in those years of tensity in Anglo-German relations Wilde could readily serve the German concepts of *Kultur* and *Volk*—France, and more notably England, being countries without those ennobling features. Leo Colze (*Die Türmer*, 1913) was able to announce that because he "lived with his head" Wilde was void of the "Gemüt," let alone "Tiefe," that make an artist immortal. Wilde's popularity stemmed from the modern generation's failure to understand that search for beauty becomes a corrupt undertaking without the required basis (and this basis, we may easily infer, is "rootedness" in German *Volk*). The attitude incidentally extends itself even to English scholars of German culture. Wilde could be used to exemplify the decadence of England, but his martyrdom could also be presented as a crystallization of British hatred of *Kultur*. With the general public, as well as with the publicists, Wilde continued to be popular in Germany; he was read widely, his plays were acted; there was Richard Strauss's opera, and, according to Schlösser, before the Second World War he was the most popular English author in Germany, more popular even than Edgar Wallace. A further symptom of his popularity was his frequent appearance as a topic for German doctoral theses. The variety of Wilde's sources might testify to his aspiration to *Kultur*, might provide discipline for the doctoral candidate, but they became in themselves a *Hauptproblem*. What identity could an author of such lavish derivations possess? This crux was not altogether resolved, but source-studies and vocabulary statistics proliferated.

Even in the Nazi period, Wilde surprisingly flourished, assisted by the fact that the *index expurgatorius* of decadent literature related only to those who had died in 1904 or after. Wilde's plays ran during the Second World War, though doctored to suit the more sturdy wit and humor of the *Volk*. Karl Schaezler's "Brief zu einem Englischen Bild" (*Hochland*, 1939–40) indicated with what facility earlier interpretations of Wilde could be turned about just sufficiently to fit the propaganda machine. Schaezler discovered *Dorian Gray* in the soldiers' library. The novel, he tells us, is good literature and like all good literature a document of its time. It is no longer the wit of the decadence which lives, but rather Wilde's observations about the English and his own time in particular (as voiced by Lord Henry). "Wir haben in unserem Wahn Körper und Seele getrennt und einen Realismus erfunden, der gewöhnlich, einen Idealismus, der leer ist" forms the basis for an argument against the "Gewaltpolitik" of the English imperialists which is a materialistic, self-seeking means to an end and therefore "seelenlos" in comparison to the *Reich*. New empires always arise when body and soul part company, and the English nineteenth-century Empire has reached that decadent low point where morals come to be founded on pragmatism. The consequence is "Machtpolitik," which reached its climax in the First World War. It cannot be claimed that Wilde attempted with *Dorian Gray* to represent the typical Englishman, to be sure, but in *De Profundis*—the controlling document once more—he does claim to be the typical product of his times and concentrates in his works all the destructive intellectual subjectivity that has poisoned the air of the Occident and of England in particular. Wilde's book is not therefore actually immoral (*unsittlich*); it portrays the consequences of immorality (*Unsittlichkeit*). Dorian did not see the light, but *The Ballad of Reading Gaol* and *De Profundis* showed that Wilde himself was able to subdue egoism and find the way to ethos. The final moral is that in the same manner, the present war must subdue the "gewöhnlichen Realismus" and "leeren Idealismus" of the British liberal civilization (as differentiated from a *Kultur* understood), and *Dorian Gray* can be safely read to understand why.

To conclude on this note would be ungenerous and indeed unfair. The Germans were the first to take Wilde as a figure seriously and to treat the man and his work in a responsibly scholarly manner. If on occasion we have fretted against what appear to be certain limitations in their *Quellenstudien* approach, we remain fully aware of what the student owes to their pertinacity. Nor do we wish to imply that the better German work was accomplished before the Second World War. So rich indeed is the German offering that we can do no more here than mention some major studies and a scattering of the many periodical and newspaper items.

The French response has been more subtle and often more skeptical. From the beginning Wilde's personality tended to interest the French more than the works. He entered Paris like a Parisian but remained splendidly himself. There is the description in Henri Mondor's *Vie de Mallarmé* (Paris, 1941–42) of Wilde at one of Mallarmé's Tuesdays: "en habit, lustré, cosmétiqué, couvert de bijoux sur sa graisse molle." Wilde came as a master in 1893, even if as a master who was prepared to learn. But a number of the young French writers had masters already; and some, like Téodor de Wyzewa and Adolphe Retté, could distinguish little more than the portentous dandy-charlatan, later tragic, buffoon figure. Especially revealing here is Wyzewa's article in the *Revue Bleue* of 2 April 1892. *Lady Windermere's Fan* appeared to him "une pièce tout à fait parisienne" —the plot was Balzacian. *Dorian Gray* was a bad novel, and Wyzewa suggested sources (e.g., Frédéric Soulie). In *Intentions*, we are told, Wilde attacks the essentially English notion that there is a positive and invariable reality. Insisting on Wilde's debt to the French in protesting against English life, Wyzewa concludes that the prediliction for the artificial over the natural is really a Berlin taste. In spite of the cool tone, here and in the paragraph Wyzewa contributed to an anonymous review in the *Revue Bleue* (17 Apr. 1892), there is evidence of Wilde's being more appreciated outside England than within it, a pattern to be repeated after the trials and again after Wilde's death. Some of the younger French writers were indeed conquered: Pierre Louÿs, Octave Mirbeau, Marcel Schwob. Stuart Merrill admired him but in his first article on Wilde in *La Plume* of 1893 denied him major status. Merrill's later articles in that same magazine included a protest against the imprisonment in 1895, an *éloge* in 1900, and some comments on Adolphe Retté's remarks on Wilde in *Le Symbolisme, anecdotes et souvenirs* (Paris) in 1904. Nonetheless, the French contribution has certainly been more sympathetic than the Anglo-Saxon, if less massive and protracted than the German.

From the Irish little could be expected, and the expectation has not been disappointed. Wilde as a Protestant Anglo-Irishman who was tactless enough to succeed in England could hardly be expected to engage the interest, let alone the energies, of DeValera's Eire. Even his final conversion to Catholicism did not arouse attention in Ireland to the extent it did among Italian critics. There have, however, been useful contributions from Irish sources on Oscar's relation to the Wilde family.

An early American appreciation of Wilde's *Intentions*, although with an uncharacteristic suggestion that he abstain from serious topics, can be found in Agnes Repplier's *Essays in Miniature* (1892). The tour of 1882 left some lingering involvement, but it is only recently that American energy has been fully brought to bear. Karl Beckson's *Oscar Wilde: The Critical Heritage* (1970) testifies to the discipline of American scholarship, and from Susan Sontag and Philip Rieff we might gather precisely how the energy is likely to be directed in contemporary criticism: on Wilde as theoretician of culture. But also perhaps on the artist as outsider (though this is yesterday's news). Or again on Wilde deployed first as precursor of the New Criticism and then as antidote to it. In this respect, perhaps, Wilde is similar to Pater. (It remains one of the curiosities of writing about Wilde and about Pater that the same author is rarely able to do justice to both figures.) It all depends on where the emphasis is put: on the autonomy of art or on the subjectivity of the critic; Wilde obligingly allows both.

Wilde's capacity to engage in image-making games is endless. He provides good fodder for Freudians, and here perhaps we should offer some explanation for our evident doubts about the Freudian approaches. That it is possible to write on Wilde without being amusing, they amply prove: but, more fundamentally, our objections to them are not merely that they overlook historical context and meanings but that they often seem harshly unaware of the historicity of their own conclusions. The early diagnoses of sado-masochism make uninspiring reading; more recent accusations of sexual chauvinism (Freud-based) are partly polemical and may already be redundant.

Which brings us finally to Wilde's appeal to the gay vanguard, Wilde as Homintern Messiah. In *De Profundis*, Wilde publicly identified himself with Christ; and his posthumous reputation falls neatly enough within the paradigms of Christian (and gay) faction. There are floating *logia*; apocryphal gospels, pious and not so pious legends, while his mode of paradoxical discussion, his prose-poem parables, all recall the reported discourse of his great model. Heresies accumulate: Lord Alfred Douglas begins as St. John and ends as Judas, aided by the crass secular arm of T. W. H. Crosland, though Wilde himself claimed the role of his own Judas. Robert Ross, whose preferred part was that of Pope, is hounded to suicide; and the structure of *Aberglaube* is completed by Frank Harris' biographical, or rather autobiographical romance, with the imprimatur of Shaw. There are reports of unpublished works which will detonate scandal; precious fragments, forgeries, pious or commercial merely, multiply. Wilde's personality, but not his work, reigns. Then demythologizing ensues.

Given the difficulties we have outlined, we have not chosen to include everything written on Wilde, that figure who is all elusive foreground. What is not specially seminal, though it may not be without its own interest, has mostly been omitted. What is repetitious, fatuous, or of purely topical interest also finds no place: the endless English discussion of Wilde's "sincerity," for example. On the other hand, where an item relates to more than one part of the oeuvre, we have occasionally mentioned it in more than one of our segments.

A clever graduate student once observed, "How can I write anything about Wilde? He is always right about everything." Some have written about Wilde, holding an opposite belief; but more truth subsists in the remark than in the notion that Wilde is insincere, shallow, immoral, irremediably minor. It needs to be said unequivocally that Wilde is a major figure, a master of the moral life. In all their dealings with Wilde, the English have been wrong about practically everything.

I. Bibliographies

"Stuart Mason" (Christopher Millard) published his *Bibliography of Oscar Wilde* in 1914 (rpt. 1967 with an introd. by Timothy d'Arch Smith, who contributes a brief biography of Millard; there are glimpses of Millard in Osbert Burdett, *Memory and Imagination*, 1955). This supersedes Mason's earlier bibliography of the poems (1907). In some ways it remains an appropriate memorial to Wilde: a rambling compendium of information—biography and bibliography intermingled, the crucial and the trivial barely distinguished. Though Owen Dudley Edwards was justifiably scathing in his review of the photo reprint (*BC*, 1967) and pointed out several significant errors, the Wilde scholar must remain grateful for its existence, not least, as Ernst Bendz pointed out (*EngS*, 1915), for its reprinting some of Wilde's anonymous early articles. Mason also includes details of early collections of Wilde's epigrams and in an appendix lists a few of the critical articles that appeared in Wilde's lifetime and soon after his death. Mason does not, however, note that four of Wilde's poems appeared in *Lyra Hibernica Uacra* (comp. and ed. Rev. W. MacIlwaine, 1878), two being published there for the first time. The William Andrews Clark Library at Los Angeles contains Mason's own annotated and revised copy of his bibliography which he was preparing for publication at the time of his death.

A. Horodisch has furnished *A Bibliographical Study of Oscar Wilde's Ballad of Reading Gaol* (1954), which cites a number of translations. Numerous translations and some articles are listed and discussed in A. Schlösser's *Die Englische Literatur in Deutschland von 1895 bis 1934* (Jena, 1937). But by far the best bibliography of early German translations is by Helmut Reige in the German edition of Hart-Davis' *Letters: Oscar Wilde Briefe II. Anmerkungen* (Hamburg, 1966). Guillot de Saix, *Les Songes merveilleux du dormeur éveillé. Le chant du cygne: Contes parlés d'Oscar Wilde* (Paris, 1942) contains an extraordinarily wide if thoroughly ravelled bibliography of Wildeana with a particular emphasis on the French response. The inaccuracy of many of de Saix's entries must be stressed. However this bibliography does suggest that a search through inaccessible French papers such as *Comœdia* and *La Rumeur* might prove rewarding.

Donald L. Lawler is strongly and justly critical of the Wilde bibliography in the *NCBEL* (1969), which is as casual about Wilde as about a number of other figures of the late nineteenth century (*PBSA*, 1973). Lawler corrects several entries and lists many additional works. Minor bibliographical items include "R. W.," "Notes for a Bibliography of Wilde" (*Books and Bookplates*, 1904–5); L. I. Heber, *The Books, Manuscripts and Autograph Letters of Wilde* (1909), and Seymour de Ricci, *The Book Collector's Guide* (1921).

The catalog of the Tite Street sale has been made available by A. N. L. Munby in *Sale Catalogues of Libraries of Eminent Persons* (*in Facsimile*), Vol. 1, *Poets and Men of Letters* (1971). The most prominent of the sale catalogs are *Two Hundred Books from the Library of Richard Butler Glaenzer* (1911); J. M. Stetson's *Wilde Collection* (1920); and Dulau & Co., Booksellers, *A Collection of the Original Manuscripts, Letters and Books of Oscar Wilde* (1928). The Glaenzer catalog has a preface by the vendor commenting on the evidence from his collection of manuscripts as to Wilde's exacting self-criticism. Some rare and fugitive items are also listed. The Dulau catalog contains several items of Wildeana not included in Mason and is useful for the bibliography of such Continental critics as Ernst Bendz and Georges-Bazile.

Sarah Augusta Dickson's introduction to the four-act version of *The Importance of Being Earnest* (2 vols., 1956), lists the known manuscripts of that play and reconstructs Wilde's preferred version.

For the major libraries with holdings of Wilde manuscripts, the following may be consulted: *The Library of William Andrews Clark, Wilde and Wildeana* (1922–31), supplemented and in general superseded by J. C. Finzi, *Wilde and His Literary Circle . . .* (1957); the catalog of *An Exhibition on the Occasion of the Opening of the T. E. Hanley Library . . .* (1958); "The Arents Tobacco Collection" by S. A. Dickson (*BNYPL*, 1950); "The Katharine S. Drier Collection of Oscar Wilde" by Donald C. Wing (*YULG*, 1953). The Bodleian has a typewritten catalog, *Collection of Original Manuscripts, Printed Books, Pamphlets and Periodicals Relating to Oscar Wilde*, the property of H. M. Hyde (n.p., 1951), containing transcripts of letters to Hyde from Douglas and others and a voluminous list of Wildeana. For the Hyde library also, see G. C. Austin's edition of *Four Oaks Library* (1967) in which H. Montgomery Hyde describes his Wilde collection, now at Four Oaks. Michael Pinhorn briefly discusses his collection in *The Private Library* (1960).

Catalogs of exhibitions include the Trinity College, Dublin, Library *Catalogue of An Exhibition of Books in Commemoration of the Centenary of the Birth of Oscar Wilde* (1954); and *Wilde and the '90s*, the descriptive catalog of an exhibition held at Princeton in 1966, which contains also a printing of Richard Ellmann's "The Critic as Artist as Wilde," an essay by E. D. H. Johnson on the nineties in general, and photographs of Wilde's manuscripts.

Lionel Stevenson discusses criticism of Wilde's poetry in *The Victorian Poets: A Guide to Research* (ed. Frederic E. Faverty, 1956); and Wendell V. Harris discusses criticism of Wilde's critical prose in *Victorian Prose: A Guide to Research* (ed. David J. DeLaura, 1973). There is a brief and distinctly inadequate entry on Wilde in Paul F. Breed and Florence M. Sniderman, *Dramatic Criticism Index* (1972).

Wilde items are included in the annual bibliographies in the following periodicals: *ELT, IUR, MD, Nineteenth Century Theatre Research, VN, VS*; and in the *MLA International Bibliography*.

N. A. Salerno is engaged on the compilation and editing of "Oscar Wilde: An Annotated Bibliography of Writings about Him," for inclusion in the Annotated Secondary Bibliographies Series under the general editorship of H. E. Gerber. H. J. Lethbridge is preparing a select bibliography of the Continental response to Wilde.

II. Editions

Of Wilde's work, there is no satisfactory edition. All editions that purport to be such are incomplete, inadequate textually, and void of proper annotation. The first attempt at collection was made in the New York edition of 1907. This was in fifteen volumes and limited to 450 copies. It includes the *Impressions of America*, edited by Stuart Mason, facsimiles of letters and of the fragment of an unpublished manuscript in prose; the public correspondence between Wilde and Whistler; "L'Envoi" to *Rose Leaf and Apple Leaf* by J. Rennell Rodd (1882), and what claims to be the "unexpurgated" version of *De Profundis* as translated from the German by Henry Zick, accompanied by four letters relating to the work from Wilde to Robert Ross. There are a few useful and indeed entertaining illustrations, and two apocryphal works: the translation from Barbey d'Aurevilly, *What Never Dies*, and *The Priest and the Acolyte* by J. F. Bloxam, republished from *The Chameleon* (1894). The last volume contains a not markedly illuminating life and critical estimate which quotes from a manuscript of *The Ballad of Reading Gaol*. The standard edition is that by Robert Ross, Wilde's literary executor (1908–22; rpt. 1969); the fifteenth volume added in 1922 contains the apocryphal *For Love of the King*. Certain material was not available to Ross; and the edition is not complete, particularly in the verse and the criticism. It can be supplemented by the Doubleday Page edition, (12 vols., 1923), which was several times reprinted. This is also useful for the introductions to the separate volumes by Richard Le Gallienne, W. B. Yeats, Sir J. Forbes-Robertson, Coulson Kernahan, Edgar Saltus, A. B. Walkley, Arthur Symons, Padraic Colum, John Drinkwater, and others (see *The Critical Heritage*). The Doubleday edition drops *The Priest and the Acolyte* but retains the supposititious *What Never Dies*. It collects some fugitive poems and the early translations from Greek drama.

A new collected edition of the works, in preparation for the Oxford University Press by Owen Dudley Edwards, will take available manuscript sources into account and will probably mark as decisive a moment in Wilde scholarship as the publication of Sir Rupert Hart-Davis' edition of *The Letters* (1962) or of Richard Ellmann's biography when that appears.

There exist numerous selections from Wilde's work. Few can be relied on in textual matters, and whatever value they possess is in general confined to the introductory matter. Such introductions are often by creative writers and so have a double interest. Among this class may be mentioned that by Richard Aldington (1946) which in America appears in the Viking *Portable Wilde*. Aldington's introduction is brisk and luminously commonsensical. A number of sound if barely original observations are purveyed: on Wilde's relation to the nineteenth-century tradition of the Dandy; on Wilde's distancing of his own earlier criticism by involving it in the more open texture of *Intentions*; and on the iterative incantatory language of *Salome*; but none of these topics is altogether developed.

The *Poems and Essays* (ed. Kingsley Amis, 1956) is judiciously selected and includes a large clutch of poems along with the *Rise of Historical Criticism*. The introduction is agreeably noisy, reflecting the esthetics of that sect of British poets of the 1950's, "the Movement," and Amis' very personal predilections. Amis' comments on the poetry are discretely outlined under the appropriate section. Amis tends to denigrate the depth or method of the criticism, part of his emphasis on Wilde the dandy. "The Critic as Artist," for example, is not "a reflective dissertation, but a cultural exhibition-bout, a jazz version of Ruskin." *De Profundis* fails: "it is a demonstration in truly pathetic detail of the impairment of the intelligence through suffering." The sincerity embarrasses (the wheel has indeed turned full circle in Anglo-Saxon criticism of Wilde). *The Soul of Man under Socialism* Amis admires as a "neo-Arnoldian" assault on Philistinism.

Richard Ellmann's introduction to the *Selected Works* (1961) presents an eloquent if somewhat narrow version of the subject. Ellman's second selection, *The Artist as Critic* (1968), contains a wide-ranging and programmatically chosen number of critical texts and reviews, some of them little known. In a dense and suggestive introduction Ellmann argues Wilde's "modernity," largely through accumulation of insights in Wilde that anticipate such later writers as Gide, Mann, Cavafy, and Genet. Wilde was one of the first to insist, for example, that exaltation of the artist involves a corresponding exaltation of the critic. In his mature work, Wilde's stance was polemical as a spokesman for the young, and he is compared with Nietzsche, though Wilde reshuffles rather than transvalues traditional ethical concepts. Wilde's view of art was double: art was disengaged from life yet deeply incriminated with it; in Wilde can be found the artist-criminal equation and the ethical justification of criminality that becomes entirely explicit in Genet. These comments are substantiated by continuous reference to Wilde's texts.

The *Essays* have been edited with an introduction by Hesketh Pearson (1950). Here, the introduction has only a moderate critical value. The *Complete Works* (ed. J. B. Foreman, introd. Vyvyan Holland; new ed., 1966), if not complete, is more complete than most.

Stanley Weintraub's *The Literary Criticism of Oscar Wilde* (1968) gives a generous and annotated selection with a solid introduction and is a good alternative to Ellmann.

Among the selections in many languages of aphorisms from Wilde's published writings and reported conversations are *Oscariana* (1895, 1910)—the 1895 volume was supposedly chosen by Mrs. Wilde: the 1910 selection differs from it; *The George Alexander Birthday Book* (1903); *Sebastian Melmoth (Oscar Wilde)* (1904); *Epigrams and Aphorisms* (1905); Oscar Herrmann and W. W. Massee, *The Best of*

Oscar Wilde (1905); Temple Scott, *The Wisdom of Oscar Wilde* (1906, 1908); Stuart Mason, *The Oscar Wilde Calendar* (1910), *Great Thoughts from Oscar Wilde* (1912); G. N. Sutton, *Aphorisms of Oscar Wilde* (1914); F. Stocchetti, *L'Amore e le donne* (Genoa, 1916); Louis Thomas, *L'Esprit de Wilde* (Paris, 1920); Léon Treich, *L'Esprit de Wilde* (1926); A. Redman, *The Witticisms of Oscar Wilde, An Anthology* (1952); L. J. C. Boucher, *Epigrammen* (The Hague, 1958); Cecil Hewetson, *Wit and Wisdom of Oscar Wilde* (1960, 1967); S. McCann, *The Wit of Oscar Wilde* (1969); D. Stanford, *Witticisms of Oscar Wilde* (1971).

Some of Wilde's prose poems appeared in *The Spirit Lamp* (1893); *FortR* (1894); *La Revue Blanche* (1899). There are further selections in *Poèmes en prose* (trans. Charles Grolleau, preface by Jacques Desroix, Paris, 1906—not in Mason), *Mercure de France* (1926) and in an undated volume, privately produced by Gabrielle Enthoven, entitled *Echoes*. The last two contain versions of "Jezebel." *Poems in Prose and Private Letters* (1919) has a brief preface by Frank Harris, six prose poems, four prison letters to Ross reprinted from the edition of 1906 along with Rennell Rodd's Italian quatrain: "Al tuo martiro cupido e feroce." Four prose poems said to be previously unpublished are contained in Vyvyan Holland's *Son of Oscar Wilde* (1954); two of these had in fact previously appeared in *Pegasus* (1915). "Phrases and Philosophies for the Use of the Young" appeared in *The Chameleon* (1894). Hart-Davis printed "A Few Maxims for the Instruction of the Over-Educated" in *The Letters*. Other aphorisms of this order remain in manuscript.

Kevin H. F. O'Brien has reconstructed Wilde's lecture "The House Beautiful" (*VS*, 1974) from fragments of manuscript and conflation of various newspaper accounts. The lecture was also used by Wilde during his intermittent lecture tours in Britain between 1883 and 1887. O'Brien comments on the sources, particularly relating Wilde's text to Morris, but perhaps rather mutes Wilde's indebtedness to the various manuals of the Aesthetic movement, Mrs. Haweis, Loftus, and others. O'Brien is at present working on an edition of the American lectures based on his 1973 dissertation (Notre Dame). An 1882 San Francisco lecture delivered by Wilde entitled "Irish Poets and the Poetry of the Nineteenth Century," identical presumably with "Irish Poets '48," has been lavishly reconstructed by Robert D. Pepper from manuscript sources and newspaper reports and printed as a monograph (1972). The unpublished notes for this same lecture have been edited by Michael J. O'Neill (*UnivR*, 1955). An annotated edition of the anonymous criticism has been compiled in a 1970 dissertation by C. Markgraf (Univ. of Calif., Riverside).

The title of Thomas Moult's "A Newly Discovered Essay on Poetry by Oscar Wilde" (*Voices*, 1920) is misleading—it is in fact a reprint of "L'Envoi" to *Rose Leaf and Apple Leaf*.

Some Early Poems and Fragments (ed. Alan Anderson, 1970) contains eight uncollected items from the W. A. Clark Library; and *Remorse: A Study in Saffron* (1961) with a note by Majl Ewing is from the same source. The poem is dated 10 November 1889, though that is not necessarily the date of composition, but the date on which the manuscript was given to a friend. "Rabboni" appeared in *The*

Papyrus (1909), while *To M[argaret]. B[urne-]. J[ones].* (1920) appeared in *Coterie* (1920–21) and in an edition of 65 copies. Both printings have a note by Mason appended which gives the *terminus ad quem* as September 1888, the date of the lady's marriage.

DUBIA AND APOCRYPHA

A fairly extensive list could be compiled of apocryphal works attributed to Wilde. The translation of d'Aurevilly's *Ce qui ne meurt pas* (1902), is sometimes falsely ascribed to him (see *RAA*, 1927), as is Petronius' *The Satyricon* (1902). (The Widow of Ephesus episode was reprinted in *The Golden Book Magazine* of 1933.) *For Love of the King* (1922) is discussed under drama. *Teleny*, which is attributed to Wilde and some of his circle, was published by Leonard Smithers in 1893; in an expurgated edition with introduction by H. Montgomery Hyde (1966); in an American paperback edition (1966).

"Reconstructions" based on ideas attributed to Wilde should also be used with caution. Examples are "Jezebel" or as it sometimes appears "Ahab and Isabel" (so Wilde pronounced the latter name), "Drame inédit en un acte" put together by Guillot de Saix on the basis of plans that Wilde discussed with Ada Leverson and Ross in Paris (*Mercure de France*, 1937), and *La Femme couverte de joyaux*, "inédite établie" by de Saix (*L'Age Nouveau*, 1938), which is related to *La Sainte Courtisane*. Also see G. P. Monkshood, "Oscar Wilde's only unpublished play," *Reynold's Weekly Newspaper*, 23 Aug. 1903, and Georges-Bazile, "*La Sainte Courtisane*" (*Mercure de France*, 1911). Some of de Saix's reconstructions are taken from recognizable sources; about the origins of others, he is silent. "Une Tragédie de femme par Wilde" (*Mercure de France*, 1938) is de Saix's translation of *A Woman's Tragedy*; and he produced congregations of stories and prose poems attributed to Wilde (*Nouvelle Revuen Française*, 1939; *Mercure de France*, 1940; *Les Oeuvres libres*, 1949). His *Les Songes merveilleux du dormeur éveillé* is the summation of de Saix's eccentric activities: it contains nearly a hundred short stories reputedly told by Wilde, many of them with annotation and commentary. "Cupid and the Lion" (*The Golden Book Magazine*, 1934) is a piece without distinction and without source. The Germans, active in all fields of translation, have not neglected the apocryphal writings: Schlösser lists five volumes appearing between 1906 and 1925, the most elaborate being *Der Priester und der Messnerknabe, und andere Apokryphe Erzählungen* (also includes *Die Orangenschale* and *Old Bishops*), translated by Sybille and Franz Blei (1925).

III. Letters

The publication of Sir Rupert Hart-Davis' magnificent edition of *The Letters of Oscar Wilde* (1962) may yet come to be seen as the start of a new era in Wilde studies. While it does not include every lunch invitation issued by Wilde, the achievement is immense: of the

1,298 letters that Hart-Davis collected, 1,008 are reproduced. The book is divided chronologically into sections, each with its own introduction. *The Letters* includes the definitive transcription of *De Profundis*, and there are appendices containing additional letters from such figures as Campbell Dodgson and Otho Holland Lloyd. Hart-Davis standardizes spelling and the text generally; the volume is splendidly illustrated, its apparatus is flawless, and the footnotes, the fruit of intensive research, in themselves contain more information on Wilde than is available in any other single work. So while it may not be true to assert, as did the *TLS* (29 June 1962), that this edition supplants the need for a biography, nevertheless the overall presentation of the material is so thorough that it will continue to stand as the primary bibliographical and biographical source for all aspects of Wilde scholarship.

The Letters subsumes earlier collections such as *Children in Prison and Other Cruelties of Prison Life* (1898), which reprinted the *Daily Chronicle* letters; *Four Letters (to Robert Ross) . . . Which Were Not Included in the English Edition of "De Profundis"* (1906); *Outlook* (1913); *Resurgam*: unpublished letters with a foreword by C. K. Shorter (1917); the two sets of letters edited by More Adey: *After Reading* (1921) and *After Berneval* (1922)—editorial background given in Hart-Davis; *Some Letters from Oscar Wilde to Lord Alfred Douglas* (1924) with illustrative notes by Arthur C. Dennison, Jr., and Harrison Post and an essay by A. S. W. Rosenbach; *Sixteen Letters from Oscar Wilde to William Rothenstein* (ed. John Rothenstein, 1930); and the thirty-three Oxford letters included in Vyvyan Holland, *Son of Oscar Wilde* (1954). The two Adey volumes were sympathetically reviewed by "Bernard Lintot" (*Today*, 1924; *Littell's Living Age*, 1924).

The Letters can be supplemented by *Whistler versus Wilde*, privately printed in 1906, which usefully juxtaposes the public letters and telegrams between the two strategists of publicity; and *Letters to the Sphinx* (1930), which has reminiscences of Wilde by the "Sphinx" herself, Ada Leverson.

The extraordinary nature of *The Letters* inspired many reviewers to respond to it with what amounted to full-scale essays. It not only revived questions about the relationship between the life and the work, but provided at last the evidence for those questions to be properly addressed. A most honest response came from W. H. Auden (*NY*, 9 Mar. 1963; rpt. *De Profundis*, ed. Hart-Davis, 1964; *Twentieth Century Views*; and *Forewords and Afterwords*, 1973). Consistent interest is shown throughout the reviews in *De Profundis*, the letters on prison reform, and the lifestyle of the post-prison years. Most readers of the letters perceived an apparently inevitable progression in a career which struck them as containing elements of genuine tragedy. (See *Commonweal*, 1962; *QR*, 1962; *SAQ*, 1964; *NewS*, 29 June 1962; *NL*, 1967.) Not that everyone emerged from the experience of reading the letters with renewed admiration for Wilde. George Steiner compared them unfavorably with the letters of D. H. Lawrence (*KR*, 1963), and Cyril Connolly displayed an impatience with the man and his milieu (*Previous Convictions*, 1963). Simone de

Beauvoir was more generous in her comments (*All Said and Done*, 1974). A fairly full list of reviews can be found in the annual bibliographies of *VS* for 1962 and 1963.

Since Hart-Davis a few additional letters have appeared. They include "Oscar Wilde and the People's Palace" (*East London Papers*, 1963); a letter to Edward Rose (*BNYPL*, 1964); "Oscar Wilde and Gabriel Sarrazin: A New Wilde Letter" (*EA*, 1965); three letters to George Macmillan (*Letters to Macmillan*, ed. Simon Nowell-Smith, 1967); a letter to Elizabeth Marbury (*ELN*, 1971); letters to E. T. Cook and W. T. Stead, very inaccurately annotated by Joseph O. Baylen (*The Serif*, 1971); and a letter to Cunninghame Graham (*N & Q*, 1976). Four letters to Douglas written in April and May 1895, which were translated into French for an abortive article and subsequently translated by Stuart Mason back into English, the language in which they appear in Hart-Davis, were finally published in French (*NRF*, 1966). A letter from Constance to Wilde, written just before their marriage, has been printed in *The Golden Book Magazine* (1933). There are two letters from Constance to Sherard in "Oscar Wilde en prison d'après des lettres inédites" (*Figaro Littéraire*, 27 Jan. 1966).

IV. Manuscripts

After the sack of No. 16 Tite Street, Chelsea, Wilde's home in April 1895, his effects, including manuscripts, were widely scattered. Some disappeared and have never been recovered; some have emerged from time to time at sales and become available to inspection if purchased by major libraries or public-spirited individuals; others Wilde gave to friends, and certain of these are not so readily traceable.

The most complete record survives of the plays in various drafts. The New York Public Library has a shortened version of the first draft of *The Importance of Being Earnest* and an earlier draft of Acts III and IV of the four-act version; manuscripts of parts of *The Duchess of Padua* and of *A Florentine Tragedy*; seven poems, including an early draft of *The Sphinx* and "The Harlot's House." Of the critical prose, there is a manuscript of "The Function of Criticism," the draft of "The Irish Poets of '48," and part of an unpublished essay on "Hellenism," of which a further part is to be found in the William Andrews Clark Memorial Library at Los Angeles.

The Clark Library possesses two fragments of unpublished plays, "Beatrice and Astone Manfredi" and "A Wife's Tragedy." Of *The Duchess of Padua*, there is a manuscript with corrections, additions, and annotations; of *An Ideal Husband*, an early original draft, a typescript with holograph corrections and emendations of 1894, and proofs containing revisions of some additions in holograph, while some fragmentary passages from this play are to be found in a notebook containing also a text of *La Sainte Courtisane* identical with the published version. Of *Lady Windermere's Fan* there is a typescript under the earlier title "A Good Woman," another typescript, and an acting version in manuscript (not Wilde's). A typescript of "Mrs. Arbuthnot," the earlier title of *A Woman of No Importance*, has corrections and emendations in Wilde's hand. Of *Vera, or the Nihilists*, there is an early manuscript version in a notebook which contains other miscellaneous writings. Of the fiction, there is a manuscript draft in 23 pages of *The Picture of Dorian Gray* with many corrections and alterations; an autograph leaf from Chapter v with erasures and corrections; and a typescript of 231 pages with corrections and emendations in Wilde's hand. Among the numerous poems, published and unpublished, in typescript and manuscript, there are three drafts of *The Sphinx*, all fragmentary, one with fourteen verses set out in the *In Memoriam* stanza form, and a manuscript of 90 stanzas of the poem. Of the criticism, there is a manuscript of "The True Function and Value of Criticism" of 1890; a considerable fragment in 70 pages of an 1886 essay on Chatterton designed for *The Century Guild Hobby Horse*; and a commonplace book with unpublished personal notes.

Material at the University of Texas includes an acting typescript of *A Woman of No Importance* with manuscript revisions and notes by Wilde, Beerbohm Tree, and others; a notebook of 1891 containing a manuscript of *Salome* extensively revised and corrected; a typescript with authorial corrections of "A Good Woman"; another early typescript; and an acting version in manuscript (not Wilde's). Additionally, Texas is rich in letters to and from Wilde.

The British Museum contains an autograph and typescript of *Epistola in Carcere et Vinculis* (*De Profundis*) (Add. Ms. 50141 A & B); poems, in particular *The Sphinx* with designs by Charles Ricketts (Add. Ms. 37942); and a number of early autograph drafts and typescripts of the plays. *Lady Windermere's Fan* (Add. Ms. 37943) is. a first draft with corrections and additions. This version is incomplete and distinctly differs from the published version, while of "Mrs. Arbuthnot" there are two typed versions with autograph corrections, the second of 92 folios being nearer to the published version (Add. Mss. 37944 and 37945). Of *An Ideal Husband* there are a number of drafts of which Act iv appears to represent the earliest version (Mabel Chiltern appears as Violet). The title in this version is "Mrs. Cheveley." Acts i, iia, and iii belong to a later version, and iib to one still later (Add. Ms. 37946). A typed copy of this play involves autograph corrections and is nearer than any of the other drafts to the printed version (Add. Ms. 37947). Of "Lady Lancing," as *The Importance of Being Earnest* was first entitled, there is an early draft of Acts iii and iv which in the printed version were conflated into Act iii. At f.1 is a draft in pencil of part of the final passage of Act i (Add. Ms. 37948). Acting versions of the plays are to be found among the Lord Chamberlain's papers (Add. Ms. 53707). They are listed in the Register, Vol. iv, 1887–1897. There are also letters to Mrs. C. C. Stopes, 13 from Constance Wilde and 14 from Oscar, dictated on *Woman's World* notepaper (Add. Ms. 58454); these reveal Constance's strong involvement both with *Woman's World* and with the *Rational Dress Society Gazette*.

At the Houghton Library, Harvard, is to be found a typescript with extensive autograph corrections dated London 1893–94 of two versions of *An Ideal Husband* along with four diagrams of stage settings. Harvard also holds letters and telegrams.

The Beinecke Library at Yale has poems, lectures, "The Star Child," and an early draft of *Vera*; the Huntington Library, San Marino, California, has poems and manuscripts of two of Wilde's American lectures. Other sources are Princeton; the Rosenbach Foundation, Philadelphia, which has manuscripts of "The Portrait of Mr. W. H.", the sonnet "On the Sale by Auction of Keats's Love Letters," and some other letters along with a late manuscript of *Salome* with corrections by Pierre Louÿs and re-corrections by Wilde; the Bodmer library, near Geneva; and the Pierpont Morgan Library, New York, which has an autograph of *The Picture of Dorian Gray*. The private collection of Mrs. Donald F. Hyde contains what was the collection of H. Montgomery Hyde, including an early draft of *The Sphinx*; "The Function of Criticism," the earlier version of "The Critic as Artist," the draft of a lecture on "The Irish Poets of '48"; and part of an essay on "Hellenism," of which another portion is to be found at the Clark Library. The Bodleian, Oxford, contains mostly transcripts, including a version of *De Profundis*, *Epistola in Carcere et Vinculis*, the source being in most cases Robert Ross.

Sale catalogs still constitute a useful source for our knowledge of unpublished and variant material. Some of these catalogs have already been listed in section 1; here, the Benet and Anderson Galleries New York and Maggs Brothers and Sotheby's of London may be mentioned.

This cursory list of some of the major manuscripts will sufficiently indicate the importance of a proper study of manuscript material. The dramatic manuscripts, in particular, indicate the care with which Wilde worked.

V. *Biography*

Few literary figures can have had as much written about their lives as Oscar Wilde, and yet until the publication of *The Letters* essential information was repeatedly obscured by inaccuracy and distortion. The need for an authoritative biography remains as urgent as ever. For instance, the early biographies—especially those of Douglas and Sherard—tend to suffer from vested interests. All are highly partisan and bedeviled by feuds and jealous bids for possession.

Lord Alfred Douglas wrote four separate books on his relationship with Wilde, but they are all characterized by petulant defense of himself and vindictiveness toward others. Douglas' own monstrous ego always overshadows his descriptions of Wilde; his views are of no help or even interest to the literary critic, and extremely dubious biographically. Douglas' career never escaped the taint of 1895, and as the years went by he became more of a social anomaly; his books remain a sad monument to a squalid episode. Invariably he returns to the Ransome libel case of 1913 as the most typical instance of the persecution that he felt he had always suffered and as the most important suit in a lifetime of litigation. The facts of the matter are these. In the course of writing his book on Wilde, Arthur Ransome was given access by Robert Ross to certain documents which included the unpublished parts of *De Profundis* and correspondence between Wilde and Douglas. On the basis of this material Ransome seemed to imply in his book that Douglas had been in part responsible for Wilde's downfall. Douglas then sued Ransome but lost his case when the documents, including the passages from *De Profundis* (which Douglas claimed never to have seen), were read out in court. The suspicion was that Ross had unfairly withheld documents earlier and had supplied them to Ransome only in order to blacken Douglas' name. This suit provoked another in which Douglas was accused of libeling Ross by calling him a blackmailer and a homosexual. The full history of these and other cases can be read in *Bosie* (1963) by Rupert Croft-Cooke. The experience in court recharged Douglas' compulsion to clear himself of guilt, although from then on he had to take account of the damaging evidence from *De Profundis*. The important point for Wilde scholars is that it seems unlikely that Douglas, who was paranoid and deceitful by nature, ever felt sufficiently confident to tell plainly what had occurred between himself and Wilde.

Douglas contributed a signed review of *Salome to The Spirit Lamp* (Oxford, 1893, rpt. *The Critical Heritage*). An article intended for *Mercure de France* never appeared there, so that Douglas' first comments on Wilde published after the trial (but made before he had knowledge of *De Profundis*) are in "Introduction à mes poèmes avec quelques considérations sur l'affaire Oscar Wilde" (*La Revue Blanche*, 1 June 1896; also see 15 June 1896.) *Oscar Wilde and Myself* (1914) is the most notorious and indefensible of the books that bear Douglas' name. Produced in collaboration with the journalist T. W. H. Crosland, whose free verse tirade *The First Stone* (1912) had been written in response to *De Profundis* (see W. Sorley-Brown, *Lord Alfred Douglas: The Man and the Poet*, 1918 and *The Life and Genius of T. W. H. Crosland*, 1928), *Oscar Wilde and Myself* has as its main plank that Douglas was "a mere child," an innocent, when he met Wilde. It also contains Douglas' most sustained attempt to denigrate Wilde's achievements as an artist. The book was thoroughly, and probably definitively, reviewed by Ernst Bendz (*EngS*, 1915–16). For an account of a meeting that took place before the First World War see Max Meyerfeld's "Bosies Quittung" (*Das Literarische Echo*, 1916). In "All's Well with England," a sonnet, Douglas attacks Ross, but there are slight signs of a warmer attitude toward Wilde's work in an article in *Plain Speech* (1921). Much of the *Autobiography of Lord Alfred Douglas* (1929; in America as *My Friendship with Oscar Wilde*, 1932) is taken up with attacks on Harris, Ross, and Sherard, but there are some details of Douglas' subsequent life and of his financial dealings with Wilde. In *Without Apology* (1938) he expresses his regret over *Oscar Wilde and Myself* and tells the story of the collaboration over *Mr. and Mrs. Daventry* in a further attempt to run Harris down. Finally in *Oscar Wilde* (1940) Douglas goes to some lengths to make amends for his initial treachery. The tone is mild and conciliatory, and Douglas allows himself to make a personal statement of opinion about homosexuality. He comments on other books about Wilde and his own statements about Wilde's writings are more moderate than before. But whether Douglas' sequence of books is evidence as a whole of growing self-knowledge remains an open question.

A number of obscurely produced pamphlets appeared over the years in connection with Douglas' quarrels. They include Harris and Douglas, *New Preface to "The Life and Confessions of Oscar Wilde"* (1925) and R. H. Sherard, *A Letter from Lord Alfred Douglas on André Gide's Lies about Himself and Oscar Wilde* (Calvi, 1933). Also see *The Academy* (1908, rpt. *The Critical Heritage*); Douglas' doggerel poem *The Rossiad* (2nd. ed., 1916); *Mercure de France* (1 Feb. 1929); *Carmina* (1931, 1932).

The most thoroughly researched life of Douglas is *Bosie*. The particular strength of this book, apart from its detail, is that the author knew his subject personally, although he is perhaps too generous to him in consequence. Croft-Cooke tried hard to be fair to Ross at the same time but hardly succeeds; nor is *Bosie* of much interest to the literary critic. Patrick Braybrooke's *Lord Alfred Douglas: His Life and His Work* (1931) is an absurd attempt to rehabilitate Douglas by exalting his poetry, and William Freeman's *The Life of Lord Alfred Douglas, Spoilt Child of Genius* (1948) is full of basic errors.

The main events of the relationship are recounted again in *ContempR* (1962), and, in Dutch, in *NVT* (1970). Percy Colson and the Marquess of Queensberry's *Oscar Wilde and the Black Douglas* (1948) is a history of the Queensberry family and most notable for its revealing introduction by Montgomery Hyde and copious quotation from the Queensberry family papers. There are appendices, "The Portrait of Mr. W. H." and "Oscar Wilde and the Problem of Sexual Inversion." The book was, however, harshly reviewed in the *TLS* by John Sparrow (24 Nov. 1950) along with other works concerning Douglas. Sparrow's essay is reprinted with some revisions in his *Independent Essays* (1963).

If Douglas never transcended his bitter resentments, Robert Harborough Sherard, a loyal friend to Wilde in his later years, never broke free of a dog-like devotion. The determination to protect Wilde at all costs results in some bizarre omissions. For instance, *Oscar Wilde: The Story of an Unhappy Friendship* (1902, 1905) contains no reference to Douglas and no indication as to the nature of Wilde's offense. Instead there is fulsome praise ("Oscar Wilde, as I knew him, was the purest man in word and deed that I have ever met") and only the safest of anecdotes, many to do with Wilde's stays in Paris. *The Life of Oscar Wilde* (1906) puts forward the thesis that Wilde's weaknesses (still unspecified) were caused by a hereditary susceptibility to alcohol and, to a lesser extent, exposure to corrupt environments. Sherard is scathing about Wilde's youth in Oxford and London, although he includes useful information on the early lectures and the visit to America, as well as on Wilde's family background. ("Jacta Alea Est" is reprinted in this volume.) Wilde's reputation is defended against English contempt by reference to his Continental admirers. But the overall chronology of the book is unclear, and the estimations of Wilde's character, including a comparison with Napoleon, remain preposterous. Sherard's version of events was discussed at some length by Max Meyerfeld in *Berlinische Zeitung* (30 Sept. 1906). *The Real Oscar Wilde* (1917) was intended as a supplement to *The Life* and was apparently prompted by the Ransome case and Douglas' behavior. Much of it is taken up with minor quibbles such as Wilde's hairstyle and dress, but the influence of Swinburne is stressed and there is information about Wilde's freemasonry and friends such as Hermann Vezin and Ellen Terry. The account of Wilde's final years is more detailed. Sherard also discusses Wilde's last phase in *Reynold's Newspaper* (21 June 1903), *Twenty Years in Paris* (1905), and *Modern Paris* (1921). Sherard continued his self-appointed role as custodian of Wilde's memory in *Oscar Wilde, "Drunkard and Swindler". A Reply to George Bernard Shaw* (Calvi, 1933); *André Gide's Wicked Lies about the late Mr. Oscar Wilde in Algiers in January, 1895, as Translated from the French and Broadcast by Dr. G. J. Renier* (Calvi, 1933); *Oscar Wilde Twice Defended* (1934), in which he replied to Gide, Harris, and Renier; and *TLS* (15 Oct. 1938). In his review of Sherard's *The Real Oscar Wilde* (*EngS*, 1916) Ernst Bendz remarked on its "apologetic vein," which he suggests was the result of Sherard's lack of real intimacy with Wilde. There is no doubt some truth in this. (Also see *SatR*, 2 June–28 July 1928.) The student of Wilde's *Nachwirkung* should not neglect the Sherard papers in the University of Reading archive. These include letters written to Sherard by Alfred Douglas, Vyvyan Holland, Robert Ross, Frank Harris, Warder Martin of Reading Gaol, A. J. A. Symons, Reginald Turner, and numerous others. There are copies of letters written by Sherard himself over thirty years; newspaper cuttings 'and photographs, while among the diaries is one specifically relating to *Oscar Wilde Twice Defended* and covering the years 1933-39.

Though no doubt well intended, the activities of Robert Ross have always been historically suspect, particularly when they concerned the handling of Wilde's papers. The main source of information about him is *Friend of Friends* (ed. M. Ross, 1952); it collects letters to Ross and selects from Ross's papers, which await further study. In 1908 Ross issued a circular warning of unauthorized and apocryphal editions of Wilde's works, *re Oscar Wilde Deceased.*

Two early biographical works by Leonard Cresswell Ingleby ("C. Ranger Gull"), *Oscar Wilde* (1907), which has a slight critical emphasis; and *Oscar Wilde: Some Reminiscences* (1911) are inhibited both by the comparative recentness of Wilde's fall and by Ingleby's lack of insight.

By far the most notorious life of Wilde is Frank Harris' *Oscar Wilde: His Life and Confessions* (1916). Harris is not to be trusted on any subject, and much of what he says about Wilde amounts to pure fabrication, yet some critics still repeat his stories without skepticism. And it must be conceded that Harris' book has its uses, if only when read as a kind of fantasia improvised around the basic events; in modern jargon, it might even be classed as a psychohistory. Harris understands a good deal about Wilde's personality, and his choice of anecdote (whether factually accurate or not) is often significant for the way in which it indicates a psychological truth. In fact Harris does tend to qualify the veracity of his stories of his own accord—but frequently after he has told them—and readers of his book should be warned of this technique. The great influence that Harris' biography has had is a tribute to his mythmaking powers and to his ability to construct an engaging narrative. The book was greeted with resentment by both Douglas (see Horace Brodzky, *Henri Gaudier-Brzeska*, 1933) and the faithful, although Douglas later made some accommodation with Harris. It also gained in stature through the later inclusion of Shaw's comments—although these in themselves caused controversy (Hugh Kingsmill, *FortR*, 1938), which takes us into the remoter areas of Wilde's afterlife. For additional matter concerning Harris' relationship with Wilde, see *Contemporary Portraits* (1915); various letters to Harris in *Pearson's Magazine* (1918, rpt. *The Critical Heritage*); *My Life and Loves*, which has appeared in various stages of completeness; his intro. and essay for *De Profundis* (1926); a letter to *Mercure de France* (15 March 1929); Gerald Hamilton's obituary of Harris in *Berliner Tageblatt* (3 Sept. 1931), A. I. Tobin and E. Gertz, *Frank Harris* (1931), Vincent Brome, *Frank Harris* (1959), and Philippa Pullar, *Frank Harris* (1975).

It was not until 1946 and Hesketh Pearson's *The Life of Oscar Wilde* (rpt. 1975 with an intro. by Peter Quennell) that anything like a competently organized and professional biography became available. Pearson included many personal reminiscences that had not been collected before, but even he failed to draw a sufficiently clear line between established fact and reported anecdote; and his treatment of Wilde's homosexuality is so discreet as to make all his comments on his subject's personality seem naïve. Pearson's book succeeded in directing some attention to Wilde's pre-1895 career, but as a determinedly noncritical work it concentrates on Wilde's activities rather than his writing. (See Edmund Wilson, *NY*, 29 June 1946.) There are some grounds for saying that this remains the most sensible and trustworthy biography, although its reliability has come under attack in the *TLS* (3 Feb. 1950; 26 June–19 Oct. 1962).

It is depressing to record that a recent attempt at a full biography does little to alleviate the clouds of gossip and scurrilous hearsay that have gathered over the years. Yet for all its pretentiousness and inaccuracy, Philippe Jullian's *Oscar Wilde* (1969) is a stylish work and innovatory to the extent that it draws upon the unpublished papers of the Hope-Nicholson family. Jullian is able to apply his knowledge of French culture to Wilde and has some interesting suggestions about the relevance of Paul Bourget's *Dialogues esthéthiques* to *Intentions*, and a variety of French novels to *Dorian Gray*. He also confirms the influence of French dramatists. But the howlers are frequent, and many important matters are overlooked entirely. A final section deals with apocryphal material, and there is an authoritative appendix by Brian Reade on the authenticity of *Teleny*. All in all, Wilde deserves a good deal better than this.

H. Montgomery Hyde, *Oscar Wilde. A Biography* (1975) draws to a large extent on Hyde's several previous works, and is therefore of most value for its provision of yet another account of the trials and for the use that Hyde makes of his own acquaintance with Douglas. There is some new information, on Carlos Blacker and on Ross; and there are some tantalizingly brief quotations from the memoirs of Sir Edmund Trelawney Backhouse (in the Bodleian) which are, according to Hyde, "unpublished as well as unpublishable." Hyde is a distinguished bibliophile and legal historian but he has few pretensions as a literary critic and this new book is not the biography that the prospective student of Wilde's work requires. There is a good bibliography and a descriptive list of manuscript sources.

Apart from these major biographies, there are a large number of popular works, none of them at all satisfactory in themselves, yet each possibly containing the stray remark or piece of information not found elsewhere and perhaps deserving to be followed up. Into this category falls Boris Brasol, *Oscar Wilde: The Man—the Artist* (1938), which was influential in its time and is reasonably thorough although interspersed with amateur psychologizing. Francis Winwar, *Oscar Wilde and the Yellow Nineties* (1940), is a vivaciously novelletish biography, which attempts to convey a sense of period by bringing in Beardsley, Smithers, Lionel Johnson, *et al.* The book is most noticeable for a thinly disguised attack on Douglas, and in fact the second edition (1940) has a blustering foreword by the victim himself. Winwar's article in the *SatR* (17 Aug. 1940) recounts the row over Epstein's memorial, the rumor of Wilde's return in 1913, and other posthumous incidents. James Laver's monograph (1954) is unremarkable and unreliable. There is little to be said for Lewis Broad, *The Friendships and Follies of Oscar Wilde* (1954), which is largely based on Sherard, and even less for Frank Brennand, *Oscar Wilde* (1960).

Vyvyan Holland's autobiography, *Son of Oscar Wilde* (1954), has a good deal of information about his father: there is a notable description of Tite Street and its decorations, appendices containing material from Wilde's Oxford days, four "unpublished poems in prose, and correspondence with Douglas.

The best of the picture books is also by Holland: *Oscar Wilde: A Pictorial Biography* (1960), which has a concise factual account of the life and a good if unenterprising range of pictures. In comparison Martin Fido's *Oscar Wilde* (1973) is marred by shoddy and sometimes irrelevant reproductions and a text that is over-reliant on dubious secondary sources. Nevertheless Fido writes pleasantly enough and is unusually detailed on Wilde's involvement with the *Woman's World*.

The French have been particularly assiduous in writing biographies of Wilde. L. F. Choisy (Paris, 1927) has some slight critical emphasis, but L. Lemonnier (Paris, 1931 and 1938) gives orthodox popular versions of the old stories. G. J. Renier (1933) presents a liberal case for homosexuality, and this attitude is more firmly held by Robert Merle (Paris, 1949), who offers some incidental information on Wilde's debt to the French well-made play and attempts to analyze his style on Bergsonian lines. In his second book, *Oscar Wilde; ou la "Destinée" de l'homosexuel* (Paris, 1955), Merle presents the homosexual in an existential definition as the "suicidal hero," backed up with some statistical evidence. (Also see *La Revue de Paris*, 1954.) Lucie Delarue-Mardrus, *Les Amours d'Oscar Wilde* (Paris, 1929) is an elegantly flimsy reconciliation of diverse sources: Ransome, Renaud, Sherard, Harris, Douglas. Constance Wilde and Douglas are the justification for the title.

There is a choice of books on the family background. P. Byrne, *The Wildes of Merrion Square* (1953); T. G. Wilson, *Victorian Doctor: Being the Life of Sir William Wilde* (1942); Horace Wyndham, *Speranza: A Biography of Lady Wilde* (1951); and Eric Lambert, *Mad with Much Heart* (1967): all have been largely superseded by Terence de Vere White, *The Parents of Oscar Wilde* (1967), a detailed work which is of particular interest for Lady Wilde's comments on her son's activities. The role of Lady Wilde has always attracted conjecture. In *Oscar Wilde and His Mother: A Memoir* (1911), Anna, Comtesse de Brémont, puts forth a complicated theory of hereditary "genius" in order to attribute Wilde's "feminine soul" to his dominant mother. Such speculation was less uncommon in its own time than now, although the eccentricity of this particular book is confirmed by its author's belief in spiritualism. However, the descriptions of Wilde's appearance and conversation do have an authentic ring. W. W. Kenilworth also took a mystical approach in *A Study of Oscar Wilde* (1912). Those with a taste for psychic research will, like James Joyce, enjoy Hester Travers Smith, *Psychic Messages from Oscar Wilde* (1924; in America *Wilde from Purgatory*, 1926; also see *The Occult Review*, 1923–24; *Studies (Dublin)*, 1924; and Frank Harris' review in *Haldeman-Julius Monthly*, 1925), in which an eerily disembodied Oscar announces that "being dead is the most boring experience in life." Similar feats are achieved in a splendidly produced volume, *The Ghost Epigrams of Oscar Wilde as taken down through automatic writing by Lazar* (1928) and in Werner Weist, *Geisterepigramme* (Leipzig, 1929).

Owen Dudley Edwards writes about "Wilde and Henry O'Neill" (*IB*, 1959), and the fullest description of the relationship with Mahaffy is in W. B. Stanford and H. B. McDowell, *Mahaffy: A Biography of an Anglo-Irishman* (1971). T. G. Wilson writes on "Oscar Wilde at Trinity College, Dublin" in *The Practitioner* (1954), and Wilde's Oxford days are recalled by G. T. Atkinson in the *Cornhill Magazine* (1929); in Shane Leslie's *Memoir of J. E. C. Bodley* (1930); and by D. C. H. Blair in *The Dublin Review* (1938). Wilde's long skirmish with Catholicism is traced by Shane Leslie in *The Month* (1962).

As the foremost personality of two consecutive cultural moments Wilde can hardly fail to involve everyone who writes on either the Aesthetic Movement or the Decadent 90s. But the question remains: Where precisely does Wilde stand in relation to his contemporaries, on the distorting edge or at the defining center? Walter Hamilton's *The Aesthetic Movement in England* (1882), written when the movement emerged, avoided judgment, mainly because it was too close for a completed historical definition. Hamilton remains a useful source for parodies and reports of the American lectures but is unreliable on almost everything else. He voiced considerable admiration for the poems. William Gaunt, *The Aesthetic Adventure* (1945), and Elizabeth Aslin, *The Aesthetic Movement: Prelude to Art Nouveau* (1969), are important histories. Both note, as major incidents in the publicity campaign, the many satirical attacks in *Punch* (du Maurier's caricatures were not initially inspired by Wilde, as Leonée Ormond makes clear in *George du Maurier*, 1969, but increased in their resemblance to him as they continued); *Patience* and the Aesthetic burlesques that preceded it; the extraordinary response to the American tour. In all this hullabaloo it is not easy to draw the line between Wilde as instigator and Wilde as victim. Gaunt weaves a biography of Wilde into a much larger scheme but with indiscriminate expertise; a fascinating panorama, his book lacks any detailed etiology. Although erudite on matters of interior decoration and lavish in her use of illustration, Aslin chooses to concentrate on the American tour yet again and could surely have told us more about Wilde's use of Morris and perhaps E. W. Godwin. The relation of Wilde's earlier essays and reviews to Godwin awaits examination, though the difficulties are formidable: much of that influence was oral, and Godwin's writings are for the most part fugitive. The chapter on Godwin in John Stokes' *Resistible Theatres* (1972) has some preliminary findings. The most recent book, *The Aesthetic Movement* (1972) by Robin Spencer, starts a new and not wholly welcome trend by stressing the importance of Whistler, but at Wilde's expense. John Dixon Hunt passes some harsh judgments on Wilde's use of Pre-Raphaelite traditions in *The Pre-Raphaelite Imagination 1848–1900* (1968). In *Health, Art and Reason* (1974), Stella Mary Newton places Wilde's contribution to a single aspect of Aestheticism: the polemics of dress reform. Also see Alison Adburgham, *Liberty's: A Biography of a Shop* (1975).

Osbert Burdett, *The Beardsley Period* (1925), and Richard Le Gallienne, *The Romantic '90's* (1925, new ed. 1951), considered subsequent developments. Burdett disapproved of the theatricalism which he saw running through the whole of Wilde's career, although he allowed that a period of histrionic decadence was perhaps the necessary prologue to a new era; Le Gallienne was unexpectedly objective but also noticed that Wilde symbolized the phenomenon of change: "Out of 1890s chaos emerged an astonishing, impudent microcosm." Le Gallienne had in fact reviewed *Intentions* in *The Academy* (1891, rpt. *The Critical Heritage*) and, pseudonomously, *Salome* in *The Star* (22 Feb. 1893).

Holbrook Jackson's *The Eighteen Nineties* (1913) remains indispensable reading for any student of the decade. Wilde appears in four chapters of the book, but appears curiously isolated, an embarrassment in a volume whose theme is that the *fin-de-siècle* figures represent "a dash for life" in the valley of the shadow of High Victorianism. Since the emphasis tends to be on the talented Playboy of the West End, Wilde cannot be quite accommodated.

The treatment of Wilde in Ellen Moers, *The Dandy* (1960), is for the most part adverse. She complains that his public flamboyance debased the privacy of the true Dandy; by underestimating Wilde's own background, she attributes his success to a general cheapening of society. Moers makes too much of *A Rebours* in her discussion of *Dorian Gray*, and she fails to comprehend the intellectual basis for Wilde's high estimation of the critic. In all these general books there is a tendency to overrelate disparate figures—connections between Wilde and the art of Beardsley in particular are often very much simplified. The most reliable account of this relationship is in Stanley Weintraub's *Beardsley* (1967). Guy Deghy and Keith Waterhouse, *Café Royal. Ninety Years of Bohemia* (1955) has no originality.

The fullest record of Wilde's lecture tour of North America is still Lloyd Lewis and Henry Justin Smith, *Oscar Wilde Discovers America* (1936; rpt. 1967, reviewed by C. K. Hyder in *SatR*, 23 May 1936), which contains many amusing anecdotes and parodies as well as a large number of illustrations. The most famous of these is probably Charles Kendrick's cover for *Ye Soul Agonies in ye Life of Oscar Wilde* (1882). Stuart Mason's edition of *Wilde's Impressions of America* (1906) includes poems and articles. Mason's *Oscar Wilde and the Aesthetic Movement* (1920) is a small collection of parodies and caricatures—many of them American. These books can be supplemented by *The Bookman*, New York, 1911, 1920; *Colophon*, 1932, 1935 (the meeting with Whitman); *Minnesota History*, 1936; *Palimpset*, 1937; *California Historical Society Quarterly*, 1940; *NEQ*, 1940; *PrS*, 1940, 1947 (the meeting with George Edward Woodberry), 1967; *Bulletin of the Historical and Philosophical Society of Ohio*, 1957; and *TQ*, 1967. Most of these articles are culled from newspaper reports. See also Mary Watson, *People I Have Met* (1890); Lilian Aldrich, *Crowding Memories* (1920); and William Hogan and William German, *The San Francisco Chronicle Reader* (1962). Kevin O'Brien's "Oscar Wilde and Canadian Artists" (*AntigR*, 1971) pays particular attention to Homer Watson and Frances Richards.

Records of Wilde's earlier stays in Paris include Jacques Daurelle in *Echo de Paris* (6 Dec. 1891); Anatole France in *Univers Illustré* (1893); *The Bookman*, New York, 1911, and *T. P.'s Magazine* (1911), with illustrations; Henri Mazel in *Everyman* (1912); Ernest Raynaud in *La Mêlée symboliste*, Vol. II (Paris, 1920); and G. Le Rouge in *NL* (3 & 10 Nov. 1928): most make reference to the composition of *Salome*. Also see Jacques de Langlade, *Oscar Wilde, écrivain français* (Paris, 1975).

Wilde's career as a journalist has only been documented in part. There is a little information about the *Woman's World* in Simon Nowell-Smith, *The House of Cassell 1848–1958* (1959). Arthur Fish, a colleague, describes Wilde as editor in *Harper's Weekly* (4 Oct. 1913) and *Cassell's Weekly* (2 May 1923). Horace Wyndham's articles on his editorship (*Life and Letters*, 1947; *TC*, 1958) lack detail. A letter to the *TLS* (11 Aug. 1972) notes one of his last contributions to newspaper controversy, the recommendation of Swinburne for the laureateship.

Wilde's relationship with Ricketts, who designed a number of Wilde's books and entertained him at "The Vale," is briefly touched on in Denys Sutton's "A Neglected Virtuoso: C. S. Ricketts" (*Apollo*, 1966). Michael Brooks (*Criticism*, 1970) covers Wilde's own views on book design and the comparative styles and iconographies of editions illustrated by Crane and Ricketts. The same relationship is discussed by Giles Barber with a surer sense of the tradition to which Ricketts' designs belong in "Rossetti, Ricketts, and Some English Publishers' Bindings of the Nineties" (*The Library*, 1970). *The Early Nineties: A View from the Bodley Head* (1971) by James G. Nelson treats Wilde in relation to the publishers Elkin Mathews and John

Lane, and to Ricketts and Beardsley. There is also useful comment on Wilde's friendship with John Gray. The circulation, distribution, and financial aspects of Wilde's books are discussed. The importance of the book derives largely from the fact that it is based on manuscript material. Nelson uses the files of the present firm of Bodley Head and the Elkin Mathews papers at Reading University but makes no noticeable use of the Lane archive at Westfield College, University of London. Nelson supersedes J. Lewis May, *John Lane and the Nineties* (1936). Wilde's dealings with another publisher, Leonard Smithers, are remarked on by Jack Smithers in *The Early Life and Vicissitudes of Jack Smithers* (1939).

Some of Wilde's friendships have been described individually. H. Montgomery Hyde discusses Wilde's association with E. W. Godwin (*Architectural Review*, 1951; rpt. *Cases That Changed the Law*, 1951), but confines this to the decoration of Tite Street. Also see *Country Life* (1972). W. T. Going (*VN*, 1958) refers to Wilde's acquaintance with Wilfrid Scawen Blunt and briefly compares the writing that the two men produced as a consequence of their experiences in prison. For the relationship with Florence Balcombe see Daniel Farson, *The Man who Wrote "Dracula"* (1975); and for that with Lily Langtry see James Brough, *The Prince and the Lily* (1975). In his book on Curzon (*Superior Person*, 1969), Kenneth Rose refers to his subject's slight acquaintance with Wilde. There is information about Wilde's friendship with Ada Leverson, remembered for her parodies of his plays in *Punch* as well as for her loyalty after the catastrophe, in an essay by Colin McInnes (*Encounter*, 1961); in Violet Wyndham, *The Sphinx and Her Circle* (1963); and in Charles Burkhardt (*ELT*, 1970). Roy Harrod has recorded the esteem in which Wilde was held by the Forbes-Robertson family (*TLS*, 27 July 1962). In *ELT* (1971) Welford Dunaway Taylor discusses the portrait of Wilde in *Shadows of Flames* (1915) by Amelia Rives, an American who knew Wilde between 1889 and 1894. J. Joseph Renaud recalls his meetings with Wilde in the preface to his translation of *Intentions* (1905; also in *La Grande Revue*, 1905). Two famous and not too stringent satires are Robert Hichens' *The Green Carnation* (1894) and "Y. T. O." (L. C. Amery and others), *Aristophanes at Oxford* (1894). Wilde had already been presented on stage as Lambert Stryke in F. C. Burnand's *The Colonel* of 1881 (not printed, but available in the Lord Chamberlain's papers, British Museum), but this avatar was soon eclipsed by the resonant success of Gilbert and Sullivan's *Patience* (1881) though the identity of Bunthorne, the Aesthetic poet, remains debatable and is probably composite. *The Poet and the Puppets* (1893) by Charles Brookfield and Charles Hawtrey (both of whom tradition credits with assisting Queensberry with his prosecution) is also comparatively genial, though with hints of plagiarism.

There are full transcripts of both trials, together with appendices on related subjects and excerpts from contemporary comment, in H. Montgomery Hyde, *The Trials of Oscar Wilde* (1948; new and enl. ed., 1962; rpt. 1973). Hyde tells some of the same story in *Carson* (1953); also see Edward Marjoribanks, *The Life of Lord Carson* (Vol. 1, 1932). Also see Derek Walker-Smith and Edward Clarke, *The*

Life of Sir Edward Clarke (1959) and Sir Travers Humphreys, *A Book of Trials* (1953). Mason gives details of a pamphlet called *The Life of Oscar Wilde* which was sold in the streets during the trial: this and similar items are now extremely rare; there are long excerpts from the shorthand reports of the second trial along with material relating to Douglas in another rare book, *The Trial of Oscar Wilde* (anon., Paris, 1906) which mysteriously reappeared as *The Shame of Oscar Wilde* (n. p., ca. 1950), a photographic reprint of the 1906 volume with the little running titles altered and omitting pages 127–34; Hilary Pacq, *Le Procès d'Oscar Wilde* (Paris, 1953), also contains transcripts; Christopher Millard, *Oscar Wilde Three Times Tried* (1912) includes details of subsequent petitions as well as of the trials. Douglas G. Browne, *Sir Travers Humphreys: A Biography* (1960), relies on Hyde to a large degree. *Public Opinion* of 1895 gives extracts from four American papers' reactions to the trials. F. K. Kaul (*Die Weltbühne*, 1961) points out that Wilde was punished according to the class justice of Victorian society. The names of upper-class figures involved in the same scandal were suppressed, and they were left unpunished. The legal implications of the libel suit against Queensberry are usefully defined in A. D. Austin's "Regina versus Queensberry" (*UnivR*, 1966).

Dalhousie Young's brave *Apologia pro Oscar Wilde* (1895); Ernest Newman in *The Free Review* (1895, rpt. *The Critical Heritage*); and an excessively rare pamphlet by "I. Playfair" produced in Newcastle-on-Tyne immediately after the trials and entitled *Gentle Criticisms of British Justice* shine out among the surrounding vilification. Colby College, Maine, possesses Mason's copy of the last, with his marginalia. The author is identified as J. H. Wilson, who issued the book, and the paragraph alluding to the well-known actor assisting the prosecution has the word "Brookfield" written against it. (John Boon, who knew Brookfield well, has the fullest account in *Victorians, Edwardians and Georgians*, 1927.) These three defenses of Wilde can be compared with J. M. Stuart-Young's later and more ambivalent efforts in *Osrac, the Self-Sufficient* (1905), *The English Illustrated Magazine* (1905), *An Urning's Love* (1905), *The Antinomian* (1909) and *Out of Hours* (1909). In the course of the first trial an attempt was made to smear Wilde by associating him with a childishly blasphemous and prurient story which had been anonymously published in *The Chameleon* in 1894, "The Priest and the Acolyte." This was reprinted in 1907 with the author named as John F. Bloxam (by that time a clergyman) and an introductory protest by Stuart Mason that recalled parts of the cross-examination relating to the story. For the responses of W. T. Stead and others to the trials see *Studies in English* (University of Mississippi, 1965).

In *AN&Q* (1963) W. White revealed an American plan to bribe the governor of Pentonville to connive at Wilde's escape. Hyde described the arrest in *Waterloo Review* (1959) and provided an account of the years in jail and after in *Oscar Wilde: The Aftermath* (1963), a useful but sometimes controversial book (see *MLR*, 1964; *VS*, 1965; and *TLS*, 21 June–12 July 1963). Hyde has disagreed with C. H. Norman over such matters as the conduct of the trial, the payment of Wilde's counsel, and the failure of the Court of Criminal Appeal to reconsider the case in 1905 (*TLS*, 29 Sept.–14 Nov. 1963). Information on Wilde's relationships with Warder Martin and others is available in *The Story of Oscar Wilde's Life and Experience in Reading Gaol*, with a tribute by Rose Freeman Ishill (*Bruno's Weekly*, 1916; rpt. 1963), and from H.-D. Davray in *Mercure de France* (1926). There is nothing new about Wilde in Peter Southerton, *The Story of a Prison* (Reading, 1975), but Penelope Fitzgerald, *Edward Burne-Jones* (1975) includes some brief descriptions of Wilde in jail.

Sophisticated research into the homosexual mores of the late nineteenth century is a comparatively recent development, although the German pioneer Magnus Hirschfeld (*Die Homosexualität des Mannes und des Weibes*, 1914) frequently cited Wilde as a case-history and his immense work is valuable bibliographically. François Porché, *L'Amour qui n'ose pas dire son nom* (Paris, 1927) took Wilde as his main example, noted the opinion of Zola, and ended with a discussion of Gide. An interesting bibliography on the subject is included in Noel I. Garde, *Jonathan to Gide: The Homosexual in History* (1964). Clifford Allen (*International Journal of Sexology*, 1949) and Macdonald Critchley (*Medical History*, 1957, and *Medico-Legal Journal*, 1962; both rpt. in *The Black Hole*, 1964) do not commit themselves much beyond a provisional diagnosis. A. Hoffer suggests that Wilde's homosexuality and his behavior at the trials were caused by a personality change resulting from "insidious cerebral syphilitic processes" (*Amer. Journal of Psychiatry*, 1957). In a chapter in *Feasting with Panthers* (1967) and a complete book, *The Unrecorded Life of Oscar Wilde* (1972), Rupert Croft-Cooke traces Wilde's sexual journey from Oxford Uranians to Piccadilly renters. The two treatments duplicate each other to some extent, and the title of the second suggests more than it contains. In any case one should not turn to Croft-Cooke for new material so much as for a sense of milieu. The only asset of Croft-Cooke's work is his evident lack of sympathy with Wilde's writings, a point made by G. A. Cevasco in his review of *The Unrecorded Life* (*ELT*, 1973). Mason's gloss on *Gentle Criticisms of British Justice* slightly undercuts Croft-Cooke's assertion that the report of Brookfield's assisting the prosecution is a late fabrication. In an article on the polarities of homosexual writing in England (*CE*, 1974) David Jago draws an interesting comparison between the sensibilities of Wilde and of E. M. Forster: Wilde seeks confrontation with heterosexual society and expresses himself through the theater; Forster desires integration, and his chosen medium is a developed version of the English school story. But Jago perhaps underestimates the Uranian tone of Wilde's Oxford and even of his relationship with Douglas. This whole issue of *CE* is devoted to "The Homosexual Imagination"; there is a bibliography. Three books, although not specifically on Wilde, contain enlightening background material on this aspect of his life: H. Montgomery Hyde, *The Other Love* (1970), Timothy d'Arch Smith, *Love in Earnest* (1970), and Brian Reade, *Sexual Heretics* (1970). Two issues of *Le Crapouillot* (Paris) are notable primarily for their curious illustrations: "Les Homosexuels" (1955) and "Les Pédérastes" (1970).

Marc André Raffalovich, who inspired Wilde's famous remark that he came to London to create a salon, but only achieved a saloon, made his own contemporary contribution to the field of pseudo-pathology with an essay written in French which is now extremely rare: *L'Affaire Oscar Wilde* (Lyons, 1895), but reprinted in his *Uranisme et unisexualité* (Lyons and Paris, 1896), and in Le Docteur Laupts (G. Saint-Paul), *L'Homosexualité et les types homosexuels* (Paris, 1910). This work and the Wilde case in general were referred to by Havelock Ellis (incorporating the work of John Addington Symonds): *Sexual Inversion* (1897). In 1927 Raffalovich contributed a malicious account of Wilde to *Blackfriars* under the pseudonym of Alexander Michaelson. This has been reprinted by Fr. Brocard Sewell in *Footnote to the Nineties* (1968). Further information about Raffalovich and his companion John Gray, who had of course been a friend of Wilde in earlier days, is available in this book and in a collection of essays entitled *Two Friends* (ed. Sewell, 1963). The correspondence between Louÿs and Gray and that between Gray and Louÿs is extant, but neither has as yet been fully edited (see *RLC*, 1953). Both could throw more light on Wilde.

The career of an even more crepuscular figure of the *fin de siècle*, Count Eric von Stenbock, is traced by John Adlard in *Stenbock, Yeats and the Nineties* (1969). However, Adlard merely notes intermittently that Stenbock's activities were contemporaneous with those of Wilde and can prove little interaction between them, apart from a mutual friendship with More Adey.

Stenbock's passion for animals would have come under the category of "zoophilia" in the diagnoses of decadent behavior offered by Max Nordau in his sensational book *Degeneration*. The publication of an English translation of *Degeneration* in 1895 only confirmed and strengthened the Philistine backlash expressed by leader writers at the time of the trial. But in fact Nordau's recognition of Wilde's centrality can now be read in a painfully ironic light as an anticipation of Wilde's own claim of "symbolic relationship to his age." In Book III of *Degeneration* Wilde is isolated as the chief representative of the English Decadence, and Wilde's criticism serves as prologue to Nordau's extended attack on the "egoism" of late Romantic esthetics in general. Again, viewed from a distance, the scathing connections that Nordau later makes between Wilde and Nietzsche are not entirely beside the point. But Nordau's work remains above all the prime example of that very hysteria which he himself condemned in others, and its impact in England provides a model instance of the mythmaking power of modern publicity.

Wilde's time at Berneval is described by André Germain in *La Revue Européenne* (1923); by Jacques Emile Blanche, *Portraits of a Lifetime* (1937); by S. Pakenham, *Sixty Miles from England: The English at Dieppe, 1814–1914* (1967); by Marius David, *Paris-Normandie* (22 Nov. 1967); and by Alin Caillas in *Oscar Wilde tel que je l'ai connu* (Paris, 1971). Ernest Dowson's friendship with Wilde developed largely in Dieppe (see *The Letters of Ernest Dowson*, ed. Desmond Flower and Henry Maas, 1967).

For French responses to Wilde's career a very helpful article by L. Lemonnier should be consulted: "La Condemnation de Oscar Wilde et l'opinion française" (*Revue Mondiale*, 1931) as well as de Saix's maddening bibliography to *Les Songes merveilleux du dormeur éveillé* and the earlier sections of Jacques de Langlade, *Oscar Wilde, écrivain français*. The trials were closely followed by the French papers: see in particular *Echo de Paris* (29 May 1895); *Figaro* (9–13 April 1895); *L'Illustration* (23 Mar. and 13 April 1895); *La Revue Blanche* (throughout 1895 but especially Henri de Regnier, 15 Dec.). In addition to the items already cited describing Wilde's early visits to Paris there are innumerable French memoirs which contain allusions to the early and late periods in France as well as to reactions to the trials. Among the more prominent are: André Billy, *La Muse aux besicles* (n.d.); Adolphe Brisson, *Le Théâtre* (1909); P. Champion, *Marcel Schwob et son temps* (1927); François Coppée, *Mon Franc-Parler* (1906); Léon Daudet, *Ecrivains et artistes* (1929), *Souvenirs des milieux littéraires* (1915); Louis Delluc, *Chez de Max* (n.d.); Edmond et Jules de Goncourt, *Journal* (1956); Charles du Bos, *Journal* (1949, esp. Tome III, 1926–27); André Fontainas, *Mes Souvenirs du symbolisme* (1928); Edmond Jaloux, *Les Saisons littéraires 1893–1903* (1904–1914) (1942); Ernest La Jeunesse, *Les Nuits, les ennuis et les âmes de nos plus notaires contemporains* (1896); Jean Lorrain, *Sensations et souvenirs* (1895), *Poussières de Paris* (1896), *La Ville empoisonnée* (1936); Lugné-Poc, *La Parade: Acrobaties* (1931); Camille Mauclair, *Servitude et grandeur littéraires* (1922); Stuart Merrill, *Prose et vers* (1925); F. de Miomandre, *Figures d'hier et d'aujourd'hui* (1911); Octave Mirbeau, *Les Ecrivains 1884–1894* (1926); P. Morand, *Tendres Stocks* (1921); Henri de Regnier, *Figures et caractères* (Paris, 1901); Jules Renard, *Journal inédit* (1925); Adolphe Retté, *Le Symbolisme, anecdotes et souvenirs* (Paris, 1903); L. Tailhade, *Quelques Fantômes de jadis* (1920); Octave Uzanne, *Visions de notre heure* (1899). In *Oscar Wilde: La Tragédie finale* (1928) Henry-D. Davray includes an essay about his dealings with Wilde when he translated the *Ballad* as well as biographical sketches based on late correspondence. Also see Davray in Mercure de France (1901, rpt. *The Critical Heritage*). In "Abraham France: Traducteur du Virgile: Oscar Wilde" (*Rev. Politique et Littéraire*, 1929), M. Yourcenar focused on Wilde on Capri. There are poignant images from the last phase in Wilfrid Hugh Chesson, "A Reminiscence of 1898" (*The Bookman*, London, 1911); Leo Clarétie (*Figaro*, 1 April 1907); Laurence Housman, *Echo de Paris* (1923); Ernest La Jeunesse (*La Revue Blanche*, 1900 and *Cinq ans chez les sauvages*, 1901); Louis Latourette (*Nouvelles Littéraires*, 5 Dec. 1925); Henri de Regnier (*Annales Politiques et Littéraires*, 29 Nov. 1925); Paul Wiegler, *Genius in Love and Death* (1926; trans. 1929). For a highly dramatic account of Wilde's last days and death see the interview with the proprietor of the Hôtel d'Alsace in *Intransigeant*, 30 Nov. 1930. In *Rev. Hebdomadaire*, 1925, Georges-Bazile reports information from Ross clarifying the circumstances of the death; also see *Le Temps*, 11 June 1912. Terence Cawthorne (*Proceedings of the Royal Society of Medicine*, 1959) suggests that Wilde died of "nothing less than an intercranial complication of suppurative otitis media." The long uncertainty about the deathbed conversion was resolved by Father Edmund Burke in *The London Magazine* (1961) and by Rupert Croft-

Cooke in *Books and Bookmen* (1974). Also see André Billy, *L'Epoque 1900* (Paris, 1951) and "Louis Wilkinson," "Oscar Wilde: Some Hitherto Unpublished Letters" (*NewS*, 3 Jan. 1914).

Franz Blei's *In Memoriam Oscar Wilde* (Leipzig, 1905) contains essays by Ernest La Jeunesse, Arthur Symons and Blei himself, as well as some of Wilde's *Phrases and Philosophies*. A similar book is *Recollections of Oscar Wilde* (1906), trans. with an intro. by Percival Pollard, in which he quotes from E. Gómez Carrillo's important notes on the inspiration for *Salome*. However this volume only contains the essays by Ernest La Jeunesse, Arthur Symons and Blei himself, as *The Papyrus* (1908) together with an offering from Michael Monahan: "Oscar Wilde's Atonement" (rpt. from *The Papyrus*, 1906). Monahan reprinted this essay frequently, sometimes with additional comment: see *Palms of Papyrus* (1908); *An Attic Dreamer* (1922); *Adventures in Life and Letters* (1925). Monahan's *Nemesis* (1926, rpt. 1968) contains two related essays which defend Wilde through reference to *De Profundis*. "Arthur Cravan" was the pseudonym of Wilde's nephew by marriage, the poet and pugilist Fabian Lloyd: *Maintenant* (1912–13, rpt. 1957) contains inferior portraits of Wilde, some descriptions of his appearance entitled "Documents inédits sur Oscar Wilde," and Cravan's own short fantasy "Oscar Wilde est vivant," in which he imagines Wilde's reappearance in 1913. The items from *Maintenant* were translated and printed in *The Soil* (1917) together with a description of Tite Street and some letters to Smithers. Edgar Saltus first met Wilde in 1882 and in his *Oscar Wilde: An Idler's Impression* (1917, rpt. 1968) recalls their relationship mainly through reconstructed conversation and in a style which at times resembles that of Arthur Symons. In a book of reprinted essays, *Oscar Wilde: A Retrospect* (Vienna, 1921), Ernst Bendz considered the memoirs of Sherard, Harris, and Shaw, the Ransome case, and French influence on *Salome*. *Oscar Wilde: Recollections* (1932) by "Jean Paul Raymond" and Charles Ricketts is valuable for its transcriptions of prose poems and details of the proposed staging of *Salome* as well as for more personal memories. Ricketts' *Self-Portrait* (1939), based on his journals and letters, is also of some relevance to Wilde. Also see "Jean Paul Raymond" (Ricketts' pseudonym), *Beyond the Threshold* (1929). Ford Madox Ford's reminiscences are unfortunately hard to credit (*Ancient Lights*, 1911; *Return to Yesterday*, 1931; *The March of Literature*, 1938; *SatR*, 27 May 1939) but the voluminous memoirs of Sir Compton Mackenzie (*My Life and Times*: Octaves 2, 1963; 3, 1964; 10, 1971) and Sir William Rothenstein (*Men and Memories*, 3 vols., 1931–39) estimate Wilde's impact both on their own careers and on the age. A privately printed collection of essays, *In Memory of Dorothy Ierne Wilder*. "Oscaria" (1951) commemorates Oscar's niece by his brother Willie's second marriage; there are a few Oscar stories in Janet Flanner's contribution. A special edition of *Adam* (1954) was largely devoted to Wilde and brought together short tributes from a dozen or so French writers; memorial essays by Lady Emily Lutyens and "Louis Marlow" (L. U. Wilkinson); a 1912 essay by Stuart Merrill (with details on the composition of *Salome*); and a prose poem, "Le Miracle du masque," "texte recueilli par Guillot de Saix." Vincent O'Sullivan, *Aspects of Wilde* (1936), has been the source for many stories subsequently incorporated into formal biography. O'Sullivan is often acute about other people's interpretations of Wilde and has a good sense of surrounding personalities. In a posthumously published collection of essays, *Opinions* (1959), he amplified his own portrait of Wilde and stressed the importance of William Morris. Earlier, O'Sullivan had defended Wilde's status as a writer against Shane Leslie (*New York Evening Post*, July 1917) and against George Moore (*Pearson's Magazine*, 1918; rpt. *The Critical Heritage*). A. J. A. Symons died before completing his biography, but three chapters are preserved in *Essays and Biographies* (1969): on Wilde as conversationalist, at Oxford, and on the trip to America; all benefit from Symons' eye for the significant detail. Also see *Some Letters of Vincent O'Sullivan to A. J. A. Symons*, ed. Alan Anderson (Edinburgh, 1975).

Otherwise the list of books and contributions to periodicals that contain some odd reference to Wilde is immense, but the following are all established, although not necessarily reliable, sources for anecdote and reminiscence: Douglas Ainslie, *Adventures Social and Literary* (1922); anon., *Echoes of the Eighties* (n.d.); anon., 1871–1935, untitled (1936); F. Anstey, *A Long Retrospect* (1938); Charles Archer, *William Archer* (1931); Dame Helen Porter Armstrong (Nellie Melba), *Melodies and Memories* (1925); Margot Asquith, *More Memories* (1933); Gertrude Atherton, *Adventures of a Novelist* (1932); James S. Bain, *A Bookseller Looks Back* (1940); Sir Squire Bancroft, *Empty Chairs* (1925); Sir Squire and Lady Bancroft, *The Bancrofts, Recollections of Sixty Years* (1909); Natalie Clifford Barney, *Aventures de l'esprit* (1929); Mrs. Claude Beddington, *All That I Have Met* (1929); E. F. Benson, *My Memories* (1930), *As We Were: A Victorian Peep Show* (1930), *Final Edition* (1940); Sir Frank Benson, *My Memoirs* (1930); Bernard Berenson, *Sunset and Twilight* (1963); F. G. Bettany, *Stewart Headlam* (1926); Martin Birnbaum, *Wilde: Fragments and Memories* (1914; trans. as the 2nd essay in *Beardsley et Wilde*, Paris, 1939); Sir Chartres Biron, *Without Prejudice* (1936); David C. H. Blair, *In Victorian Days* (1939); Wilfrid Scawen Blunt, *My Diaries* (2 vols., 1919–20); J. Comyns Carr, *Some Eminent Victorians* (1906); Mrs. J. Comyns Carr, *Reminiscences* (1925); Evan Charteris, *Life and Letters of Sir E. Gosse* (1931); Cheiro (Count Louis Hamon), *Cheiro's Memoirs* (1912); John Connell, *W. E. Henley* (1949); Walter Crane, *An Artist's Reminiscences* (1907); Sir Arthur Conan Doyle, *Memories and Adventures* (1914); Lady Augusta Fane, *Chit Chat* (1916); "Michael Field" (Emma Cooper and Katharine Bradley), *Works and Days* (1933); Sir Johnston Forbes-Robertson, *A Player under Three Reigns* (1923); James Glover, *Jimmy Glover His Book* (1911); Lord Ronald Gower, *My Reminiscences* (2 vols., 1883); Roger Lancelyn Green, *A. E. W. Mason* (1952); Lady Gregory, *Lady Gregory's Journals, 1916–1930* (1946); Richard Burdon Haldane, *An Autobiography* (1929); Charles Hawtrey, *The Truth at Last* (1924); Chris Healy, *Confessions of a Journalist* (1904); Robert Hichens, *Yesterday* (1947); Seymour Hicks, *Twenty-Four Years of an Actor's Life*

(1910), and several other volumes; C. Lewis Hind, introd. to Stephen Phillips' *Christ in Hades* (1917); E. A. B. Hodgetts, *Moss from a Rolling Stone* (1924); C. J. Holmes, *Self and Partners (Mostly Self)* (1936); Laurence Housman, *The Unexpected Years* (1937); Desmond Chapman Houston, *The Lost Historian: A Memoir of Sir Sidney Low* (1936); Sidney Huddleston, *Back to Montparnasse* (1937); Violet Hunt, *The Flurried Years* (1926); Horace G. Hutchinson, *Portraits of the Eighties* (1920); Augustus John, *Chiaroscuro* (1952); Louise Jopling, *Twenty Years of My Life* (1925); Coulson Kernahan, *In Good Company* (1917); Lily Langtry, *The Days I Knew* (n.d.); Georgette Leblanc, *Maeterlinck and I* (1932); Shane Leslie, *Sir Evelyn Ruggles-Brise* (1938); W. H. Leverton, *Through the Box-Office Window* (1932); E. V. Lucas, *The Colvins and their Friends* (1928), *Reading, Writing and Remembering: A Literary Record* (1932); Lady Emily Lutyens, *A Blessed Girl* (1953); Elizabeth Marbury, *My Crystal Ball* (1924); "Louis Marlow" (L. U. Wilkinson), *Seven Friends* (1953); W. B. Maxwell, *Time Gathered* (1937); Sir Peter Chalmers Mitchell, *My Fill of Days* (1937); Bernard Muddiman, *The Men of the Nineties* (1920); Luther Munday, *A Chronicle of Friendships* (1912); Julia Neilson, *This for Remembrance* (1940); Ralph Nevill, *The Reminiscences of Lady Dorothy Nevill* (1906); Sir Henry Newbolt, *My World as in My Time* (1932); Mrs. T. P. O'Connor, *I, Myself* (1910); E. R. Pennell, *The Life and Letters of Joseph Pennell* (1929); E. T. Raymond, *Portraits of the Nineties* (1921); Ernest Rhys, *Everyman Remembers* (1931); Grant Richards, *Memoirs of a Misspent Youth* (1932), *Author Hunting* (1939); W. Pett Ridge, *I Like to Remember* (1925); Arthur Roberts, *Fifty Years of Spoof* (1927); W. Graham Robertson, *Time Was* (1931); Elizabeth Robins, *Both Sides of the Curtain* (1940); Sir James Rennell Rodd, *Social and Diplomatic Memories 1884–1893* (1922); John Rothenstein, *The Life and Death of Conder* (1938); Frank Rutter, *Since I was Twenty-Five* (1927); Walter Sichel, *The Sands of Time* (1923); "Sigma" (J. O. Field), *Personalia* (1903); Osbert Sitwell, *Noble Essences* (1950); Sacheverell Sitwell, *For Want of the Golden City* (1973); Douglas Sladen, *Twenty Years of My Life* (1914); Lincoln Springfield, *Some Piquant People* (1924); H. M. Swanwick, *I Have Been Young* (1935); Laura Troubridge, *Life Amongst the Troubridges* (1966); Katharine Tynan, *Twenty-Five Years: Reminiscences* (1913); Dame Irene Vanbrugh, *To Tell My Story* (1948); Bertha Vyver, *Memoirs of Marie Corelli* (1950); L. B. Walford, *Memories of Victorian London* (1912); A. Ward, *Recollections of A Savage* (1923); Sir Algernon West, *Private Diaries* (1922); Frederic Whyte, *William Heinemann* (1928); Esmé Wingfield-Stratford, *The Victorian Sunset* (1932); and Maud Wynne, *An Irishman and His Family* (1937). Also see *Libre Parole* (24 June 1909) and *L'Action d'Art* (1 Apr. 1913).

Some of the major controversies that have obscured Wilde's memory are described in a helpful book by H. Montgomery Hyde, *Cases That Changed the Law* (1951). These include the Ransome case, the Pemberton Billing trial, and Millard's suit over the forgery *For Love of the King*. In *The Critic* (1905) George S. Viereck presents the case for Wilde's messianic reappearance on the streets of New York. An account, with documentation, of the protests, particularly French, which greeted his memorial sculpture is to be found in Jacob Epstein, *Let There Be Sculpture* (1940).

Among the many biographies in languages other than English and German are: S. Juan Arbó (Madrid, 1960); C. Van Balen (Haarlem, 1910); J. Antonio G. Blasquez (Madrid, 1969), which also contains some criticism, notably of the prose, with a brief but useful bibliography; F. Balmaceda Cardozo, *Oscar Wilde, Estudio Bio-Bibliográfico* (Porto Allegre, 1935); M. T. Dainotti Cerutti, *Oscar Wilde e il suo problema religioso* (Modena, 1958); C. M. Franzero, *Vita di Oscar Wilde* (Florence, 1938). Alcalá Galiano has a long essay which first appeared in *La Revista Quincenal* (Feb. & Mar. 1918), as part of *Conferencias y Ensayos* (Madrid, 1919). The celebrations in London are described in "El Centenario de Oscar Wilde" in *Esqueletas Divinos* of Patricio Gannon (Buenos Aires, 1971), which contains also two pieces on John Gray. *Król Zycia* (Warsaw, Cracow, 1948) is a biographical novel in Polish by J. Parandowski. José Nava has mediated Wilde's personality to the Portuguese with a few poignant inaccuracies and a useful brief bibliography in *Uma Tragedia Anglo-Florentina* (n.p., 1969).

VI. *Major Critical Studies*

It is impossible in Wilde's case to draw a distinct line between biographical and critical treatments. But Arthur Ransome's *Oscar Wilde: A Critical Study* (1912) might be classed as the first genuinely critical book, if only because its slight biographical emphasis was justified on the grounds that Wilde saw "art as self-expression and life as self-development." Ransome has a firm grasp of Wilde's intellectual systems; he respects the paradox and makes a good attempt to place *Salomé* in the context of the symbolist drama. The most obvious weakness of the book is the lack of interest in the later plays and the failure to relate these to the overall pattern—but this was an oversight that was not to be rectified for many years and is noticeable in quite recent work. The first edition of Ransome contains some remarks about Douglas and *De Profundis* which led to the famous court case. The offending passages were removed in the second edition (1913).

R. T. Hopkins' *Oscar Wilde: A Study of the Man and His Work* (Jan. 1913; rev. ed., June 1913; rpt. 1970) also offered itself as a critical study rather than a biography, but it is heavily dependent on Sherard, ignores the plays except for *Salome*, and rarely rises above plot summary of the other works. There is an appendix by George Berrien on *The Soul of Man*. *Wilde: A Study* (1930) by Patrick Braybrooke was a full-scale attempt at rehabilitation but has no critical acumen except for the recognition that *The Importance* contains elements of satire.

The bibliography of Arthur Symons is densely snarled, consequent partly on his habit of embodying parts of earlier works, whether books or reviews, in later works, particularly after his crackup in 1908. His *A Study of Oscar Wilde* (1930) is typical (see *Speaker*,

1891 and *SatR*, 1898, rpt. *The Critical Heritage*; the 1901 obituary which was also printed in *Studies in Prose and Verse*, 1904; *La Plume*, 1905; *Athenaeum*, 1908, rpt. *The Critical Heritage; The Bookman*, New York, 1920; the introd. to the vol. devoted to *Intentions* in the Doubleday ed., 1923, etc.). The most curious quality of *A Study* is its ambivalence. Symons is troubled by Wilde's pretensions to have been an artist when what survives is his "personality." He returns obsessively to one of Wilde's most famous statements: "I took the drama, the most objective form known to art, and made it as personal a mode of expression as the lyric or the sonnet. . . . I treated art as the supreme reality, and life as a mere mode of fiction," and notes that this takes Wilde "no nearer to reality." Symons is uneasy even with his own paradoxical formulation that Wilde was at his most sincere when striking poses. He is more sympathetic to the criticism, most sensitive in response to the *Ballad* and *De Profundis*. This book can still be recommended, with the proviso that some previous acquaintance with Symons' critical approach is probably necessary. And it would help to read at the same time a contemporary review of it in the *TLS* (8 Jan. 1931). This short notice signals the arrival of a rudimentary history of ideas to replace Symons' impressionism and elevates Wilde the thinker to the company of Schopenhauer and Hegel. English critics were at last beginning to see that Wilde's ideas had a respectable pedigree.

Oscar Wilde (1947) by Edouard Roditi is concerned primarily to place him in the tradition of the dandy, which requires that attention be given to the historical origins and context of Aestheticism. This emphasis produces a chapter on Wilde's poetry relating it to his preoccupations with synesthesia and, in rather sketchy terms, with the visual arts, but it prevents an appreciation of Wilde's plays apart from *Salome*—for instance, Roditi sees *The Importance* as a bid for popularity and a betrayal of the principles of dandyism as he understands them. However, he successfully compares *Dorian Gray* with *Melmoth the Wanderer*, notes some telling inconsistencies in Wilde's handling of the underworld, and relates the book's main characters to other dandies in fiction. The rest of the book considers Wilde's role as dandy as it affected his politics, his ethics, and his esthetics. Roditi largely vindicates his thematic approach, although the insights are sometimes weakened by the absence of general knowledge—whether of art history, of psychology, or of philosophic tradition.

St. John Ervine, *Oscar Wilde: A Present Time Appraisal* (1951), has much familiar material, often highly colored by its author's evident disapproval of his subject. Ervine becomes most involved when he pits Wilde against Shaw for the title of supreme individualist, but his book ends with the kind of superior moral distaste that characterizes its literary judgments throughout: "What punishment is fitting for the man who takes his gift from God and drops it in the mire? That was the sin committed by Oscar Wilde. It was the sin against the Holy Ghost." Ervine takes the same sanctimonious attitude to Wilde in *Bernard Shaw: His Life, Work and Friends* (1956).

The first book which applies recognizably modern critical methods is Aatos A. Ojala's *Aestheticism and Oscar Wilde* (Helsinki, 1954–55), yet even this now appears an odd mixture of the adventurous and the anachronistic. "Aestheticism" is understood to refer to an expressive mode that derives from certain kinds of perception and, in the case of Wilde, a certain psychology. In Part I of his work, *Life and Letters* (1954), Ojala shows how Wilde's "Narcissism" made him write plays which, although realizing the "objective" form of his thought as he claimed, nevertheless fail because characters turn out to be puppets, mouthpieces for ideas, and not fully integrated into plot and situation. In Part II, *Literary Style* (1955), Ojala is mainly concerned with the part played by synesthesia in Wilde's prose. *The Laocoon* is used to fairly good effect, but Ojala's seemingly uncritical appropriation of the bizarre terminology first made well known by Max Nordau ("echolalia" and so on) is deeply suspect. He practices an analytical method based on word counts and the tabulation of recurring stylistic elements that is tedious to follow and predictable in its conclusions. In this respect Ojala's approach had been anticipated by Stephen von Ullmann (*EngS*, 1938), who had also tried to rationalize Wilde's uses of synesthesia and to offer a psychological explanation for the mixing of otherwise disparate sense impressions. The time is now perhaps ripe for a properly equipped scholar to bring this work up to date with a more scientific inquiry into the psycholinguistic origins of Wilde's style.

The Paradox of Oscar Wilde (1949) was offered by George Woodcock as a critical companion to Hesketh Pearson's biography. Woodcock recognizes Wilde as an important figure in literary history but is at something of a loss as to why; the final judgment is conventional, if it does not actually contradict the book's premise: Wilde was a greater personality than he was a writer. Indeed, the book is characterized as a whole by a failure to deliver what it promises; its "dialectical" method, chosen to suit the Wildean paradox and the "continual rivalry of paganism and Christianity, of the gospel of hedonism and the gospel of suffering " turns out to rely far too heavily on biographical gossip. Nor does Woodcock approve at heart of epigram and wit which he sees mainly as the trivialization of serious matters. He is right to point to the significance of Wilde's interest in Chaung Tzu (although this has been taken much further by later scholars), but his suggestion that cabbalistic thought may have played its part in Wilde's intellectual development is greatly overstated. Woodcock is eager to claim Wilde as an anarchist (also see his *Anarchism: A History of Libertarian Ideas and Movements*, 1962); he is at his best when he pays tribute to the courageous spirit of the prison letters, and Ellmann was surely right to reprint the section on *The Soul of Man* in his *Twentieth Century Views* collection, since here Woodcock's appreciation of Wilde's "humanism" is most obviously justified. W. H. Auden, however, was prompted to issue a witty and sophisticated riposte against all such attempts to turn Wilde into a prophet ("A Playboy of the Western World: St. Oscar, the Homintern Martyr," *PR*, 1950; rpt. *New Partisan Reader 1945–53*, ed. Phillips and Rahv, 1953). Woodcock summarized his own approach in a later article (*New Republic*, 12 July 1954) but added nothing new.

In a review of Epifanio San Juan's *The Art of Oscar Wilde* (1967), Thomas Flanagan wrote: "Mr. San Juan cherishes solemnity as Wilde cherished wit" (*VS*, 1967). The judgment is too harsh, but one can see Flanagan's point. San Juan has read almost everything available about Wilde, an achievement the reader is never allowed to forget, although this does mean that his book serves incidentally as a useful working bibliography. The method is principally to describe Wilde's work in the common vocabulary of contemporary criticism, which in itself reinforces Wilde's claim to be taken seriously; the disadvantage is that its subject is finally smothered by jargon. Moreover, the theoretical base, when it is disclosed, turns out to be unambitious: the artist projects a world in which experience is transformed, and form and content are united. There are chapters on the poetry, the criticism (this particularly overladen with paraphrase), the poetic drama, and a survey of "the action of the comedies." San Juan is best on *Dorian Gray*, where he stresses the spatial qualities of the novel and the significance of theatrical gesture, though the importance of Lord Henry and Hallward is consequently underestimated. *The Art of Oscar Wilde* has the stale air of a thesis *réchauffée*. The extent to which this opinion is generally held can be judged from the reviews listed in VS (1968).

Kevin Sullivan's pamphlet *Oscar Wilde* (1972) is careless in its use of facts and often embarrassing in its trite attempts to make Wilde relevant to contemporary society. A basic error in dating Wilde's introduction to Douglas nullifies many of the points made about *Dorian Gray*. Michael Hardwick, *The Drake Guide to Oscar Wilde* (1973), is a rudimentary biography with plot summaries of the major works; its one novelty is the inclusion of a discography.

The deposition of biography must involve its replacement by critical thesis. Christopher Nassaar's *Into the Demon Universe* (1974) never wanders far from its controlling idea and is occasionally at its mercy. Stressing the demonism latent in the romanticism of the early part of the century, Nassaar claims that Wilde "elevated the demonic to the status of a religion and tried to terminate the nineteenth century with a religion of evil, an unholy worship of evil beauty." But the pursuit of evil is an ambivalent motivation in decadent literature; what seems to be necessary for art may turn out to be entirely destructive in life; evil may take full possession of the self. The point of departure is 1886, the moment when Wilde's writing becomes original and when he was probably first initiated into the world of homosexuality. Lengthy analyses of "Lord Arthur Savile's Crime" and the fairy tales show how innocence confronts evil dialectically so that a higher innocence may ultimately be attained. Subsequent works (*Dorian Gray, Salome* in particular) are increasingly demonic in that their protagonists are irrevocably given over to evil. Nassaar's most important achievement is to have related this progression to the context of Victorian art movements; indeed, with a sometimes picturesque sense of chronology he suggests that Wilde's writings are actually engaged in debate with the surrounding culture. Thus he stresses the significance of Tennyson to the early stories and the presence of Pre-Raphaelitism in *Dorian Gray*, making comparisons with nineties poetry throughout. In a central chapter, "The Daughters of Herodias," he makes new connections between *Salome* and Frazer's *Golden Bough* and relates *A Woman of No Importance* to *The Scarlet Letter*. The consequent treatment of *The Importance* comes as a disappointment: Nassaar's argument that in this play Wilde is preoccupied with parodying his own previous works smacks of too neat a resolution of his earlier themes. Nor is objectivity fully recovered in the concluding discussions of *De Profundis* and *The Ballad*. However, in our view this is one of the better critical books on Wilde even if some judgments of it have been hostile (see *NCF*, 1974; *SEL*, 1974; *Criticism*, 1975; *VN*, 1975; *YES*, 1975; *N&Q*, 1976).

VII. Shorter Critical Studies

If Wilde has suffered longer than most from the biographical approach, then the reasons for this need to be acknowledged. In Wilde's case the life and the work do inevitably seem interdependent: indeed, many of his own pronouncements point out that no absolute division between the two can ever be made. But the wholeness, the sense of progression throughout the career, despite the many kinds of writing attempted, also make it very difficult to group criticism of Wilde under generic headings. A recent tendency has been to concentrate on his criticism, but commentators have still stressed its autobiographical nature, sometimes presenting Wilde as critic of his own work. Students of Wilde should therefore be warned that many of the books and articles that we mention overlap each other in their frames of reference, and that, for instance, a piece ostensibly on the plays may also contain remarks on the fiction, poetry, or criticism.

Such factors complicate the question of Wilde's "reputation." Karl Beckson's excellent *Oscar Wilde: The Critical Heritage* is helpful in charting Wilde's stock until the 1920's, especially with regard to the plays. In his introductory discussion Beckson goes beyond the scope of his printed selections. Similarly, *Oscar Wilde: A Collection of Critical Essays*, ed. Richard Ellmann (*Twentieth Century Views*, 1969) is more valuable than is often the case with such volumes and is particularly strong on other writers' responses to Wilde in their creative as well as their critical work. We discuss most of Ellmann's selections individually; but mention should be made now of his introduction, a concise critical history in itself.

Together, Ellmann's essays on Wilde compose a prelude to his full-length study. His previously mentioned introduction to *Oscar Wilde: Selected Writings* (1961) proposes Wilde as an innocent "only varnished with corruption." His "Romantic Pantomime in Oscar Wilde" (*PR*, 1963) is a wide-ranging discussion of Wilde's literary personality that moves toward a historical placing. It is infused, though sympathetically, by the perception of waste. Ellmann agrees with Wilde's own judgment on himself that he held a symbolic relation to his age. But unable to direct his own talents, every aspect became ambivalent; his sins and his passions no less than his protest. The product of a post-Romantic age, he turned to paradox and wit, and his theme was exile. The doctrine of the mask "is itself a mask," unlike that of his great pupil Yeats. It was Wilde's essential innocence always shadowed by guilt that accounted for his need to expose and confess. Like all Ellmann's pieces, this is a wise and highly developed application of a biocritical approach.

In England biographical knowledge at first raised only moral embarrassments, intensified by the revelations of *De Profundis*. But there were some exceptions—for instance, Walter Frewen Lord ("Some Noticeable Books," *Nineteenth Century*, 1905) and W. M. Leadman (*Westminster Review*, 1906, rpt. *The Critical Heritage*), who forgave Wilde on the basis of the letter. Other instances of a more flexible attitude can be found in H. J. Birstingl (*Westminster Review*, 1910); K[enneth] F[ord] C[allaghan] (*The Caian*, the magazine of Gonville and Caius College, 1911); Mrs. Havelock Ellis (*FortR*, 1917).

In America among the earlier reactions were Willis Vickery's *Oscar Wilde* (1906), published in Cedar Rapids, Iowa, which together with inaccuracies and provincial moralizing did specify the charges against Wilde from the court proceedings; Lewis Piaget Shanks in *The Dial* (1910, rpt. *The Critical Heritage*); Alfred Newton's slim volume in his defense, *Oscar Wilde* (1912; see also Newton's *The Amenities of Book-Collecting and Kindred Affections*, 1920); two contributions from Kansas by Charles J. Finger: "The Tragic Story of Oscar Wilde's Life" (*Ten Cent Pocket Series*, n.d.) and "An Outline of the Works of Oscar Wilde" (*Life and Letters*, 1923); Sylvestre Dorian, "The Plagiarism of Oscar Wilde" (*Haldeman-Julius Monthly*, 1925). Finger is not stupid, though not precisely original. Frank Harris spent some years of his youth in Lawrence, Kansas, and his lingering presence partially accounts for the curious incidence of items about Wilde published from there. However all these are mostly interesting for their very distance from the Wilde milieu—they provide another instance of the power of his example. In an eccentric but spasmodically perceptive essay G. R. Throop (*Mid-West Quarterly*, 1915) first saw Wilde as attempting to synthesize romanticism with classicism and then drew an extended comparison with Gautier. Throop failed, however, to allude to the English Parnassian context: Dobson, Lang, and so on.

More typical in both England and America were essays such as Homer E. Woodbridge's "Oscar Wilde: A Study in Decadent Romanticism" (*Harvard Monthly*, 1905) and William Chislett, Jr., in "The New Hellenism of Oscar Wilde" (*SR*, 1915). Both Woodbridge and Chislett were characterized by the kind of moral doubts of the opposition in the nineties, and they thought that Wilde had corrupted the classical ideal. Gilbert Coleridge (*Nineteenth Century*, 1922) is a more extreme instance of the same prejudice, and E. T. Raymond (*Outlook*, 4 Dec. 1920) is largely Philistine. H. L. Mencken was ambivalent in his intro. to *A House of Pomegranates* (1918, rpt. *The Critical Heritage*). Lewis Melville presented a balanced case in *The New World* (1919) and made some commonsense points about the plays. Richard Le Gallienne tried to draw attention to Wilde's intellectual powers and the charitable spirit of his wit (*Munsey's Magazine*, 1919). Caution, both moral and literary, is expressed in such books as Harold Williams, *Modern English Writers* (1919); Robert Lynd, *The Art of Letters* (1920); S. M. Ellis, *Mainly Victorian* (1924); G. K. Chesterton, *The Victorian Age in Literature* (1925);

Edward Shanks, *Second Essays on Literature* (1927); Arnold Bennett, *The Savour of Life* (1928). A. Devoe's *The Portrait of Mr. Wilde* (1930) is slim, elegant, and empty—a series of imagistic paragraphs. Compton Mackenzie's acknowledgment that Wilde's trial "did more to destroy the Victorian idea than anything else" was counteracted by his remark that "a foolish and artificial book like *Dorian Gray* seemed corrupt enough to have been written by Satan himself" (*Literature in My Time*, 1933).

However, in 1932 Patrick Braybrooke (*Essays by Divers Hands*) and A. C. Wilson (*Papers of the Manchester Literary Club*) both noted a renewal of interest in Wilde. This had perhaps already been reflected by the publication of the 1930 "Everyman" edition of his writings. Braybrooke qualified his own approval of the plays with very English doubts about the dangers implicit in Wilde's "cleverness," though he admitted to an admiration for *Dorian Gray* and the short stories. Wilson made the unusual point that *De Profundis* belonged with the critical essays, since its principal concern was art; but he also noticed "a stream of vulgarity" in Wilde's stories and dismissed most of the plays.

An early attempt to discuss Wilde's "afterlife" is offered by Percival Pollard (*Their Day in Court*, 1909), who reprints among other things his appreciation of Wilde written for *The Papyrus* of 1908. Pollard suggests a gruesome parallel between Wilde's life and that of T. G. Wainewright. More importantly he provides some mild documentation of Wilde's influence in Germany. The year is 1905; the place, Berlin; and the influence is asserted, though barely demonstrated, on the "thought-modes" of Dehmel, Bierbaum, and Wedekind (cf. Jules Huret, *En Allemagne. Rhin et Westphalie*, Paris, 1907). The 1969 photo-reprint of *Their Day in Court* has an informative introduction by Douglas C. Stenerson: Pollard sometimes wrote on Wilde using the nom-de-plume "The Ringmaster" (e.g., *Town Topics*, 15 June 1905). Pollard correlated with enthusiasm the reception of *Salome* in Germany. Another American critic of the same school, James Huneker (*Unicorns*, 1918) praises Wilde the conversationalist and personality but finds the works *pasticcio*; the plays "fascinating as fireworks and as remote from human interest"; *Intentions* remains Wilde's best work, for it is his most "spoken" prose. Huneker's views can be compared with those of Symons. There is little to detain the student of Wilde in the elegantly evasive essay by the "New Humanist" Stuart Sherman that first appeared in *Books*, the literary supplement to the *Herald Tribune*, on 19 July 1925 (rpt. *Critical Woodcuts*, 1926). These three Americans at least abstain from crass moralizing.

Many French critics are legitimately concerned with the *personnalité* of the writer as it infuses his work: examples are Louis Thomas (*Revue de Belgique*, 1913); Paul Chauvet in *Sept essais de littérature anglaise* (Paris, 1931); and Robert André (*NRF*, 1966). At the same time they naturally draw parallels with French writers of the period, in terms of lifestyle. In *Les Fous de 1900* (Paris, Geneva, 1954) André Germain compares Wilde and Douglas with Verlaine and Rimbaud. The same comparisons are made by C. Bronne in "Parallèlement: Wilde et Verlaine en prison" (*Synthèses*, 1955). Verlaine may have benefited from his prison experiences, but the harsher treatment accorded to Wilde "fit sombrer . . . en lui-même. Au dessus de lui-même, elle éleva Verlaine. Autant comparer l'enfer et le purgatoire."

Other French critics, however, put the accent on the intellectual milieu. Paul Souday's "L'Esthétique d'Oscar Wilde" (*Les Livres du Temps*, 1913) is primarily a comparison with Ruskin as an influence and as one superseded. Souday goes on to make what was to become a standard point: that Wilde failed to maintain his own esthetic theory in his life (more doing than being). The essay on Wilde that forms part of Raymond Laurent's *Études anglaises* (Paris, 1910) constitutes a remarkable early attempt to place its subject in a "philosophic" tradition: Coleridge, the Pre-Raphaelites, Pater; it is the composition of a critic who died at the age of twenty-one. Laurent finds the life more significant than the art, and *The Importance* goes unmentioned. In "L'Intellectualisme d'Oscar Wilde" (*RAA*, 1935), J. Charbonnier was confident enough of Wilde's achievement to show that he adopted a scientific attitude to the ancient division between body and soul (Lord Henry, for instance, is a behaviorist), and that his concept of language anticipated Bergson. Three offerings from Georges-Bazile are of less significance: *Portraits d'hier* (Paris, 1911) has an almost purely biographical stress, based on Sherard, Gide, and La Jeunesse; *La Route* (1912) notes Millard's *Oscar Wilde Three Times Tried* and prints Louÿs' "Hyacinthe!"; also see *Comoedia* (11 Dec. 1912). Some French books on Wilde were reviewed together in *Le Temps* (25 Sept. 1931). C. Campinchi, *Conférencia* (1 Sept. 1934), gives a cursory account of the life. Charles Dédéyan's *Le Nouveau Mal du siècle* (2 vols., Paris, 1968, 1972), if not quite extending its theme from China to Peru, does manage to include South America and the Soviet Union. Wilde's birth date is incorrectly given, and a few perfunctory comparisons are instituted between Wilde and Verlaine as prison penitents.

Italian critics tend to seek out spirituality and to stress the importance of *De Profundis*. Aurelio Zanco's *Oscar Wilde* (Genoa, 1934) is typical in this respect. Zanco virtually ignores the later plays, showing interest mainly in *The Duchess of Padua*, *Salome*, and *A Florentine Tragedy*, and is otherwise concerned with the criticism and poetry. There are a few errors of fact, and Zanco's own Crocean esthetic has naturally dated, but his book is reasonably conscientious bibliographically. In *Rivista d'Italia* (1904) G. Gamerale made an intelligent attempt to connect Wilde's esthetic with the conduct of his trial. Other Italian critics—such as G. A. Borghese, *Studi di letteratura moderne* (Milan, 1920); Carmelo Sgroi, *Saggi e problemi di critica letteraria* (Catania, 1933); and Augusto Guidi, "Aspetti letterari della cosidetta reazione antivittoriani: Wilde" (*Humanitas*, 1952)—draw attention to Wilde's eventual conversion when they discuss *De Profundis* and, like Sgroi, may conclude that Wilde's progression demonstrates that "la moralità non basta"; Mario Praz's 1925 essay (published in *Il patto col serpente*, Milan, 1972) is an agreeable exception, which relates to his *Romantic Agony*.

The German fascination with Wilde has been uninterrupted, although the emphasis of the books has often, regrettably, been on source studies. More distinguished are the articles and in particular the translations. So numerous are the offerings here that only a few can be noted. In P. Aronstein's *Oscar Wilde: Sein Leben und Lebenswerk* (Berlin, 1922), the subject is presented as "Prophet der Schönheit"; the wit and the fairy stories are praised. The inevitable comparison between Wilde and Goethe (*Dorian Gray* with *Werther!*) is drawn. Wilde emerges as a dangerous case of the separation of life and art. R. Defeiber's *Oscar Wilde: Der Mann und sein Werk im Spiegel der Deutschen Kritik und sein Einfluss auf die Deutsche Literatur* (Heidelberg, 1934) dominated German discussion for at least two decades, largely as a consequence of its laborious paraphrase of the numerous magazine and newspaper responses to Wilde in the years immediately following his death. Wilde's influence, mainly through *Salome*, on Hofmannstahl and Eulenburg is touched on. Defeiber's own historical moment emerges in his comment that Hofmannstahl was probably attracted to Wilde's "Orientalismus" because of his ostensibly Jewish origins. Defeiber's book, like a number of other German studies, is born out of resentment at Wilde's influence: however, the consoling conclusion is drawn that it was limited to a small sect of Aesthetes and was mostly negative.

Felix P. Greve belongs to the transcendental wing of the Teutonic genius. A "creative critic," and no lover of method, sources, or evidence, he furnishes two pamphlets, *Oscar Wilde* (Berlin, 1903) and *Randarabesken zu Wilde* (Minden, 1903). In the second work, Greve develops a theory of the artist as the rested "Bauer" married to the Wandering Jew. This union produces an individual who can only become a criminal or an artist. Wilde is viewed as a typical modern artist in his rootlessness. Unable to concentrate his talents on a single great work, he diffuses them in the immediate acts of living, wit, and the pleasures of society. Returning at least to the area of speculation, if not to the subject, Greve contributes an essay to *Porträts* (Berlin, 1911) in the context of a collection whose theme is preparation for the coming of a "Menschendämmerung" to end the long decline in value of the human soul. Once more Greve uses Wilde as an emblem of the modern artist torn between the desire to produce great art and the impossibility of fulfillment, conditioned as he is by the historical moment. Wilde's career, says Greve, is divided into two sharp phases, though the division is not pre-Reading and post-Reading; the Pre-Raphaelite phase characterized by the search for form and the struggle between cynicism and artistic ambition. The second phase transcends the limits of Pre-Raphaelitism (at this point *Dämmerung* enters) and Wilde becomes truly "free." The major works are *Salome*, *The Sphinx*, and *The Ballad*. It is easy to mock Greve, and indeed he was criticized as confused and wild-eyed both in his essays and in his translations of Wilde by one of the better earlier German critics, Max Meyerfeld, in an account of the Wilde renaissance in Germany (*Das Literarische Echo*, 15 Jan. 1904). Greve's freedom of approach is not uninteresting, but he is void of method.

Carl Hagemann (*Oscar Wilde*, 1904, 1925) makes some attempt to relate Wilde to his Continental contemporaries, including Wedekind. Among other early treatments Ernst Weiss in *Psychologische Streifzüge über Oscar Wilde* (Leipzig, 1908) reveals an interest in *The Soul of Man*; Wilde's essay had previously been reviewed by

Josef Bloch in *Dokumente des Sozialismus* (1904). Os. Sero, *Der Fall Wilde und das Problem der Homosexualität* (Leipzig, 1896) and Dr. Numa Prätorius, *Jahrbuch für sexuelle Zwischenstufen* (1901) consider Wilde's homosexuality. In *Zeitschrift für Sexualwissenschaft* (1918) L. Hamilton discusses the relationship between Wilde and Douglas in the light of the Ransome trial.

Many of the German works of the inter-war period are *Quellenstudien*. K. Lück's *Die Französische Fremdwort bei Oscar Wilde als Stilistisches Kunstmittel* (Griefswald, 1927) is highly characteristic. Lück performed the arduous and largely superfluous task of listing Wilde's every use of a French word or phrase. More useful offerings are Alice Herzog's *Das Märchen Oscar Wildes* (Mulhouse, 1930), which paid some attention to the French symbolists and to Hans Christian Andersen; and Edward Schön's *Französische Einflüsse in Oscar Wildes Werken* (Hamburg, 1949). One should not forget Luise Schnapp, "Oscar Wilde und die Bibel" (*Germanisch-Romanische Monatsschrift*, 1933), of some relevance, conceivably, to *Salome*.

Wilde makes a considerable appearance in Otto Mann's *Der Dandy: Ein Kulturproblem der Moderne* (Heidelberg, 1925), where the general argument is that in countries without "Kultur," conspicuously England, secondarily France, the cultural void resulted in the counter-movement of the dandy, a type characterized by Aestheticism, negativity, and a longing for the ideals of the past. (Friedrich Muckermann discussed Mann's book together with other recent German work on Wilde in *Der Gral, Monatsschrift für Schöne Literatur*, Essen, 1926.) In "Der Dandy und sein Untergang" (*Stimmen der Zeit*, 1962–63), Gisbert Kranz relates Wilde both to the traditions of the dandy and to comments passed by other writers.

Notable early treatments with a mainly biographical emphasis include Carl Dietz, "Oscar Wilde" (*Preussische Jahrbücher*, 1906); Johann F. Hahn, *Oskar Wilde* (Munich, 1906); Halfdan Langgard, *Oscar Wilde* (Stuttgart, 1906); Helene Richter, "Oscar Wildes Kunslerische Personlichleit" (*Englische Studien*, 1912); and T. Brucauff, "Oscar Wilde," *Die Neueren Sprachen* (1916). Also see "H. V. E.," *Freistadt* (Munich, 23 May 1903); Walter Friedemann (*Frankfurter Zeitung*, 29 Aug. 1903); G. Weiss, *Der Alte Glaube* (24 Mar. 1905); Victor Klemperer, *Aus Fremden Zungen* (1906); and Alois Stockmann, *Stimmen aus Maria Laach* (1908). Fritz Engel's *Oscar Wilde und seine besten Bühnenwerke* (Berlin, 1921), however, barely rises above plot summary. Alexander von Gleichen-Russworm, *Dandies and Don Juans* (1927, trans. 1928) has a chapter on Wilde, superficial and biographical. Otto Flake, *Versuch über Oscar Wilde* (Munich, 1946) is a short critical biography which goes some way toward placing Wilde in a European context. E. Ebermayer's *Das ungewöhnliche Leben des Oscar Wilde* (Bonn, 1954) concentrates on the trials but relies on Harris and is organized like a morality play. K. Konkoly's *Oscar Wilde in der Anekdote und Gesammelt* (Würzburg, 1963) is an illustrated pocket-book made up of anecdotes and epigrams from familiar sources. P. Funke's *Oscar Wilde in Selbstszeugnissen und Bilddokumenten* (Hamburg, 1969) is solidly researched and inventively illustrated and has a formidable bibliography.

Stylistics are another German preoccupation: Elisabeth Müller,

Oscar Wilde: Wesen und Stil (Zurich, 1934) tabulates Wilde's vocabulary, syntax, and rhythms; Erwin Ihrig categorizes the paradox (Marburg, 1934) with allusion to nineteenth-century manuals on the figure; Elizabeth Schirmann, "Die Literarischen Strömungen in Werke Oscar Wildes" (*Griefswalder Beiträge zur Literatur und Stilforschung*, 1935) breaks down the oeuvre according to mode: "Romantik," "Realismus," and so on. A dissertation by Ursula Risse, *Kunstanschauung und Kunstschaffen bei Oscar Wilde* (Freiburg, 1951) continues tradition by seeking out synesthesic elements and also gives an excellent bibliography. Wilde makes a number of appearances in Lothar Hönnighausen's *PreRaphaeliten und Fin de Siècle* (Munich, 1971), an ambitious and impressively ranging study of imagery from the emblemata of the sixteenth century via the Oxford Movement and the Pre-Raphaelites to the *symboliste* version of *correspondances*. The main evidence is culled from Wilde's poetry.

It is to the early phase in Wilde's "afterlife," of articles and reviews in magazines and newspapers that *Oscar Wilde* by Hedwig Lachmann (later Landauer) belongs (Berlin, 1905?). It concentrates primarily on *Salome* (of which Lachmann made a commendable translation), has little to say of *The Ballad*, and ignores *The Importance*. The illustrations include one plate from Althea Gyles' series on "The Harlot's House." That poem is translated—"Das Hurenhaus"—along with two of Wilde's sonnets. The reception of the early translations of Wilde forms a literature of its own. Perhaps the most magisterial review is "Wilde, Wilde, Wilde" by Max Meyerfeld (*Die Literarische Echo*, 15 April 1905). As outlined in our introduction and elsewhere, the main clusters of articles relate to *De Profundis* in its 1905 and 1925 versions. Even when they do not deal directly with that work, it remains a focal point for generalization. One may begin with an elegant and impressive critic, Franz Blei. In "Oscar Wilde" (*Die Zeit*, 1903), Blei's accent falls on Wilde the dandy in his general relationship to British society, which Blei condemns for not permitting itself to be tyrannized over by a dandy and then crucifying him. Wilde's dandyism—artistry of personality—informs all his works with the exception of *The Ballad*. In a second article, "Das Ästhetische Leben" (*Österreichische Rundschau*, 1906), Blei voices an impatience with the anecdotal approach to Wilde and with critical judgments on individual works. Wilde's life should be interpreted in the broader context of intellectual history, Blei says. Wilde sought to give the impression that he lived for art alone, but actually lived an attempt to deny the importance of morality, and his central problem was of a moral nature.

Johannes Gaulke is one of the earliest German critics to discuss Wilde (see our intro). In his "Oscar Wilde" (*Das Magazin für Literatur*, 1901) Gaulke continued to find Wilde typical of the *fin de siècle*, relating the paradoxes underlying Wilde's wit to abnormal sexuality and to conflict with a society which had itself lost any sense of naïve feeling. Later Gaulke suggested that Wilde might have become a contemporary Aristophanes were English society (or German for that matter) worthy of him (*Bühne und Welt*, 13 May 1903). In this instance it could be said that Gaulke was at least trying to introduce Wilde's comedies to a wider public. But other German critics are more rewarding. Arthur Sewett, "Oscar Wildes seelische Kämpfe" (*Die Nation*, 1905) argues that Wilde's works, though grotesque, display a tendency to the morally serious. The end of Wilde's life and work was the pursuit of self, and in that Wilde reveals himself simultaneously as Aesthetic idealist, naïve romantic, and "der moderne Mensch" whose aim is to assert personality without moral or didactic intent. *Dorian Gray*, Wilde's "deepest" work, is dominated by the notion of self-realization at any cost. Dorian becomes a prime example of dualism, division of body and soul. In Reading Gaol, similarly, Wilde was forced to view his own "portrait," but unlike Dorian's, Wilde's act of self-recognition led to unified being. For S. Lublinski (*Zeitschrift für Französischen und Englischen Unterricht*, 1904–05), all Wilde's works grew out of a longing for "Kultursehnsucht." Unlike the Athenians of Pericles' age or the poets of German classicism, Wilde pursued beauty to the exclusion of all other values and at the expense of unity of being. Tragic lives such as those of Byron, Shelley, and Wilde result from the inability of England to produce a universal *Kultur*. Wilde's popularity, Lublinski tells us, was a consequence of German youth reacting against naturalism which also overemphasized a single value, technical reality; but the longing for the universal human ideal will soon relegate Wilde to obscurity. Another critic makes much the same point about the reaction to naturalism, but Carl Dietz in *Die Schöne Literatur* (11 Sept. 1909) also discusses the translations of Wilde, finding only the Lachmann-Landauer and the Insel edition from Vienna satisfactory and only the former excellent. Walter Heymann (*Xenien*, 1911) is more positive. Admitting Wilde's shortcomings, he declares himself fascinated by the division between feeling and conscience on the one hand and intellect on the other in "The Fisherman and His Soul" and *Dorian Gray*. Richard Meyer in a more generalized piece (*Velhagen und Klasings Monatshefte*, 1913) finds Wilde essentially a figure of transition. His rise and fall is explicable only in the peculiar English context, for English society tolerates writers only if they are gentlemen and normally treats them disdainfully even then. The result is the dilettante who, while writing little (and so keeping his amateur status), becomes notorious through wit and gimmickry. To this tradition belongs the dandy, Wilde himself, a materialist Aesthete who adjusts his ideals to the views of others. Meyer makes an early comparison of Wilde and Nietzsche: both in their way tried to be supermen. What at first glance might appear a serious comparative study, Ernst Groth's "Oscar Wilde und Walter Pater" (*Beiblatt zur Anglia*, 1914) turns out to derive from Bock's book, while the date of the article has its significance. Groth condemns the exaggerated enthusiasm of the German public not merely for Wilde but for modern English literature in general. For the style of criticism initiated by Pater and Wilde, Groth coins the amusing term "Kapriolismus." Pater advances an unoriginal Aesthetic hedonism which is perfectly impractical; Wilde, who borrows from everyone, attempts to put Pater's ideas and theories into practice. More enthusiastic is Fred A. Angermayer in an article contributed to *Die Literatur* in 1926, which was written in response to Meyerfeld's translations of the letters to Robert Ross of Wilde's last years. (Also see Angermayer in *Berliner Tageblatt*,

1938.) H. Temborius, "Neuromantische Wesenszüge bei Wilde" (*Zeitschrift für Französischen und Englischen Unterricht*, 1928) is a short and trivial survey of some of Wilde's more famous pronouncements. In 1940, once more silhouetted by war, Karl Schaezler in "Brief zu einem Englischen Bild" (*Hochland*) neatly transposes previous interpretations for purposes of propaganda but does not condemn Wilde, who after all was a critic of his own society. This article has been discussed in greater detail in our introduction.

Further contributions in foreign languages include A. A. Vasseur's *Gloria aventuras peregrinas* (Madrid, 1919), which translates five of the prose poems and "The Happy Prince," suggesting that "The Doer of Good" has analogues with the "Lazarus" of Léon Dierx (1868) and the "Lazaro" of José Asunción Silva; César González Ruáno, *Notas sobre Oscar Wilde* (Madrid, 1925); an early essay by René Wellek in Czech (*Listy pro Uměni a kritiku*, Prague, 1935); Ayala Ramon Perez includes an essay on *De Profundis* and has two essays on the implications of the Pemberton Billing affair in *Las mascaras*, Vol. II (Madrid, 1940); N. T. Thomsen, *Oscar Wilde: Literaturbilleder fra det moderne England* (Copenhagen, 1920) concentrates on the drama and the criticism; also in Danish, Ole Vinding, "Oscar Wilde's Breve" (*Perspektiv*, 1962); in Dutch there is H. Kapteign's *Autonomie Dichters Typen: Van Poets Maudits* (Utrecht, 1949); in Icelandic, G. Kamban, "Wilde" (*Ithunn*, 1929); and in Polish, S. J. Imber, *Pieśń i dusza Oskara Wilde'a* (Warsaw, 1934).

Signs at last of a more sophisticated application of biography in English and American criticism begin to appear in Desmond Mac-Carthy's essay in *English Wits* (ed. Leonard Russell, 1940); Arthur H. Nethercot (*PMLA*, 1944); Noel Annan (*New Statesman*, 2 Oct. 1954); Joseph Wood Krutch (*Nation*, 1954); Vivian Mercier ("The Fate of Oscar Wilde," *Commonweal*, 1955); and A. G. Woodward (*ESA*, 1959). Most contain intuitions that were to be explored more deeply by later critics: Aestheticism as an antecedent of the New Criticism; the confessional urge; the importance of the sinner and the centrality of a "secret" that presumably has to do with homosexuality. Yet none follow through the implications of what they see, no doubt because of uneasiness with the notion of Wilde as a serious writer. Among journalists, at all events, this inhibition is still not always overcome and perhaps never will be; examples are Michael Harrison's silly and vulgar piece on the occasion of Wilde's centenary (*Courier*, 1954) and Richard Pine (*DM*, 1971-72).

Reconsiderations of Wilde's historical significance can be found in several postwar books that survey the major figures of the late nineteenth century, although approaches vary according to the intellectual origins of each. Graham Hough's *The Last Romantics* (1949) is arguably the most important, although Wilde himself plays a comparatively minor part in his overall scheme. Hough claims that *Dorian Gray* is an abuse of the examples of Pater and Huysmans because it substitutes melodramatic devices for moral experience. In *The Listener* (1954), Hough further questions Wilde's originality but makes the more subtle point that Wilde's critical theory does not entirely suit his own works, where autobiographical fantasy is the key.

In America Wilde's claims have been strengthened by a propensity to view him as a precursor of Freud, an emphasis that partly compensates for a vitiating caution in matters of politics. This is true of Gaylord C. Leroy's *Perplexed Prophets* (1953), which argues that Wilde was a believer in the "free expansive forces of the personality" liberating him from "the distrust of human potentialities" common to the High Victorians; an affinity with Rossetti prevents him from matching the achievements of Morris and Shaw. But Leroy underestimates the political potential of Aestheticism, which he contrasts with modernism *tout court*—his omission of Pater is in part to blame for this distortion.

Attempts to formulate a working definition of Decadence have always been unsatisfactory, especially when they attempt to distinguish it from Aestheticism. A. J. Farmer, *Le Mouvement esthétique et 'décadent' en Angleterre 1873–1900* (*Bibliothèque de la Revue de Littérature Comparée*, Paris, 1931), traces an overall direction in Wilde's writings but only on the basis of a very loose definition. Decadence here is associated with "une vision intérieure," which Wilde derived in rather uncertain terms from Pater. *Dorian Gray* and *Salome* are inevitably seen to be the central texts, though Farmer has some relevant analyses of the shorter fiction. The work has all the characteristics of the older French theses: it is immensely thorough and contains a great deal of bibliographical information but remains deficient in critical argument. Though imprecise, it is probably of most lasting value for its identifications of French influences —Baudelaire, Flaubert, Gautier. Not that Anglo-Saxon surveys of Decadence are any more conclusive. Two early books of literary history saw Wilde as entirely symptomatic of the decay of Romanticism: R. A. Scott-James, *Modernism and Romance* (1908, rpt. in part *The Critical Heritage*) and J. M. Kennedy, *English Literature 1880–1905* (1912), although Kennedy also alluded to the influence of Jowett's editions of Plato, an area that has yet to be fully explored. For one contributor to Orage's *New Age* Wilde was to be seen only as a reaction to Victorianism, his mind "a drugged and stupefied slave" to his body, and not therefore as the true herald of Nietzschean modern man (Edward Moore, *We Moderns*, 1918). In more recent comment on Decadence, Wilde has invariably played a part, but not always a major one (Clyde de L. Ryals, *JAAC*, 1958; Robert L. Peters, *JAAC*, 1959; Clyde de L. Ryals, *TSL*, 1959; Richard A. Long and Ira G. Jones, *CE*, 1961; *ELT*, 1974).

Wilde now holds a more secure position in the books that survey the transition from Decadence to Modernism, especially when the emphasis is on the doctrine of the mask and the figures of the Aesthete and the dandy, major symptoms of the age's concern with the fragmentation of the self. Janko Lavrin recognized the signs well enough in his study of European writers, *Aspects of Modernism from Wilde to Pirandello* (1935), but damned Wilde for hedonism nonetheless. G. Masur includes Wilde in his large scale survey *Prophets of Yesterday* (1961) but is entirely unoriginal and apparently unperturbed by questions of historical and comparative method. Both Barbara Charlesworth (*Dark Passages: The Decadent Consciousness in Victorian Literature*, 1965; a version of the Wilde chapter in *Spectrum*,

1963) and John Lester (*Journey through Despair*, 1968) locate Wilde's place in a tradition that runs from Rossetti and Swinburne through Pater to Symons. Charlesworth makes an interesting comparison between *The Ambassadors* and *Dorian Gray*, refers to Baudelaire, notes Wilde's predilection for sexual fantasy, and decides that by the time he comes to write *The Importance* mask and reality have proved to be one and the same thing. Lester uses Wilde as a buttress for numerous topics: his section on the mask is the most substantial, although the originality of Wilde's ethics is insufficiently stressed.

Alick West's chapter on Wilde in *The Mountain and the Sunlight* (1958) is one of the most incisive examinations of Wilde the social thinker but, unfortunately, one of the least known. West concentrates on the poems and early criticism to expose the contradictions in Wilde's socio-esthetic program. The underlying theory is shown to be compromised because it is based on a naïve sense of historical process, which is connected in turn with Wilde's preoccupation with the form rather than the content of art. West is particularly acute about *Dorian Gray*, where he finds evidence of "the division of mind in a divided society," and he notes that Wilde's attitudes inevitably lead to a complete separation between art and people, which William Morris, for instance, avoids. The assumptions behind this reading are strictly Marxist, but the motives are sympathetic; for while West accuses Wilde of capitulating finally to sentimental fatalism, he adds that to dismiss him as merely decadent would be to align oneself with Carson. An earlier Marxist reading by Granville Hicks in *Figures of Transition* (1939) has dated much more severely.

A constructive article by Birgit Borelius (*Scripta Minora*, 1966–67) falls into three interconnected parts. First, she questions the conclusions reached by Ojala and the earlier German scholars about the part played by color in comparisons between the arts, and proves that Wilde's sources for his poetry were almost undoubtedly literary. In a careful analysis of his intellectual relations with Whistler, Wilde is revealed as a "Judas": his critical ideas owe a great deal to Whistler, but he transcends his master by taking his attitudes as a starting-point in "The Critic as Artist" and then refining and refuting them. This discussion replaces that of Gerda Eichbaum (*EngS*, 1930–31). In the final sections, Borelius demonstrates how Wilde took the motif of "whiteness" from Pater and Swinburne and used it in the creation of Salome, who embodies necrophilia, perversity, and sterility. A further suggestion connects Salome with the figure of Diana of Ephesus.

Wilde and Henley were linked by Yeats, and comparisons between the great Aesthete and imperialist poets are frequent. They run through Holbrook Jackson's admirable *The Eighteen Nineties* (1913) to, for instance, Alan Rodway's 1958 essay in *The Penguin Guide to English Literature*, Vol. VI, ed. Boris Ford. The opposition surfaces again in David Daiches' *Some Late Victorian Attitudes* (1969) in the formula: "Aestheticism and stoic activism can be seen as opposites of the same medal." Daiches makes specific comparisons first among Wilde and Kipling and Henley and then between Wilde and Butler. William Empson has made a different point about Wilde's place in the national culture, complaining that his fascination with the aristocracy "leaves a rather bad taste in the mouth because it is slavish; it has something of the naive snobbery of the high-class servant" (*Some Versions of Pastoral*, 1935). Empson also has some pertinent comments on the nineteenth-century cult of the artist as criminal and the figure of the innocent upper-class girl.

In conclusion it must be said that the application of psychoanalytic techniques to Wilde's case has so far brought only feeble results; examples are Clifford Allen, *Homosexuality and Creative Genius* (ed. Hendrik Ruitenbeek, 1967), Louis Aubrun, *Paris Soir* (10 June 1931), and Edmund Bergler, *Fashion and the Unconscious* (1953). Biographical sources are uncritically utilized in A. Stocker, *L'Amour interdit: Trois anges sur la route de Sodom* (Geneva and Annemasse, 1945), where Wilde appears in company with Gide and Claudel in an analysis from a Latin Catholic point of view.

VIII. Plays

An examination of the reviews collected by Beckson and of the dramatic criticism of the time (particularly that of Archer, Grein, and Walkley) shows how the response to Wilde's plays was governed by the contemporary atmosphere. Two principal issues emerged: Did these plays have French models, and if so, what were they? Was Wilde capable of writing a "serious" play? Even Shaw in his generally respectful comments was unsettled by the second question—as is evidenced by his dislike of *The Importance* (see *Our Theatres in the Nineties*, 1948). Max Beerbohm never ceased to pay tribute to Wilde's genius in his worldly and dispassionate journalism (*Around Theatres*, 1959; *More Theatres*, 1969; *Last Theatres*, 1970). Although Beerbohm did not consider Wilde to have been an instinctive writer, nobody has better appreciated the brilliance of his stage technique or judged more succinctly his innovative contributions to dramatic history.

Immediately after the conviction various publishers and theatrical managers expediently withheld all reference to Wilde; even the adverse comments in Augustin Filon, *Le Théâtre anglais* (Paris, 1896) were entirely omitted from the English translation (*The English Stage*, 1897). Yet the public commitment of Beerbohm and others is some indication that the period of silence was shorter than is sometimes supposed. Certainly it was not too far into the new century before it became possible to write about Wilde again, although many of the surveys of modern drama published in the first three decades tend to denigrate his achievement and, for instance, frequently rank Pinero above him. The most influential of these was Archer's *The Old Drama and the New* (1923), but see also Mario Borsa, *The English Stage of Today* (1908); F. W. Chandler, *Aspects of Modern Drama* (1914); Ludwig Lewisohn, *The Modern Drama* (1915); T. H. Dickinson, *The Contemporary Drama of England* (1917); Storm Jameson, *Modern Drama in Europe* (1920); Gilbert Norwood, *Euripides and Shaw with Other Essays* (1921); Nellie Burget Miller, *The Living Drama* (1924). In an excellent survey written in 1908 (*FortR*; rpt. *Twentieth Century Views* and *The Critical Heritage*), St. John

Hankin was still referring back to the French—"in the age of Ibsen and Hauptmann, of Strindberg and Brieux, he was content to construct like Sardou and think like Dumas fils"—but he also identified *The Importance*, along with *Arms and the Man* and *The Philanderer*, as a specimen of "farcical comedy." Equally notable is C. E. Montague's essay in *Dramatic Values* (1911). Montague's analysis of Wilde's technique is convincing not only because of his critical acumen but also because of his capacity to recognize and explain the styles of social behavior portrayed in the comedies. With a little intelligent hindsight Wilde's modernity became more apparent to others. Recognitions of it can be found in chapters by P. P. Howe (*Dramatic Portraits*, 1913), who made some use of "The Truth of Masks" when he demonstrated Wilde's desire to make use of the theater's ability to draw upon all the arts; and by Archibald Henderson (*European Dramatists*, 1913), who again made comparisons with Shaw and, less satisfactorily, with Ibsen. Henderson's conclusions are, however, spoiled by his old-fashioned ("philistine") attitude, which connects the art of paradox with egoism and therefore judges that Wilde lacks the human sympathy necessary for a dramatist. The same prejudice dominates the treatment of Wilde in his earlier *Interpreters of Life and the Modern Spirit* (1911). Also see *Arena* (1907, rpt. *The Critical Heritage*).

Moral doubts continued to burden discussions until the Second World War, although Hesketh Pearson (*Modern Men and Mummers*, 1921) tried to argue that Wilde was a subjective artist because an audience laughs with his characters, rather than at them, as is the case with Sheridan and Congreve. In *The Comedy of Manners from Sheridan to Maugham* (1931), N. W. Sawyer was genial if patronizing about Wilde and fitted him rather insecurely into the tradition. Rose Snider (*Satire in the Comedies of Congreve, Sheridan, Wilde and Coward*, 1937) and Henry Ten Eyck (*Masters of Dramatic Comedy and their Social Themes*, 1000) both emphasized how Wilde's talent to amuse concealed an underlying sentimentality. John Mason Brown drew more stimulating comparisons between the social comedy of Wilde, Maugham, and Coward in his *Seeing More Things* (1948); and in *The Tight-rope Walkers* (1956) Giorgio Melchiori referred to Christopher Fry and the late plays of T. S. Eliot.

It was probably not until the 1950's that there came the beginning of a revaluation. Louis Kronenberger attempted to justify the uncertain comedy of Wilde's problem plays, but his case was spoiled by an incomplete understanding of the nineties theatrical scene (*The Thread of Laughter*, 1952). Although unduly censorious about the early work (and *Salome* in particular), Allan Harris ("Oscar Wilde as Playwright: A Centenary Review," *Adelphi*, 1954) at least acknowledged the social implications behind Wilde's apparent frivolity and accepted that, for all the surface glitter, his personal involvement in his plays might in itself challenge established morality. In this context the comments of Tyrone Guthrie appear condescending (introd. to *Plays*, 1954). Guthrie was still applying naturalistic criteria to prove Wilde's immaturity.

It took an experienced commitment to the full social reference of the genre for Wilde's method of comedy to be given the serious analysis that it deserved. Eric Bentley's brief but brilliant remarks on *The Importance* in his *The Playwright as Thinker* (1955) are seminal, whatever play is being studied. Bentley credited Wilde with the creation of a new kind of comedy, a "variant of farce" in which the dialogue is a "pseudo-irresponsible jabbing at all the great problems"; so that "witticisms are, not comic, but serious relief." His perception that Wilde's bohemian mask anticipated Pirandello's juggling with role and identity opened the way for many new approaches.

Perhaps only one other general discussion deserves to be put alongside Bentley's although, significantly, it is an attempt to refute some of Bentley's claims. In "Comedy and Oscar Wilde" (*SR*, 1966) Ian Gregor argues that the main problem that Wilde faced as a dramatist was to find "a world fit for the dandy to live in; fit, in the sense that such a world would help to make clear the meaning of the dandy." The early solution was for the dandy to be "voluntarily displaced," a process that operates in all the plays until *The Importance*, when Wilde creates a world inhabited by dandies only. By making the point that paradox is at heart a self-delighting mode of expression, Gregor can claim against Bentley that Wilde had finally written the pure Aesthetic play. Arthur Ganz comes to a not dissimilar conclusion in "The Divided Self in the Society Comedies of Oscar Wilde" (*MD*, 1960), though with less elegance; moreover, Ganz bases his argument on the only partially documented suggestion that until his last comedy Wilde was uncertain whether or not to cast in his lot with the dandy—the moralism of philistine society still held a claim on him through much of the earlier work. Unfortunately, despite its avowed intention, E. K. Mikhail's "Oscar Wilde and His First Comedy" (*MD*, 1968) fails to enlighten us as to why Wilde turned to comedy in the first place. In their editions of *The Importance* (1959) and *Lady Windermere's Fan* (1960) V. F. Hopper and G. B. Lahey include the same general essay on Wilde the playwright. This is based on a witty but mildly inaccurate biographical comparison with Byron, and the plays are approached via dandyism and the function of wit: "In all the comedies except *The Importance* Wilde has tried to mix the water of a too-easy sentimentalism and the oil of a glassy cynicism." Louis Kronenberger's introduction to the 1962 paperback edition of *Lady Windermere's Fan* and *The Importance* makes a similar point, noting that the mixed modes of the earlier play (mawkish soliloquies and brilliant epigrams) make it seem altogether schizoid, whereas *The Importance* represents a triumph of manner in which "the wildly fanciful circumstance is matched by the madly literal-minded social reaction to it." G. Wilson Knight is as idiosyncratic as ever in *The Golden Labyrinth* (1962) where, in a brief discussion, he shows a marked enthusiasm for *Vera*.

Radical approaches have since been stimulated by the wish to relate Wilde to the preferred modes of the contemporary theater. Morris Freedman has considered Wilde together with O'Casey as a precursor of modern tragicomedy (*CE*, 1964; rpt. *The Moral Impulse*, 1967, with a faintly startled introduction by Harry T. Moore); but these connections remain tenuous despite Freedman's attempt to relate what he sees as Wilde's overdetermined social environments with the world of the absurd. In *British Drama Since Shaw* (1972)

Emil Roy suggests that Wilde was closer to Yeats than Shaw in that he supported an idealist theater characterized by imaginative rather than mimetic possibilities. Roy makes his point with some very intelligent readings that explain behavior in psychological terms: Wilde's characters, for instance, are "isolated individuals surrounded by incompatible choices, each mode of conduct as farcically incomplete as it is compelling." B. H. Fussell (*SR*, 1972) has little patience with most of Wilde's plays but has some good points about their structure nonetheless: the dandy is a kind of Vice or jester, the world of London society is urban-pastoral, and Wilde's achievement is to combine Nature and Art, good and evil, within a single character. She is original also about the two plays that she does admire, offering *Salome* and *The Importance* as an antithetical pairing: masque and antimasque. *Salome* prefigures Artaud because it has some of the hieratic ritualism of a Black Mass but is tinged with comedy; and *The Importance* foreshadows the absurd or even Genet in the absolute dominance of its comic symmetry.

There remains the persistent question of Wilde's use of the drama of his own time, although M. Ellehauge made a start in "Initial Stages in the Development of the English Problem-Play" (*EngS*, 1932). The French example is probably more crucial. Stephen Stanton drops a few hints about this in his introduction to *Camille and Other Plays* (1957) but fails to follow them through; while John Russell Taylor in *The Rise and Fall of the Well-Made Play* (1967) refers only to Wilde's own influence upon H. A. Jones, Shaw, Maugham, and others and entirely ignores the question of a specific debt to France. In "The Influence of Dumas fils on Oscar Wilde" (*FR*, 1933) Stanley Schwarz attempted to prove Wilde's dependence on a single French playwright, but weakened his account by imprecise methods of comparison and some glaring misreadings. He juxtaposed *An Ideal Husband* with *L'Ami des femmes*, and *A Woman of No Importance* with *La Fille naturel*. E. H. Mikhail (*BLG*, 1968) broadened the enquiry to include Scribe, Sardou, and Augier, whom he had obviously studied in detail, but unfortunately his conclusions (e.g. about Wilde's attitudes to women) offer little improvement on Schwarz. "The Importance of Reading Alfred: Oscar Wilde's Debt to Alfred de Musset" (*BNYPL*, 1971) by Charles B. Paul and Robert D. Pepper stands out as a rare attempt to trace a specific source for one of Wilde's plays. Very detailed documentation is accumulated in order to prove that the genre to which *The Importance* belongs is that of the *comédie-proverbe*, that its precise model is *Il ne faut jurer de rien*. But this argument further depends on an acceptance of Wilde's consciously "doubling" the characters and situation of de Musset's play (the comparison is with Shakespeare's use of Plautus in *A Comedy of Errors*). The parallels are by no means equally convincing and there is no doubt that Paul and Pepper overstate their case, but the basic suggestion is intriguing (also see *ELT*, 1972). More work is still required in this area.

Further attention needs to be paid also to the day-to-day world of the London theater in which Wilde lived and worked, although a welcome "reconstruction" of the first performance of *The Importance* is already under way. A little preliminary information is available from James Agate (*Masque*, 1947; rpt. *James Agate, An Anthology*, 1961), from Hesketh Pearson (*Theater Arts*, 1961), and from such books as A. E. W. Mason, *Sir George Alexander and the St. James Theatre* (1935); but prolonged research into newspapers, memoirs, accounts, etc., all the residue of theatrical activity, as well as more information about social history, is what is required. It would be valuable to know if, for instance, the financial arrangements involving the plays that are detailed by J. B. Booth in *London Town* (1929) are at all accurate.

Not surprisingly, there is little of interest on *The Duchess of Padua*. R. Fischer in "Oscar Wilde, *Die Herzogin von Padua . . .*" (*Archiv für das Studium der Neueren Sprachen*, 1905) was written in response to Meyerfeld's translation. Fischer finds the work immature, but proleptic of *Salome*: romanticism will become eroticism and language lyrical rather than dramatic. However "Alfr. B." (*Beilage zur Allgemeinen Zeitung*, 12 Oct. 1904) was rhapsodic: the play could be mistaken for the work of Shakespeare.

Cleanth Brooks and Robert B. Heilman printed *Lady Windermere's Fan* in *Understanding Drama* (1945), using it mainly as a vehicle for the exposition of their pedagogic method. They surround the text with questions and comments intended to direct the student toward the specific evaluation that what starts off well as serious drama ends up in a losing battle with melodrama. While in sympathy with the indictment of Lady Windermere's inadequate moral experience, which they take to be Wilde's aim, they object that her development is inhibited early on when Wilde becomes wholly concerned with rescuing his character from the situation in which he has placed her. This judgment has been questioned by Morse Peckham (*CE*, 1956). Peckham shows that the "non-fulfillment" of traditional plot and Lady Windermere's never learning the truth makes a dramatic point: although she comes to see that people are a mixture of good and bad, she does not learn to question moral categories, only moral conclusions. The analysis provided by Hopper and Lahey in their edition (1960) has more in common with Brooks and Heilman than with Peckham. Relating the play to the traditions of the well-made play and of English comedy, they judge Wilde to be generally conservative and therefore socially irresponsible, although, more unusually, they do allow that his depiction of the fallen woman figure is less sentimental than those of Pinero and Shaw.

The problem of determining the circumstances in which *Salome* came to be written has been summed up by Clyde de L. Ryals (*N&Q*, 1959), who distinguished three separate "legends" of its composition. The sources for these are Adolphe Retté, *Le Symbolisme, anecdotes et souvenirs* (Paris, 1903); Stuart Merrill's review of Retté's section on Wilde (*La Plume*, 1904); and Ernest Raynaud, *La Mêlée symboliste*, Vol. II (Paris, 1920), which fills in something of the Parisian context that affected the play. The anonymous *Things I Shouldn't Tell* (1924) contains the quite unauthenticated story that *Salome* was translated into French by a student named Pelissier. A detailed scholarly examination of the texts that survive has yet to be conducted. The 1909 Methuen edition has a preface by Ross and a bibliography of editions and translations compiled by Walter Ledger.

In *El libro de los mujeros* (Paris, 1909; see also *La Plume*, 1902)
E. Gómez Carrillo recalls the various images of Salome around which
Wilde's imagination played before he began the actual composition.
An earlier article in *Almas y Cerebros* (Paris, 1892; see also *Esquisses*,
Madrid, 1892) refers to *Salome* and other works by Wilde.

Salome is a special case in Wilde's oeuvre in that it invites an
approach through a particular myth, and any study of its nineteenth-
century variations must begin with Mario Praz's classic study of the
Fatal Woman, *The Romantic Agony* (1933), and Frank Kermode's
more theoretical *Romantic Image* (1957). Yet Praz was unac-
countably disparaging about Wilde's play, finding it of interest
mainly as a parody of Decadent material. Those critics who have
placed Wilde's handling of the figure of Salome in that narrower
tradition which embraces Heine, Flaubert, and Gustave Moreau have
been generally more appreciative. A long anonymous survey of nineteenth-century treatments, which refers also to Renaissance depictions, appeared as early as 1912 in *The Edinburgh Review* and still
provides a good introduction to the topic. Maurice Vaucaire in *La
Nouvelle Revue* (1907) and Ernest Gaubert in *Mercure de France*
(1910) supplied less thorough surveys of the same and related material in French.

The hinterland of German Salome scholarship is immense and has
only partly been explored. A standard resource is Hugo Daffner's
Salome. Ihre Gestalt in Geschichte und Kunst (Munich, 1912) with
its extraordinary range of illustrations. The mature thoughts of
Reimarus Junior may be found in the new edition of his work on
Salome in the New Testament and later literature, *Stoffgeschichte der
Salome-Dichtungen* (Leipzig, 1913). Of mainly historical interest is
an essay by F. P. Greve, "Wilde und das Drama," published in *Oscar
Wildes Werke* (Berlin, ca. 1903). Notable from the early period are
Luise Becker's "Salome in der Kunst des letzten Jahrtausends" (*Bühne
und Welt*, 1902); J. Abraham's *Salome oder über die Grenzen der
Dichtung* (Berlin, 1907); and, for more remote areas of the Salome
legend, Waldemann Kloss, "Herodias, the Wild Huntress in the Legend of the Middle Ages" (*MLN*, 1908). In *Oscar Wildes Salome:
Eine Kritische Quellenstudie* (Munich, 1913) F. K. Brass discusses
the play's relationship to biblical sources, Heine's *Atta Troll*, Flaubert's *Herodias*, William Wilde's sonnet "Salome," and Maeterlinck's
Princesse Maleine. Those who wish to relate Wilde further to the
French treatments may consult Hertha Bren's *Die Gestalt der Salome
in der Französischen Literatur (Mit Berücksichtigung der Nicht-
französischen Versionen des Salomestoffes)* (Vienna, 1950). Roland
Schaffner also provides a comparative study in *Die Salome-Dichtungen von Flaubert, Laforgue, Wilde und Mallarmé* (Würzburg,
1965), with a useful bibliography.

Many attempts have been made to locate specific sources for
Wilde's play. Jacob N. Bean indicated how both Wilde and Suder-
mann (in his *Johannes*, 1889) may have drawn on Heine (*MLN*,
1907). The influence of Maeterlinck, which has never been in doubt,
was acknowledged by Michel Arnaud (*La Grande Revue*, 1907) and
again by Clayton Hamilton (*Seen on the Stage*, 1920). The influence
of Flaubert was further discussed by Ernst Bendz (*EngS*, 1917). In

the most recent full-scale survey in English (*The Legend of Salome and the Principle of Art for Art's Sake*, Geneva, 1960) Helen Grace Zagona devotes a chapter to Wilde in which she makes a comparison with Flaubert, but the critical content is thin. F. Zaic draws attention to Henry Rich's *The Daughters of Herodias* of 1831 (*Anglia*, 1960). An influence suggested by Z. Raafat is Sardou's *Théodora* (*RLC*, 1966). There are also many treatments connecting Wilde's *Salome* with the work of his contemporaries and later writers. Herbert Salu relates the play to A. H. Tammsaare (*Commentationes Balticae*, 1959); L. Dieckmann makes an interesting comparison with Hofmannstahl's *Elektra* (*TSLL*, 1960); and a rather moderate piece by M. G. Rose traces the myth through the treatments by Mallarmé and Wilde to Yeats in his *Full Moon in March* (*CompD*, 1967). Other speculations are offered by Holbrook Jackson in his introduction to the play (1938) and in a very cultivated article by Merritt Y. Hughes (*University of California Chronicle*, 1928), who refers to Arnold's *Merope* and goes on to consider Wilde's thought more generally in the light of Nietzsche's attack on Euripidean paradox.

The sensational debut of Strauss's opera inevitably prompted further discussions of Wilde's work. In Germany reviews of early productions of the play are themselves of some interest. Eugen Zabel's "Oscar Wildes Drama 'Salome'" (*Illustrierte Zeitung*, 5 Mar. 1903) has a good photograph of the production at the Kleinen Theatre, Berlin. In *Neue Freie Presse* (15 Sept. 1903) "Sch.F." reviewed a performance at the Deutschen Wolfstheater, compared Wilde with Byron, alluded to Zola and Flaubert, and remarked on "die Puritaner Englands." Alfred Kerr bracketed Wilde with Strindberg and Wedekind (*Das Neue Drama*, 1905). Adam Röder's *Salome* (Wiesbaden, 1908) was polemical about both Wilde and Strauss. In *The Craftsman* (1907) K. R. Roof compared the play with the opera and provided pictures of two German actresses in the title role; in *Poet-Lore* (1913) Arthur Row reviewed a New York production, and in *The Drama* (1922) William Saunders considered Wagnerian influences on *Salome*. *The Salome Motive* by John S. White (n.d.) is a brief but competent history of the myth also in the context of the opera. *Comœdia* (19 Mar. 1923) has an illustrated account of Taïrov's Kamerny Theatre production.

Some recent approaches to the myth employ new and ambitious methods. Bertrand d'Astorg (*RDM*, 1971) connects the sacrilegious myth of Salome with Judaic law and modern versions with the new meanings that the myth took on after the French Revolution (a king beheaded) as well as new freedoms that made it possible to draw overt sexual connections between the dance and the beheading. But even in this account Wilde is seen as restrained, resting finally with a conviction that he will voice in poetry: "each man kills the thing he loves." In a genuinely comparative article Nicholas Joost and Franklin E. Court (*PLL*, 1972) reinforce their analysis of the play with allusions to the transformations that the fatal woman has undergone previously. They argue that Herod forms an image of Salome that is based on surfaces, on his subjective view of her, while Iokanaan sees through to her passionate soul, but only by ignoring her flesh. Entrapped between these opposing views Salome emerges as something of a tragic heroine, a mystic sacrifice with which Wilde must necessarily identify. But significantly the most distinguished recent analysis of *Salome* concentrates almost exclusively on a conjectured English field of reference. In "Overtures to Salome" (*YCGL*, 1968; *Twentieth Century Views*, 1969; *Golden Codgers*, 1973) Richard Ellmann explains the play in terms of an opposition between the "tutelary presences of Pater and Ruskin," casting Wilde in the role of a vacillating Herod as he attempts to compound a Ruskinian moral earnestness (Iokanaan) and a Paterian sensual passion (Salome). It has yet to be seen whether Ellmann's intricate exposition can be reconciled with the larger mythic and literary context of the Salome story; but it should be noted that he does observe two outside sources that are possibly significant—the remarks reported by E. Gómez Carrillo and the *Salome* of J. C. Heywood, which Wilde reviewed.

Since a majority of commentators have longed to equate Wilde with at least one of his characters, it is hardly surprising that psychoanalytic critics should have determined to find evidence of concealed autobiography. The earliest attempt was made by Isador H. Coriat (*PsyR*, 1913) who put forward the unattractive thesis that this play (and others of his works) contains evidence of Wilde's polymorphous perversity—both homosexual and sadistic. More than four decades later Edmund Bergler (*PsyR*, 1956) tried a more sophisticated approach, though it was based on a similar premise: cruelty is dominant in *Salome*, therefore Wilde probably identified masochistically with the "castrated" male. Also see J. H. Plokker, *Nederland Tijdschr Psychologische* (1940). Kate Millett has recently taken the play to task in her *Sexual Politics* (1970). Starting with an original comparison with *A Doll's House*, she argues that *Salome* is a dream of homosexual guilt and thus irrelevant to the real sexual battle of the period, which is dramatized by Ibsen. Wilde tries to conceal and divert his secret desires by approving of a castrating woman within the conventions of the myth. But this contains within itself a double revenge, for both Iokanaan and Salome are destroyed. Although it is difficult to sustain Millett's thesis in the context of Wilde's whole output and of other versions of Salome, it remains one of the more challenging readings of the play. Otto Rank, *Das Inzest-Motiv in Dichtung und Sage* (Leipzig and Vienna, 1926) found evidence of a father-daughter complex in *Salome*. Robert Rogers in *A Psychological Study of the Double in Literature* (1970) wields a blunt Freudian instrument briefly if amusingly in a discussion of *Salome* as an example of "latent object doubling"; Father Decomposition (into a virtual gallery) from the point of view of the female protagonist: Salome's actual father strangled by her stepfather Herod; Iokanaan (who also does duty for the superego) condemning Salome's incestuous impulses. By dancing for her stepfather Salome achieves symbolic incest with him, acquires Iokanaan's head (the penis), and revenges herself on the prophet for thwarting her incestuous desires. Involved in this, according to blueprint, is jealousy of and revenge on Herodias. The latent doubling permits simultaneous dramatization of overt denial and covert satisfaction within the incest taboo which may be "bad logic but good theatre and good psychology."

The storm that surrounded Strauss's opera is an example of Wilde's "afterlife," and so too, in a minor way, is the notorious Pemberton Billing case of 1918, when the organizers of a performance of *Salome* were persecuted and libeled by a rabidly patriotic Member of Parliament. This unsavory occasion (during which Douglas pronounced Wilde "the greatest force for evil in Europe for the last 350 years") was reported in *Mercure de France* (1918). It accounts for the discussion about Wilde and *Salome* in *Current Opinion* during 1918, accentuated by the publication of Harris' biography. (See also Vincent O'Sullivan's letter to Harris, *Pearson's Magazine*, 1918; rpt. *Critical Heritage*; Frank Hackett, *New Republic*, 1918; *The Vigilante*, *passim*; and Sir Travers Humphreys, *Criminal Days*, 1949.) Harris was editor of *Pearson's* between 1917 and 1921, which accounts for the Wildeana appearing there; this should also be set in the context of Harris' pro-German and anti-British sentiments. More recent discussions can be found in *QJS* for 1966 by O. J. Brockett and in N. H. G. Schoonderwoerd's *J. T. Grein, Ambassador of the Theatre 1862–1935* (1963).

Of *An Ideal Husband* there is little criticism. The best offering is a brief essay by E. H. Mikhail (*MD*, 1968), in which the point is made that Wilde identifies both with Sir Robert Chiltern and, more obviously, with Lord Goring. Eric Rhode makes a similar point in the transcript of a BBC "Critics" discussion of the 1966 production (*The Listener*, 1966).

Inevitably it has been *The Importance* that has received the bulk of critical attention. Sarah Augusta Dickson's edition (2 vols., 1956) provides one of the most thorough and useful records of any Wilde text, and her introduction contains the essential information on its history, in particular of the original four-act version. H. Montgomery Hyde also reprinted the "lost scene" in the *Listener* (1954). Vyvyan Holland's four-act version (1957) is based on the 1903 German translation, *Ernst Sein*, although Holland says in his intro. that almost everything is contained in one or another of the manuscripts or transcripts. Dickson's edition was welcomed by the *TLS* (1 March 1957) and by Theodore Bolton (*PBSA*, 1956). A review in *BNYPL* (1956) regretted that it was still not possible to study how the manuscript version of Act II came to be abbreviated; and in general opinions about the quality of the four-act version vary (*SatR*, 12 May 1956; *EA*, 1959; *MD*, 1968). The most serious investigation of the theoretical issues involved when considering pre- and post-production scripts is by L. A. Beaurline (*Papers in Dramatic Theory and Criticism*, ed. David M. Knauf, 1960), who takes *The Importance* as his main example. Beaurline puts up a strong defense of the four-act version, in terms of its thematic coherence. Yet despite Dickson's excellent edition the spate of articles over the last twenty years or so has often included criticism that is dry, repetitious and that reaches familiar and obvious conclusions with a depressing frequency. Franz Zaic (*Das moderne Englische Drama*, ed. Horst Oppel, Berlin, 1963) summarized some of this conventional wisdom for the German audience.

Certainly it is now agreed that the play is among the greatest of all English comedies. The most prominent of a small group of dissidents from this opinion has been Mary McCarthy. Reviewing a performance in 1947 (*PR*, 1947; rpt. *Sights and Spectacles, 1937–1958* and *Twentieth Century Views*) McCarthy went so far as to suggest that the experience of watching the play might drive one to sympathize with the Marquess of Queensberry. Wilde has created a Sartrean hell, "a ferocious idyll," an "infernal Arcadia," peopled by the insensible and the depraved. Deliberately provocative as these jibes may have been, one looks in vain for such an engaged response in more academic discussions of the play.

A popular approach is the attempt to fix the play in its relationship to previous schools of English comedy. Richard Foster (*CE*, 1956) has distinguished *The Importance* from both farce and the comedy of manners and associated its "extra-rational world" with that of romantic fiction. Only Lady Bracknell, who expresses outright scorn, escapes the alternative roles of sentimentalist or schemer; Foster sees Wilde's purpose as to satirize society by exposing the literature it produces. While agreeing that the play measures the decay of aristocratic sensibility, James A. Ware (*ELT*, 1970) connects it with the Etheregean comedy of manners. Algernon, like Dorimant in *The Man of Mode*, is "both shallow and serious," characterized simultaneously by self-indulgence and moral earnestness; qualities that are momentarily reconciled through farce. For this aspect the most thorough and convincing treatment is by David Parker (*MLQ*, 1974). Drawing upon Empson's analysis of the "Natural Man," Parker concedes that Algy is similar to a Restoration blood in that his very roguishness is proof of his moral freedom, but makes the further point that Wilde's play is in fact superior to Restoration drama because its "farcical structure helps distance what we see." Wilde's method also looks forward to the Absurd, but it has the added virtue of satirizing the manners of a particular class. Parker's approach is notable for the large perspective that it holds over dramatic history, as well as for the close attention to the nineteenth-century meanings of such key words as "serious" and "earnest." Interestingly, Lady Bracknell emerges in this account as the embodiment of feminine strength: her creative imagination builds a solid world that operates according to her own laws. In *EIC* (1976) Geoffrey Stone analyzes the play in terms of "metalanguage," the relation of language to underlying meaning structures, but this produces few fresh insights.

The critical articles that remain are best taken in the order in which they appeared, since to some extent they represent an ongoing debate about the play's structure and in particular its ironical technique. In 1956 Otto Reinert (*CE*) claimed that the satiric strategy of *The Importance* developed Wilde's earlier pattern of ironic inversion to the point where epigram participted in the total meaning of the play and that the only true ironist was therefore the playwright himself. Sacrificing naturalism completely, Wilde wrote a play that was all farce and thus "a lucid image of the non-farcical reality that is kept strictly outside the play." It is, however, peopled by cynical realists: Bunburyists by necessity, for Bunburying was the only escape from Victorian convention. How the art of Bunburying can be related to Wilde's pronouncements on the importance of lying is demonstrated by E. B. Partridge (*BuR*, 1960). First he identifies the style of the Wildean hero as a form of *sprezzatura*, for it includes the ability to mock itself; then he shows how the play's structure effectively parodies that of classical drama. That both Wilde and Algy assume the mask of the dandy for their own ends is a related point made by Harold E. Tolliver (*MD*, 1963), though he ends with disappointing clichés about serious triviality. Arthur Ganz (*MD*, 1963) also reiterates established ideas about the function and motives of the dandy but makes the original, if questionable, point that both Chasuble and Lady Bracknell share aspects of this subversive spirit because they too make ordinary morality seem ridiculous. Ganz puts forward an argument similar in essence to that of his earlier article in order to claim that the world of the play is one of pure Aesthetic form. Attempting to sum up this particular critical history, Robert J. Jordan (*ArielE*, 1970) distinguishes between two schools: that which sees the play as satire or social criticism (Bentley, Foster, Reinert) and that which finds its fantasy "an expression of the author's aesthetic creed" (Tolliver, Ganz). The division is probably too facile, for it seems to have hindered Jordan's own attempt at mediation, which is largely on the side of "fantasy." His half-hearted researches, mainly through the columns of *Punch*, in pursuit of the New Woman as the type to which Gwendolen belongs, bring him to the quixotic conclusion that since the objects of the play's humor were well established at the time, then its strength must lie elsewhere than in social satire. He concludes that it is in the "dream of elegance" and the exhibition of innocent childlike games or fantasies. Jordan is best on the inversion of sexual roles, and his preliminary inquiries into the play's contemporary reference have some value, although we can expect that they will be taken much further by others. L. A. Poague (*MD*, 1973) manipulates an armory of sub-Empsonian categories of irony in order to come to the opposite conclusion: the play is so intellectually dense that we don't notice that it contains elements of sentimental wish fulfillment. Poague counts four hundred examples of comic inversion in order to justify his claim that the play demands intellectual exertion. J. L. Styan has made a technical comparison with *Rosmersholm*, noting Wilde's manipulations of the formal modulation of dramatic speech in the tea-party scene (*The Elements of Drama*, 1960). In *The Divine Average* (1971) William G. McCollom analyzes Wilde's ironic technique to demonstrate a general law of comedy: "Wit, even by association, is better than good behaviour," and he makes some suggestive comparisons with Shaw; while in *Comedy, the Irrational Vision* (1975) Morton Gurewitch concludes that "however delightful and psychically emancipatory Wilde's nonsense is, it has become somewhat old-fashioned by now."

Contributions that fall beyond this grouping include Werner Vordtriede's suggestion (*MLN*, 1955) that the second act parallels the garden scene in Goethe's *Faust*. Vordtriede also draws attention to the structural echoes of classical drama and Italian comedy. Otto Reinert made a brief foray into an unexplored area when he showed (*MD*, 1959) how the stage directions in Act III compose a kind of dance, "a visual image of the artifice of sophisticated courtship and a major device in the play's aesthetic distancing." Arthur Nethercot has suggested (*MD*, 1963) that Miss Prism's name (a frequently exaniined topic) derives from exercises intended to form a young girl's lips correctly; these exercises are referred to in *Little Dorrit*.

Several editions contain useful critical introductions. Hopper and Lahey (1959) in their essay on the play stress contradictions between what the characters do and what they say, and detail Wilde's manipulation of traditional plot elements. Their suggestions for set design, however, are bizarre, owing as much to New York in the 1900's as to London in the 1890's. Henry Popkin summarizes previous opinion and alludes to the various versions in his 1965 edition. Popkin's own verdict is that the play operates as social criticism by implying the absence of style in the real world. The thoughts of one of Wilde's greatest interpreters can be found in John Gielgud's *Stage Directions* (1963) and in his introduction to the Hereford edition (1970): "The decorum, the deadly importance of the triviality is everything—they are greedy, determined, but exasperatedly polite."

The most important line of inquiry is that of Joseph W. Donohue, Jr., who has been engaged in tracking down records of the original production (see *N&Q*, 1970). The fruits of this effort are to be found in *Nineteenth Century British Drama* (ed. Kenneth Richards and Peter Thomson, 1971). By collating all possible information Donohue plans to establish the cultural ambience in which the play was first received. This is a valuable and to some extent innovatory method, although it has been slightly hindered by the absence of a prompt-book, causing Donohue to rely largely on the rehearsal text. Some of his most interesting conclusions so far concern the ways in which business developed in rehearsal modified the text itself, a discovery that should probably be linked with Paul C. Wadleigh's inference from his study of contemporary reviews (*QJS*, 1966) that the biggest laughs came not at the epigrams so much as at particular actions on stage.

Frank Harris' *Mr. and Mrs. Daventry* was belatedly published in 1956 with an introduction by H. Montgomery Hyde. Hyde tells how Wilde wrote to George Alexander in 1894 with an idea for a play, how he sold the same idea to Frank Harris, and how Mrs. Patrick Campbell agreed to act in a play based on it if Harris should write it. Hyde's edition is taken from the text used in 1900 and found among Mrs. Campbell's papers. Also see Alan Dent, *Mrs. Patrick Campbell* (1961). Wilde's dissatisfaction with Harris' version has been recorded by T. H. Bell (*The Bookman*, New York, 1930), who acted as an intermediary between the two at the time of composition. Bell's papers are now in the British Museum, Add. MS. 58079b; his unpublished "Oscar Wilde without Whitewash" is in the Clark Library. Hyde's edition can be compared with *Constance*, a reconstruction by Guillot de Saix and Henri de Briel based on the same story, which was published with a preface by Vyvyan Holland in 1954 (*Les Oeuvres libres*). De Saix and Briel claim to have worked from an outline given them by Mrs. Brown Potter, an American actress to whom Wilde had also sold the story.

The extraordinary and comic story of Mrs. Chan Toon's half-successful attempt to hoax Wilde's publishers with a forged Wilde play called *For Love of the King* has been authoritatively told by George Sims (*BC*, 1958; *TLS*, 9 Oct. 1969). This led to a famous libel case between Christopher Millard and Methuen & Co. in 1922. Millard himself brought out a pamphlet containing correspondence between the major figures involved, *Who Wrote "For Love of the King"?* (1926).

IX. Fiction

Wilde's short stories and fairy tales have received little attention beyond the major critical studies, and among these only Nassaar devotes much space to them. Philippe Jullian's article on the Aesthetic background is superficial (*RDM*, 1961). A slight piece by Vyvyan Holland on the fairy stories (*Adelphi*, 1954) at least recognizes their potential interest. Also see Dorothy Scarborough, *The Supernatural in Modern English Fiction* (1917). In his introduction to *The Young King and Other Tales* (1962), John Updike comments on the parabolic significance of fairy tales. Although directed at children, Updike's apothegms, like those of Wilde himself, are also instructive for adults. Walther Fischer comments on the close parallels between "The Canterville Ghost" and Louise Falconer's *Cecilia de Noel* but admits that the priority of Wilde's story precludes the possibility of its being influenced by Falconer's *nouvelle* (*Neophilologus*, 1925).

Holland published the complete text of *The Portrait of Mr. W. H.*, with an introduction, in 1958 (an edition of ten copies had been published in 1921). A complete text was also printed by Edward Hubler in *Shakespeare's Sonnets and the Commentators* (1962). A review of Holland's edition in the *TLS* (21 Nov. 1958) noted elements of proleptic autobiography. Both this reviewer and Hilary Corke (*The Listener*, 1958) accepted Holland's account of how the manuscript disappeared, but H. Montgomery Hyde complained that Holland had not told the full story (*TLS*, 5 Dec. 1958). The best critical essay is Lewis J. Poteet, "Romantic Aesthetics in Oscar Wilde's 'Mr. W. H.'" (*SSF*, 1970), which connects it with Wilde's critical methods in general. An early example of German appreciation is Richard Schaukal's "The Portrait of Mr. W. H. by Oscar Wilde" (*Österreichische Rundschau*, 1905): the charm of Wilde's style dissolves the literary hypothesis.

The starting point for a study of *The Picture of Dorian Gray* is likely to be Stuart Mason's *Art and Morality* (1908; rev. 1912), which reproduces newspaper controversies resulting from the original publication, a transcript of the relevant portions from Carson's long cross-examination at the trial, and other bibliographical material. William Edener's critical edition (1964) is based on the *Lippincott's* printing of July 1890 and has full variorum notes along with an introduction. Paul Goetsch compared the two versions (*Die Neueren Sprachen*, 1966); and in *Die Romankonzeption in England 1880–1910* (Heidelberg, 1967) he related *Dorian Gray* to *Marius*. Also see *Der Englische Roman, Interpretationem* (ed. Goetsch et al., 1973). Isobel Murray's edition (1974) is based on the April 1891 Ward Lock edition, although it includes a short list of variants. Throughout her polished introduction Murray stresses the relevance of Pater, who reviewed the novel in 1891 (*Bookman*, London; rpt. *Sketches and Reviews*, 1919). She also draws some slight attention to the fiction of Edward Heron-Allen. Her notes reveal the many sources of Wilde's apparent erudition. However, Murray's explanation of the motives behind Wilde's revisions was at once strongly challenged in the *TLS* (26 June–13 Sept. 1974). In an earlier essay Murray compared the 1890 and the 1891 texts (*DUJ*, 1972) to show that Wilde's revisions tend to stress the moral significance of the story by giving more details about Dorian's career of sin and by making him into a more active protagonist. Murray also indicated that these new emphases tend further to distinguish Dorian from superficially similar heroes such as Des Esseintes and Marius; and she made another contribution to the long list of Wilde's possible sources—Lefébure's *Embroidery and Lace*. Donald L. Lawler has examined the manuscripts in the Pierpont Morgan and Clark libraries, and has concluded that an even earlier manuscript than these must have existed and that Wilde revised his novel not twice but three times before its original publication in *Lippincott's* (*SB*, 1972).

Whereas French critics in the first decades after the publication of *Dorian Gray* tended to have a sense of *déjà lu*, the novel was a popular success in Germany. But critical reaction was mixed, with unfavorable judgments predominating. Johannes Gaulke translated portions in 1901 (*Das Magazin für Literatur*, also see *Jahrbuch für sexuelle Zwischenstufen*, 1901) and in his commentary stressed the problem of homosexuality. Paul Gutmann (*Südwestdeutsche Rundschau*, 15 June 1902) devoted half his article to arguing that criminals could be tragic figures but that modern civilization had lost any real sense of tragedy. *Dorian Gray*, being based on modern Aesthetic assumptions, was necessarily inferior, its only interest documentary. Philipp Frey's review of the 1907 Olschlögel translation (*Österreichische Rundschau*, 1908) stressed the mediocrity of *Dorian Gray* but found the book fascinating as the autobiographical confession of a wonderful sinner. Reaction to the book in Germany is said to be polarized: to some pious, extraordinarily cheap sensationalism with a moral to the other. Karl Hans Bühner (*Berliner Börsenzeitung*, 1939) found the esthetic view expressed by Wilde in *Dorian Gray* to be self-contradictory owing to Wilde's fluctuations between the extremes of art as senseless and art as useful. For Bühner, only art with redeeming social value could survive: that meant Schiller and excluded Wilde.

The most notable of prewar discussions of *Dorian Gray* is now sometimes overlooked. Madeleine L. Cazamian, *Le Roman et les idées en Angleterre* (Paris, 1935) remains the most extensive account of its philosophic content. She argues that Wilde was attracted throughout his work, and in *Dorian Gray* in particular, to opposed philosophic traditions: one empirical, skeptical, Darwinist; the other Platonic, idealistic, above all Hegelian. It is regrettable that these soundings have not been taken further, but the failure can be explained. For what emerges from Mason's compendium is the excessive confusion that followed upon Wilde's prefatory remarks about the morality of art, and this has persisted. Indeed, much criticism has been given over to the single difficulty that this of all Wilde's works should be so very moral in its implications. An astute modern commentator, Morse Peckham, has couched his own views, fittingly, in the form of a social paradox: *Dorian Gray*, like the best Decadent art, is morally responsible because it acknowledges the illusion that inevitably accompanies eroticism, whereas a middle-class morality tale is to be associated with the genuinely pornographic because it insinuates that gratification can somehow be fully achieved (*Beyond the Tragic Vision*, 1962).

The question of Wilde's personal involvement in the novel follows from the issue of its morality. Arthur Nethercot cited an 1894 letter to show that Wilde was himself divided in his identification with the main characters (*PMLA*, 1945). Ted R. Spivey argued (*BUSE*, 1960) that, in damning Dorian, Wilde was also condemning the cult of sensation that had been preached by Pater and practiced by himself. Sensation depends upon curiosity and ultimately upon egoism; but although Lord Henry encourages Dorian to pursue sensation he himself, like an artist, remains intellectually distanced from his subject and, like a scientist, only shapes the life of his creation. Opposed to Dorian's egoism are the love and primitive instincts of Sibyl and James Vane. The ultimate paradox is that Wilde, the Aesthete, should defend the superiority of the natural over the artificial. Spivey supports his argument with the perhaps superfluous suggestion that Lord Henry, like Mephistopheles, may be more than mortal.

Otto Rank's essay on the double was first published in 1914 but has since been reprinted in several versions, most recently as *The Double: A Psychoanalytic Study* (1971). Rank's work is certainly of historical importance: *Dorian Gray* is cited in the course of a discussion of the homosexuality and the ambivalent attitudes to the self that accompany narcissism. Havelock Ellis mentions Rank's approach to the novel in his *Studies in the Psychology of Sex*, Vol. VII (1928). Ralph Tymms follows on from Rank in *Doubles in Literary Psychology* (1949) but in this, as in later treatments of the *Doppelgänger* theme, *Dorian Gray* does not benefit greatly from the wider context. The recent books on the subject are likewise probably symptomatic of the rise of psychoanalytical methods in criticism, although, ironically, the best tend to be those that are least doctrinally Freudian. None are particularly notable for originality of insight. In *The Divided Self* (1969) Masao Miyoshi remarks yet again on the indecisive quality of *Dorian Gray*. Wilde (like some of his characters) is Faustian, but in a late nineteenth-century way: unable to choose, he resorts to a random selection of masks. It took the moderns to show that mask and mirror, for Wilde "performer's tools," might become "precision instruments in service of the science of the self." Robert Rogers in *A Psychoanalytic Study of the Double in Literature* (1970) briefly discusses the novel as an example of "manifest subject doubling," offering little that is new. Hallward is suggested as an allegorical artist-surrogate of Wilde himself, whose integrity complements Dorian's hypocrisy. While, in a possibly Jungian treatment (*The Literature of the Second Self*, 1972), C. F. Keppler notes that Dorian gets some satisfaction from the portrait's hideousness, although as the representation of the dark side of his psyche, of "Death in Life," his primary response to it is one of revulsion.

Jacob Korg ("The Rage of Caliban," *UTQ*, 1967) calls *Dorian Gray* "an uncommitted work." The Victorian interest in dualism is a response to a dichotomy between two dominant views of the self: the idealistic and the pragmatic. Like other versions of the same theme, *Dorian Gray* finally confirms a belief in the uniqueness of a self that is still dependent upon external circumstances; yet the end of the book also suggests some "new and unimagined metaphysical framework," hence its "uncommitted" nature. In "Hebraism, Hellenism, and *The Picture of Dorian Gray*" (*VN*, 1967) Jan B. Gordon reads the novel in terms of an Arnoldian cycle, which he connects with Dorian's double nature. But in " 'Parody as Initiation': The Sad Education of Dorian Gray" (*Criticism*, 1967) Gordon approaches the *Doppelgänger* theme from a different aspect by drawing attention to the process of initiation that goes with the confusion between art and life. Dorian is a Paterian threatened by determinism and an associationist forced to reconcile his spiritual beliefs with scientific language and theory. Gordon draws attention to the many images of labyrinthine enclosure which indicate the dangers of intellectual compartmentalization. Dorian does become a work of art, although an overall identity is finally denied him. Gordon returns to *Dorian Gray* in *UWR* (1970) and in *ELT* (1972) but widens the discussion to include many other nineteenth-century writers, the Victorian detective story, 1890's pornography, and, most interestingly, Freud's *Studies in Hysteria*. Another example of the possibilities of an ambitious approach is Charles Altieri's "Organic Models in Some English *Bildungsroman*" (*JGE*, 1971). A comparison between *Dorian Gray* and *Rasselas* turns out to be more fruitful than might be expected. Altieri puts forward the startling but largely vindicated claim that Wilde "was probably the first literary figure to concern himself almost exclusively with the state of man in a post-technological society" and that he anticipated Marcuse. The argument is conducted in terms of educational models: Dorian's post-Romantic "organicist" cultivation of the individual self does not allow him to become involved in history, yet he is reduced to a fixed image through art, Lord Henry survives because he alone speaks the language of society. In contrast, throughout *Rasselas* education is still to be seen as the realization of community.

Like Spivey, Houston A. Baker, Jr. (*NCF*, 1969) identifies Lord Henry as a Mephistophelean figure when he compares *Dorian Gray* with Goethe's *Faust*. He is more original in his concentration upon Hallward: he sees him as a tragic example of the self-conscious artist who by putting too much of himself into the portrait corrupts the original ideal of physical beauty. As a result of this attention Dorian becomes vain and hedonistic and has to be destroyed in order that the canvas may regain its beauty. In his discussion of *Dorian Gray* (*Comedy, the Irrational Vision*, 1975) Morton Gurewitch decides that Lord Henry transforms the sin of wit into the wit of sin. Gerald Monsman (*UTQ*, 1971) has made some sound distinctions between the moral temperament and the emotional control of the Paterian hero, who is revealed as the living personality behind works of art, and Wilde's dandies, who are entirely concerned with the metamorphosis of life into art.

Most critics rightly pay attention to the presence of Wilde's favorite myth of Narcissus, and Robert Keefe (*SNNTS*, 1973) has made especially good use of it. By stressing Hallward's importance as a serious artist, Keefe replaces Baker's moralistic reading with esthetic preoccupations. Dorian is a passive Narcissus in whom Hallward observes an image of himself that he is unable to integrate with his own way of life. At the final ironic confrontation Hallward becomes the artist as hunter while Dorian is the murderer as victim.

John Pappas (*ELT*, 1972) has shown how images of flowers and animals compose a complex pattern of natural process and order in which no clear role is offered for the human protagonists; but Pappas' insight is insufficient in itself and should have been expanded to take evolutionary theories more fully into account. More to the point is the discussion of the novel by A. Dwight Culler in "The Darwinian Revolution and Literary Form" (*The Art of Victorian Prose*, ed. George Levine and William Madden, 1968).

A good deal of writing on *Dorian Gray* is taken up with the hunt for Wilde's sources. The most frequently cited works are probably Balzac's *Peau de Chagrin*, Poe's *The Oval Portrait*, and of course above all *À Rebours*, which Walther Fischer discussed in *EngS* (1917–18). Bernard Fehr systematically examined the book's many other literary references (*EngS*, 1921) and Lucius H. Cook reviewed the French sources (*RR*, 1928). But since then Oscar Maurer, Jr., has put forward the claims of a short story by George Sala (*PQ*, 1947), and R. D. Brown has identified three works of history that Wilde drew upon ("Suetonius, Symonds and Gibbon in *The Picture of Dorian Gray*," *MLN*, 1956). D. C. Rose has drawn attention to a story about a portrait by Sir Joshua Reynolds (*TLS*, 13 June 1968)— although he finds it difficult to explain how Wilde might have heard about it—and Charles G. Nickerson incidentally cleared up some confusion about a supposed model for Hallward when he presented the most detailed case so far for the importance of Disraeli's *Vivian Grey* (*TLS*, 14 Aug. 1969; see also 21 Aug.–9 Oct.). Dominick Rossi has attempted to indicate further parallels with Goethe's *Faust* (*CLAJ*, 1969). Poteet has remarked yet again on Wilde's admiration for Maturin's *Melmoth the Wanderer* (*MFS*, 1971), and W. E. Portnoy has noted Wilde's use of Tennyson, particularly "The Lady of Shalott" (*ELT*, 1974).

Since it appears in bibliographies of Wilde, the student should be warned against perusal of Lady Gargiles' *Petit Essai sur Portrait de Dorian Gray d'Oscar Wilde* (Paris, 1917). This is a series of letters addressed to a presumably imaginary friend in defense of some ideas of life and art inspired by Wilde's preface. Lady Gargiles' thoughts are maundering and serenely pedestrian.

Criticism that traces the influence of *Dorian Gray* on other writers is less common, but Kenneth M. Rosen has connected the book with Eugene O'Neill's *The Great God Brown* (*MD*, 1971).

X. *Criticism*

Paul Elmer More's well-known essay "Criticism" (*Shelburne Essays*, 1910; rpt. *Selected Shelburne Essays*, 1935) belongs to a dull phase in literary criticism, but it retains its importance as a sign of reengagement with Wilde. More set out to demonstrate that Wilde exploited the dichotomy in Matthew Arnold's theory between the moral and esthetic senses in an even more extreme way than Pater had done. What had resulted from Wilde's modification of Arnold was a dangerous view of culture as a kind of deterministic race-experience, entirely opposed to the original concept of culture as self-discipline. More decided that Wilde lacked moral responsibility because he discounted the element of personal judgment that must be part of our sense of the past.

However pious his dismissal, More had tried to place Wilde in a specific tradition. And it is the problem of tradition that matters: Wilde can be seen as either a transitional or a catalytic figure in the history of English criticism, as either a synthesizer of current ideas or an important theoretician in his own right. Whatever the final verdict, it has always seemed essential to establish as precisely as possible his relationship to those who were unquestionably the main influences upon him: Arnold, Ruskin, Pater.

Finding exact evidence of Wilde's adumbration of the English tradition was a Continental, largely German, preoccupation at first. The early German studies are rigorously detailed, always based on textual data; what they lack is a sense of the larger cultural issues or of literary quality. But even in the German context Edouard J. Bock's *Walter Paters Einfluss auf Oscar Wilde* (Bonn, 1913) is unusually dependent upon juxtaposed quotation. Bock traces dozens of echoes of Paterian vocabulary and phrase in Wilde's writing, from the earliest poetry through *De Profundis*; and he compares their critical theory, noting especially a concept of the historical imagination. Surprisingly, he has least to say about the Paterian sources for "The New Hedonism" as it appears in *Dorian Gray*. *The Influence of Pater and Matthew Arnold in the Prose Writings of Oscar Wilde* (Göteburg, 1914) by the Swedish critic Ernst Bendz was equally pioneering and remains one of the best introductions to the subject. Bendz credits Wilde with "a quite feminine instinct of adaptability and imitation." His comparative analyses of prose styles are again highly detailed, although sometimes ponderous and unsophisticated by modern standards. Bendz reveals his commitment to Wilde in his opinion that Arnold became a powerful inspiration only late on and in his preference for Wilde's use of antithesis and epigram. Bendz's earlier *Some Stray Notes on the Personality and Writings of Oscar Wilde* (Göteburg, 1911) amounted to an act of homage in which he managed to be thoroughly Paterian while hardly mentioning Pater and to defend both Wilde's extreme Aesthetic position and a new mystical philosophy of nature which he thought to have been implied in *De Profundis*. This work was translated into French by Georges-Bazile (*La Vie des lettres*, 1914). A. J. Mainsard held slightly Jesuitical opinions about the morality of Aestheticism (*Études*, 1928) but those became intrusive only at the conclusion of his competent discussion of the Heraclitean subjectivism adopted by Pater and later manipulated by Wilde: "Tout ce que Pater avait rêvé du style, Wilde le réalise dans sa propre vie." G. Duthuit, *Le Rose et le noir de Walter Pater à Wilde* (Paris, 1923) is less detailed and more fanciful than the earlier treatments. David DeLaura briefly discusses the relationship with Arnold (*TSLL*, 1962). The presence of Ruskin in Wilde's esthetic has been less thoroughly explored—André Maurois in *Études Anglaises* (1927; also see *Conférencia*, 1926) is superficial on the subject—except by Ellmann in his "Overtures to *Salome*," a creative interpretation of a creative relationship. German dedication to source studies is still apparent in Fritz Carl Baumann, *Oscar Wilde als Kritiker der Literatur* (Zurich, 1933), which is significant mainly for the attention it pays to Wilde's early reviews.

There have been other suggestions about Wilde's critical mentors; for instance, Disraeli has been put forward as a model for the dialogue technique (see J. C. Squire, "Solomon Eagle," *Essays at Large*, 1922, and Hesketh Pearson in his introduction to *Essays by Oscar Wilde*, 1950). And the inquiry has been broadened to include Continental thought absorbed either through direct exposure or in some more vicarious manner. Leonard A. Willoughby (*PEGS*, 1964–65, also printed as a pamphlet) says that Wilde "proclaims Goethe right at the start as the *fons et origo* of the idea that art is to be regarded, not only as the reflection of Life, but as the central and organising principle of Life considered as an Art." Willoughby shows how Wilde's esthetic doctrines are based on a misinterpretation of Goethe's position (although they incorporate much of its complexity) and how they often contradict themselves. Thus Wilde is linked via Pater and Mahaffy with a German tradition, although Willoughby concedes that Wilde's own tastes are more mystical than transcendental. Unfortunately the only English discussion of "Wilde and Heine" is entirely speculative and unscholarly (Coulson Kernahan, *DM*, 1940). Suggestive, but only in a general way, is the novelist Lion Feuchtwanger's "Heinrich Heine und Oscar Wilde: ein Psychologische Studie" (*Der Spiegel*, 1908; rpt. *Centum Opuscula*, 1956). Parallels rather than sources are offered. Heine and Wilde shared the same tragic internal conflict between heart and head that led them to long for totality and harmony of the person (this is religion, rather than Goethe, as in so much German criticism). Both writers have an elegant aristocratic tone; both prefer the unusual, the pose, the perverse. Both "borrow" material, giving it a new twist; are most adept at short forms and lack humor and feeling, though not wit. Along with Nietzsche and Hugo, Wilde and Heine are the great virtuosi of Romanticism; all are part of a chain which includes and concludes with Wilde.

On the French influence, an important and much cited work, which goes beyond Enid Starkie's superficial *From Gautier to Eliot* (1960), is Kelver Hartley's *Oscar Wilde: L'Influence française dans son œuvre* (Paris, 1935). This is particularly useful for French newspaper reports of Wilde's crucial 1891 stay in Paris and for contemporary comment on *Salome*. Hartley also relates *Vera* to Sardou's *Fédora* and *The Duchess of Padua* to Hugo's *Lucrèce Borgia*. The presence of French Symbolist doctrine in *Intentions* is perhaps overemphasized, but the influence of Renan's *Vie de Jésus* on Wilde's concept of Christ is well documented. Two subsequent articles have discussed the importance of Renan: Joan Harding (*ContempR*, 1953), who cites the *Dialogues philosophiques* and *La Vie de Jésus*; and Brian Nicholas, "Two Nineteenth-Century Utopias: The Influence of Renan's *L'Avenir de la science* on Wilde's *The Soul of Man under Socialism*" (*MLR*, 1964). Nicholas' is the more detailed treatment, but both stress the obvious attractions for Wilde in Renan's trust in the multiplicity of experience rather than in the older notions of unchanging human nature. Louise Rosenblatt devotes considerable attention to Wilde in her exhaustive survey "L'Idée de l'art pour l'art dans la littérature anglaise pendant la période victorienne" (*Bibliothèque de la Revue de Littérature Comparée*, Paris, 1931) and decides that Wilde's contribution to a powerful Anglo-French tradition was not originality but theatricality and extremism. Contradictions innate in Wilde's ideas are shown to account for his seemingly absolute commitment to form, leading eventually to "l'art pour l'artificialité" and "l'artiste en vie." Rosenblatt also provides some useful but minor documentation of the Aesthetic Movement. W. Schrickx has contributed "Oscar Wilde in Belgium in 1879 and his early interest in Théophile Gautier," (*RLV*, 1971): the visit to Belgium took place in the company of Rennell Rodd; the influence of Gautier was, predictably, via Pater and Swinburne.

The exotic influence of the Taoist Chaung Tzu, long noted by critics, is most thoroughly assessed by Isobel Murray (*DUJ*, 1971). J. Curling corrects some of Wilde's errors of fact in "Pen, Pencil and Poison" (*James Weathercock, The Life of Thomas Griffiths Wainewright, 1794–1847*, 1938). In "Oscar Wilde as a Shakespearean Critic" (*Shakespeare Commemoration Vol.*, Calcutta, 1966) Jyotsna Bhattacharjee explicates "The Truth of Masks" with copious quotation but no mention of E. W. Godwin, who almost certainly provided Wilde with both inspiration and documentation.

In 1915 Alice Wood published a remarkably prescient essay (*North American Review*; rpt. *The Critical Heritage*) showing how Wilde's notion of "creative criticism" differed from Pater in its refusal to identify the art object with any larger external reality. She claimed that in this respect Wilde anticipated the modern approach, and she referred to the esthetics of Post-Impressionism, even of Cubism. But a new Anglo-American orthodoxy, derived from T. S. Eliot and engaged with Arnold in particular, tended to dismiss Wilde's importance along with that of Pater; this is nowhere more clearly indicated than in Eliot's own aside that the *Renaissance* "propagated some confusion between life and art which is not wholly irresponsible for some untidy lives." Even arguments against Eliot were not necessarily to Wilde's advantage: Leonard Brown testified in 1934 that Wilde's special "psychology" exonerated Arnold from the responsibility of having spawned decadent progeny (*SR*). More recently Wilde has benefited from the growing consensus that acknowledges Pater's stature. New interest in the complex shifts of Pater's thought has brought about an awareness of Wilde's position in relation to it— even to the point where he is accorded the rank of an equal partner. Signs of this process can be traced in the following: John Pick's rather superficial "Divergent Disciples of Walter Pater" (*Thought*, 1948); Ruth Z. Temple, "The Ivory Tower as Lighthouse" (*Edwardians and Victorians*, ed. Richard Ellmann, 1960); Wendell V. Harris, "Arnold, Pater and Wilde and the Object As in Themselves They See It" (*SEL*, 1971). In a succint comparison with Pater, however, R. V.

Johnson (*Aestheticism*, 1969) is less enthusiastic about Wilde's modifications to Aesthetic principles and suggests that his theory potentially
reduced all art to a level of banality.

Contemporary studies of Wilde's criticism may be said to begin
with reappraisals from two distinguished scholars. René Wellek surveys the whole of Wilde's critical output in Vol. IV of *A History of
Modern Criticism* (1965), where he notes three sometimes contradictory strands in Wilde's theory: "Panaestheticism, the autonomy of art,
and a decorative formalism." Perhaps the most significant moment in
a discriminating analysis is marked when Wellek reconciles Wilde's
sense of the historical imagination with Eliot's own "tradition," although his conclusion is still somewhat reductive: Wilde is left only
as "the representative figure of the English aesthetic movement."
Richard Ellmann's superbly organized "The Critic as Artist as Wilde"
(*Wilde and the Nineties*, ed. Charles Ryskamp, 1966; rpt. *Encounter*,
1967; *The Poet as Critic*, ed. F. P. W. McDowell, 1967; *The Artist as
Critic*, 1968; *Golden Codgers*, 1973) has been mentioned earlier.
Blending textual analysis and biographical inference, Ellmann ac-
cords Wilde a key place in the modern tradition and attempts a
synthesis of the internal contradictions that Wellek finds so troubling.

The title of an essay by A. E. Dyson, "Oscar Wilde: Irony of a
Socialist Aesthete" (*The Listener*, 1961; rev. in *The Crazy Fabric*,
1965), draws attention to the central concerns of some recent criticism. Dyson is anxious to reconcile Wilde's witty Aestheticism with his
avowedly radical social views; he attempts this by indicating the
moral force of the inverted cliché or paradox and by placing Wilde's
individualism in a tradition that includes Blake and Lawrence. But a
compulsion to present his case at the court of Dr. Leavis inhibits the
unqualified expression of enthusiasm for Wilde that his essay otherwise implies. Masolino d'Amico was on safer ground ("Oscar Wilde
between 'Socialism' and Aestheticism," *EM*, 1967) in concentrating
on *The Soul of Man* as the only full exposition of Wilde's social
theory. But d'Amico's allusions to Fabianism, to the teachings of
Ruskin and Morris, to the anarchism of Kropotkin, had already been
taken further by J. D. Thomas (*RUS*, 1965). In a balanced argument
Thomas shows how Wilde's essay benefits from a close historical placing, particularly where it relates to contemporary dichotomies between
individualism and socialism. The remarks about the role of Shaw are
of considerable interest. Qualified admiration for *The Soul of Man* has
been expressed by George Orwell (*Collected Essays, Journalism and
Letters*, Vol. IV, 1968) and by Raymond Williams (*Culture and Society
1780–1950*, 1958).

Seymour Migdail (*DR*, 1967) has passed some unfashionably
harsh judgments upon Wilde's fondness for epigram and dissents
from the growing consensus that tries, like Dyson, to find social
significance in a witty expression of *l'art pour l'art*. For Migdail,
Wilde's posturing was primarily a response to a philistine age, con-
cealing contradictions that can no longer be justified. Wilde's belief in
the autonomy of art is defended by Hilda Schiff (*E&S*, 1965) on the
grounds that it posits the idea that "Art, once created, has a metaphysical worth above and beyond mere human description." She
connects this with the doctrine of impersonality put forward by mod-

erns such as Eliot, Hulme, and Yeats. Frank Kermode in *Romantic Image* is of course the prime exponent of this line, but R. J. Green (*BJA*, 1973) takes the argument further when he distinguishes between Wilde's method in his early reviews and in *Intentions*. The later criticism allows for the inconsistencies that result from a breakdown in shared beliefs; it is "iconic." Green rushes breathlessly past Pound, Joyce, and Beckett to rest rather precariously with McLuhan; but he makes little of the dramatized structure of the later criticism that he admires. J. D. Thomas (*ELT*, 1969) makes some good points about this aspect. He stresses the etymology of the word "intention" itself and, very sensibly, connects the telling of partial truths with the relativities of dramatic form. If further evidence is needed of the theatrical nature of Wilde's criticism, there is Charles Marowitz' dramatization "The Critic as Artist" (*Plays and Players*, 1971), although Marowitz chooses to present the dialogues in the form of a seduction scene between an older and a younger man. Stanley Weintraub's introduction to his selection *The Literary Criticism of Oscar Wilde* (1968) gives a sound résumé of Wilde's critical position as it is now generally defined and pays some attention to the circumstances under which the reviews were written.

It is agreeable to note the fascination that Wilde now holds for the avant-garde critic and the relevance his thought is assumed to have for contemporary culture. Susan Sontag's famous "Notes on Camp" (*Against Interpretation*, 1966) takes Wilde as both premise and example: his epigrams are "camp" because they are wholly self-conscious and playful. Sontag's definition of "camp" as "the relation to style in a time in which the adoption of style—as such—has become altogether questionable" provides a nice insight into the place Wilde held in his own culture, as much as it applies to figures in our own time. A rather more demanding exploration of the appropriateness of Wilde's ideas to the present is Philip Rieff's long essay (*Encounter*, 1970). Rieff's method is a species of cultural Freudianism: he argues that although Wilde created a type that is now exploited commercially, yet his aspirations for the artist can never be fulfilled. For Wilde wished that the artist as a consummate individualist be able to "express everything," which is impossible, since culture depends for its very existence upon repression. Rieff's tortuous argument ultimately defies summary, but it is remarkable if only as a portent of what Wilde's criticism might inspire in the future.

Jan B. Gordon's long review of Richard Ellmann's *The Artist as Critic* and *Twentieth Century Views* volumes (*KR*, 1970) can serve as an introduction to his own sophisticated approach to Wilde. Gordon objects to some of the items collected in *Twentieth Century Views* because they underestimate the profundity and modernity of Wilde's thought. He claims, for instance, that Wilde's epigrammatic method points forward to Norman O. Brown and McLuhan. It is, as always, the phenomenology of the *fin de siècle* that really interests Gordon, but he has some provocative asides on pornography and Wilde's attitudes to America and manages fairly successfully to connect Wilde's "closed circuit" linguistic system with R. D. Laing's researches into schizophrenia.

Keith Connelly is less carried away by Wilde's dazzling use of the seemingly impersonal epigram. In his sober review of Beckson's *Critical Heritage* and Ellmann's *The Artist as Critic* (*CQ*, 1972) he doubts that Wilde's control over his ideas was any firmer than over his life. Connelly wonders about the connection between "ornamental" writing and a chaotic existence and questions the circular argument that justifies Aesthetic criticism: "the critic must apply his personality to art, and yet receive it from art in the first place." What kind of fulfillment can we find in Wilde's criticism when he himself failed to find any valuable alternative to art in experience? Connelly's argument strikes a cautioning note that probably derives its force from a Leavisian skepticism.

It is true, as J. E. Chamberlin has remarked (*HudR*, 1972), that Wilde's reputation has been strongest on the Continent, and this may account for the resurgence of interest in his criticism now, when Continental traditions are becoming more widely known in England and America. Chamberlin points out that Wilde was respected by such figures as Klee, Kandinsky, and Schlemmer, and he equates the Taoist notion of the "still point of the turning world," with which Wilde was presumably familiar, with modern poetics. But it is the comparisons that Chamberlin makes with Worringer and Veblen that are most provocative, especially since, he assures us, this links Wilde to Adorno in terms of sociological discourse. Would Wilde have been surprised to have found the cult of idleness associated with the New Left? Perhaps not. In any case Chamberlin's essay, like the others, is testimony to the continuing vitality of his ideas.

XI. De Profundis

A complete and accurate printing of *De Profundis* is in Hart-Davis' edition of *The Letters*, which should be consulted for a concise résumé of a complicated bibliographical history. (Also see H. Montgomery Hyde in the London *Sunday Times*, 3 Jan. 1960.) *De Profundis* began its public career in Germany with Max Meyerfeld's translation of 1905, which was serialized in *Neue Deutsche Rundschau* in January and February of 1905 and appeared in book form later in that year, but before the English publication and in a somewhat fuller form. In the preface to the serial publication, Meyerfeld expressed the view that *De Profundis* was destined to surpass all of Wilde's other works. Later in 1905, the German translation was itself translated into French, Spanish, and Italian (where the four letters to Ross first appeared in their original English, with a few minimal suppressions of the German text). As we have mentioned in our introduction, Meyerfeld's translation conditioned Wilde's image on the Continent for a number of years. The incomplete parts of the letters were made available by Meyerfeld in 1925 in German while prohibited passages appeared in part of a volume by Georges-Bazile, *Clamavi ad Te, suivi d'un choix de pensées* (Paris, 1925). This volume, according to Mason, whose copy is in the University of Toronto Library, was itself suppressed. Vyvyan Holland's edition (1949) is not the "first complete and accurate version" that he claims; see Hart-Davis, *The Letters*.

German reactions to the Meyerfeld translation and to Wilde's new work were favorable. A. Sewett in *Deutsche Monatsschrift für das Gesamt Leben der Gegenwart* of 1905 argued against Shaw's view that *De Profundis* was merely another mask. Sewett found in the work a reflection of Wilde's discovery of his own true humanity, a view shared by J. J. David (*Die Nation*, 1905), though with a biographical and evangelistic bias. A. Brandl in *Archiv für das Studium der Neueren Sprachen* (1905) found the book odd and fascinating because of Wilde's philosophy of art elaborated in prison and solitude to maintain his spirits. Perhaps the most interesting of the early German reactions was that of Oscar Bulle in "Das *De Profundis* eines Aestheten" (*Beilage zur Allgemeinen Zeitung*, 5 March 1905). Wilde, Bulle said, had a clever knack for presenting paradoxes and form as truth but had no faith in the truth of objects or concepts. His pursuit of art was not modified by prison; he continued to perfect his art through the discovery of suffering and his new esthetic understanding of Christ. But there was, according to Bulle, a fundamental contradiction in Wilde's position. He complained about the world's hardness and his own folly while praising suffering and pain as a source of inspiration. But Bulle's general reaction was favorable, as was that of "W.," *Protestantenblatt* (Bremen, 1905), and Alois Wurm (*Literarische Handweiser*, 1906). H. Hauck in "Oskar Wilde über die Englischen Gefängnisse: Ein Beitrag für Psychologie des Gefangniswesens" (*Monatsschrift für Kriminalpsychologie und Strafrechtreform*, 1910) granted that *De Profundis* was a distinguished work of art, but for him it was equally valuable as a firsthand source for evaluating the British penal system. Citing also some of Wilde's letters, Hauck's conclusion was that the inhumane treatment of children and the physical and psychological neglect of adult prisoners embittered rather than rehabilitated. Further examples of the German reaction are given in the bibliography to Defeiher's *Oscar Wilde: Der Mann und sein Werk*.

After the publication in 1925 of the full text in German translation, Günther Hildebrandt (*Die Bücher-Stube*, 1925) suggested that a revision of the uncritical glorification of Wilde would now ensue. Alois Stockmann discussed the relationship between Wilde and Douglas in *Stimmen der Zeit* of that same year and decided that whether or not an actual homosexual liaison existed, the friendship was unhealthy. But if the recriminations and money details led some in the direction of revisionism, Otto Zarck's reaction in *Neue Deutsche Rundschau* of 1925 was hyperbolic: *De Profundis* was addressed not to Douglas but was rather a hymn to "Geist." Also see Leonhard Wolff, "Oskar Wilde und seine Konversion" (*Werk und Wert*, 27 Jan. 1927).

Elsewhere in Europe the polemics of Douglas and Crosland, the libel suits and suggestions of forgery provoked further comment. H.-D. Davray, reviewing the French translation of 1905 in the June issue of *Mercure de France*, attacked the annotation and the spelling of proper names. The novelist "Rachilde" in a review of the French translation of *Oscar Wilde and Myself*, "Oscar Wilde et lui" (*Mercure de France*, 1918) protested against the reservation of the letter in the British Museum until 1960. The most rigorous post-war French commentary comes from Albert Camus, who relates Wilde, via *De*

Profundis, to his own existential definition of the Dandy (*Essais*, 1965).

In America, the contributions to *The Papyrus* have been noted. Henry Savage, *Book Notes* (1925), gave a brief account of the circumstances of the letter and at least sensed the ambivalences in Wilde's attitudes to himself, to Douglas, and to society. Perhaps the most interesting of the immediate British reactions was that of Hugh Walker, "The Birth of a Soul" (*Hibbert Journal*, 1905). Walker interpreted *De Profundis* as an orthodox expression of *pecca fortiter* at its most extreme (Wilde's unnatural vice). Walker detected a shift in Wilde's position: in *De Profundis* he accepts society's punishment as a means of purification; in the *Ballad* he rejects it, prefiguring by that the moral collapse of the last years. Wilde had to die to society and almost to himself to achieve self-recognition and personal purification. Walker still makes simplistic distinctions, however, between "sincerity" and "affectation" and assumes that Aestheticism is by definition a pose. J. Tyssul-Davis (*The Inquirer*, 12 Aug. 1905) also stressed the importance of both punishment and religious faith.

Information about the protracted and undignified quarrels that surrounded *De Profundis* is available in the books by Douglas and others, in *Two Worlds* (1926), and in a privately printed pamphlet by Frederick Peters, *The Riddle of De Profundis* (1945). The strong likelihood of Douglas' never having received his copy of the letter and the role of Robert Ross in this matter have been discussed in the *TLS* (30 Aug.–27 Sept. 1963).

Hart-Davis' text was reprinted in a paperback edition in 1964, with his original notes; Auden's "An Improbable Life"; *The Ballad*; and a few letters to Ross, Douglas, and others that bear on *De Profundis*. In that same year appeared Jacques Barzun's paperback edition, Barzun placing the letter in the context of Wilde's whole oeuvre. The emphasis is on the criticism: Wilde's central insight was that the individual's relation to himself defines the nature of society. Barzun can then offer *De Profundis* as a document which "neither disgusts by the painful detail nor shames our humanity by its exposure of the ego stripped."

Wilde's identification of himself with Christ touches on sensitive areas of taste and personal response: Margot Asquith remarked that "to read Wilde upon Christ is like reading Wordsworth in a brothel." However, *De Profundis* continued to attract the attention of theologians. Hans Ording (*Kirke og Kultur*, 1941) discussed "Oskar Wildes esteticke Kristusbilde" in relation to Renan and Christianity (the article is in Norwegian).

The ambiguous nature of Wilde's letter as both public manifesto and personal address continues to present real problems for the literary critic. G. Wilson Knight has some deeply felt observations in *The Christian Renaissance* (1962; rpt. *Twentieth Century Views*). He traces Wilde's use of jewel imagery in his early work. Jewels serve as a metaphor for the fundamental dilemma: "How may the 'soul' and its jewelled and seemingly infertile Eros be related to love and Christian values?" Wilson Knight then suggests that *Dorian Gray* is a critique of the Platonic Eros from this standpoint and that later in *De Profundis* Wilde finally confronts the issue through "a martyrdom, a crucifixion, a self-exhibition in agony and shame." By concentrating on the figure of Christ as sinner, Wilde is able to equate his own life with that of the Savior: a work of art with a tragic form.

Jan B. Gordon pursues the literary function of the public confession in his "Wilde and Newman: The Confessional Mode" (*Renascence*, 1970), where the comparison is made between *Apologia pro Vita Sua* and *De Profundis*. Gordon argues that both men write from prison, literally for Wilde, metaphorically for Newman, and that they have as a common purpose the justification of a conversion. Wilde has to explain his conversion to "hedonism" in the light of his apparent fall into philistine grossness. Like Newman, his defense embodies a version of *felix culpa*, offering his behavior as a "natural" act that will lead eventually to redemption. Gordon's analysis of the temporal and dramatic structure that Wilde uses to estheticize his own career is ingenious, and he makes some suggestive references to other contemporary works of autobiography as further examples of what was in effect a new genre. Wilde emerges from his self-confessional as a saint, as passive martyr, as androgyne; guilty of the sins of life yet free of the defects of art, he redeems his identity by undertaking a labyrinthine journey backward, from his humiliating end to a new beginning. Gordon's essay is the most subtle treatment yet of *De Profundis*, and perhaps his most valuable and original contribution to Wilde studies. Two subsequent readings of *De Profundis* are less impressive: Meredith Cary (*TSL*, 1971) claims that Wilde identified with Christ in order to acknowledge his sin: the life of pleasure had to be forsworn primarily because it was incomplete. Joseph Butwin (*VN*, 1972) suggests that the character of Christ was yet another role for Wilde to play, "more Shakespearean that Christian," and notes his frequent use of the very theatrical image of the brokenhearted clown.

XII. Poetry

In England, Wilde's poetry has never been highly regarded. The general attitude was wittily prefigured by Oliver Elton's comments on *Poems* (1881) when the author's presentation copy was (unprecedentedly) rejected by the Oxford Union. The first ground then (and since) was that *Poems* was shamelessly derivative, though Wilde's work is perhaps no more derivative at this earlier stage than that of most other poets. It was rather the self-conscious programmatic element in the homage to a gallery of masters that seemed suspicious. But, more gravely yet, the poems Elton observed were "this" and "that," vaguely sinister pronominal forms pointing doubtless to the wavering sexual tastes exhibited in such a work as "Charmides." *Punch*, however, found the poetry tame, even if the poet were Wilde.

The minor place that the poetry has tended to assume has been partly reinforced by Wilde's versatility. That his talent as a poet developed long went unrecognized, for the later lyrical poems remained uncollected for many years (there are still a number of fugitives), while *The Sphinx* could hardly expect an unbiased response in England, since its avowed aim was to "destroy domesticity." The exception to general indifference or condemnation was *The Ballad of Reading Gaol*, for the Anglo-Saxon could point to its "sincerity" and could read it as a return to "life" and a disavowal of the Aesthetic and decadent past. Yet the poem could still be reduced by complaints that its literary language deranged the plain ballad style or, alternatively, that the leaner realism betrayed the more studied and ethically generalized areas of the poem.

German appreciation of Wilde's poetry was consistently generous, particularly in the years from 1903 on. Otto Hauser (*Die Nation*, 1905), for example, ranked Wilde along with Rossetti and Swinburne as one of the best modern English poets; the narrative and dramatic works, Hauser regarded as overrated. He praised Wilde's gift for reproducing plastic qualities. Rather surprisingly, he declared that the manner of *The Ballad* is perfectly in keeping with that of the earlier poetry; the real change is in the starkness of the context and the unqualified truth of personal experience. But with Wilde even naked reality takes on "the deep beauty of symbol."

Apart from *The Ballad*, English and American criticism in the years after the First World War was adverse. Even anthologists of the 1890's found Wilde an embarrassment. *The Ballad* is reprinted in C. E. Andrews and M. O. Perceval's *Poetry of the Nineties* (1926), but the editors found the poem overlong and the rhetorical intensification faltering. A glance at Housman reveals Wilde as a less true poet. *The Sphinx* has an element of joy in terror: "the esthete in his search for beauty has gone beyond the visible world of the Greeks . . . in wonder at exotic forbidden things." Only *The Ballad* is actually embodied, however, in the anthology. As to Donald Davidson, editor of *British Poetry of the Eighteen Nineties* (1937), one can only speculate why he capitulated to the assignment since he had such a patent distaste for his subject. This distaste may, nonetheless, have sharpened his generalizations: Wilde, to whom he gave a greater representation than Andrews and Perceval, "seems to have stepped into a role already created and only awaiting a player." Other roles available to Wilde were those of Hellenist, poet of the Irish renaissance, and so forth. "English society permitted Wilde to state the death of morality as boldly as he pleased, but when Wilde as citizen acted on that principle, punishment was swift and condign. It was as if De Quincey, inflated with the popularity of his essay 'On Murder as One of the Fine Arts' had gone out and cut somebody's throat." *The Ballad* is excepted from the low estimate of Wilde's other poetry; it was as serious a retort as that of Byron upon a society which had punished its author with exile for being true to his principles.

The freezing point of Wilde's reputation in England arrived in the gray 1930's. Many contemporaries who had responded to the personality were dead, and Wilde himself had become a cliché, imprisoned in the socially conscious 1930's image of the 1890's. MacNeice did not mention Wilde in his manifesto *Modern Poetry* (1938), subsuming him, presumably, under the routine sneer "the dead hand of Walter Pater." Herbert Palmer's ideal in *Post-Victorian Poetry* (1938) was the poetry of the Georgians, so it is barely surprising that for him Wilde's poetry was chiefly "flowery pastiche." However, Palmer took *The Sphinx* to be one of the chief technical feats of the last sixty years; Wilde had "operatively proved that Tennyson's rhymes are much more effective as internal and cross rhymes than as end rhymes, signs pointing too, to a more flexible stanza and greater speed and resonance in the metrical beat." Palmer also noted that Wilde's Decadent pessimism is similar to that of Hardy and Housman. In the introduction to L. Vivante's *English Poetry and its Contribution to the Knowledge of a Creative Principle* (1950), a quasi-philosophic offering, T. S. Eliot remarked with a familiar mandarin weariness that Wilde's poetry was "inferior . . . on grounds of literary criticism (as well as because of personal taste)" and proceeded to appeal confidently to a consensus: the reader might be surprised to find a critic recommended by Eliot bothering with a poet "whom he had always regarded as second-rate." Even Auden, who admired Wilde with discrimination, thought the poetry no good.

A later generation, concerned less with any threat that Wilde and his generation might pose to literary identity, could afford a more detached look at Wilde the poet. Some general historians of poetry may serve as markers. In 1944 H. J. C. Grierson in *A Critical History of English Poetry* glided over Wilde in one sentence without mentioning the *Ballad*. Sir Ifor Evans in *English Poetry in the Later Nineteenth Century* (1933; rev. ed., 1966) found the life more significant than the literature, though he persisted in misdating Wilde's birth. About the poems he was relaxed, defending *Poems* (1881) from any charge of crude plagiarism and noting the breadth of interest that volume displays. However, the various and incompatible political stances cause Sir Ifor to doubt whether any of them "represent a sincere conviction." A closer look at the poems is evident in H. N. Fairchild's *Religious Trends in English Poetry*, Vol. v (1962), though Fairchild hardly liked what he saw. The 1881 was essentially a volume of "engagement": Wilde was always anxious to live his theories; a man "of the ivory megaphone rather than of the ivory tower." The image of the crucified, loosely associated with the sufferings of man in *De Profundis* and *The Ballad*, derived from Winwood Reade's *The Martyrdom of Man*. On *The Ballad* the judgment was that "not many poems so factitious have been so deeply felt." Fairchild had some sympathy with Wilde's protest against Christian inhumanity to "weaker or less fortunate brothers . . . despite some confusion between the idea that prisons are stupidly brutal institutions and the idea that nobody should ever be punished for anything." The fundamental analogy between suffering man and suffering Christ, Fairchild dismissed as theologically inaccurate and the notion that the trooper's fellow prisoners "took his guilt into their own guilty hearts with penitent love" humanly implausible. V. De Sola Pinto in *Crisis in British Poetry 1880–1941* (1951; 3rd ed., 1958), commenting briefly, found more poetry in Wilde's prose than in his verse. De Sola Pinto finally reverted to more conventional judgments: "If Wilde could have outgrown the shallow hedonism which he mistook for a philosophy of art, he might have become the poet of the social conscience of his age."

From the beginning American no less than Anglo-Saxon criticism of Wilde was readily distinguishable from the Continental. Where the Germans took the verse seriously and gave it serious scholarly attention, the Anglo-Americans tended to be strong in opinion and in moral tone. Precisely that approach is illustrated by Homer E. Woodbridge in "Oscar Wilde as a Poet" (*Poet Lore*, 1908). Wilde's "criticism of life" is limited to "passion and weariness of passion," a somewhat unfair instance of borrowing one's criticism of Wilde directly from Wilde himself. As poet, Wilde had genius, but his lack of "spiritual vision" proved an "insurmountable barrier" to greatness. Four poems emerge as major: "Charmides," "The New Helen," *The Sphinx* (not unintelligently described as a "reverie in grotesque word-sculpture"), and *The Ballad*, "passionately felt" but with less imaginative strength and finish than the other major poems.

If German criticism has taken Wilde's poetry with some gravity, its sources have been taken even more gravely, and these extend far beyond Shakespeare and the English Romantics and Victorians. For the Germans, the presence of such sources, particularly when Continental, indicate Wilde's status as a figure in world literature.

Regrettably, however much one is grateful for the quantity of German writing on Wilde, its tendency is often to amass sources simply for those sources' sake rather than to discover something new or unexpected in Wilde's text. The 1920's and 1930's were the golden age of the thesis that depended on source studies, and Wilde was established as one who provided rich evidence for *Quellenstudien*. Few of these German scholars troubled their analysis with any general literary theory or manifested any acute desire to place Wilde's poems in wider contexts; with all their devoted scholarship such articles tend now to be of limited usefulness.

Bernhard Fehr's "Studien zu Oscar Wildes Gedichten" (*Palaestra*, 1918) is a classic 212 pages and essentially consists in remorseless comparison of one poem with another; there is little historical or even biographical detail. Literary sources only are adduced, and the content of the article in proportion to its length is somewhat tenuous. Fehr's piece, however, is still a necessary point of departure and much Continental criticism, in particular, derives from it. One of the first was H. Mutschmann, who, in *Beiblatt zur Anglia* for 1919, duly vulgarized Fehr's findings by declaring Wilde to be a plagiarist pure and simple. Mutschmann demonstrated to his own satisfaction that verses, patterns, meters, metaphors, and even whole lines had been transferred from Palgrave's *Golden Treasury*. The only interest that remained was the pathological. Fehr answered Mutschmann in "Über Oscar Wildes Gedichten und anständige Kritik" (*Beiblatt zur Anglia*, 1920). Mutschmann's findings supported Fehr's own theories of word-echoes, but Fehr objected to Mutschmann's moralizings and hyperboles, the consequence being that neither Fehr's book nor Wilde's poetry was justly evaluated. In a sense Mutschmann had properly raised the question of whether Wilde's poetry was worth scholarly effort if it was so derivative, and the onus was certainly on the purveyors of *Quellenstudien* to make a case. Mutschmann returned to the topic in "Nachtrag zu Oscar Wildes Gedichten" (*Beiblatt zur Anglia*, 1921) and extended his list of borrowings, now favoring the Romantics as prime material. Helene Richter's "Oscar Wildes Persönlichkeit in seinen Gedichten" (*EngS*, 1920) made its points in a mere 75 pages. The poems were usefully discussed in order of periodical publication; "The Rise of Historical Criticism" was related to the oeuvre, and "Speranza" herself brought to bear on it. Richter also used "The Critic as Artist" in comment on individual poems. Gerda Eichbaum (*Die Neueren Sprachen*, 1932) noted the type of language used of Whistler's painting so that it could be related to Wilde's poetry. There are numerous references to "die Palette" of both. This perhaps is the most balanced of such articles, but remains light on theoretical content and has probably been superseded by R. L. Peters's article discussed below. The Germans, had they exhibited more curiosity about manuscript material, or had such material been generally available, were well placed to produce a proper edition of the poems with a convincing apparatus.

Edouard Roditi's "Wilde's Poetry as Art History" (*Poetry*, 1946) was adapted as the second chapter of his *Oscar Wilde* (1947). Roditi also rehearsed the confusion of literary genres, while Wilde's various poetic manners, changing tastes, and use of imagery were related with a laconic vagueness to the literary and art history of the nineteenth century ("Charmides" takes one back—does it not?—to Flaxman, but it never does to neglect Leighton). Roditi admired "The Harlot's House" for its "modern simplicity," no less than *The Ballad*, but in general the poetry was warmly dismissed as an admirable preparation for Wilde's prose. Wilde went "far towards the awareness of all cultural history, and the appreciation of all art was one of the philosophic aims of Benedetto Croce and Henry Adams." Interesting: but though Roditi omitted the fact, it was one of the aims also of Walter Pater. Wilde, however, like Browning, was still only able to view different periods of art disparately. This whole piece is densely generalized and, in spite of its namesmanship, not always impeccably informed.

With J. D. Thomas' "Oscar Wilde's Prose and Poetry" (*Rice Institute Pamphlet*, 1955) we re-enter the moral world of the Anglo-Saxons or Anglo-Americans. This began life as a lecture and is elegantly, sometimes wittily written, though censorious about Wilde's defects of character and somewhat derivative in matter. Thomas attempts the analysis of *Poems* (1881) as a logically structured volume along the line of Hugh Kenner's analysis of Yeats's *Collected Poems* as a single "Sacred Book of the Arts," though the analogy here is with musical composition; and Thomas makes no attempt to claim for Wilde that ironized dialectic and dramatic unfolding of themes and selves present in Yeats. A pattern of loose but definable "movement" from esthetic withdrawal through sensuous religiosity to the statement of some putative higher wisdom—the choice in "Humanitad" of Athene rather than Aphrodite—is evident. Thomas notes Wilde's response to machinery, though without relating that to Wilde's contemporaries, to a Huysmans, a D'Annunzio, or a Kipling, for example. "The Harlot's House" is placed in the context of the controversy with Whistler (that old *topos* indeed of the hierarchy of the arts, poet versus painter, as exemplified in the *Ten O'Clock* and Wilde's review of that work). "The Harlot's House" marks also the transition from Impressionism to Symbolism. *The Sphinx* is overtly symbolic: the veiled subject may be Wilde's possible syphilitic infection. *The Ballad* fittingly closes Wilde's career with paradox. The apostle of "Beauty" rests his surest poetic fame on a ballad of ugliness, of "the unlacquered truth," though this critic ignores the Decadent notion that the beautiful should be found in the ugly.

Kingsley Amis' introduction to his selection from Wilde's *Poems and Essays* (1956) is refreshingly no-nonsense, free from moral prejudice and fashionable literary stock response, but empirical and not precisely profound. Wilde's poetry may be difficult to take for admirers of Eliot and Empson, but "an ideal reader . . . will find other grounds for condemning 'The New Helen' than that it proves no whetstone for the ratiocinative faculty." *The Ballad* fails in its mixture of plain and direct with archaic language. Wilde is the most *literary* of all Victorian poets: "Nearly all his verse shows, not merely a preference for literary subject-matter and attitude, but a remarkably determined attempt to exclude, in all departments of language: (diction, syntax, morphology, etc.) any feature that could primarily be associated with speech rather than with writing, anything that might seem informal, let alone colloquial, rather than literary." Amis does not deny that literary poetry can be good, but he remains uneasy with Wilde's archaism. The best poems are those with French rather than British connections, "Impression du matin" and "Symphony in Yellow," where Wilde extends the scope of literary scenic description to include urban properties. Romantic verse about London remains the least faded of the types of poetry written by the poets of the English Decadence. If its very remote ancestor is Wordsworth's sonnet written on Westminster Bridge, its barely recognizable descendants are imagism and Eliot's "Preludes." *The Sphinx* remains Wilde's finest poem with its assortment of visual, tactile, and olfactory images; its cunningly placed extreme epithets; and its polysyllabic nouns suggesting transliteration from some Eastern tongue.

W. Y. Tindall in *Forces in Modern British Literature 1885–1956* (1956) focused more strongly than Amis on Wilde as a precursor of the twentieth century, and his volume should be consulted for its comments on other parts of the oeuvre. Of *Poems* (1881) he observed that they anticipate Eliot's summary of the past by theft and allusion, while in such poems as "The Harlot's House" the macabre, the urban, and the grotesque combine "with a sudden disconcerting prettiness more horrible than what preceded it." Tindall's comments were acute in spite of the perpetuation of a few howlers.

Wilde (along with Henley, Symons, and William Sharp) was discussed in an important article by R. L. Peters, "Whistler and the English Poets of the 1890s" (*MLQ*, 1957). Wilde's "painterly" poems were precisely related to Whistlerian simplified outlines, evasion of anecdote, titles taken from musical terms, the use of single color imagery, and Whistler's version of Japanese art. Peters does not perhaps sufficiently attend to Gautier as prime influence on Wilde, and his unsympathetic comments on Wilde's verse tend to confuse judgment with assertion. In " 'On the Sale by Auction of Keats's Love Letters.' A Footnote to Wilde's Sonnet" (*Keats-Shelley Journal*, 1958) Brooks Wright discussed the context of the poem.

A. E. Rodway's remarks on Wilde as poet appeared in a general survey of what was termed "The Last Phase," forming part of *The Penguin Guide to English Literature*, Vol. VI (1958). This aggregation is dominated by sub-Leavisian judgments, so that any committed response to the period or its representative figures was barely to be expected. Rodway's responses, however, were intelligent and unbiased. He made a sustained comparison with Kipling which revealed, under the surface distinctions, strong similarities between the authors. As a poet, Wilde developed steadily, and in *The Sphinx* managed effects of surreal synesthesia and a humorous turn of imagery that suggested some distancing by Wilde of his own mannerisms (but Rodway perhaps should have stressed that such equivocations of tone are not unusual in Decadent writers). Rodway agreed with Amis that the most satisfying poems were those which resembled Whistlerian painting. Yet with all Wilde's Aestheticism and Kipling's mastery of the colloquial and the popular culture of the music hall, it was Wilde who produced the one major poem, in a popular kind, of the *fin de siècle*. In *The Ballad*, Wilde used whatever diction was tactically useful (though this again, the critic might have noted, marks the poem as Decadent). *The Ballad* involved not merely feeling but the hard thinking that went into "The Soul of Man under Socialism" (Rodway's favorite Wilde text) along with an intelligent use of refrain. In a survey, Rodway must make rapid generalized points, but within such limits this remains a sensitive and persuasive piece.

There are few German periodical articles of importance on the poetry in the years preceding and after the Second World War. Joachim von Helmersen in "Oscar Wildes Gedichttitel" (*Die Literatur*, 1935) expressed enchantment with the titles of Wilde's poems; first, because they conjure up associations which provide the key to the thematic sphere of each poem and, second, because they announce an "eternal humanism" that is generally European rather than restricted to one *Volk*. It was unfortunate, Helmersen concluded, that the poems did not live up to the promise of their titles. In "Heckels Holzschnitte zu Wildes 'Zuchthausballade'" (*Philobiblon*, 1962), Gottfried Sello offers an absorbing study of the encounter between the young Expressionist Heckel of the "Die Brücke" group and Wilde's poem.

In Italy, Wilde has aroused less interest than in France and Germany, and Italian responses tend to amount to mere *rifacimenti* of earlier European criticism. Mario Vinciguerra in *Romantici e decadenti inglesi* (Foligno, 1926) concentrated mainly on the later career, analyzing *De Profundis* and *The Ballad*, but went little further than elegant generalities. Agostino Lombardo's *La poesia dall'estetismo al simbolismo* (Rome, 1954) antedated much of the recent Anglo-Saxon interest in the topic, but actually offered an Italian source study based on German source studies, though Lombardo professed the laudable aim of demonstrating the positive aspects of the Decadence. *Poems* (1881) were presented as a programmatic arrangement, a species of anthology from Milton to Arnold, the Aesthetic "imaginary museum" and as anticipating Decadent sensitivity and linguistic devices. There was also a long, convincing, though not altogether original, comparison of *The Sphinx* with Flaubert's *Tentations* and with Baudelaire's "Le Chat."

Among detailed discussions of individual poems is Bernhard Fehr's "Oscar Wildes 'The Harlot's House'" (*Archiv für das Studium der*

Neueren Sprachen, 1916). Sources predominate once more: Pater, Poe, Chaucer, Shakespeare, Rossetti, Gautier, Whistler, the Goncourts, Baudelaire's "Danse Macabre," and, lest we forget, Tennyson's "Charge of the Light Brigade" (though there remains the little matter of meter even if both poems are heavily mimetic). Then there is Mark Twain and a ballad called "The Public House" from *The Sporting Times* of 1885. Dance rhythms are of course important, and Fehr concludes with comment on how certain words should be stressed. How the poem survives this Alexandrian tesselation, he does not altogether explain. This article, however, must still be read for its fertility of detail and splay of source material. J. D. Thomas' "The Composition of Wilde's 'The Harlot's House' " (*MLN*, 1950) owes much to Fehr, but is superseded by the author's essay on the poetry in general, already cited. Among the glosses on various poems in David R. Clark's *Lyric Resonance* (1972) is a close critical reading of Wilde's "Requiescat." Clark's conclusion is that the delicate beauty of the poem when examined becomes an example of Wilde's fatal facility for imitation.

The Ballad of Reading Gaol has attracted more comment than any other individual poem. The better criticism has attempted to meet the general problem *The Ballad* poses. This can be broadly summarized as the apparent fissure between the "I" as sufferer and the "I" as commentator; between narrative and ethical generalization; between the objectivity of the ballad form and the propagandist element in the poem; between the often effective realism and the ornate diction found in particular in section III.

R. B. Glaenzer (*The Bookman*, New York, 1911), however, deals as much with *De Profundis* as with *The Ballad*. The hanging of Trooper Woolridge is juxtaposed with the Henley Regatta as a festival of fashion taking place barely ten miles away. Glaenzer quotes Wilde's comment on the law in an interview of 1895. *The Ballad* is preferred above *De Profundis* with its "false notes and grating discords." *The Ballad*, though, is "a quaint exposition of ever-present anguish and inconsolable self-pity." The main inspiration is to be found in Housman (suggested already by Stuart Mason), also Hood's "Eugene Aram"; the importance of Coleridge's *Rime of the Ancient Mariner* is doubted, in spite of the obvious verbal echoes. A list of editions is given. This article contains atypically little biographical material, suggesting deliberate abstention. In contrast John T. Winterich (*Publishers Weekly*, 1931) is nothing but biographical.

The third section of Arthur Symons' *A Study of Oscar Wilde* deals with *The Ballad*. This is late and rambling Symons, but still worth remark: not solely because it is by Symons, and Symons was a contemporary. Of the sources Symons observes that not Hood but W. E. Henley's "In Hospital" should serve as control, since there "a personal experience and personally observed surroundings are put into verse as directly and with as much precise detail as possible." But *The Ballad*, unlike Henley's sequence of poems, does not fuse modernity and firsthand subject with new form, nor does it escape poetic diction. Didactic and realistic details are not in themselves art, and the grim concreteness of "the hangman with his gardener's gloves" that attracts praise in more recent criticism for Symons remains "fine prose, not poetry." The poem remains fixed near the level of raw document, an angry interrupted reverie; it is the asides that count, not the story. The theme that unifies a poem not altogether homogenous, the moral truth that "all men kill the thing they love," is a symbol of the "obscure deaths of the heart," the "violence done upon souls." Symons reminds us of Alfred Douglas' claim in *Oscar Wilde and Myself* (1914) that Douglas, as the more experienced writer of ballads, was prominent in the composition of the poem. That Douglas could have given assistance is possible, but on past form it seems more likely that his presence was a hindrance rather than a help. Symons, however, merely repeats Douglas' claim without comment. If the ninth poem in *The Shropshire Lad* had any influence, the comparison remains in Wilde's favor. Symons' piece then collapses into a jagged history of the ballad form, drawing a comparison, in passing, with "Eugene Aram" (after telling us that such a comparison was irrelevant)—Hood and Wilde as masters of splendid horror. As a creature of extremes, Wilde takes both the humanitarianism and the realism of his poem to their limits. *The Ballad* was necessarily the end of Wilde's career. Wilde had, Symons concludes, in some sense no self, he was all attitude; wit, the least personal form of speech, remained with him to the end.

For another contemporary and acquaintance, W. B. Yeats, it is the story, not the asides, that count. In the vivid introduction to his eccentric *Oxford Book of Modern Verse 1892–1935* (1936) Yeats dismisses all of Wilde's poetry except *The Ballad*: a "young man," himself, "would have felt nothing but contempt for the poetry of Oscar Wilde, considering it an exaggeration of every Victorian fault, nor, except in the case of one poem not then written, has time corrected the verdict." The "stark realism" of *The Ballad*, once its "foreign feathers" are plucked from it, is akin to that of Thomas Hardy. Even famous lines "effective in themselves" are excised from the version Yeats prints, for they become in their context artificial, trivial, arbitrary; a work of art can have but one subject." Only in this poem does Wilde, who otherwise shared the admirations of his older Victorian contemporaries, achieve a great, or "almost great" poem; though disaster did not wholly clear his soul, there at least he was enabled to become antithetical to the age. Yeats's view of Wilde, particularly in relation to *The Ballad*, was examined by R. Stamm in "W. B. Yeats und Oscar Wildes 'Ballad of Reading Gaol'" (*Wiener Beiträge zur englischen Philologie*, 1957). The background of *The Oxford Book of Modern Verse* is also discussed. C. J. Dixon (*Fin de Siècle. Poetry of the late Victorian period. 1860–1900*, 1968) includes *The Ballad* in the version furnished by Yeats but misleadingly describes it as "revised by W. B. Yeats."

An anonymous writer in *Reading and Collecting* for 1937 offered a suavely belletristic piece ostensibly on *The Ballad* but really consisting in generalized observations of Wilde, who we gather has "known every adventure except a private life and every sensation except peace." An editorial comment in *The Explicator* (1943) distinguishes two types of moral statement in *The Ballad*. The first is the murderer as epitome of all mankind; the second, that of prison reform, issuing finally in the notion that Christ's forgiveness, not man's, comes with remorse. The three major themes enrich one another: social reform, the guilt of all men, and Christ's forgiveness of all. "Much apparent inconsistency may be explained by the paradoxical logic of the prisoners' judging God's justice by the standard of man's." Epifanio San Juan in *The Art of Oscar Wilde* (1968) relies mainly on the elaborate redaction of earlier criticism for his comment on the poems, though for *The Ballad* San Juan furnishes an interesting solution to the problem of how to relate the ballad form to the acutely personalized area of comment. "Wilde moulds a metrical convention into an organic pattern. . . . He uses a poignantly repetitive, circular pattern in matter and narration. Its center of authority is the 'I,' alternately the elegaic chorus and the protagonist. The 'I' acts as a variable *persona*: spokesman or typical figure. His personal impressions, conditioned by the prison, bear no individualising trait. Escaping from phantasy, the speaker directs the progression of his feelings towards involvement with the victim's end."

According to C. S. Nassaar in *Into the Demon Universe* (1974), *The Ballad* is a flawed masterpiece. Where *De Profundis* ends on a note of hope, in the poem all is horror and damnation, for it is written in dialectical opposition to *The Rime of the Ancient Mariner*. Like the mariner, the guardsman commits an *acte gratuit* and falls as a consequence into a two-fold demon universe—an internal Hell of spiritual foulness and an external Hell of punishment. Unlike the mariner, the guardsman never escapes from his double Hell: death is the only release. The guardsman's experience, moreover, is symbolic of the human situation. All human beings, beginning in innocence, at some point willfully murder the innocent self, "the thing they love." But Wilde sometimes forgets that his prison *is* symbolic and confusingly attacks human injustice, on occasion turning the poem into a propagandist tract; he fails, in other words, to subscribe to the thesis of Nassaar's entertaining book. Burton R. Pollin (*RLV*, 1973/4) also compares *The Ballad* with *The Rime* and tells us that *The Rime* is the greater poem: it is difficult to see why this article was either written or published.

The present state of criticism of *The Ballad* is usefully summarized by Derek Stanford in "Facets of Reading Gaol" (*Books and Bookmen*, 1974).

XIII. *Wilde among His Contemporaries and Later Writers*

By according him a determining role in the drama of his *Autobiographies*, Yeats created a lasting image of Wilde that was compounded when he placed him firmly in Phase 19 of *A Vision* as "essentially a man of action" (the key passages are reprinted in *Twentieth Century Views*; also see *The Critical Heritage*). In *Eminent Domain* (1967) Richard Ellmann explores Yeats's affiliation with the older man with some graphic descriptions of their meetings. He tracks the direct line of influence: Yeats's use of images of Christ, his interest in the Salome myth, above all the modifications that he made to the idea of the mask. An important supplement to Ellmann's work is W. Schrickx, "On Giordano Bruno, Wilde and Yeats" (*ES*, suppl., 1964). Schrickx

details the interest shown by both writers in the Renaissance panthe-
ist and suggests the powerful influence upon Yeats of *Dorian Gray*,
which he described in an 1891 review of *Lord Arthur Savile's Crime*
as "with all its faults of method, . . . a wonderful book." A minor
contribution to the field is contained in George Bornstein, "A Borrowing from Wilde in Yeats's *The King's Threshold*" (*N&Q*, 1971); and
Wilde's review of two Yeats books has been reprinted (*IB*, 1962).

Shaw's views of Wilde depend on self-identification: he looks for
an ally; the Puritan co-opts the Hedonist, and Shaw discovers a Wilde
that is like himself: triumphant enemy of English hypocrisy. There
are two main statements of reminiscence. In the first, which was
published in German (*Neue Freie Presse*, 1905; rpt. *The Matter with
Ireland*, ed. David H. Greene and Dan J. Laurence, 1962), the literary defense is characteristically heterodox (*De Profundis* is but another comedy) and Wilde's confidence in the superiority of his own
pose is overestimated, perhaps intentionally. The main distinction is
between Wilde the anachronistic Romantic and the moderns, among
whom, of course, Shaw includes himself. The second statement was
made in response to Harris' biography and is included in later editions of it (also rpt. Shaw's *Pen Portraits and Reviews*, 1931; and
Twentieth Century Views); and it contains some much stronger criticisms: Wilde was lazy, was sometimes a coward and always a snob;
the suppressed part of *De Profundis* shows Wilde "at his worst and
weakest." But can Shaw have changed his mind only on the basis of
what he had learned from Harris, or was it that time had elapsed and
the audience had changed, permitting more than a display of loyalty?
Critics of the drama often make comparisons between the two playwrights but as yet they have looked at the surface only. (Manlio
Miserecchi, *Nuova Antologia*, 1957, is inadequate about the relationship; in Japanese there is H. Hira, "Bernard Shaw and Wilde,"
Eibungaku Kenkyu, 1952.) What might Shaw's comment on *The
Importance* "his finest really heartless play" tell us about his own
work?

Yeats and Shaw (and Wilde himself) have left us their own cultural histories, which are inevitably self-directed and self-concealing.
A comparative study of their versions of the nineties should go beyond casual talk of "influence" and might among other things disclose
a Wilde who is much more than an acknowledged father loyally
remembered, but in the harsh light of his own disgrace.

Attempts to relate Wilde and Henry James have been largely unsuccessful. It has often been supposed, for instance, that there is a
connection between Wilde and the figure of Gabriel Nash in *The
Tragic Muse*. However, a recent essay denies a specific identification
and suggests that the only valid grounds for comparison between the
real and the fictional Aesthete lie in their mutual derivation from Pater
(D. J. Gordon and John Stokes, *The Air of Reality: New Essays on
Henry James*, ed. John Goode, 1972; all previous discussions of the
topic are also listed here; see, e.g., *NCF*, 1957; *PMLA*, 1958; Oscar
Cargill, *The Novels of Henry James*, 1961). The failure to acknowledge Pater also debilitates Edouard Roditi's argument (*UKCR*,
1948). Roditi discovers an oblique reference to James in one of
Wilde's early reviews, but otherwise his article has more to do with

James's attitudes to Aestheticism in general than with Wilde. George Monteiro (*AL*, 1964) notes that the two men were in Washington in July 1882; but the records of their coinciding paths, although amusing, are hardly significant. Similarly, the references to Wilde made throughout the five volumes of Leon Edel's biography of James (1963–72) are often intriguing but inconclusive and sometimes even questionable; for instance: "The Wilde case had dearly brought release to James; he could now deal more directly with sex."

Stephen Daedalus is a variety of Aesthete, and Joyce wrote an important essay on Wilde as Irish scapegoat (*The Critical Writings of James Joyce*, ed. Ellsworth Mason and Richard Ellmann, 1959; rpt. *Twentieth Century Views*). Beneath Wilde's shining Aestheticism, itself the rebellious product of Anglo-Saxon puritanism, Joyce discovers a private and strictly Catholic sense of sin. Further connections between Wilde and Joyce have been suggested by Herbert Howarth in *A James Joyce Miscellany* (ed. Marvin Magalaner, 1959); Donald J. Weinstock (*AN&Q*, 1969); and Archie K. Loss (*JML*, 1973). Also see *The Critical Heritage*.

A. E. Housman's response to the trial and condemnation of Wilde can be gathered from the poem "O who is that young sinner," which was printed as No. xviii of the "Additional Poems" in *A. E. H.* by Laurence Housman (1937). Housman regarded Wilde highly: "from a European point of view the three great English poets are Shakespeare, Byron, and the late Mr. Wilde" (*Cambridge Review*, 1915); but for a more reserved comment see *The Letters*, ed. Henry Maas (1971). Mario Praz (*The Romantic Agony*) cites without reference a parody of *Dorian Gray* by Swinburne: *The Statue of John Brute*. Edward Gordon Craig frequently referred to Wilde, see in particular *The Mask*, Oct. 1908.

The major theme of Jacques de Langlade, *Oscar Wilde, écrivain français* is Wilde as "ce prodigieux personnage, qui a laissé dans la littérature française une trace fulgurante." Developing ideas present in his Preface to the *Oeuvres* (1975), de Langlade shows how the outline of Wilde's career became a paradigm for French writers from Louÿs, Barrès, Mirbeau, and Charles du Bos to Montherlant, Sartre, Camus, and Genet. That exotic French amalgam of English characteristics, *le snobisme* (to which Wilde made a major contribution), the prophetic modernity of Wilde's esthetics, and the changing images of the homosexual are all given due attention; particularly in extended treatments of Gide, Proust, and Cocteau. Although it follows the irritating French mode of having neither index nor bibliography, this book partly satisfies a need that has long been apparent; it is discussed by Jacques de Ricaumont in *RDM* (1975).

André Gide's essays on Wilde are collected in *Oscar Wilde* (1949), although they had appeared previously in separate editions in both English and French (see Mason). The best treatment in English of these and of the other works by Gide on which Wilde has a bearing is Richard Ellmann's "Corydon and Menalque" (*Golden Codgers*, 1973; see also his introd. to *Twentieth Century Views*). Ellmann explicates Gide's view of Wilde as his "spiritual seducer" and shows how Wilde's "New Hellenism" offered him a way out of Aestheticism by exchanging the sacred for the secular and by infusing esthetics with experience. Françoise J. L. Mouret has dated their first meeting (*FS*, 1968) and Michael Albeaux-Fernet has composed a rhapsodic appraisal of the part played by the Narcissus myth in Wilde, Gide, and Valéry (*RDM*, 1972). Also see Charles du Bos, *Le Dialogue avec André Gide* (1929), *Cahiers André Gide* (1969), *Revue des Lettres Modernes* (1970), and a brief discussion of Gide's personal impressions of Wilde's development in Karl Hellwig's "André Gide und Oscar Wilde" (*Kleine Bund*, 1929).

Wilde's impact on other Continental writers has begun to be documented. The first meetings with Mallarmé and the possibility of his influence on Wilde have been discussed by Eileen Souffrin (*RLC*, 1959) and H. P. Clive (*FS*, 1970). In "Barbey d'Aurevilly et Oscar Wilde" (*RLM*, 1970) John Greene perpetuates the fallacious story that Wilde translated *Ce qui ne meurt pas* and indicates vaguely what he and d'Aurevilly have in common. Connections with Stefan George are made by Victor A. Oswald, Jr. (*MLQ*, 1949) and Guido Glur (*Sprache und Dichtung*, Berne, 1957). R. Breugelman's challenge to Glur's source study takes the form of a "confrontation" between Wilde and George. But although informative, his two articles (*Proceedings of the Pacific Northwest Conference on Foreign Languages*, 1964, 1966) are sometimes too complex in their metaphysics. He first examines the "Bios Theoretikos" and compares the two writers' common characteristics as Aesthetes with homoerotic tendencies, noting the fundamentally escapist Narcissism of their "Ich-Du" relationships, and their attitudes to authority. Wilde is shown to have less willpower than George, as driven by impulses rather than by purpose. The second article concentrates on a comparison of the esthetics of the two authors, claiming that both Wilde and George are concerned with form that creates its substance and is "Geist." Breugelmans rehearses a similar comparison in *Mosaic* (1968), arguing that both authors are precursors of twentieth-century alienation in their simultaneous commitment and disgust. Hugo von Hofmannsthal's 1905 essay (*Gesammelte Werke in Einzelausgaben*, Prose II, 1951, trans. *Selected Prose*, 1952) is notable for its refusal to distinguish between Wilde's nature and his fate: to be an Aesthete is itself to be a tragic figure: when Wilde sued Queensberry he merely replaced the mask of Bacchus with the mask of Oedipus or Ajax; all roles were contained within the man. The two authors themselves are brought together in Eugene Weber's "Hofmannstahl und Oscar Wilde" (*Hofmannstahl-Forschungen*, 1971).

Thomas Mann's brief remarks on Wilde and Nietzsche (*Last Essays*, 1958; relevant portions rpt. *Twentieth Century Views*) possess an interest that goes far beyond the fact of their authorship; and the strange similarities between the two might claim attention in any history of nineteenth-century ideas—Lionel Trilling suggests some possible collocations in *Sincerity and Authenticity* (1971). Adolf Mayer, *Die Wartburg* (Leipzig, 25 Feb. 1910) briefly confessed himself to be ashamed of the influence of the twin evil spirits of Wilde and Nietzsche upon his culture. At present the only extended treatment of the intellectual relationship with Nietzsche is in Dutch: Norbert Loeser, *Nietzsche en Wilde en Anders Essays* (Haarlem, 1960), although it is at least acknowledged in David S. Thatcher's *Nietzsche in*

England (1970). J. C. Powys also invoked Nietzsche, but to Wilde's disfavor; yet he did allow that Wilde's frivolity and worldliness may have best served his cause (*Suspended Judgements*, 1916; rpt. *The Critical Heritage*). Powys' aim appears to have been to cut Wilde down to an appropriate size with some powerful phrase-making; his disdain, nonetheless, is more impressive than that of George Moore (*Moore versus Harris*, 1925). There is some information about the rivalry between the Irish exiles in Gerald Griffin, *The Wild Geese* (1938). The relationship between Whistler and Wilde has generally been presented in terms of *The Gentle Art of Making Enemies* (1890), particularly by those supine Boswells, the Pennells, in their biography (1911).

Rubén Darío's *éloge*, "Purificaciones de la Pieded," written in Paris in December 1900, is reprinted in *Obras* (Vol. III, Madrid, 1919). Wilde appears as martyr of the British bourgeoisie. The Nicaraguan poet describes Wilde's conversation at a gathering at the bar Calisaya. The Flemish writer Georges Eekhoud dedicated a story to Wilde in *Le Cycle patibulaire* (1896). There are many pieces which make connections between foreign authors and Wilde: for example, "José Asunción Silva and Wilde" (*Hispania*, 1962), where C. W. Cobb notes Silva's presence in London in 1884 at a moment when Wilde was attracting notice and points out a few echoes of Wilde in Silva's verse. The influence, however, was passing, but witnesses to the early as well as the wide range of Wilde's image and his work. A. Casemiro de Silva in *Eça a Wilde* (Rio, 1962) confronts and compares Eça de Queiros, the nineteenth-century Portuguese novelist, and Wilde. R. Breugelmans has recorded Wilde's reputation in the Low Countries (*Studia Germanica Gandensia*, 1961); Walter W. Nelson, *Oscar Wilde in Sweden* (Dublin, 1965) has two essays on his influence on Swedish writers; B. S. McDougal has interestingly traced Wilde's reception in the "new" China of the 1920's (*Journal of the Oriental Soc. of Australia*, 1972–73); Lisa E. David has shown how he inspired modernists and anarchists in Spain (*CL*, 1973). A. L. Volynsky published an essay in Russian on Wilde (St. Petersburg, 1900) and there are no doubt other Russian contributions. There are even connections to be made with Jorge Luis Borges, who has commented that to mention Wilde is "also to evoke the notion of art as a select or secret game," and that his syntax is always very simple and that the "fundamental spirit of his work is joy" (*Other Inquisitions*, 1937–52, 1964, rpt. *Twentieth Century Views*).

It has been suggested that the outline of Wilde's downfall is apparent in the plot of John Galsworthy's *Loyalties* (*ETJ*, 1958); and Franz Zaïc has written "Zu Anouilhs Bearbeitung von Oscar Wildes 'The Importance of Being Earnest'" (*Die Neueren Sprachen*, 1959).

An early sympathetic appearance of Wilde in fiction occurs in "George Fleming" (Constance Fletcher), *Mirage* (1877). The scene is Egypt and Wilde is Davenant, indolent, full of dreamy paradox, a lover of Greek antiquity. Wilde makes only one appearance, but his martyred presence resounds through Roger Peyrefitte's partial *roman à clef* of homosexual life, *L'Exil du Capri* (Paris, 1959; trans. 1961). Images of Wilde in French fiction generally are discussed in H. Jäckel, *Der Engländer im Spiegel der Französischen Literatur von der Romantik bis zum Weltkrieg* (Breslau, 1932). Among the many French novels that contain allusions to Wilde or characters based upon him are: Octave Mirbeau, *Le Journal d'une femme de chambre* (Paris, 1900); Jean Lorrain, *Monsieur de Phocas* (Paris, 1901) and *Coins de Byzance: Le Vice errant* (Paris, 1902—Lorrain disliked Wilde personally: see Philippe Jullian, *Jean Lorrain ou le satiricon 1900*, Paris, 1974); Jacques d'Adelsward, *Lord Lyllian* (Paris, 1904); Maurice Barrès, *Un Jardin sur l'Oronte* (Paris, 1922); Abel Hermant, *Le Cycle de Lord Chelsea* (Paris, 1923); Georges Maurevert, *L'Affaire du grand plagiat* (Paris, 1924); René Boylesve, *Le Parfum des Iles Borromées* (Paris, 1925). Jäckel also cites Paul Damby, *Mylord l'Arsouille* (Paris, 1928). More amusing than most is Jean Fayard's *Oxford et Margaret* (Paris, 1924; trans. 1925), whose high point of Wildery is a private performance of *Salome*, the main part played by "the famous Huntley, a freshman from Marlborough," who has a marvellous bust: "People were not worrying much whether Salome was acting well or not."

The many adaptations of the works and scenarios on Wilde's life are in general without distinction. Daniel Farson alludes to the suggestion that the downfall of Wilde and the dancing *putains* influenced Bram Stoker's account of the gloating of the Vampire Women at Castle Dracula (*The Man Who Wrote Dracula*, 1975). There is a novel in Portuguese, *A Noiva de Oscar Wilde* by "Sérgio Espínola" (Gastão Cruls), which appeared in *Revista do Brasil* (1919). L. Cohen's *Oscar Wilde* (1928) is a gauche fantasy that looks like a bid to reclaim Wilde for the heterosexual world; this is certainly not the case with Clement Wood's novel *The Sensualist* (1942). Desmond Hall's *I Give You Oscar Wilde* (1965) is a biographical novel and generally cozy but for an unwarranted emphasis on Wilde's supposed syphilis. Carl Sternheim's play *Oscar Wilde* (1925) is somewhat better, fluently mingles fact and fiction, and presents Wilde's homosexuality as something of a revolutionary fervor. Ernst Heilborn (*Das Literatur*, 1925) criticized Sternheim for diluting the real Wilde by imposing the revolutionary image and creating instead a plucked chicken without talent, passion, or depth. Sternheim concentrates on the Wilde of the last phase. The characters include Ross, Taylor, Atkins, and Parker, described as "jockeys": and "Lord Tusby aus dem Haus des Earl of Dunmore," who is generally referred to as "Tubby" perhaps in allusion to G. S. Street's comic Aesthete in *The Autobiography of a Boy* (1894) or perhaps to Reggie Turner. At all events Tubby speaks for the author as well as himself when he robustly cries: "Halt! Gott strafe England—und seine schnöden Henker!" Arthur H. C. Prichard's *Conversations with Oscar Wilde* (1931) is unamusing and entirely fictitious; John Furnell's *The Stringed Lute* (1955) is faintly more authentic; the play *Oscar Wilde* (1957) by Leslie and Sewell Stokes carries a preface by Douglas; Maurice Rostand's dramatization of the trials, *Le Procès d'Oscar Wilde* (reviewed in *L'Européen*, 1 Mar. 1935), has been translated into German (1951). In 1960 two British films appeared simultaneously: *Oscar Wilde* and *The Trials of Oscar Wilde*; reviewers generally agreed that *The Trials* was the more serious treatment. *The Picture of Dorian Gray* has been dramatized by G. C. Lounsbury (1913) with a dull fidelity,

S. Mercet (Paris, 1922), M. M. Miller (1931), C. Cox (1948), and John Osborne (1973). It is nothing less than a tragedy that there should be no known copy of the 1916 Russian film of *Dorian Gray* directed by Vsevolod Meyerhold, although some stills survive. Critics have claimed that it anticipated *The Cabinet of Doctor Caligari*. Wilde's relevance to the cinema is estimated by J. G. Simoes in *Estado di Saó Paulo* (16 Jan. 1965). M-G-M produced an inferior film of *Dorian Gray* in 1945 directed by Albert Lewin; the more recent version issued in 1970 from American International Pictures, produced by Massimo Dellamano with screenplay by Marcello Coscia and Dellamano, is base camp with the natty idea of casting a Dorian who speaks in thick German-American. It is discussed in *The Film Annual* (1971). Constance Cox based a comedy on *Lord Arthur Savile's Crime* (1963). Tom Stoppard's sparkling play *Travesties* (1974) reflects Wilde's brilliance; and in *An Oscar of No Importance* (1968) the actor Micheál MacLiammóir discusses his own interpretation of Wilde with professional insight. Ellmann includes some famous poems on Wilde by Behan, Betjeman, Crane, and Lionel Johnson in *Twentieth Century Views*. (Another poem by Johnson entitled "A Friend," which begins "All that he came to give," may also be about Wilde.) Lesser known poems to and about Wilde written in his lifetime can be found in Anon., *The Silver Domino, or Side Whispers, Social and Literary* (1892) and in G. F. Reynolds Anderson, *The White Book of the Muses* (1895). Robert Buchanan's "The Dismal Throng," which attacks Wilde along with Ibsen and Tolstoy, is included in his *Complete Poetical Works* (1901). *The Papyrus* has poems by R. B. Glaenzer (1906) and Charles Hanson Towne (1908) on Wilde's works and three poems addressed to Wilde by G. S. Viereck, Richard Le Gallienne, and R. B. Glaenzer, all of 1905, the year of *De Profundis*. There is a pious sonnet to Wilde by L. Macnamara in *Westminster Review* (1912); three poems to Wilde by Allen Norton in *Saloon Sonnets* (1914); a short poem by Dwight Taylor, "Fat Wilde," in *Some Pierrots Come from Behind the Moon* (Boston, 1923); and "Oscar Wilde and Aubrey Beardsley," by John Waller, in *The Kiss of Stars* (1948). "A Monsieur de Reul," by Jacques Perk (*Brieven en dokumenten*, Amsterdam, 1959) contains what is possibly an early allusion to Wilde. Dino Campana's "Oscar Wilde a San Miniato" (*Canti Orfici*, 1914) is eloquently surrealistic but not altogether Oscar. Richard Howard's dramatic poem (*New American Review*, 1973) on Wilde's meeting with Whitman attempts empathy with both men, but gives us an Oscar less witty and a Walt less wild than might have been hoped for.

More knowing than all these is Max Beerbohm's "A Peep into the Past" (*Two Worlds*, 1926; rpt. *A Peep into the Past*, ed. Hart-Davis, 1972, together with two later tributes: "A Lord of Language," 1905, and the speech read at the unveiling of a commemorative plaque at Tite Street in 1954). Beerbohm's first published article, "Oscar Wilde by an American," is printed in *Letters to Reggie Turner* (1964), which also contains much information about Wilde; as does Stanley Weintraub's *Reggie* (1965). There are a few vivid references in *Max and Will* (ed. Mary M. Lago and Karl Beckson, 1975). David Cecil, like most who write on Beerbohm, is dismissive about Wilde's influence on Beerbohm and in general about Wilde (and Pater) in *Max* (1964). There are additional anecdotes in S. N. Behrman, *Conversations with Max* (1960), and a more analytical treatment of the relationship between the two in J. Felstiner, *The Lies of Art* (1973). Max's caricatures of Wilde are listed in *A Catalogue of the Caricatures of Max Beerbohm*, compiled by Hart-Davis (1972), Nos. 1778–95.

GEORGE MOORE

Helmut E. Gerber

As a private person, as a public figure, and as an artist, George Moore was a complex person who compounded his natural condition with artfully contrived self-contradictions. Small wonder, then, that biographers and critics, anecdotists and reviewers have often been at odds in portraying the man and the writer. Before one assays a detailed review of research, it is useful to set forth a broad context for some of the major problems.

One of the central problems in the views we get of Moore results from his multiple self-exiles. Born in Ireland with a sense of the Irish landlord, touched quite deeply by the Irish political and theological situation, almost unconsciously having absorbed a sense of the Irish landscape and the associated mythology, Moore nevertheless grasped the opportunity in 1873, when he was twenty-one, to go to Paris. He became a lifelong Francophile. About 1880, the deteriorating condition of the Moore estate in Ireland necessitated his arranging to have it competently looked after. He took up residence in London, with frequent visits to Ireland, and began his first English period. The French period, though much discussed in later reminiscences by scholars and by those who knew him then, has still not been fully clarified. Questions still persist about how well Moore really knew some of the novelists, poets, and painters with whom he later claimed intimacy. The really important matters, however, about the educative experience of this early French period are fairly well known. However well he knew some of the prime movers among the Naturalists, the Symbolists, and the Impressionists, there is no doubt that Moore was an attentive listener at the Nouvelle Athènes and that he went on to enrich the lessons he learned in France. He learned enough about the major movements in the literary and painterly arts to become a significant ambassador of the arts between England and France. He translated some Symbolist poems, wrote prefaces for Naturalist novels and appreciations of the French painters, and, above all, made use of French artists' technical innovations in his own work. By 1880 he had tried his hand at painting, poetry, and the drama. Using material from his French experience, he soon went on to write reviews, real and imaginary conversations, and novels more or less in the French manner. He went on for fifty-three years making frequent visits to French friends and adding more to his circle. Throughout his life France remained his cultural fountain of youth.

Although he lived mainly in London from about 1880 to 1901, when he took up residence at Ely Place, Dublin, he was already making more frequent visits to Ireland than usual by 1898 and was already involved with Martyn and Yeats in efforts to establish an Irish theater movement. Just as France was never to be wholly out of mind, so Ireland remained a compelling lodestone for him. There, too, despite what he may have said publicly at various times, he found imaginative stimulation to the day of his death.

During the first period of twenty-one years Moore spent in London, he made a respectable reputation as a novelist; short-story writer; playwright or, better, knowledgeable theater man; memoirist; art, music, and literary critic; polemicist; and raconteur. Moreover, his work in all these areas was extraordinarily diverse. But partly because of Moore's own self-portraits and his public flamboyance, the dominant view of him was more a caricature than a portrait, and this distorted view has informed almost everything written on Moore, with only a few exceptions along the way and especially in recent years. As a writer he was quickly labeled a Naturalist or "Zola's ricochet," despite the fact that *A Drama in Muslin* (1886), *Esther Waters* (1894), *Celibates* (1895), *Evelyn Innes* (1898), and *Sister Teresa* (1901) really have little resemblance to the works of the French novelists said to have inspired them. As a man who kept himself much in the public eye and who was leading a very active social life, he is mainly remembered for his "naughtiness" or even as a middle-aged lecher. The view of him as austere in his artistry, sincerely concerned about the tenants on his estate, morally and ethically opposed to the British attitude in the Boer War, always ready to help younger writers find publishers, and capable of severe self-criticism has only begun to emerge in fairly recent years. These were the aspects of his personality he did not flaunt and that many of those who knew him either ignored or rather grudgingly noted.

Disgruntled with the state of novel criticism and with the situation in the English theater, even after his flirtation with the Independent Theatre movement, and apparently sensing that his creative impulse was in danger of being exhausted, he allowed Edward Martyn, Arthur Symons, and W. B. Yeats to persuade him to devote his energies to the Irish theater movement. Moore went to Ireland with a well-established reputation as a novelist and essayist, but especially, for the immediate purpose, as a man with a practical knowledge of the theater. He had authored or co-authored some six plays. In addition, alone or with collaborators, he had translated plays by others, dramatized short stories by others, and written a number of one-acters which were not published but were produced (see Gilcher, M5, M6, M8, M10, and M12; all references to Gilcher are to Edwin Gilcher's *A Bibliography of George Moore*, 1970). He had been one of the defenders of the production of Ibsen's plays in London; he had worked with J. T. Grein in connection with the Independent Theatre; he had written one or more articles or reviews on the Théâtre Libre and on specific plays nearly each year from 1885 on; he knew many actors and theater-managers; he had ready access, for propaganda purposes, to various newspapers and periodicals; and, of course, he was an Irishman. With such credentials, he could be useful.

Writers on Moore during this Irish period have left no doubt that Moore made good use of his opportunities and his associations for selfish ends, but his real contribution to the Irish literary movement was for many years belittled. Yeats, Lady Gregory, and others involved in the Irish literary movement soon discovered that Moore was not about to be "managed." He unquestionably had a better practical knowledge of the theater than anyone else active in the early stages of the Irish theater movement, at least until the Fays became the prime movers; he insisted on being in charge; he was rather more interested in the theater of Ibsen than in the kind of poetic drama Yeats had in mind; he had a curious obsession with the revival of Gaelic, which Yeats did not share; he was too individualistic to commit himself to political movements, as Douglas Hyde and others could; he was divisive in his tendency to make flamboyant public utterances about the suppressive influence of the Church; and Yeats and Edward Martyn soon discovered, as had Pearl Craigie before them and as would others after them, that Moore was a difficult collaborator.

During the ten years he spent in Ireland, Moore made a number of lifelong friends, John Eglinton (i.e., William Magee), Kuno Meyer, and Richard Best being the most important. At the same time, with the publication of *The Untilled Field* (Gaelic, 1902; English, 1903), *The Lake* (1905), *The Apostle: A Drama in Three Acts* (1911), and with the writing of the three volumes that were to make up *Hail and Farewell* (1911, 1912, 1914), Moore added a new dimension to his art, the prelude to his increased interest in myth, biblical materials, and, generally, the past and the development of his later style.

After his falling out with Yeats, Lady Gregory, and others, not a sudden, catastrophic event but a slow process of attrition that began some time in 1904, Moore in 1911 settled at 121 Ebury Street, London, for the rest of his life. Ireland had served him well and was to continue to serve him in, for example, *A Story-Teller's Holiday* (1918) and *Ulick and Soracha* (1926). His farewell to Ireland was not absolute and final, nor was it bitter.

The last twenty-two years of Moore's life have often been regarded as a period of withdrawal, a retirement into a kind of Elysium where Moore sat like a careless god as life went by. At this time in his life he is often characterized by such epithets as the Sage of Ebury Street, frequently with the suggestion that he devoted himself to fussing over revisions of his published work at the expense of any genuine creative energy. The facts, however, belie this view of Moore. Undoubtedly he gave much time and energy to revising his works and preparing collected editions, but the work was no mere editorial tinkering; it was often a task of drastic rewriting to bring the older works closer to that perfection of style he felt he had begun to attain during his Irish period. He also went on to write some distinctly original material, the volumes of *Hail and Farewell*, begun in Ireland; *The Brook Kerith* (1916); *A Story-Teller's Holiday; Avowals* (1919), perhaps half of which had been written before 1910, the rest after the departure from Dublin; *Conversations in Ebury Street* (1924); *Héloïse and Abélard* (1921), Moore's own retelling of the love story; *The Pastoral Loves of Daphnis and Chloë* (1924), based on a sixteenth-century French translation of Longus' story, but more Moore's version than a translation; *Ulick and Soracha; Aphrodite in Aulis* (1930), which, despite the care he took to be accurate on historical matters and in the description of setting by consulting a number of classical scholars, is largely Moore's invention; and *A Communication to My Friends* (1933), which he was polishing at the time of his death.

Nor was this all. He prepared for publication and production five plays; drastically rewrote or rearranged four earlier works; prepared *An Anthology of Pure Poetry* (1924); continued to publish in periodicals and to engage in debates on all kinds of subjects—censorship, vaccination, religion, Irish Home Rule, hand-set books, electric sky-signs, and, as usual, the misinterpretation of his books. He visited Palestine in order to see the scene of *The Brook Kerith*; went to France frequently to visit Edouard Dujardin and other friends; made annual pilgrimages to the Wagner festival in Beyreuth; visited friends in Ireland and England; welcomed admiring visitors; and corresponded voluminously with publishers, printers, friends, his agents, American readers, and young writers seeking advice. Even in the late twenties, when he was often ill, there was no abatement of work.

He was surely far from a recluse during the last twenty-two years of his career, nor was he content to rest on such laurels as he had won. No doubt at age fifty-eight or so there was evidence that Moore had less physical energy. There was an occasional melancholy sense that the world around him was shabbier, that contemporary life lacked style, that his era was over. Yet he went on practicing his art and perfecting it with a great deal of creative energy. There was no retirement, but a change of attitude and emphasis. That he was less concerned with the larger reading public is most evident in his choice of subjects and style. The subject and style of, say, *The Brook Kerith* or *Héloïse and Abélard* can hardly be called fare for the same audience of "common readers" that bought and read *Esther Waters*. No doubt, like Pater, Flaubert, and Henry James before him, he concentrated his energies more on the execution, the style, than ever before. In subject matter he had always been concerned with what he considered the universal aspects of human nature, a mother's love for her child or a passion for God. In the earlier work, however, he had cast his characters and themes in a contemporary scene. In his later work he most often evaded the limitations of immediacy and found his subject in myths and in the historical past. The general emphasis on producing enduring, beautiful books is evidenced in many ways. He was more deeply concerned about the quality of paper, the design of the title page, the decorations, the beauty of the typography than he was about the money he would make from limited editions. In passionate notes to his publishers and to the printers he argued the superiority of hand setting over Monotype, quarreled about a minor irregularity in the printing of one character, and objected to the shade of blue used for a binding.

It is this later George Moore with whom the critics and the scholars, until very recently, could not seem to come to grips. The man who had written *Esther Waters* had somehow eluded them; many of Moore's readers, common and uncommon, could not seem to follow him beyond this novel. A smaller number could follow him only through *The Untilled Field* and *The Lake*, and still fewer cared to go further than *The Brook Kerith*. Even now he is mainly remembered for *Esther Waters*, with an occasional nod toward *A Mummer's Wife*; for such imaginative autobiographies as *Confessions of a Young Man*; perhaps for the curious mixture of essays, reminiscences, and fictions in *Avowals*, *Memoirs of My Dead Life* (1906), *Conversations in Ebury Street*, and *Hail and Farewell*, although it is doubtful that many actually read this remarkable literary symphony.* As a writer he was too restless and too much on the move, and as a person he was too self-contradictory to be easily and happily labeled and categorized.

I. Bibliographies and Manuscript Locations

Edwin Gilcher's definitive *A Bibliography of George Moore* (1970) supersedes I. A. Williams' *Bibliographies of Modern Authors, No. 3, George Moore* (1921) and Henry Danielson's "George Moore, A Bibliography [1878–1921]" in *A Portrait of George Moore in a Study of His Work*, by John Freeman (1922). A. J. A. Symons' intention to prepare a comprehensive bibliography with Moore's assistance never came to fruition. Gilcher's work, based on his own outstanding collection, but each entry "checked against as many other copies as possible," is a model of bibliographic detective work. Gilcher describes in considerable detail the many variant editions that Moore produced, and copious notes provide all kinds of information on Moore and publishing history. The compiler lists books and pamphlets, including collections of letters; contributions to work by other writers, including prefaces, poems, essays, short stories, plays, letters, and excerpts; periodical appearances; translations; and miscellanea, including uncompleted works, unpublished plays, and erroneous attributions. For any future scholarship on George Moore, especially textual studies, Gilcher's bibliography must be the starting point. Also useful, although not so accurate or complete as Gilcher's work, are the primary and secondary bibliographies in Jean C. Noël's *George Moore: L'Homme et l'œuvre* (1852–1933) (Paris, 1966).

The most complete bibliography of writings about Moore, with abstracts, has appeared in *English Fiction* (later *Literature*) in *Transition: 1880–1920*, 2, No. 2, Parts 1 and 2 (1959), 1–91; 3, No. 2 (1960), 34–46; 4, No. 2 (1961), 30–42; and supplemented by further items in succeeding numbers of the same publication. The 1,100 or

---

* Stanley Weintraub has in preparation a one-volume synthesis of all of Moore's memoirs, on the order of his earlier *Shaw: An Autobiography*. This volume, *Confessions of a Young Man Grown Old*, will contain annotations of places and persons to which Moore alludes.

more items that have been listed to date are a fairly representative
sampling of the bulk of what has been written on Moore. These
listings of secondary materials are being thoroughly revised and supplemented for inclusion, eventually, in a volume in the Annotated
Secondary Bibliography Series in progress at the Northern Illinois
University Press.

Manuscript holdings of Moore's works are widely scattered, partly
because Moore sold some of his manuscripts, proofs, and printed
volumes with marginal notes, sometimes with Harry Spurr acting as
agent; partly because one of his secretaries allegedly stole some
manuscripts and sold them; and partly because some publishers' files
(e.g., T. Fisher Unwin's) were sold at auction. Moore himself seldom
saved letters or even copies of his own books. In any event, among
major holdings, most of which have been combed by Joseph Hone,
Malcolm Brown, Sir Rupert Hart-Davis, Jean C. Noël, H. E. Gerber,
and others, important materials may be found in the Berg Collection
of the New York Public Library; University of London Library; Special Collections, University of Kansas Libraries, Lawrence; National
Library of Ireland, Dublin; Humanities Research Center, University
of Texas; University of Washington, Seattle. Smaller holdings may
also be found at the Henry E. Huntington Library; Lilly Library,
Indiana University; Princeton University; University of Florida,
Gainesville; University of Illinois, Urbana; The Brotherton Library,
University of Leeds; Carl H. Pforzheimer Library; The Fales Collection, New York University Library; Bibliothèque Nationale; and the
private collection of Dr. Lafayette Butler. The most complete collections of editions of Moore's works are those of Frank Fayant, now in
the Rare Book Department, Cornell University Library; and Edwin
Gilcher's collection, now in Special Collections, Charles Trumbull
Hayden Library, Arizona State University.

II. Editions and Textual Studies

There is no complete collected edition of Moore's works. Unless
such an edition were a variorum edition or at least a fairly heavily
annotated edition, little more purpose would be served than is already served by the several existing collected editions Moore himself
supervised. The two major editions, not identical in titles included,
are the American Carra Edition in twenty-one volumes and two supplementary volumes in the same format, and the English Uniform
Edition in twenty volumes (Gilcher, A36–n2 and A6–n9, respectively). The latter edition was reissued as the Ebury Edition in 1937
and has, since 1942, been called the Uniform Edition.

Since Moore revised most of his books several times and since he
concerned himself throughout his career with the perfection of style,
a few variorum and annotated editions must be cited as well as
several of the more important textual studies that attempt to deal
with Moore's complex revisions. In dealing with matters of this kind,
Gilcher's bibliography, again, is an absolutely essential reference
work. Luckily, many of the works listed below are accurate because
their authors had the advantage of Gilcher's advice even before his

book saw print. Royal A. Gettmann's "George Moore's Revisions of *The Lake,* 'The Wild Goose,' and Esther Waters" (*PMLA,* 1944), although it does not make use of all the variants Gilcher has cited, is an important early study which apparently stimulated other scholars to undertake variorum editions and textual studies on a large scale. Gettmann was the first scholar to point out that Moore was in the habit of revising his novels quite early in his career, not only in his old age. As we now know, even the second edition (1885) of *A Modern Lover* (1883) contained revisions and additions; *A Drama in Muslin* was wholly rewritten as *Muslin* (1915); *A Mere Accident* (1887) was also wholly rewritten as "John Norton" for inclusion in *Celibates,* which in its turn went on to a variety of revisions and rearrangements of its contents as *In Single Strictness* (1922) and *Celibate Lives* (1927). The complex textual history of *Confessions of a Young Man* is dealt with in Susan Dick's "*Confessions of a Young Man* by George Moore: A Variorum Edition" (Diss. Northwestern 1967), which served as the basis of Dick's annotated edition (1972).

Dick's dissertation gives a fuller account of the variants based on a comparison of nine texts than her published critical edition of the work.* *Evelyn Innes* also illustrates Moore's early obsession with revising his work in that the first edition appeared in May, a revised second edition in August, and a "trial revised edition" (Gilcher, A22-c) of twelve copies in October, a third edition in 1901, and a fourth in 1908. John Denny Fisher's "*Evelyn Innes* and *Sister Teresa* by George Moore: A Variorum Edition" (Diss. Illinois 1959) most fully deals with the revisions in Moore's "double novel."

Several other works deal with textual variants on a larger scale. William A. Perkins' "George Moore's Realistic Novels; Roots, Achievements, Influence" (Diss. Stanford 1954) lists and comments briefly on revisions in a number of works. More important and more detailed, Jay Jernigan (Diss. Kansas State 1966) deals with *A Modern Lover, A Mummer's Wife, A Drama in Muslin, A Mere Accident, Spring Days* (1888), *Mike Fletcher* (1889), *Vain Fortune* (1891), and *Esther Waters.* Part of this dissertation is the basis for Jernigan's "The Bibliographical and Textual Complexities of George Moore's *A Mummer's Wife*" (*BNYPL,* 1970). Jernigan has also dealt with an early serial version of some chapters of *Esther Waters* (*NCF,* 1968). Still another study of revisions is Graham Owens' Leeds dissertation (1966). The editor's commentary and Moore's letters in H. E. Gerber's *George Moore in Transition: Letters to T. Fisher Unwin and Lena Milman, 1894–1910* (1968) contain much information on Moore's revisions in the books from *Celibates* through *The Lake,* particularly on the revisions of the stories in *The Untilled Field.* A second volume of letters and commentary by the same editor, now nearing completion, will contain much new material on the revisions in Moore's books after about 1910.

While each textual scholar draws some conclusions pertinent to his

* For a more detailed account see my review of Dick's edition in *HAR* (1972). In " 'I am still a young man': George Moore's Last Revisions of *Confessions of a Young Man,*" *BNYPL* (1975), W. Eugene Davis and Mark J. Lidman study Moore's unpublished revisions of the 1926 Heinemann edition of *Confessions of a Young Man.*

immediate thesis and while there are several unpublished dissertations on Moore's style, no full-scale study of his stylistic experiments making use of research on his revisions has been published. The scholar who makes the effort of examining Moore's revisions in many novels over the course of his whole career will at least recognize that all this revising was not merely a matter of correcting punctuation, tenses, and diction but a carving out of what Moore came to call his "melodic line," the flowing rhythmic style one associates with *The Brook Kerith, Héloïse and Abélard, Daphnis and Chloë,* and *Aphrodite in Aulis.* In fact, one suspects that the creation of an original work, an original story, became less important to Moore than the creative translation of known stories into his own style. The style became his personal signature, his creative act, his invention. Thus, he took Pater's and Wilde's remarks on style, on manner or execution, to be the basis of the creative act. Less concerned about the moral principle or content than Henry James, Moore indeed made execution everything.

III. *Autobiographies, Letters, and Biographies*

AUTOBIOGRAPHIES

In the strict sense, George Moore wrote no autobiography; in a more flexible sense almost everything he wrote, excepting perhaps the novels, short stories, and plays, was autobiographical. It is even possible to make a case for such a play as *The Coming of Gabrielle* (1920) and such a story as "Euphorion in Texas" (1914) containing sly autobiographical allusions. On the other hand, of such an autobiographical work as *Confessions of a Young Man,* in the first edition of which the "hero" was called Edward Dayne, one can say that it includes a good deal of fiction and a great deal of imaginative distortion. His "confessions," "memoirs," "opinions," "avowals," "impressions," "hails and farewells," "conversations," and "communications" are less in the line of St. Augustine's *Confessions* or Cardinal Newman's *Apologia pro Vita Sua,* or of Dickens' *David Copperfield* and *Great Expectations,* or of Samuel Butler's *The Way of All Flesh* than they are in the line of such imaginary portraits as Pater's "A Child in the House" or Charles Lamb's "Dream-Children" and "The Superannuated Man." His autobiographical writings are not reliable factual records, and no one title gives us a full and reliable impression of his personality. These writings borrow from and blend many genres. They record the mood of the moment and are often concerned more about being interesting or provocative than about being accurate. We should probably take Moore's wax-plate image in *Confessions of a Young Man* seriously, for his process of "becoming" did not end until his death. He assumes diverse poses or masks as they serve his immediate purposes, but the poses or masks are themselves genuine facets of Moore. Throughout his imaginative autobiographies and his essays, as in his multiple revisions, what the reader sees happening is what Walter Pater called "brain-building by which we are, each one of us, what we are."

The works having some bearing on Moore's life can be arranged in priority groups. Most nearly autobiographical are *Parnell and His Island* (1887); *Confessions of a Young Man*; *Hail and Farewell*; George Moore's preface to Colonel Maurice Moore's *An Irish Gentleman George Henry Moore, His Travels, His Racing, His Politics*, (1913); and *A Communication to My Friends*. Of these titles, two may seem a little peripheral and require brief comment. *Parnell and His Island* provides useful background on the condition of Ireland as Moore saw it. It is in some ways a book of scenes and characters like Dickens' *Sketches by Boz*. Fairly representative are such sketches as "Dublin—The Castle, The Shelbourne Hotel, The Kildare Club, Mrs. Rushville," "The Tenant Farmer," and "The Priest." This volume has been perceptively discussed in Malcolm Brown's *George Moore: A Reconsideration* (1955). *Parnell and His Island, A Drama in Muslin*, and the known facts of Moore's actions as an Irish landlord suggest, as Joseph Hone has said, that the "antihumanitarian principles of the Rue de la Tour des Dames were not put into practice on the estate." Maurice Moore's life of his and George's father has obvious bearing on the autobiography, particularly in light of George Moore's preface, where he rewrites the cause of his father's death as suicide, and in light of George Moore's repeated disclaimers that the family was of Catholic origin. Maurice's book helps to explain George's self-view in the early pages of *Confessions of a Young Man*.

A second priority group of publications that have some autobiographical interest, perhaps as records of Moore's moods and of the development of his imagination, consists of six major titles. *Literature at Nurse; or Circulating Morals* (1885), for example, is an important document in the history of censorship, a subject to which Moore returned many times throughout his career as his books were refused wide circulation, banned, or criticized on moral grounds. *Impressions and Opinions* (1891) is important as a subsequent record of some of the echo-auguries Moore first announced in *Confessions of a Young Man*. There are important essays and revealing musings on Balzac; Turgenev; Zola; Théâtre Libre and Ibsen; and Meissonier, Degas, and painting. In *Modern Painting* (1893) Moore gathered essays from the *Speaker*, of which he had been art critic from 21 March 1891 to 23 November 1895. This volume is important not only insofar as it was an effective introduction of the French painters to England and supported the development of the English art movement, but also because it reveals the development of Moore's esthetic principles and his interdisciplinary interests, which were to influence significantly his fiction and his literary criticism. *Memoirs of My Dead Life* is more a collection of essays than is *Confessions of a Young Man*. It reprints material, usually in revised form, some of which he had published in *Dana* under the appropriate title "Moods and Memories" and in *The Hawk* as "Notes and Sensations," as well as pieces from other periodicals. *Avowals* is particularly valuable as autobiography for the revealing "imaginary conversations" with Edmund Gosse and John Lloyd Balderston, most of these having in fact been composed by Moore. This collection of essays and conversations Moore himself relates to *Confessions of a Young Man* in the essay originally published as "Avowals: Being a New Series of the Confessions of a Young Man" (*Lippincott's Magazine*, Sept. 1903–Feb. 1904), which is the basis of Chapters 4–6 in *Avowals*. Like *Avowals*, *Conversations in Ebury Street* also gathers a number of conversations, these with John Freeman, Edmund Gosse, and Granville Barker, and includes revisions or at least echoes of works published earlier, among them part of the prefatory "The Thesis" which became the introductory conversation to *Pure Poetry*.

In a third and more speculative degree of priority one might put some of the novels, short stories, and plays in which specific persons or amalgamations of persons Moore knew are the basis of fictional portraits. Among the fictions that include portraits of people Moore knew, one may single out "Mildred Lawson" in *Celibates*, in which the titular heroine may be an amalgamation of aspects of Pearl Craigie, Lena Milman, and probably other women; *A Mere Accident*, *Mike Fletcher*, "John Norton," and "Hugh Monfert," for all of which Edward Martyn seems to have been a model; *Evelyn Innes*, in which A. E. and Yeats apparently share the role of model for the character of Ulick; *Euphorian* [sic] *in Texas*, which contains several portraits of women whom Moore had met or with whom he had a fairly extended correspondence. Although some of these identifications have been tentatively suggested in Gerber's *George Moore in Transition*, Hone's *Life*, and Rupert Hart–Davis' introduction to the Moore–Lady Cunard letters, a fruitful study might be made of the real-life sources of many of Moore's fictional portraits. Such a study could add significantly to our knowledge of Moore's personal relationships and the imaginative process by which he translated fact into fiction.

LETTERS

The many letters from Moore to various correspondents that have been published already and those now being prepared for publication are far more useful for an understanding of both the "bürger" and the "künstler" than any of the biographies, reminiscences, appreciations, or anecdotes in which Moore figures. In Section II ("Contributions") of his definitive bibliography, Gilcher lists small groups of letters, single letters, and excerpts from letters that have been published in various works by others than Moore; in Section III ("Periodical Appearances"), he lists published letters to editors of various newspapers and periodicals; and in Section I ("Books and Pamphlets"), he lists major collections of published letters. Among six major collections, four have been published, one is available only in an unpublished dissertation, and one is now in preparation.

The first of these to be published is *Letters from George Moore to Ed. Dujardin 1886–1922*, selected, edited, and translated by John Eglinton (1929). The volume included 124 letters out of a larger extant number. The letters suggest the characteristic way in which Moore often used his friends, but they also suggest that the relationship between Moore and Dujardin was genuinely warm. Dujardin, as a biblical exegete, eventually Professor of the History of Primitive Christianity at the Sorbonne, and as a knowledgeable Wagnerite, was most useful to Moore as an adviser on biblical history and music. His studies in connection with his major book, *La Source du fleuve chrétien*, led to many talks with Moore and undoubtedly influenced the writing of *Evelyn Innes, Sister Teresa, The Lake, The Apostle*, and more significant, *The Brook Kerith*. In fact, in Moore's *The Lake*, Ralph Ellis (later renamed Walter Poole) writes a scholarly work called *The Source of the Christian River*. It is also possible that Dujardin may, as he later claimed, indeed have influenced Moore's style, what Dujardin in his *Le Monologue interieur* (1931) calls "free association." Dujardin also occasionally corrected Moore's French, helped to get Moore's works translated into French, and was Moore's confidant in such personal matters as the novelists' problems with Pearl Craigie during the collaboration on *The Peacock's Feather*. (For discussion of Dujardin's influence see Francesco Cordasco, *MLN*, 1947.)

The second collection of letters to be published is *Letters of George Moore*, "with an introduction by John Eglinton, to whom they were written" (1942). This volume contains 119 letters, dated 1909–32, out of a probable five to six hundred. Moore probably met Eglinton in the late nineties, at the time the novelist was being more and more drawn to Ireland. Eglinton, like Richard Best, because of his association with the National Library in Dublin, was particularly well situated to act as a resource person for Moore, one who could verify information Moore needed in connection with a novel he was working on, one who could recommend books for the novelist to read, or, more often, who could talk to Moore about books the novelist was too impatient to read himself. Moore and Eglinton, though the latter was not nearly so rash as Moore, shared similar views on the negative effect of the Church on Irish politics and the economy. In fact, Moore so respected Eglinton's scholarship that he wanted Eglinton to write his biography. It was Eglinton who suggested that Moore write about Irish life in the manner of Turgenev's *Tales of a Sportsman*; the result was the stories of *The Untilled Field*. Moore, in turn, as a gesture of friendship gave Eglinton the article that became *Memoirs of My Dead Life* to publish in *Dana* when Eglinton founded that periodical, and it was Eglinton who supplied the name "Orelay" for one of the stories in the volume.

The third major collection of letters, probably the most charmingly written, is *George Moore: Letters to Lady Cunard, 1895–1933* (ed. Rupert Hart-Davis, 1957). The volume includes 247 letters out of the thousands that may have been written. Sir Rupert Hart-Davis in his introduction and notes has provided a balanced discussion of the relationship of the two correspondents. Lady Cunard (née Maud Burke) was undoubtedly the only real love in Moore's life. She was a witty, intelligent, and brilliant hostess; well read; and an accomplished pianist. To her Moore could confide without pose his disappointments, his problems in the writing of a particular work, and his moods of depression when a new work was completed. He could use her as a sounding board when he had doubts about a story he was writing. Throughout his life she appears to have remained his vision of the unattainable ideal of womanhood. One mystery concerning their relationship still intrigues biographers: Was Nancy Cunard

George Moore's daughter? Various people who knew Nancy have remarked on a resemblance, and Nancy Cunard herself has alluded to the suggestion without confirming it. There is, however, no firm evidence. The chief significance of the suggestion is the bearing it may have on the charge that Moore was impotent, that his stories of his love affairs are largely fictions, and that his portraits of women in the novels and stories are influenced by his alleged impotence.

Another important collection of letters of a quite different kind is *George Moore in Transition: Letters to T. Fisher Unwin and Lena Milman, 1894–1910*, edited with a commentary by Helmut E. Gerber (1968). Of the 298 letters, 183 are to Unwin, 94 to Milman, and 21 to various other recipients. The letters to Unwin are mainly business letters, often rather cantankerous and generally hurriedly dashed off without regard to stylistic niceties. Their importance lies mainly in what they tell us, sometimes from day to day, about Moore's revisions of works from *Celibates* through *The Lake*, and particularly about *The Untilled Field;* second, in these letters we see the shrewd businessman in Moore at work; and third, we get some interesting insights into author-publisher relationships.

The letters to Lena Milman bring to light a relationship not commented on before in any work on Moore. Milman, the daughter of the Commandant of the Tower of London, was a talented hostess, an adept translator from Russian, an accomplished violinist, and apparently quite knowledgeable in the painterly arts. Like Clara Lanza at about the same time, Milman was a responsive sounding board for Moore's artistic interests. He took her to art galleries and performances of plays given by the Independent Theatre Society; he sought her reactions to *Modern Painting* and had her read proof for *Esther Waters*; he encouraged her to write and to translate from Russian. Eventually he contributed an important preface to her translations of Dostoevsky's *Poor Folk*. His letters to her are perhaps best described as discreet, he is careful not to offend her moral sense. The relationship, which ended about the time Pearl Craigie came on the scene and his fascination with the more sophisticated Lady Cunard became more ardent, was certainly a quite platonic one. Lena Milman is important in Moore's life mainly because she encouraged or revitalized his interest in Turgenev and other Russian writers.

Unfortunately, one group of letters is available only in an unpublished dissertation, Charles Burkhart's "The Letters of George Moore to Edmund Gosse, W. B. Yeats, R. I. Best, Miss Nancy Cunard, and Mrs. Mary Hutchinson" (Maryland 1958), comprising 170 to Gosse, 14 to Yeats, 39 to Best, 20 to Nancy Cunard, and 59 to Mary Hutchinson, a total of 302 letters dated 1890–1933. Burkhart gives us many completed and carefully dated letters that had not been published at all or that were merely excerpted by others, often published undated, and sometimes carelessly dated. These letters fill some of the gaps in the more major published correspondence and should be consulted in conjuction with such works as Evan Charteris' *The Life and Letters of Sir Edmund Gosse* (1931); Hone's *Life of George Moore* (1936); *The Letters of W. B. Yeats* (ed. Allan Wade, 1954); Nancy Cunard's *GM: Memories of George Moore* (1956), and Charles J. Burkhart's "George Moore and *Father and Son*" (*NCF*, 1960).

Nearing completion is a volume of approximately 1,200 letters, edited with a commentary by Helmut E. Gerber. These will include significant runs of letters to T. Werner Laurie; the Pinkers (Moore's agents); Richard Clay and Sons (printers); John Freeman; Hildegarde Hawthorne, whose relationship to Moore has not been previously noted; Virginia Crawford; Colonel Maurice Moore; several of Moore's secretaries; various critics, book collectors, and representatives of publishing firms; and many others. The emphasis in these letters is on the publication and revisions of Moore's books from about 1910 to his death, but the letters also reveal many personal aspects of his life. With the publication of this volume and the smaller groups of letters listed in Gilcher's bibliography, approximately 2,000 letters will be in print. It is probably a fairly small percentage of the many thousands Moore wrote.

Finally, the commentary in Gerber's *George Moore in Transition* and in the volume now in progress takes into account nearly all the published letters written between about 1895 and 1933 and culls from them what is pertinent to Moore's private life and his career as an artist.

BIOGRAPHICAL STUDIES

Among the biographical works on Moore, the standard is still Joseph Hone's *The Life of George Moore*, further supplemented by Hone's *The Moores of Moore Hall* (1939). Though Hone is not meticulous about recording dates for events and letters, though few letters are given in full, and though there is almost none of the kind of documentation modern scholars generally like to have, the portrait of Moore is fairly accurate and the book, above all, is readable. Hone's volume can be supplemented with the letters that have been published since 1936 and with different perspectives provided by such works as Susan Mitchell's negative view in *George Moore* (1916), John Freeman's sympathetic treatment in *A Portrait of George Moore in a Study of His Work* (1922), Geraint Goodwin's sometimes quite revealing imitation of one of Moore's "conversations" in *Conversations with George Moore* (1930), Humbert Wolfe's appreciative *George Moore* (1932), and Charles Morgan's impressions of the style of the writer and of his creative mind in *Epitaph on George Moore* (1935). The considerable bulk of pre-1936 material is trivial, pleasant, but not very informative anecdote, and much that is a mixture of undistinguished biographical and critical commentary. Most of this material is given in the annotated secondary bibliographies which have appeared in *EFT* and *ELT*. Only a small number of somewhat specialized works need be cited here.

Moore's life in France and his lifelong relationships with French friends were dealt with abundantly in the obituary columns in the large number of centenary reminiscences that appeared in 1952. The matter is summed up in George-Paul Collet's *George Moore et la France* (Geneva, 1957). Collet gives some fifty pages to Moore's relationships with such French friends as Blanche, Dujardin, Firmin Roz, and many others; another fifty pages, not of direct biographical importance, deal mainly with the image of France in Moore's work; about eighty pages deal with the influence on Moore of such French writers as Gautier, Zola, Flaubert, the Goncourts, Balzac, Huysmans, and Dujardin. The book's greatest value is perhaps its treatment of Moore's later French friendships, especially since some of the supporting evidence (oral reminiscences and correspondence) is new.

Since the publication of Collet's book, the best book by a Frenchman has undoubtedly been Jean C. Noël's *George Moore: L'Homme et l'œuvre* (*1852–1933*) (*1966*). It, too, deals concisely with the French period from 1873 to 1880 in Chapter iii ("Un auteur en quête d'une personnalité"). Much of Noël's book, however, is not a mere recitation of the biographical facts, but an interpretative psychological study, and therein lies its superiority to many other books on Moore. Appendix ii ("George Moore á Paris") is especially useful for its three short notes: "George Moore et les rues de Paris," "Les Domiciles parisiens de George Moore," and "La Vente." Also especially useful for further information on George Moore's relationship to France is Section v ("Etudes en langue française. Documentation française ayant servi à l'étude de l'œuvre, de l'auteur et du milieu") of Noël's bibliography. Among the most useful items listed there are those by Paul Alexis, Auriant, André Billy, J. E. Blanche, G. P. Collet, Edouard Dujardin, Louis Gillet, Charles Guyot, Daniel Halévy, G. Jean-Aubry, Paul Morand, Jean C. Noël, and George Rivière.

The biographical aspects of Moore's first London period, from about 1880 to about 1895, have been somewhat less thoroughly and certainly less coherently treated than other phases of Moore's career; Gerber's commentary in *George Moore in Transition* attempts to bring some order to this period for the years 1895 to 1901. For the first fifteen years, Hone's *Life* is still the most useful source available. A few minor pieces touch on various specific activities of Moore during the first London period: Anna I. Miller's *The Independent Theatre in Europe, 1887 to the Present* (1901) gives glimpses of Moore as advocate of the free theater in England and his part in the founding of the Irish National Theatre; John Stokes's *Resistible Theatres: Enterprise and Experiment in the Late Nineteenth Century* (1972) discusses Moore's role in the Independent Theatre Movement; William Rothenstein's *Men and Memories* (3 vols., 1931–39) is a mine of information on Moore's relationship with members of the English art colony and many other matters; Ernest A. Vizetelly's *Emile Zola: Novelist and Reformer* (1904) provides information on Moore's campaign against censorship, a subject he wrote on vigorously all his life; A. I. Tobin and Elmer Gertz's *Frank Harris: A Study in Black and White* (1931) comments on Moore's testimony at the Pennell-Whistler trial and the threatened duel with Whistler; and, more recently, Stanley Weintraub's *Whistler* (1974) has dealt with the Whistler-Moore friendship and feud; Vineta Colby's *The Singular Anomaly* (1970) has excellent material on Moore's personal relationship and collaboration with Pearl Craigie ("John Oliver Hobbes"); John Bennion Booth's *Pink Parade* (1923) provides some rare information on Moore's association with such experimental newspapers as *The Pink 'Un, The Bat,* and *The Hawk*; Heinrich Felberman's *The Memoirs of a Cosmopolitan* (1936) testifies to

Moore's being on the *Examiner* staff early in 1880; and various items in Noël's bibliography also bear on Moore's involvement in the English theater movement: William Archer (p. 620), Oswald Crawford (p. 621), Clarence Decker on Ibsen (p. 621), Edmund Gosse (p. 622), James Joyce (p. 623). Additional material on Moore's involvement in theatrical enterprises and with English artists during the nineties may be gleaned from the annotated listings in *EFT* and *ELT*.

Biographical comments on Moore's relationship with Ireland during the period from about 1901 to about 1911 number in the hundreds. They are often trivial and repetitious; the identical anecdotes, or variations on them, are told over and over again. The comments fall into two distinct camps: those that see Moore as an opportunist exploiting his Irish friends and the literary movement, as an amoralist (if not immoralist), as an agnostic (if not an atheist), and generally as a most unpleasant and unwelcome person; and those who picture him as essentially kind, if a bit naughty, as a much needed energetic and knowledgeable organizer of Ireland's theatrical and literary talents, and as a man of lively and amusing, although perhaps mercurial, character.

William Archer's "Conversation V: With George Moore" (*Critic*, 1901), reprinted in *Real Conversations* (1904), gives the opportunist case for Moore's leaving London to participate in the Irish literary movement; Lady Isabella Augusta Gregory's *Our Irish Theatre* (1913) gives a rather grudging account of Moore's role; Gerald Griffin's *The Wild Geese* (1938) depicts Moore as exploiting his friends and the Celtic Renaissance for selfish ends. A more sympathetic view is taken by Denis Gwynn's *Edward Martyn and the Irish Revival* (1930), which portrays Moore as enthusiastically and effectively contributing to the literary revival; Sister Marie-Thérèse Courtney's *Edward Martyn and the Irish Theatre* (1956), which interestingly explores Moore's relationship with Edward Martyn and their influence on each other, on the whole presents a moderate Catholic view of Moore; Una Ellis-Fermor's *The Irish Dramatic Movement* (1939; 2nd ed., 1954) draws a critical comparison between Moore and Martyn to Moore's advantage; Nancy Cunard's *GM: Memories of George Moore* (1956), as might be expected, draws a sympathetic portrait of the author's childhood friend, her mother's lover and frequent house guest, and a brilliant raconteur; John Eglinton's *Irish Literary Portraits* (1935), which brings together some reminiscences of earlier date, provides a reasonable and balanced account of Moore's role in the literary revival; A. E. (George Russell), for whom Moore had kind feelings, in *Some Passages from the Letters of AE to W. B. Yeats* (1936) surprisingly provides evidence that A. E. may have sided with Yeats in considering Moore a dupe, for in 1899 he wrote to Yeats, "I want Moore to be the martyr"; Walther Gilomen's survey of the Yeats-Moore relationship (*ES*, 1937), on the whole at the expense of Moore, is balanced by St. John Gogarty's anecdotal but good-humored view in *As I Was Going Down Sackville Street* (1937).

Many of the reminiscences of the Moore-Yeats relationship published after about 1935 appear to have been propelled into print as a result of Yeats's published responses about that time to Moore's *Hail and Farewell* of twenty years before. On the whole, Yeats appears to have disliked Moore the man and was somewhat divided in his opin- ion of the artist. In "Commentary on a Parnellite at Parnell's Funeral" (*The King of the Great Clock Tower, Commentaries and Poems,* 1935), Yeats groups Moore with Wilde and Shaw as Irish writers "too conscious of intellectual power to belong to poetry," and as "the most complete individualists in the history of literature, abstract, isolated minds, without a memory of a landscape," men different from those, like Joyce and Synge, who have a passion for reality and satiric genius. In *Dramatis Personae, 1896–1902* (1935), included in *The Autobiography of William Butler Yeats* (1938), Yeats views Martyn as the typical "peasant saint" and Moore as "the peasant sinner." Within certain limits, according to Yeats, Moore had a technical understanding of painting and the theater and, when possessed by an idea, he had "courage and explosive power; but sacrificed all that seemed to other men good breeding, honour, friendship, in pursuit of what he considered the root facts of life." Moore was "a man carved out of a turnip," he "was never to attain the discipline of style," he "had but blind ambition," yet in his collaboration with Martyn, Yeats concedes, Moore was often all self-abnegation. Yeats's paradoxical view of Moore in the following comment is probably justified: "He was all self and yet had so little self that he would destroy his reputa- tion, or that of some friend, to make his audience believe that the story running in his head at the moment had happened, had only just happened." *The Letters of W. B. Yeats* also reveal a mixed view of Moore. Yeats admits to admiring Moore's *Esther Waters* but also sees Moore as a difficult collaborator, as a "preposterous person." Even *Hail and Farewell* is seen as "the first book for ten years where he has not been petulant. It is curiously honest." On the whole, Yeats tends to underrate Moore's energetic effectiveness in getting the Irish the- ater movement launched in its early stages. The view of Moore pre- sented in Yeats's letters is somewhat further modified in John Butler Yeats's *Letters to His Son W. B. Yeats and Others* (ed. Joseph Hone, 1944), in which the older Yeats is seen attempting to soften his son's growing hatred for Moore. Yeats's *Memoirs* (ed. Denis Donoghue, 1972) expresses the poet's dislike of Moore more emphatically.

A number of articles on the Yeats-Moore relationship published in the 1960's attempt objective reassessments, which in the main depict the two writers as equally important contributors to the Irish literary movement. Patrick Kavanagh (*Irish Times,* 10 June 1965) defends Moore's portrait of Yeats in *Hail and Farewell* and holds that Moore was "truly Irish and Catholic and European, and with Joyce and Yeats deserves to be remembered equally." T. R. Henn (*DM,* 1965), citing Yeats's "slanderous" allusions to Moore in *The Cat and the Moon* and elsewhere, goes on to point out that "malicious gossip" was characteristic of Dublin society. He suggests that, among other rea- sons, the quarrel between Yeats and Moore also arose "because each saw himself as a leader of the literary-political wing of the Irish *risorgimento.*" Ann Saddlemyer (in *The World of W. B. Yeats,* ed. Robin Skelton and Saddlemyer, 1965; rev. ed., 1967), after noting the difficulties of collaboration with Moore, insists that Moore provided much energy and enthusiasm during the early stages of the Irish literary movement and contributed seriously to the dramatic work of Edward Martyn and Yeats, that his Irish experience also contributed to his own "technical virtuosity," that "he had a more profound grasp of Ibsen's technical accomplishment" than Martyn, and that he had "a clearer grasp of stagecraft than either Yeats or Martyn."

The quarrel over Moore's role in the composition of Yeats's *Where There Is Nothing* is extensively reviewed by Jack Wayne Weaver (*Éire*, 1968), generally with a sympathetic leaning toward Moore; the same problem is further touched on by David S. Thatcher (*MD*, 1971) and Patricia Ann McFate and William E. Doherty (*IUR*, 1972). Meredith Cary (*Éire*, 1969) makes the point that Yeats did not understand Moore's essentially literary intentions in *Hail and Farewell* and thus in his response to Moore "sulked through his irrelevant complaint against Moore's artistic portraiture." The tendency to see Moore in a more favorable light is also borne out in the following commentaries: Padraic Colum (*DM*, 1962); Augustine Martin (*Studies*, 1965); Lady Beatrice Glenavy (*DM*, 1966); and *Nancy Cunard: Brave Poet, Indomitable Rebel, 1896–1965* (ed. Hugh D. Ford, 1968). A fairly favorable view of Moore's plays is given in Philip M. Armato's "Theory and Practice in George Moore's Major Drama, 1879–1930" (Diss. Purdue 1970). Patricia McFate presents a fairly objective and interesting analysis in *"The Bending of the Bough* and *The Heather Field*: Two Portraits of the Artists" (*Éire*, 1973). She notes that Moore portrays two versions of the artist (Kirwan and Dean), based on George Russell and himself; Edward Martyn portrays two other versions (Carden Tyrrell and Barry Ussher) based on George Moore and himself. On the other hand, several other critics have taken more negative views, especially on the plays written in collaboration. Thus Mireille Schodet, in "The Theme of Diarmuid and Grainne," in *Aspects of the Irish Theatre* (ed. Patrick Rafroidi, Raymonde Popot, and William Parker, Paris, 1972), maintains that the two different sets of mind of the collaborators result in a play of divided purpose. Paul A. Newlin's negative comment (*Éire*, 1973) is even more sweeping. Moore's plays, he maintains, fail for various reasons: "inability to determine a subject and stick to it," heavy use of melodrama, and inability to transform readable prose into stageable action.

Benedict Kiely (*Irish Times*, 14 Jan. 1971) seems to sum up the importance of the Irish period when he writes of Moore that "Ireland revived him, helped him to perfect the prose that he desired. He brought it with him to the Paris of Abelard, to the desert of the time of Christ and in the dying fall of 'Aphrodite in Aulis,' to the Greece of Pericles." Kiely also seems to point to the tendency to upgrade Moore's position as a writer when he refers to him as Ireland's "second-greatest novelist."

Biographical material on the later period of Moore's life, from 1911 to 1933, has been slight, and for good reason. When at fifty-nine Moore left Ireland to live at 121 Ebury Street, London, he had won several reputations for himself; he no longer had need of flamboyant self-advertisement; he had explored nearly all the genres and a considerable variety of techniques; and he had found his *métier*. More ardently than ever, he devoted himself to his art, to the refinement and perfection of style, to the making of beautiful books. Most of his battles, except for a few appearances in the public arena against censorship, were with his publishers and the printers about his revisions and about the appearance of his books. On the whole, Hone's *Life* adequately provides the essential information on his continuing friendships with such people as Lady Cunard, John Eglinton, Edouard Dujardin, and others; his journey to Palestine; his visits with English and French friends; his nearly annual trips to Beyreuth; his entertaining visitors, although less frequently; and so on. During the twenties he was occasionally ill, sometimes spending several weeks at a time in a nursing home, but always correcting proof, making revisions, thinking of another project to undertake.

The considerable space given to this highly selected survey of autobiographical and biographical writings is more or less proportionate to the amount of such comment that has been published. More important, however, as Charles Burkhart (*Bibliotheca Bucnellensis*, 1967) suggests, is the fact that the "biographical heresy" has been profitably used to inform major critical works on Moore, such as those by Malcolm Brown and Jean Noël.

IV. Criticism

Rather than list even a selection of reviews of Moore's books, most of which seem rather monotonously to play the same tune over and over again, it is more economical to direct the student and researcher to the abstracts published in the various issues of *EFT* and *ELT* referred to earlier and, for the period from about 1894 to 1910 to Gerber's survey of the critical reception of Moore's works in *George Moore in Transition*. Another survey for the period from 1910 to 1933 will be included in the commentary of Gerber's forthcoming volume of letters. A similar study has also been made by James R. Hodgins in "A Study of the Periodical Reception of the Novels of Thomas Hardy, George Gissing, and George Moore" (Diss. Michigan State 1960). In addition, in recent years two collections of essays on Moore, described later, have been published.

Throughout Moore's career, reviewers tend to praise his character portraits and often his style; the same reviewers, however, then frequently damn the work under review for its lack of humor, its dubious morality, or its vulgarity. Some reviewers who condemned the early books for their realism in the French manner condemn some of the later books for their lack of realism and contemporaneity. In any event, there is little serious extended criticism of Moore's work until the 1950's. The increased amount and quality of such criticism and the growing number of dissertations during the last twenty years suggest that Moore's position in literature is being reevaluated and that he is likely to be given a more important position.

Some of the major books on Moore have already been touched on in other connections earlier in this chapter; because, in works on Moore, biography and criticism almost inevitably interweave, it may be assumed that some titles referred to earlier also contain critical commentary. To avoid a great deal of repetition, only some eight or

nine major book titles, another dozen or so important general articles
or chapters in books, and, finally, a larger group of representative
articles arranged more or less according to emphasis need be dealt
with here.

Among the major book-length studies of Moore, the earliest is John
Freeman's *A Portrait of George Moore in a Study of His Work*
(1922), which incorporates material from an article published in the
London Mercury two years earlier. On the whole, Freeman gives
some of the works from *The Lake* on and Moore's later style far more
favorable attention than most critics have. He also recognizes the fine
qualities in some of the earlier books which many writers had condemned. Even in *Memoirs of My Dead Life*, Freeman admires the
half imperceptible blending of the true with the false and, in *Hail
and Farewell*, Moore's "perfect detachment" made him "all eyes for
others' humours and weaknesses, all ears to every echo, and all ice to
every little naked imp of pity." As a critic, however, Moore showed a
"failure in detachment." As a novelist, Moore overcame "the evil Victorian tradition of the formless." *A Modern Lover* and *Lewis Seymour*
(1917) Freeman briefly dismisses, but *A Mummer's Wife* reveals
"the transient and brilliant triumph" of the naturalistic formula,
Lennox admirably exemplifying "the stability of animal vigour when
a finer [moral] activity has died." Freeman especially singles out *A
Drama in Muslin*, "a sort of small comédie humaine" by intention, for
a place in the canon. *Spring Days* and *Mike Fletcher* are dismissed,
the latter because it is spoiled by Moore's "strange fondness for the
corrupt and wanton." *Vain Fortune*, however, demonstrates proper
artistic restraint; and *Celibates*, perhaps a little strangely, is defective
because it illustrates "a theme." *Evelyn Innes*, a "luxurious uphol-
stered" period piece, is "not a novel of passion, but of intellectual
sensualism." *Esther Waters* is praised for having been conceived in
the naturalistic tradition "lightly observed and sparingly infringed"
and for being marked by an "easy, harmonious development" that
ends quietly in beauty. *The Lake*, "a beautiful creation, of clear outline and sparse colour," points to the magnificent later style. Despite
fairly conventional religious views, Freeman can write of *The Brook
Kerith* that Moore approaches the material purely "as a man of letters," though with sincerity, that he joins imagination with reason and
gains a major artistic triumph. Finally, *Héloïse and Abélard* is "monotonous" only in the sense of being "monotoned"; it is never tedious;
it is a masterpiece that prompts a "quickening of spirit."

Freeman is a sensitive, though not profound, critic of Moore; he
does not explore many of the general observations he makes, but he
touches tentatively and very generally on judgments that critics were
only to begin to make more significantly thirty years later. But though
Freeman often saw Moore and corresponded with him steadily while
the book was being written, he did not allow Moore to dictate his
critical responses; to Moore's credit, the letters also indicate that the
novelist allowed Freeman free rein. In fact, after the book was published, Moore complained about some biographical material and
some critical remarks that seemed like moral judgments.

After Freeman's book there is no significant book-length study of
Moore until Sonja Nejdefors-Frisk's *George Moore's Naturalistic*

Prose (Lund, 1952). It does not, as the title might suggest, deal with Moore's prose style as such, but with subject matter, methods, characterization, and so forth. Chapter i concerns Moore's discovery of naturalism, his eventual break with Zola, and his subsequent adherence to Pater, Huysmans, and Yeats; Chapters ii–v present detailed discussions of *A Modern Lover, A Mummer's Wife, A Drama in Muslin,* and *Esther Waters.* On the whole, the critic leans too heavily and naïvely on Moore's *Confessions of a Young Man* for her developmental thesis. She does not recognize that Pater and Huysmans or other writers of the same kind are already in evidence in the "naturalistic" novels of the 1880's, including *Confessions of a Young Man,* and that fictional devices learned from Zola and others continue to be evident in later works. By comparison, Freeman's study is considerably more sensitive and unconventional.

The first thoroughly modern scholarly work on Moore is Malcolm Brown's influential *George Moore: A Reconsideration* (1955). The strength of Brown's book rests in part on his cogent use of the "biographical heresy" to inform his critical revaluation, especially in the first chapter on "The Irish Landlord." Also particularly astute is Chapter viii on "The White Birds of Recollection," in which Brown discusses Moore's later style and his concern with myth, folklore, the past, and universal themes. Perhaps the weakest part of the book is the oversimplified discussion of Moore's Parisian period and the influence of Zola. Most suggestive is Brown's seeing Moore as a significant transitional figure in a massive cultural revolution, as recording both "the painful demise of the Victorian age and the equally painful birth of the age which succeeded." He judges *Esther Waters* and *A Mummer's Wife* to be "two of the dozen most perfectly wrought novels to appear in the English realistic tradition since the high noon of Victorian genius, novels not out of place in the company of the best novels of the language"; *A Modern Lover* and *A Drama in Muslin,* even, deserve to be remembered as transfusing "French realism into the ailing late-Victorian English novel"; and at least four of his later novels (*The Lake, The Brook Kerith, Héloïse and Abélard,* and *Ulick and Soracha*) deserve rediscovery "after today's dominant tastes have passed with the mutation of things."

With the publication of A. Norman Jeffares' *George Moore* (1965) in the widely used Writers and Their Work Series, the novelist appears to have been more generally recognized as a major writer. Jeffares, interestingly, gives more attention to some of Moore's less well-known novels than, say, to *Esther Waters.* Thus, *A Drama in Muslin, The Brook Kerith,* and *Héloïse and Abélard* receive fairly lengthy discussion supported by long illustrative quotations. *The Lake* and *The Untilled Field* are treated perhaps too skimpily, although Jeffares singles out such stories as "The Wedding Gown," "The Window," and "So On He Fares" as "masterly pieces of storytelling, spare, economical but highly emotive." Despite Malcolm Brown's "reconsideration" of ten years earlier, Jeffares still finds it necessary to conclude that "Moore's achievement needs reconsideration," that "his merits should not be ignored," and that "he was a man in whom imagination and narrative skill, capacity for industrious work and artistic conscience so fused that he produced fiction and fictionalized autobiography which has the timeless quality of all great art."

Jean C. Noël's *George Moore: L'Homme et l'œuvre* (1852–1933) (1966) is the most thorough full-length critical study of Moore that also makes use of the "biographical heresy." Much of the biographical information is drawn from Hone, but it is here significantly interpreted in the light of Moore's creative production. Noël properly places influences and borrowings in perspective; as Charles Burkhart wrote (*ELT*, 1967), "Fidelity to self is the center of Noël's interpretation of Moore." Almost all of Moore's works are discussed in great detail, even *Flowers of Passion* (1877) and *Pagan Poems* (1881); *Evelyn Innes, The Lake*, and other works of the middle period are aptly considered as "psychomusicale"; and he astutely examines Moore's criticism as essentially in the manner of confessions. He traces minutely the development of Moore's late style from hints of it in the early works through its full-fledged form in *Héloïse and Abélard*. Reworked and somewhat reduced in length, Noël's book should be translated into English.

Although it is ostensibly an edition of letters, Gerber's commentary in *George Moore in Transition: Letters to T. Fisher Unwin and Lena Milman, 1894–1910* (1968) culls out of all published works and letters for the period under consideration the essential elements of a biographical narration and traces the critical reception of Moore's work. In the main, like some other recent writers on Moore, Gerber sees Moore as evolving his later style more consciously between 1894 and 1910, while not discarding everything he had learned earlier. The history of Moore's development as an artist is more a history of absorption and discovery than a history of discarded masters and manners. The volume Gerber now has in progress, besides providing about 1,200 more letters, will continue to trace Moore's career and the critical reception of his works from 1910 to his death.

Two recent books have usefully collected articles on George Moore: *George Moore's Mind and Art* (ed. Graham Owen, 1968) and *The Man of Wax* (ed. Douglas A. Hughes, 1971). Some of the essays in Owen's book are new and some are reprinted; they cover the whole range of Moore's career. Milton Chaikin, for example, discusses "George Moore's Early Fiction"; Bonamy Dobrée discusses "George Moore's Final Works"; Brendan Kennelly deals with the short stories, Herbert Howarth with the Dublin period, Norman Jeffares with *A Drama in Muslin*, Graham Hough with "George Moore and the Novel"; and others deal with special aspects—Blisset on literary Wagnerism, William C. Frierson on Moore's compromise with the Victorians, Graham Owen on the "melodic line." (For abstracts and references to abstracts in earlier issues, see *ELT*, 1971.) Douglas Hughes's volume, which includes three of the pieces also in Owen's collection, reprints a number of reminiscences, for example by John Eglinton, W. B. Yeats, and Austin Clarke. In addition, it provides some critical comment by Frank Swinnerton and Virginia Woolf, Peter Ure's "George Moore as Historian of Conscience," Enid Starkie on Moore and French naturalism, two essays on *Esther Waters*, one article on the short stories, one on *Hail and Farewell*, one on *The*

Brook Kerith, and Malcolm Brown on Moore as critic. (For abstracts and references to abstracts, see *ELT*, 1973.)

The most recent book on Moore is Janet Egleson Dunleavy's *George Moore: The Artist's Vision, the Storyteller's Art* (1973), based on her dissertation (New York 1969). Dunleavy modestly claims no more for her book than its being a "brief introduction to the prose, drama, and poetry of George Moore." She bases her reexamination on Malcolm Brown's observation that Moore's career is "an incomparable aesthetic journey, ranging more widely than the careers of Shaw, or Bennett, or Wells, or even Joyce and Yeats, though he did not always return from his expeditions as enriched as they." Dunleavy traces the various influences on Moore in his esthetic journey toward its culmination in what she calls his mastery of "the poetic-symbolist novel."

Since most of the books cited above have taken into account much of the important material that has appeared in periodicals and as chapters in books, only a few titles of this kind need be noticed. Although he admires Moore's *A Mummer's Wife* and *Esther Waters* and concedes that the heroine of *Evelyn Innes* and *Sister Teresa* is "powerfully drawn," Edward Wagenknecht in *Cavalcade of the English Novel* (1943; with expanded bibliography, 1954) concludes that Moore is a minor novelist because there is little passion in his work. Further, though the style of Moore's later books is beautiful, "It creates a soporific effect." In his *The Victorian Conscience* (1952), Clarence R. Decker brings together a number of articles on Moore's relationship to French naturalism in which he recognizes that the novelist's affection for naturalism was a "passing fancy" and that Moore was in fact pointing the way to twentieth-century judgments on many artistic matters. Ruth Temple in *The Critic's Alchemy* (1953) gives a fine account of Moore's role in making the new French literature and painting and the theory of art for art's sake known in England, defends Moore's impressionistic criticism, and suggests that Moore, with Gosse and Symons, may be regarded as a precursor of later critical theories. The same general idea is explored by H. E. Gerber (*JAAC*, 1967). It may be noted here that during recent years a number of unpublished dissertations have dealt with Moore's theory of fiction and stylistic practice: Thomas C. Ware, "George Moore's Theory and Practice of the Novel" (North Carolina 1969); Clyde Patrick White, "George Moore: From Naturalism to Pure Art" (Virginia 1970); Vera Paula Krieger, "The Quest for a Totally Aesthetic Realism: A Study of the Major Fiction of George Moore" (Bowling Green State 1971); Phyllis H. Duckworth, "Naturalism and Romanticism in the Novels of George Moore" (Tennessee 1972); Douglas A. Hughes, "George Moore's Art of Fiction" (Colorado 1971); and James C. Wilcox, "Rhythm, Structure and Style in George Moore's Later Novels" (Northern Illinois 1972).

Herbert Howarth's chapter on Moore in *The Irish Writers, 1880–1940* (1959) is an important examination of much of Moore's work in the light of Moore's biography and of cultural history. Howarth shows Moore absorbing painterly impressionism in *A Modern Lover, Confessions of a Young Man, Modern Painting, A Mummer's*

Wife, and *Esther Waters*; and Wagnerism in *Evelyn Innes*, *Sister Teresa*, and *Hail and Farewell*. He praises the truthful and artistic representation of Ireland in *The Lake* and *The Untilled Field* and Moore's "subversion of the Villa" in the battle for greater artistic freedom. Howarth concludes by predicting greater interest in Moore's late style, which is decorative and human and vital. Graham Hough, in "George Moore and the Nineties," *Edwardians and Late Victorians* (ed. Richard Ellmann, 1960), sees Moore's *Confessions of a Young Man* as a particularly representative work of the 1880–1914 period. It is a comment on and demonstration of "a greatly increased range and a new freedom in the choice of subjects from actual life," it depicts the "confused set of tendencies that cluster around the notion of art for art's sake," and it illustrates a "conscious reaction against the English literary tradition." Hough cogently observes that naturalism "did not drive out aestheticism, it substituted a new aestheticism of an extended kind," and Moore hinted that form and style were the common ground between the two theories. Hough adds to this discussion (*REL*, 1960) and insists that Moore's "triumph is to have combined vividness of presentation with a prose whose rhythm and texture is itself beautiful to contemplate." Raffaella M. Uslenghi's "Una prospettiva di unita nell'arte di George Moore" (*EM*, 1964) is an ambitious and important article on Moore, a lengthy English abstract of which may be found in *ELT* (1971). At the crux of this writer's essay is the thesis that Moore's work is unified by a constant artistic integrity, by his primary loyalty to his art and to beauty, not to creeds and theories.

Richard Cave's "The Quest of George Moore" (*Cambridge Review*, 1968) is a suggestive essay which regards Moore's novels as seeking a moral center in life. By combining Balzac's vitality and moral sense and Wagner's theory of the life-force, reflected in *Esther Waters*, *The Lake*, and *The Brook Kerith*, Moore achieved a new moral stance. Along similar lines, Peter Ure's "George Moore: A Historian of Conscience," in *Imagined Worlds* (ed. Maynard Mack and Ian Gregor, 1968), deals with Moore's concern with the necessary oneness of conscience and deeds as revealed in *A Mummer's Wife*, *A Drama in Muslin*, and *Esther Waters*.

Although there have been a number of psychologically oriented discussions of Moore, Martin Seymour-Smith's (*Encounter*, 1970) is more specific than most such studies have been. Moore's themes, the author maintains, are "the existential consequences of 'art for art's sake'; the sexual nature of women; the relationship between art and life." Moore exploits his voyeurism and femininity and in John Norton presents the most acute study of homosexuality in English during the century, but even more successful is the portrait of Joseph of Arimathea as a homosexual type in *The Brook Kerith*. Moore, the author concludes, used his own difficulties with sexuality and artistic selfishness to create a meaningful world in his novels.

In recent years a growing number of explications and revaluations of individual works has begun to appear. Among these are two on *Esther Waters*: Carol Ohmann's (*NCF*, 1970) and Brian Nicholas' (in *The Moral and the Story*, by Ian Gregor and Brian Nicholas, 1962). Both essays tend to denigrate the novel on the grounds that

Moore was either straddling two stools or writing a novel on principles he no longer believed in. Thus, according to Nicholas, the novel
is illogical in presenting Esther both as victim on naturalistic principles and as victor. Ohmann also proposes that the novel reveals
"Moore's disaffection from his contemporary subject" and that he
wrote his best fiction when he turned to Irish subjects in *The Untilled
Field* and *The Lake*. Lionel Stevenson's excellent introduction to the
Riverside Editions reprint of *Esther Waters* (1963) is a fine corrective to the negative views of the novel. Stevenson compares the texts
of 1894, 1899, and 1920, relates scenes and persons to real-life models,
compares Moore's novel with Hardy's *Tess*, surveys early reviews, and
on the whole praises Moore's independent accomplishments. Kenneth
B. Newell has examined closely the stories of *The Untilled Field*
(*ELT*, 1971), and Meredith Cary has written a short piece on "The
Window" in "Saint Biddy M'Hale" (*SSF*, 1969). *The Lake* also has
been closely studied in two important articles: Max Cordonnier's
(*DM*, 1967) and Eileen Kennedy's (in *Modern Irish Literature*, ed.
Raymond J. Porter and James D. Brophy, 1972). Kenneth B. Newell's
close reading of "The 'Wedding Gown' Group in *The Untilled Field*"
(*Éire*, 1973)will be incorporated in his book on *The Untilled Field*
and *The Lake*, now in progress.

Finally, it remains to take into account source studies, studies of
Moore's autobiographical writings as art forms, studies of the influence of music on Moore's works, and studies of Moore's influence on
other writers. Moore's borrowing from French writers is probably the
most frequently discussed subject among source studies. The fullest
treatment of this subject is by Milton Chaikin, first in his 1954 New
York University dissertation, "The Influence of French Realism and
Naturalism on George Moore's Early Fiction," and then in some four
articles based on the dissertation: "Balzac, Zola, and George Moore's
A Drama in Muslin," (*RLC*, 1955); "The Composition of George
Moore's *A Modern Lover*" (*CL*, 1955); "A French Source for George
Moore's *A Mere Accident*" (*MLN*, 1956), and "George Moore's *A
Mummer's Wife* and Zola" (*RLC*, 1957). In general, Chaikin finds
resemblances in scenes, characters, narrative techniques, and language between Moore's early novels and the work of Balzac, Zola,
and the Goncourts. On the whole, Zola most often provides the narrative method and Balzac the modification of the more extreme aspects
of French Naturalism. In recent years critics have suggested that the
extent of the French influence even on Moore's early novels may have
been exaggerated. Calvin S. Brown, in "Balzac as a Source of George
Moore's *Sister Teresa*" (*CL*, 1959), recognizes a correspondence of
some details in Moore's novel with details in Balzac's *La Duchesse de
Langeais*, but also notes that Moore excised these Balzacian parallels
in a later edition. Two articles on *Esther Waters* suggest the kind of
homegrown sources he was just as likely to adapt to his purpose as
French literary sources. Lynn C. Bartlett (*ELT*, 1966), for example,
makes a convincing case for a servant called Maggie Younghusband
as one of several models for Esther. Miss Younghusband is the purported author of "From the Maid's Point of View" in the *New Review*
(1891), a periodical in which Moore and his friend Mrs. Bridger had
published. Paul Sporn, in "*Esther Waters*: The Sources of the Baby-

Farm Episode" (*ELT*, 1968), while granting that Flaubert's *Madame Bovary* and *L'Education sentimentale* may have suggested the idea for the famous scene, argues cogently for a more immediate source in Benjamin Waugh's "Baby-farming" (*ContempR*, 1890).

Michael W. Brooks (*ELT*, 1969) traces the influence of Schopenhauer in such early works as *Confessions of a Young Man, A Mere Accident, Mike Fletcher, A Drama in Muslin,* and *Spring Days* to its profound expression in *The Brook Kerith*, in which Moore shows "that pessimism can be interpolated as a wise and humane attitude toward life." Schopenhauer, Brooks maintains, provided the framework in which Moore could account for "both the power of the will and its futility," a thesis which might resolve the problem Brian Gregor finds in *Esther Waters*, i.e., a heroine who is both victim and victor. Brooks convincingly suggests that Moore may not have been quite so incapable of philosophical depth of understanding as has generally been thought. This is not to say that Moore himself read in philosophy very deeply, but he did make use of the knowledge of F. MacCurdy Atkinson and E. V. Longworth. In any event, many students of Moore are now beginning to recognize that much of Moore's pretense of ignorance was a hoax.

Two short notes on source materials suggest the kind of investigations of Moore's sources that might be explored further: Eileen Kennedy's "The Source for Moore's Title, *The Untilled Field*" (*ELT*, 1969), and John Cronin's "George Moore's *The Lake*: A Possible Source" (*Éire*, 1971). Eileen Kennedy, granting that Moore may have had Turgenev's *Virgin Soil* in mind as well as Psalm 65 ("the untilled meadows overflow with a rich harvest"), suggests that a more likely source is Shelley's "England in 1819": "A people starved and stabbed in the untilled field." Curiously, Roland Duerksen's *Shelleyan Ideas in Victorian Literature* (The Hague, 1966) makes no mention of Moore. A thorough study of Moore's knowledge of and use of Shelley's ideas would be most worthwhile. John Cronin suggests that an undated pamphlet by Thomas Connellan may have influenced the denouement of *The Lake*, another novel that warrants close study for the sources of characters, scenes, and ideas. Jack Wayne Weaver's "Moore's Sainted Name for Gogarty in *Hail and Farewell*" (*ELT*, 1971) also suggests a need for a carefully annotated edition of Moore's remarkable "autobiography." Weaver points out that Gogarty is directly referred to twice but that he is also portrayed as Conan. Since there are some sixty Irish saints of this name, it becomes evident that Moore is having a good deal of fun at the expense of Oliver St. John Gogarty, whose pranks Moore had had to endure on a number of occasions. Two important source studies appeared in *ELT* in 1975: Eileen Kennedy's "Turgenev and George Moore's *The Untilled Field*" and Francis L. Nye's "George Moore's Use of Sources in *Héloïse and Abélard*."

While there are scattered generalizations about Moore's method of writing autobiography, relatively few close studies exist. A good starting point is Wayne Shumaker's *English Autobiography: Its Emergence, Materials, and Form* (1954), especially the chapter called "The Narrative Mode: Moore's *Hail and Farewell*"; with some changes, this chapter has also appeared in *The Man of Wax* (ed.

Douglas A. Hughes, 1971). Shumaker's work is marred by such over-simplifications as the comments that in *Confessions of a Young Man* Moore "dissipates energy" by violating structural unity and that *Hail and Farewell* is unified through its theme or mission "to destroy the Roman Catholic Church and bring Art to Ireland." Shumaker then goes on to suggest some aspects of Moore's handling of the genre: novelistic handling of time, skillful omission or concealment of transitions, alternation and blending of reverie with physical actions, and adroit foreshadowing of his unifying images. John Firth's "George Moore and Modern Irish Autobiography" (*Wisconsin Studies in Literature*, 1968) is also more suggestive than conclusive. Firth notes that the importance of *Hail and Farewell* rests on the fact that it became the impetus behind the development of Irish autobiography; that, like other Irish autobiography, Moore's story is one of disenchantment and exile; and that it challenged the traditional idea that autobiography is factual. Firth then interestingly suggests Moore's use of narrative masks, the central character being alternately An Egotist, A Modest Man, A Ladies' Man, A Misogynist, An Iconoclast, A Dandy, A Cultural Chauvinist, A Champion of Irish Genius, A Fraternal Writer, A Messiah, and A Ridiculous Man. More technically oriented is Michael M. Riley's "Persona and Theme in George Moore's *Confessions of a Young Man*" (*ELT*, 1976). The article is based on Riley's "The Sculptor and the Statue: George Moore as Autobiographer" (Diss. Claremont Graduate School 1970) which analyzes Moore's work in order to establish a critical basis for autobiography as a genre. Also valuable is Robert Michael Scotto's "Self-Portraits of the Apprentice Artist: Walter Pater's *Marius*, George Moore's *Confessions*, and James Joyce's *A Portrait of the Artist*" (Diss. City Univ. of New York 1970) emphasizing Pater's influence on Moore and Joyce. The three writers are said to share three techniques: a heightened moment of learning about artistic temperament and/or artistic life, thematic use of a set piece, and thematic use of style.

George Moore's interest in music and its use in a number of his novels has long been recognized. There is an ample record of his talks with Edward Martyn and Edouard Dujardin about music, especially that of Palestrina and Wagner, and his annual visits to the Wagner performances in Beyreuth are well known. So, also, his repeated offers to write libretti for various composers have been noted. The index to Gerber's *George Moore in Transition*, for example, lists references to J. S. Bach, Johannes Brahms, Chopin, Arnold Dolmetsch, Paul Dukas, Sir Edward Elgar, Michael Esposito, Reynaldo Hahn, Nellie Melba, Mozart, Paderewski, Palestrina, Scarlatti, Richard Strauss, and, of course, Wagner.

Two major articles deal with Moore and music: William F. Blissett's "George Moore and Literary Wagnerism" (*CL*, 1961) and Sara Ruth Watson's "George Moore and the Dolmetsches" (*ELT*, 1963). In his detailed discussion of Moore's leading "the way in the writing of Wagnerian novels," Blissett argues that the Wagnerian discussion in *Evelyn Innes* is "skillfully integrated with the theme of the book and the life of its characters." Blissett goes on to trace Moore's absorption of Wagnerism from literary Wagnerism in his Paris days to the social Wagnerism of the first London period, to the Wagnerism combined with Irish myths of his Irish period. The chief cause of Moore's failure to do in literature what Wagner did in music is the lack of an orchestra, an "emotion of multitude." Moore's work, Blissett concludes, is too monochromatic. Fred Sinfelt (*Studies in the Humanities*, 1969) provides a broad survey of the influence of *The Ring* on most of Moore's novels and supplements Blissett's discussion.

Watson, in her closely argued essay, shows that much of the musical knowledge and some of the characters in Moore's *Evelyn Innes* were derived from his attendance at the Dolmetsch concerts of old music and his membership in the "Dolmetsch circle," which included Arthur Symons, Yeats, William Rothenstein, Ellen Terry, Florence Farr, Margaret Mackail, Lawrence Binyon, William Morris, Shaw, and, later, James Joyce and Ezra Pound. Dowlands, Mr. Innes' house in the novel, was also the name of Arnold Dolmetsch's house in Dulwich; Mr. Innes is probably drawn after Dolmetsch; the descriptions of concerts in the novel are fairly accurate descriptions of concerts at the Dolmetsch establishment. Blissett, Sinfelt, and Watson have provided a solid foundation for further investigations of Moore's use of music in his novels. In this connection, a careful comparison of Moore's use of music with Gabriel D'Annunzio's use of it would make quite fruitful study.

Relatively little has been written on Moore's influence on others. Most commentaries get little further than the biographical peripheries of the subject, as, for example, the bulk of what has been written about the relationships of Moore, Martyn, and Yeats. A few general comments have appeared on Moore's influence on Arnold Bennett, but these are almost all based on Bennett's public admission of indebtedness. Perhaps little has been done with the subject on the assumption that Moore changed his style and his material so often that there was nothing typical to imitate or to be influenced by. Yet many writers, whether they like Moore personally or not, have written respectfully of his artistry, his technical accomplishments, so that one has the impression that Moore is often regarded as a writer's writer. Actually, only one major writer has been discussed frequently in the light of Moore's influence: James Joyce.

Most discussion of Moore's influence on Joyce focuses on *The Untilled Field* and *Dubliners*. Eileen MacCarvill (*ALM*, 1958) cites parallels between Moore's and Joyce's short stories and discusses the relationship of Joyce's *The Day of the Rabblement* to Moore and the Irish theater. Richard Ellmann (*KR*, 1958) shows that Joyce borrowed the ending for "The Dead" from Moore's *Vain Fortune*, a book which Joyce in *The Day of the Rabblement* praised as "fine original work"; Moore, however, disliked all the stories in *Dubliners* except "The Dead," of which he said, "I regretted I was not the author of it." Eileen Kennedy, in "Moore's *Untilled Field* and Joyce's *Dubliners*" (*Éire*, 1970), notes that Joyce read *The Untilled Field* in 1904 and that there are similarities of themes of exile, repression, mordant piety, and artist-as-priest, as well as similar incidents and symbols. Karl Beckson, in "Moore's *The Untilled Field* and Joyce's *Dubliners*: The Short Story's Intricate Maze" (*ELT*, 1972), maintains that the recurring themes, images, and characters and the novelistic structure of Moore's volume provided Joyce with methods for organizing his own stories. Patricia Ann McFate, in " 'A Letter to Rome' and 'Clay': Similarities in Character and Conclusion" (*SSF*, 1972), notes that both stories are informed by the paralysis theme and Turgenev's style. Moore's *Evelyn Innes* and *Sister Teresa*, according to Albert J. Solomon's "The Backgrounds of 'Eveline' " (*Éire*, 1971), influenced Joyce's story. Phillip L. Marcus' "George Moore's Dublin, 'Epiphanies' and Joyce" (*JJQ*, 1968) argues that the vision of Dublin in *Parnell and His Island* and in *A Drama in Muslin* parallels that of Joyce in *Dubliners, Stephen Hero*, and *A Portrait of the Artist as a Young Man*. Albert J. Solomon (*JJQ*, 1973) discovers portraits of Moore in *Ulysses* and notes passages that recall *A Mummer's Wife, Confessions of a Young Man*, and *Parnell and His Island*. In two other articles Solomon makes a case for the influence of Paul Blouet's *John Bull and His Island* on Moore's *Parnell and His Island* and on Joyce's "Eveline" (*N & Q*, 1973, and *Costerus*, 1973, respectively). It should be noted that much of Solomon's published work on Moore and Joyce derives from his "James Joyce and George Moore: A Study of a Literary Relationship" (Diss. Pennsylvania State 1969).

In the light of the above studies of Moore's influence on Joyce and the observation of a number of critics that Moore provided a stimulus for the development of the modern Irish short story, one hopes that more thorough studies will be undertaken. Moore's influence on J. M. Synge, for example, has been suggested, and the likelihood of his influence on Sean O'Faolain, James Stephens, and Frank O'Connor might well be explored. Arnold Bennett often indicated his indebtedness to Moore, yet no detailed study has been produced. Similarly, there have been general suggestions of Moore's influence on Theodore Dreiser, Sinclair Lewis, Charles Morgan, David Garnett, and James Huneker, yet his influence on these writers has not been treated in any detail. Moore's correspondence and the reviews of his work clearly indicate that he was a writer much respected by the literary community in America, Ireland, England, France, Germany, and perhaps Italy. As Gilcher's bibliography shows, Moore's works were widely translated into Czech, French, German, and Italian, and less widely into Chinese, Danish, Dutch, Japanese, Norwegian, Russian, Spanish, and Swedish. George Moore was no parochial writer, especially not in his later works. His place in world literature, his influence on writers of various nationalities, and his critical reception on the Continent justify thorough study.

A survey of scholarship on George Moore shows that many subjects warranting investigation have been only rather superficially treated. Much needs to be done: a modern scholarly biography that takes into consideration much correspondence published since Hone's life, Noël's interpretative biographical commentary, and Gerber's additions to the biographical record; studies in Moore's reading and the philosophical concepts derived from various informants and his fictional representation of this material; studies of his use of music and painting in his fiction for purposes of structure, characterization, and thematic development; studies of Moore's imaginative processes based on textual research; investigations of Moore's uses of myth and folklore, especially in such works as *The Untilled Field* and *A Story-*

Teller's Holiday; investigations of his critical work in terms of ideas and techniques; and studies of his impact on other writers. Most useful as a basis for much of the work that still needs to be done on Moore would be annotated editions of, especially, such works as *Hail and Farewell, Memoirs of My Dead Life, Conversations in Ebury Street,* and *Parnell and His Island.*

The time has surely come when critics and scholars can penetrate the many masks Moore assumed mainly for artistic purposes and can appreciate the complex artist in whom these masks merge, the man in whom "craft and innocency were mingled strangely."

BERNARD SHAW

Stanley Weintraub

Bernard Shaw is an artist of classical standing, although his death occurred in 1950. Because of his long life, the usual centenary revaluations occurred only six years later, when the temporary eclipse which often follows the demise of a major writer had yet to run its brief course. But G. B. S. has survived. His books are read; his plays are produced; his personality is of compelling interest; his every work either is being scrutinized by scholars or inevitably will be as manuscripts emerge from private hands.

Shaw's letters and manuscripts have survived in great quantity not only because he saved most scraps himself but because he was a public figure for so long—perhaps the most influential writer of his time—recipients of the many thousands of his letters often preserved them, and his manuscript writings were marketable early in his career. His own papers—including much of his correspondence and the largest collection of his play manuscripts—are now largely at the British Museum, one of the three residuary legatees of his will. Many of his play drafts and the largest collection of his letters are at the University of Texas. His diaries and some business records as well as his letters to the Webbs are at the British Library of Political and Economic Science (London School of Economics); however, two of his three income ledgers, covering the most productive years of his career (through 1928), are at Texas. The manuscripts of four of his novels and the fragment of an uncompleted novel are at the National Library of Ireland. Substantial collections of Shaw manuscripts, letters, and printed materials exist also at the New York Public Library (Berg Collection), the University of North Carolina at Chapel Hill, the Houghton Library at Harvard University, the Burgunder Collection at Cornell University Library (especially rich in rehearsal copies, leaflets, and pamphlets), Yale University, the Mugar Memorial Library at Boston University, and the library of Nuffield College, Oxford University, which houses the Fabian Society archive. Few major Shaw collections remain in private hands.

I. Bibliographies

The only practical bibliography of Shaw will be that of Dan H. Laurence (2 vols., in preparation). It features full collations and a detailed history of each publication, notes on textual variations between editions and between printings of a single edition. Included, too, are Shaw's rehearsal copies, contributions to books by others, and a listing of every periodical publication located, including letters to editors and self-drafted interviews and questionnaires. The full texts of Shaw's printed-message postcards are included, and all identified silent editings and rewritings are described—Fabian tracts, biographies, and other publications. Archival sources of all scarce items are identified.

Earlier bibliographical attempts were at best skimpy, partial, and dated and have only historical interest. The best of these are Earl Farley and Marvin Carlson, "George Bernard Shaw: A Selected Bibliography (1945–55), Part One and Part Two" (*MD*, Sept. and Dec. 1959); Lawrence C. Keough, "George Bernard Shaw, 1946–1955, A Bibliography" (*BB*, Sept.–Dec. 1959 and Jan.–Apr. 1960 and May–Aug. 1960). In progress, as part of the Annotated Secondary Bibliography Series, is a three-volume Shaw, the segments edited, respectively, by John R. Pfeiffer, Elsie B. Adams, and Donald C. Haberman. "A Continuing Checklist of Shaviana," which lists new editions of Shaw as well as secondary bibliographical items from books and periodicals to theses, dissertations, films, and recordings, continues to appear thrice yearly in *The Shaw Review*, which began its checklists in 1950.

The contemporary response to Shaw is documented in the *Critical Heritage* volume (ed. T. F. Evans, 1976), which begins with the early plays and closes its extracts from printed as well as diary and letter sources with obituary notices and tributes.

II. Editions

The *Bodley Head Edition of Collected Plays and Their Prefaces* (7 vols., 1970–74) contains not only all the plays and prefaces published by Shaw in his lifetime in their finally revised texts* but (in the 7th volume) fragments of the *Passion Play* (1878), *The Cassone* (1889), and *The Garden of the Hesperides* (ca. 1930's), plus the full texts of a dramatization of Ethel Voynich's *The Gadfly* (1898) and a number of short plays and exercises in dialogue, some hitherto unpublished or uncollected, which Shaw frugally elected not to discard altogether. The edition (in the U.S., entitled *Collected Plays with Their Prefaces*, 1975) also contains data regarding composition, publication, and first

---

* Also crucial to any study of Shaw's dramaturgy are not only the earlier published texts but Shaw's printed rehearsal proof copies of his plays in wrappers for actors, directors, translators, and other theater uses. The practice began with *Blanco Posnet* in 1909 and provides variant texts—sometimes the only record of some dialogue—since Shaw amended his texts frequently from standing type before first publication.

performances in English as well as miscellaneous Shavian pronouncements on each play in the form of press releases, self-drafted interviews, program notes, and letters to editors. It supersedes all previous
collections. Shaw's screenplays are being collected and edited for a
future volume by B. F. Dukore.

In Shaw's lifetime the limited Collected Edition (33 vols.,
1930–37), called the Ayot St. Lawrence Edition (30 vols., 1930–32)
in the United States, was followed in England by the Constable
Standard Edition. Each published the five novels followed by the
plays to date, and nonfictional prose collections and compilations
such as the three volumes each of *Our Theatres in the Nineties* and
*Music in London, What I Really Wrote about the War, Doctors'
Delusions, Crude Criminology, Sham Education, Essays in Fabian
Socialism*, and *Short Stories, Scraps and Shavings*. These were supplemented through Shaw's remaining career by additional Standard
Edition titles (*Sixteen Self Sketches*, 1949, was the last), including
volumes of new plays.

Not included in the collected works was his *Table Talk of G. B. S.
Conversations on Things in General between George Bernard Shaw
and His Biographer, Archibald Henderson* (1925). Originally a
ninety-five-page manuscript, it was never a dialogue except on paper.
Among Shavian publications of note that appeared separately from
the Collected and Standard editions in his last decades were his last
(1948) edition of *Fabian Essays*, which he had first edited and contributed to in 1889, and of which he had overseen additional augmented editions in 1908 and 1920.

A valuable adjunct to the Shavian dramatic texts is the ten-volume
Concordance to the Plays and Prefaces of Bernard Shaw, by E. Dean
Bevan (1971), which is in effect a dictionary of Shavian quotations as
well as a concordance that uses a computerized "key-word" system
which places each word centrally in a substantial context. But the text
used is the Collected Edition, which means (since another concordance soon is unlikely) that cross-references to it from the Bodley
Head text will continue to be needed.

Posthumous collections of Shavian writings have continued to enlarge the prose canon: *Shaw and Society, An Anthology and a
Symposium* (ed. C. E. M. Joad 1953), extracts from Shaw's writings
on society; *Shaw on Theatre* (ed. E. J. West, 1958), uncollected
writings on drama; *How to Become a Musical Critic* (ed. Dan H.
Laurence, 1961), uncollected writings on music; *Platform and Pulpit*
(ed. Dan H. Laurence, 1961), uncollected speeches; *The Matter with
Ireland* (ed. Dan H. Laurence and David H. Greene, 1962), uncollected writings on Ireland; *The Religious Speeches of Bernard Shaw*
(ed. Warren S. Smith, 1963), lay sermons and speeches; *The Ration-
alization of Russia* (ed. Harry Geduld, 1964), Shaw on his U.S.S.R.
trip; *Selected Nondramatic Writings of Bernard Shaw* (ed. Dan H.
Laurence, 1965); *Shaw on Religion* (ed. Warren S. Smith, 1967);
G. B. S. The Road to Equality: Ten Unpublished Lectures and Essays
(ed. Louis Crompton, 1971), lectures, mostly early, on socialism and
economics; *The Nondramatic Literary Criticism of Bernard Shaw*
(ed. Stanley Weintraub, 1972), including an early—1887—and
lengthy Shaw lecture on realism in fiction.

Other Shavian writings, particularly early efforts, have been published in journals. Among the most notable (ed. Louis Crompton and Hilayne Cavanaugh) is his 1884 lecture on Shakespeare's *Troilus and Cressida*, which exceeds in length among Shaw's writings on the Bard even Shaw's Preface to *The Dark Lady of the Sonnets (ShawR,* 1971). More cullings of the archives are in progress, the most recent of them *Practical Politics: Twentieth Century Views on Politics and Economics* (ed. Lloyd Hubenka, 1976), post–1906 lectures and articles.

Shaw's private letters have been appearing in newspapers, journals, and books of biography and memoirs since his earliest public years. It is likely that the number he wrote in seventy years of public life is well into six figures and that tens of thousands are still extant, many now in public and private library collections. The first and only substantial publication of the correspondence is the *Collected Letters of Bernard Shaw* (ed. Dan H. Laurence, 1965–   ), which will bring together in four volumes fewer than three thousand of the letters (I: 1874–97; II: 1898–1910; III: 1911–25; IV: 1926–50). Earlier collections—several of them incomplete or with slightly flawed texts—have been primarily those addressed to a single correspondent: *Letters from George Bernard Shaw to Miss Alma Murray (Mrs. Alfred Forman)* (1927), *More Letters . . .* (1932); *Ellen Terry and Bernard Shaw: A Correspondence* (ed. Christopher St. John, 1931); *Florence Farr, Bernard Shaw, W. B. Yeats: Letters* (ed. Clifford Bax, 1941; a useful supplement is Josephine Johnson, *Florence Farr: Bernard Shaw's "New Woman,"* 1975); *Bernard Shaw and Mrs Patrick Campbell: Their Correspondence* (ed. Alan Dent, 1952); *Advice to a Young Critic* [R. Golding Bright] and *Other Letters* (ed. E. J. West, 1955); *In a Great Tradition: Tribute to Dame Laurentia McLachlan, Abbess of Stanbrook* (ed. the Nuns of Stanbrook, 1956), where a chapter is devoted to her correspondence with Shaw; *Bernard Shaw's Letters to Granville Barker* (ed. C. B. Purdom, 1957); *To a Young Actress: The Letters of Bernard Shaw to Molly Tompkins* (ed. Peter Tompkins, 1960).

It is likely that full exchanges of letters between Shaw and other correspondents will appear in the years following the completion of the *Collected Letters* and the authorized biography. As far as accurate texts of Shaw letters are concerned, all transcripts prior to the Laurence edition must be accepted with great caution, even—perhaps especially—those edited, vetted, or made by Shaw himself, who rewrote his letters when circumstances were propitious. (Compare those to T. D. O'Bolger in *Sixteen Self Sketches*, 1949, with their originals in *Letters*, III; and the notorious letter on sex to Frank Harris in *Bernard Shaw*, 1931, with its revision in *Sixteen Self Sketches*.) In some correspondences the editors' readings are at fault (as with the letters to Barker); in other cases, especially in Shaw's lifetime (as with the letters to Harris and Ellen Terry), Shaw himself did the excising and bowdlerizing. One examination in point is O. M. Brack, Jr.'s "Miss Gambogi and the Terry-Shaw Correspondence" (*PBSA*, 1972), which notes differences even between the first and second editions of the correspondence with Ellen Terry.

III. Biographies and Autobiographies

Although Shaw never wrote an autobiography, he put vast segments of memoir material into his prefaces, pamphlets, essays, lectures, lay sermons, tracts, private letters, and other writings, collecting some of the autobiographical pieces, with a few new essays, into his *Sixteen Self Sketches* and in the process silently censoring or amending old articles and letters. Several of his prefaces were substantial contributions to the memoirs he would never write, particularly those to the novel *Immaturity* (written 1921) and *London Music in 1888–89* (written 1935). The *Sketches* and the two prefaces form the core of *Shaw: An Autobiography 1856–1898*, which with its sequel (subtitled *The Playwright Years: 1898–1950*), both edited by Stanley Weintraub (1969, 1970), form a continuous narrative created by stitching together hundreds of extracts from Shaw's autobiographical writings drawn from almost as many sources and concluding with Shaw's will. All the words are Shaw's, even the chapter titles.

Shaw contributed lavishly to biographical books about him done in his lifetime, thus furnishing them with a below-the-surface autobiographical dimension. He provided a young Irish-American scholar, T. D. O'Bolger, with thousands of words of memoir-detail for the updating of his dissertation, "The Real Shaw" (Pennsylvania 1913), into a book, then prevented its publication. (The manuscript is at Harvard.) Prudently keeping copies of his letters, Shaw eventually used many of the details himself, particularly for the preface to *Immaturity*. For Frank Harris, Shaw not only composed a Harrisian parody, "How Frank Would Have Done It," which appeared in his former editor's *Contemporary Portraits* (1919), but later helped complete a biography of himself of which Harris, at the end of his life, had managed only the first sixty-five pages. Privately Shaw considered it mostly his book, although Harris' paid ghost-writer, Frank Scully, computed the printed text of *Bernard Shaw* (1931) as seventy-two percent Scully (often through rewriting G. B. S.'s letters), and twenty-two percent Shaw (the remainder, apparently, Harris).

"How Frank Would Have Done It" was not the first of Shaw's autobiographical writings produced in the third person, most of these taking the form of self-interviews purporting to record live and spontaneous give-and-take. Among the more elaborate third-person attempts, some of them serious efforts to control his history, others only elaborate private jokes, is the chapter (xxvii) Shaw wrote in November 1902 for Cyril Maude's *History of the Haymarket Theatre* (1903) describing the ill-fated rehearsals for a Maude production— which never came off—of Shaw's comedy *You Never Can Tell*. Forty years later Shaw spent months rewriting and adding to Hesketh Pearson's *G. B. S.* (1942), first making penciled corrections and interpolations which Pearson could rewrite and rub out and then writing red-inked comments meant for background rather than publication. His efforts, Shaw told Pearson afterward, took the time in which three plays might have been written.

In Shaw's lifetime his biographers were often saddled with the autobiographer as collaborator. Authorized biographer Archibald

Henderson had his first of three Shavian biographies held up while Shaw insisted that the book needed more work; and he benefited from Shavian dissertations on biographical writing as well as dozens of autobiographical letters, many of which Henderson turned largely into the third person. One (3–17 Jan. 1905, in *Letters*, II) was fifty-four holograph pages—more than twelve thousand words. Later biographers were assisted by mail. Even into Shaw's nineties, as was the case with William Irvine, the biographee provided interlinear emendations for a typescript (chs. i and ii of *The Universe of G. B. S.*, 1949).

Most of the books about Shaw published in the first three decades of the twentieth century were commentaries and elucidations, few of them with any substantial or reliable biographical data. The first major biography was Archibald Henderson's mammoth (and authorized) *George Bernard Shaw: His Life and Works* (1911), perhaps the largest such volume ever produced about a contemporary hardly more than halfway through his career. It was augmented by his *Bernard Shaw: Playboy and Prophet* (1932) and his *Bernard Shaw: Man of the Century* (1956), each indispensable for its detail (the three overlap, but later volumes necessarily cut back on earlier material) yet sometimes unreliable because Henderson—a mathematician by training—often uncritically accepted information Shaw gave him in such overwhelming profusion and in addition faced the myriad other problems of every authorized biographer dealing with a living subject.

Frank Harris' *Bernard Shaw: An Unauthorized Biography* (1931) had the handicaps of Harris' flair for sensation and Shaw's ostensible desire to supply it for the faltering biographer. Hesketh Pearson's *G. B. S.: A Full-Length Portrait* (1942), the text of which Shaw revised and augmented, was deliberately, in the Pearson manner, long on anecdote and short on documentation. After Shaw's death it was revised as *George Bernard Shaw: His Life and Personality* (1963), to include Pearson's *G. B. S.: A Postscript*, published immediately after Shaw's death in 1950 to capitalize on the event and to utilize material compiled since the book and/or withheld from print as a matter of delicacy in Shaw's lifetime.

Also produced in Shaw's lifetime were William Irvine's *The Universe of G. B. S.* (1949), still the standard account of Shaw's intellectual development; R. F. Rattray's handbook-chronology, *Bernard Shaw: A Chronicle* (1950); Shaw's secretary Blanche Patch's valuable source book *Thirty Years with G. B. S.* (1951); and Stephen Winsten's *Days with Bernard Shaw* (1949). Winsten, once Shaw's Ayot St. Lawrence neighbor, also produced a second book of purported conversations, *Shaw's Corner* (1952), and *Jesting Apostle: The Life of Bernard Shaw* (1956); however, the factual dubiousness of the latter suggests that all three Winsten books should be used with caution.

Although the 1950's was too close to Shaw's passing for publication of biographies not begun in his lifetime, in the anniversary year itself came the two major full-length biographies which still await successors. Henderson's *Man of the Century* (1956), while less readable than

St. John Ervine's *Bernard Shaw: His Life, Work and Friends* (1956),
is more reliable, since the Ervine book, although by an Irish biographer
and playwright once personally close to Shaw, lacks not only documentation but also objectivity, warped as it is by the author's antipa-
thies toward Fabianism and Shaw's many Fabian friends. A later, less
ambitious, biography, particularly useful with respect to Shaw's
music-critic years but entirely leaning on standard sources, is Audrey
Williamson's *Bernard Shaw: Man and Writer* (1963); while a gossipy
and unreliable biographical source (rather than biography) is R. J.
Minney's *Recollections of George Bernard Shaw* (1969). Other books
in the decades since Shaw's death have been built about the author's
authentic or indirect—or assumed—relationship to Shaw. Lawrence
Langner of the Theatre Guild, for example, produced a *Bernard
Shaw and the Lunatic* (1963; largely a rehash, with augmentations,
of his Shaw chapters in *The Magic Curtain*, 1951), and Valerie Pascal
Delacorte's *The Disciple and His Devil* (1970) concerned Shaw's film-
director Gabriel Pascal, who brought *Pygmalion* and *Major Barbara*
to the screen. Two books edited by Allan Chappelow fall roughly into
the same category, his *Shaw the Villager and Human Being. A Biographical Symposium* (1961), a collection of memoir-pieces by
Shaw's friends and neighbors emerging out of Chappelow's visits to
Ayot St. Lawrence in 1950 to photograph Shaw. One of the photographs, showing the ninety-four year-old G. B. S., walking-stick in
hand, Shaw christened "The Chucker-Out," thus giving Chappelow
his title for a sequel volume, which he subtitled "A Biographical
Exposition and Critique." *Shaw—"The Chucker-Out"* (1969), mis-
represented as the most detailed account available of Shaw's social,
moral, and political views, is disabled by the editor's analyses but
remains valuable for its biographical source material—extracts from
Shavian speeches, provincial newspaper cuttings, and other pronouncements lifted from obscure locations. (Unfortunately few are
fully transcribed, identified completely, or represented accurately.)

In the 1960's, with the beginnings of accessibility of archival material from the Shaw estate, biographical interest in Shaw increased
strikingly. Stanley Weintraub's *Private Shaw and Public Shaw: A
Dual Portrait of Lawrence of Arabia and G. B. S.* (1963) analyzes
the intersecting lives of Shaw and the war hero who became his
surrogate son over the period from their meeting in 1922 to "Shaw's"
(T. E. changed his name legally in 1927) death in a motorcycle
accident in 1935. Later, in another close biographical analysis of a
crucial period in Shaw's life, *Journey to Heartbreak* (1971), Weintraub probes the war years 1914–18 and their aftermath, the two
books linked by *Saint Joan*, the culmination of the latter and the
beginning of the former. (*Heartbreak* is also particularly useful with
respect to the origins of *Back to Methuselah* and *Heartbreak House*,
while *Private Shaw* has considerable detail on *Too True to Be Good*,
in which "T. E. Shaw" is "Private Meek.") Also in the early 1960's came
Janet Dunbar's *Mrs. G. B. S.* (1963), a biography of Charlotte Shaw
which emphasized her strikingly unhappy although affluent childhood and premarital life (the Shaws married in their early forties in
1898) and scanted the long years of her poor health and decline

(1932 to 1943). Her impact upon Shaw's creativity remains to be explored, while her success in her self-appointed role as guardian of Shaw's private and professional life now appears less simplistic.

Ample documentation now exists to appraise Shaw's earliest years, which appear far more complex than Shaw's lighthearted view of them in his memoir-writings. B. C. Rosset's *Shaw of Dublin: The Formative Years* (1964) is a massive exploration of Shaw's childhood, the *ménage à trois* in which it was largely lived, and its implications in Shaw's playwriting, while John O'Donovan's thin *Shaw and the Charlatan Genius* (1965) examines young Shaw's relationship with the interloper in the household, music teacher George John Vandeleur Lee. Paralleling this period although moving chronologically beyond it is Henry George Farmer's hostile *Bernard Shaw's Sister and Her Friends* (1959), which seems to have the apparatus of genuine research but is primarily an axe-grinding polemic aimed at demonstrating that Shaw was jealous of his older sister Lucy, lacked affection for her, and kept her out of his life. Another study of the years of apprenticeship, which extends the formative years into Shaw's forties—J. Percy Smith's *The Unrepentant Pilgrim: A Study of the Development of Bernard Shaw* (1965)—utilizes British Museum and London School of Economics archival material up to that point unavailable in print but is unreliable as analysis, however valuable for the documentary material excerpted, especially for extracts from Shaw's shorthand diary of 1885–94, which although translated by Stanley Rypins remains without a publisher.

More journalism than biography is C. G. L. DuCann's *The Loves of George Bernard Shaw* (1963), which treats in separate Sunday-supplement chapters G. B. S.'s amorous (and other) relationships with the women in his life; yet even so it is more reliable than Tullah Hanley's *The Strange Triangle of G. B. S.* (1956), a "novel" based upon the Shaw-Janet Achurch correspondence. Still another book about Shaw's relationship with a young woman is Peter Tompkins' *Shaw and Molly Tompkins* (1961), about a Shavian effort to play Pygmalion (or Henry Higgins) toward an aspiring but untalented American actress in the 1920's and 1930's; while Vincent Wall's small study, *Bernard Shaw: Pygmalion to Many Players* (1973), reviews G. B. S.'s activities as self-appointed mentor to actresses over two generations. Two other biographical books deal with Shaw's relationships with individual artists. C. B. Purdom's *Harley Granville Barker* (1956), although a full life of the actor-director-playwright, derives much of its interest from Shaw's earliest relationship with a surrogate-son figure; William B. Furlong's *Shaw and Chesterton: the Metaphysical Jesters* (1970) explores the interrelationships of the writer-debaters who were public enemies and private friends all their lives.

A biography in several volumes by Michael Holroyd was authorized by the Bernard Shaw Trustees in 1970, but it is unlikely to be available within the decade.

IV. *Early Criticism*

In the decade before the First World War a considerable library of Shaw criticism began to appear. In his introduction to the first of what would be a flood of books, American journalist H. L. Mencken wrote (in *George Bernard Shaw: His Plays*, 1905), "Pick up any of the literary monthlies and you will find a disquisition upon his technique, glance through the dramatic column of your favorite newspaper and you will find some reference to his plays." By assiduous self-advertisement as well as by the apparent novelty of his plays, Shaw had begun to be written about in the periodical press; however, Mencken's book—the first entirely on Shaw—appeared only in Shaw's fiftieth year. (The table of contents of Mencken's study advertised chapters on the novels and on the major plays from *Widowers' Houses* to *Major Barbara*, but no chapter on the latter play was printed.) Holbrook Jackson's *George Bernard Shaw* (1907), the first G. B. S. study to be published in England, emphasized the playwright as "a leader of thought," the integrator of philosophy and drama, and compared him in relation to his era with Swift and Carlyle. In the same year appeared Desmond MacCarthy's *The Court Theatre*, a review of the 1904–07 seasons at the Court under the J. E. Vedrenne–Harley Granville Barker management. Of the 988 performances, 701 had been of eleven Shaw plays. MacCarthy's criticism, insisting that Shaw's plays aimed at forcing men to examine their pretensions, their emotions, and their consciences, stands up well in its scrutiny of the plays' theatrical values, with his review of *Major Barbara* still one of the best analyses of that complex work. MacCarthy's *Shaw* (1950) collects all of his reviews of Shaw's plays he wished to preserve, while *The Court Theatre* has been reprinted (1966, ed. Stanley Weintraub) in augmented form.

Another early study which remains useful, although ideologically hostile to Shaw, is G. K. Chesterton's still provocative *George Bernard Shaw* (1909; enl. 1935). While Chesterton praised Shaw's gaiety and wit he deplored his extravagantly "heartless" view of human relations, which meant that it failed to coincide with G. K. C.'s conservative near-medievalism. On the Continent two books on Shaw appeared before the war, in opposing camps. Augustin Hamon, French translator of Shaw's plays, produced the admiring *Le Molière du xxᵉ siècle: Bernard Shaw* (1913, English trans. 1916); H. Richter, in Leipzig, published *Die Quintessenz des Shawismus* (1913). A final prewar book, Joseph McCabe's *George Bernard Shaw* (1914), was, in its author's view, "a critical interpretation of the man and his message" and an overt, rationalist response to Chesterton's strictures. For a survey of the range of pre-1914 critical opinion, the T. F. Evans *Critical Heritage* volume (1976) is most useful.

In the journals, the best prewar writing on Shaw was that of a young critic who would be a war casualty, Dixon Scott, whose *Bookman* article (1913) was a balanced appraisal of Shaw's dramatic method ("the tyranny of technique over temperament") and prose style ("one of the most remarkable verbal weapons ever forged . . . , an instrument built expressly for cut-and-thrust platform work"). More than any other critic of his time, Scott probed intelligently into

Shaw's shortcomings as a dramatist yet concluded that "once the limitations of the plays are realized they cease to possess any," recognizing that the force propelling his dramatic prose was "a passion for purity, gentleness, truth, justice and beauty." In 1916 Scott's essay reappeared in a posthumously issued collection of his essays, *Men of Letters*, by which time John Palmer had published a long article in the *Fortnightly Review* (Mar. 1915), "Bernard Shaw: An Epitaph." With the outbreak of war, and Shaw's unpopular points of view regarding it, it was fashionable to consider Shaw's influence as thinker as on the wane—thus the title—yet Palmer continued to give Shaw high marks as thinker as well as playwright, foreshadowing the change in public opinion that would recognize Shaw as sage by war's end. (The transition is treated biographically in Weintraub's *Journey to Heartbreak: Bernard Shaw 1914–1918*.)

Three book-length wartime critical studies were less than fully admiring. Harold Owen's *Common Sense about the Shaw* (1915) hysterically attacked *Common Sense about the War* and G. B. S. in general; Percival P. Howe (1915) castigated the "publicist's unreality" of Shaw's plays, the product of a view of life limited to "the Fabian Society and the cart and trumpet"; and Richard Burton (1916) saw a theatrical sensibility beyond the capability of any other contemporary but also an ambivalence which left him suspicious of overt meanings in Shaw. Most wartime writing about Shaw, during his most unpopular period, suggested that books about him would have then been a hazardous commercial enterprise. Newspaper attacks were frequent and emotional. Considered opinion largely awaited the release of his new plays, products of the war that had inhibited major dramatic statement.

The publication of *Heartbreak House* (1919) and *Back to Methuselah* (1921) did little to advance Shaw's reputation, nor did their performances, although both works, particularly the former, have gained respect in time through performance and later criticism. As Graham Sutton observed in *The Bookman* in March 1924, Shaw's detractors often based their arguments on mutually exclusive points of view: "Half of them complain that Mr Shaw is too serious, the other half that he is not serious enough." Performances (New York, 1923; London, 1924) of *Saint Joan* reversed the trend of criticism, the public (with criticism rushing to follow) seeing in the play a contemporary classic. The Nobel Prize for Literature followed in 1926; a decade later Winston Churchill referred to Shaw in *Great Contemporaries* as "the greatest living master of letters in the English-speaking world." Although Shaw's later plays (once he was past seventy) showed an inevitable weakening of his dramaturgical hand and his political views as a new war approached fell into increasing disfavor, criticism thereafter largely accepted the premise that he was the most significant English playwright since Shakespeare as well as a master at many of the other literary trades. In his last full decade, the 1940's, his ninetieth birthday and its aftermath precipitated a shelf of books and other works, from biographies and memoirs to works of substantial criticism. A number of these, to be described below, remain among the most lasting contributions to an understanding of the man and his work.

V. General Critical Evaluations

Once the Shavian canon was relatively established, in the late 1940's, the first real flowering of criticism occurred. Eric Bentley followed up his discussions of *Candida* and other early plays in *The Playwright as Thinker* (1946) with *Shaw: A Reconsideration* (1947; rev. 1957 as *Bernard Shaw*), still useful particularly for its analyses of the "newness" in Shaw's dramaturgy. William Irvine's *The Universe of G. B. S.* (1949) benefited from Shaw's own reading of the text and remains a solid foundation for the study of the ideas in Shaw's plays and his general intellectual development as a child of Victorian radicalism. Similar in intent, but structured about particular concepts, is Julian Kaye's *Bernard Shaw and the Nineteenth-Century Tradition* (1958), its approach identifiable from such chapter headings as "The Rebellion against Mid-Century Mechanism" and "Shaw and Nineteenth-Century Political Economists." Also probing Shaw's cultural inheritance, but from the perspective of the live drama rather than ideas, is Martin Meisel's *Shaw and the Nineteenth-Century Theatre* (1963), which relates Shaw's playwriting techniques and subjects to his experience, as spectator and drama critic, of Victorian dramatic genres and their conventions of character, action, and setting.

A different approach to the canon is taken in Arthur Nethercot's *Men and Supermen: The Shavian Portrait Gallery* (1954; rev. 1966), which examines and classifies Shaw's characters first from the standpoint of Shaw's *Quintessence of Ibsenism* division of people into Philistine, Idealist, and Realist and then by occupation, sex, race, and aspiration. The *Theatrical Companion to Shaw* (ed. Raymond Mander and Joe Mitchenson, 1955) surveys the plays as performances, with photographs, lists of casts, plot summaries, sketchy extracts from early reviews, and valuable reprintings of Shavian program notes. (The program notes, supplemented by additional such notes, reappear in the *Bodley Head Bernard Shaw*.) Other "companions" to Shaw exist but have little to recommend them. Short accounts vary so widely in quality that pamphlets should be noted if only to be described as dated (Ward, 1951, and some later revisions) or unreliable (Matthews, 1969); however, A. M. Gibbs's *Shaw* (1969) is a good short account, and the sixty-five pages in J. I. M. Stewart's Oxford History of English Literature volume, *Eight Modern Writers* (1963), are incisive, insightful, unidolatrous criticism.

A shelf of general critical evaluations of the plays in book form exists, some of the volumes focused (at least titularly) about a thesis and some restricted to particular segments of the canon. Thus Arland Ussher's pungent *Three Great Irishmen: Shaw, Yeats, Joyce* (1952) looks at G. B. S.'s Irishness and, going beneath the sod, sees a Socrates who was also an Aristophanes. Restrictive in another sense, Charles A. Carpenter, in *Bernard Shaw and the Art of Destroying Ideals* (1969), is concerned with the plays through *Man and Superman* and their dramatic strategies, which the critic sees as the destruction of audience delusions and preconceptions, leading (Shaw hoped) to popular reassessment of personal and societal values. J. M. Wisenthal's *The Marriage of Contraries* (1974) begins with *Man and*

Superman and concludes with the first postwar plays and demonstrates Shaw's dramatic use of the tension (and often, then, the harmony) of opposites. Charles A. Berst, scrutinizing the texts of ten major plays from *Mrs Warren* to *Saint Joan* (but not *Methuselah*) in *Bernard Shaw and the Art of Drama* (1973), explores Shaw's "complex and penetrating aesthetic sensibility." Louis Crompton's *Shaw the Dramatist* (1969), one of the most solid of the general books, examines twelve major plays through *Saint Joan* from the standpoint of their social, philosophical, and historical backgrounds—and thus becomes a source study for Shaw's themes, characters, and situations, Crompton relying for his clues not only upon internal and secondary evidence but upon the study of Shaw's extant play manuscripts. Another volume that uses the manuscripts to examine the plays is Bernard F. Dukore's (1973), which probes Shaw's theory and practice as a playwright, often by studying his revisions and his intentions as seen in his published prefaces and private letters. (Both Dukore and Crompton use the *Major Barbara* manuscripts to good effect and demonstrate the values of close study of the play manuscripts largely at the University of Texas and the British Museum.) Margery Morgan, in an uneven but often insightful book, *The Shavian Playground* (1972), suggests an interest in Shaw's backgrounds in her title; however, except for republication of valuable articles (to be referred to in their appropriate places), is under-researched and addicted to hasty generalization, particularly about Shaw's use of myth. Colin Wilson's confessedly "existential" *Bernard Shaw: A Reconsideration* (1969) is sporadically interesting for its flashes of insight but disabled by Wilson's inadequate scholarship and theatrical understanding and his all-encompassing, scriptural dedication to Shaw's Creative Evolution concepts. "I see him," Wilson insists of Shaw, "as an *evolutionary* portent." Equally weak are Homer Woodbridge's *G. B. Shaw: Creative Artist* (1963), a series of apparently unrefurbished classroom lectures; and Leon Hugo's *Bernard Shaw: Playwright and Preacher* (1971), a general review of Shaw's thought which loses force as the critic loses interest in Shaw (who fails to measure up to his standards). Yet for this somewhat disenchanted view alone Hugo's study is a useful corrective. Maurice Valency's *The Cart and the Trumpet: The Plays of George Bernard Shaw* (1973) is a sound play-by-play examination of the canon, based less on Valency's scholarship than on his experience as play translator and critic of European drama. Thus he brings to a view of Shaw his study of the late nineteenth-century philosophers and literary experimentalists and attempts (intriguingly yet not always convincingly) to see Shaw as Symbolist and to discover his relations—as Symbolist—with Strindberg, Wagner, Mallarmé, and other Continental influences.

Other book-length studies of the plays have, even more confessedly, special critical axes to grind and sometimes succeed in enlarging our perspectives. No confessedly feminist critic has improved upon Barbara Watson's *A Shavian Guide to the Intelligent Woman* (1964), for example, but additional critiques from a feminine perspective are now burgeoning. From Sweden comes Sonja Lorichs' *The Unwomanly Woman in Bernard Shaw's Drama and Her Social and Political Background* (1973); and the January 1974 *ShawR*, in an

BERNARD SHAW / *Stanley Weintraub* 179

oversized special edition entitled "Shaw and Woman" (ed. Rodelle Weintraub, rev. and enl. as *Fabian Feminist: Bernard Shaw and Woman*, 1976), contains critiques crediting Shaw both with pioneering balanced characterizations of women and with continuing nineteenth-century female stereotypes. (Possibly the most extreme denunciation of Shaw by a feminist has come from Germaine Greer in "A Whore in Every Home," her program-essay for the National Theatre, London, production of *Mrs Warren's Profession*, which indicts Shaw for using as his example of the "profession" a competent and successful businesswoman rather than one of the far more numerous women brutalized by poverty and by her trade. "Whore" is reprinted in *Fabian Feminist*.)

Paul A. Hummert's *Bernard Shaw's Marxian Romance* (1973) sees Marx in almost every Shavian play and loses credibility in overstatement; yet many plays become better understood in the light of the Marxian grip on Shaw, which may have slackened at times but was never lifted. The grip of the Aesthetic Movement, particularly that of the Pre-Raphaelites (Shaw called *Candida* his Pre-Raphaelite play), is scrutinized through the canon in Elsie Adams' *Bernard Shaw and the Aesthetes* (1971), which is especially thorough on Shaw's views on art and artists in his plays. The interaction of nineteenth-century ideas and movements in Shaw's plays remains a fertile area for Shavian critics, as beneath the surface of Shavian drama is a battlefield of conflicting and overlapping Victorian ideologies often transformed by twentieth-century experience.

Several book-length examinations of the plays observe them as manifestations of language, a subject in which Shaw expressed profound interest all his life and which he made, Shaw insisted, the basis of his most popular high comedy. (A collection of his relevant pronouncements, *Bernard Shaw on Language*, 1963, is edited by Abraham Tauber.) *Shaw: The Style and the Man* (1962), by Richard Ohmann, is a lively and thorough analysis of Shaw's characteristic linguistic modes in his nondramatic prose, especially the prefaces to the plays. John A. Mills, in *Language and Laughter* (1969), extends linguistic analysis to the plays themselves and is particularly useful in examining Shaw's employment of dialect, automatism and word-play, and linguistic satire. Fred Mayne, in *The Wit and Satire of Bernard Shaw* (1967), limits his study to the methods and subtleties of Shavian satire. Its isolation as a functional element has the drawback of disembodying Shaw's intellect from the rest of the playwright; however, this is the drawback of many of the special studies enumerated here. The most searching linguistic analysis of Shaw appears as the lengthiest chapter in *Six Dramatists in Search of a Language* (1975), where Andrew Kennedy sees Shaw's attempts at linguistic naturalism "deflected by his emphatically different use of language," and concluding in the later plays—as a reflection of the breakdown of values —with a language that is only the thin edge between life and despair.

Book-length collections of general Shavian criticism by several hands are relatively few. Stephen Winsten's *G. B. S. 90: Aspects of Bernard Shaw's Life and Work* (1946) was the only one to appear in his lifetime and was of uneven critical value although of enduring value biographically for its recollections by G. B. S.'s contemporaries.

A few essays go beyond that, notably Lord Keynes's on Shaw and Isaac Newton, and Dean Inge's on Shaw as theologian. Louis Kronenberger's *Shaw: A Critical Survey* (1952) gathered articles and book extracts from 1901 (Max Beerbohm) through an obituary tribute (Thomas Mann) and remains one of the most useful single books on Shaw. A number of the articles and books referred to here are represented in it, wholly or in part.* The only collection still in print is R. J. Kaufmann's *G. B. Shaw: A Collection of Critical Essays* (1965), which is largely post-1950. A number of critics referred to in this survey of research are extracted,** while the anthology is additionally valuable for its reprinting of G. Wilson Knight's otherwise neglected study, "Shaw's Integral Theatre," on Shaw's visionary satire. Critical anthologies focused from special perspectives are a likely possibility for the future, for the mass of writing about Shaw has become so great that such screening and collating of criticism may become the only way to make the best general criticism accessible.

Criticism of the Shavian canon as individual chapters of more general books, or as articles or reviews, will largely be treated separately below under specific play titles; however, a dozen or more authors should be singled out for their range of coverage. Although Max Beerbohm retired as dramatic critic of *The Saturday Review* in 1910, he had reviewed every Shaw production in London since 1898, as well as published texts of plays not yet produced, and emerged from hostility and skepticism into grudging admiration for the theatrical qualities of Shaw's work. The selected reviews, published as *Around Theatres* in 1924, were supplemented posthumously into a complete run of the *SatR* contributions via *More Theatres* (1969) and *Last Theatres* (1970) and have the added value of enabling one to view Shavian drama in the context of Edwardian theater. An even greater range is visible in Desmond MacCarthy's *Shaw* (1951), although only G. B. S.'s plays are seen in review, for MacCarthy was active as a critic for nearly half a century of Shavian theater.

American critical journalism emerged nearly as early, in the work of H. L. Mencken and then of his colleague George Jean Nathan; however, the best American criticism in Shaw's lifetime came from Edmund Wilson, who began reviewing Shaw in *The New Republic* just after the First World War and produced his most thoughtful analysis in "Bernard Shaw at Eighty," first in the *New Yorker* in 1936 and then in book form in *The Triple Thinkers* (1938), where he saw the principal pattern in Shaw ("aside from the duel between male and female") as "the polar opposition between the type of the saint and the type of the successful practical man." Writing for *The Nation* at the same time was Joseph Wood Krutch, who saw Shaw's dilemmas as those of the playwright who must fight his audience, rather than accept its prejudices, and then attempt to transcend in his later dramas (and in revivals of earlier ones) the fact of his ideas and techniques becoming "the general background of twentieth-century thought" rather than "the esoteric possession of a few." As drama critic and play-reader for the Theatre Guild, John Gassner covered

* Palmer, Howe, Chesterton, Huneker, Nathan, Krutch, Wilson, Auden, Barzun, Peacock, Joad, Bentley, Young, Spender, Pritchett, Brown.
** Ohmann, Bentley, O'Donnell, Crompton, Morgan, Martz, Fiske.

the same span of years, his views on Shaw culminating in his "Saint George and the Dragons" (in *The Theatre in Our Times*, 1954), in which he saw Shaw's achievement as reconciling preacher and dramatist—that it was often in his preachment that he found his art. Shaw, Gassner declared in many contexts over the years, "enriched the realistic substance of the drama by bringing economics and sociological realities into the theatre, and by turning the British drawing room into a forum, actually liberated the stage from the limitations of realism. He recalled the theatre to its classic and Elizabethan heritage of freedom from picayune illusionism; in other words, he drew close to the freedom of presentational as against representational art" ("Bernard Shaw and the Making of the Modern Mind," rpt. in *Dramatic Soundings*, 1968).

The most provocative criticism on the other side of the Atlantic at the same time was Marxist. "Christopher Caudwell" (Christopher St. John Sprigg) produced an invective-filled chapter on Shaw in his *Studies in a Dying Culture* (1936) in which G. B. S. is identified as the victim of "bourgeois illusions" despite his claims of identity with socialism. "From this . . . springs the unreality of his plays, their lack of dramatic resolutions, the substitute of debate for dialectic, the belief in life forces and thought Utopias, the bungling treatment of human beings in love, the lack of scientific knowledge and the queer strain of mountebank in all Shaw says." E. Strauss, in *Bernard Shaw: Art and Socialism* (1942), with slightly more sympathy, examined the relationship between Shaw's plays and his politics and found them wanting as ideology although—for that very reason—successful as drama. More Marxist was Alick West, in *Bernard Shaw: A Good Man Fallen among Fabians* (1949—the title taken from a remark by Lenin which Caudwell had quoted), who saw Shaw's greatest weakness as "his isolation from the force that will make the future, the working-class movement of socialism." Yet he also saw G. B. S. as the first playwright to "break through the barrier, which most playwrights were too awed even to approach, . . . [of] the imaginary world of the drama against the forces of change in the world of reality; he had to create the means to express dramatically that the men and women on the stage were members of a society based on exploitation. He created these means."

In Shaw's last decade, overviews of his work came more and more to resolve, or at least blur, the complexities in his life and work. W. H. Auden in "The Fabian Figaro" (*Commonweal*, 23 Oct. 1942) noted in referring to "the famous Shavian humor" that "at the bottom of everything comic lies a contradiction," one of these contradictions —despite Marxist objections—being that Shaw was "the only writer who has read Karl Marx with real profit." In the last analysis, however, he saw Shaw in musical terms—not as the Mozart of English drama described earlier by Edmund Wilson but as "the Rossini. . . . He has all the brio, the humor, the tunes, the clarity, and the virtuosity of that great master of Opéra Bouffé." Jacques Barzun's "Bernard Shaw in Twilight" (*KR*, 1943) saw Shaw at 87 as no longer having "a living reputation" but rather the legendary one of a classical artist, his criticism being likely to endure long after the works criticized were forgotten, with the "salt of satire" the "great preservative" likely to keep his plays on the stage. To Louis Kronenberger, publishing his dramatic lectures just after Shaw's death (*The Thread of Laughter*, 1952), balance was needed in any immediately post-humous appraisal, and he arrived at it by reminding readers of Shaw's "repetition, unevenness, self-indulgence, frivolity, exhibition-ism," before he cited his successes, notably the brilliant vigor of writing Shaw brought to the dramatization of people and ideas. "What should be said at least is simply that here is one of the great masters of dialogue, one of the ablest writers of prose, in the whole range of English writing, whether drama or literature."

Although overviews continued to be written, even after the inevitable obituary notices in 1950–51 and centenary summations in 1956–57, the most useful writing about Shaw since this period lies in criticism of, and researches into, the individual plays and in approaches to the canon from special perspectives. Thus Donald Costello's *The Serpent's Eye: Bernard Shaw and the Cinema* (1965) ranges over plays from *How He Lied to Her Husband* to the screen triumphs of *Pygmalion* and *Major Barbara* and failures of the on-site spectacle *Caesar and Cleopatra* and the posthumous *Androcles and the Lion*. Sidney P. Albert's "Bernard Shaw, Philosopher" (*JAAC*, 1956) is the best of the synthesizing studies from that angle; while a seminal study which identifies Shaw as part of a philosophical tradition that has speculated on the role of Will in evolution is Daniel J. Leary's "The Evolutionary Dialectic of Shaw and Teilhard [de Chardin]: A Perennial Philosophy" (*ShawR*, 1966). An erratic and idiosyncratic study of Shaw as religious prophet is Colin Wilson's *Bernard Shaw: A Reconsideration* (1969), but the least trustworthy of all such studies is the earlier C. E. M. Joad *Shaw* (1949), which cribs in haste from a variety of unacknowledged sources, particularly Dixon Scott. (See Julian Ross's "A Piece of Literary Shoplifting," *ShawR*, 1968.) Religious perspectives toward the canon are utilized by Gerald Weales in a survey chapter in *Religion in Modern British Drama* (1961) and—in dealing with Shaw as existential thinker—in Bernard F. Dukore's *Bernard Shaw, Playwright* (1973) and in entire books in Anthony Abbott's *Shaw and Religion* (1965) and Alan Barr's *Victorian Stage Pulpiteer: Bernard Shaw's Crusade* (1973). The best work on Shaw as a religious thinker is by Warren Sylvester Smith, in his two anthologies of Shavian writings (some previously unpublished) on the subject, *The Religious Speeches of Bernard Shaw* (1963) and *Shaw on Religion* (1967), and most notably in the major portion of his important and much underrated *The London Heretics 1870–1914* (1968), which definitively examines liberal religious movements in London in late Victorian and Edwardian London, Shaw's influential role in them, and their influence upon Shaw's thinking and writing.

In *Bernard Shaw, Director* (1971), Bernard F. Dukore examines Shaw's intrusion into directing his own plays, and their meaning derived therefrom, and his contribution toward modern directorial style. Earlier, in W. A. Armstrong's "George Bernard Shaw: The Playwright as Producer" (*MD*, 1966) and in Sidney P. Albert's "Shaw's Advice to the Players of *Major Barbara*" and "More Shaw Advice to the Players of *Major Barbara*" (*ThS*, 1969, 1970), a start had been made toward such analysis; while in "The Avant Garde Shaw" (*Shaw* [Festival] *Seminar Papers*—'65 and later anthologized reprintings) Stanley Weintraub examines Shaw's playwriting as foreshadowing developments later considered (in other playwrights from Brecht to Beckett) avant garde and even "absurd." A number of critics have since developed this concept further. Imaginative perspectives toward the plays are likely to continue to enable us to view the canon from fresh yet valid angles and enlarge our vision of Shavian drama.

VI. The Novels; and Early Musical, Dramatic, and Literary Journalism

Although all five of Shaw's novels have been published—the first, *Immaturity* (written 1879) only in the collected editions—not all of them have been reprinted since, and only *Cashel Byron's Profession* (written 1882) and *An Unsocial Socialist* (written 1883) are currently in print. *Cashel Byron* has been republished (ed. S. Weintraub, 1968) in a text that reproduces the first (1886) Modern Press edition with an appendix of variants from the *To-Day* serial text. *Socialist* appears in the 1888 cheap edition text in *Selected Non-Dramatic Writings of Bernard Shaw* (ed. Dan Laurence, 1965) and in the similar Collected Edition text (with 1930 preface) in a Norton Library volume (introd. R. F. Dietrich and B. B. Watson, 1972). The fragment of Shaw's sixth novel (written 1887–88) was published as *An Unfinished Novel by Bernard Shaw* (1958), edited and with a biographical introduction by Weintraub. Manuscripts of the novels, except for *Love among the Artists* (inadvertently carted off by the dustman, except for scattered pages retrieved and sold by the British bookseller Dan Rider), were presented by Shaw to the National Library of Ireland in 1946.

Studies of the novels, individually and collectively, have had from the start the competition of "Bernard Shaw's Works of Fiction: Reviewed by Himself," *The Novel Review* (Feb. 1892), which brilliantly analyzed all four published novels. An early bibliography is Maurice Holmes's *Some Bibliographical Notes on the Novels of George Bernard Shaw* (ca. 1928), and a detailed pamphlet on *An Unsocial Socialist* itself is F. E. Loewenstein's *The History of a Famous Novel* (1946). The best of the studies of the novels published in Shaw's lifetime is Claude Bissell's (*UTQ*, 1947), while the only book on the novels is R. F. Dietrich's *Portrait of the Artist as a Young Superman* (1969), which examines the fiction as the maturing of the Shavian personality, in the process focusing heavily upon the first novel, *Immaturity*. As a study of Shaw's developing prose style Richard Ohmann's *Shaw: The Style and the Man* also utilizes the novels. The two most substantial studies of the novels, both of monograph length and both emphasizing the novels as intimations of the plays, are Weintraub, "The Embryo Playwright in Bernard Shaw's Early Novels" (*TSLL*, 1959); and R. Hogan, "The Novels of Bernard Shaw" (*ELT*, 1965). Useful articles on individual novels are Weintraub, "Bernard Shaw, Charles Lever and *Immaturity*" (*ShawR*,

1957); Phyllis Goodman, "Beethoven as the Prototype of Owen Jack [in *Love among the Artists*]" (*ShawR*, 1965); and John Rodenbeck, "The Irrational Knot: Shaw and the Uses of Ibsen" (*ShawR*, 1969).

Dan H. Laurence's introduction to *How to Become a Musical Critic* (1961), a collection of reviews and essays Shaw had not collected in his own *Music in London* and *London Music*, is the most thorough analysis of Shaw as music critic. Biographically, the best sources remain Shaw himself and Rosset's *Shaw of Dublin* (for the Lee relationship). Useful on the music criticism itself is George S. Barber (*PMLA*, 1957).

The art criticism is little known. As "G. B. S." in *The World*, Shaw in the late 1880's inveighed against academic painting and praised the later Pre-Raphaelites and the Impressionists, while earlier he had championed the same causes in "Art Corner" columns in Annie Besant's socialist monthly *Our Corner*. Four *World* reviews are reprinted by Jack Kalmar in "Shaw on Art" (*MD*, 1959) and two 1886 "Art Corner" reviews in *ShawR* (1972). Shaw's "exploitation" of his immersion in art to create scenes, situations, and characters in his plays is explored by Stanley Weintraub (*MD*, 1975).

An 1887 lecture, "Fiction and Truth," appears in *The Nondramatic Literary Criticism of Bernard Shaw* (ed. S. Weintraub, 1972), the introduction to which is one of the few extended evaluations of Shaw as literary critic. Book criticism from the *PMG* also appears in Laurence, "G. B. S. and the *Pall Mall Gazette*: A Bibliographical Study" (*ShawR*, 1960). Shaw's press controversies (several of these reprinted in *ShawR*) and letters to editors will be collected in *Agitations* (ed. Laurence, forthcoming).

Shaw's best-known criticism, *The Quintessence of Ibsenism* (1891), has been scrutinized in a number of articles, notably Daniel C. Gerould's (*CL*, 1963), which takes to task Edmund Wilson, Eric Bentley, Raymond Williams, and other critics for accusing Shaw of misrepresenting Ibsen. Shaw analyzes the plays as exposures of sham ideals, in his preface even declaring that his intention is not to examine the dramatics or poetics of the plays, Gerould writes, for Shaw was introducing Ibsen to a *reading* public at a time when there was "no valid dramatic tradition" in which to visualize the playwright. Another useful study is John Gassner's "Shaw on Ibsen and the Drama of Ideas," in *Ideas in the Drama* (English Institute Essays, 1964), reprinted in *Dramatic Soundings*. Again the charge that Shaw created Ibsen in his own image is refuted, his "provocative definition of Ibsenism" rather an introduction to "that considerable portion of the modern drama that exemplifies modern social and moral thought." However, Alan P. Barr's persuasive "Diabolonian Pundit: G. B. S. as Critic" (*ShawR*, 1968) examines Shaw's use of his criticism in general to proselytize, *The Quintessence of Ibsenism* not excluded.

The "other" major critical essay, *The Perfect Wagnerite* (1898), has received less critical attention but is the subject of a thorough examination by William Blisset (*UTQ*, 1957–58), who concludes that as long as Shaw found a kindred intellectual and spiritual soul in Wagner he was contentedly Wagnerian but that Shaw ignored his hero's shift to conservatism and love-worship. Janice Henson (*ShawR*, 1961) also notes that "It is curious that the very point at which

Shaw boggles is the one most typical of Wagner's operas as a whole, and the one which his interpreters generally find easiest to accept, . . . the search for redemption through love."

Criticism and research have largely neglected the other polemical writings—the political, philosophical, social, and economic articles, treatises, and books. Emil Strauss's *Bernard Shaw: Art and Socialism* (1942) remains the standard Marxist account of Shaw's social and economic writings, with no comparable examination from another perspective. Weintraub's *Journey to Heartbreak* analyzes the origins and impact of the World War I writings, many but not all of them reprinted in the Collected Edition volume (XXI), *What I Wrote about the War*; and Dan H. Laurence and David H. Greene have collected most of the writings about Ireland into *The Matter with Ireland* (1962), which annotates biographical and historical obscurities. Shaw's interest in and use of psychology is explored by Sidney Albert (*MD*, 1971), who augments and corrects Arthur H. Nethercot (*MD*, 1969). Daniel Dervin's *Bernard Shaw: A Psychological Study* (1975) is the first attempt at a book-length analysis of Shaw's psychology. Predecessor studies are few, notably Philip Weissman's chapter, "Shaw's Childhood and *Pygmalion*," in *Creativity in the Theater: A Psychoanalytic Study* (1965); and Erik H. Erikson's "The Problem of Ego Identity" (*Jour. of the Amer. Psychoanalytical Assn.*, 1956), which incautiously takes Shaw's tales about his childhood in the prefaces to *Immaturity* and *London Music* at face value. Shavian polemical and critical writings provide an almost inexhaustible vein for future exploration, and much of this side of his multifarious output offers perspectives upon the creative side of the enormous Shavian canon.

VII. Criticism of Individual Plays

The quantity and range of criticism of individual Shavian plays seem to be a reflection of the depths critics feel can be sounded rather than an index to their popularity in performance, although in a few cases—*Candida, Pygmalion*, and *Man and Superman*, for example—critics and audiences seem equally bemused. More and more research and criticism are being directed toward the later, less produced plays, partly because the soil is less tilled but partly, too, because their political, philosophical, and technical complexities were in advance of their time and can now be better understood. Additional incentives to study the later plays are the release and publication of letters and documents relating to this phase of Shaw's life, although the seventh volume of the *Bodley Head Shaw*, with its addition of early play fragments to the canon as well as its completion of the previously known canon with the final plays, is likely to spur new interest as well in Shaw's apprentice period as a playwright.

Shaw's first serious play attempt, a blank verse biblical parable begun in 1878, was first published in 1971 as *Passion Play* (ed. Jerald Bringle) and has had too limited an exposure for extensive criticism. Beyond the editor's brief prefatory account of its composition and abandonment in the second act, there is an analysis of its autobiographical content in Rodelle Weintraub's "Shaw's Jesus and Judas" (*ShawR*, 1972), and additional biographical probing in Ishrat Lindblad's "The Household of Joseph: An Early Perspective on Shaw's Dramaturgy" (*ShawR*, 1974). Shaw's first completed play, *Widowers' Houses* (produced 1892), has been the subject of little useful research and criticism other than in book-length studies, although Charles Shattuck's "Bernard Shaw's 'Bad Quarto'" (*JEGP*, 1955), which studies the 1893 and 1898 printed text versions of *Widowers' Houses*, remains a model of its kind, and in it Shaw's developing professionalism as a playwright is palpable. (Few other studies of the printed texts exist, among them H. M. Geduld's on *Back to Methuselah, ShawR*, 1962, and B. F. Dukore's "Toward an Interpretation of *Major Barbara*," *ShawR*, 1963.) The best critical analysis of Shaw's dramatic strategy in the play remains C. A. Carpenter's in his *Art of Destroying Ideals*. *The Philanderer*, Shaw's second completed, and perhaps least produced, play of normal length, has provoked little research and less useful criticism, Brian F. Tyson being responsible for the only studies of its development. "Shaw's First Discussion Play: An Abandoned Act of *The Philanderer*" (*ShawR*, 1969) describes an abandoned 88-page draft of a discursive act on the marriage question and the problem of divorce, questions later taken up in the discussion-play *Getting Married*. "One Man and His Dog: A Study of a Deleted Draft of Bernard Shaw's *The Philanderer*" (*MD*, 1967) describes an abandoned "Gilbertian plot." Shaw had difficulties developing a play in which his ideas would cohere; thus the largely unsuccessful finished work, which both critics and producers have shied away from.

Shaw's third play has attracted researchers and critics from the start. Tyson, in "Shaw among the Actors: Theatrical Additions to *Plays Unpleasant*" (*MD*, 1971), has examined revisions Shaw made in all three "unpleasant plays" prior to publication in 1898, particularly in sharpening stage directions; while an enlightening study of Shaw's development as a dramatist as he wrote *Mrs Warren's Profession* in 1893 is B. G. Knepper's "Shaw Rewriting Shaw: A Fragment" (*ShawR*, 1969), which compares versions of the third (and last) act, finding "little more than unrelieved melodramatic mawkishness" in the first version, while "the second moves toward genuine dramatic force," and the third "achieves it." Shaw's development of the well-made play inherited from French masters and English imitators into a dramatic form uniquely his own is described in Stephen Stanton's "Shaw's Debt to Scribe" (*PMLA*, 1961) and in Eric Bentley's standard "The Making of a Dramatist (1892–1903)" (*TDR*, 1960). Bentley's analysis of Shavian structure and the "emotional substance" that fleshes it out demonstrates how Shaw's use of reversal and anticlimax transforms the Scribean method and creates thinking audiences by upsetting their expectations. The literary background of the play in French fiction is established by Geoffrey Bullough in "Literary Relations of Shaw's Mrs Warren" (*PQ*, 1962), which also discusses sources from life. From the literary standpoint a major omission is repaired in Betty Freeman Johnson's "Shelley's *Cenci* and *Mrs Warren's Profession*" (*ShawR*, 1972), which validates Shaw's declaration to Archer in an 1893 letter that he had "skilfully blended the plot of the Second Mrs Tanqueray with that of the Cenci." Stephen R.

Grecco adds several suggestions from life in Shaw's own strong-minded and independent mother and sister in "Vivie Warren's Profession" (*ShawR*, 1967), suggesting, too, lesbian tendencies in Vivie Warren—an allegation countered by Marlie P. Wasserman (*ShawR*, 1972). In Charles Berst's "Propaganda and Art in *Mrs Warren's Profession*" (*ELH*, 1966), the drama is seen as a morality play, with Vivie tempted, but spurning the bait for freedom; contemporary morality is examined with respect to the first U. S. production in 1905 (and the verdict is harsh) by George A. Wellwarth (*ShawR*, 1959). Few "modern" commentators are likely to agree with Percival P. Howe's 1915 assessment that the preface to *Mrs Warren* renders the play unnecessary.

Arms and the Man, completed and produced in 1894, has been performed far more than it has been examined. The standard study of its sources is Louis Crompton's chapter on the play in *Shaw the Dramatist*, where the play is described as having thrown overboard "the whole of Victorian moral rhetoric . . . for a utilitarian, naturalistic ethic." Charles A. Berst's "Romance and Reality in *Arms and the Man*" (*MLQ*, 1966), like his other periodical contributions adapted into his *Bernard Shaw and the Art of Drama*, suggests penetratingly that the comedy "expresses the interlocking relationship and mutual dependence of romanticism and realism." As in so many other instances, the most probing look at a Shaw play is Shaw's own, in this case his partly tongue-in-cheek "A Dramatic Realist to His Critics" (*New Review*, July 1894), several times reprinted and crucial to all critics.

Candida, also completed in 1894, has mesmerized researchers and critics from the start. A useful collection of criticism is Stephen Stanton's *A Casebook on* Candida (1962), which brings together commentary by Shaw and others and extracts portions of texts influential in the intellectual background of the play from De Quincey to Carlyle and Nietzsche. (Stanton's "Debt to Scribe" article is also predominantly an analysis of *Candida*.) Other studies of the play's intellectual background, with emphasis upon character prototypes, include Arthur H. Nethercot's "Who Was Eugene Marchbanks?" (*ShawR*, 1972), which sums up the cases for various prototypes from life and awards the palm to Shelley on the basis of echoes and analogues in the play; Louis Crompton's *Shaw* chapter on *Candida*, which makes a case for the effete young Yeats Shaw knew in the early 1890's; and Barbara Peart's "De Quincey and Marchbanks" (*ShawR*, 1974), which upholds Shaw's contention that Marchbanks is based upon the young De Quincey via analogues with the David Masson 1887 biography of De Quincey owned by Henry Salt and very likely read by Shaw. In "Pre-Raphaelite Drama: *Candida*," in Elsie Adams' *Shaw and the Aesthetes* (original essay in *PMLA*, 1966), the play is seen as a "Shavian mystery play about Madonna and Child"—a viewpoint Shaw gave cause to accept in a famous letter to Ellen Terry—and also as about the Pre-Raphaelite idealizing of woman and of artistic purpose. The standard critique of *Candida* remains Eric Bentley's, elaborated in many places but first set forth in detail in *The Playwright as Thinker* (1946), which sees the play in its ambiguities as more than the "life-illusion of Ibsenic proportions" of Candida's husband Morell. Arthur Nethercot's provocative thesis ("The Truth about *Candida*," *PMLA*, 1949) that the three major characters represent Shaw's dramatizing of the three basic character types he formulated in *The Quintessence of Ibsenism* (Realist, Idealist, Philistine) offers insights into Shaw's early dramaturgy that appear useful if not applied too rigidly. Charles Berst (in his *Art*) provides a persuasive defense of the gentle Morell and concludes that his "smug" wife Candida "is not quite worth the fuss." And he escapes the shyness of previous critics by elaborating upon the obvious imagery in the opening tableau and subsequent confrontation scene in Act III. "Such extensive and pointed sexual innuendo is unique in Shaw," according to Berst. "One would like to speculate that Shaw, still burning over the censor's rejection of *Mrs Warren's Profession*, is, incidentally, mocking that man's obtuseness, sailing by him with a smile." The sexual double entendres seem unquestionable; however, their inspiration may have appeared obvious to Janet Achurch, the Ibsenist actress for whom Shaw created the role of Candida and in whose marital life Shaw played a more persuasive Marchbanks.

The Man of Destiny, Shaw's short play about the young Napoleon written in 1895 for Henry Irving (who never played it), has elicited little research and less criticism. The standard account of its backgrounds may be Martin Meisel's analysis of its strain of Scribe-Sardou romance, in which Shaw—in effect—remakes Sardou's *Madame Sans-Gêne*, a play he reviewed the year he wrote his own, observing in the process that Napoleon was "inscrutable, . . . as becomes a Man of Destiny" (*Shaw and the Nineteenth Century Theater*). *The Devil's Disciple*, another product of Shaw's then-active penchant for rewriting history, has been produced far more often, but has apparently been considered almost equally lacking in such subtleties as are attractive to critics. His confessed indebtedness to Blake (in his remarks prefacing the play) is briefly examined by Irving Fiske (*Shavian*, 1951; rpt. in R. J. Kaufmann, *G. B. Shaw. A Collection of Critical Essays*, 1965) who says little about the Blakean element in *The Devil's Disciple*. Two useful background studies of the play are Walter L. Royall's (*ShawR*, 1967), on Shaw's reliance on DeFonblanque's 1876 biography for his acerbic yet admiring portrait of General Burgoyne, and Raymond F. Nelson's (*ELT*, 1969), comparing the devil-hero of Robert Buchanan's narrative poem "The Devil's Case: A Bank-Holiday Interlude" (1896) with Dick Dudgeon, who, however derivative —Shaw had read the verses—is rather an agent of vitalism. Meisel's study is the best between book covers, covering nineteenth-century melodramas Shaw knew in which attractive scapegraces get in and out of familiar predicaments, from Dion Boucicault's stage success *Arrah-na-Pogue* (1864) to Charles Dickens' novel *A Tale of Two Cities* (dramatized in 1860), the ending of which Shaw quickly confessed he had satirized. Shaw himself provided background on the development of the play in "Trials of a Military Dramatist," *Review of the Week* (4 Nov. 1899), while the most useful general critical study in book form—and one of the rare extended studies of the play—is a chapter in Crompton's *Shaw*, which includes material from play manuscripts.

You Never Can Tell (1896), Shaw's subversive venture into fashionable West End comedy, completed before his inversion of popular melodrama in *The Devil's Disciple*, has seldom had its stageworthiness tested and has been unpopular with critics and scholars. A rare background study is Stanley Weintraub's "G. B. S. Borrows from Sarah Grand: *The Heavenly Twins* and *You Never Can Tell*" (*MD*, 1971), which concludes that the forgotten but once scandalous Ibsenite novel, despite sentimental and obtrusive moralizing, "seems to have provided Shaw with some of what he needed to develop a comedy which went beyond the illusions of conventional love to show its biological and irrational truth, and went beyond the illusions of fast-fading Victorian parent-child relationships to show them unsentimentally and unsparingly." A pedantic and unconvincing chapter in Margery Morgan's *The Shavian Playground*, "Making the Skeleton Dance" (earlier the preface to a 1967 Australian reprint of the play), suggests *commedia dell'arte* origins (in particular seeing the comic twins, Philip and Dolly, as Harlequin and Columbine) as well as patterns of Dionysiac ritual. More satisfactory is Maurice Valency's analysis in *The Cart and Trumpet*, which, although dating completion of the play a year too early, observes that Shaw aimed at "a level of comedy in which farcical situations would be given something like tragic weight. In some sense this was the contrary of Ibsen's method. The improbabilities of *You Never Can Tell*, its extraordinary encounters and coincidences, are acceptable only on the level of farce; but they were intended to have the force of parable. The *reductio ad absurdum* of the norms of social behavior would then have a moral connotation, and the jest would imply a sermon."

The historical basis of Shaw's first major history lesson, *Caesar and Cleopatra*, has been researched with thoroughness. Gordon W. Couchman's "Here Was a Caesar: Shaw's Comedy Today" (*PMLA*, 1957) examines how and if the playwright used the classical source material he publicly credited (such as Plutarch and Suetonius); and Gale K. Larson (*ShawR*, 1971), using G. B. S. correspondence not available earlier to Couchman, traces the development of Shaw's search for and use of historical material. Couchman's expansion of his Caesar essay is *This Our Caesar. A Study of Caesar and Cleopatra* (1974). Larson's edition of *Caesar and Cleopatra* in the Bobbs-Merrill Shaw Series (1974) includes an introductory discussion of Shaw's sources and reprints a number of Shavian commentaries on the play, including extracts from letters, articles, a rebuttal to a review of the play, and a 1945 letter to the editor of the *Times* of London. One of Shaw's major sources for his *Caesar*, and his likely justification for Cleopatra's youth and Caesar's asexual relationship with her (both useful for his purposes but violations of fact), is Theodor Mommsen's *History of Rome* (English trans. 1862–66); Shaw's use of it is explored by Stanley Weintraub in "Shaw's Mommsenite Caesar" (*Anglo-German and American-German Crosscurrents*, Vol. II, ed. P. A. Shelley and A. O. Lewis, 1962), findings afterward confirmed by several pages of notes by Shaw on Mommsen dated 1898 and reproduced in Crompton's *Shaw* from University of Texas holdings. Another perspective upon Shaw's use of history is Otto Reinert's "Old History and New: Anachronism in *Caesar and Cleopatra*" (*MD*, 1960), the author finding amid all the apparent anachronisms that it

is progress that is a myth and that the only real anachronism is
Caesar, who is a human being ahead of his time, the incipient
Übermensch. Two studies point to Shaw's use of pictorial materials in
his research: George W. Whiting's "The Cleopatra Rug Scene: An-
other Source" (*ShawR*, 1960) and Martin Meisel's "Cleopatra and
'The Flight into Egypt'" (*ShawR*, 1964).

Critical studies of the play are numerous, particularly those involving Shakespeare and Shaw. Accepting the carefully question-marked
bait G. B. S. offered in the title to one section of the preface to his
Three Plays for Puritans: "Better than Shakespear?" Couchman has
produced two studies of the play worth referring to, one on the
Shakespeare-Shaw theme: "*Antony and Cleopatra* and the Subjective
Convention" (*PMLA*, 1961); and "Comic Catharsis in *Caesar and
Cleopatra*" (*ShawR*, 1960). C. A. Berst (*JEGP*, 1969) examines the
artistic devices used to convey a sense of Caesar's greatness; H.
Ludeke, in "Some Remarks on Shaw's History Plays" (*ES*, 1955),
takes the point of view that Shaw's own need for a hero-image made
creative demands upon the portrait he received from history which
were too great to resist. Perhaps the most penetrating analysis is by
Daniel J. Leary (*ShawR*, 1962), who formulates a theory of "dialectic
action" in Shavian drama in which—in this case—the antithesis, "the
commonsense sphere of practical consideration" (closed morality),
collides with the thesis, "The poet-philosopher's longer view of life"
(open morality), to produce as its synthesis an incarnation of "ideal
values," here seen but fleetingly in the Life Force's occasional Supermen, but someday to be seen in the "long-desired social millenium."
Leary applies his post-Bergsonian "dialectical action" theory to other
plays, including *Major Barbara* and *Heartbreak House*.

Captain Brassbound's Conversion, Shaw's last nineteenth-century
play, has been examined little more often than it has been performed.
G. B. S., punning upon Shelley's poem, once noted that a tentative
title for the play had been "The Witch of Atlas." Roland Duerksen
studies the suggestion seriously (*ShawR*, 1972) and finds Lady Ceci-
ly's success in making

> All harsh and crooked purposes more vain
>   Than in the desert in the serpent's wake
> Which the sand covers . . .

one of the many parallels of the effect of Shelley's witch and Shaw's
lady. (On Shelley and Shaw in general see Duerksen, *PMLA*, 1963,
and the Shaw/Shelley issue of *ShawR*, 1972.) G. B. S. himself detailed his indebtedness to R. W. Cunninghame Graham's travel book
Mogreb-el-Acksa, in his *Plays for Puritans* preface and his further
indebtedness to the personality of his friend Graham (particularly for
the character of Sergius in *Arms and the Man*) has also long been
known. His relations with Graham and their impact upon his plays
are summed up in "Bernard Shaw and Don Roberto," by John
Walker (*ShawR*, 1972).

Of the few extended studies of this comic melodrama two are
particularly valuable—Bentley's in *The Playwright as Thinker*, analyzing its central ironies, and Maurice Valency's in *The Cart and*

Trumpet, which sees the play as a surprisingly successful "mixture of styles," Shaw's "workmanship in fitting together these random elements . . . of the rough-and-ready sort appropriate to a type of drama not intended for close scrutiny."

Man and Superman (written 1901–02) has inspired a critical bibliography of immense proportions, with Shaw's own prefaces to the play and to the later *Back to Methuselah* among the most useful glosses. No textual study of the play exists, because Shaw has frightened off most textual critics through his own passion for accuracy in seeing his work through the press; however, James Redmond has noted in "A Misattributed Speech in *Man and Superman*" (*TLS*, 18 Jan. 1974) that Act I lines by Octavius run into a two-sentence speech which must be spoken by Ann Whitefield. The printing error has persisted into the now standard *Bodley Head Shaw*, as has a misprint in the preface (*Bodley* II, 494) quoting the *mille e tre* (a thousand and three) in the *Don Giovanni* "catalogue aria" of Leporello as "*mille etre* adventures" (Robertson Davies, *TLS*, 15 Feb. 1974). Such textual slips are rare in Shaw; however, it is inevitable that others will be identified.

For Shaw's use of the Don Juan myth good evaluations of the evidence are Oscar Mandel's *The Theatre of Don Juan* (1963), R. J. Blanch's (*RLV*, 1967), and Carl Mills's (*CL*, 1967). These (as well as many other publications) describe Shaw's inversion of the archetypal virile lover and seducer into the prey of the female, but none refer to earlier Shavian suggestions of the plot and theme, as does S. Weintraub (in *Shaw: Seven Critical Essays*, ed. N. Rosenblood, 1971), who examines both Shaw's 1887 autobiographical short story "Don Giovanni Explains" and 1883 novel *An Unsocial Socialist* as early working models for *Man and Superman*. Charles Loyd Holt's "Mozart, Shaw and *Man and Superman*" (*ShawR*, 1966) is a reliable investigation into how Shaw used the opera *Don Giovanni*, including close approximations of actual lines from the libretto, to arrive at his "deliberate inversion, . . . shaping *Man and Superman* out of the world's memory of Don Giovanni." Joseph Bentley (*ShawR*, 1968) goes even further by demonstrating that even the collapse of Tanner's resistance in the last act is an echo out of his mythic past, an allusion to the last act of *Don Giovanni*, where the statue gives the hero a final chance to repent before dragging him off to hell.

Numerous studies examine the theoretical basis of Shaw's play, the fullest of these being two by Carl Henry Mills, "Shaw's Debt to Lester Ward in *Man and Superman*" (*ShawR*, 1971), where sociologist Ward's "gynaeocentric" theory on female selection and evolution is seen as central to Shaw's ideas on Creative Evolution; and "Shaw's Theory of Creative Evolution" (*ShawR*, 1973), which examines the evolution of Shaw's thinking on the subject in general.

Shaw himself observed (Preface to *Back to Methuselah*) that his ingenuity in *Man and Superman* may have been counter-productive. "The effect was so vertiginous, apparently, that nobody noticed the new religion in the centre of the intellectual whirlpool." Louis Kronenberger in *The Thread of Laughter* (1952) refers to the Hell scene's "defects of logic, its perversities of temperament," and Berst (in *Art*) sees Shaw as compromising his argument through the very dramatic controls he exerts over his dialectic in the debate in Hell. "While the wit and drama render the cosmology vital, the philosophy seems more dramatic than sound, the beauty of the rhetorical pyrotechnics more satisfying than the logic of the discourse."

The standard critical study of *Man and Superman* may be Frederick P. W. McDowell's "Heaven, Hell and Turn-of-the-Century London: Reflections upon Shaw's *Man and Superman*" (*DramaS*, 1963), to which Crompton, Valency, Morgan, and others acknowledge indebtedness for its interpretations of the relationships between the frame play and the play-within-the-play. Much the same area is covered by J. L. Wisenthal (*MD*, 1971). Little has been done to examine Shaw's appendices to the play, "John Tanner's *The Revolutionist's Handbook and Pocket Companion* and *Maxims for Revolutionists*"; however, Charles A. Carpenter, in "Notes on Some Obscurities in 'The Revolutionist's Handbook'" (*ShawR*, 1970), has made a start toward rendering the topical allusions in the *Handbook* intelligible to modern readers, while Richard Ohmann's *Shaw: The Style and the Man* analyzes the prose of the *Handbook* as well as Shaw's method of developing "Tanner's" argument.

John Bull's Other Island (1904) has been receiving more stage and scholarly attention in recent years, after decades of undeserved neglect. Warren S. Smith (*ETJ*, 1951), writing on the preoccupation with salvation in the play despite its comedic texture, began its rescue from academic oblivion. The three archetypal leading male roles—the practical man, the romantic, and the saint—are, according to Smith, crucial to an understanding of Shavian drama, for overtones of them and of their final trio reappear throughout Shaw. (Edmund Wilson discussed the practical man-and-saint polarity in his "Bernard Shaw at Eighty" in *The Triple Thinkers*, 1938.) A study of Shaw's playwriting techniques using *John Bull's Other Island* as model is Jere Shanor Veilleux, "Shavian Drama: A Dialectical Convention for the Modern Theatre" (*TCL*, 1958), where the dialogue is examined in terms of the Socratic pattern of contradiction. But it was much longer before another sound study focused entirely on *John Bull* appeared—F. P. W. McDowell's "Politics, Comedy, Character and Dialectic: The Shavian World of *John Bull's Other Island*" (*PMLA*, 1967), which analyzes English and Irish types and the subjects of Shaw's satire. Books on G. B. S. have continued to neglect *John Bull*, although Valency provides an enlightening background analysis, Morgan in a chapter on the play roughly parallels points made in the McDowell article, and Wisenthal in *The Marriage of Contraries* examines this play of opposing temperaments as the first of Shaw's "in which characters are overtly symbolic."

Little research on the play exists in print. M. J. Sidnell (*MD*, 1968) extracts from Yeats's correspondence with Shaw and Lady Gregory over the Abbey rejection of the play engineered by Yeats, defending less Yeats's esthetic positions than his political ones justified by the later *Playboy* hysteria, but failing in the process to understand the comic exuberance in Shaw's satire. The Sidnell article has been revised and expanded in his "Hic and Ille: Shaw and Yeats," in *Theatre and Nationalism in Twentieth-century Ireland* (ed. Robert O'Driscoll, 1971), which prints seven letters from W. B. Y. to G. B. S.

Meisel's chapter on Irish romance reviews *John Bull*'s inheritance from (and satire upon) the "stage Irishman" farce, and Raymond S. Nelson (*ShawR*, 1970) suggests that the prototype for the unfrocked Father Keegan was not only Shaw's friend the modernist Catholic priest George Tyrrell, who was unfrocked in 1906—after the play— but also another Shaw friend, Edward Carpenter, whose unorthodox ideas and simple life had resulted in his leaving the Anglican priesthood. Much additional scholarship and speculation can be anticipated concerning *John Bull* as it moves toward recognition as a major Shavian play.

One of the handicaps in esteem that have faced *John Bull's Other Island* since it was succeeded by *Major Barbara* (written 1905) is that it was closely sandwiched in time between two of Shaw's most profound and provocative dramas. More scholarship and explication of high quality has been devoted to *Major Barbara* than to any other play by G. B. S. The texts have been examined scrupulously for hints of elusive meaning to be gleaned from changes in the printed versions or the later film script and from the much more substantial alterations made in manuscript as Shaw wrote the play. Crompton's chapter on the play (in earlier form published as "Shaw's Challenge to Liberalism," *PrS*, 1963) studies it from the standpoint of Shaw's cynicism about liberal idealism and utilizes among other Shaw manuscripts the first ("Derry") manuscript of the play (8/9/05) to define the character and philosophy of Andrew Undershaft, as he is portrayed with less subtlety in the earlier text. Bernard Dukore in *Shaw the Playwright* and earlier articles has also studied the manuscript and printed texts, and Sidney P. Albert (*ETJ*, 1968) examines how Act III was rewritten under the impetus of Gilbert Murray's criticisms and how much the play owes in characterization to Murray and the aristocratic family into which he had married. Albert enlarges understanding of Shaw's own perspectives toward the play in his "Shaw's Advice to the Players of *Major Barbara*" and "More Shaw Advice to the Players of *Major Barbara*," (*ThS*, 1969, 1970).

Studies of the complex origins of the play have added dimensions to its meaning. Albert has completed a lengthy essay on the play in terms of Euripides' *Bacchae*, a play Shaw knew in Murray's own adaptation, and has published another on the philosophical backgrounds of the play, "The Price of Salvation: Moral Economics in *Major Barbara*" (*MD*, 1971), and still another on the real-life distillery aspect of the play, " 'Letters of Fire against the Sky': Bodger's Soul and Shaw's Pub" (*ShawR*, 1968). Margery Morgan, as does Crompton in "Shaw's Debt," looks at the religious aspect of the play through the Nietzschean concept of Dionysius that Shaw knew from *The Birth of Tragedy* in "Shaw, Yeats, Nietzsche and the Religion of Art" (*Komos*, 1967) as well as in her *Shavian Playground* chapter on the play. Joseph W. Frank had earlier explored the idea of the play as religious allegory (*PMLA*, 1956); Stanley Weintraub has supplied a corroborative "Addendum" (*ShawR*, 1958) on the Church of St. Andrew Undershaft in London and its pertinent history; and in Weintraub's "Four Fathers for Barbara," *Directions in Literary Criticism* (ed. S. Weintraub and P. Young, 1973), the four munitions-maker antecedents for Andrew Undershaft are related to the character and the play, as are other probable sources and prototypes of one of Shaw's most challenging characters. Additional source studies of more limited scope but of great penetration are Julian B. Kaye's in *Shaw and Nineteenth Century Tradition*, where the Carlylean aspects of the play are demonstrated and Undershaft seen as possibly derived from "Plugson of Undershot," owner of a firm located in the parish of St. Dolly Undershot; David H. Bowman's "Shaw, Stead and the Undershaft Tradition" (*ShawR*, 1971), on the Andrew Carnegie element in Barbara's father; and J. L. Wisenthal's "The Underside of Undershaft: A Wagnerian Motif in *Major Barbara*" (*ShawR*, 1972), on Shaw's equation of Alberich with industrialists of the Krupp, Cadbury, and Lever variety—and thus with Undershaft.

Critical studies of the play as theater and as literature have been proliferating. One of the most provocative—and unflattering—remains Francis Fergusson's chapter in *The Idea of a Theater* (1949), "On Shavian Theatricality: The Platform and the Drawing-Room." More philosophical is Charles Frankel's "Efficient Power and Inefficient Virtue," in *Great Moral Dilemmas in Literature Past and Present* (ed. R. M. MacIver, 1956), which examines the way Shaw attempts to synthesize virtue and power. Barbara B. Watson's "Sainthood for Millionaires" (*MD*, 1968) takes up the same theme, seeing as Shaw's point that the world must be saved by its worldly saints and by worldly means; while B. F. Dukore (*MD*, 1966) again examines the problem of joining virtue to power, this time imaginatively via the working maxims of the six previous Andrew Undershafts as well as the laconic one ("Unashamed") of the seventh armaments czar, Barbara's father. The "Mephistopheles-Machiavelli" side of Undershaft is explained by Charles Berst (*PMLA*, 1968; also in his *Art*), who points out that "In his social role Undershaft is quite like Milton's Satan, forced by circumstance to make a religion of his surroundings. He is a prose picture of the assertion that 'The mind is its own place, and in itself / Can make a Heav'n of Hell, a Hell of Heav'n.' " Shifting literary metaphors to the Blakean, Berst goes on to suggest that the denouement is a "Marriage of Heaven and Hell." Still, few explanations of the play's dramatic and intellectual effectiveness improve upon two brilliant reviews of the first production—those by Desmond MacCarthy (rpt. in his *Court Theatre* and in his *Shaw*) and by Max Beerbohm (rpt. in *Around Theatres*). MacCarthy sees *Major Barbara* as "the first English play which has for its theme the struggle between two religions in one mind," and Beerbohm, in "Mr Shaw's Position," recants his own position on the stageability of Shavian drama by conceding that the Court Theatre production of *Barbara* had convinced him that he had read the plays without "theatrical imagination."

The fifth (and last) act of *The Doctor's Dilemma* (written 1906) has inspired much of the most interesting writing about the play. Crompton has published extracts from a British Museum manuscript first draft of the act as an appendix to his discussion of the backgrounds and composition of the play. Norbert F. O'Donnell (*ShawR*, 1959) examines Ridgeon's misunderstandings of art, love, and ethics, all three themes of the play, and all three of which lead him into assuming a medical dilemma where none existed. Alfred Turco is similarly concerned with the legitimacy of the dilemma in "Sir Colenso's White Lie" (*ShawR*, 1970), seeing Ridgeon's "ten men in a lifeboat" dilemma as moral posturing and a fabrication and the play as a black comedy in which the lovesick Ridgeon succeeds in killing his rival (for a woman) and discovers that he has—in his own words— "committed a purely disinterested murder." More general analyses are J. Percy Smith's in *The Image of the Work* (1955), which denies, however, Ridgeon's self-interest, and Margery Morgan's discussion in *The Shavian Playground*, which concludes that the play is "Shaw's tribute of loyalty to the socialist movement in all its vagaries—including the rascality of (Edward) Aveling, the suffering of Eleanor Marx, the dreams of the Pre-Raphaelites, the robust humor and power of the work of William Morris, his public dedication and private unhappiness, and the magnificence of Jane Morris at her husband's funeral—all absorbed into a remarkable aesthetic affirmation." The esthetic element—particularly the Pre-Raphaelite aspect—absorbs Elsie B. Adams in "The Unscrupulous Artist" chapter of *Bernard Shaw and the Aesthetes*, where Louis Dubedat, because of his amoral love life, personal charm (both of these equally applicable to the scientist Aveling), and cynical attitude toward his patrons, is identified with Dante Gabriel Rossetti. In a sidelight on this question Stanley Weintraub in *Beardsley: A Biography* (1967) suggests that Beardsley provided Shaw with Dubedat's profession, youthful genius, and fatal illness. As for the basic situation of the play, Martin Meisel sees not only a Shavian bow to Molière but to two Victorian dramatic genres, "Domestic Comedy" and Comedy of the Professions"; and Stanley Weintraub sees (in "The Embryo Playwright") characters and situations ripening for the play in the early novels (*TSLL*, 1960).

The medical side of the drama—Shaw wryly subtitled it a tragedy, writing about doctors and medicine in general—has elicited surprisingly little serious research and criticism, although Roger Boxill has devoted an entire book, *Shaw and the Doctors* (1969), to a thorough airing of the subject. That the medical profession did not take seriously his implicit and explicit injunctions to examine and heal itself must have irritated Shaw all his life.

The seldom performed—and at first censored—*The Shewing-Up of Blanco Posnet* (written 1909), which Shaw first subtitled *A Sermon in Crude Melodrama*, is seldom examined in Shaw studies apart from those particularly interested in his religious plays, where the impact of Tolstoy's *The Power of Darkness* is noted. Valency writes that Shaw's Western frontier allegory, despite its weaknesses, "has nevertheless aroused some scholarly interest," but the nontheological interest seems centered almost entirely in Meisel's study, where each of Shaw's plays is found to have some Victorian theatrical antecedent. The Bret Harte-David Belasco American mining camp melodramas are late nineteenth century in date but owe little to the contemporary English stage on which they sometimes appeared. The best account of its notorious first production—in Dublin to evade the Lord Chamberlain's suppression in London—is Dan H. Laurence's (*ShawR*, 1955) which includes comments by Yeats and a review by Joyce.

Getting Married (written 1907–08), although antedating *Blanco Posnet*, fits closely in Shaw's developing dramaturgy with the conversation-comedies which followed *Blanco Posnet, Misalliance* (written 1909) and *Fanny's First Play* (written 1910–11). "The *Getting Married* Controversy" (*ShawR*, 1966) reprints the exchanges between Shaw and Lord Alfred Douglas in *The Athenaeum*, which Douglas then edited, in which circulation motives may be surmised but in which Wilde's former intimate expressed his moral outrage about Shaw's views on marriage and divorce. The innovative nature of Shaw's playwriting technique in the play has inspired more scholarly interest than the social heresies, although these, too, have received attention, particularly since the newest phase of feminist activity. Eric Bentley in *Bernard Shaw* (1947) examines the "disquisitory" plays from the standpoint of the structural and thematic interrelationships, seeing one of their common but less obvious characteristics as their lack of protagonist. William Sharp (*ETJ*, 1959) and Stanley J. Solomon (*ShawR*, 1962) analyze the integration of theme and structure in Shavian discussion-drama. Alan J. Downer's "Shaw's First Play" (in *Shaw: Seven Critical Essays*) contrasts the techniques of *Widowers' Houses*—in point of time Shaw's first completed play—and *Getting Married*, which he sees as "the first completely Shavian play." Conversely, Margery Morgan's "The Greek Form Again: *Getting Married*" chapter of *The Shavian Playground* finds more that is Grecian than the classical unities the play observes, pointing especially to Aristophanic burlesque, in which are discovered tenuous Shavian affinities. (Other scholars, too, have located Aristophanic elements in various Shaw plays, just as Morgan and others have also seen *commedia dell'arte* elements in Shaw; although it is unlikely that he was free from their direct or indirect influence, claims about their impact seem exaggerated.)

Misalliance and *Fanny's First Play* have received far less scholarly attention, although the latter had Shaw's longest initial stage run in London and the former has become since Shaw's death one of his most successful plays in revival. B. C. Rosset in *Shaw of Dublin* sees in *Misalliance* more profound and disturbing biographical links with Shaw's family life in Dublin than the superficial ones noted by other biographers (often with Shaw's assistance) and suggests that Shaw may even have considered himself "daring" for having put them into print, making the play "his chief vehicle for transferring something of the fascinating drama of the Shaws of Dublin to the stage." Morgan (in *MD*, 1962, prior to book form) relates elements of the play to Shaw's reading of Granville' Barker's *The Madras House* in manuscript; B. F. Dukore, in "*The Madras House* Prefinished" (*ETJ*, 1972), printing Shaw's revised third act from the (University of Texas) manuscript written by Shaw to spur Barker to complete and produce the play, observes in effect that the relationship between plays may have been symbiotic. Dukore (in *Bernard Shaw, Playwright*) is one of the few critics to comment at length on *Fanny's First Play*, which opens and closes with a frame-play in which London critics, thinly disguised, scrutinize the play and are themselves caricatured by Shaw, an aspect of the play examined by C. A. Carpenter (*ShawR*, 1964).

Androcles and the Lion (written 1912) has been written about in depth primarily by researchers into Shaw's religious work (e.g.,

Smith, Weales, Abbott, Barr). It might be said of a number of Shaw plays, but especially of *Androcles*, that the best writing about it remains the original review by Desmond MacCarthy (*NewS*, 6 Sept. 1913, rpt. in *Shaw*), who noted his "discovery" after seeing the first production that the playwright's "most striking" intellectual qualities "spring from his being extraordinarily free from all forms of spiritual snobbery." Its origins in Victorian Christmas pantomimes are so palpable that Meisel devotes a chapter, "Christian Melodrama and Christmas Pantomime," entirely to the play, and Berst in his *Art* observes that "conceptually" it does not matter that "in a spiritual sense the happiness at the end is bogus: [that] if the Christians' cause has gained ground, it has not gained on its own merit." The Happy Ending is poetic justice, which pantomimes must have, but "in reality, the reformers are usually eaten [by the lions]." What is crucial is the interior of the parable. Little other serious study has been given to *Androcles*, although Valency finds interesting European analogues in Maeterlinck and in J. R. Planche's "fairy extravaganzas" as well as later in Anouilh. Even less research appears to have been accomplished on Shaw's *Dark Lady of the Sonnets* (written 1910), which has little subtext to explicate and about which the origins are clear from Shaw's lengthy preface. But an entire literature exists on Shaw and Shakespeare, to be examined in a later section.

Shaw's other short plays written in the first two decades of the century, from curtain-raisers to—as he rightly described them—"tomfooleries," have attracted little scholarly attention, although *The Admirable Bashville* (written 1902), because of its obvious derivation from the novel *Cashel Byron's Profession*, is discussed by Weintraub and Hogan; and the trivial *Passion, Poison and Petrifaction* (written 1905) has been examined provocatively by Paul Silverstein in "Barns, Booths, and Shaw" (*ShawR*, 1969) not only for its own brand of satire but as an anticipation of Ionesco-like absurdism. D. G. Dossot in *Shaw of Dublin* sees *The Fascinating Foundling* and *Press Cuttings* (both written 1909) and the many other plays and playlets of Shaw's in which a foundling is crucial or bastardy or doubtful parentage is involved (as in *Misalliance*) not as mere satirizing of an old plot device but as part of the playwright's compulsion to send a particular "biographical rabbit" through the "warrens" of his work—his alleged concerns about his mother's relationship with G. J. V. Lee, and thus with his own parentage. S. Weintraub has described the composition (and, in some cases, production) of the wartime playlets in *Journey to Heartbreak*, observing that one of them, *Annajanska; or The Bolshevik Empress* (written 1917), is an "embryonic suggestion" of *Saint Joan*. Bernard Dukore in *Bernard Shaw, Playwright* demonstrates that Shaw's claim to have permitted himself "variations" in the postwar *Jitta's Atonement* (written 1920–21), his free adaptation of his German translator Siegfried Trebitsch's *Frau Gittas Sühne*, is "disingenuous" since they "pervade and alter the entire play."

The scholarly literature on *Pygmalion* has been stimulated mainly by controversies over the arbitrariness or inevitability of Shaw's ironic unsentimental conclusion; analyses of its structure in general have often resulted from attempts to build a case for a particular thesis about the ending of the original play, the film script, or the musical version in which Shaw had no hand, although the adapter of the latter, Alan Jay Lerner, has described its text in *"Pygmalion* and *My Fair Lady"* (*ShawR*, 1956) as having in it "sixty percent of the original play." Whatever Shaw's contributions to the screenplay, the stage version remains the text by which to understand Shaw's methods and motives, for the exigencies of a different medium and audience required a different (as well as *ex post facto*) treatment, and Charles Berst (in *Art*) is correct to insist, in discussing the "tightness of context and economy of detail" which typify most Shavian dramatic patterns, that a good example of Shaw's "economy and aesthetic discipline is his elimination (in the pre-cinema text) of what might be the triumphal climax of *Pygmalion*—the Ambassador's party scene."

Eric Bentley in his *Bernard Shaw* has provided the standard analysis, perceiving the play as "a singularly elegant structure. . . . It is a good play by perfectly orthodox standards and needs no theory to defend it. It is Shavian, not in being made up of political or philosophic discussions, but in being based on the standard conflict of vitality and system, in working out this conflict through an inversion of romance, in bringing matters to a head in a battle of wills and words, in having an inner psychological action in counterpoint to the outer romantic action, in existing on two contrasted levels of mentality, both of which are related to the main theme, in delighting and surprising us with a constant flow of verbal music and more than verbal wit." Stanley J. Solomon (*ETJ*, 1964) defends Shaw's ending on structural grounds—that it is not "an arbitrary imposition of the author's temperament" for Shaw could not have intended a "sentimental and one-dimensional" play. Pygmalion must lose his Galatea for he has created (beyond his expectations?) a person with "independence of spirit and vitality of mind." Such examinations of the play—and this is the best of many—are often either implicit or explicit responses not only to the film or musical versions of the play but to the unfortunately influential article by Ronald Crane, *"Pygmalion*: Bernard Shaw's Dramatic Theory and Practice" (*PMLA*, 1951), which appears largely responsible for the respectability of the misconception that Shaw sanctioned the sentimental ending of the film and took his own epilogue as "something less than serious," a concept further explored by Bernard F. Dukore's " 'The Middleaged Bully and the Girl of Eighteen': The Ending They *Didn't* Film" (*ShawR*, 1971). Dukore here has had the opportunity to examine the film script, which Donald R. Costello in *The Serpent's Eye* (which both reviews the history of the film and prints portions of the dialogue) was able to reconstruct only from the printed screen version and a transcript of the sound track.

Crompton provides an excellent background study in his *Shaw*, emphasizing Shaw's unsentimental and unromantic characterization of Higgins. Recognizing Shaw's irony, Berst observes (in *Art*), "As Eliza misconstrues her predicament as a seduction peril, Higgins oversimplifies the situation as a fascinating experiment. The Cinderella dreams and Pamela fears have their counterpart in the Pygmalion obsession." Similarly, Crompton concludes that the insistence upon having Eliza and Higgins "end as lovebirds" shows "how popular sentiment will ignore any degree of incompatibility between a man and a woman once it has entertained the pleasant fancy of mating them." Freudian analyses—supported by Shaw's own state-ments, in and out of the play—suggest a further complication, that Higgins' mother-complex has disabled him from marital aspirations; and Philip Weissmann, in *Creativity in the Theatre* (1965), relates the play to oedipal feelings from Shaw's own childhood and its writ-ing to the death of Shaw's mother and his contemporaneous—and futile—erotic pursuit of Mrs. Patrick Campbell. Henry R. Richardson (*PsyR*, 1956) classifies Higgins' problem as a "Pygmalion-reaction"— the suppression of love through esthetics. But the critical controversy is for that reason alone likely to continue.

Pygmalion has also attracted studies of language, in particular John A. Mills in *Language and Laughter: Comic Diction in the Plays of Bernard Shaw* (1969) and Fred Mayne in *The Wit and Satire of Bernard Shaw* (1967). Joseph Saxe's *Bernard Shaw's Phonetics: A Comparative Study of Cockney Sound-Changes* (1936) is the most exhaustive analysis of the flavorsome diction of Eliza and her father.

There are numerous accounts, anecdotal and otherwise, of the events leading up to the writing and production of *Pygmalion*, both in Shavian biographies and memoirs and in biographies of Mrs. Shaw, Mrs. Patrick Campbell, and Herbert Beerbohm Tree. Richard Huggett's *The Truth about Pygmalion* (1970) is an entertaining journalistic potpourri of all of them.

Heartbreak House (written 1916–17) is one of Shaw's most com-plex creations, with its origins literary and philosophical as well as rooted in actuality. Arthur Nethercot, in "Zeppelins over Heartbreak House" (*ShawR*, 1966), describes the events over Ayot St. Lawrence on the night of 30 September–1 October 1916 that provided G. B. S. with the apocalyptic climax and conclusion to the play; and Stanley Weintraub in *Journey to Heartbreak* (1971) traces not only the de-velopment of the play but Shaw's own transition from the optimism that had generated *Pygmalion* to the despair of the war years that culminates in *Heartbreak House* and the two major plays that fol-lowed. In the process Shaw's own words in his preface to the play (1919) that "when the play was begun not a shot had been fired" and his equivalent words to Archibald Henderson quoted in *Playboy and Prophet* (1932), both of which had caused the composition of the play to be ascribed to 1913–16, are shown to be at odds with the facts. Actual writing appears to have been begun on 4 March 1916 and completed late in May 1917; but it is possible that Shaw's thoughts about the play began to form on his seeing Chekhov's plays in a Moscow Art Theatre touring production in London in 1913, the inspiration for the subtitle, *A Fantasia in the Russian Manner on English Themes*. Michael Mendelsohn (*ShawR*, 1963) sees the play as a redistillation of *The Cherry Orchard* (and earlier Chekhov plays); while Robert Corrigan (*ShawR*, 1959) sees the play as a pessimistic view of the contemporary scene.

Other literary and philosophical approaches to the play are by Louis Crompton in *Shaw*, where "the spirit behind *Heartbreak House*" is thought to be Old Testament–Carlylean, particularly the books of Micah, Jeremiah, and Exodus; by Stanley Weintraub (*MD*, 1972—a revised and augmented version of an earlier essay in *Ariel*,

1970, and in *Journey to Heartbreak*) who views the play as Shaw's attempt to provide a *Lear*-dimension of echoes and reverberations; and by Daniel J. Leary (*MD*, 1972), who sets out to show Shaw's connections with the "whole mythopoetic content of English art" with special reference to Blake. (Despite Leary's essay, the earlier by Fiske noted under *The Devil's Disciple* and Julian Kaye's *Shaw and the Nineteenth Century Tradition*, Blake's impact upon G. B. S. remains insufficiently studied.) A pregnant observation by Colin Wilson in his *Bernard Shaw: A Reassessment* about the philosophical tone of the play is that it "anticipates Eliot's *Waste Land* in its tone and in its analysis of the problem of a civilization undermined by triviality and 'nihlism.' But Eliot arrived at the conclusion that the answer lies in a return to traditional Christianity, and Shaw was quite certain that it did not." In *Homage to Daniel Shays: Collected Essays 1952–1972* (1972), Gore Vidal, however, sees a curious paradox emerging from Shaw's despair. "*Heartbreak House* is a moonlight play, suitable for recapturing the past. Elegy and debate cancel one another out. Nor is the work really satiric, an attack on 'folly and worthlessness.' These people are splendid and unique, and Shaw knows it. He cannot blow them up at the end."

The dimension of actuality in the play is noted in suggestions for the prototypes of its leading characters. Crompton puts forward Mrs. Patrick Campbell for Hesione (as Shaw had confided to her), Cunninghame Graham for her husband Hector (who has also been thought to contain elements of Shaw's womanizing Fabian friend Hubert Bland), and businessman Hudson Kearley (Lord Devonport) for "Boss" Mangan (this also established from Shaw's correspondence). His suggestion that Shaw's idealistic city-planner friend Ebenezer Howard is the basis for the weak Liberal dreamer Mazzini Dunn seems tenuous. Weintraub adds actress Lena Ashwell's father Captain Pocock, whom Shaw identified as Captain Shotover (Julian Kaye notes Carlyle's Plugson of Undershot); and Virginia and Leonard Woolf as the imperious Lady Ariadne Utterword and her absent colonial governor husband Sir Hastings; and Weintraub also sees the Webbs's rented country house in Sussex, where the Shaws and Woolfs weekended in 1916, as the original of *Heartbreak House* itself.

Critical perspectives upon the play have been numerous and at wide variance with one another. Stark Young's disappointed review of a thirties revival (rpt. in *Immortal Shadows*, 1938), had some influence in inhibiting productions; and Mary McCarthy's essay on the same performance (rpt. in *Sights and Spectacles*, 1956), in which she discerned "the terror of the play's lost author, who could not, in conscience, make his story come out right, or indeed, come out at all," was misunderstood at the time as being in the same vein, although its aim was to stress the ominousness in the play. Soon afterward this was understood. *Heartbreak House* found its time in the shattered world that was the legacy of the Second World War.

Frederick P. W. McDowell's "Technique, Symbol and Theme in Shaw's *Heartbreak House*" (*PMLA*, 1953) remains the standard examination of Shaw's dramatic devices, improving upon William Irvine's explication of the allegory in *The Universe of G. B. S.* A useful supplement is Michael W. Kaufman's "The Dissonance of Dialectic: Shaw's *Heartbreak House*" (*ShawR*, 1970), which analyzes the structural elements as possibly derived from the musical fantasia and sees the drama as evolving "from the decacaphony produced by the [ten] counterpointed characters. . . . Form and meaning coalesce." Both Margery Morgan (in *The Shavian Playground*) and Berst (in *Bernard Shaw and the Art of Drama*) see *Heartbreak House* as a dream-play, an insight which has come strikingly late to critics, since Ellie Dunn falls asleep at the beginning of the play and Hesione Hushabye (her charactonym itself should have awakened readers and viewers) dozes offstage, while Boss Mangan is put into a hypnotic sleep in a later act; and talk of sleep and dreams permeates the dialogue. The dream atmosphere helps explain the dislocations and the illogic others have seen in the play and gives weight to "mad" old Captain Shotover's cursing "the happiness of yielding and dreaming instead of resisting and doing, the sweetness of the fruit that is going rotten." Perhaps the Strindbergian vein in the play should be examined.

Viewing the play from a theatrical angle, Harold Clurman (*TDR*, 1961) finds subtleties in characterization and meaning that may escape a purely literary reading. D. C. Coleman (*DramaS*, 1966–67) looks at the play from the perspective of a work "strikingly similar in setting and structure," Edward Albee's *Who's Afraid of Virginia Woolf?* (1962). With surprisingly little strain Coleman elaborates on his thesis that "the action of both [plays] advances by means of domestic sport, called by Albee 'fun and games.'" Thus the suggestion advanced in *Journey to Heartbreak* of a Virginia Woolf component to *Heartbreak House* becomes a strange irony.

The five-play cycle *Back to Methuselah* (written 1917–20) is likely to elicit more research and criticism than almost any other Shavian play; however, the aggregate is currently small. The beginnings of research into Shaw's sources were in H. M. Geduld's six-volume variorum edition of the play submitted as a doctoral thesis at Birkbeck College, University of London (1961). From it Geduld has taken two useful articles: "The Textual Problem in Shaw" (*ShawR*, 1962) concerns the need to reconcile changes made silently in subsequent printings of the play as well as to correct errors in the American editions G. B. S. did not proof. "The Lineage of Lilith" (*ShawR*, 1964) seeks to explain where Shaw sought his information on the apocryphal character who appears only in the final pages of "As Far as Thought Can Reach" (v) and his motives in introducing her "during the last moments before the final curtain." H. M. Geduld provides a useful stage history of the first performances in England (*MD*, 1959), including newspaper accounts, letters, and reminiscences of participants. (Lawrence Langner's *The Magic Curtain* and *G. B. S. and the Lunatic* detail the American opening from the perspective of the Theatre Guild management.) B. G. Knepper's "*Back to Methuselah* and the Utopian Tradition" (Diss. Nebraska 1967), relates the play to the utopias of Plato, More, Swift, and Bulwer-Lytton, the latter material published by Knepper as "Shaw's Debt to the Coming Race" (*JML*, 1971). This science-fiction aspect of *Methuselah*, its origins and its impact upon subsequent writers in the genre, is the major, although not the only, theme of scholars in the "Shaw and Science Fiction" issue of *ShawR* (1973), ed. John R. Pfeiffer.

That Shaw may have received his ideas about death resulting from "discouragement" in "The Tragedy of an Elderly Gentleman" (IV) from Sir Francis Galton as well as from Bulwer-Lytton is one of the theses advanced by Crompton in *Shaw the Dramatist*; while Margery Morgan in "*Back to Methuselah*: the Poet and the City" (*E&S*, 1960, rpt. in *The Shavian Playground*) analyzes the cycle largely in terms of Plato's *Republic* and Swift's *Gulliver's Travels*, cautioning that "Once we cease to be deluded by the fable of longevity," which serves only as a vehicle for the play's essential structure, the cycle becomes not a "straggling chronicle-play" but a "total image of man." Much has been done on a dissertation level on mythic elements in the play, but the only useful study in print in this area is Richard Foster and Daniel J. Leary's "Adam and Eve: Evolving Archetypes in *Back to Methuselah*" (*ShawR*, 1961). Weintraub's *Journey to Heartbreak* traces *Methuselah*'s use of contemporary people and events and the evolution of the play from idea to four-play cycle and then to five-play cycle. As Shaw often pointed out, he was the best authority on himself, and the long preface to the play, incorporating elements from lectures and lay sermons delivered as early as 1906, remains the most important critical commentary. It is supplemented by Shaw's 1944 Postscript to the Oxford World's Classics edition of the play (1945). Several of the addresses which enunciated the theories Shaw would dramatize are printed in W. S. Smith's *The Religious Speeches of Bernard Shaw* and Dan H. Laurence's *Platform and Pulpit* or extracted in *Journey to Heartbreak*.

Saint Joan (written 1923) is the subject of a considerable critical literature. Its initial reception and performance history have been documented in detail. Alice Griffin (*ShawR*, 1955) extracts press reaction to the first New York production and two subsequent revivals, and Irving McKee (*Shavian*, 1964) also surveys the 1923–24, 1936, and 1939 American productions. E. J. West (*QJS*, 1954) reviews English as well as American productions and critiques. Daniel C. Gerould (*ShawR*, 1964) examines French press reaction to the Paris premiere in 1925 as well as the continuing reputation and influence of the play in France.

Fidelity to or departure from history, chronicle, legend, and religion in the play has been scrutinized from a variety of perspectives. An early attacker was Shaw's old friend John Mackinnon Robertson, once a declared "Rationalist," who disputed the veracity of Shaw's portrayal in a small and small-minded book, *Mr Shaw and "The Maid"* (1925) and was upheld by T. S. Eliot (*Criterion*, 1926), an ironic position in the light of Eliot's later cribbing from *Saint Joan* for his *Murder in the Cathedral*. A denunciation similar to Robertson's was published by another Shaw friend, Charles Sarolea, as "Has Mr Shaw Understood Joan of Arc?" (*Eng. Rev.*, 1926), where Shaw is accused of making a brilliant play by turning a pious, mystical maid into a heretic; while J. van Kan (*FortR*, 1 July 1925) denies that Joan could be considered a premature Protestant. The best balanced and most informed analysis of Shaw's treatment of the historical Joan remains that of the Dutch medieval historian Johan Huizinga, originally in *De Gids* (1935) and later in English translation in *Men and Ideas* (1959). "The task that Shaw has set himself," Huizinga observes, "approximates the highest task the human mind has succeeded, a few times, in accomplishing: the creation of tragedy from history."

More recent studies of the play as history include Hans Stoppel's examination of assertive mystics (*ES*, 1955) and William Searle's "Shaw's Saint Joan as 'Protestant' " (*ShawR*, 1972), the latter describing Shaw's Joan as "irrationalist" and "quite as much of an absolutist as her judges." Crompton reviews the historical sources Shaw appears to have used in addition to the T. Douglas Murray translation of Quicherat's transcription of the trial records, making a strong case for the *Catholic Encyclopaedia* (1910) section on "Inquisition" as the basis for the Inquisitor's rationalizations. A cautionary approach to *Saint Joan* and sainthood from the standpoint of contemporary production is Albert Bermel's "The Virgin as Heretic," in *Contradictory Characters* (1973), which warns that overly reverent direction has been turning what Shaw had written into an "anti-Shaw play. . . . If the play is to have its effect, the audience must feel the force of Joan as Shaw conceived it. To start with, they must take her as a nuisance. A heroic nuisance, to be sure, . . . but a fanatical woman who gives her friends and enemies alike no peace."

The play as tragedy—classical, modern, or "Shavian"—has been the subject of several studies. John Fielden sums up the evidence (*TCL*, 1957), concluding that the playwright aimed at classical tragedy, while Louis Martz (in *Tragic Themes in Western Literature*, 1955), maintains that although this may have been Shaw's intention, he reaches only "the very rim of tragedy." However, Stanley J. Solomon (*MD*, 1964) defines the play not in Aristotelian terms but as pre-Brechtian "epic tragedy," explaining that "The chronicle structure becomes necessary to the epic play in order to build up *both* forces of contention to formidable size, not just to increase the hero's reputation. . . . The scope of the material handled in the epic play is generally of greater social significance than that of the tragedy, which is generally concerned with the fall of a single person."

Other studies of Shaw's attitudes toward tragedy lean heavily upon his principles in the Preface to *Saint Joan* and his practice in the play. Sylvan Barnet, in "Bernard Shaw on Tragedy" (*PMLA*, 1956), questions whether Shaw's Life Force concept is compatible with the ideas of tragedy. Critics examining the play as tragedy inevitably point to Shakespearean models as well as Greek ones, Shaw himself observing the need to save the Maid from the Bard's scurrilous and jingoistic portrayal of her as a witch. Here Frederick S. Boas's "Joan of Arc in Shakespeare, Schiller and Shaw" (*SQ*, 1951) is an authoritative expansion of Shaw's own prefatory remarks on the subject.

How the idea to write a St. Joan play matured in Shaw is the subject of S. Weintraub's introduction to his edition of the play in the Bobbs-Merrill series (1971); and his "Bernard Shaw's Other Saint Joan" (*SAQ*, 1965) illuminates a living prototype, T. E. Lawrence, whose person and personality intruded into Shaw's life the year the play was written. Shaw's state of mind as he prepared the play for production is best seen in Lawrence Langner's *G. B. S. and the*

Lunatic (1963), where a chapter details Shaw's long-distance involvement in the first production of the play (by the Theatre Guild in New York), with much useful biographical and background material, including Shaw letters and cables. Shaw's writing of a screenplay version in the 1930's is the subject of the introduction to *Saint Joan: A Screenplay* (ed. B. F. Dukore, 1968), which includes the full text as well as alternate matter. The attempted censorship of the script led to Shaw's withdrawal from the project. (The film was finally produced posthumously, with a grotesquely warped script by Graham Greene, whose theology apparently was passport to noncensorship.) Shaw's own protest, "*Saint Joan* Banned: Film Censorship in the United States," appeared in the *New York Times* (14 Sept. 1936) and the *London Mercury* (Oct. 1936). Harry W. Rudman provides a survey of the film censorship problem as it related to Shaw (*ShawR*, 1958).

Criticism of the play has usually taken shape from a particular approach based upon Joan, her faith, or the dramatic form into which Shaw put her triumph and travail. Several excellent, and brief, critiques avoid compartmentalizing the play. Edmund Wilson's early review of the published play ("Bernard Shaw since the War," *The New Republic*, 27 Aug. 1924) observes that "what is unexpected in Shaw" is that "we find the forces of tradition and authority represented as equally intelligent and morally admirable with the heretic and rebel" and not left with "the reassuring inference that the catastrophe of Joan—like the disillusionment of Major Barbara or the embitterment of Vivie Warren—is merely a sacrifice which will bear fruit in a more intelligent program of social reconstruction." Desmond MacCarthy's review of the London premiere (*NewS*, 5 & 12 Apr. 1924; rpt. in his *Shaw*) notes this aspect as one of the two extraordinary intellectual merits of the play, which he sees as "the force and fairness with which the case of her opponents is put" as well as "the startling clarity with which each one states it;" and "the intensity of its religious emotion and the grasp the playwright shows of the human pathos of one who is filled with it, as well as . . . her immunity from requiring anything like pity." An unusual reaction to the New York opening—primarily because of its source, another major playwright—was that of Luigi Pirandello, who wrote in the *New York Times Sunday Magazine* (13 Jan. 1924) of the "half-humorous melancholy which is peculiar to the disillusioned idealist. Shaw has always had too keen a sense of reality not to be aware of the conflict between it and his social and moral ideals."

Criticism from the start has fixed often upon the relevance of the Epilogue, about which even some of Shaw's admirers have complained, William Irvine (in *Universe*) labeling it "a vulgarization and a lengthy elucidation of the obvious." But among the most cogent later appraisals of the play is that of Gerald Weales in *Religion in Modern English Drama* (1961), who includes a staunch defense of the Epilogue, with its ambivalences and ironies, as the "heart" of the drama, dependent "for its irony on the Shavian assumption that Joan's death is an unnecessary horror. Yet for Joan the Catholic, her death is not a misfortune, but a triumph." J. I. M. Stewart's Shaw chapter in *Eight Modern Writers* (1961) considers *Joan* "conceivably the finest and most moving English drama since *The Winter's Tale* or

The Tempest." And A. N. Kaul in *The Action of English Comedy: Studies in the Encounter of Abstraction and Experience from Shakespeare to Shaw* (1970)—in effect a response to Martz—sees *Joan* as "the tragedy of an historical hero rather than a saint." Some critics have complained of lapses in taste in Shaw's prose poetry, particularly where Joan is given lines deemed too sophisticated for a young country girl, criticism better applied to a realistic or naturalistic play. The most apt response appears to be that of Arthur Mizener in "Poetic Drama and the Well-Made Play" (*English Institute Essays 1949*, 1965), where *Saint Joan* is described as having—"like the work of all great poets—the inexhaustible fascination of thought and feeling dramatically suspended in a controlled medium. . . . Every great moment in the play echoes the whole play, exactly as do the great moments in a poem."

Interesting special approaches include that of S. John Macksoud and Ross Altman (*QJS*, 1971), who analyze the play's dialogue according to the principles of Kenneth Burke's *Philosophy of Literary Form* to explain how Shaw succeeds in "making the audience tolerant of heresy." From the rhetorical to the political is a small jump, and from the latter perspective some of the most curious scrutinies of the play occur. Alick West in *A Good Man Fallen among Fabians* sees Joan through a Marxist lens, finding the saint of the Epilogue a violation of the revolutionary spirit of the first six scenes. Arland Ussher in the perspicacious and underrated *Three Great Irishmen: Shaw, Yeats, Joyce* (1952) sees Joan as "an anticipation of the superhumanity which, in Shaw's biological vision, is to replace man in an unforeseeable future. She is an unhappy Trotskyist—whose place, unfortunately, is before the Stalinist firing squads." Yet the play, paradoxically, has been highly successful in print and performance in Russia, A. Obraztsova very likely echoing the Soviet position in her *Dramatturgicheskii metod Bernarda Shou* (1965)—that Joan, coming from the lower orders, is "a people's heroine," with "her strength as the strength of the people, and her reason as the reason of the people."

A convenient gathering of much useful criticism and research is *Saint Joan Fifty Years After: 1923/24–1973/74* (ed. S. Weintraub, 1973), which includes a number of the critiques noted above* as well as other approaches to the play.

A start toward textual study of *Saint Joan* is made in the Bobbs-Merrill edition of the play (ed. S. Weintraub) with the first page of the Preface, where the editor notes that Shaw after referring in the first (1924) printing to "obscure heroines who have disguised themselves as men to serve as soldiers" silently substituted for one of them (in the 5th impression)—the "Chevalier d'Eon"—a reference instead to the even more obscure Catalina de Erauso. Shaw had discovered that the Chevalier—a French secret agent—was actually a man who, depending on the assignment, dressed as either man or woman, but had been thought by the English to be a woman. A minor matter, yet it is another indication—witness Redmond's *TLS* note on *Man and Superman*—that Shaw's texts need closer scrutiny.

---

* Pirandello, MacCarthy, Wilson, van Kan, Huizinga, Robertson, Eliot, Sarolea, A. West, Ussher, E. J. West, Martz, Stoppel, Fielden, Stewart, Gerould, Obraztsova, Weintraub, Kaul.

The Apple Cart (written 1929) broke a long playwriting hiatus for Shaw and was a box office success, despite the mixed press that has continued through each revival. Although the first of Shaw's political fantasies, it was preceded by the highly political and controversial *Gospel of the Brothers Barnabas* (Pt. 2) in the *Methuselah* cycle, which mixed political prophecy and satire with immediate postwar reality. That *The Apple Cart*, too, has its origin in the wartime atmosphere of 1914–18 is observed by S. Weintraub in *Journey to Heartbreak*; while G. Wellwarth in "Gattie's Glass of Water" (*ShawR*, 1969) expands our knowledge of the man after whom Shaw's "Breakages, Ltd." concept in the play was fashioned, Shaw having identified Alfred Gattie and told part of the story in his preface. A possible source for the play in another play is the subject of Margery Morgan's "Two Varieties of Political Drama: *The Apple Cart* and Granville Barker's *His Majesty*" (*Shavian*, 1962; and *The Shavian Playground*). Reliable criticism of the play is rare, as most books on Shaw's dramaturgy stop with *Saint Joan* and few critiques appear in the journals. As a result Edmund Wilson's paragraphs in "Bernard Shaw at Eighty" (also in *The Triple Thinkers*) remain valuable as do Eric Bentley's in his *Bernard Shaw*; and, among later studies, McDowell's " 'The Eternal against the Expedient': Structure and Theme in Shaw's *The Apple Cart*" (*MD*, 1959) expertly relates the play to earlier Shavian themes and shows how the developing new themes are dramatized with "technical dexterity and dialectical skill." That it is Shaw's best comedy, as Colin Wilson has declared in *Religion and the Rebel* (1957), is nevertheless an overstatement, although it is likely to find a higher place in the Shavian canon as the later plays are more fully explored.

Among the more curious pieces on *The Apple Cart*, more a footnote to the play than criticism, is Lord Altrincham's "Reflections on *The Apple Cart*" (*National and Eng. Rev.*, 1958), which examines Shaw's political views and speculates upon what would have happened had King Edward VII adopted King Magnus' strategy with his ministers.

The making of *Too True to Be Good* (written 1931) is described in Weintraub's *Private Shaw and Public Shaw* (1963), where "Private Shaw"—T. E. Lawrence—is shown to have had a direct hand in the development of the "Private Meek" role, which travesties his service situation. Weintraub's "The Two Sides of 'Lawrence of Arabia': Aubrey and Meek" (*ShawR*, 1964) supplements the findings in *Private Shaw* by explaining *Too True* as in part an analysis of Lawrence's motives and nature, which both he and G. B. S. understood to represent T. E. L.'s duality, with Meek the surface image, and Aubrey Bagot the deeply disturbed inner T. E. L. Both Norbert O'Donnell (*PMLA*, 1957) and E. E. Stokes (*ShawR*, 1965) examine Bunyan as a major force in Shaw's intellectual development—with special reference to *Too True* (with its Bunyanesque Sergeant), where Stokes sees Shaw giving Bunyan contemporary application, while O'Donnell sees Shaw as "Shavianizing" Bunyan to "present his own views under the guise of championing those of others." Another Shaw-Bunyan study of note is Scott McMillin's (*ShawR*, 1966), a close study of a copy of *The Life and Death of Mr Badman* "with copious annotations in Shaw's hand" that demonstrates that Shaw's admiration for the writer must have been founded on *The Pilgrim's Progress* alone.

Too True has been given short shrift by critics, although revivals have demonstrated a stageability and relevance not apparent to its earliest reviewers. The only useful extended analysis of the play remains McDowell's " 'The Pentecostal Flame' and 'the Lower Centers' " (*ShawR*, 1959), which explains the apparently diffuse play as evidence of Shaw's increasing interest in stylization yet sees it as a dramatic unity, belying the assertion of The Microbe at the close of the first act that although the play was now over, the characters would discuss it for two more acts.

Little of consequence can be noted regarding two one-act Shavian plays of the early 1930's, *Village Wooing* (written 1933) and *The Six of Calais* (written 1934), although S. Weintraub reminds in *Journey to Heartbreak* that the latter playlet owes its origins to Shaw's journey to Flanders as war correspondent in 1917.

On the Rocks (written 1933), although seldom performed, has elicited a considerable although only fitfully illuminating bibliography, McDowell calling it (*ETJ*, 1961) "one of the more satisfying of Shaw's later plays" and "a coda to *Heartbreak House*." On the other hand, Paul Hummert (*Drama Critique*, 1959, incorporated into his *Bernard Shaw's Marxian Romance*) sees Marxist thinking so predominant "that the great playwright even sacrifices his usually fine dramaturgy to economics, resulting in a poor but important play," indeed the "most cynical and vicious of Shaw's plays." Few other critiques of the play apart from general assessment of the "political extravaganzas" of this period of Shaw's output merit consideration; and among general books on Shavian drama only the "Eschatological Plays" chapter of Morgan's *Shavian Playground* covers this period with any thoroughness, Morgan ending with the striking Genet-like concept of a "true perception" inherent in the political plays from *The Apple Cart* through the 1930's—"that the power enjoyed by leaders of men is like an actor's power, equally dependent on a public stage and the imaginative investment of massed humanity in the figures that perform on it. This is not only the culmination of Shaw's long concern with idealism; it is the furthest reach of his understanding of the relation of his own identity as dramatist to his political mission: that he had come to understand political realities as themselves forms of theatre; and to see the fate of democracy, and humanity's control of its own destiny, as dependent on men's understanding of the determining part that the audience plays in the theatrical event."

The Simpleton of the Unexpected Isles: A Vision of Judgment (written 1934), its setting the product of a Shaw voyage to New Zealand and its eugenic and apocalyptic thesis the culmination of interwar years despair, has been seen largely as a failure, Shaw even replying to the assertion of Joseph Wood Krutch in *The Nation* (6 March 1935) that the play was meaningless vaudeville, like other recent Shaw plays, with a lengthy rejoinder in the *Malvern Festival Book*, 1935 (rpt. West's *Shaw On Theatre* and *The Bodley Head Bernard Shaw*, 6). McDowell (*MD*, 1960) sees the play as lacking "an adequate center—a commanding protagonist" but finds a coherence to the whole in the form of an "ideological rather than a purely dramatic organization." Daniel Leary also visualizes the play as more a drama of ideas than anything else Shaw had yet put on the stage. He describes the play (*ETJ*, 1972) as "a dialectic of inept evolution and allegorical timelessness. The synthesis . . . is not despair but an open-ended Nothing."

The ebullient *Millionairess* (written 1932–34), subtitled "A Jonsonian Comedy," has, surprisingly, been examined in print only glancingly from the standpoint of Jonsonian comedy and in fact hardly examined at all. (A long aside in Albert H. Silverman's fine "Bernard Shaw's Shakespeare Criticism," *PMLA*, 1957, looks at the play as Jonsonian "moralistic satire.") Although critics should have been teased by the curious existence of two endings for the play (both printed), one for communist countries and another (the standard conclusion) for noncommunist countries, this oddity has provoked little discussion. Dukore, in *Bernard Shaw, Playwright*, observes that Shaw in his old age thus had done "what his Marxist critics had since virtually the beginning of his career asked him to do, provide an upbeat ending." But his earlier stratagems prove by this experiment to have been "artistically far more rewarding." Hummert's *Shaw's Marxian Romance* ignores the perverse alternative ending and devotes its *Millionairess* space to a discussion of the pro-Mussolini "Preface on Bosses."

The relatively minor *Cymbeline Refinished* (written 1936), Shaw's provision of an alternative ending for one of Shakespeare's last successful plays, has evoked scholarly interest because of its associations with the Bard and with critical controversies concerning Shaw's ambivalent attitudes toward him. In *Studies in Honor of T. W. Baldwin* (ed. Don Cameron Allen, 1958), Rudolph Stamm reviews the history of Shaw's attitudes toward the play and toward contemporary performances, including correspondence about the Irving (Lyceum) production with Ellen Terry, concluding with an assessment of the "refinishing" and of Shaw's virtues and limitations as a Shakespeare critic. (He treats the latter aspect more fully in *SJW*, 1958.) Earlier E. J. West had analyzed the "refinishing" from approximately the same angles (*TA*, 1950), using the same background material, but analyzing the Shavian fifth act in greater detail. Dukore, in *Bernard Shaw, Playwright*, has also compared the original with the suggested replacement, concluding that Shaw's abridgments and alterations are "in order to make the action less unbelievable, and this negative phrase is purposeful. In comedy the preposterous may be accepted if treated as obviously comic." Edwin Wilson anthologized the *Cymbeline* material—reviews, letters, and the act itself—in *Shaw on Shakespeare* (1961), which includes all the major (and much of the minor) Shavian statements on the Bard with the exception of the 78 manuscript pages of an 1884 lecture to Furnivall's New Shakspere Society on *Troilus and Cressida*, since published in the "Shaw/ Shakespeare" issue of *ShawR* (1971). This issue also includes critiques and a useful Shaw-Shakespeare bibliographical checklist by John Rodenbeck. Chronologically the last word is Jerry Lutz's thin *Pitchman's Melody: Shaw about "Shakespear"* (1974), which con-

cludes, unsurprisingly, that for Shaw—missionary and progenitor of
the new drama—Shakespeare was "the means, not end."

Geneva (written and revised 1936–38; further revised 1946) was
Shaw's final contemporary political play, one that embroiled him in
controversy not only with the critics but prior to production with
Theatre Guild director Lawrence Langner. Langner published his
side of the story and his exchange of letters with Shaw (which led to
rewriting parts of the play Langner—with reason—found offensive)
in *The Magic Curtain* (1951). An entire monograph-length study has
since been published on the play, G. E. Pilecki's *Shaw's "Geneva"*
(1965), which examines the evolution of the text through its successive revisions (to keep up with affairs in Europe). Susan C. Stone
(*ShawR*, 1973) attempts to disprove charges that in the play Shaw
drew an apologia for strongmen in his belief that they were a necessary (and temporary) expedient en route to the Superman, or the
ideal society of the future. To Stone the Hitler, Mussolini, and Franco
figures are antiheroes—defective dictators, uncurbed because our social institutions are stagnant and powerless.

"*Geneva* is as close to Aristophanic comedy as any Shaw play gets,"
Morgan has written in *The Shavian Playground*. "The fact may be
connected with the publication in 1933 of [his friend] Gilbert Murray's *Aristophanes*, dedicated to G. B. S." Aristophanic tendencies in
Shaw long predating the Murray book are seen in Robert R. Speck-
hard's two studies, "Shaw and Aristophanes: How the Comedy of
Ideas Works" and "Shaw and Aristophanes: Symbolic Marriage and
the Magical Doctor Cook in Shavian Comedy" (*ShawR*, 1965); however, these do not invalidate the thesis that later Aristophanic impetus to Shavian drama may have resulted from the 1933 book. Sister
M. Corona Sharp took another look at the dramaturgical side of the
play (*ShawR*, 1962), using the term *mask* to explain the ironic dialectic structure of the play—that "the catchwords and ambitions of each
character are his or her individual mask; while the characters themselves are masks of human beings; and finally, the whole political
game is a giant mask worn over the face of humanity." The "political
game" which formed the living and shifting background of the play is
described in S. Weintraub's *The Last Great Cause: The Intellectuals
and the Spanish Civil War* (1968), where Shaw, during the period of
the writing of the play, is shown as one of the "Aloof Olympians" of
literature who claimed to stand above the battle. ("Spain must choose
for itself: it is not really your business.")

Shaw's last prewar play was *In Good King Charles's Golden Days*
(written 1938–39, revised 1946), which shifted his dramatizations of
ways by which the world might be better governed backward in time
to the period of Charles II. J. M. Keynes, in "G. B. S. and Isaac
Newton" (in *G. B. S. 90*, ed. S. Winsten, 1946), observes that Shaw
places the action of the play in 1680 and "with wild departure from
the known facts he describes Newton as he certainly was not in that
year. But with prophetic insight into the possibilities of his nature he
gives us a picture which would not have been very unplausible thirty
years later—*In Dull King George's Golden* (much more golden)
Days." Norbert O'Donnell (*ShawR*, 1958) suggests that the focus of
the lengthy first-act discussion is the problem of knowledge and that

what it reveals is "the possibility of a degree of harmony in the world of intellectual discussion which is ironically contrasted with the discord prevailing in the world of political action. . . . Read in this way, *Good King Charles* is not only a unified whole but a significant revelation of the state of mind and spirit in which Shaw wrote his last plays."

Extended studies of the later plays by Katherine Haynes Gatch and more recently by Hansruedi Kamer are likely to be the basis for additional scrutiny of the last period of Shaw's playwriting; and to these may be added the several seminal studies of individual plays by Frederick P. McDowell, in time to be part of a major book. In "The Last Plays of Bernard Shaw: Dialectic and Despair," in *English Stage Comedy* (English Institute Essays, ed. W. K. Wimsatt, 1954), Gatch, having said earlier—in " 'The Real Sorrow of Great Men': Mr Bernard Shaw's Sense of Tragedy" (*CE*, 1947–48)—that the last plays have no obvious dramatic analogues, goes on to suggest that Shaw used "a dialectical structure derived from Hegel and Marx," modified by "the solvent of the comic spirit." In the later plays she sees a calculated ironic relationship between the magnitude of the themes and the triviality of the treatment, concluding that the plays are Shaw's response to a compulsion to find "new modes for our time." (It has been noted earlier that Huizinga saw a Hegelian approach to tragedy in *Saint Joan*; and that Shaw's method generally resembles Hegelian synthetic dialectic is also one of Albert's observations in "Bernard Shaw: The Artist as Philosopher.") Hansruedi Kamer's *Kunsterliche und politische Extravaganz in Spatwerk Shaws* (Swiss Studies in English, 73, 1973) examines the plays from *The Apple Cart* to *Farfetched Fables* as experiments in political and philosophical extravaganza, expressions of the interwar and immediate postwar years disregarding realistic requirements and exploring new dramatic dimensions including allegory and symbolic action.

Separate studies on Shaw's surprisingly sprightly first postwar play (begun 1936–37; re-begun in 1945, and completed when he was 90, in 1947) are few, the fullest of them McDowell's "The World, God, and World Bettering: Shaw's *Buoyant Billions*" (*BUSE*, 1957). "The continuity of Shaw's intellectual life" is demonstrated by the play, McDowell asserts. *Buoyant Billions* "should not be so much dismissed as a derivative work as studied for its apical significance in Shaw's development. Its forthright elaboration of long-held ideas and attitudes enables us, too, to glance backward and reinterpret the twentieth-century [Shavian] plays more surely in its mirrored image." Richard Nickson's "The World Betterer: Shaw versus Shaw" (*ShawR*, 1959) analyzes the father-son conflict in the play as one between Shaw the pragmatist and Shaw the prophet.

No useful separate or extended analyses of *Farfetched Fables* (written 1948) or the brief satirical puppet play *Shakes versus Shav* (written 1949) exist; but there is a study of Shaw's last play, *Why She Would Not* (written 1950). Dan H. Laurence's "The Facts about *Why She Would Not*" (*Theatre Arts*, Aug. 1956) examines the shorthand manuscript numbered LIV in the canon by Shaw and defends its completeness, noting that the last page is dated "23/7/50 Ayot" and "End of Scene 5 and of the play."

VIII. *Influence and Reputation*

The range and depth of Shaw's literary and extraliterary impact cannot be measured by research in this area of Shaw studies, which is insubstantial. In playwriting, the drama of his own native Ireland has been profoundly affected; and although Sean O'Casey and Brendan Behan pointed to this aspect of their own work, the former (in his memoirs in particular) with profound reverence, there are no useful studies. Shaw's stormy relationship with the Abbey Theatre is the only pertinent subject touched upon by scholars. With respect to England the status of research into Shaw's influence is little better. Shaw's attempts to entice major writers in other genres to write for the theater is well known, and his awkward involvement with James's theatrical ventures is told by Leon Edel in the fourth and fifth volumes of his *Henry James*. His attempts to lure Conrad, Galsworthy, Moore, Wells, Bennett, Chesterton, and other contemporaries into playwriting are less well known, although Kinley E. Roby's "Arnold Bennett: Shaw's Ten O'Clock Scholar" (*ShawR*, 1970), examines one of the results and William B. Furlong's "Shaw and Chesterton: The Link Was *Magic*" (*ShawR*, 1967) examines another. G.B.S.'s impact upon the younger generation is also inadequately researched. His close, two-way relationship with Granville Barker is analyzed by Margery Morgan in her study of Barker, *A Drama of Political Man* (1961), but—among Edwardians—no study of the Shavian impact upon St. John Hankin, or even W. Somerset Maugham, appears to exist. Noel Coward confessed how much he owed to G. B. S. in his early work, especially to *You Never Can Tell*, in his memoir *Present Indicative* (1937), but critics have not ranged beyond repeating Coward. James Bridie was known as the "Scottish G. B. S.," but again no extended criticism has evaluated the observation; and J. B. Priestley's own comments about his indebtedness to Shaw have evoked no corroborative studies. Among writers in the post-World War II generations several have been identified with Shaw for one reason or another, among them Nigel Dennis, John Whiting, and John Osborne, with Katherine J. Worth's article, "Shaw and John Osborne" (*Shavian*, 1964), and her book, *Revolutions in Modern English Drama* (1973), perhaps the best connections of Shaw with Osborne; while Gabriele Scott Robinson's (*ShawR*, 1974) is the only close examination of relationships between Shaw and Whiting.

Shavian influence has been identified in a number of European playwrights, notably Bertolt Brecht (whose own 1926 "Ovation for Shaw" made the fact of his Shavian interests clear), Friedrich Durrenmatt, Max Frisch, Günter Grass, and Peter Weiss, among German-language playwrights; however, thorough studies remain to be done. That Shaw's impact in European theater was both early and profound is evident not only from his having been widely translated and performed (Shaw even encouraged world premieres of several of his plays in Berlin, Vienna, and Warsaw) but from a thorough scrutiny of that early impact in John J. Weisert's "Shaw in Central Europe before 1914," in *Anglo-German and American-German Crosscurrents*, II (1962). (A worldwide scanning of Shaw performances appears in

212 ANGLO-IRISH LITERATURE *A Review of Research*

Lucile K. Henderson's "Shaw around the World" appendix to Archibald Henderson's *George Bernard Shaw: Man of the Century*, 1956.) Shavian influence in France, particularly in the impact of his *Saint Joan* on French historical drama, has been noted by Daniel Gerould (*ShawR*, 1964); while Judith R. Calvin (*ShawR*, 1962) analyzes the traces of Shavian thought and dramatic structure that "permeate" the works of Giraudoux. Curiously, this latter element has resulted in a forty-year time reversal in Maurice Valency's *The Cart and the Trumpet: The Plays of George Bernard Shaw*, where the critic—a translator of Giraudoux—observes of certain lines in *Major Barbara* that they "oddly recall the Ragpicker's wry speech in . . . *La Folle de Chaillot*." The Shavian impact upon Jean Anouilh has been profound, but remains uninvestigated, nor do relationships between Shaw and Sartre appear to be usefully scrutinized, an exception being Ruby Cohn's "Hell on the Twentieth-Century Stage" (*WSCL*, 1964), which sees resemblances between *Don Juan in Hell* and *No Exit*, both pleasant "Palaces of Lies." In general, despite the unsuccess of Shaw's plays (other than *Joan*) in France, his impact upon French playwrights has been substantial, although examined only superficially.

Shaw's influence in America largely remains to be explored. Elmer Rice has discussed his own early interest in Shaw (*ShawR*, 1957). Shaw's considerable impact upon Eugene O'Neill is noted by Arthur and Barbara Gelb (*ShawR*, 1962, and in their biography, *O'Neill*, 1962); while Louis Shaeffer examines that impact more substantially, particularly in the second volume of his biography, *O'Neill: Son and Artist* (1973). S. N. Behrman, called by some the most notable American writer of high comedy, knew his Shaw and knew Shaw himself; but no study of that relationship exists other than Behrman's own memories of Shaw in *The Suspended Drawing Room* (1965; originally in *NY*, 1945) and in *People in a Diary* (1972). Perhaps the most substantial examination of Shavian influence upon an American playwright remains Anne N. Lausch's "Robert Sherwood's Heartbreak Houses" and "The Road to Rome by Way of Alexandria and Tavazzano" (*ShawR*, 1963). His impact upon Thornton Wilder, Arthur Miller, Tennessee Williams, and Edward Albee is largely unexplored, although a brief note by Gerald Weales, "Tennessee Williams Borrows a Little Shaw" (*ShawR*, 1965), and D. C. Coleman's "Games" article in *DramaS* (1966–67; see under *Heartbreak House*) suggest that there is more to be done. A book-length study of Shaw and (and in) America by Dan H. Laurence, now in progress, may be the real beginning.

Examination of Shaw's literary and stage impact, however preliminary, is further along than other, perhaps more essential, Shavian research. Political and social changes, accelerated even more in the twentieth century than heretofore, have accelerated changes in diction, idiom, and language in general, making Paul Kozelka's pioneering *A Glossary to the Plays of Bernard Shaw* (1959) the merest scratching of the surface. Variorum editions of the plays are thus one of the many needs in Shaw scholarship yet to be achieved. Satisfactory texts of the novels are another as is the restoration to print of many of the other works now unavailable. More complete texts of his literary and art criticism are needed to supplement the samplings which are all we currently have; the salvaging of all of his drama criticism (some pseudonymous) not in the collected volumes may be one of the earliest fruits of the *Bibliography*. Much ephemeral writing remains in manuscript, particularly drafts of lectures; and these are likely to appear piecemeal rather than in any logical context. Many thousands of Shaw's extant letters remain unpublished because it was not economic to issue a selection of his correspondence in more than four volumes. The canon is likely both to increase and to become more accessible, the latter to occur especially as Shavian copyrights (to work published by the time of his death) expire in Berne Convention countries in the year 2000.

Shaw's influence in areas not literary or theatrical has been extensive although little re-evaluated since the events themselves. As an act of public statesmanship his pioneering battle for a National Theatre has been posthumously successful. He liked to think of himself as a municipal citizen, and his public pronouncements on international affairs often show—with the First World War very likely the exception—that he was more of a man of vision closer to home. In 1933, on his first American visit, he maintained to the mayor of San Francisco, "People think of me as a theatrical man, but I am really proud of having served six years as a municipal councillor." He had been awakened to civic issues by the same problems which evoked his early plays and wrote usefully on subjects such as municipal ownership of utilities (*The Common Sense of Municipal Trading*, 1904), now widespread; however, he was also an effective local officeholder for the London borough of St. Pancras from 1897 to 1903, an experience surveyed by H. M. Geduld in "Bernard Shaw, Vestryman and Borough Councillor," in the now-defunct *California Shavian* (1962) and—in shorter form—in *The Shavian* (1964). Shaw's contributions to national politics resulted initially from his leadership role in the Fabian Society, which led inevitably to the larger stage of the infant Labour Party. Both are imbrovely described in the autobiographical prefaces Shaw contributed to sixty years of succeeding editions of *Fabian Essays*, the first of which, in 1889, he edited.

Nothing more useful has yet appeared for evaluating Shaw's various extraliterary influences than *G. B. S. 90*, essays collected by Stephen Winsten to honor Shaw's ninetieth birthday. Included are J. B. Priestley on Shaw as social critic, J. D. Bernal on Shaw as scientist, Dean W. R. Inge on Shaw as theologian, Maurice Dobb on Shaw and economics, A. S. Neill on Shaw and education, Emil Davies on Shaw and local government, Sir William Haley and Val Gielgud on Shaw and the growth of radio. There is little else by political or economic historians to isolate Shaw's genuine impact upon wage and hour legislation, municipalization of utilities and transportation, tax equalization, censorship, women's rights (but for *Fabian Feminist*), the National Health Acts, and other changes in the relationships between man and his government.

Shaw's practical role in political affairs is very likely underestimated. S. Weintraub's *Journey to Heartbreak* demonstrates how seriously the government viewed him during the 1914–18 war and the reality of his impact, from gadfly to the architect of a real shift in opinion—through his chairmanship of the Fabian Research Committee—in creating serious interest in international organization (and thus the postwar League of Nations). Perhaps his efforts in attempting to mold opinion about Ireland are also underestimated, for the Laurence and Greene edition of *The Matter with Ireland* shows that, however abortive and frustrated were Shaw's attempts to play a larger role than events permitted, he did help make Irish interests better known and more respectable. But his major public role may have been, in the longer view, on a smaller stage, although Emil Davies' wry forecast of a schoolgirl essay in the Shavian bicentenary year of 2056 deliberately exaggerates: "George Bernard Shaw was noted as an authority and pioneer in regard to municipal affairs. He was a London Borough Councillor and wrote a book entitled *The Common Sense of Municipal Trading* which has become a classic. He also wrote some plays."

That the adjective *Shavian* has gone into the language, and appears in all major dictionaries, is a clue not only to the extent of Shaw's influence, but to the solidity of his reputation. Retiring as theater critic for the *Saturday Review* in 1898, just after he had begun *Caesar and Cleopatra*, Shaw in his forty-second year (and bedridden with a serious foot infection) joked in a valedictory column, "I may dodder and I may dote; I may potboil and platitudinize; I may become the butt and chopping-block of all the bright, original spirits of the rising generation; but my reputation shall not suffer: it is built up fast and solid, like Shakespeare's, on an impregnable basis of dogmatic reiteration." In his preface to the play he was then writing he again invoked the Bard in the "Better than Shakespeare?" title to a section in which he made no such claims except as he referred to Shakespeare as having wrongly given (in *Antony and Cleopatra*) "theatrical sublimity" to a "wretched" business, sexual infatuation—a passion of less than tragic weight—and having failed to visualize Caesar (a demagogue in *Julius Caesar*) as a man who embodied the best possibilities of the human race. A half century later Shakespeare remained to him the supreme dramatic poet, however unoriginal the ideas or the ethic he dramatized; and in the puppet play *Shakes versus Shav* (1949) the ninety-four year-old Shaw's alter ego appeals to "Shakes,"

> Peace, jealous Bard.
> We are both mortal. For a moment suffer
> My glimmering light to shine.

The comparison continues to be made. Although each master used the stage in his own way, each was without peer as creator of a lasting canon. J. I. M. Stewart in the twentieth-century volume of the *Oxford History of English Literature* (*Eight Modern Writers*) invokes the Bard in calling *Saint Joan* "conceivably the finest and most moving English drama since *The Winter's Tale* or *The Tempest*." Gore Vidal in *Homage to Daniel Shays* sought the same figure of speech in writing, "I should put quite plainly here at the beginning that I regard Bernard Shaw as the best and most useful dramatist in English since the author of *Much Ado about Nothing* turned gentleman and let fall the feather."

Such invocations refer to Shaw's reputation as playwright alone;

however, without mentioning Shakespeare other than by inference, the 1974 edition of the *Encyclopaedia Britannica* also begins its *Shaw* section with the Bard, then going on to nondramatic aspects of his work.

Among brief general evaluations, the bleakest is Angus Wilson's thoughtful "The Living Dead—IV: Bernard Shaw" (*LonM*, 1956); more balanced is F. P. W. McDowell's "Another Look at Bernard Shaw: A Reassessment of His Dramatic Theory, His Practice and His Achievement" (*DramaS*, 1961), which examines the dramatic tension the playwright secures between realism and artifice, his "sensitivity to the manifold resources of language," and the vigorous life given to large ideas—the "fusion of comic inventiveness with probing intelligence" in the service of "ethical idealism." But serious critics sometimes cavil at the kind of life given to particular Shavian ideas. According to Allardyce Nicoll in *English Drama 1900–1930: The Beginnings of the Modern Period* (1973), Shaw was as incautious in his thinking as he was brilliant and scintillating, and "apt to seize upon conclusions without considering their implications, inclined to lose sight of humanity in the process of ratiocination. . . . Fortunately, however, Shaw's rather jejune but dangerous personal philosophizings were accompanied by other qualities, and especially by his effervescent sense of fun, by his innate theatrical skill and, perhaps most important of all, by his idiosyncratic treatment of his stage figures." On balance, nevertheless, G. B. S. remains to Nicoll "this dramatic colossus," an epithet inapplicable in his terms to any other figure in English drama since 1616. With less caviling *TLS* (24 May 1974) observed that "Shaw can combine psychological generosity with merciless social analysis (not to mention exhilarating theatricality). . . . Shaw seems old fashioned [only] because he allows both sides their most persuasive arguments and their human dignity."

Perhaps the Chairman of the Nobel Committee of the Swedish Academy, Per Hallström, summed up Shaw as well in his lifetime as has been done since, in awarding him the Prize for Literature (1925), finding "beneath all his sportiveness and defiance . . . both idealism and humanity, [his] stimulating satire often being infused with a singular poetic beauty." Combining caution with encomium he added that although Shaw's "criticism of society and his perspective of its course of development may have appeared too nakedly logical, too hastily thought out, too unorganically simplified, . . . his struggle against traditional conceptions that rest on no solid basis and against traditional feelings that are either spurious or only half genuine, has borne witness to the loftiness of his aims." More than a half-century later the evaluation stands up.

W. B. YEATS

Richard J. Finneran

Bald heads, forgetful of their sins,
Old, learned, respectable bald heads
Edit and annotate. . . .

("The Scholars")

In March of 1885 a young man not quite twenty years of age, known
to most of his friends as "Willie," made his first appearance in print
with two poems in the *Dublin University Review*. Those fortunate to
have a copy of that rare item possess the beginning of a very remarkable career. For almost the next fifty-five years Yeats continued to
forge his achievement, producing a body of work extraordinary not
only in its significance but also in its variety: poems, plays, short
stories, a novelette (and an unfinished novel), autobiographical
pieces, journals, diaries, essays, speeches, criticism, reviews, and that
volume that defies a single-word description, *A Vision*. And Yeats not
only wrote; he also lived—more fully than most, and with a spectrum
of roles sufficient for several lifetimes. The range of his life can be
seen in the distance from the celibate figure of the 1890's, shying
away from a prostitute in the Hammersmith Railway Station because
he was in love with "the most beautiful woman in the world," to the
"wild wicked old man" of the 1930's, undergoing a sexual rejuvenation operation which, if fraudulent physically, was apparently successful psychologically; or from the investigator of psychical
phenomena, journeying to France in 1914 to observe a bleeding picture, to the Irish senator, vehemently defending the rights of his
Protestant minority in 1925. Some of these and other activities have
been an embarrassment to some of his critics, but nothing Yeats did is
altogether irrelevant to his achievement. Throughout the life and the
works we find both constant development *and* continual identity.

Modern literary scholarship has not been remiss in responding to
Yeats. One's first impression in surveying this material is of sheer

numbers. In 1948, the compiler of one of the first surveys of Yeats criticism noted with a touch of Anglo-Irish pride "an average of six scholarly articles appearing on the subject every year." Nostalgia indeed: the latest (forthcoming) bibliography of secondary material, necessarily selective, will list about 6,000 items. A second impression, especially when looking at the work of recent years, is of the narrow scope of many of the studies. For example, we have lately been presented with full-length studies of four poems and of five plays, as well as another study which does little more than summarize selected interpretations of a single lyric.

Where, then, is a student to begin? Certainly not with the minutiae of literary scholarship: where, that is, a naïve reader of the correspondence columns of *TLS* (25 Feb. 1965, 28 Nov. & 12 Dec. 1969) might conclude that of the refrain to "Easter 1916" ("All changed, changed utterly: / A terrible beauty is born") Yeats can take credit only for "All"; thus neglecting the imaginative facility with which he was able to draw on the various sources—if indeed he knew them (O. Henry's "A Fog in Santone" seems less than likely). Rather, an ideal student, one with a firm grounding in the primary material, should perhaps begin with one of the standard biographies and a selection of the better studies cited under "General Works" (x), and thence to the most provocative examinations of the poetic and dramatic writings. By then many of the standard issues in Yeats criticism will have surfaced, and this chapter may serve a useful purpose in directing further study. It is also not redundant to suggest that most of the best Yeats criticism has been done by Yeatsians: casual visitors to the oeuvre have seldom left substantial tracks.

A word about the chapter itself. It is of course a radical selection, anything like a complete survey requiring not only several volumes but also what one critic has somewhat disdainfully called "a committee of his exegetes" (conditions certainly unobtainable and probably undesirable). Excluded altogether are works not in English, unpublished studies (including dissertations), and most explications of individual poems and plays. Only a small sample of the mass of material in periodicals is cited. Some of these articles of course found their way into longer studies, and with a good portion of the rest it is difficult to disagree with T. R. Henn's comment: "much . . . is fruitful, more is sheer ingenuity." Important and substantial chapters in books are included; and, so far as I know, I have cited all books and monographs in English published through 1974.

Almost all the early full-length studies have been reprinted, occasionally by more than one publisher; these reprints have been mentioned only if they include new material. A number of individual volumes by Yeats have been reprinted in America after the expiration of the original copyrights. A more disturbing trend is the republication —at exorbitant prices—of recent critical studies from Europe or, especially, India.

I. *Bibliographies, Catalogs, Concordances*

PRIMARY BIBLIOGRAPHIES

Given the complexity of Yeats's publication history, it is difficult to overestimate the importance of the standard work: Allan Wade, *A Bibliography of the Writings of W. B. Yeats* (3rd ed., rev. Russell K. Alspach, 1968). Wade began this work in 1908, when he contributed a bibliographic section (also printed separately) to the *Collected Works in Verse & Prose*. The *Bibliography* itself was first published in 1951; a second edition (rev. Rupert Hart-Davis) in 1958. Earlier works are of historical interest only: A. J. A. Symons, *A Bibliography of the First Editions of Books by William Butler Yeats* (1924), William M. Roth, *A Catalogue of English and American First Editions of William Butler Yeats* (1939), and P. S. O'Hegarty, "Notes on the Bibliography of W. B. Yeats" (*DM*, 1939, 1940) are the main examples.

In addition to a list of Yeats's books and contributions to books and periodicals, the Wade/Alspach *Bibliography* includes sections on translations, the Cuala Press, books about Yeats, and Yeats and broadcasting (by George Whalley, added to the second edition). Many of Yeats's inscriptions are reproduced, and the book is filled with much other information.

The most extensive list of additions and corrections to Wade/Alspach is by K. P. S. Jochum (*BB*, 1971), to be expanded in his forthcoming *Classified Bibliography*. Colton Johnson has listed and reprinted three early items (*N&Q*, 1972). Other additions have been made by Shirley W. Vinall (*N&Q*, 1973), George Monteiro (*N&Q*, 1974), and Colin Smythe (*Long Room*, 1974). A few other items will be cited in section II.

SECONDARY BIBLIOGRAPHIES

The most comprehensive work is, or will be, *W. B. Yeats: A Classified Bibliography of Criticism including Additions to Allan Wade's* Bibliography of the Writings of W. B. Yeats *and a Section on the Irish Literary and Dramatic Revival* by K. P. S. Jochum, with the publisher at the time of this writing. Jochum's volume will cover most work on Yeats (excluding that in Japanese or Irish) and everything of importance on the Revival from the beginnings through 1971, with a number of items from 1972 and 1973 added. For later publications the most accurate listing is of course the *MLA International Bibliography*; also useful are the Annual Review Number of *JML*, which annotates or reviews many of the entries, and the annual bibliography in *IUR*.

The *Classified Bibliography* supersedes all previous works, but some of the major ones may be briefly noted. Although lists of research began to appear as early as 1903, the first extensive compilation was published in *The Permanence of Yeats* in 1950. George

Brandon Saul provided a very selective list in *Stephens, Yeats, and Other Irish Concerns* (1954). A fairly large bibliography was printed in 1965 in *Centenary Essays on the Art of W. B. Yeats* (ed. D. E. S. Maxwell and S. B. Bushrui). Donna Gerstenberger's list of material on the plays (MD, 1965) was selective and partially annotated. Much more extensive was K. P. S. Jochum's *W. B. Yeats's Plays: An Annotated Checklist of Criticism* (Saarbrücken, 1966). John E. Stoll's *The Great Deluge: A Yeats Bibliography* (1971) was extremely selective and grossly inaccurate. The list of studies in E. H. Mikhail's *Dissertations on Anglo-Irish Drama: A Bibliography of Studies, 1870–1970* (1973) was incomplete and not confined to work on the plays. The most important volume prior to the *Classified Bibliography* was K. G. W. Cross and R. T. Dunlop, *A Bibliography of Yeats Criticism, 1887–1965* (1971). This work, which attempted to include all studies except those listed in Shotaro Oshima's *W. B. Yeats and Japan,* had a number of valuable features, including an admirable index and the listing of reviews of books both by and about Yeats; however, its value was undercut by errors and omissions.

Bibliographies of criticism of individual works have so far concentrated on "Sailing to Byzantium" and "Byzantium." A. Norman Jeffares' somewhat cursory discussion (*ESA*, 1962) and the selective listing in *William Butler Yeats: The Byzantium Poems* (ed. Richard J. Finneran, 1970) have been superseded by two recent works by James Lovic Allen: "Yeats's Byzantium Poems and the Critics, Reconsidered" (*CLQ*, 1973), a discussion and selected bibliography; and "Charts for the Voyage to Byzantium: An Annotated Bibliography" (*BNYPL*, 1973), also somewhat selective but the more useful of the two. In both instances one must be cautious in accepting Allen's evaluations.

The following generally accessible essay-reviews often comment on the direction of Yeats scholarship and should be consulted by the careful student for judgments on individual studies that in many cases differ from those in this essay: A. Norman Jeffares (*Hermathena*, 1948); Ian Fletcher (*LHY*, 1961); Hazard Adams (*TSLL*, 1962); K. G. W. Cross in *In Excited Reverie* (ed. A. Norman Jeffares and K. G. W. Cross, 1965); August W. Staub, (*QJS*, 1966); George Mills Harper (*SR*, 1966); Helen Vendler (*MR*, 1966); Brian John (*JGE*, 1967); Richard M. Kain (*Éire*, 1967): Ian Fletcher (*SoR*, 1968; and *NewS*, 27 June 1969); Hazard Adams (*GaR*, 1970); George Mills Harper (*CEA*, 1971); James L. Allen (*JML*, 1971); Jon Stallworthy in *English Poetry: Select Bibliographical Guides* (ed. A. E. Dyson, 1971); Michael J. Sidnell (*UTQ*, 1972); Hazard Adams (*GaR*, 1972); Richard J. Finneran (*JML*, 1973); A. Norman Jeffares (*SR*, 1974); K. P. S. Jochum (*Anglia*, 1974); Graham Hough (*TLS*, 14 Feb. 1975); George Mills Harper (*SoR*, 1975); Richard J. Finneran (*ConL*, 1976); Edward Engelberg (*SR*, 1976); and A. Norman Jeffares (*SR*, 1976).

CATALOGS

Catalogs of library holdings and of exhibitions are valuable not only for tracing a rare item but also for the annotations and inscriptions that are often supplied. Excluding sales catalogs, the most important of which are the *Complete Catalogue of the Library of John Quinn* (1924) and the Parke-Bernet Sales Catalogue No. 281 (1941), the earliest is *W. B. Yeats: Manuscripts and Printed Books Exhibited in the Library of Trinity College, Dublin* (comp. R. O. Dougan, 1956). The account of the exhibition in "Books and Manuscripts of W. B. Yeats" (*TLS*, 4 May 1956) is a useful supplement, but it should be noted that much of the material, including almost all the manuscripts, was on loan and is not held by Trinity. Hester M. Black's *William Butler Yeats: A Catalog of an Exhibition from the P. S. O'Hegarty Collection in the University of Kansas Library* (1958) describes some items from a very important collection; further information can be found in Frank C. Nelick, "Yeats, Bullen, and the Irish Drama" (*MD*, 1958). *William Butler Yeats, 1865–1939: Catalogue of an Exhibition, 13th–22nd May 1965* (1965) is a short list of some material from the University of Newcastle-upon-Tyne. One of the largest collections of Yeats materials in America is listed by Michael J. Durkan in *William Butler Yeats 1865–1965: A Catalogue of His Works and Associated Items in Olin Library, Wesleyan University* (1965). Some of the material in the Sligo County Library and Museum is described by Nora Niland in *Jack B Yeats and His Family* (1971). Other collections which have been more briefly noted or described include those at Wellesley (*Bull. of the Friends of Wellesley Coll. Lib.*, 1952), Texas (*LCUT*, 1957, 1959), Yale (*YULG*, 1958), and Kenyon (*Kenyon Coll. Lib. Acquistions Bull.*, Feb. 1959, Nov. 1961). Colby College also has an extensive collection of books by Yeats, many from the library of Ernest A. Boyd. The University of Massachusetts has recently acquired the important collection of Russell K. Alspach.

CONCORDANCES

Particularly because of Yeats's habit of repeating words, images, and symbols, concordances are an especially valuable research tool. *A Concordance to the Poems of W. B. Yeats* (ed. Stephen Maxfield Parrish, programmed by James Allan Painter, 1963) and *A Concordance to the Plays of W. B. Yeats* (ed. Eric Domville, 1972) are both in the Cornell series and are alike in most ways: they were done by computer and are thus (one hopes) infallible; they are keyed to the *Variorum* editions and list (with certain exceptions) words appearing in the variant lines; and they include a frequency list for Yeats's vocabulary. The respective introductions are more lively reading than one might expect, the first listing the animals and birds that appear in the poems and the second commenting on the differences in diction between the poems and the plays. The concordance to the plays has the advantage of distinguishing between upper- and lower-case letters.

II. Editions

It was rare indeed for Yeats to republish any of his work without revision. Occasionally these changes produced what is essentially a new work; seldom were they insignificant. Thus critical editions are of paramount importance in Yeats studies. The appearance of a uniform, edited "Works" is unlikely for at least several decades. We are now fortunate in having authoritative editions of the poetry and the plays. The textual condition of the prose may be described as chaotic but improving.

POETRY

The standard edition is *The Variorum Edition of the Poems of W. B. Yeats* (ed. Peter Allt and Russell K. Alspach, 1957; corrected 3rd printing, 1966). This edition uses as copy-text the two-volume "Definitive Edition" of the *Poems* (1949), the proofs of which Yeats is said to have corrected shortly before his death; the exact accuracy of that statement awaits the discovery and examination of the proofs (a few pages have recently surfaced in the Macmillan Archive at Basingstoke). *The Variorum* includes the substantial number of poems Yeats excluded from *Poems* as well as two posthumously published works. All variants from earlier printings are listed at the foot of each page. Thus one can reconstruct a poem as it appeared in any given printing and, by use of the important appendix on the "Order and Placement of Poems," the contents of any given volume. The *Variorum* also contains over sixty pages of notes, prefaces, and dedications to the poems, many of which are essential aids in interpretation.

A future revision of this edition will have to involve a few previously unrecorded printings of poems: of "What Then?" noted by Robin Skelton (*IB*, 1963); of "When You are Old" and "The Sorrow of Love," pointed out by George Monteiro (*PBSA*, 1966); and of "Remembrance," cited by K. P. S. Jochum (*N&Q*, 1971). A more complex and important concern is that of the contents, order, and text of the section of "Last Poems." In *Yeats's 'Last Poems' Again* (1966) Curtis Bradford has argued cogently that the section as it now stands should be divided into two parts: "New Poems" (all the poems up to and including "Are You Content?") and "Last Poems" (the remainder, minus three poems published only in *On the Boiler*). Moreover, this new "Last Poems" section should be completely re-ordered, to begin with "Under Ben Bulben" and conclude with "Politics." Bradford's most important piece of evidence is a manuscript table of contents (first published *MLN*, 1961) for *Last Poems and Two Plays* (1939). Bradford's monograph also suggests some minor textual corrections and provides a reading of the reconstructed "Last Poems," demonstrating the significance of the new order. Whether Yeats would in fact have maintained this structure may always be a matter for speculation; but in the absence of other evidence, Bradford's proposals seem conclusive.

The *Collected Poems* is an acceptable reading edition only in the eighth (1956) and later impressions of the American edition.

Plays

The standard edition is *The Variorum Edition of the Plays of W. B. Yeats* (ed. Russell K. Alspach, 1966; corrected 2nd printing, 1966). Since Yeats did not prepare a final revision of his plays, the copy-text is the English edition of the *Collected Plays* (1952); the American edition (1953) has numerous errors (some of which are noted by G. B. Saul in his *Prolegomena to the Study of Yeats's Plays*) not corrected in later impressions. The *Variorum Plays* follows the format of the *Variorum Poems* in listing all the variant readings and reprinting the lengthy notes, prefaces, and dedications. However, some of the plays presented special problems in collation, and Alspach was forced to adopt varying solutions. With *The Countess Cathleen*, for instance, the final version and the variants are printed on the recto pages, the earliest version on the verso pages. Though somewhat awkward, this procedure may be the best possible. The edition also includes a valuable appendix on first performances, an index to characters, and a general index.

In addition to prose versions of three plays, the *Variorum Plays* contains six works not in the *Collected Plays*: four early poetic dramas (also in the *Variorum Poems*); *Where There Is Nothing*, a collaboration with Lady Gregory and Douglas Hyde; and *Diarmuid and Grania*, a collaboration with George Moore not published in Yeats's lifetime. A separate edition of *Diarmuid and Grania*, with an introduction by Anthony Farrow, was published in 1974. Unfortunately, this printing uses the same text (*DM*, 1951, ed. William Becker) as the *Variorum Plays* and does not refer in any detail to the manuscript material at Texas (see Ray Small, Diss. Texas 1958) and elsewhere. Thus its only value is for the introduction, which offers an interesting discussion of both the play itself and the process of collaboration and is particularly good in relating the themes of *Diarmuid and Grania* to Moore's earlier works.

Yeats worked on three other plays that were not published until after his death, one of which is now available in full. Hazard Adams has quoted from and discussed a typescript of "The Country of the Young" (*PMLA*, 1957), a variant of Lady Gregory's *The Travelling Man* (1906). Adams notes that Yeats's version "eliminates the simple moral of Lady Gregory" and centers on "the failure of the imagination." In *Yeats's Iconography* F. A. C. Wilson provides a synopsis of an unfinished dance-play, which he entitles "The Bridegroom"; Wilson comments that "the play is clearly about the doctrine of the image." "Heads or Harps," a brief political satire written with Lady

Gregory, has recently been published in *The Translations and Adaptations of Lady Gregory and Her Collaborations with Douglas Hyde and W. B. Yeats* (ed. Ann Saddlemyer, 1970; vol. IV of the *Collected Plays*; vol. VIII of the "Coole Edition").

A separate edition of *Sophocles' King Oedipus* (1969) includes a selection from Aristotle's *Poetics* and an introduction by Balachandra Rajan, which only briefly discusses Yeats.

From an editorial standpoint, the crucial question about Yeats's plays—particularly the early ones—is their authorship: that is, the extent to which they were written in collaboration with various figures. George Moore's contribution has been noted above. Douglas Hyde not only worked on *Where There Is Nothing* but also, according to Vivian Mercier (*MD*, 1965), had a small share in *The Unicorn from the Stars*. Edward Martyn, George W. Russell (A. E.), and Arthur Symons may have helped with *Diarmuid and Grania*. Lady Gregory was of course Yeats's major collaborator. Indeed, in the printings before the *Collected Plays* (1934) she was listed as the co-author of *The Unicorn from the Stars*; in all, she appears to have contributed in some way to ten of Yeats's published plays, beginning with *Cathleen ni Houlihan* and ending with *Sophocles' King Oedipus*.

The exact nature of the Yeats-Gregory collaboration has long been a matter of rumor, anecdote, and debate. In *A Short History of Irish Literature* (1967), for example, Frank O'Connor reports that Yeats took credit for the use of a barrel in her *The Rising of the Moon*. Writing with some hostility toward Yeats in *Lady Gregory: A Literary Portrait* (1961; 2nd ed., 1966), Elizabeth Coxhead concentrates on refuting the charges that Lady Gregory "interfered with and spoilt Yeats's plays, and that he really wrote the best of hers." The largest claims for her contribution to Yeats's plays have been made by Daniel J. Murphy (*MD*, 1964; and *Modern Irish Literature*, ed. Raymond J. Porter and James D. Brophy, 1972). Discussing *Cathleen ni Houlihan* in the latter essay, Murphy claims that "all the evidence clearly indicates that Lady Gregory wrote the play in its entirety." A more thoughtful evaluation of the collaborative process can be found in Saddlemyer's foreword to the volume of Lady Gregory's plays cited above. It is likely that the issue will have to be resolved (to the extent that it ever can be) on a play-by-play basis, and only after the publication of the relevant manuscript material and correspondence.

PROSE

To move from the splendid *Variorum Poems* and *Variorum Plays* to the prose is indeed to enter the fallen world. The bulk of Yeats's prose, excepting *A Vision*, can be found in a four-volume uniform edition issued by Macmillan in London from 1955 to 1962; three of these volumes were issued simultaneously by Macmillan in New York. These editions contain numerous minor variants from the last versions published in Yeats's lifetime, some of which are noted by Marion Witt in "Yeats: 1865–1965" (*PMLA*, 1965). Though the authority of these variants will have to be determined for each individual work, they can be accounted for generally by one or more of the following sources: Mrs. W. B. Yeats, who was the "silent" editor of the first three volumes; Thomas Mark, Yeats's editor at Macmillan, London; corrected copies of some books in Yeats's library; and, most importantly, the proofs for the Coole Edition, a limited, collected edition which Yeats worked on around 1931–32 and later but which was never published (an advertisement can be seen in the Yeats issue of *The Arrow*, 1939; this edition must not be confused with the current Coole Edition of Lady Gregory). For the time being, then, these Macmillan volumes must be accepted as the best available texts.

Autobiographies (1955), not published in America, contains the three sections of the autobiography proper—"Reveries over Childhood and Youth," "The Trembling of the Veil," and "Dramatis Personae"—which treat Yeats's life from childhood to about 1902; two extracts from a 1909 diary, "Estrangement" and "The Death of Synge"; "The Bounty of Sweden," an account of his visit to accept the Nobel Prize in 1923; and "The Irish Dramatic Movement," his Nobel lecture. An index has been furnished for this edition, but the treatment of Yeats's notes is inconsistent, only two of the six to "The Irish Dramatic Movement" being reprinted. The American version, misleadingly entitled *The Autobiography of William Butler Yeats*, was first published in 1938 and reissued in 1953. This edition omits "The Irish Dramatic Movement" and is defective textually, since the jacket of *Autobiographies* states that "Yeats himself read the text of this edition shortly before his death, and it embodies the last corrections he made in matters of detail." The 1965 paperback edition of *The Autobiography* (not noted in Wade/Alspach) restores "The Irish Dramatic Movement" but is still lacking a footnote to "Ireland after Parnell." In short, *Autobiographies* remains the only acceptable text.

An important supplement to this volume is *Memoirs* (ed. Denis Donoghue, 1972). This edition contains the draft of an autobiography written in 1915–17 covering the period from 1887 to about 1898 and the full text of the journal which Yeats excerpted for *Autobiographies* and of which a further selection was published as *Reflections* (ed. Curtis Bradford, 1972). Most of the journal entries are from 1909–14, but among the few later ones are some drafts for "Leda and the Swan" (unfortunately not transcribed with complete accuracy). Although *Memoirs* is elegantly edited, only two of the appendices are really necessary. Since Donoghue was for a time engaged on the authorized biography of Yeats (see his statement in the "Viewpoint" column of *TLS*, 16 Feb. 1973, and the forceful replies of Michael B. Yeats and G. S. Fraser in letters in the two following issues) his copious notes are almost always accurate. The overly brief introduction should be supplemented by Ian Fletcher's "Yeats's Quest for Self-Transparency" (*TLS*, 19 Jan. 1973), a brilliant essay-review.

Mythologies (1959), the second volume in the Macmillan series, contains *Per Amica Silentia Lunae* and the bulk of the prose fiction— *The Celtic Twilight, The Secret Rose, Stories of Red Hanrahan,* and the "Rosa Alchemica" stories. All the fiction except *The Celtic Twilight* is included in a critical edition of *The Secret Rose* (ed. Warwick Gould, Phillip L. Marcus, and Michael J. Sidnell, forthcoming). The major revisions to *The Celtic Twilight* have been discussed by Richard J. Finneran (*TSE*, 1972). A critical edition of *Per Amica* is in progress by Warwick Gould.

The major supplement to *Mythologies* is *John Sherman and Dhoya* (ed. Richard J. Finneran, 1969), which contains the 1908 text of a novelette and short story; the variants from the early printings are also provided. The introduction is a generalized sketch of the composition, publication, and themes of the works. This edition should be supplemented by Ian Fletcher's review (*N&Q*, 1971), which notes a textual correction and suggests Lionel Johnson as a partial model for one of the main characters in *John Sherman*.

The third volume in the Macmillan uniform edition, *Essays and Introductions* (1961), contains the most important of the critical prose: *Ideas of Good and Evil, The Cutting of an Agate*, some scattered introductions and a broadcast, and three seminal essays Yeats wrote in 1937—the Introduction to the volume, "A General Introduction for My Work," and "An Introduction for My Plays." Jon Lanham is preparing a critical edition of *Ideas of Good and Evil* which may now be available. A useful supplement to *Essays and Introductions* is *Letters to the New Island* (ed. Horace Reynolds, 1934; rpt. 1970), which reprints Yeats's early (1888–92) prose contributions to *The Providence Sunday Journal* and *The Boston Pilot*. Yeats contributed an interesting preface to the collection; Reynolds' introduction is a valuable summary of the main ideas of the articles, quite perceptive for its time. The volume is otherwise unedited.

Explorations (1962), selected by Mrs. W. B. Yeats and the final volume in the Macmillan series, is something of a miscellany, apparently designed to reprint material not readily available elsewhere. It includes introductions to Brian Merriman's *The Midnight Court* and to two works by Lady Gregory; "Swedenborg, Mediums and the Desolate Places," an important essay first published in Lady Gregory's *Visions and Beliefs in the West of Ireland; If I Were Four-and-Twenty* and *Pages from a Diary Written in Nineteen Hundred and Thirty*; the introductions to the plays in *Wheels and Butterflies* (also included in *Variorum Plays*); and most of the prose and two of the three poems from *On the Boiler*. But the largest section of *Explorations* consists of Yeats's early dramatic criticism, selected primarily from *Samhain* and *The Arrow*.

The most important supplements to *Explorations* are the recent facsimile reprints of *Beltaine* (1970) and *Samhain* (1970), both with introductory notes by B. C. Bloomfield. *Beltaine* contains perhaps ten pages of Yeats material not reprinted elsewhere. *Samhain* reprints about the same amount of uncollected material but also includes the first of the three states of a 1909 *Samhain*, in this instance entitled "Paragraphs from the Forthcoming Number of 'Samhain'" and signed by Yeats only. The second state, entitled "Paragraphs from Samhain, 1909" and signed by Yeats and Lady Gregory, can be found in Lady Gregory's *Our Irish Theatre: A Chapter of Autobiography* (1972), foreword Roger McHugh (vol. IV of the Coole Edition), which also collates the third state, entitled "Paragraphs Written in November 1909" and signed by both writers. (Wade/Alspach is incorrect in citing only two states of this pamphlet.) This edition also prints a similar item from 1910, "The Irish National Theatre: Its Work and Its Needs," not cited by Wade/Alspach.

Yeats's most important prose work—in terms of the amount of time he devoted to it, if not in the estimation of all his critics—is *A Vision*, first published in a limited edition in 1926 (title page dated 1925) and substantially revised for the commercial edition of 1937. A corrected edition, described as incorporating "the author's final revisions," was published in New York in 1956 and reprinted in London in 1961. However, in "A Preliminary Note on the Text of *A Vision* (1937)" (in *Yeats and the Occult*, ed. George Mills Harper), Richard J. Finneran has noted that the 1962 London edition embodies further corrections and should be considered the best available text. M. B. Decker has pointed out an unresolved inconsistency (*N&Q*, 1973). Craig Wallace Borrow's index to *A Vision* (*BNYPL*, 1973) is keyed to the 1956 text but can be used with any of the editions from 1937 on. George Mills Harper and Walter K. Hood are preparing critical editions of both versions of *A Vision*; the 1926 text will be published first.

The recent edition of *Fairy and Folk Tales of Ireland* (1973), foreword Kathleen Raine, reprints *Fairy and Folk Tales of the Irish Peasantry* (1888) and *Irish Fairy Tales* (1892), both of which Yeats edited and contributed to. (To compound the titular confusion, the 1888 volume has been reprinted various times as both *Irish Fairy and Folk Tales* and *Irish Folk Stories and Fairy Tales*.) Raine's foreword is a brief defense of the fairy faith; the volume is otherwise unedited.

Quite different from this early work is *The Senate Speeches of W. B. Yeats* (ed. Donald R. Pearce, 1960), which gives an interesting picture of Yeats's activities in the Irish Senate from 1922 to 1928. However, the volume is rather inadequately edited and should not be used without reference to W. B. Stanford's "Yeats in the Irish Senate" (*REL*, 1963). *Tribute to Thomas Davis* (1947; rpt. 1965) includes Yeats's speech at the 1914 Davis centenary celebrations, a letter from A. E. to Yeats, and a foreword by Denis Gwynn providing the context for the material.

Most—but not all—of the remainder of Yeats's prose first published in newspapers or periodicals can be found in the two volumes of *Uncollected Prose by W. B. Yeats*. Volume I (ed. John P. Frayne, 1970) covers the period 1886–96 and includes a bibliography. Volume II (ed. Frayne and Colton Johnson, 1975) reprints work from 1897 to 1938 (as well as two earlier items omitted from the first volume) and has the index to both volumes. Each volume includes some items not cited in Wade/Alspach. The copious notes are usually accurate, the introductions to each volume informative, if wordy. Since these important editions will be of interest primarily to specialists, the exclusion of some appropriate items is disturbing.

Although all the Yeats material in *Davis, Mangan, Ferguson?: Tradition and the Irish Writer* (1970), foreword Roger McHugh, is available elsewhere, this slim volume retains some interest for the two essays by Thomas Kinsella, in the first of which he comments, "Yeats stands for the Irish tradition as broken; Joyce stands for it as continuous, or healed—or healing—from its mutilation."

Despite the number of volumes discussed in this section, a significant amount of Yeats's published prose remains uncollected. The recent (1970–71) reprinting of the entire series of the Dun Emer and Cuala Press books has made available a number of prefaces and introductions. An important item which has fortunately remained in print is *The Oxford Book of Modern Verse* (1936), with its long introduction. Other scattered items have been reprinted in various critical studies and will be noted below. But other essays, prefaces, and introductions, as well as miscellaneous material, remain uncollected; for the serious student there is no substitute for a careful study of the Wade/Alspach *Bibliography* and its several additions.

SOME SELECTED EDITIONS

The Celtic Twilight and a Selection of Early Poems (ed. Walter Starkie, 1962) is most valuable for reprinting the 1902 text of *The Celtic Twilight*; the poems are also presented in their early versions. *Running to Paradise: Poems by W. B. Yeats* (ed. Kevin Crossley-Holland, 1967) is an introductory selection designed for younger readers.

Editions intended for use in university courses differ in availability between the United States and other countries. Outside the United States these editions have been prepared by A. Norman Jeffares. In each instance they include a brief introduction of the life-and-works variety and informative, if occasionally inaccurate, notes. Both *Selected Poetry* and the volume of selected *Poems* were published in 1962. They have identical introductions but different selections of poems. *Poems* has the larger selection but also some inexplicable omissions (such as "Lapis Lazuli"). The notes are also more detailed in *Poems*. *Selected Plays* (1964) includes eleven works. The text of *Cathleen ni Houlihan* is taken from *Samhain* (1902) and is "therefore" (?) placed at the end of the volume. The text for the other ten plays is somewhat ambiguous, as Jeffares acknowledges the assistance of Mrs. W. B. Yeats "in correcting the text of *Collected Plays*" but does not indicate what corrections, if any, were made. The division of material between *Selected Criticism* (1964) and *Selected Prose* (1964) is not easy to justify, but together they provide a representative sampling. The selected bibliographies in these editions inexplicably fail to cite any of Richard Ellmann's studies.

In the United States Jeffares' *Selected Plays* was reprinted as *Eleven Plays of William Butler Yeats* (1964). The most important American selection is *Selected Poems and Two Plays of William Butler Yeats* (ed. M. L. Rosenthal, 1962). Though it, too, has some curious omissions (such as "Mohini Chatterjee"), it is the best of the selected editions. The text of the poems follows that of the *Variorum Poems*; unfortunately, *Calvary* and *Purgatory* are taken from the defective American edition of the *Collected Plays* and thus have some minor errors. Rosenthal's introduction is intelligent, the notes and glossary useful and accurate. Also available in the United States are paperback editions of the *Autobiography* (but see above), *Essays and Introductions, Explorations, Mythologies*, and the second version of *A Vision*.

III. Correspondence

To date less than half of Yeats's extant correspondence has been published. The forthcoming *Collected Letters of W. B. Yeats* (ed. Eric Domville and John Kelly) will be a complete edition, including all the letters, postcards, telegrams, and so on that can be located. Projected for approximately eight volumes, with the first to appear perhaps as early as 1977, this monumental edition will be a major contribution to Yeats studies.

The most important collection now available is *The Letters of W. B. Yeats* (ed. Allan Wade, 1954). Although there are major gaps—including Maud Gonne, Mrs. W. B. Yeats, Ezra Pound, George Moore, and G. B. Shaw, for instance—Wade's selection is excellent. The brief introductions to the six sections of the collection also constitute a fine short biography of Yeats. Wade's transcription of Yeats's difficult handwriting is to be commended. However, by contemporary editorial standards Wade's edition has serious deficiencies: many letters are excerpted, often to present Yeats in a more favorable light; the notes, though generally accurate, are too few; and the index is inaccurate and incomplete. Although most readers are doubtless grateful for the standardization of Yeats's erratic spelling, something of the flavor of the letters is lost. And, of course, two decades of continued scholarship have brought to light various errors in facts and dating, one of which is noted by David S. Thatcher in "A Misdated Yeats Letter on Nietzsche" (*N&Q*, 1968).

The Wade edition includes all of the Yeats material from *Florence Farr, Bernard Shaw and W. B. Yeats* (ed. Clifford Bax, 1941) and *Some Letters from W. B. Yeats to John O'Leary and His Sister* (ed. Allan Wade, 1953). It also includes all the letters from *W. B. Yeats: Letters to Katharine Tynan* (ed. Roger McHugh, 1953); however, this collection is still of interest for the introduction discussing the relationship, the notes (only some of which are included by Wade), and the printing of an essay on John Todhunter not found in *Uncollected Prose*.

There are three other important collections of the correspondence. *Letters on Poetry from W. B. Yeats to Dorothy Wellesley* (1940), reissued in 1964 with an introduction by Kathleen Raine, includes Yeats's late (1935–38) letters to Wellesley (some of which appear in the Wade edition), some letters from Wellesley to Yeats, and scattered comments by Wellesley. The edition is an important supplement to a study of the "Last Poems," particularly "The Three Bushes." Incidentally, Wellesley's *Beyond the Grave: Letters on Poetry to W. B. Yeats* (n.d. [1949?]) is a series of letters addressed to Yeats after his death; he does not seem to have replied. Edward O'Shea's "Yeats as Editor: Dorothy Wellesley's *Selections*" (*ELN*, 1974) is a useful account of the changes Yeats made in her poems.

W. B. Yeats and T. Sturge Moore: Their Correspondence 1901–1937 (ed. Ursula Bridge, 1953) is best known for the long discussion about the reality of John Ruskin's phantom cat; in effect, this was a three-sided exchange, as Sturge Moore would pass on the ideas of his brother G. E. Moore, a leading English philosopher. Many of the other letters concern Sturge Moore's designs for book-covers for Yeats. A useful supplement to the edition is an exhibition catalog, *T. Sturge Moore (1870–1944): Contributions to the Art of the Book & Collaboration with Yeats* (ed. Malcolm Easton, 1970), which includes a brief essay on the Moore-Yeats relationship and has numerous illustrations.

Ah, Sweet Dancer: W. B. Yeats–Margot Ruddock, A Correspondence (ed. Roger McHugh, 1970) prints both sides of the 1934–37 correspondence and is relevant to several of the "Last Poems." The edition also includes an unpublished poem, "Margot," and a discussion of Yeats's emendations to Ruddock's poems, seven of which he included in the *Oxford Book of Modern Verse*.

Numerous letters of Yeats have been published in critical studies and will be noted below. A few other major collections may be cited here. Volumes II and III of the *Letters of James Joyce* (ed. Richard Ellmann, 1966) contain both sides of the Yeats/Joyce correspondence, as well as a few letters by Yeats to Ezra Pound and Edward Marsh. *Letters to Macmillan* (ed. Simon Nowell-Smith, 1967) prints some letters to Yeats's main publisher. *Frank Pearce Sturm: His Life, Letters, and Collected Work* (ed. Richard Taylor, 1969), includes almost all of the exchange between Yeats and Sturm, the most important part of which concerns *A Vision*. Taylor's introductory essay provides a summary of the relationship. An important set of letters is rather poorly summarized and quoted from in Christiane Thilliez, "From One Theatrical Reformer to Another: W. B. Yeats's Unpublished Letters to Gordon Craig," in *Aspects of the Irish Theatre* (ed. Patrick Rafroidi, Raymonde Popot, and William Parker, Paris, 1972). *The Wonder and Supernatural Plays of Lady Gregory* (ed. Ann Saddlemyer, 1970; vol. III of the *Collected Plays*; vol. VII of the Coole Edition) includes a 1915 letter from Yeats to Lady Gregory. Lady Gregory's *Sir Hugh Lane: His Life and Legacy* (1973), foreword James White (vol. X of the Coole Edition), contains a number of Yeats's letters to the press about the Lane affair, as well as his unpublished "Clairvoyant Search for Hugh Lane's Will." Yeats's letters to J. M. Synge will be published in Ann Saddlemyer's forthcoming edition of *Theatre Business, Management of Men: The Letters of the First Abbey Theatre Directors*.

Numerous letters have been published in periodicals. H. W. Haeusermann's "W. B. Yeats and W. J. Turner, 1935–37" (*ES*, 1959, 1960) contains eighteen letters of only passing interest. A more important set is found in Donald T. Torchiana and Glenn O'Malley, "Some New Letters from W. B. Yeats to Lady Gregory" (*REL*, 1963), twenty-three superbly edited letters from 1912–14 and 1920. Ronald W. Ayling has published a total of fourteen letters (ten reprinted from periodicals) in different combinations in several journals (*Theoria*, 1963; *Threshold*, 1965; *MD*, 1966) without indicating the double or triple use of the material. Most of these letters concern the theater. A smaller number of letters include the following: to an anonymous correspondent (*N&Q*, 1958); to William Rose (*GL&L*, 1961); to Thomas MacDonagh (*MLN*, 1961); to John O'Leary (*IB*, 1963); to R. B. Cunninghame Graham (*N&Q*, 1967); to John Masefield (*MR*, 1970); to Arthur Quiller-Couch (*N&Q*, 1971); and to M.

Clifford Harrison, Herbert Horne, Elkin Mathews, and Ernest Radford (*YeatsS*, 1971). Except for a few projects approved some years ago, the publication of the full text of any Yeats letter is now reserved for the *Collected Letters*.

In addition to those already mentioned or cited elsewhere in this chapter, a substantial number of letters to Yeats have been published. Of the first importance are those from his father. A selection can be found in *Passages from the Letters of John Butler Yeats* (1917; rpt. 1971), selected by Ezra Pound; *Further Letters of John Butler Yeats* (1920; rpt. 1971), selected by Lennox Robinson; *J. B. Yeats: Letters to His Son W. B. Yeats and Others, 1869–1922* (ed. Joseph Hone, 1946), which also includes a letter from Yeats to his sister Elizabeth not in the Wade collection; and *Letters from Bedford Park: A Selection from the Correspondence (1890–1901) of John Butler Yeats* (ed. William M. Murphy, 1972). Numerous letters from George W. Russell and one from C. P. Curran are found in *Letters from AE* (ed. Alan Denson, 1961); this edition should be supplemented by *Some Passages from the Letters of AE to W. B. Yeats* (1936; rpt. 1971). A few letters to Yeats are included in *Letters of James Stephens* (ed. Richard J. Finneran, 1974). More significant is volume I of *The Letters of Sean O'Casey* (ed. David Krause, 1975), which covers the period 1910–41. This includes not only the Yeats-O'Casey correspondence but also several letters to or from Yeats and various correspondents, as well as Yeats's reader's report on *The Crimson in the Tri-Colour*. Synge's letters to Yeats will be included in Saddlemyer's *Theatre Business, Management of Men* and also in her forthcoming edition of Synge's *Collected Letters*. A selection is now available in her *Some Letters of John M. Synge to Lady Gregory and W. B. Yeats* (1971).

Daniel J. Murphy is preparing a selection from the exchange of correspondence between Yeats and Lady Gregory, which should be available shortly. Also near completion is a two-volume edition of unpublished *Letters to W. B. Yeats* (ed. Richard J. Finneran, George M. Harper, and William M. Murphy).

IV. *Biographies and Related Studies*

An authorized biography is in preparation by F. S. L. Lyons (*TLS*, 11 Jan. 1974). Until it is published, which is unlikely for several years, there are three main alternatives for a life of Yeats, none entirely satisfactory.

The first authorized biography was Joseph Hone, *W. B. Yeats, 1865–1939* (1943, title page misdated 1942; 2nd ed., 1962). Hone apparently had access to all of Yeats's papers; unfortunately, he frequently paraphrases both published and unpublished material without indicating he is doing so. Nevertheless, Hone's biography presents the largest number of facts about Yeats's life and is still standard on that level; it also includes a good number of unpublished letters from and to Yeats not yet reprinted. Aside from correcting a few details, A. Norman Jeffares' *W. B. Yeats: Man and Poet* (1949; 2nd ed., 1962) adds little biographical information. Jeffares shares Hone's penchant for the "copious use of quotation" (often the same passages) and paraphrase. His interpretations of the poems are based on a simplistic view of the relationship between biography and literature and often substitute summary and quotation for analysis. Jeffares was the first to publish Yeats's "Genealogical Tree of Revolution" but does little to explicate it. K. L. Goodwin (*N&Q*, 1965) corrects Hone and Jeffares on the date of the meeting with Ezra Pound and the composition of "The Grey Rock" and "The Three Hermits."

A better biography than either Hone's or Jeffares' is Richard Ellmann's *Yeats: The Man and the Masks* (1948), a critical biography which concentrates on the sense of division that Yeats constantly felt and his equally constant search for unity. The first major critic to study Yeats's occult activities with the seriousness they deserve, Ellmann provides excellent introductory chapters on Theosophy and the Order of the Golden Dawn. He also devotes considerable attention to Yeats's conflicts with his father, without undue exaggeration or Freudian analysis. The main fault of *The Man and the Masks* is its relative brevity and the undue proportion devoted to the early career. Ellmann is too harsh on some of the early work, describing *The Wind among the Reeds*, for instance, as "poetry where one sinks down and down without finding bottom."

A necessary addition to the three major biographies is William M. Murphy, *The Yeats Family and the Pollexfens of Sligo* (1971). Murphy draws heavily on unpublished material to trace the histories of the two families, showing how traits from both were combined in Yeats. He includes a helpful genealogical table and fourteen drawings by John Butler Yeats, mainly of various members of the family. Murphy also gives the fullest account of Yeats's mother. A shorter and somewhat different version of this work can be found in Murphy's "The Ancestry of William Butler Yeats" (*YeatsS*, 1971).

A general, sometimes provocative biographical sketch is the chapter in Arland Ussher's *Three Great Irishmen: Shaw, Yeats, Joyce* (1952), basically a study of Yeats's temperament, with some attention to the Irish background. Ussher argues that Yeats presents "the complete life-cycle of the subjective man in our time" but criticizes him for a lack of attention to the objective world. Indeed, Ussher is not especially sympathetic toward Yeats's achievement: "The author's feat of remaining young in spirit . . . really implies a lack of true growth, and a deliberate choice of adolescent crudity and bravado." The chapter in Dudley Barker's *Prominent Edwardians* (1969) covers the period of about 1891–1904; it is well written but adds no new information.

There are numerous studies of Yeats's contacts with individuals; those which operated primarily on the literary level will be cited in Section XIV. Of the remainder, one of the most significant is clearly that with his father. William M. Murphy's important "Father and Son: The Early Education of William Butler Yeats" (*REL*, 1967) includes extensive quotations from the father's unpublished *Memoirs* and basically supports Richard Ellmann's thesis. Though it does not refer to Murphy's article, unpublished material, or Yeats's *Memoirs*, Douglas N. Archibald's "Father and Son: John Butler and William Butler Yeats" (*MR*, 1974) is a well-written summary of the relationship, dividing it into three phases and arguing that "the most substantial legacy is probably that strong sense of intellectual freedom and artistic independence—the one unequivocal commitment that both men made." Studies of the father himself include James White's *John Butler Yeats and the Irish Renaissance* (1972), a brief account of his major ideas and artistic technique, with numerous plates; Douglas N. Archibald's *John Butler Yeats* (1974), a good introductory survey; and William M. Murphy's forthcoming full-scale biography.

Also central in Yeats's life was Maud Gonne. The most detailed treatment is Curtis Bradford's (*TSLL*, 1962). In addition to providing a good sketch of the relationship, Bradford argues that in 1909 (20 years after their first meeting) it was consummated, though the affair itself was short lived. In *Golden Codgers: Biographical Speculations* (1973), Richard Ellmann provides a long note on the relationship and posits a physical encounter, though he dates it "about 1907" (the later date appears to be correct). The most extensive study of Maud Gonne available is the chapter in Elizabeth Coxhead's *Daughters of Erin: Five Women of the Irish Renaissance* (1965), which includes two letters to Yeats.

Little is known about Mrs. W. B. Yeats besides the brief accounts in the various biographies. The most extended study is Curtis Bradford's "George Yeats: Poet's Wife" (*SR*, 1969), an essay written in 1955; unfortunately, it does not offer much beyond the story of Bradford's work with the Yeats manuscripts and a few anecdotes.

John Unterecker's *Yeats and Patrick McCartan: A Fenian Friendship* (1967), an exemplary monograph, traces the Yeats-McCartan friendship of the 1930's. Unterecker includes twenty-five letters from Yeats to McCartan as well as much related correspondence, including letters of Oliver St. John Gogarty, Lennox Robinson, and Mrs. Yeats; he also reprints (from *A Speech and Two Poems*) Yeats's address at the Irish Academy of Letters banquet in 1937. An appendix contains passages from McCartan's writings on Yeats.

The number of modern biographies of other writers which touch on Yeats is of course excessive even to list here. Of particular importance, though, is B. L. Reid, *The Man from New York: John Quinn and His Friends* (1968). Quinn was for many years Yeats's foremost American patron and more or less the caretaker of John Butler Yeats while he lived in New York. Reid's definitive study has a significant amount of material on Yeats, including quotations from many unpublished letters.

The most recent extended biographical study of Yeats is Brenda S. Webster's *Yeats: A Psychoanalytic Study* (1973). At times this work reads like a parody of its genre, as when Michael Robartes is compared to Timothy Leary. Webster concentrates her attention on Yeats's Oedipal complex, though she does not neglect his fears of castration and his "primal-scene fantasies, that is, fantasies of parents' intercourse reconstructed from early childhood memories or fantasies" (one can only speculate on how a fantasy can be reconstructed from a fantasy). For the dedicated student there are some interesting ideas in this study, particularly in her discussion of the revisions in *The Shadowy Waters* in relation to Yeats's involvements with Olivia Shakespear and Maud Gonne; Webster also quotes from the unpub-

lished letters to Mabel Dickinson, described as a "masseuse" and
Yeats's "gymnastics teacher and friend." However, too much of the
study is based on rather inane mis- or over-readings of a selected
body of work. Yeats's occult activities, which were surely a significant
part of his personality, are not mentioned; nor did Webster apparently have access to the unpublished journals and diaries. One hesi-
tates to consider what she would have made of Bradford's analysis
of the Yeats-Maud Gonne relationship, had she been aware of it.

An important background work for the study of Yeats's life is Richard M. Kain's *Dublin in the Age of William Butler Yeats and James
Joyce* (1962), which provides a cogent and witty exposition of the
milieu in which Yeats worked for the greater part of his career. Kain's
chapter "Politics" is the clearest guide available through the maze of
events from 1916 to 1922. The chronology, covering the period from
Yeats's first publication to the death of Joyce, is detailed and free
from error. A related but less rewarding work is Estella Ruth Taylor's
The Modern Irish Writers: Cross Currents of Criticism (1954), a
rather dated survey of the remarks of selected writers on each other
and on various topics. Also of less interest to the Yeats student is
Herbert A. Kenny's *Literary Dublin: A History* (1974), which is
neither centered on the Revival period nor especially accurate in its
details.

MEMOIRS

Reminiscences of Yeats are almost a genre in themselves. One does
not read many of the abundant examples before concluding that
there are as many images of Yeats as there are observers. Of contemporary versions, two of the most important are the sentimentalized
sketch in Katharine Tynan's *Twenty-Five Years* (1913) and *The
Middle Years* (1916) and George Moore's satiric vignettes in the
three volumes of *Hail and Farewell* (1911–14), especially the first
volume, *Ave*. The accounts of Tynan and Moore may have been
instrumental in Yeats's decision to begin his own autobiography.
Lady Gregory's memories are found primarily in *Our Irish Theatre*
and *Sir Hugh Lane*, cited above; *Lady Gregory's Journals, 1916–1930*
(ed. Lennox Robinson, 1946), which should be available shortly in
the Coole Edition; and the recently discovered *Seventy Years: Being
the Autobiography of Lady Gregory* (ed. Colin Smythe, 1974; vol.
XIII of the Coole Edition), which contains information on Yeats for
the period 1896–1922 and includes numerous passages from the exchange of correspondence. Regrettably, this last volume required
more extensive editing than it received and must be used with caution.

A. E. has written on Yeats primarily in *Some Irish Essays* (1906;
rpt. in *Imaginations and Reveries*, 1915) and *Song and Its Fountains*
(1932); many of his reviews of Yeats volumes have been collected in
The Living Torch (ed. Monk Gibbon, 1937). In a chapter in *Some
Impressions of My Elders* (1923) St. John Ervine stresses Yeats's
essential loneliness. An interesting interview with Yeats is included
in Louise Morgan's *Writers at Work* (1931). In *Discovery: Being*

the Second Book of an Autobiography, 1897–1913 (1933), John Drinkwater discusses Yeats at Woburn Buildings and two performances of *The King's Threshold*. The essay "Yeats and His Story" in John Eglinton's *Irish Literary Portraits* (1935) is a general appreciation which includes some memories of Yeats at the High School in Dublin. Unfortunately, Maud Gonne MacBride's *A Servant of the Queen* (1938) ends with her marriage in 1903 and says relatively little about Yeats. Other short contemporary accounts can be found in Wilfrid Scawen Blunt, *My Diaries: Being a Personal Narrative of Events, 1888–1914* (1919–20), foreword Lady Gregory; Gerald Griffin, *The Wild Geese: Pen Portraits of Famous Irish Exiles* (1938); the two volumes of Sir William Rothenstein's *Men and Memories* (1931–32) and his *Since Fifty* (1939); and Ethel Mannin, *Privileged Spectator: A Sequel to 'Confessions and Impressions'* (1939; rev. 1948). Mrs. Patrick Campbell's *My Life and Some Letters* (1922) contains only two letters from Yeats, which are reprinted by Allan Wade.

Collections of reminiscences began to appear almost immediately after Yeats's death. The earliest was the special Yeats issue of *The Arrow* (1939), which contained brief memorial tributes from John Masefield, Austin Clarke, and Oliver St. John Gogarty; a note by Richard Hayes praising Yeats's nationalism; brief essays by Edmund Dulac and F. R. Higgins, reprinted in *Scattering Brenches*; some impressions of Sir William Rothenstein and W. J. Turner, the latter also discussing Yeats's alterations of his poems for the *Oxford Book of Modern Verse*; and a facsimile of a letter to Lennox Robinson, whose essay sees Yeats as a "complete man of the theatre." The most important item is Gordon Bottomley's "His Legacy to the Theatre," which argues that Yeats's plays offer new techniques for contemporary dramatists.

Scattering Branches: Tributes to the Memory of W. B. Yeats (ed. Stephen Gwynn, 1940), reissued in 1965 as *William Butler Yeats: Essays in Tribute*, is the most important collection of contemporary memoirs. Gwynn briefly presents his memories of a long friendship. Maud Gonne's "Yeats and Ireland" is again reticent on their relationship but pays tribute to his nationalist activities. The first part of Lennox Robinson's essay is on Yeats's personality; this material is repeated and extended in his essay in *In Excited Reverie* (ed. Jeffares and Cross). The second part treats Yeats's dramatic skills and is also in effect reprinted and somewhat lengthened in his *Curtain Up: An Autobiography* (1942). Sir William Rothenstein's chapter adds little to his accounts cited above. W. G. Fay remarks on Yeats's skill as a producer; a few more memories are found in W. G. Fay and Catherine Carswell, *The Fays of the Abbey Theatre: An Autobiographical Record* (1935). Edmund Dulac briefly studies Yeats's essential wholeness of personality and his nobility. C. Day Lewis likewise comments on Yeats's nobility and defends his fondness for aristocratic traditions; the same arguments are made in his *Notable Images of Virtue* (1954). F. R. Higgins provides some anecdotes and also remarks on the techniques of Yeats's poems in relation to Gaelic poetry. L. A. G. Strong presents a summary and in passing defends Yeats's occult activities; fuller accounts by Strong can be found in the chapters in *Personal Remarks* (1953), a general appreciation with some reminiscences; and *Green Memory* (1961), mainly about Yeats at Oxford.

John Masefield's brief *Some Memories of W. B. Yeats* (1940) is in prose and verse, the latter rather poor. Masefield concentrates on his first meeting with Yeats, Yeats at Coole Park, and his rooms at 18 Woburn Buildings—"That curved stair, lit by a little lamp at the curve, was trodden by all who made our world." The various comments of Sean O'Casey, first published 1945-52, are gathered in the two volumes of his *Autobiographies* (1963); some essays on Yeats are collected in *Blasts and Benedictions: Articles and Stories* (1967), selected by Ronald Ayling. Mary Colum's *Life and the Dream* (1947; rev. 1966) contains some interesting memories of both Yeats and Maud Gonne. Clifford Bax suggests in *Some I Knew Well* (1951) that "there were at least six personalities in Yeats" and that he "never harmonized the complicated contents of his mind." In *Brave Spirits* (1952), Georgina Sime pictures Yeats at Bedford Park in the 1890's and on two visits to Montreal. The material on Yeats in Dorothy Wellesley's *Far Have I Travelled* (1952) repeats much of the commentary from the *Letters on Poetry*. The relevant lecture (given "about 1938") in Richard Aldington's *A. E. Housman and W. B. Yeats: Two Lectures* (1955) offers a general commentary on Yeats's character and poetry but is most interesting for the biographical information. Aldington's account of Yeats at Rapallo in 1928-29 can be supplemented by the memories of another visitor, found in *My Friend When Young: The Memoirs of Brigit Patmore* (ed. Derek Patmore, 1968), which also includes some other anecdotes.

Monk Gibbon's *The Masterpiece and the Man: Yeats as I Knew Him* (1959) is the most hostile of the extended reminiscences. Gibbon professes to appreciate Yeats's literary achievements, but his study gives scant attention to the "masterpiece." His view of the "man" is colored by his unswerving loyalty to A. E. and by his impressions of the elder Yeats (they met in 1923) as prideful and aloof. The book recounts many slights at the hand of Yeats, not the least of which was Gibbon's exclusion from the *Oxford Book of Modern Verse*. He is impatient with Yeats's thought, claiming he was "not a scholar, not a mystic, not a metaphysician." Gibbon's volume is most valuable for the four unpublished letters of Yeats it contains, including an important one on G. M. Hopkins, and the detailed account of Yeats's sisters, whom he knew much more intimately than he knew Yeats. Gibbon also gives a fairly detailed, if prejudiced, account of the relationship between A. E. and Yeats.

Oliver St. John Gogarty has written on Yeats at some length. His *William Butler Yeats: A Memoir* (1963), preface by Myles Dillon, was projected as a chapter in his unfinished *The Nine Worthies*; thus the text was not in a final form at his death. The volume as published is basically a collection of anecdotes, including the well-known remark of Joyce to Yeats, "You are too old for me to help." Gogarty also acknowledges the assistance Yeats gave him with his poems. However, the *Memoir* is by no means a complete collection of Gogarty's anecdotes, and so the earlier volumes are still important: *As I Was Going Down Sackville Street* (1937), *Mourning Became Mrs Spend-*

love (1946), *Rolling Down the Lea* (1950), and *It Isn't This Time of Year at All!: An Unpremeditated Autobiography* (1954). In addition, there are some interesting passages on Yeats in *Many Lines to Thee* (ed. James F. Carens, 1971), which contains twenty-nine letters from Gogarty to G. K. A. Bell, dated 1904–07.

The most recent full-length collection of reminiscences is *The Yeats We Knew* (ed. Francis MacManus, 1965), which contains the texts of five of the six Thomas Davis Lectures on Radio Éireann in 1965. Padraic Colum supplies some memories of Yeats, particularly at the Abbey; this is almost identical with his "Reminiscences of Yeats" (*TriQ*, 1965). Francis Stuart (Maud Gonne's son-in-law) discusses the unhappiness of Yeats's later years and his own inability to become intimate with him. Monk Gibbon does little more than repeat his attacks from *The Masterpiece and the Man.* Earnán de Blaghd (Ernest Blythe) discusses Yeats's management of the Abbey toward the end of his career. Austin Clarke recounts his memories of Yeats at the Abbey, the Thomas Davis celebration in 1914, and Coole Park. Clarke's account of the Thomas Davis episode is almost identical to that in "A Centenary Celebration" (*MR*, 1964; rpt. in *Irish Renaissance*, ed. Robin Skelton and David R. Clark); he adds a few more reminiscences in "Glimpses of W. B. Yeats" (*Shenandoah*, 1965) and "The Cardinal and the Countess" (*ArielE*, 1972).

In *Memories, 1898–1939* (1966), C. M. Bowra concentrates on Yeats at Oxford; he includes two unpublished letters, in one of which Yeats denies that he "was really much influenced by French Symbolists." *Irish Literary Portraits* (ed. W. R. Rodgers, 1972) contains an edited script of a 1949 BBC broadcast on Yeats (a shorter version had been previously published in *In Excited Reverie*). The contributors include Sean O'Faolain, W. K. Magee ("John Eglinton"), Austin Clarke, Dossy Wright, Brinsley Macnamara, Richard Best, Iseult Stuart, Lennox Robinson, Maud Gonne MacBride, Bertie Smyllie, Arthur Hannah, Anne Yeats, Norah McGuinness, Sean MacBride, Isabelle MacNie (better known as the Irish artist "Mac"), Mrs. W. B. Yeats, and Frank O'Connor. O'Connor's important recollections are brought together in *A Short History of Irish Literature: A Backward Look* (1967), more anecdote than history in the Yeats chapters, and *My Father's Son* (1968). Most of the *Audio Arts* cassette devoted to Yeats (1974) consists of Anne Yeats's memories of her father; the other important item is Gogarty's 1949 talk on "Yeats and George Moore."

Briefer reminiscences of some interest include Ella Young, *Flowering Dusk: Things Remembered Accurately and Inaccurately* (1945); R. F. Rattray, *Poets in the Flesh* (1961); some broadcasts in *James, Seumas and Jacques: Unpublished Writings of James Stephens* (ed. Lloyd Frankenberg, 1964); Lady Beatrice Glenavy, 'Today We Will Only Gossip' (1964); Walter Starkie, "Yeats and the Abbey Theatre," in *Homage to Yeats: 1865–1965* (1966), introduction Majl Ewing (a slightly revised version was published in *SoR*, 1968); Horace Gregory, *The House on Jefferson Street: A Cycle of Memories* (1971); and Micheál MacLiammóir, "How Yeats Influenced My Life In the Theatre," in *Yeats and the Theatre* (ed. Robert O'Driscoll and Lorna Reynolds).

ICONOGRAPHIES AND RELATED STUDIES

Because of the pictorial emphasis of Yeats's work, collections of photographs and pictures have a special value in Yeats studies. The most important of these is also the earliest, *Images of a Poet* (1961) by D. J. Gordon and others. This work far transcends its origins as a catalog (published as *I, the Poet William Yeats*, 1957) of an exhibition first shown at the University of Reading and later expanded for presentation in Manchester and Dublin. With the exception of brief notes by Frank Kermode on the image of the Dancer and by Robin Skelton on the books and manuscripts, the essays are collaborations by Gordon and Ian Fletcher. "The Image of the Poet" discusses Yeats's opinions of the several portraits made of him. "Persons and Places" centers on Yeats's Irish friends and offers an especially full sketch of Robert Gregory. "The Poet and the Theatre" is primarily on the Noh drama and includes an important discussion of the extent to which Japanese drama was known in England prior to the efforts of Ezra Pound. "Byzantium" is a brilliant exposition of most of Yeats's sources and of the development in England of an attitude toward Byzantium. "Symbolic Art and Visionary Landscape" is possibly the most seminal chapter in tracing Yeats's views of various artists with a scholarly awareness of the English art scene in the 1890's. The essays are illustrated by twenty-six plates. *Images of a Poet* is essential reading for any serious student.

Images and Memories (ed. S. B. Bushrui and J. M. Munro, 1970) is a useful collection of photographs, though the brief discussions accompanying them contain many inaccuracies. The volume also provides a convenient year-by-year chronology 1884–1939. *W. B. Yeats and His World* (1971) by Micheál MacLiammóir and Eavan Boland is a commentary illustrated by 138 plates. Though not free from error, it is generally accurate. But the account of Yeats's life and relationships is somewhat marred by a tendency to overdramatize and by a too easy acceptance of Yeats's own reminiscences.

Related items include *Yeats at the Municipal Gallery* (introd. Arland Ussher, 1959), which reproduces the paintings mentioned in "The Municipal Gallery Revisited"; and *W. B. Yeats: A Centenary Exhibition* (1965), foreword James White, which has only a few plates but contains valuable biographical information on some of Yeats's friends. Yeats's handprints have been reproduced (*TQ*, 1965) and await their palmist.

Sheelah Kirby's *The Yeats Country: A Guide to Places in the West of Ireland Associated with the Life and Writings of William Butler Yeats* (ed. Patrick Gallagher, 1962; 2nd ed., 1963) is the most valuable work of its kind. Kirby includes a useful list of place names in Yeats's work and provides translations of the Irish. The volume has maps and drawings but no photographs. Mary Hanley's *Thoor Ballylee—Home of William Butler Yeats* (ed. Liam Miller, 1965) is a good account of Yeats's tower, with extensive quotations from the correspondence. It is perhaps most interesting for some photographs of the tower in 1926. *Yeats and Sandymount* (comp. David R. Clark and Noel Kavanagh, 1966) consists of selections from the writings of

Yeats and others on his birthplace; there is little commentary by the compilers. Colin Smythe's *A Guide to Coole Park, Co. Galway, Home of Lady Gregory* (1973), foreword Maurice Craig, contains many interesting photographs made before Coole Park was razed and extensive quotations from Lady Gregory's writings. *A Literary Guide to Ireland* (1973) by Susan and Thomas Cahill, primarily designed for tourists, is less detailed than the above guidebooks.

V. *Manuscript Materials*

HOLDINGS

The most extensive collection of manuscript material is in the National Library of Ireland and is briefly listed in Volume IV of *Manuscript Sources for the History of Irish Civilisation* (ed. Richard J. Hayes, 1965), which also notes material in a few other libraries. Generously donated by Mrs. W. B. Yeats, the National Library collection includes essentially all the working drafts for the poems and the plays and many other items. The remainder of the manuscripts retained by Yeats is preserved by the Yeats family in Ireland; this collection includes notebooks, proofs, essays, and speeches as well as a mass of occult materials and incoming correspondence. Yeats's library is also maintained by the Yeats family in Ireland; a catalog is in preparation and may now be available. A third major collection is found in the Berg Collection, New York Public Library, which obtained most of the Yeats manuscripts by acquiring the Lady Gregory Papers, noted by Lola L. Szladits (*BNYPL*, 1969); a complete listing is provided in Volume IV of the *Dictionary Catalog of the Henry W. and Albert A. Berg Collection* (1969). Another extensive collection is in the Houghton Library of Harvard University; this includes both original manuscripts and five reels of microfilm of much of the material from Mrs. Yeats's collection. Arrangements have recently been completed for the State University of New York at Stony Brook to acquire microfilms of all the material in both the Yeats family collection and the National Library of Ireland; the National Library will also receive microfilms of the material from the family collection which it now lacks.

There are smaller holdings in numerous other libraries, including the following: Bibliothèque de l'Arsenal; Bodleian Library; Boston University; British Library (Reference Division) (*BC*, 1964; *BMQ*, 1972); Brown University; Bucknell University; University of California, Berkeley; University of California, Los Angeles; Cambridge University Library; University of Chicago; Colby College; Columbia University; Cornell University (*Yeats and the Theatre*); Huntington Library (*HLQ*, 1968); Indiana University; University of Kansas; Kenyon College; Leeds University (*A Catalogue of the Gosse Correspondence in the Brotherton Collection*, 1950); Liverpool University; Macmillan Archive, Basingstoke; Mills College, Oakland; National Library of Scotland; Northwestern University; Princeton University (*PULC*, 1955); University of Reading; Southern Illinois University; University of Texas (*LCUT*, 1957); Trinity College, Dublin; University

College, Dublin (Richard M. Kain, "The Curran Library," *Éire*, 1972); Wellesley College; and Yale University (*YULG*, 1952). Some important material is of course held by private collectors. A census of Yeats's manuscripts would be most welcome; some "Suggested Guidelines for Catalogue of Yeats Manuscripts" have been provided in *Yeats and the Theatre* (ed. Robert O'Driscoll and Lorna Reynolds).

While working on his several studies of Yeats, Curtis Bradford made transcriptions of much of Yeats's unpublished prose and gathered his partially edited typescripts into six black binders. In "Transcriptions of Yeats' Unpublished Prose in the Bradford Papers at Grinnell College" (*Serif*, 1973), James Lovic Allen and M. M. Liberman have noted that a set of these binders is available in the United States and have described the material that remains unpublished, which they estimate at about 450 typewritten pages. However, a number of the items described as unpublished are in fact available in various critical studies, as acknowledged by Allen in a list of corrections (*Serif*, 1975).

Two cautions are in order in a discussion of Yeats's manuscripts. First, one must be careful to distinguish between actual working manuscripts and what Bradford has called "concocted" manuscripts— in effect, almost a fair copy which Yeats prepared after a work was essentially completed. Many of the manuscripts from the collection of John Quinn, for instance, are of the latter kind (it is amusing to observe the neatness of Yeats's handwriting on such occasions). Second, publication of any Yeats manuscript material (and in some libraries, access to the material) is carefully and judiciously controlled by the Yeats Estate and its literary agent. At the time of writing, most of the important material is being used in various major projects.

STUDIES

A number of the critical works cited elsewhere, particularly those of Richard Ellmann and Thomas Parkinson, have of course made good use of manuscript materials. Of the full-length studies, the most generally useful is Curtis Bradford's *Yeats at Work* (1965). Bradford discusses selected poems, plays, and prose writings from their early beginnings (usually a prose "subject" for a poem, a scenario for a play) to their final printed versions. His transcriptions of the material are less complex than those of Stallworthy or other scholars. Bradford's introductions to the three sections of his study should be read by any serious student; the discussions of the individual works are valuable mainly for those interested in the particular work or in Yeats's creative process. Bradford's study should be supplemented by his article on the Byzantium poems (*PMLA*, 1960), found in revised form in *Yeats: A Collection of Critical Essays* (ed. John Unterecker).

The other major scholar of Yeats's manuscripts is Jon Stallworthy. *Between the Lines: Yeats's Poetry in the Making* (1963; corrected 2nd impression, 1965) examines eighteen poems from various periods of Yeats's career. Stallworthy provides a complete transcription of all the important manuscripts. Again, for the general reader the main interest comes in the first chapter, a discussion of Yeats's habits of composition, and the last chapter, a good summary of Yeats's techniques and subject matter. Stallworthy has published revised versions of two of his chapters: that on "The Second Coming" in the Yeats issue of *Agenda* (1971–72) and that on "The Black Tower" in his casebook *Yeats: Last Poems*. Stallworthy's *Vision and Revision in Yeats's Last Poems* (1969) uses the format of his earlier book to trace the development of some thirteen late poems. Although not completely related to the rest of the book, the opening essays are valuable. "The Dynastic Theme" shows Yeats as the first English poet to emphasize the theme and includes an extended comparison with Robert Lowell. "The Prophetic Voice" shows the influence of Spenser, Blake, Shelley, and the Irish bardic tradition on Yeats's attainment of a prophetic vision.

The other extended discussion of the manuscripts of an individual poem is not equal to the careful work of Bradford and Stallworthy. In "A Corrected Typescript of Yeats's 'Easter 1916'" (*HLQ*, 1963), George Mayhew provides a transcription of the Huntington typescript and lists the variants from a manuscript then held by Mrs. Yeats and now in the National Library of Ireland. However, Mayhew is apparently unaware that the manuscript of the poem used by Clement Shorter for the first private printing is in the Berg Collection (as noted by Marion Witt, *PMLA*, 1949); thus his study is incomplete and also contains a number of forced conjectures and inaccurate statements. Incidentally, a letter from Yeats to Shorter quoted by D. T. Torchiana in *W. B. Yeats and Georgian Ireland* seems to establish clearly that the private printing was not issued until the spring of 1917, rather than the 1916 date suggested in the Wade/Alspach *Bibliography* and accepted by Mayhew.

EDITIONS

Many individual items have been published in various critical studies. An early manuscript of "The Sorrow of the World" (later "The Sorrow of Love") is given in facsimile in *Douglas Library Notes* (Summer 1962). In "English Literary Autographs XLIX" (*BC*, 1964), T. J. Brown prints a facsimile of the British Library (Reference Division) manuscript of "The Rose Tree," dated April 1917 and quite close to the published text. P. J. Croft's *Autograph Poetry in the English Language* (1973) includes a facsimile of the University of Texas manuscript of "The Wild Swans at Coole."

An important collection of manuscript material is found in *Irish Renaissance: A Gathering of Essays, Memoirs, and Letters from the Massachusetts Review* (ed. Robin Skelton and David R. Clark, 1965). This includes editions by Curtis Bradford of "Modern Ireland: An Address to American Audiences, 1932–33" and of "Discoveries: Second Series," some brief essays from 1908–09. John Unterecker also presents eleven 1918 letters from Yeats to Mrs. Duncan, curator of the Municipal Gallery in Dublin. Another volume to contain some significant material is *Yeats and the Theatre* (ed. Robert O'Driscoll and Lorna Reynolds). O'Driscoll's "Yeats on Personality: Three Unpublished Lectures" gives the texts of three 1910 items; the notes for one of them are provided by Joseph Ronsley in "Yeats's Lecture Notes for 'Friends of My Youth.'" Colin Smythe's "A Note on Some of Yeats's Revisions for *The Land of Heart's Desire*" gives some 1911 corrections in a copy of the play from the Abbey Theatre archives. More important is "Yeats's Versions of Sophocles: Two Typescripts" by David R. Clark and James B. McGuire, which prints the variants from one typescript of *Sophocles' King Oedipus* and one of *Sophocles' Oedipus at Colonus*. A useful supplement to the first part of this essay is Frederic D. Grab's "Yeats's *King Oedipus*" (*JEGP*, 1972), which offers a good comparison of Yeats's version with the Jebb translation.

The first edition of the manuscripts of a play was *A Tower of Polished Black Stones: Early Versions of* The Shadowy Waters (ed. David Ridgley Clark and George Mayhew, 1971), which contains selected manuscripts from the Huntington Library and the National Library of Ireland and lucid commentary by the editors; it also includes four drawings by Yeats. As a scholarly text, this volume was essentially superseded by *Druid Craft: The Writing of* The Shadowy Waters (ed. Michael J. Sidnell, George P. Mayhew, and David R. Clark, 1971), which publishes all the extant manuscripts and drawings and includes a bibliographical description of the material. *Druid Craft* not only provides a running commentary on the development of the play but also has chapters on "Structure and Plot in the Manuscript Versions," "Mythical Allusion, Symbol & Vision in the Early Versions," and "The Published Versions," the last of which notes for the first time the differences in the two 1900 printings.

Druid Craft is invaluable for anyone with a strong interest in either the play or Yeats's creative process. A careful student will observe that there are both minor differences in transcription and major differences in the dating of the manuscripts between *A Tower of Polished Black Stones* and *Druid Craft*. Most of these discrepancies are to be understood as representing the different views of the several editors rather than the correction of earlier errors. Anyone who has attempted to decipher Yeats's handwriting will understand the possibilities for disagreement.

Druid Craft is the first volume in the Manuscripts of W. B. Yeats series, under the general editorship of David R. Clark. Curtis Bradford's edition of *The Writing of* The Player Queen should now be available. Virginia Rohan's *The Manuscripts of* Deirdre is scheduled for publication in the "Yeats Studies Series" in 1977. Michael J. Sidnell's *The Writing of* The Countess Cathleen also awaits publication; a description of the manuscripts is provided by Sidnell in *PBSA* (1962). Other editions of play manuscripts are in progress or projected.

W. H. O'Donnell's edition of *The Speckled Bird*, an unfinished novel Yeats worked on from 1896 to about 1903, was published in a two-volume limited edition by the Cuala Press in 1974 (one must ignore the optimistic 1973 date on the title page of Vol. 1.) This sparsely annotated edition is based in the main on the typescript. A full-scale study of the manuscripts by O'Donnell will be published shortly in the "Yeats Studies Series."

VI. *Some Early Studies (to 1940)* *

Although contemporary accounts of Yeats's career are most useful in tracing the history of his critical reputation and in assessing the literary milieu in which he worked, they may also include insights that are still valuable.

The first historian of the movement was W. P. Ryan in *The Irish Literary Revival: Its History, Pioneers and Possibilities* (1894). At the time Yeats was but one voice among many. Ryan's brief sketch emphasizes the dreamer in Yeats and recommends "that he . . . shake himself free from the passing craze of occultism and symbolism, and realise that the universe is not tenanted solely by soulths and sheogues." Another account of some interest is by Yeats's friend Arthur Symons in *Studies in Prose and Verse* (1904); Symons praises Yeats's style and argues that the poems express "the elemental desire of humanity, the desire of love, the desire of wisdom, the desire of beauty."

The honor of writing the first full-length study of Yeats fell to an American, Horatio Sheafe Krans. The title of his brief study indicates the change in Yeats's stature since 1894: *William Butler Yeats and the Irish Literary Revival* (1904). In his chapter on the Revival, Krans rightly sees the "break-up of Parnell's political ship" as giving impetus to the movement (one suspects a borrowing from Yeats's lectures on his 1903–04 tour). As a whole, the study offers little beyond summaries of the works. Krans attempts to explain Yeats's symbolism while admitting that "a not inconsiderable part of his work . . . is darkened by a recondite imagery, which for him no doubt has a meaning . . . but to the rest of mankind conveys no idea, induces no mood, and is at most perspicuous gloom."

Forrest Reid's *W. B. Yeats: A Critical Study* (1915) is a more important contemporary examination. Reid believes that Yeats is a good but not "a universal poet," and his study is distinguished by objectivity. He is impatient, for example, with Yeats's theory of symbolism and his mystical thought, which lacks the "spirit of love." He also argues that Yeats's poetic powers are declining and that "it is not likely that his style, now as austere as any style could well be, will undergo much further modification." Reid was one of the first critics to stress the importance of Yeats's revisions. He generally sees them as detrimental, as in the post-1900 changes in *The Shadowy Waters*. This work illustrates the dangers to modern scholars of ignoring the early criticism: Reid anticipates, for instance, both Harold Bloom and the editors of *Druid Craft* in his comments on the revisions to *The Shadowy Waters*; more curiously, his conclusion that Yeats's prosody is based not on standard versification but on "natural speech-stress" looks forward to Thomas Parkinson's analysis.

The year of the Easter Rebellion was a prolific one in Yeats studies. Patty Gurd's *The Early Poetry of William Butler Yeats* (1916) is primarily a study of sources and influences, touching on Irish mythol-

* This section treats the full-length studies and a few scattered items. A selection from the early essays and chapters in books is found in Sections VII and VIII, and from early studies of the plays in Section XII.

ogy, Spenser, Blake, Shelley, and Maeterlinck. Her identifications of
sources are often egregiously wrong, as when she argues that Yeats
must have used Lady Gregory's manuscripts for "The Wanderings of
Oisin." Of more interest is J. M. Hone, *William Butler Yeats: The
Poet in Contemporary Ireland* (1916). This study by Yeats's future
biographer devotes some attention to his life, particularly to the influence of John Butler Yeats; but in the main it is a general survey of the
poems, plays, and prose. The book is especially valuable for the
account of Yeats's reception by his Irish audience. Hone was more
willing than most early critics to take Yeats's occult activities with
seriousness; indeed, his remark that "we would like to know more of
Mr. Yeats' psychical experiences, his habit of magical practices, his
belief in alchemy, and what the astrologers call the 'true science'" is
still relevant. *Ireland's Literary Renaissance* (1916; rev. 1922) by
Ernest Boyd remains the most detailed account of the movement.
While admitting the importance of the poetry, Boyd gives equal
space to the plays and the prose. He is hostile to Yeats's mystical
thought, which he calls "obscure and weak," and argues that the
plays are not dramatic, *Deirdre* being a single exception. In some
brief but interesting comments in *Literature in Ireland: Studies Irish
and Anglo-Irish* (1916), Thomas MacDonagh is critical of Yeats's
lack of knowledge of the Irish language but praises the "peculiar
musical quality of his early verse," suggesting that it derives from
"that Irish chant which at once saves Irish speech from too definite a
stress and from an utterance too monotonous and harsh."

C. L. Wrenn's *W. B. Yeats: A Literary Study* (1920, rpt. from
DUJ, 1919) is brief but valuable. Among other topics he treats the
influence of Blake ("without Blake there could have been no Yeats as
we know him"), prints the Ronsard sonnet which is the basis for
"When You are Old," and sees that in *The Countess Cathleen* "Aleel
belongs, not to the parable to be set forth or the original legend, but
is rather the expression of a certain definite artistic tendency of the
'90's, introduced, it may be, as a convenient outlet for the moods
and sentiments of the writer." Wrenn reserves most of his praise for
the early poems, especially those collected in *The Rose* section.

H. M. Green provides a general sketch of Yeats's life and development in *The Poetry of W. B. Yeats* (Sydney, 1931), dividing the
career into four segments. He discusses many of the influences, including Spenser, Blake, Coleridge, Shelley, and Keats; and makes the
unusual claim that "Yeats's most obvious direct ancestor is Keats,
whose rhythms and imagery do now and then introduce themselves
among his own." He argues that Yeats was too concerned with the
poetry of escape and that his final stature is not equal to that of
Milton or Wordsworth.

L. A. G. Strong's *A Letter to W. B. Yeats* (1932) includes a basic
account of Yeats's development but is primarily a laudation. The only
fault that Strong notes is an occasional obscurity in symbolism. He
includes an interesting analysis of the differences between Yeats's
private and public personalities.

More representative of the attitude toward Yeats by many younger
writers in the 1930's is Stephen Spender's chapter in *The Destructive
Element: A Study of Modern Writers and Beliefs* (1935), in which

Yeats suffers in comparison with Eliot and Auden: although Yeats "has much wisdom, he offers no philosophy of life" and his poetry is "devoid of any unifying moral subject." Yeats received a more sympathetic treatment in Spender's *The Creative Element: A Study of Vision, Despair and Orthodoxy among Some Modern Writers* (1953). Spender there argues that Yeats's "theme is the transformation of imperfect and subjective man into his objective aims" and that he "succeeds in identifying the noblest achievement with a higher form of existence which remains human."

William Butler Yeats (1935) by J. H. Pollock is a general survey which stresses Yeats's claim to be a national poet and charts his development from "objective diffuseness to subjective intensity." Pollock finds little value in the plays and less in Yeats's occult activities or *A Vision*. He concludes that Yeats is an artist of "exquisite technique, but limited appeal." Joyce Mayhew, *Ad Multos Annos: William Butler Yeats in His Seventieth Year* (1935) is a tribute of no interest. Only slightly more memorable are the chapter in Cornelius Weygandt's *The Time of Yeats: English Poetry of To-Day against an American Background* (1937), a general sketch of the career which locates Yeats's best work in the early poems; and F. R. Higgins's "Yeats and Poetic Drama in Ireland," in *The Irish Theatre: Lectures Delivered during the Abbey Theatre Festival Held in Dublin in August 1938* (ed. Lennox Robinson, 1939), a general appreciation of Yeats's dramatic activities.

J. P. O'Donnell's *Sailing to Byzantium: A Study in the Development of the Style and Symbolism in the Poetry of William Butler Yeats* (1939) hardly merits its title, as it contains more quotation than analysis and says little on the Byzantium poems themselves.

VII. *Special Issues of Periodicals; Yeats Journals**

SPECIAL ISSUES OF PERIODICALS

With the exception of the 1939 Yeats issue of *The Arrow* (cited above), the first important special issue of a periodical was the winter 1941–42 number of *The Southern Review*. As well as any other single publication it marks the beginning of modern scholarship and criticism of Yeats (indeed, ten of the fifteen articles have been reprinted in one or more anthologies of Yeats criticism).

R. P. Blackmur's "Between Myth and Philosophy: Fragments of W. B. Yeats" (*Language as Gesture*, 1952) is a difficult but important study of how the tension between the two kinds of thought prevented Yeats from creating "except in fragments, the actuality of his age"; Blackmur nevertheless sees him as "the greatest poet in English since the seventeenth century." L. C. Knights (*Explorations*, 1946) provides sympathetic readings of the Byzantium poems but considers the career as a whole "a heroic failure." T. S. Eliot's influential essay,

---

* To avoid repetition, articles are not cited here if they are mentioned elsewhere in the chapter, either individually or as part of a full-length study. Titles of books which reprint articles but are not discussed in the chapter have been provided in parentheses.

reprinted from *Purpose* (1940) and later included in his *On Poetry and Poets* (1957), closes with the famous pronouncement that Yeats "was one of those whose history is the history of their own time, who are part of the consciousness of an age which cannot be understood without them." F. O. Matthiessen (*The Responsibilities of the Critic*, ed. John Rackliffe, 1952) offers a somewhat rambling essay on Yeats's development, with comparisons to Synge and Eliot. Delmore Schwartz (*Selected Essays*, ed. Donald A. Dike and David H. Zucker, 1970) notes the areas of Yeats's work that need study but rejects his ideas as too Romantic. Horace Gregory (*The Shield of Achilles*, 1944) treats Yeats's use of a parallel between himself and Swift and also comments briefly on Crazy Jane. Donald Davidson (*Still Rebels, Still Yankees*, 1957) notes the connection between popular lore and the artist. John Crowe Ransom's "The Irish, the Gaelic, the Byzantine" contains some scattered analyses of poems but does not justify its title, Ransom being more concerned with theories of criticism than with Yeats. Kenneth Burke's article centers on *A Vision* and offers some provocative psychological speculations. Morton Dauwen Zabel's commentary on the identity between Yeats's life and his art, as seen in the *Autobiographies*, is not especially valuable. In "Yeats's Romanticism: Notes and Suggestions" (*On the Limits of Poetry*, 1948) Allan Tate suggests the basic unimportance of *A Vision* and prophesies— with more than a little wisdom—that "the coming generation is likely to overdo the scholarly procedure" and that "Yeats's special qualities will instigate special studies of great ingenuity." Arthur Mizener provides an early recognition of the root continuity of Yeats's career despite changes in style. Austin Warren's important "Religio Poetae" (*Rage for Order*, 1949) is a sympathetic and learned defense of Yeats's occult interests. In "Domes of Byzantium" Howard Baker traces a few recurring symbols but says little on the Byzantium poems. Randall Jarrell discusses Yeats's development and sees *A Vision* as the work that allowed Yeats to write his greatest poetry; he also provides lists of the typical early and late diction of the poems.

The *Irish Library Bulletin* (1948) is now of little interest. It includes a chronology of Yeats's life by Joseph Hone, the text of a speech by Robert Farren at the Abbey in 1941, suggestions by T. R. Henn about why Yeats wanted to be buried at Drumcliff, and memories by Lennox Robinson of the 1948 funeral service.

A more important Yeats issue was the 1955 number of *Irish Writing*. Peter Allt's brief but perceptive essay "Lady Gregory and Yeats's Cult of Aristocracy" notes some comparisons between Yeats and Ben Jonson. Curtis Bradford prints an excerpt from *The Speckled Bird*, supplementing the one by Joseph Hone (*The Bell*, 1941). Donald Davie is unconvincing in discussing Yeats's understanding of Berkeley and arguing that the late Yeats is not Romantic. Peter Ure gives a reading of "Demon and Beast" in terms of the relationship between the artist and nature. Valentin Iremonger suggests that Yeats's plays are valuable as poems but not as dramas. The most important article is Hugh Kenner's "The Sacred Book of the Arts" (*SR*, 1956; *Gnomon*, 1958), a seminal statement on the unity and order of the individual collections of poems. Although Kenner was not the first critic to note the organic unity of all the poems, his statement is forceful and provocative: Yeats "was an architect, not a decorator; he didn't accumulate poems, he wrote books."

Other than the introductory note by A. Norman Jeffares, the essays in the Yeats number of *A Review of English Literature* (1963) are cited elsewhere. *The Irish Book* (1963) includes a note on the collections in the Sligo County Library and Museum by Nora Niland, and Peter Faulkner's "W. B. Yeats as Reviewer: *The Bookman* 1892–1898," which traces Yeats's growing commitment to a Symbolist view of literature. Though described as a "W. B. Yeats Commemorative Issue," the *Amherst Literary Magazine* (1964) contains only the uncollected "Crazy Jane on the King" and a brief note on the poem by Archibald MacLeish; slightly different texts of the poem had been printed as "Cracked Mary's Vision" in Richard Ellmann's *The Identity of Yeats* and as "Crazy Jane and the King" in Oliver St. John Gogarty's *Start from Somewhere Else* (1955).

The appearance of a Yeats issue of *Modern Drama* (1964) perhaps indicated that the plays had been unjustly neglected by most critics. Peter Ure's excellent article discusses the plays written in a mixture of prose and verse, with particular attention to *The Green Helmet*. Marjorie Lightfoot's "*Purgatory* and *The Family Reunion*: in Pursuit of Prosodic Description" is no more useful than Aloyse Scanlon's "The Sustained Metaphor in *The Only Jealousy of Emer*." Not much more perceptive is Sidney Warschausky on "Yeats's Purgatorial Plays." In a brief note David R. Clark discusses Aubrey Beardsley's lost drawing for *The Shadowy Waters*. Marilyn Gaddis Rose's "A Visit with Anne Yeats" is of little interest. Helen Hennessy Vendler is perceptive in "Yeats's Changing Metaphors for the Otherworld," relating the various images to Yeats's views on the relationship between life and art. Gabriel Fallon offers some reminiscences of Yeats at the Abbey in the early 1920's, especially of his speech during the riots over O'Casey's *The Plough and the Stars*. In a valuable essay John Unterecker uses *Purgatory* to show the link in the plays between "a dominant imagery and a passionate action," also arguing that the plays are performable drama. The material in the *Massachusetts Review* (1964) was reprinted in *Irish Renaissance*, cited above.

The centenary year elicited a flood of special Yeats numbers. *The Dublin Magazine* (1965) contains an important article by George Mills Harper, tracing Yeats's development of "intellectual nationalism" and demonstrating that he never abandoned his concern with Irish nationality. Muriel C. Bradbrook's "Yeats and Elizabethan Love Poetry" is a somewhat rambling essay that includes comparisons with Spenser, Ralegh, and Shakespeare. T. R. Henn presents a cogent summary of George Moore's career and a sketch of the Moore-Yeats attacks and counterattacks.

The most important article in *English* (1965) is Peter Ure's "The Hero on the World Tree: Yeats's Plays," in which he writes that Yeats believed "the heroic act was the act that combined the greatest degree of self-sacrifice with the greatest degree of self-realization." There is little of note in A. Norman Jeffares' brief "Yeats as Critic" or in the excerpts from a speech by Cleanth Brooks on Yeats's "distrust of abstraction." Hermann Peschmann briefly treats the exclusion of the war poets from the *Oxford Book of Modern Verse*; more information on one of the exclusions can be found in Joseph Cohen's "In Memory of W. B. Yeats—and Wilfred Owen" (*JEGP*, 1959). *Hermathena* (1965) contains an important essay by Philip Edwards on "Yeats and the Trinity Chair" (given to W. F. Trench), including two letters from Yeats to John Pentland Mahaffy. Brendan Kennelly discusses the basic heroic nature of Cuchulain in the plays; and H. E. Shields incorrectly locates the source of "Down by the Salley Gardens" in an Anglo-Irish broadside, "The Rambling Boys of Pleasure."

The most provocative article in the Yeats issue of *Phoenix* (Seoul, 1965) is G. S. Fraser's "Yeats as a Philosopher," which contrasts the approaches to Yeats of Kathleen Raine and John Wain and also discusses Yeats's exchange of letters with T. Sturge Moore. Fraser concludes that Yeats should be understood as a "spiritual pluralist." William Empson's rambling "The Variants for the Byzantium Poems" (rpt. from *Essays Presented to Amy G. Stock*, ed. R. K. Kaul, Jaipur, 1965) uses the drafts of the poems to argue that neither work is concerned with a transcendent realm. A commentary by Jeffares on Yeats's criticism contains more quotation than analysis. E. W. F. Tomlin briefly suggests that the continuity of Yeats's career is apparent in his diction. Kim U-Chang provides an account of the developing sense of reality in the poems but adds little to previous studies. Kim Jong Gil's note on "The Topography of Yeats's Poetry" is of no interest. This difficult-to-locate special issue also includes an article in Korean by Yi Ch'ang-pae on the later poetry.

The Review of English Literature (1965) contains a posthumous article by Lennox Robinson on the early poems which criticizes some of the revisions but offers little of value. Pronoti Baksi's "The Noh and the Yeatsian Synthesis" argues that Yeats had been developing many of the characteristics of the Noh before he came in contact with it—hardly an original thesis—and then trails off into plot summary. In "Yeats and the Rhetoric of Defilement" Jean Alexander traces some images in the late poems and provides comparisons with Marvell, Swift, and Baudelaire. Though cited by Cross and Dunlop as a special Yeats issue, *Revue des Langues Vivantes* (Brussels, 1965) contains only reviews by T. R. Henn and Irène Simon and A. Norman Jeffares' "Notes on Pattern in the Byzantine Poems of W. B. Yeats," an uninspired discussion of repetition and other rhetorical devices.

The "Yeats and Ireland" issue of *Shenandoah* (1965) includes John Unterecker's "An Interview with Anne Yeats," in which she mentions some memories of her father. The best article is John Montague's "Under Ben Bulben," which stresses Yeats as a professional poet but argues that "his *direct* influence on Irish poetry has been disastrous." M. Bernetta Quinn's "Symbolic Landscape in Yeats: County Sligo" adds little to previous accounts. The special number of *Threshold* (1965) concentrates on Yeats and the theater. Roger McHugh's short survey of the plays has little value. Austin Clarke offers some comments on verse drama in English and remarks on Yeats's and his own verse plays. John Jay outlines some of the problems in producing the Cuchulain cycle and his own solutions. In an article of some importance, "The Plays of Yeats through Beckett Coloured Glasses," Ruby Cohn shows the influence of Yeats's plays on Beckett and suggests that the two writers share a "purgatorial view of earthly life." Mary O'Malley discusses the productions of Yeats's plays by the Lyric Players Theatre in Belfast. Raymond Warren illustrates the practical problems in composing music for the plays. Pronoti Baksi and Frederick Kalister both write on the Noh, Baksi sketching the basic characteristics and Kalister explaining the use of rhythm and music. Shotaro Oshima's "Yeats and the Japanese Theatre" is primarily a history of Japanese productions of Yeats.

The Yeats section of *Tri-Quarterly* (ed. Colton Johnson, 1965) opens with a brief note by William P. Fay, then Ambassador of Ireland, on Yeats's place in Ireland. Stephen Spender's valuable "The Influence of Yeats on Latter English Poets" demonstrates that Yeats's position in the 1930's was similar to that of the younger poets, though their beliefs differed; moreover, "Yeats expressed better than anyone in this century the dilemma of the man of imagination who feels bound through principles, loyalties, beliefs to support a particular kind of political action." Moody E. Prior provides a brief and elementary study of "Yeats's Search for a Dramatic Form," essentially a summary of his account in *The Language of Tragedy* (1947; 2nd ed., 1966). John V. Kelleher's "Yeats's Use of Irish Materials" is a brilliant essay, concentrating on "lebeen-lone" and "Clooth-na-Bare"; Kelleher issues an important warning that although Yeats's knowledge of Irish materials was not scholarly, it was often more extensive than has been assumed. Roger McHugh offers little new on *The Celtic Twilight* and *The Secret Rose*. More interesting is B. Rajan's "Yeats and the Absurd," arguing that Yeats "says he has chosen to live with absurdity . . . but also to live with the recognition that there is that in him which no absurdity can touch." The issue also includes a rather abortive panel discussion among Spender, Thomas Kinsella, W. D. Snodgrass, and Patrick Kavanagh; and Donald Torchiana's humorous account of organizing the 1965 conference at Northwestern University from which most of the articles derived.

The *University Review* (Dublin, 1965) contains a sympathetic reminiscence of Yeats by Thomas MacGreevy. John J. O'Meara's case for the influence of Catullus on "The Lake Isle of Innisfree" will not convince many. Brian Coffey contributes a brief and almost incoherent defense of the same poem against the attack of Robert Graves in *The Common Asphodel* (1949); Graves's more general disparagement of Yeats can be found in the chapter "These Be Your Gods, O Israel!" in *The Crowning Privilege* (1955). Robert O'Driscoll prints some inadequately edited letters to Herbert Grierson and others and some lecture material, taken in the main from newspaper reports; the speech in defense of Synge's *Playboy* had been previously published in *The Arrow* (1907).

The *James Joyce Quarterly* (1966) includes a discussion by Russell K. Alspach of the editorial problems and solutions in the variorum editions. Thomas Parkinson's "Yeats and the Love Lyric" is a seminal treatment of the important women in Yeats's life and work, arguing that 1917 is the dividing line between two kinds of love poems. Richard M. Kain discusses the centenary activities in Ireland in 1965 and adds some incidental comments on Yeats's politics; Robert

Friend briefly reports on the Yeats International Summer School in Sligo in 1965.

The section "W. B. Yeats: Critical Perspectives" in *The Southern Review* (1969) contains a moving defense by T. R. Henn of the basic values in Yeats's work. Michael Yeats writes with authority on Yeats's political activities. Thomas Parkinson's "The Modernity of Yeats" is a cogent analysis of the value of Yeats's example to contemporary poetry—essentially "to hold before us a traditional ideal of artistic responsibility." Daphne Fullwood writes perceptively on "Balzac and Yeats" but is sometimes unclear on the question of parallels versus sources. Northrop Frye's important essay is cited elsewhere.

The only valuable article in the Yeats section of *Agenda* (1971–72), by Jon Stallworthy, is discussed elsewhere. Peter Dale attacks Yeats's system and the poems related to it, arguing that he is more a "realist" than a "symbolist." "The Conscious Mind's Intelligible Structure" by Geoffrey Hill is a mass of confusion and quotation; it appears to be about Yeats's relationship with objective reality, but one cannot be certain. C. H. Sisson writes on "Yeats and Swift" without citing the standard study by Donald Torchiana. Cal Clothier offers a paraphrase of "A Prayer for my Daughter" and an attack on Yeats's attitudes. Kenneth Cox provides some assorted comments on Yeats's style and sees the 1916 rebellion as inaugurating Yeats's "bad period."

The most important article in the Yeats number of *ArielE* (1972) is Maurice Elliot's "Yeats and the Professors," which offers detailed sketches of Edward Dowden and Frederick York Powell and discusses Yeats's ambivalent attitudes toward formal education. "W. B. Yeats and Gordon Craig" by Alan Tomlinson deals with the influence of Craig on Yeats but offers little new information; he does not refer to the correspondence on either side. Richard Londraville prints a facsimile of an early draft of "The Cap and Bells" but does not provide a transcription; the manuscript is clearly not "quite a rough version," as Londraville describes it, but almost a fair copy. Fred L. Milne's note on the "probable indebtedness" of "The Cap and Bells" to Tennyson's *Maud* is tenuous and overstated. Daphne Fullwood contributes some rather discontinuous comments on the early poems. Augustine Martin, in an essay marred by errors, attempts to show that creating the character of Red Hanrahan brought Yeats into contact with eighteenth-century Ireland.

The leading contemporary scholars in the field are conspicuous by their absence in the Yeats number of the *Journal of Modern Literature* (1975). Marjorie Perloff's interesting but tedious essay shows the relation between the stylistic techniques in the three main sections of *Autobiographies* and some of the later poems. Thomas Rees's article on Yeats and Pound ignores all the considerable scholarship on the subject; also neglecting most of the relevant earlier work is Enoch Brater's "W.B. Yeats: The Poet as Critic," which concentrates on the Spenser essay and the *Oxford Book of Modern Verse*. More significant is Edward Callan's study of the influence of Spengler on *A Vision* and the later poetry. Neither Robert S. Ryf's "Yeats's Major Metaphysical Poems," which centers on the Byzantium poems and "Among School Children," nor Barton R. Friedman's "*On Baile's*

Strand to *At the Hawk's Well*: Staging the Depths of the Mind"
offers any significant insights. Even less important, because less com-
prehensible, is Gayatri Chakravorty Spivak's "Some Theoretical Aspects of Yeats's Prose." D. E. S. Maxwell's perceptive "Time's Strange
Excuse: W.B. Yeats and the Poets of the Thirties" would have profited by reference to Samuel Hynes's essay in *Modern Irish Literature*
(ed. Raymond J. Porter and James D. Brophy). Drawing on the
Bradford transcription of the "Leo Africanus" material, James Lovic
Allen argues in "Belief versus Faith in the Credo of Yeats" that Yeats
had a "literal acceptance of several major occult doctrines" and a
"complete prepossession by . . . spiritism and mediumship"; Allen's
over-simplified position is not strengthened by his constant attempts
to refute the views of Richard Ellmann (who is even accused of
quoting from a "relatively rare book").

In addition, there were special Yeats numbers of the *Irish Times* on
13 June 1935 (also printed as a pamphlet) and 10 June 1965.

YEATS JOURNALS

At the time of writing, there is no journal being published devoted
to the work of Yeats. Considering the amount of research on Yeats
and the general proliferation of academic journals, this fact is both
surprising and puzzling.

The *Yeats Association Bulletin* (1967–70) issued only three numbers, the major aim of the Association being the erection of a Yeats
monument in Sandymount (now accomplished). The only item of
interest is a comment in No. 2 (1968) by Micheál Ó hAodha on
Yeats's contribution to *The Voice of Ireland* (ed. W. J. Fitzgerald,
1924). *The Annual Report* of the Yeats Society of Japan has been
issued since 1966. The report has some articles in Japanese, but most
are in English. Many of the essays and notes are of course on Yeats
and the Noh, though various other topics are also discussed.

What was to have been the major journal was *Yeats Studies* (ed.
Robert O'Driscoll and Lorna Reynolds), first published in 1971. The
first issue was devoted to Yeats and the 1890's. Karl Beckson's "Yeats
and the Rhymers' Club" provides a valuable sketch of the group,
stressing the dominance of Irish affiliations and the diversity of their
literary theories. Beckson also corrects the dates of the club from the
usual 1891–94 to 1890–95/96 and discusses the two anthologies the
Rhymers published. Ian Fletcher's "W. B. Yeats and Althea Gyles" is
a seminal study, making good use of Gyles's letters to Yeats and
containing much incidental information on Yeats and the 1890's. The
article also constitutes a virtual anthology of Gyles's writings. George
Mills Harper's "From Zelator to Theoricus: Yeats's 'Link with the
Invisible Degrees' " describes in detail one of Yeats's Golden Dawn
notebooks; Harper's other article is essentially included in his *Yeats's
Golden Dawn*. William M. Murphy's essay is cited elsewhere. The
editorial work in this issue by Robert O'Driscoll and Michael J. Sidnell is superseded by the new edition of *The Secret Rose*.

The second issue (1972), on John M. Synge and Jack B. Yeats, was
the last number of *Yeats Studies*, which was thereafter transformed to

the hard-cover Yeats Studies Series (with the same general editors). The first volume in the new format is *Yeats and the Theatre* (ed. Robert O'Driscoll and Lorna Reynolds, 1975), cited in section XII and elsewhere. Forthcoming volumes are mentioned in appropriate places in this chapter.

Though the Yeats Studies Series is a welcome addition, it is unfortunate that we are left without a journal. The need for a Yeats periodical on the order of, say, the *James Joyce Quarterly*—to include brief notes, reviews, supplemental checklists of criticism, and scholarly exchanges through letters, as well as traditional articles—is indeed pressing.

VIII. Collections of Criticism*

COLLECTIONS OF ARTICLES

After the memorial volume *Scattering Branches* (cited above), the first collection of previously unpublished essays was *The Integrity of Yeats* (ed. Denis Donoghue, 1964), which contains the scripts of some Thomas Davis lectures on Radio Éireann. Donoghue praises Yeats for his involvement with common life. A. Norman Jeffares briefly notes Yeats's activities as a "Public Man." T. R. Henn concentrates on Yeats's use of symbolism with particular reference to the swan and the tower. In the most provocative essay, "Players and Painted Stage," Frank Kermode argues that Yeats's "habits" of common sense and irony saved him from complete indulgence in the dream of an ultimate theater (which would be, in theory, the ballet) and thus gave his drama a firm grounding in the objective world. Donald Davie notes the ways Yeats can and cannot be an influence on younger poets; his positive contributions are seen as a "reversion to metre" and the "*ovvto* upeech" of his poetic diction.

The most uniformly perceptive of the four collections published in the centenary year is *An Honoured Guest: New Essays on W. B. Yeats* (ed. Denis Donoghue and J. R. Mulryne, 1965), which includes an essay on each of the volumes of poems starting with *The Green Helmet* as well as four other articles. Charles Tomlinson's comment on the influence of Nietzsche and the idea of "nobility" Yeats offers to younger poets is the weakest item in the collection. Northrop Frye's brilliant study of *A Vision* is cited elsewhere. T. R. Henn's remarks on *The Green Helmet* and *Responsibilities* center on the background events and the stylistic developments in the volumes. Graham Martin's important essay on *The Wild Swans at Coole* shows the differences between the 1917 and 1919 editions and argues against seeing each volume of poems as a tightly knit unity. Donald Davie tries to show that *Michael Robartes and the Dancer* concentrates on "woman's role in society." John Holloway's interesting "Style and World in 'The Tower'" treats Yeats's creation in his poems of a self-contained world and the style necessarily involved in such a process. In a somewhat loosely constructed essay, Denis Donoghue analyzes *The Wind-*

* See note to Section VII, which also applies here.

ing Stair as centered on the claims of Self and Soul; he also includes numerous remarks on Wallace Stevens and an entire section on *The Resurrection*. J. R. Mulryne writes well on the sculptural imagery and the concept of "tragic joy" in *Last Poems*. Peter Ure provides assorted comments on some of the plays. Ian Fletcher's "Rhythm and Pattern in 'Autobiographies' " is a seminal account of Yeats's attempts to place his life in some kind of organized scheme, rightly stressing the basic differences in the approaches employed.

The World of W. B. Yeats (ed. Robin Skelton and Ann Saddlemyer, 1965; rev. 1967) gives a valuable account of much of the background of Yeats's work. The two opening essays by Saddlemyer examine briefly the Celtic movement in the 1890's and place Yeats's nationalism in the context of his age. Joan Coldwell comments on the little magazines with which Yeats was associated and also remarks on his relationship with Charles Ricketts. David R. Clark's " 'Metaphors for Poetry': W. B. Yeats and the Occult" is somewhat mistitled, as it ranges beyond the occult in outlining Yeats's philosophical interests. Gwladys W. Downes briefly attempts to show that Yeats was not heavily influenced by the Tarot pack. Two other essays by Saddlemyer are important: "The Heroic Discipline of the Looking-Glass: W. B. Yeats's Search for Dramatic Design" is a lucid discussion of Yeats's dramatic esthetic and also comments on the influence of Edward Gordon Craig and Ricketts; " 'Worn Out With Dreams': Dublin's Abbey Theatre" is a scholarly treatment of the Abbey and its predecessors, showing the tension between art and nationalism. In "A Literary Theatre: A Note on English Poetic Drama in the Time of Yeats," Skelton provides a useful context for Yeats's efforts and also argues that Gordon Bottomley enjoyed some success in the genre. Coldwell provides a brief note on Yeats's book covers. David R. Clark's "Vision and Revision: Yeats's *The Countess Cathleen*" centers on the final scene and suggests that not all the changes were improvements. Skelton writes on the basic differences between A. E. and Yeats. *The World of W. B. Yeats* also includes some essays on other Anglo-Irish writers.

W. B. Yeats, 1865–1965: Centenary Essays on the Art of W. B. Yeats (ed. D. E. S. Maxwell and S. B. Bushrui, 1965) is a mixed collection. J. Kleinstück contributes some miscellaneous comments on "Yeats and Shakespeare" with attention to "Lapis Lazuli" and Yeats's theories of art. Maxwell's article on the influence of Swift on Yeats's thought and style is generally superseded by the work of Donald Torchiana. In "Oriental and Celtic Elements in the Poetry of W. B. Yeats," F. F. Farag overstates the influence of Indian thought on Yeats's handling of Irish matter. R. M. Kain gives a general sketch of Yeats's conflicts with the Irish public. Ian Fletcher's "Yeats and Lissadell" is a brilliant study of "In Memory of Eva Gore-Booth and Constance Markiewicz" and includes a sketch of the lives of the two sisters. Another important essay is Edward Engelberg's account of what university students find in Yeats and of how his work might best be taught. MacDonald Emslie exaggerates Yeats's scorn and hatred of the middle class and treats the rhetorical devices which accompany his attitudes; a more reasoned examination of Yeats's feelings toward the middle class is provided by D. E. S. Maxwell in "Yeats and the

Irishry" (*Canadian Jour. of Irish Studies*, June 1975). B. A. King notes the influences of Irish speech and some eighteenth-century rhetorical devices on Yeats's discursive prose. George Brandon Saul engages in the rather pointless activity of ranking the plays. J. R. Moore outlines the essential movement of a Yeats play, with emphasis on the kind of heroism evoked. M. J. Sidnell's "Yeats's First Work for the Stage: The Earliest Versions of 'The Countess Cathleen'" discusses the prepublication manuscripts and shows that Maud Gonne's refusal of marriage resulted in a weakening of the play's basic structure. R. Fréchet briefly compares "Sailing to Byzantium" and Keats's "Ode to a Nightingale." In "Yeats and Blake: The Use of Symbols," W. H. Stevenson argues that Yeats is more definite and precise in his symbols.

In *Excited Reverie: A Centenary Tribute to William Butler Yeats 1865–1939* (ed. A. Norman Jeffares and K. G. W. Cross, 1965) contains a number of important studies. Jeffares' biographical account of John Butler Yeats is a valuable sketch, though his attempts to minimize the influence of the father on the son are not convincing. In "The Earlier Poems: Some Themes and Patterns," David Daiches posits the value of the early verse both on its own terms and for the anticipation of Yeats's later concerns. Edward Engelberg's perceptive "'He Too Was in Arcadia': Yeats and the Paradox of the Fortunate Fall" concentrates on "The Island of Statues." A. G. Stock provides a somewhat superficial account of Yeats's work on an edition of Spenser. In an essay not up to his usual standards, T. R. Henn treats the various kinds of rhetoric in the poetry. Donald T. Torchiana's important "'Among School Children' and the Education of the Irish Spirit" shows the background to the poem in Yeats's thinking on education and especially in his reading of Gentile. Hazard Adams cogently argues that the neglected comic elements in Yeats, as seen in *Autobiographies* and *A Vision*, stem from his sense of the "fundamental irrationality of life." Equally important is Jon Stallworthy's careful tracing of the publication history of the *Oxford Book of Modern Verse* through references to the publisher's files. Russell K. Alspach's essay is essentially identical with his introduction to the *Variorum Plays*. One of the most controversial articles in Yeats studies is Conor Cruise O'Brien's lengthy "Passion and Cunning: An Essay on the Politics of W. B. Yeats" (rpt. *TriQ*, 1972), which examines Yeats as a political opportunist and, in the late career, a pro-Fascist. Though well written and impressively argued, O'Brien's essay nonetheless places an undue emphasis on what was at best a temporary attitude; of the numerous replies, one of the best is Patrick Cosgrave's "Yeats, Fascism and Conor O'Brien" (*LonM*, July 1971). In "Yeats's Arabic Interests," S. B. Bushrui concentrates on the influence of the *Arabian Nights* and Charles Doughty's *Arabia Deserta* on *A Vision* and other works.

The *Dolmen Press Yeats Centenary Papers* (ed. Liam Miller) were originally published as monographs from 1965 to 1968 and are so treated elsewhere in this chapter; they were reprinted in one volume in 1968, with a preface by Jon Stallworthy and the addition of an index. *Tributes in Prose and Verse to Shotaro Oshima* (1970) contains brief notes by A. Norman Jeffares, Brendan Kennelly, Sheelah Kirby,

James Kirkup, Roger McHugh, and Frank Tuohy, none of more than passing interest.

Though not restricted to Yeats, two recent collections of articles include some significant essays on his achievement. *Theatre and Nationalism in Twentieth-Century Ireland* (ed. Robert O'Driscoll, 1971) contains a perceptive article by George Mills Harper on the tensions in Yeats's mind between participation in and withdrawal from politics, with particular reference to Maud Gonne. O'Driscoll's "Two Lectures on the Irish Theatre by W. B. Yeats" actually consists of typescripts of a 1913 rehearsal for one of the lectures used on the 1914 American tour and of the "Letter to the Students of a Californian School," published in *The Voice of Ireland* (1924). David R. Clark's "Yeats, Theatre, and Nationalism" is a disappointing string of quotations which concludes with a few remarks on *The Dreaming of the Bones* and *The Death of Cuchulain*. More significant is M. J. Sidnell's "Hic and Ille: Shaw and Yeats" (expanded from his earlier article, *MD*, 1968), which carefully traces the relationship and includes seven letters from Yeats to Shaw; two letters from Shaw to Yeats and a quotation from an unpublished Yeats letter can now be found in Shaw's *Collected Letters 1898–1910* (ed. Dan H. Laurence, 1972). The opening essay in *Theatre and Nationalism*, "Stars of the Abbey's Ascendancy" by Ann Saddlemyer, is not centered on Yeats but provides a cogent sketch of the beginnings of the Irish dramatic movement.

The most important Yeats article in *Modern Irish Literature: Essays in Honor of William York Tindall* (ed. Raymond J. Porter and James D. Brophy, 1972) is Samuel Hynes's forceful "Yeats and the Poets of the Thirties." Hynes demonstrates that Yeats "created for younger men a model of a possible relation between a poet and his world, between the life of poetry and external reality." His comment on Yeats's political poems is a valuable corrective to the work of Conor Cruise O'Brien: "the politics they offer is the politics of tragedy, a way to face disaster. It is a stance that is of no value while one believes in the efficacy of action." James F. Carens provides a reasonable account of the relationship between Yeats and Oliver St. John Gogarty, showing in the main what Gogarty took from Yeats; a somewhat exaggerated account of the influence in the other direction can be found in D. J. Huxley's "Yeats and Dr Gogarty" (*ArielE*, 1972). Grover Smith rather cryptically treats the sources and handling of the legend of the "Leap Castle Ghost" by both Gogarty and Yeats. E. L. Epstein gives an interesting analysis of Yeats's manipulation of syntax to produce a merger of stillness and action, though his remarks on "Leda and the Swan" add little to previous accounts. David H. Greene's "Yeats's Prose Style: Some Observations" is elementary.

COLLECTIONS OF CRITICISM AND CASEBOOKS

The earliest collection of previously published criticism was also the first separate publication devoted to Yeats's work. Prepared by John Quinn for Yeats's first American lecture tour and thus entitled *Some Critical Appreciations of William Butler Yeats as Poet, Orator and Dramatist* (1903), it contains sixteen brief selections, ranging in date from Robert Louis Stevenson's 1894 letter (pub. 1899) in praise of "The Lake Isle of Innisfree" to an October 1903 review in the *Atlantic Monthly*. It is almost certainly the rarest item in Yeats criticism.

The Permanence of Yeats (ed. James Hall and Martin Steinmann, 1950) is a superb gathering of much of the best early criticism. The volume raises many of the questions that still loom large in Yeats studies, including the relevance of *A Vision* to the poetry and plays and the significance of Yeats's occult interests; and for most students it provides a sufficient sampling of the early studies. After an introduction by the editors outlining some of the major critical approaches, J. Middleton Murry (*Aspects of Literature*, rev. ed., 1934) writes on the failure of the late career, seeing *The Wild Swans at Coole* as "eloquent of final defeat." Edmund Wilson's influential essay (*Axel's Castle*, 1931) overstates Yeats's relationship to the French Symbolist movement and is impatient with *A Vision*. In another important essay R. P. Blackmur (*The Expense of Greatness*, 1940) gives an intelligent and qualified criticism of the "magical philosophy" of the later poems, arguing that it "prevents his poetry from reaching the first magnitude." Cleanth Brooks (*Modern Poetry and the Tradition*, 1939) stresses the importance of *A Vision* and explicates several poems by reference to it (thus abandoning his usual New Critical attitudes). John Crowe Ransom (*The Critical Performance*, ed. S. E. Hyman, 1956) treats Yeats's success in giving his symbols an aura of religious significance. The first chapter on Yeats in David Daiches' *Poetry and the Modern World* (1940) emphasizes the importance of Ireland in Yeats's early career; the second chapter, not included by Hall and Steinmann, gives an intelligent sketch of the work beginning with *In the Seven Woods*, though Daiches is not happy with the "crazy esoteric system" of *A Vision*. F. R. Leavis (*New Bearings in English Poetry*, 1932) also gives a sketch of the career and suggests that Yeats's Irishness partially saved him from "disillusion and waste." D. S. Savage (*The Personal Principle*, 1944) presents a harsh attack on Yeats as "inhuman" and an "aesthete all his life"; Savage was partially answered by Ransom in "The Severity of Mr Savage" (*KR*, 1945). Joseph Warren Beach (*A History of English Literature*, ed. Hardin Craig, et al., 1950) provides a brief and mixed account of Yeats's career. In an important study Eric Bentley (*In Search of Theater*, 1953) uses *A Full Moon in March* to substantiate his claim that Yeats is "the only considerable verse playwright in English for several hundred years." W. Y. Tindall (*Forces in Modern British Literature 1885–1946*, 1947) demonstrates that Yeats's symbols are more related to his occult studies than to the French tradition. Elder Olson (*Five Approaches to Literary Criticism*, ed. W. S. Scott, 1962) uses "Sailing to Byzantium" as an example to support his thesis that the "argument" is the informing principle of a lyric poem. A. Norman Jeffares notes the importance of the study of Yeats's manuscripts. W. H. Auden (*The Kenyon Critics*, ed. J. C. Ransom, 1951) writes of Yeats's potential influence on the occasional poem and on metrical variation. Morton Dauwen Zabel pays tribute to the integrity and inherent courage of Yeats's career. Walter E. Houghton argues that *Words for*

Music Perhaps, especially in the figure of Crazy Jane, presents Yeats's "amoral faith in the heroic man." *The Permanence of Yeats* also reprints the essays by Burke, Davidson, Eliot, Mizener, Schwartz, and Warren from the 1941–42 *Southern Review*, cited above.

Perhaps the most important critic not represented in this collection is C. M. Bowra, whose chapter in *The Heritage of Symbolism* (1943) places too much emphasis on Yeats's indebtedness to French Symbolist practice but also offers a useful sketch of Yeats's stylistic changes and some perceptive readings of selected poems. Another item related to *The Permanence of Yeats* is G. S. Fraser's "Yeats and 'The New Criticism'" (*Colonnade*, 1952; rpt. his *Vision and Rhetoric*, 1959); primarily a response to the essays of Houghton and Schwartz, the article also touches on the inadequacies of New Criticism when applied to Yeats.

The more recent collections of criticism naturally draw heavily on books discussed elsewhere in this chapter. In briefly citing these collections I will focus on those essays not readily available in other places. The least important of these gatherings is *Yeats* (Delhi, 1961) by B. R. Mullik, which reprints selections from seven books, beginning with Geoffrey Bullough's *The Trend of Modern Poetry* (1934) and concluding with David Daiches' *The Present Age* (1958).

Yeats: A Collection of Critical Essays (ed. John Unterecker, 1963) is a valuable reprinting of sections from seven books; three essays from *The Permanence of Yeats* (Tindall's is slightly revised); and three important articles, R. P. Blackmur's "W. B. Yeats: Between Myth and Philosophy" and Hugh Kenner's "The Sacred Book of the Arts," both noted above, and Curtis Bradford's "Yeats's Byzantium Poems: A Study of Their Development" (rev. from *PMLA*, 1960), a transcription and discussion of the drafts of the poems. Unterecker's introduction notes Yeats's efforts to make his life and work a "grand, organic whole."

The casebook on *Yeats: Last Poems* (ed. Jon Stallworthy, 1968) contains the introduction to and a generous selection from the Dorothy Wellesley correspondence, Curtis Bradford's *Yeats's 'Last Poems' Again*, and chapters from six books. It also includes a selection of the reviews of the relevant volumes from 1939–40; A. Norman Jeffares' paraphrase and cross-referencing of "Lapis Lazuli" (rev. from *MLN*, 1950); and T. R. Henn's important "The Accent of Yeats's *Last Poems*" (rev. from *E&S*, 1956), which argues against the view that "lust" is a dominant theme in the volume and shows the background to and complexity of the collection. Arra M. Garab's essay was later essentially included in his *Beyond Byzantium*. The introduction by Stallworthy comments on the critical reception of the late poems.

The casebook *William Butler Yeats: The Byzantium Poems* (ed. Richard J. Finneran, 1969) contains excerpts from ten books and seven articles: A. Norman Jeffares' pioneering "The Byzantine Poems of W. B. Yeats' (*RES*, 1946); studies of sources and parallels by Frederick L. Gwynn (*PQ*, 1953), F. N. Lees (*N&Q*, 1957), and Ernest Schanzer (*ES*, 1960); William Empson's response to the work of F. A. C. Wilson (*REL*, 1960); a brief note on the use of "musical form" by David I. Masson (*N&Q*, 1953); and G. S. Fraser's perceptive reading of "Byzantium" (*CritQ*, 1960). Finneran's introduction argues for the basic thematic similarity of the two poems.

Of the three most recent collections, the best is the most extensive, *W. B. Yeats* (ed. William H. Pritchard, 1972). Very little of the material is taken from books on Yeats. Part I covers 1886–1939 and includes not only some of the standard notices but also some more obscure comments, such as reviews by Lionel Johnson and John Todhunter; some excerpts from Yeats's own writings are also included, a requirement of the series in which the volume appears. Part II goes from 1940 to 1971 (or later, since Helen Vendler's interesting "Sacred and Profane Perfection in Yeats" was reprinted in *SoR*, 1973) and is also a nice mixture of the familiar and the unfamiliar. Yvor Winters' *The Poetry of W. B. Yeats* is included in full. The two introductions by Pritchard provide a useful sketch of some of the trends in Yeats criticism, the first one also effectively summarizing essays by F. R. Leavis and T. S. Eliot that could not be included because of problems with permissions. One may regret the editor's cavalier attitude toward the texts—"added some footnotes and dropped out a few when they didn't seem relevant"—but the collection is the most important volume of its kind.

In contrast, *Critics on Yeats* (ed. Raymond Cowell, 1971) is a rather perfunctory collection. Brief excerpts from some early commentaries and reviews are followed by selections from sixteen "modern critics," beginning with F. R. Higgins. This material will be familiar to most students; the only item taken from a periodical, Denis Donoghue's "The Vigour of Its Blood: Yeats's *Words for Music Perhaps*" (*KR*, 1959) is essentially reprinted in his *The Ordinary Universe*. The brief introduction by the editor makes some strange value judgments.

Somewhat more important is *William Butler Yeats: A Collection of Criticism* (ed. Patrick J. Keane, 1973), which includes selections from nine critics ranging from 1954 to 1969 and an original essay by Keane, "Embodied Song." With the exception of the poems by M. L. Rosenthal and the editor, the only item likely to be unfamiliar is a brief comment from Frank Kermode's *Continuities* (1968). The introduction includes some cogent remarks on the trends in Yeats studies, and the bibliography is especially useful.

A volume on Yeats in the Critical Heritage series is in preparation by A. Norman Jeffares and should now be available.

IX. *Introductory Studies; Handbooks and Guides*

Many of the works discussed in this section (as well as others cited elsewhere) make one or more of the most common errors in Yeats studies, which it may be appropriate to lay to rest: (1) Iseult Gonne (later Mrs. Francis Stuart) was Maud Gonne's daughter by Lucien Millevoye, not her "adopted daughter," "niece," or "adopted niece," a fact Yeats seems to have learned in December 1898 or shortly thereafter; (2) *Crossways* and *The Rose* were never separate volumes of poems but were rather headings first used for sections of lyrics in the

1895 *Poems*; (3) Yeats was married on 20 October 1917, not the 21st.

In addition, many of these studies will not identify the "Diana Vernon" of Yeats's unpublished memoirs. She was Olivia Shakespear, a novelist and the future mother-in-law of Ezra Pound. Yeats had a liaison with her in 1896 (his first sexual relationship). After what he calls "the breaking between us for many years," they became devoted friends, and many of the most important late letters in the Wade collection are written to her.

INTRODUCTORY STUDIES

Although Richard Ellmann doubtless exaggerates when he claims in the preface to the 1967 reissue of Louis MacNeice's *The Poetry of W. B. Yeats* (1941) that it "is still as good an introduction to that poet as we have," the study has worn rather well. MacNeice is concerned not so much with individual poems—he provides no detailed explications—as with the development of Yeats. He includes interesting chapters on the dual backgrounds of estheticism and Ireland. His study crystallizes many of the trends in Yeats studies that remained dominant for perhaps two decades, including (1) the preference for the late work ("a study of his development is a study in rejuvenation"); (2) close attention to the revisions, MacNeice being a little unusual in seeing some of them as harmful; and (3) a downgrading of the plays, the fiction, and Yeats's occult activities. MacNeice also includes comparisons between Yeats and Eliot, Lawrence, Housman, A. E., Joyce, and Rilke (whom he finds a greater poet); he remarks on the influence of Yeats on the younger generation, including Auden, Spender, and himself. He gives a valuable discussion of Yeats's use of the refrain and the ballad form in some of the late poems. If one ignores such occasional blunders as the description of the verse of *Purgatory* as "awkward," MacNeice's study can still be read with profit.

G. S. Fraser's brief *W. B. Yeats* (1954; rev. 1962), reprinted without the bibliography in his *Vision and Rhetoric: Studies in Modern Poetry* (1959), is a good but not outstanding study in the "appreciation" genre. Concentrating almost exclusively on the poetry, Fraser is more intent on presenting a picture of Yeats's "broad and deep humanity" than on providing a chronological account of the career. M. L. Rosenthal's chapter "Yeats and the Modern Mind" in *The Modern Poets: A Critical Introduction* (1960) locates Yeats's modernism in his belief in the "interrelationship of opposites" but fails to offer much beyond explications of some poems.

The intended audience for A. G. Stock's *W. B. Yeats: His Poetry and Thought* (1961) remains obscure. As an introductory study it gives scant attention to the life, ignores the plays except for an entire chapter on *The Countess Cathleen* and *The Land of Heart's Desire*, and devotes two chapters to *A Vision*—the first a rather convoluted explanation and the second a more eloquent defense of Yeats's right to his own ideas (a theme that runs throughout the study). The first chapter attempts to establish some distinctions between the English and the Irish traditions, but these are thereafter touched on only occasionally. The early chapters ignore the poems and concentrate on the thought; the latter chapters reverse the balance, providing line-by-line summaries of the major poems. Beginning students will find that the book assumes too much, as in the claim that "Sailing to Byzantium explains itself"; advanced students are likely to be disconcerted by the lack of much reference to previous studies and by such remarks as the description of the middle plays as "romantic and poetic." Stock's work, however, is considerably more important than B. P. Misra's W. B. Yeats (Delhi, 1962), which contains an unacceptable number of errors. The commentary is little more than paraphrase interspersed with remarks such as "as dramas go, Countess Cathleen is a small drama."

J. I. M. Stewart's chapter on Yeats in Eight Modern Writers (Vol. XII of the Oxford History of English Literature, 1963) is a sketch of the career by a hostile critic who finds it difficult to admit or explain Yeats's stature. Stewart is impatient with much in Yeats, including his concepts of nobility and his occult activities. Stewart's numerous witticisms directed at Yeats are seldom successful. The bibliography has more interest than the chapter itself.

W. B. Yeats (1963) by Peter Ure is good but brief. The biographical introduction is sound, though it says little about Yeats's activities at the Abbey, his relationship with Synge, and other items of some importance. The chapters on the poems and plays occasionally offer some provocative insights, but they are so organized as to be difficult for a beginning student to follow—the treatment, for instance, in one chapter of the poems dating 1904–33. The chapters on the plays are superior to the others. Though he does not attempt to impose any definite thesis on Yeats's achievement, Ure does deny the overall unity of the Collected Poems. The discussion of "Yeats and the Critics" is perceptive.

Balachandra Rajan's W. B. Yeats: A Critical Introduction (1965; 2nd ed., 1969, revised only in the bibliography) is the most satisfactory of the introductory studies. Although on that level it suffers from a lack of information on the Anglo-Irish background and on Yeats's life, Rajan effectively outlines Yeats's career as a poet and a dramatist, with some attention to the prose, particularly A Vision. Rajan places Yeats in the mainstream of English poetry and rejects any more limited label, such as occultist or Irish nationalist. He cogently combines summary and explication in his comments on almost all the major poems and plays. His repeated warnings not to accept Yeats's critical pronouncements at face value are salutary. Rajan concludes that "the driving force in Yeats's poetry is the assertion of man's creative power against the strength of circumstance, embodied even in the destructive distortions of that strength. It is also a deep sense of man as the continuing battleground and of tension and combat as the springs of his being."

William York Tindall in his pamphlet W. B. Yeats (1966) does not appear in complete sympathy with his subject. He divides the career into four phases and treats some representative poems from each phase. He has little to say on A Vision—"his business none of ours."

The usually unsuccessful attempts at wit, as in the description of "He Bids His Beloved Be at Peace" as the "hairiest of hairy poems," are more numerous than the occasional perceptive comments.

Raymond Cowell's *W. B. Yeats* (1969) is written for the "ordinary man who reads for pleasure" but will offer little to anyone but the pure novice. It treats only the poems, and the explications are usually naive simplifications. The remark by a critic writing in 1969 that the "early and late work tends to be ignored" is difficult to understand. Of some interest are the comparisons between Yeats and Keats and the appendix on "Yeats at Work," which cogently discusses the development of six poems. A. Norman Jeffares' first introductory study was *The Poetry of W. B. Yeats* (1961), a sketch of the life and works. This was followed by his *W. B. Yeats* (1971), a cross between an introduction to the poems and an anthology. After a brief outline of the career and an interesting section on Yeats's critical reception, the volume is divided into topics such as "Yeats and Ireland," "Yeats and Friendship," and so on. Both volumes are elementary and are intended for the relatively uninformed. A third introductory statement by Jeffares is his chapter in *Irish Poets in English* (ed. Seán Lucy, 1973).

The most impressive brief essay on Yeats's achievement is the chapter by Thomas Parkinson in *The Twentieth Century* (ed. Bernard Bergonzi, 1970; Vol. VII of the History of Literature in the English Language). Of much less interest is the sketch of Yeats's career by James V. Baker in *British Winners of the Nobel Literary Prize* (ed. Walter E. Kidd, 1973).

Denis Donoghue's *Yeats* (1971) was published in the Modern Masters series and is this cited here, although it is by no means satisfactory as an introduction. Donoghue sets out to discover "Yeats's sensibility . . . so far as it manifests itself in the poems and plays" and concludes that Yeats is preoccupied with "power" and "conflict." Donoghue believes that the emphasis on power derives in the main from Nietzsche; and he considers the Yeats-Nietzsche relationship, which is almost the subtheme of the study, "a more telling relation than that between Yeats and Plato, Plotinus, or Blake." The influence of the Romantic poets is generally discounted, except in the final chapter where the Romantic concept of the autonomy of the imagination is used to explain and partially defend Yeats's late political ideas. Although the study contains numerous perceptive remarks, *Yeats* is loosely constructed; and many of the texts have been selected for, and interpreted by, the thesis of Nietzsche's seminal influence. Moreover, Donoghue shares with Harold Bloom not only the title *Yeats* but also a fondness for hieratic and undemonstrated pronouncements: "*The Wild Swans at Coole* is history, consistent with symbolism; *The Tower* is symbolism, consistent with history."

A Preface to Yeats (1974) by Edward Malins contains some useful information and interesting photographs; but it is arbitrarily and awkwardly divided into various sections and lacks an index. The discussion of "Easter 1916," for example, is found in the chapter "Yeats's Family, Friends and Acquaintances," in the section on Pearse. This chapter itself includes such figures as James Connolly and Junzo Sato but not Edward Gordon Craig or T. Sturge Moore. The volume has a substantial number of errors and is defective in the bibliography. More modest in aim is Gayatri Chakravorty Spivak's *Myself Must I Remake: The Life and Poetry of W. B. Yeats* (1974). Designed for pre-university students, it provides an effective sketch of the life and major works and is almost free from error.

HANDBOOKS AND GUIDES

George Brandon Saul's *Prolegomena to the Study of Yeats's Poems* (1957) was a pioneering effort to supply the necessary annotations for the poems. Saul provides the publication record, indicating dates of composition, changes in title, and the first printing in which the poem attained essentially its final form; he also gives cross-references to other works and often cites criticism (his idiosyncratic evaluations of other critics must not be taken too seriously). Saul is especially good in explaining references to Irish mythology and folklore.

Saul's work is basically but not completely superseded by A. Norman Jeffares' *A Commentary on the Collected Poems of W. B. Yeats* (1968). Jeffares always indicates the first publication and the date of composition (if known) for each poem; what other information is supplied often seems a matter of chance. The entries range from a single line ("To an Isle in the Water") to sixteen pages ("Parnell's Funeral"). Jeffares usually quotes from Yeats's prose and letters at excessive length; critical views are sometimes included, as are manuscript versions. At times cross-references within the *Commentary* substitute for meaningful analysis or annotation. The introductory headnotes are perfunctory for the first four sections but are more interesting thereafter. Though the *Commentary* is the logical starting point for the study of any individual poem, one must bear in mind that it contains numerous factual errors.

A different but better book is John Unterecker's *A Reader's Guide to W. B. Yeats* (1959), an excellent example of its genre. As he admits, Unterecker accepts the views of Donald Stauffer on Yeats's use of symbols and of Hugh Kenner on the ordering of the *Collected Poems*. Unterecker's introductory account, "The Major Themes," is an effective statement. He is particularly good in tracing the bird and tree images in "The Wanderings of Oisin" and in insisting that the poem is symbolic and not allegorical. Unterecker is less lucid on the remainder of the early poetry, which he tends to oversimplify (especially *The Wind Among the Reeds*). Half the study is devoted to the poems from *The Tower* on. Although no one will agree with all of Unterecker's readings, they are generally perceptive.

George Brandon Saul's *Prolegomena to the Study of Yeats's Plays* (1958) follows much the same format as his volume on the poems. Likewise, *A Commentary on The Collected Plays of W. B. Yeats* (1975) by A. Norman Jeffares and A. S. Knowland is similar to the earlier handbook to the poems by Jeffares—useful but imperfect. Based on the British edition of the *Collected Plays* without cross-references to the page numbers in the American edition, the book contains an excessive amount of quotation from Yeats's notes and prefaces; the handling of criticism is inconsistent, ranging from lengthy quotation to brief referral. Once past the numerous errors in the chronology, the *Commentary* is generally accurate in its details.

There are three entries in the undergraduate *vade mecum* genre: Sandra Gilbert's *The Poetry of William Butler Yeats* (1965), which also discusses the Cuchulain plays, in the American Monarch Notes series; Richard Morton's *An Outline of the Poetry of William Butler Yeats* (1971), also published as *Notes on the Poetry of William Butler Yeats*, in the Canadian Coles Notes series; and D. J. Murphy's *William Butler Yeats: A Student's Guide to his Work* (1974), in the Irish Mercier Commentary series. There is little to choose among them.

X. General Studies

V. K. Narayana Menon's *The Development of William Butler Yeats* (1942; 2nd ed., 1960) contains little of interest except some anecdotes in the preface by Herbert J. C. Grierson. The text itself is superficial in content and consists in the main of quotation or paraphrase. Menon is more than a little impatient with the "fantastical philosophy" of Yeats. There are very few revisions in the second edition. Since Abinash Chandra Bose admits in *Three Mystic Poets: A Study of W. B. Yeats, A. E. and Rabindranath Tagore* (1945) that Yeats "belongs less to the class of mystics who also happen to be poets than to the class of poets who, owing to the special bent of their genius, come to be regarded as mystics," his study is likewise unenlightening. However, Bose had met Yeats in 1937 and quotes a few interesting remarks. In the introduction James Cousins also recalls a 1912 visit with Yeats, Maud Gonne, and Tagore in Normandy and reports Yeats's comment that "Myth is vision in action."

Peter Ure's *Towards a Mythology: Studies in the Poetry of W. B. Yeats* (1946) still merits a careful reading. Ure argues that Yeats used myth to unite "the abstract idea with the personal passion and the personal meaning" and correctly suggests that *A Vision* gave Yeats a "metaphysical order" which allowed him to write the major poems of his later career. Ure begins with a study of the Cuchulain plays, showing that the myth makes possible a union of the individual and the type. The second chapter centers on "In Memory of Major Robert Gregory" and treats Yeats's mythologizing of his family and friends. After a discussion of *A Vision* and some related poems and plays, Ure concludes with an extended commentary on the Crazy Jane poems. He sees Yeats's work as defined by the "Otherness" of his thought and by the process through which "the poetic images have the solidity of sense objects."

Marion Witt's "William Butler Yeats," in *English Institute Essays: 1946* (1947) demonstrates with some effectiveness that Yeats provided "a heavy scaffolding of biographical information" necessary to a full understanding of his work. The chapters on Yeats in Graham Hough's *The Last Romantics* (1949) likewise retain some value. After treating Yeats's place in the 1890's and his attempts to purify his poetry of "impurities and miscellaneous rubbish," Hough discusses Yeats's various mythologies and traces the main ideas of *A Vision*. His

final chapter outlines "The Beliefs of Yeats" and posits their continued viability. The epilogue is an interesting "Conversation in Limbo"
between Yeats and H. G. Wells. The section on Yeats in John Heath-
Stubbs's *The Darkling Plain: A Study of the Later Fortunes of
Romanticism in English Poetry from George Darley to W. B. Yeats*
(1950) is an acceptable general sketch of Yeats's development, suggesting that "the greatness of Yeats as a poet lay in his reassertion
and rediscovery of the concrete; and this arose mainly from his enlarging the aesthetic scheme to bring the Irish political crisis within
its scope." Less persuasive is his claim that the Byzantium poems
present "a deliberate and heartless régime of oppression in the cause
of beauty."

T. R. Henn's important *The Lonely Tower: Studies in the Poetry of
W. B. Yeats* (1950; 2nd ed., 1965) is a work of much wisdom, tact,
and modesty. Henn draws effectively on his immense knowledge of
not only all of Yeats's writings but also Western literature and painting in general. The eighteen chapters offer a chronological study of
the poems as well as discussions of the plays, *A Vision*, and other
topics. Though methodologically suspect, Henn's chapter "Painter
and Poet" is the pioneering work in the examination of Yeats's visual
sources. Henn is eloquent though not invariably accurate in his defense and explanation of Yeats's occult interests and *A Vision*. Of
perhaps the greatest interest are the opening chapter on the Anglo-
Irish background (which can be supplemented by Henn's "W. B.
Yeats and the Irish Background," *YR*, 1953), essential reading for any
non-Irish student; the two chapters on Yeats's style; and the discussions of "Image and Symbol" and "Myth and Magic." But there is
little in the volume that can be neglected.

Richard Ellmann's *The Identity of Yeats* (1954; 2nd ed., 1964) is a
brilliant study which constantly refers to unpublished material to
trace the development of Yeats's thought; the emphasis is on the
poems, but numerous other works are discussed. Since, as Ellmann
rightly argues, for Yeats "style" is inseparable from "thought," the
book also treats the changes in the poetic style. The preface to the
second edition, first published as "Yeats without Analogue" (*KR*,
1964), defends the uniqueness of Yeats and is an important essay in
its own right. The first chapter suggests that Yeats adopts three basic
roles—seer, victim, and assessor. "The Search for Limits" deals with
the Irish level and the tapestry-like qualities of the early poems, and
with the use of occult symbolism, particularly the four elements. Ellmann then posits the inapplicability of the term "belief" when applied to Yeats and argues that the doctrine of the "Moods" was a
substitute for "belief." The study of Yeats's iconography centers on
the Rose, Tree, and Cross and demonstrates that *The Shadowy
Waters* was a culmination of the early symbolism. "The Pursuit of
Spontaneity" notes the influence of Nietzsche in the movement toward a new kind of simplicity. The chapter on "Style and Rhetoric"
discusses the changes themselves, noting that Yeats was never as close
to "the natural words in the natural order" as he claimed. Ellmann
then outlines the major ideas of *A Vision*, shows their use in some
poems, and touches on the presence of mythic rituals. "The Final
Form of Experience" contrasts Yeats's attitudes toward Asia and Eu-

rope, discusses the late style by reference to Yeats's work with translations of Irish poems by Frank O'Connor, and comments on the ballads with special reference to the refrains. Ellmann concludes by suggesting that the art of Yeats is characterized by "affirmative capability." *The Identity of Yeats* includes not only the unpublished "Seven Propositions" but also two important appendices. The first provides explications of thirty-four selected poems; the readings are supported by various kinds of material but are not consistently persuasive. The other appendix gives "A Chronology of the Composition of the Poems." (In *Yeats at Work*, Curtis Bradford has noted that these dates are usually taken from intermediate drafts, and that "often many months elapsed between intermediate and final drafts.") In short, although *The Identity of Yeats* is perhaps not a tightly knit unity, there is no better place to begin a serious study of Yeats than this seminal work.

Archibald MacLeish's short *Yeats and the Belief in Life* (1958), reprinted in his *A Continuing Journey* (1967), deserves to be better known. MacLeish shows that the belief for which Yeats "thirsted and to which he eventually attained was a belief in man, a belief in man's life, *in spite* of misery and *in spite* of death." The pamphlet contains some perceptive remarks on "The Magi," "The Second Coming," and a few other poems. MacLeish's suggestive chapter on Yeats in his *Poetry and Experience* (1961) praises the poems that are involved with the public world and presents an allegorical reading of "The Grey Rock." In contrast, the chapter on Yeats in Vivian de Sola Pinto's *Crisis in English Poetry* (1951; 3rd ed., 1958) centers on the early career and has little of note, arguing that Yeats was "an isolated and therefore incomplete genius."

The Vast Design: Patterns in W. B. Yeats's Aesthetic (1964; with revisions to the bibliography, 1974) by Edward Engelberg is a valuable study, closely written and carefully organized. He examines Yeats's esthetic as based on various pairs of antitheses, occasionally unified by means of the "single image." Engelberg cogently places Yeats in the European tradition as a whole, treating the relationship between Yeats's esthetic and his views of history and philosophy, along with his opinions on painting and sculpture. Yeats's indebtedness to Pater is remarked but inadequately pursued. Engelberg begins by showing that Yeats's esthetic is based on such oppositions as lyric/drama and personal passion/anonymity; he also comments that Yeats's imagination was "primarily . . . epic." "Market Cart and Sky: The Two Ways of Art" centers on the tension involved in the choice of subject matter. The third chapter notes how the experience in the theater led Yeats toward a reconciliation of stillness ("picture") and motion ("gesture"); Engelberg then discusses the attempt to enlarge this reconciliation into an "epic vastness" and provides a lengthy discussion of Yeats's symbolism. The concept of "tragic joy" is analyzed as a union between passion and reverie. The final chapter centers on "The Statues." Engelberg concludes that the "single image in Yeats's aesthetic is an heroic image, one of the 'heraldic' images which it was his aim to restore to literature. . . . He remains the last of the great European poets."

The four related works are quite unsatisfactory when compared with *The Vast Design*. In *Zeami, Bashō, Yeats, Pound: A Study in Japanese and English Poetics* (1965), Makoto Ueda relies heavily on quotation and paraphrase to present Yeats's views on "Imagination, Symbol, and the Mingling of the Contraries." He avoids any reference to previous studies and offers little new. In *Coleridge's and Yeats's Theory of Poetry* (Delhi, 1967), Satya Dev Jaggi fails to consider the chronological development of Yeats's theories and thus finds more confusion than exists (there is no comparison with Coleridge's theories). The chapters on Yeats in Frank Lentricchia's *The Gaiety of Language: An Essay on the Radical Poetics of W. B. Yeats and Wallace Stevens* (1968) show only a superficial acquaintance with previous criticism. The commentary on Yeats's "explicit poetics" tries to demonstrate that he moves from early transcendent and magical theories to an esthetic involving impersonality (the mask) and the immersion in history. The chapter on "implicit poetics" treats the Byzantium poems as expressions of antinomy and "Lapis Lazuli" as a resolution through art. The method is paraphrase-explication, the conclusions unoriginal. A final critic who is apparently ignorant of Engelberg's study is Marvel Shmiefsky, whose chapter on Yeats in *Sense at War with Soul: English Poetics 1865–1900* (1972) contains little more than summaries of the essays in *Ideas of Good and Evil*. Of some interest are the parallels he finds between Yeats and Arnold.

Thomas R. Whitaker's *Swan and Shadow: Yeats's Dialogue with History* (1964) is a major contribution to Yeats studies. It is a difficult and complex book, not for beginners; it is also a work of vast scholarship and erudition, sometimes exposed a bit too self-consciously (as in the six epigraphs which open the study). Whitaker is most perceptive in his general thesis and in his documentation of Yeats's sources, including not only the familiar figures (Blake, Shelley, Nietzsche) but also a large gallery of more obscure writers (often from the occult traditions). He is less uniformly successful in his readings of individual works, where occasionally he overreads the work to fit his thesis and obscures the reading itself with a host of source citations. Also less successful are the numerous references to analogues, ranging from Jung to Allan Tate, which often interrupt and make more difficult an already subtle argument.

In the cogent introduction Whitaker argues that Yeats sees history variously as "a bright reflection of the poet's self" (swan) or "a shadowy force opposed to that self" (shadow); stated another way, Yeats employs either a "God's-eye view of the panorama of history" or "the perspective of dramatic experience." Each vision is continually qualified by the other (a process somewhat obscured by the two-part structure of *Swan and Shadow*), the continuing dialogue between them ultimately issuing in Yeats's insistence on embracing the full self to achieve transcendence. The section on "History as Vision" treats such matters as the appearance of cyclical theory in the early Yeats and in other writers of the 1890's; Yeats's views on "apocalypse"; the influence of Nietzsche; and the "Dove or Swan" chapter of *A Vision*. It concludes with a study of the various visionary speakers and poems. The less valuable section on "History as Dramatic Experience" begins by showing Yeats coming to terms with Ireland and moving toward a poetry "not of sancity but of tragic self-knowledge" but thereafter resolves into explications of individual poems with only a tangential relationship to Whitaker's primary concerns. But as a whole *Swan and Shadow* is essential for the advanced student.

The same cannot be said of the chapter on Yeats in Harvey Gross's *The Contrived Corridor: History and Fatality in Modern Literature* (1971), which ignores Whitaker and is neither original nor stimulating. Gross discusses Yeats's use of the myth of "Eternal Recurrence," with some reference to the influence of Nietzsche, and concludes that Yeats is a "secular apocalyptist."

In *A Vision of Reality: A Study of Liberalism in Twentieth-Century Verse* (1965), Frederick Grubb sees Yeats as "a child of the Enlightenment: hard, reckless, quick to seize the logic and passion of ideology." Grubb's chapter is primarily a rather incoherent attempt to demonstrate Yeats's "liberalism." Of no more interest is Brian Farrington's *Malachi-Stilt-Jack: A Study of W. B. Yeats and His Work* (1965), a pamphlet which grudgingly admits that Yeats is "the greatest poet of our age" but then attacks his beliefs, particularly in regard to politics and the aristocracy. A third short study of little note is George Brandon Saul's *In . . . Luminous Wind* (1966), which contains sections disparaging the prose fiction, praising the poems before 1933 and attacking those after, and discussing the use of bird imagery (only the swan is seen as an important symbol). The essays are marred by Saul's constant attacks on the anonymous "analysts" and his "rating" of poems according to his rather idiosyncratic tastes.

Charles Berryman's *W. B. Yeats: Design of Opposites* (1967) offers little of value. The book contains far too much quotation and shows little knowledge of previous criticism. Berryman begins by summarizing the possible sources of *A Vision* and commenting on Yeats's theory of opposition. He then applies this theory to Yeats's personality, to historical design, to sex, to esthetics, and to ontology (in a few pages each). In the third chapter he argues at length with F. A. C. Wilson—citing only *W. B. Yeats and Tradition*—over whether Yeats's poetry is visionary or dramatic, concluding that it is dramatic and that the drama centers on Yeats's inability to attain a completed vision. In the section on "Explication" Berryman finds opposites in selected works (chosen with no clear rationale). Occasional insights vie with the more numerous thesis-inspired misreadings.

Of greater perception are the two chapters on Yeats in *The Ordinary Universe: Soundings in Modern Literature* (1968) by Denis Donoghue. "The Human Image in Yeats," put together from several periodical articles, is not convincing in placing Yeats's greatest achievement in *The Wild Swans at Coole*. A better essay is "Yeats and the Living Voice," which suggests the value of Yeats's "commitment to an oral culture": "Yeats got from Irish sources what he needed for his poems: a sense of roots, a feeling of continuity, a sense of communal values issuing in speech and action, 'the dialect of the tribe.'" B. L. Reid's "The House of Yeats," in his *Tragic Occasions: Essays on Several Forms* (1971), discusses Yeats's concept of nobility. The chapter "Yeats: Violence, Tragedy, Mutability" in *The Edge of Impossibility: Tragic Forms in Literature* (1972) by Joyce Carol Oates is a provocative examination of the "essential ambiguity of

Yeats's imagination," noting a number of connections with Nietzsche.

The tendency of A. Norman Jeffares to be prolific through repetition is seen at its worst in his *The Circus Animals: Essays on W. B. Yeats* (1970). This volume of previously published work contains essays which date from as early as 1946, and the revisions are minimal. "Yeats's Mask" provides an inauspicious opening by attributing one of Blake's most famous statements to Denis Saurat. The other essays include "Yeats, Public Man," "Women in Yeats's Poetry," "Poet's Tower," "Yeats, Critic," and "Gyres in Yeats's Poetry." The only important article is the biographical sketch of John Butler Yeats (revised from *In Excited Reverie*, a fact not indicated). The volume also contains a 1960 essay on Oliver St. John Gogarty.

Of perhaps even less interest is Baidya Nath Prasad's *W. B. Yeats as a Literary Critic and Other Essays* (Ranchi, 1971). The title essay suggests that Yeats's major achievements as a critic are "'his reordering of tradition, the diagnosis of the disease of modern creative sensibility [and] the emphasis on the value of mythology to interpret modern experience." The longest section is on "Yeats's Concepts of Tragic Drama" and is more summary than analysis. In addition to two other essays on the drama and one on Yeats's attitudes toward the middle class, the volume includes "Vedanta and Yeats," mainly on Mohini Chatterjee and Yeats; "Yeats and Kalidas," on the influence of Sanskrit drama; and "Yeats and Prasad," a comparative study with the modern Hindi poet, not the author. This incompletely researched collection does little to advance our understanding of any of its subjects.

More significant than either of these collections is *Yeats and Anglo-Irish Literature: Critical Essays by Peter Ure* (ed. C. J. Rawson, 1974), which includes both unpublished and published work. "W. B. Yeats and the Growth of a Poet's Mind" provides a good sketch of his development, noting the importance of *A Vision* as a synthesis. "W. B. Yeats and the Irish Theme," mainly on the Cuchulain cycle, is also useful. "The Integrity of Yeats" is a defense against the attacks of T. S. Eliot, I. A. Richards, and Stephen Spender; Spender is also answered in "W. B. Yeats and the Musical Instruments," a somewhat disconnected essay. The article on the "Supernatural Songs" is interesting but treats only the first four lyrics. The collection also includes brief notes on "The Statues" and "Parnell's Funeral"; and the four essays and the monograph on Yeats and Shakespeare cited elsewhere.

XI. *Studies of the Poetry*

The chapter on Yeats in Robert Farren's *The Course of Irish Verse in English* (1947) praises Yeats's style but offers little of value. Much more significant is *The Golden Nightingale: Essays on Some Principles of Poetry in the Lyrics of William Butler Yeats* (1949) by Donald A. Stauffer; though the tone of the writing is sometimes obtrusive, the book is historically important in Yeats studies and still repays a careful reading. Stauffer defends *A Vision* as a "brilliant series of fictions" and offers a list of Yeats's beliefs. His treatment of Yeats's poetics centers on the theory of the symbol; he lists ten attributes of the Yeats symbol and then shows the gradual development of the gyre symbol. "The Reading of a Lyric" cogently argues that a New Critical approach to Yeats offers little hope of success and that "knowledge of at least the main body of his poems" is necessary to an understanding of any individual lyric. He traces the swan symbol through several poems. Stauffer concludes by offering a brief sketch of the career and classifying the poems into types. He describes the final purpose of Yeats's art as "revelation through joy." Stauffer's various lists and classifications are not satisfactory, and his study is marred by being centered on the last twenty-five years of Yeats's career: one "will not have missed much . . . if he begins his reading with *Responsibilities*." But his argument for the essential unity of Yeats's work, supported by extensive quotations in the thirty-four pages of notes, is effectively developed.

In contrast, the analysis of thirteen of the "Last Poems" by Vivienne Koch in *W. B. Yeats: The Tragic Phase* (1951) offers only scattered insights. Koch's thesis is that the poems "celebrate suffering not only as the inevitable condition of living, but as a sign that we truly live" and that "the terms in which Yeats expressed this suffering in the last seven or eight years of his life were very largely sexual." Unfortunately, the explications themselves do not always bear out these ideas, and the few remarks of value come only when Koch abandons her New Critical approach. She is also impatient with the "dubious concoction" of *A Vision*. More important is the chapter on "Yeats's Philosophical Poetry" in Raymond Tschumi's *Thought in Twentieth-Century English Poetry* (1951), which provides a basic explanation of *A Vision*, arguing that it is "a skeleton or a mere scaffold and should be understood metaphorically," and explications of the poems related to it. Though Tschumi's explanations are sometimes too simplistic, his critical approach to Yeats's poems is more fruitful than that of Koch.

Thomas Parkinson's *W. B. Yeats Self-Critic: A Study of His Early Verse* (1951; rpt. 1971 with *The Later Poetry* and a new foreword) is a lucid and well-written discussion of the development of Yeats's style and of the intimate connection between style and content. Parkinson correctly sees the Abbey experience as the most important factor in the stylistic changes. He begins by demonstrating how Yeats shaped his style in the 1890's both by excluding some poems from his collections and by revising others. Parkinson argues that by the time the early style reached its fullest development in *The Wind Among the Reeds*, Yeats realized that it could be used only on certain areas of experience. The chapter "A Poet's Stagecraft: 1899–1911" employs the revisions in *The Shadowy Waters* to illustrate the effects of Yeats's dramatic theory and practice on his style (Parkinson's account here should be supplemented by *Druid Craft*). He admits only a minor role for Ezra Pound in Yeats's development of a dramatic voice in his lyrics. Parkinson concludes by discussing the later revisions to the early poems. His work essentially supersedes Peter Allt's pioneering "Yeats and the Revision of His Early Verse" (*Hermathena*, 1944, 1945), which analyzes sixteen kinds of revision in the poems from "Crossways" and "The Rose." Marion Witt's "A Competition for Eternity: Yeats's Revision of His Later Poems" (*PMLA*, 1949) retains some interest.

Yvor Winters' *The Poetry of W. B. Yeats* (1960), reprinted from *TCL* (1960) and included in his *Forms of Discovery* (1967), is entertaining to some, irritating to most. The most famous of the hostile critics, Winters attacks Yeats on all sides: "his obscurity results from his private symbols . . . , from the confusion of his thought, and from the frequent ineptitude of his style. . . . His ideas were contemptible." Of the several refutations, the most convincing are John R. Moore's "Swan or Goose?" (*SR*, 1963), the anonymous "Yeats in Winters's Grip" (*TLS*, 18 Feb. 1965), and Ian Fletcher's "The Traffic in Yeats" (*TLS*, 2 May 1975). The two other most influential detractors of Yeats are Karl Shapiro and F. R. Leavis. In *In Defense of Ignorance* (1960), Shapiro attacks Yeats because of his "commitment to the historical role" and the "lifelong silliness" of his occult interests which "weakened his whole structure of thought." Equally unacceptable are Shapiro's labeling of Yeats a "Classicist" (a category in which he also places Eliot, Pound, and Stevens) and his conclusion that Yeats is "a master craftsman of the poem, and nothing else." In *Lectures in America* (1969), F. R. Leavis argues that Yeats "had no centre of unity" and was "unable to find one"; he admits only two examples of "major poetry" in Yeats (the Byzantium poems), though he does have a few kind words for "Among School Children."

More important than these fault-finding essays is the chapter on Yeats in George T. Wright's *The Poet in the Poem: The Personae of Eliot, Yeats, and Pound* (1960). Although the study is too brief for a full exploration of this significant topic, Wright is successful in arguing that Yeats's total vision is larger than that of his individual speakers: "The poem, taken as a whole, is the mask through which he speaks, as poet, to his reader; the poem, not the 'I,' is his voice, his persona." Wright also gives some attention to the nineteenth-century background, particularly Byron and Wilde.

Despite the lucid style and the sensitivity of many of the insights, *William Butler Yeats: The Lyric of Tragedy* (1961) by B. L. Reid is a disappointing study. Reid wants to show that the tragic sense of lyric poetry is equivalent in scope and value to the "systematic" tragedy of drama. Although the point is true in general, the attempt to equate the two genres leads Reid into such statements as "his last poems . . . have to be seen as a quite literal lyric equivalent of the satyr-play." Reid begins with an unnecessary survey of some theories of tragedy from Aristotle to Gilbert Murray and then traces some of Yeats's statements, mainly from "The Tragic Theatre." He finds only "pathos" in the early poems and emphasizes the importance of Maud Gonne's marriage in Yeats's transition to a more tragic sense. After discussing some prose statements related to the concept of "tragic joy," Reid offers some good readings of selected poems from the middle period. The chapter on "Late Theory" makes a rather artificial distinction among four forms of Yeatsian passion—"Joy, Defense, Sublimation, Transcendence." Fortunately, Reid does not press these categories in dealing with the poems themselves, but later he argues that they are equivalent to the various stages of classical tragedy. The study of the "Late Poems" is usually sensible, and he provides a cogent defense of their sexuality. He concludes with an attempt to parallel Yeats's poems "taken as a whole" with the "design of the Dionysus-mystery which is the primitive original of tragedy" and with an unnecessary argument with Walter Houghton and Stephen Spender. Reid makes few references to previous studies, and his terminology is loose. Nonetheless, the study provides some cogent explications and does not deserve the general neglect it seems to have received.

Graham Martin's study of the later poetry in *The Modern Age* (Vol. VII of the Pelican Guide to English Literature, ed. Boris Ford, 1961; 3rd ed., 1973), includes some interesting comparisons with Eliot. However, Martin is impatient with Yeats's "ideas": "Like any great poet, Yeats offers many satisfactions, but there seem to me good grounds for rating the simple direct centrality of much of his work as the most lasting." Bhabatosh Chatterjee's *The Poetry of W. B. Yeats* (Bombay, 1962), essentially unrevised after 1953, contains a sketch of the life which draws heavily on *Autobiographies*; five chapters of paraphrase-explications of selected poems; and an appendix on "Visions and Revisions" (which ignores the *Variorum Poems*). Chatterjee does not succeed in his attempt to "show the development of Yeats' mind and craft, and to examine the richness and complexity of his symbolism." Of some interest is his argument against seeing an important influence of French Symbolist poetry.

The section on Yeats in C. K. Stead's *The New Poetic* (1964) is nicely done. Stead treats Yeats's attempt in his early career to attain a balance between the conflicting demands of poetry, the audience, and the public world, commenting that "his poetry enters the public world as the work of no other Symbolist poet does." He examines Yeats's personae and concludes that he "stands alone among English speaking poets of this century in his ability to assimilate a complex political event into the framework of a poem without distortion of the event or loss of its human character in abstraction." His major example is "Easter 1916." A related essay is Graham Martin's "Fine Manners, Liberal Speech: A Note on the Public Poetry of W. B. Yeats" (*EIC*, 1961), which distinguishes between the public and the visionary modes in Yeats's poetry and concludes that the public poems succeed by "the calling into being of an audience . . . committed to certain social values."

In *Rilke, Valéry and Yeats: The Domain of the Self* (1964), Priscilla Washburn Shaw places Yeats in a mediate position between the other two writers, arguing that "his poetry communicates a more balanced awareness of self and the world, in which the irreducible existence of each is made felt." However, her analyses of selected poems are unexciting, and the book will be of little use to those without a close knowledge of Rilke and Valéry, who are given considerable attention even in the chapters on Yeats. "Leda and the Swan" receives the most extended commentary.

Thomas Parkinson's *W. B. Yeats: The Later Poetry* (1964) is a lucidly written and often brilliant study. The major thesis is that "Yeats's poetry was largely determined by his dramatic sense," but many other topics are examined and effective use made of manuscript materials. Among the topics are Yeats's theory of personality contrasted with those of Eliot and Pound; Yeats's adoption of five major poetic roles and the basic division in his career in 1917; the manuscript versions of "Speech after Long Silence" and "Among School Children"; Yeats's methods of composition; and the symbols of swan, sun, and moon as their meanings are conditioned by context. Parkinson rightly questions F. A. C. Wilson's allegorical approach and Frank Kermode's view of a poem as a "self-limited organic artifact." He relates the disappearance of Yeats's major icons after 1933 to the sense of a new beginning found in the "Last Poems" and provides an interesting discussion of Yeats's prosody, claiming that he used not accentual-syllabic verse but either a decasyllabic line or a stress line, depending on the content of the poem. In the final chapter Parkinson shows Yeats's value to contemporary poetry, suggesting that he should be "emulated rather than imitated" and that he offers a corrective to the poetry of "dandyism" or "hipsterism." Parkinson's volume is the single most important study of the later poetry.

T. R. Henn's *W. B. Yeats and the Poetry of War* (1965), reprinted from *PBA* (1965), concentrates on Yeats's poems on the Irish rebellion and the later civil war. It is useful for a sketch of the background of the events by someone who lived through them. Henn also cites some variants to "Reprisals" from a text "taken down from [Peter] Allt himself, in 1947." The chapter on Yeats in *Poets of Reality: Six Twentieth-Century Writers* (1965) by J. Hillis Miller centers on Yeats's sense of antithesis as the fundamental fact of reality and on the various solutions he posited. Miller argues that Yeats's basic choice was "the way down": "to will, with all one's passion and strength, the eternal repetition of earthly existence with all its tragic suffering." This thesis is of course not original, and one might have wished for more attention to the chronological development of Yeats's ideas and for fewer quotations of passages out of context. However, many of the details of Miller's study are provocative and are doubtless worth the struggle with his prose style.

Most of Abraham Verhoeff's *The Practice of Criticism: A Comparative Analysis of W. B. Yeats's "Among School Children"* (1966) consists of a summary of the major previous criticism and is therefore quite helpful to anyone with a strong interest in the poem. The summary is accomplished on a stanza-by-stanza basis; Verhoeff also offers his own view, which stresses that the tree is imaged in springtime and that dancing is an activity of youth: "the poem is a curse on old age and the last stanza does not hold out new hope or suggest a solution in a life beyond this life." He argues that "Among School Children" falls into two halves, with the first clearly superior. Although Verhoeff's reading of the poem is not satisfactory, the volume can still serve a useful purpose. Regrettably, the circumstances of publication (a Utrecht thesis with a limited American reprint) have made it difficult to locate. The commentary on Yeats in Patrick C. Power's *The Story of Anglo-Irish Poetry (1800–1922)* (1967) is scattered and elementary ("the poet of the fairies is no doubt W. B. Yeats"). Like Parkinson, whom he does not acknowledge, Power suggests that Yeats used syllabic verse in some of the early poems.

Four Essays on the Poetry of W. B. Yeats (Santiniketan, 1968) by

S. C. Sen is of only passing interest. The loosely constructed sections examine the diction, the Irish elements, the treatment of time, and the love lyrics. The study contains numerous errors and makes little reference to previous criticism. Arra M. Garab's *Beyond Byzantium: The Last Phase of Yeats's Career* (1969) offers an occasional insight but does not significantly advance our understanding of the period. It is of some use in providing a well-written summary of the general critical opinion on selected late poems. The first chapter is an over-simplified sketch of the treatment of time in the poems up to and including "Sailing to Byzantium," arguing that they are funda-mentally escapist. Garab then treats Yeats's movement toward ac-ceptance of the real world and points to the influence of Villon. The next four chapters offer readings of certain late poems; other topics discussed include the relationship between Yeats and Frank O'Con-nor and the influence of Gaelic poetry. Garab concludes that the condition toward which Yeats strived in his later career was "whole-ness." In *The Truth of Poetry: Tensions in Modern Poetry from Baudelaire to the 1960's* (1969) Michael Hamburger presents a sug-gestive examination of the essentially dramatic mode of Yeats's poems and of the partial nature of his political opinions: "most of the ex-treme opinions and attitudes in Yeats's work are those of his anti-self." Of less interest is the section on the later poetry in *A Map of English Verse* (1969) by John Press, which consists of an introduc-tion of no special value, a selection from the criticism and some comments by Yeats, and a small anthology of the poems.

Allen R. Grossman's *Poetic Knowledge in the Early Yeats: A Study of* The Wind Among the Reeds (1969) is a difficult but important volume for advanced students. Grossman attempts to demonstrate that the collection is "a mythological poem . . . which takes as its subject the search for poetic knowledge; and poetic knowledge in *The Wind Among the Reeds* defines itself as an account of personal origins." Grossman argues that the search is essentially for Wisdom, seen in the archetypal figure of the White Woman; the attempt to attain her involves a conflict with a Father-God figure and often results in the protagonist's death. Much of this study is devoted to identifying Yeats's sources, particularly the gnostic and cabalistic ones (with which Grossman, unlike Harold Bloom, is in sympathy). Though it unfortunately does not draw on Yeats's own Golden Dawn materials, the chapter on "The Wars of Eden" is a forceful discussion of the ways in which Golden Dawn rituals are used in the poems (in this case "The Everlasting Voices" and "The Travail of Passion"). Other interesting chapters include his discussion of the three major personae of the volume (Aedh, Hanrahan, and Roberts) and of the parallels Yeats found or invented between the Celtic and the aesthetic movements. Grossman's explications are not always convincing, and the refusal to consider biographical levels prevents his study from being a full examination of the collection. And although he remarks briefly on it, a fuller discussion of *The Shadowy Waters* would have given a more nearly complete picture of one aspect of Yeats in the 1890's.

The thesis of Bernard Levine's *The Dissolving Image: The Spir-itual-Esthetic Development of W. B. Yeats* (1970) is that Yeats's

W. B. YEATS / *Richard J. Finneran* 273

poetry moves toward a concentration on the speaking voice, with the images taking a secondary place to the sense of awareness of the psyche of the speaker. Though both its general validity and its originality are overstressed, this concept is presented with some intelligence in the opening chapter on "Yeats's esthetic and the concept of the self." Thereafter, though, the book descends into strained ingenuity and prolix writing and employs a bewildering variety of critical approaches. The occasional valid perception is lost in a maze of unfounded speculation, best seen in the elaborate misreading of "Leda and the Swan."

Vikramaditya Rai's *The Poetry of W. B. Yeats* (Delhi, 1971) consists of two introductory chapters, five chapters offering paraphrases of most of the major poems, and a concluding chapter on Yeats's style. Rai admits that he is not attempting to offer any new insights, the single exception being his reading of "Grimalkin" in "The Statues" as "referring to the Sphinx, symbol of European intellect." Although not unacceptable as an introductory study, the book contains numerous errors and often falters in its prose style. Of less use is John T. Braun's *The Apostrophic Gesture* (1971), which begins by presenting the vaguely phenomenological theory that "the gesture a poem makes" involves the three steps of "turning aside, invocation, and return." Braun then attempts to apply this thesis to ten selected poems and concludes with an appendix summarizing the readings of "several Yeats critics." The most generous response to this poorly written study would be to accept the implications of the dedication and consider it a parody, in which case it is only unsuccessful; if, as seems more likely, it is meant for serious criticism, it is an abject failure.

Lyric Resonance: Glosses on Some Poems of Yeats, Frost, Crane, Cummings and Others (1972) by David Ridgley Clark includes a discussion of the influence of some of the poets Yeats included in *A Book of Irish Verse* on his later poetry, an unsatisfactory explication of "He Bids His Beloved Be at Peace," and a cogent commentary on "Poussin & 'News for the Delphic Oracle.'" Arnold Goldman's "The *Oeuvre* Takes Shape: Yeats's Early Poetry," in *Victorian Poetry* (Stratford-upon-Avon Studies, 15, 1972), is a satisfactory but unoriginal tracing of the publication history of the volumes up to and including *In the Seven Woods*.

The basic thesis of Daniel Albright's *The Myth against Myth: A Study of Yeats's Imagination in Old Age* (1972)—that Yeats's later poetry moved toward a fuller acceptance of the real world and that this process involved coming to terms with and partially rejecting his early work—is likewise less than novel. Nor does the attempt at wit in the acknowledgments ("the only original sin is plagiarism") disguise the lack of detailed attention to previous criticism. The first chapter studies "The Tower" on the basis that the "key" to its meaning is the "act of aesthetic *composition*." Although Albright places too much emphasis on the "lechery" of Hanrahan, this chapter is indeed interesting. Unfortunately, it bears only a tangential relation to the other three, which examine various versions of paradise: "The Earthly Paradise" ("The Wanderings of Oisin"), "The Poverty of Heaven" ("News for the Delphic Oracle"), and "Earth Unparadised" ("The Circus Animals' Desertion"). Although the study contains some suggestive insights, the critical methods employed are constantly suspect. Finally, Albright's style is exceedingly pretentious; he seldom uses the right word if he can find an obscure one.

No more successful is Robert Snukal's *High Talk: The Philosophical Poetry of W. B. Yeats* (1973), though it also contains a few suggestive explications. The book includes far too much quotation, both of entire Yeats poems and of long passages from an assortment of writers ranging from A. J. Ayer to Geoffrey Durrant. "Philosophical poetry" is never defined, and Snukal by no means provides a full survey of previous scholarship. The usual technique of the study is to quote a poem, quote the analysis of either Richard Ellmann or John Unterecker, and then attempt to refute it. After a discussion of the influence of Kant, Hegel, and others, the chapter "Towards a Reading of the Poems" offers acceptable but sometimes simplistic analyses. "Symbol and Symbolism" is a fuzzy theoretical discussion of meaning in poetry, followed by an account of Yeats's theory of symbolism which ignores the work of Edward Engelberg. The remaining chapters are primarily readings of individual poems; other topics discussed include the influence of Plato, Porphyry, and especially Whitehead. Snukal concludes that "the thrust of Yeats's philosophical poems is to discover the nature of mental activity, and to develop a critique of abstraction that does justice to the importance of ideas, but which at the same time delivers us from what Whitehead called the 'fallacy of misplaced concreteness.'" The three appendices are hardly necessary (the "Genealogical Tree of Revolution" is incorrectly attributed to *The Identity of Yeats* rather than to *W. B. Yeats: Man and Poet*).

Also of little value is *Interpretations of the Later Poems of W. B. Yeats* (Dharwar, 1973) by Shankar Mokashi-Punekar, which considers four poems from *Responsibilities* and most of the later lyrics. The study is marred by the poor style, the continual attacks on formalist approaches to Yeats, and the exaggerated emphasis on Yeats's use of Indian matter. His insistence that the poems "adhere to a single significance" often results in literal readings which ignore subtleties of tone.

Colin Meir's *The Ballads and Songs of W. B. Yeats: The Anglo-Irish Heritage in Subject and Style* (1974) begins by tracing Yeats's early attempts to be a national poet and the shift around 1893 to a more esoteric subject matter; aside from the identification of some sources, little is added to previous studies (not all of which are taken into account). After commenting on the translations of Gaelic poetry available to Yeats (Callanan, Mangan, and Hyde in particular), Meir examines "Yeats's Debt to Anglo-Irish Dialect" on the basis of P. L. Henry's *An Anglo-Irish Dialect of North Roscommon* (1957). He concludes with a study of "ballad rhetoric" in various poems and suggests the indebtedness of Yeats's "passionate syntax" to Gaelic poetry. This relatively short study is more interesting for the specific details on sources and dialect devices than for the general thesis, which does not sufficiently credit the other influences on Yeats's changing style, especially his work in the theater. More information on "A Yeats Borrowing from Mangan" is provided by D. C. Sutton (*N&Q*, 1974). Georges-Denis Zimmermann's "Yeats, the Popular Ballad and the Ballad-Singer" (*ES*, 1969) is a useful chronological sketch of Yeats's various theories, arguing that "what did not change fundamentally was the conviction that good ballads, with their explosive power, had a special function in saving morals and politics from abstraction and in stirring up healthy hatred or enthusiasm." A more general essay which can still be read with profit is G. S. Fraser's "Yeats and the Ballad Style" (*Shenandoah*, Spring 1970), which shows Yeats's use of "balladic shorthand" in several poems.

The opening chapter in Daniel A. Harris' important *Yeats: Coole Park & Ballylee* (1974) deals with the change in Yeats's view of Coole from a Celtic to a Renaissance to an Anglo-Irish perspective and with the necessity he felt for a myth of place. The next two chapters concentrate on Yeats's views of the peasantry and of the Renaissance. Special attention is given to the influence of Ben Jonson, Harris concluding that "Yeats's unrelenting emphasis on dynamic energy, on movement in the mind and body of his speaker, constitute his major modification of Jonson's form." In the remainder of the volume Harris provides detailed commentary on the poems associated with the Tower and Coole Park, concluding with an excellent analysis of "The Black Tower."

It is salutary to note that *Yeats: Coole Park & Ballylee* is not only impeccably written but is also one of the most carefully researched of recent books on Yeats. At times, though, Harris descends to bickering; for instance, although his points are almost always convincing, there are far too many references to William M. Carpenter's *The Green Helmet* Poems and Yeats's Myth of the Renaissance" (*MP*, 1969) and Majorie Perloff's " '*Another* Emblem There': Theme and Convention in Yeats's 'Coole Park and Ballylee, 1931' " (*JEGP*, 1970), which might have been disposed of in a note each. Moreover, Harris almost reverts to a New Critical approach to Yeats in refusing to consider much outside of the individual poems and generally ignoring Yeats's placement of them in the individual collections. But for the eighteen or so poems that he considers in detail, Harris' readings must be the starting point for any future discussions; though sometimes overextended, they are consistently intelligent and well argued.

There are some brief comments on Harris' major topic in *Happy Rural Seat: The English Country House and the Literary Imagination* (1972) by Richard Gill. A more important supplement is the provocative account of the significance of the Tower in James Olney's comparative study, " 'A Powerful Emblem': The Towers of Yeats and Jung" (*SAQ*, 1973).

Frank Hughes Murphy's *Yeats's Early Poetry: The Quest for Reconciliation* (1975) is an academic exercise in close reading which does little to advance our understanding of the period. Murphy uses a solidly New Critical approach on selected poems from *Crossways* through *Michael Robartes and the Dancer*; he does not consider the early poems Yeats excluded from the *Collected Poems* or even "The Wanderings of Oisin." His central and unoriginal thesis is that the poems present various sets of oppositions which Yeats attempts to reconcile. No attempt is made to provide a full survey of the previous scholarship (other than those in *The Permanence of Yeats*, Murphy cites but one periodical article). Defending Yeats against the attack of D. S. Savage thirty years after it was made is perhaps less than necessary.

Stanley Sultan's interesting monograph *Yeats at His Last* (1975) reasserts Curtis Bradford's views on the order and contents of the "Last Poems" section of the *Collected Poems* and argues that the general neglect of Bradford's thesis is due to "current critical interest in the romantic Yeats and literal devaluation of his very different qualities." He discusses the significance of the reconstructed order, noting the difference between "the poetic declarations of the *seanchan* which dominate the first half of the volume and the voice of the dying man which is the chief agency of coherence in the second half." Sultan also explicates some selected poems and finds that "the relationship of life and death is the pervasive subject of *Last Poems*." Advanced students will doubtless regret Sultan's view that "documentation of all my indebtedness would be distracting more than anything else."

Dudley Young's *Out of Ireland: A Reading of Yeats's Poetry* (1975) is not based on very extensive reference to either Yeats or his critics (representative omissions include the *Memoirs* and Engelberg, Whitaker, and Bloom, the last of whom Young often resembles). Apart from two chapters outlining Yeats's esthetics and the historical development in theories of the relation of the self to the "other," this slim volume consists of close readings of a dozen poems or parts of poems, with briefer comments on several others and on three plays; all the material dates from *Responsibilities* or later. Young often creates a "problem" which he thinks Yeats faced in a certain poem and then speculates at length on the solutions he might—or should—have found; thus many of his explications are quite muddled. But on other works he is refreshing and provocative, and as a critical essay on some aspects of Yeats's poetry *Out of Ireland* should not be neglected.

XII. *Studies of the Drama*

GENERAL STUDIES

There is little of interest in *Irish Plays and Playwrights* (1913) by Cornelius Weygandt, especially since he does not consider Yeats an effective dramatist. Of some fame is an anecdote: "he told me, when I asked him which writing of his he cared most for, 'That I was last working at, and then "The Shadowy Waters."'" Ernest A. Boyd gives a more sympathetic sketch of Yeats's dramatic career in *The Contemporary Drama of Ireland* (1917). Restating his position from *Ireland's Literary Renaissance*, Boyd argues against the view that Yeats's activities with the Abbey were detrimental to his lyric poetry. Boyd also summarizes the attacks on *The Countess Cathleen* by Frank Hugh O'Donnell in *Souls for Gold!*, the text of which is now conveniently available in the Coole Edition of Lady Gregory's *Our Irish Theatre* (cited above).

In *The Irish Drama* (1929), Andrew E. Malone provides a general sketch of the dramatic career, with extensive plot summaries. Malone argues that Yeats is "the poet in the theatre rather than the poet-dramatist" but gives special praise to *Kathleen Ni Houlihan* ("one of the greatest one-act plays of the modern theatre") and *The Hour Glass* ("the greatest morality play of the contemporary theatre"). In her chapter on Yeats in *The Irish Dramatic Movement* (1939; 2nd ed., 1954), Una Ellis-Fermor concentrates on the early and middle plays and on Yeats's leading role in the dramatic movement as a whole. Most of her comments are now dated, though the chapter on "Ideals in the Workshop" gives a useful summary of the major dramatic theories of Yeats and Lady Gregory.

Perhaps the earliest account that repays reading is the brief chapter in Ronald Peacock's *The Poet in the Theatre* (1946), a balanced but on the whole sympathetic assessment. Peacock argues that "in Yeats three things work together which in creative writers had for a long time been antagonistic: spiritual, dramatic, and poetic values." Also of interest is A. N. Jeffares' *A Poet and a Theatre* (Groningen, 1946), a competent sketch of Yeats's theatrical activities, with emphasis on the early years. Unfortunately, the brief section on Yeats in T. R. Henn's *The Harvest of Tragedy* (1956) offers little more than plot summaries of selected plays. In *The Third Voice: Modern British and American Verse Drama* (1959), Denis Donoghue examines with no great insights *The Shadowy Waters*, *The Hour Glass*, *At the Hawk's Well*, and *A Full Moon in March*, which he somewhat surprisingly calls "Yeats's best play." Donoghue maintains that "none of Yeats's verse plays is a complete success" because "by the time Yeats's conception of dramatic form had moved from theory into mature practice, he had ceased to be a great poet" (that is, after *The Tower*). William L. Sharp's "W. B. Yeats: A Poet Not in the Theatre" (*TDR*, Winter 1959) is an unconvincing attempt to suggest the essential failure of the *Four Plays for Dancers*, primarily because of the difficulty of "distinguishing between voices" of the characters.

In *The Drama of Chekhov, Synge, Yeats, and Pirandello* (1963), F. L. Lucas displays little sympathy for Yeats, whom he describes as "one of the many anti-rationalists of our distracted century." His comments on the plays consist of hostile plot summaries. Lucas concludes that the plays are not successful because Yeats lacked "sufficient observation and grasp of character" and was "tempted to some rather thin dramatic theorizing." Of even less importance are the chapter and section on Yeats in H. H. Anniah Gowda's *The Revival of English Poetic Drama* (1963; enl. ed., New Delhi, 1972), which consist of little more than plot summaries.

Peter Ure's *Yeats the Playwright: A Commentary on Character and Design in the Major Plays* (1963) is a sensible and intelligent study. Ure has the modest aim of providing a "critical handbook or companion to some features of the plays," and thus his critical approach varies. With *The Countess Cathleen* and *The King's Threshold*, for instance, he pays close attention to the revisions (regrettably, he overlooks the 1913 revisions in *Cathleen*). On the other hand, he examines *Deirdre* as showing a lack of correlation between Yeats's theory and practice, as the play centers on her "character" rather than her "personality." The study contains a useful appendix, listing for each play the date of composition, first performance, and first printing. Unlike many other critics, Ure always considers the plays as

drama and is impatient with any doctrine that interferes with that
consideration. Though essentially an introductory work, *Yeats the
Playwright* should not be neglected.

The main interest of Helen Hennessy Vendler's *Yeats's* Vision *and
the Later Plays* (1963) is in the first section, an explication of *A
Vision*. Particularly valuable are the two charts of the phases in relation to historical eras (the second set is more accurate). However,
Vendler's claim that the book "is about imagination" and her desire to
present a "nonesoteric interpretation" lead her to place excessive
emphasis on the esthetic level of *A Vision*, and thus her reading is at
best partial. Her equation between Yeats's account of the states after
death and "the aesthetic process as it occurs in the creating mind" is
far fetched. She also does not sufficiently consider the differences
between the 1926 and 1937 editions. In any event, the moderate
success of the first part of the book does not continue when she
attempts to apply her reading of *A Vision* to eleven selected plays.
Since she describes the plays as "arid and contrived," "trying and
artificial," and "disconnected and jerky," one can only speculate on
why she tried to write a study of them. Moreover, her refusal to
consider Yeats's plays as drama results in the absurd stratagem of
assigning speakers to individual lines of some of the songs in the
plays. She is occasionally stimulating on plays that actually can be
read as esthetic documents (such as *The Player Queen*) but is perfectly confused about many others. Vendler's readings can be used
only with extreme caution, and students should not be misled by her
erroneous statement that *The Only Jealousy of Emer* was called "A
Sword Blade against the Foam" "in its earliest printing."

S. B. Bushrui's *Yeats's Verse-Plays: The Revisions 1900–1910*
(1965) is a competent if sometimes tedious study, useful to someone
with a particular interest in one of the five plays discussed. With *The
King's Threshold* and *Deirdre*, Bushrui wisely abandons his chronological limits and traces the plays through to their final form; it is
unfortunate that the same principle was not applied to the minor
post–1910 changes in *The Shadowy Waters, On Baile's Strand*, and
The Green Helmet. With *The Shadowy Waters* Bushrui overlooks the
differences in the two 1900 versions, a repetition of Thomas Parkinson's error, but less understandable since he uses the *Variorum Poems*
as his text. Bushrui's conclusions about the changes in Yeats's style
during the decade parallel those of earlier scholars, though he does
emphasize the possible influence of Synge. The study can be supplemented by his account of the revisions to *The Hour Glass*, in *W. B.
Yeats: Centenary Essays* (ed. D. E. S. Maxwell and Bushrui).

Thomas Parkinson's "The Later Plays of W. B. Yeats," in *Modern
Drama: Essays in Criticism* (ed. Travis Bogard and William I.
Oliver, 1965) is a perceptive but brief article, stressing again (see
CL, 1954) that Yeats only adapted the Noh form rather than imitated it; he also argues that the plays are relevant to the conditions of
the contemporary stage. Parkinson effectively demonstrates the classical structure of *The Resurrection*. In a chapter in *English Dramatic
Form: A History of Its Development* (1965), Muriel C. Bradbrook
also treats Yeats's influence on modern playwrights: "The image of
the tramp, the beggar or the blind man has become the most potent

Icon of the modern stage—in Beckett and Genet, Pinter and Ionesco, the lineaments traced by Yeats maintain their form." Thus Bradbrook's short sketch of Yeats's development in drama concludes that "a great personal achievement was also the foundation for great work to follow."

W. B. Yeats and the Theatre of Desolate Reality (1965) by David R. Clark is a brief but important study. The major interest is not in the general thesis—that Yeats's drama evolved toward a "drama of perception" and that his plays are "recognition scenes" which represent "the action and theatre of perception" (the terminology borrowed from Francis Fergusson, as Clark indicates)—but in the particular insights that Clark elicits from the texts and in his constant awareness of the plays as theatrical events. His treatment of *Deirdre* is seminal in showing the function of the chess-game and the brazier in the symbolic structure of the play. With *The Dreaming of the Bones* he treats the relationship to the Noh, the importance of place, and the differences in language (and thus modes of perception) between the soldier and the ghosts. He is also effective in showing the three different "plays" that occur in *The Words upon the Window-Pane* and in analyzing the verse of *Purgatory*. Clark concludes that Yeats "has been more successful than any other modern dramatic poet in meeting the crisis of his age." One regrets that only four plays are examined.

Another important study is Leonard E. Nathan's *The Tragic Drama of William Butler Yeats: Figures in a Dance* (1965). Quoting Yeats, Nathan argues that Yeats's plays at their best display "the war of spiritual with natural order." Unfortunately, he devotes well over half his study to tracing the development of the mature form—neatly termed the "Yeatsian No"—used to image the conflict. In discussing seven of the pre-1916 plays, Nathan often criticizes them for not being something they were never designed to be. The best part of this section (though there are cogent comments throughout) is his discussion of Yeats's estheticism, with special reference to the parallels with Villiers de l'Isle-Adam, Maeterlinck, and Pater. In his analysis of ten late tragedies, however, Nathan is always stimulating and often brilliant. Particularly lucid are his comments on the two Christ plays and *The Only Jealousy of Emer*. With *Purgatory* he makes the curious statement that it is set "in the nineteenth or early twentieth century," thus dispensing with the possible political level of the play without even considering it. Nathan often takes issue with previous critics, especially F. A. C. Wilson and H. H. Vendler, and his arguments are almost always persuasive. He concludes that at least some of Yeats's plays deserve a "place in the tradition" of performable drama.

Studies of Yeats and the Noh abound. Yasuko Stucki (*MD*, 1966) is not especially convincing in her attempt to show that Yeats deviates from the Noh to the detriment of his plays. The most satisfactory of the studies is *Yeats and the Noh: Types of Japanese Beauty and Their Reflection in Yeats's Plays* (1966) by Hiro Ishibashi, a useful account of the basic characteristics of the form and of Yeats's adaptations of it to his own purposes. The monograph is profusely illustrated with pictures of Noh masks and productions and of Japanese art. Ishibashi also provides an appendix on Yeats's interest in Zen Buddhism and prints a letter to Daisetz Suzuki (which comments on Wyndham Lewis' *Time and Western Man*).

Vinod Sena (*MD*, 1966) strings together some quotations in an ineffective attempt to prove that Yeats never believed in the possibility of a modern poetic drama. A rebuttal of some success is provided by Rupin W. Desai (*MD*, 1969). The chapter on Yeats in Raymond Williams' *Drama from Ibsen to Brecht* (1968) is an acceptable general survey of Yeats's dramatic development, with extensive quotations. In "The Same Enemies: Notes on Certain Similarities between Yeats and Strindberg" (*MD*, 1969), Frederick S. Lapisardi admits that Yeats is indebted only for "impressionistic scene painting" (a point which could easily be argued) and then proceeds to discuss some rather tenuous parallels. Stephen M. Gill's *Six Symbolist Plays of Yeats* (New Delhi, 1971) is of even less interest. A good portion of the text is given over to the "Plays in Synposis." The commentary is elementary at best; the style is on occasion unintentionally comic.

John Rees Moore's *Masks of Love and Death: Yeats as Dramatist* (1971) is the only study available to treat all the works in the *Collected Plays*, to which Moore adds *Diarmuid and Grania* but regrettably not *Where There Is Nothing*. The book assimilates much from the previous criticism and is not, with some exceptions, original. But it does provide a useful account of the dramatic career and particularly lucid readings of *The Player Queen*, *The Herne's Egg*, *Purgatory*, and *The Death of Cuchulain*. Moore stays close to the texts: the usual method is to give a plot summary with commentary and then go on to discuss some relevant special topics, such as the revisions, the use of language, problems in staging, or previous studies. The theoretical discussion of "The Uses of Drama" is not especially rich and is most useful for describing the character of Cuchulain as he is treated in the Irish sagas. The early chapters tend to be tedious and repetitious. Moore makes a strange but atypical error when he remarks that in *On Baile's Strand* Cuchulain "escapes the oath which would have been a testament to the High King's mastery" (there is no oath-taking in the first version; in the revised text Cuchulain takes it). The study becomes effective with the chapter on *The Player Queen*. It is unfortunate that Moore does not use the *Variorum Plays* (which indeed he never mentions) as his text, which would have allowed him to quote Yeats directly rather than requoting earlier studies. In short, though, for its summary aspects and inclusiveness *Masks of Love and Death* is the place to begin a study of the plays.

The chapter on Yeats in Emil Roy's *British Drama since Shaw* (1972) employs an ineffective psychoanalytical approach and concentrates on *The Player Queen* ("Yeats's first successful play"), *The Words upon the Window-Pane*, and *Purgatory*. Roy suggests that Yeats's drama "is a compressed psychodrama of compulsion, presenting an irreconcilable conflict between transformation and identity, time and immutability." Much more stimulating is the essay on "Tragic Rites in Yeats's 'A Full Moon in March'" in Joyce Carol Oates's *The Edge of Impossibility* (1972), which argues that "all Yeats's plays may be called religious dramas, celebrations of a unique kind of mass." A related and also interesting approach is taken by

Natalie Crohn Schmitt in "Ecstasy and Insight in Yeats" (*BJA*, 1971), though she overstates the extent to which Yeats believed in the primacy of language. Schmitt has applied her basic thesis to *A Full Moon in March* (*ETJ*, 1972) and, with less success, *Purgatory* (*CompD*, 1973–74). Susan R. Gorsky's "A Ritual Drama: Yeats's Plays for Dancers" (*MD*, 1974) adds little to previous accounts and fails to define its central term of "ritual drama."

Another study which ignores much of the earlier scholarship is the chapter on Yeats in Donna Gerstenberger's *The Complex Configuration: Modern Verse Drama* (Salzburg, 1973). Centering on *The Shadowy Waters, Calvary*, and *Purgatory*, Gerstenberger falls short of demonstrating that Yeats "was instrumental in actually creating on the stage a totally coherent verse drama having the vital relationship between structure and language that modern poets sought in their poetry." In "*At the Hawk's Well*: Yeats's Unresolved Conflict between Language and Silence" (*CompD*, 1973) Edna G. Sharoni presents an unconvincing attack on the late dance plays, arguing that they are marred by Yeats's "fundamental indecision about the primacy of the word versus the primacy of the dance." Two other essays which show a lack of understanding of Yeats's dramatic theories are Kathleen M. Vogt's "Counter-Components in Yeats's *At the Hawk's Well*" (*MD*, 1974) and Warren Leamon's "Yeats, Synge, Realism, and 'The Tragic Theatre'" (*SoR*, 1975).

In *The Cuchulain Plays of W. B. Yeats: A Study* (1974), Reg Skene argues that "the major patterns of meaning in the plays become apparent only when they are considered together." It is a well-written volume but adds only slightly to our understanding. Although Skene produced the five-play cycle in 1969, he offers few comments on the actual staging of the plays. The serious student will be dismayed by the lack of direct reference to previous criticism. Skene begins by tracing the relation of the plays to Yeats's mystical interests. The second chapter provides plot summaries of the plays and shows the variations from Lady Gregory's accounts. "The Burning Wheel of Love" offers an original but over-ingenious equation of the plays with certain phases in *A Vision* and with months of the year. After a discussion of the biographical level of the plays, Skene sketches the basic principles of Yeats's stagecraft, emphasizing the relationship with Edward Gordon Craig. The last five chapters explicate the plays of the cycle, almost on a line-by-line basis. Although all of his readings are generally acceptable, none is especially original. Skene is perhaps best with *On Baile's Strand*, particularly in showing the function of the subplot. There are also some interesting comments on the interconnections between the five plays.

The scattered comments on Yeats in Micheál Ó hAodha's *Theatre in Ireland* (1974) are generally accurate but elementary. Much more significant is *Yeats and the Theatre* (ed. Robert O'Driscoll and Lorna Reynolds, 1975), the first volume in the Yeats Studies Series. James W. Flannery's "W. B. Yeats, Gordon Craig, and the Visual Arts of the Theatre" traces their work together and effectively draws on the unpublished correspondence. Karen Dorn's "Dialogue into Movement: W. B. Yeats's Theatre Collaboration with Gordon Craig" concentrates on the 1912 revisions to *The Hour-Glass* while arguing that "Yeats's skill in fitting dialogue to movement was a skill he had learned from Craig." These two essays are supported by numerous illustrations; strangely, neither makes any reference to Alan Tomlinson's article on Yeats and Craig (*ArielE*, 1972). Richard Taylor's "Assimilation and Accomplishment: No Drama and an Unpublished Source for *At the Hawk's Well*" offers an excellent discussion of both the No itself and Yeats's adaptation of it; Taylor also gives the text of a No play from Pound's papers (entitled *Yoro*) which was a major source for *At the Hawk's Well*. The other items in *Yeats and the Theatre* are cited elsewhere (particularly in section V).

George Mills Harper's monograph *The Mingling of Heaven and Earth: Yeats's Theory of Theatre* (1975) argues that Yeats developed "a complete and consistent esthetic of the theatre founded upon a Romantic faith in symbolic art." Though using an unnecessary amount of quotation, Harper effectively demonstrates that Yeats's theories were based on metaphysical assumptions about the existence of a higher reality.

YEATS IN PRODUCTION

As noted by Vivian Mercier (*MD*, 1965), the most significant lacuna in the criticism of Yeats's plays is attention to their actual effect on the stage. Some of the essays in the Yeats issue of *Threshold* (cited above) were a beginning. More important is Liam Miller's "W. B. Yeats and Stage Design at the Abbey Theatre" (*MHRev*, 1970), a useful account of the problems Yeats faced in stage design and the solutions offered by Charles Ricketts, Craig, and others. It is especially valuable for the twenty illustrations. Also of interest is James W. Flannery's "Action and Reaction at the Dublin Theatre Festival" (*ETJ*, 1967), which discusses his experimental staging of *Calvary* and *The Resurrection* in 1965—"the first Stanislavskian production of Yeats ever attempted." Flannery suggests that Yeats "in more ways than one is a dramatist of the twenty-first century rather than the twentieth." In "Yeats: What Method?" (*QJS*, 1971), Josephine Johnson discusses the Flannery *Calvary* as well as her own production of the play in Miami and also draws some parallels with Brecht. The 1973 Abbey production of *Sophocles' King Oedipus*, using additions to Yeats's text by Richard Murphy, is described by Rebecca Schull in "The Preparation of King Oedipus" (*The Arts in Ireland*, 2, No. 1, 1973). Other recent productions have been briefly noted by Ruby Cohn (*ETJ*, 1969), David R. Jones (*ETJ*, 1971), and Joseph Ronsley (*ETJ*, 1972).

James W. Flannery (*Studies*, 1973) shows the relation between Yeats's practical knowledge of acting and the development of his theories. Flannery is doubtless correct when he claims that "there are few dramatists whose plays have suffered more because of misunderstandings of how to stage them than W. B. Yeats." His discussion of Yeats's requirements for an actor of "poetical culture, passion, musical speech and bodily energy" is followed by a section on "The Mechanics of Acting." Flannery concludes that "one might reasonably argue that it is by discovering the histrionic techniques necessary to perform Yeats's own plays that the theatre may rediscover an important part of its true identity and purpose." Also of some interest is R. D. Eno's "Yeats' Theatre" (*DM*, 1973), which argues that "inflexible obedience to his theatrical dicta will not help a producer make good theatrical decisions, although the dicta remain available choices. It is to the plays themselves we must turn for instruction how to stage them." Certainly one must sympathize with Eno's plea for new productions which will take into account Yeats's "sheer, non-verbal, theatrical spectacle."

YEATS AND THE ABBEY

Though one would hardly assume so from the brief treatment in Dawson Bryne's *The Story of Ireland's National Theatre: The Abbey Theatre, Dublin* (1929), the career of Yeats and the early history of the Abbey are intertwined. Indeed, in *The Story of the Abbey Theatre from Its Origins in 1899 to the Present* (1950) Peter Kavanagh verges on idolatry, admitting that his study "is intended as a serious and positive exposition of Yeats's ideal and the ultimate decline of this ideal." Somewhat more objective is Lennox Robinson's *Ireland's Abbey Theatre: A History 1899–1951* (1951). Gerard Fay's *The Abbey Theatre: Cradle of Genius* (1958) is the most objective study to date, though it is centered on the period 1902–08 and understandably pays a great deal of attention to the Fay brothers. All of these volumes are valuable for the quotations from contemporary reviews, reports of Yeats's speeches, and so forth; the studies of Robinson and particularly Fay also include unpublished correspondence to and from Yeats. As scholarly histories of the Abbey, all are likely to be superseded by *The Modern Irish Drama, a documentary history*, by Robert Hogan and James Kilroy, which draws extensively on contemporary records and avoids the factual errors of previous studies. The first volume, *The Irish Literary Theatre, 1899–1901* (1975), is now available, with further volumes scheduled to appear shortly.

The voluminous diary of Joseph Holloway, architect of the Abbey and an inveterate playgoer, contains occasional letters to and from Yeats and a great wealth of anecdotal material. Two selections have been published, both edited by Robert Hogan and Michael J. O'Neill: *Joseph Holloway's Abbey Theatre: A Selection from His Unpublished Journal* Impressions of a Dublin Playgoer (1967), and, in three volumes, *Joseph Holloway's Irish Theatre* (1968–70). Another interesting item is *Towards a National Theatre: The Dramatic Criticism of Frank J. Fay* (ed. Robert Hogan, 1970), which contains various articles and comments on Yeats and a useful 1908 lecture by Fay, "Some Account of the Early Days of the Irish National Theatre Society." Hogan notes that many of the articles "were actually exhortations, more or less unconscious, for W. B. Yeats to join with a troop of Irish amateur actors."

Even more important for the Yeats student is James W. Flannery's *Miss Annie F. Horniman and the Abbey Theatre* (1970). This monograph on the financial benefactor of the Abbey discusses her relationship with Yeats in detail and quotes from the unpublished letters on both sides. James Kilroy's *The 'Playboy' Riots* (1971) is another useful monograph, including interviews with Yeats and reports of his speeches as well as providing a valuable context for one of the most important public controversies of his career. James W. Flannery's *W. B. Yeats and the Idea of a Theatre: The Early Abbey Theatre in Theory and Practice* should be now available.

For more details on these studies and many other relevant works, see the chapter on Irish Drama in the present volume.

XIII. *Studies of Other Topics*

A VISION AND MYTHOLOGY

The most provocative study of *A Vision* is found in a series of three essays by Northrop Frye. In "Yeats and the Language of Symbolism" (*UTQ*, 1947; rpt. in his *Fables of Identity: Studies in Poetic Mythology*, 1963), Frye places Yeats's search for a "language of symbols" within the late Romantic tradition and describes *A Vision* as "among other things one of the grammars of romantic symbolism." He also maintains that the book "reflects a romantic pessimism founded on a conception of cyclic fatality." This early study is still valuable, but it is surpassed by Frye's seminal "The Rising of the Moon: A Study of 'A Vision,'" in *An Honoured Guest* (ed. Denis Donoghue and J. R. Mulryne). Though Frye argues that *A Vision* "is a fragmentary and often misleading guide to the structure of imagery in Yeats," he has nonetheless provided the most lucid analysis of its major ideas. Frye extends his commentary in "The Top of the Tower: A Study of the Imagery of Yeats" (*SoR*, 1969; rpt. in his *The Stubborn Structure*, 1970), which centers on the imagery of Yeats's "Eros vision." In both the later essays Frye stresses that for Yeats "the sources of creation were within man, in the corruption of the human heart." Thus "in Yeats the top of the tower is both the rag-and-bone shop of the heart and the translunar Paradise that the heart alone has created." No serious student can neglect these essays.

Hazard Adams has also written on some aspects of *A Vision* with exemplary insight. In "Yeatsian Art and Mathematical Form" (*CentR*, 1960) Adams argues that *A Vision* "is ultimately a commentary upon the nature of poetry, the position of the poet, and the values and limitations of the peculiar kind of knowledge which the poet can possess" and provides an interesting reading of "The Statues." In another important article, "Symbolism and Yeats's *A Vision*" (*JAAC*, 1964), Adams emphasizes the importance of the opening sections of *A Vision* and of the book itself as a work of art. He suggests that "the system of *A Vision* is a Yeatsian grammar of poetic symbolism, conforming to the categories of the literary universe or symbolic form."

The first section of Morton Irving Seiden's *William Butler Yeats: The Poet as a Mythmaker, 1865–1939* (1962) deals with "The Quest for a Faith." After a useful but not always accurate survey of sources and comments on some early works, Seiden summarizes the major ideas of the 1926 *A Vision* and then shows the changes in the 1937 printing. In "The Myth Evaluated" he is impatient with *A Vision* but recognizes its importance to Yeats. The second section of the book, "Artifacts of Eternity," begins by classifying Yeats's symbols into four types and also finding four main subjects in the late poems. He treats poems about individuals that can be related to particular phases in *A Vision* and lists ten attitudes Yeats held toward Maud Gonne. His chapter "Nature Gods, Cycles, and Antinomies" concentrates on the plays but includes a hopelessly confused argument that Yeats was (or should have been) moving toward a belief in the Orphic mysteries as his basic myth. The final two chapters examine selected poems, the critical method varying from minute close readings to brief paraphrases. There are some scattered insights in Seiden's study, but not enough to justify its length. Its major value is perhaps for showing the differences between the two editions of *A Vision*.

The chapter "Yeats and His System" in Ethel F. Cornwell's *The Still Point* (1962) is a rather simple summary of Yeats's esthetic principles, not especially well supported by a few remarks on selected major poems. One of the most extended attacks on *A Vision* is found in Laurence Lerner's *W. B. Yeats: Poet and Crank* (1963; rpt. from *PBA*, 1963). The first section sees *A Vision* as filled with "crackpot ideas" and "poppycock." The second part, which concentrates on "A Dialogue of Self and Soul" and Yeats's concept of art, is more useful.

Although Shankar Mokashi-Punekar's *The Later Phase in the Development of W. B. Yeats: A Study in the Stream of Yeats's Later Thought and Creativity* (Dharwar, 1966) has chapters on almost everything—from "Yeats's Spiritist Metaphysic" to "Thoughts on Love"—the focus is on Yeats's later beliefs, with special reference to *A Vision*. Unfortunately, what insights the book may have are buried beneath a mass of unclear writing and a labyrinth of incomprehensible figures, diagrams, charts, and tables. The major value of the study is for the appendix containing excerpts from thirty of Yeats's letters (dated 1932–38) to Shri Purohit Swami.

Of considerably greater interest is Daniel Hoffman's valuable *Barbarous Knowledge: Myth in the Poetry of Yeats, Graves, and Muir* (1967). Hoffman begins with Yeats's roots in ballad tradition and works toward his construction of myth. He offers a cogent discussion of Yeats's ballads, both early and late. The chapter on "Red Hanrahan" and "The Tower" is less successful, but he provides excellent readings of the Cuchulain plays (particularly *The Death of Cuchulain*) and shows that they form a coherent cycle. Hoffman is one of the few critics to take Yeats's fairy and folk material with the seriousness it deserves, showing Yeats's interest in it as a reaction to nineteenth-century scientific and rationalist thought.

In *Ancient Myth in Modern Poetry* (1971) Lillian Feder treats Yeats's use of myth under the three heads of "Myth and the Unconscious," "Myth and Ritual," and "Myth and History." The remarks on Yeats are not strongly original or perceptive. The study is of more value to the Yeats student for the background chapters and for the constant comparisons between the use of myth by Yeats and by Eliot, Pound, and Auden (drawn most broadly at the beginning of Ch. VI). The chapter on Yeats in John B. Vickery's *The Literary Impact of* The Golden Bough (1973) is likewise unsatisfactory. Confining himself almost exclusively to the poems, Vickery finds more allusions to *The Golden Bough* than exist and exaggerates their importance or misreads their function with some consistency. He is of course most stimulating on poems indeed indebted to Frazer, particularly "Parnell's Funeral" and "Her Vision in the Wood." He suggests that Yeats was "the first writer to register his awareness of *The Golden Bough* as relevant to the symbolic language of literature." As with the Feder book (inexplicably not cited by Vickery), this study is more important for the cogent background chapters on *The Golden Bough* than for the remarks on Yeats. Overlooked by Vickery and still of some interest is William V. Spanos' "Sacramental Imagery in the Middle and Late Poetry of W. B. Yeats" (*TSLL*, 1962), though some of his points are pressed too far.

James Lovic Allen has written a series of articles on *A Vision* and related topics. In "Yeats's Phase in the System of *A Vision*" (*Éire*, 1973), Allen is unconvincing in placing Yeats in phase 13 rather than 17. In "The Road to Byzantium: Archetypal Criticism and Yeats" (*JACC*, 1973), he takes issue with the approaches of Thomas R. Whitaker and Frye and argues for the relevance of Philip Wheelwright's study of archetypes. Allen suggests that "a simple twofold dichotomy between this world and a supernatural, often paradisal, otherworld underlies virtually all of Yeats's early work and thought, while a slightly more complicated structure of earthly world, ghostly otherworld, and remote but quite real world of supernatural perfection permeates the thought and expression of his later career." He hardly succeeds in refuting Frye, whose essay in *An Honoured Guest* is not even cited. In "From Puzzle to Paradox: New Light on Yeats's Late Career" (*SR*, 1974), Allen argues that "in his late life Yeats wholeheartedly and emphatically believed in the major ontological tenets of his esoteric system." The "new light" is that the mixture of immanent and transcendent modes in the late poems can be explained through the distance between Yeats's phase (whether 13 or 17) and the phase where release is possible (28). Finally, in "Unity of Archetype, Myth, and Religious Imagery in the Work of Yeats" (*TCL*, 1974), Allen tries to demonstrate that Yeats's "single myth" is "the union of man and God, the human and the divine, the natural and the supernatural" and that the journey is the "universal motif" of his work. The approaches of Frye and Adams are more fruitful than Allen's simplifications.

Stuart Hirschberg has offered (*ELN*, 1974) an ingenious argument that Yeats saw himself in Phase 17 because it "corresponds to the geometrical angle of the sun and moon in his own horoscope" (that is, 218.62 degrees apart). Joan S. Carberg's "*A Vision* by William Butler Yeats" (*Daedalus*, 1974) is a perceptive exposition of the basic ideas of the work, with particular reference to their relevance to our own time. Dedicated students may be interested in *Phases of the Moon: A Guide to Evolving Human Nature* (1974) by Marilyn Busteed, Richard Tiffany, and Dorothy Wergin, which is based on *A Vision*. The work of H. H. Vendler on *A Vision* is discussed in Section XII.

THE OCCULT AND YEATS'S RELIGION

Virginia Moore's *The Unicorn: William Butler Yeats's Search for Reality* (1954) is a disappointing study. Despite considerable research, access to a mass of unpublished material, and conversations with Mrs. Yeats, Pound, and Maud Gonne (among others), Moore does not provide a satisfactory treatment of any of her various topics, which include "Irish Lore and Druidism," Blake, the Order of the Golden Dawn, *A Vision*, "Spiritism," and Yeats's reading in Western philosophy. The study is marred by the sentimentality of the writing and by the failure to relate any of the sources discussed to the poetry or the plays. Moore is also intent on proving Yeats orthodox, and the chapter "Was Yeats a Christian?" answers yes with a minimum of qualification. The book is useful primarily for the extensive bibliography and for the unpublished material it prints, much of which is still unavailable elsewhere.

A more precise study of Yeats's religion is found in Peter Allt's "Yeats, Religion, and History" (*SR*, 1951). Allt provides a cogent survey of the sources for Yeats's religious feeling and defines "the mature religious Anschauung of Yeats" as "the possession of religious belief without any religious faith. He combines with a notional assent to the reality of the supernatural, an emotional dissent from its actuality." Allt is also perceptive on *A Vision* and *The Resurrection*. The chapter "W. B. Yeats: Theology Bitter and Gay" in Harold H. Watts's *Hound and Quarry* (1953) is likewise effective in contrasting Yeats's "religion" with Christianity: to Yeats, "God is, in fact, emeritus." Watts's chapter on Yeats's use of mythology is of less interest.

Vernon Watkins (*TSLL*, 1962) tries to argue that the late poems are essentially Christian but offers little evidence other than their "religious sense." The chapter on Yeats in Cleanth Brooks's *The Hidden God* (1963) is also disappointing. The statement that Yeats's "obsession" with Christian themes "tells its own story" is more evasion than enlightenment. Brooks later notes that the "restoration of the dimension of awe is the most significant thing about Yeats's treatment of Christianity." William T. Noon's chapter on Yeats in *Poetry and Prayer* (1967), which centers on the poems with "Prayer" in the title and concludes that "without poetic blight, Yeats's gift survived the refusal of religious faith," does little to advance our understanding. No more significant is the treatment of Yeats in Vincent Buckley's *Poetry and the Sacred* (1968), which argues with only partial success that "Yeats's concern with the past, racial or personal, gay or bitter, was at every stage religious in nature." Of even less value are the scattered comments on Yeats in Colin Wilson's *Poetry and Mysticism* (1969).

W. B. Yeats and Occultism: A Study of His Works in Relation to Indian Lore, The Cabbala, Swedenborg, Boehme and Theosophy (Delhi, 1965) by Harbans Rai Bachchan unfortunately does not take into account any research after 1954, when it was completed as a thesis (the "2nd ed." of 1974 is in fact a reprint). The study contains some occasional insights but is hardly a lucid examination of any of its topics. Also unsatisfactory is the chapter on Yeats in John Senior's

The Way Down and Out: The Occult in Symbolist Literature
(1968). Senior recognizes the importance of Yeats's occult activities
but judges him as not fully attaining "occult vision." The polemical
tone and general imprecision of this study also undercut its value.
Somewhat more useful is Robert M. Schuler's "W. B. Yeats: Artist or
Alchemist?" (*RES*, 1971), though it sometimes finds more alchemical
imagery than can be justified.

In *Yeats, the Tarot and the Golden Dawn* (1972; rev. 1976), Kathleen Raine presents a somewhat rambling essay on the relation between the Tarot cards and the rituals of the Golden Dawn, followed by
a discussion of Yeats's use of this material in selected works. Raine's
monograph is most valuable for the numerous illustrations, which
include some cards from Yeats's own Tarot packs and his Golden
Dawn implements as well as pages from some unpublished notebooks. Of less interest is the chapter on Yeats in Kathryn R. Kremen's
*The Imagination of the Resurrection: The Poetic Continuity of a
Religious Motif in Donne, Blake, and Yeats* (1972), which presents
and partially obfuscates the unoriginal thesis that since Yeats did
not believe in a traditional Christian God, his work is centered on
man's own sense of conflict in the world of time. Since she is less
interested in what Yeats believed than in what he disbelieved,
Kremen's incompletely researched study adds little to our understanding.

The most comprehensive account of the Order of the Golden
Dawn, Ellic Howe's *The Magicians of the Golden Dawn: A Documentary History of a Magical Order 1887–1923* (1972), contains a
significant amount of information on Yeats. But more important for
the Yeats student is George Mills Harper's lucid *Yeats's Golden Dawn*
(1974). Somewhat mistitled, the study is essentially a detailed and
scholarly examination of Yeats's participation in the two quarrels in
the Golden Dawn from April 1900 to February 1901—although chapters providing the background for Yeats's occult activities and tracing
the fate of the Order after 1901 are included. Harper quotes extensively from unpublished materials, including numerous letters to
Yeats. The lengthy appendices make available much uncollected or
unpublished material by Yeats and others, the most important being
the two rarest items in the Yeats canon: *Is the Order of R. R. & A. C.
to remain a Magical Order?* and its postscript (both 1901). Harper is
perceptive in showing the relation of those essays to the important
article on "Magic." Although *Yeats's Golden Dawn* concentrates on
the political rather than the mystical side of Yeats's occult experiences, it is essential reading for the advanced student.

Philip Sherrard's brief *W. B. Yeats and the Search for Tradition*
(1975) discusses Yeats's investigations of various religious and philosophical doctrines; it is elegantly written, if unoriginal.

Yeats and the Occult (ed. George Mills Harper, 1975), a collection
of uniformly excellent essays which also includes numerous uncollected or unpublished documents, is of the first importance in Yeats
scholarship; with it, doubt as to the seriousness or extent of Yeats's
occult activities becomes untenable. The editor begins with a survey
of the major manuscript materials. In " 'A Subject of Investigation':
Miracle at Mirebeau," Harper edits Yeats's report of a 1914 investiga-

tion of a bleeding oleograph. Harper and John S. Kelly present the text of the "Preliminary Examination of the Script of E[lizabeth] R[adcliffe]," which describes one of Yeats's most sustained experiences with mediumship. Arnold Goldman's essay provides a general survey of these types of investigations, with emphasis on the "Leo Africanus" correspondence. Walter Kelly Hood edits rejected sections from both versions of *A Vision*, "Appendix by Michael Robartes" and "Michael Robartes Foretells." Two complementary essays examine Yeats's major occult personae, Michael J. Sidnell tracing the function of Michael Robartes throughout the canon and Warwick Gould concentrating on the sources for Owen Aherne. Biographical studies of Yeats and MacGregor Mathers by Lawrence W. Fennelly and of Yeats and W. T. Horton by Harper and Richard J. Finneran are included, the latter reprinting the rejected section of Yeats's introduction to *A Book of Images* (1898). William M. Murphy's article establishes that other members of the Yeats family were subject to visionary experiences and shows John Butler Yeats's contrasting attitudes to the psychic activities of Lily Yeats and the mystical studies of W. B. Yeats. James Olney's "The Esoteric Flower: Yeats and Jung" is a comparative study concentrating on common sources, especially in Platonic and Neoplatonic traditions. William H. O'Donnell comments on the tension between art and "adeptship" in some of the early poems and fiction. *Yeats and the Occult* also includes a defense of Yeats's thought by Kathleen Raine, a commentary on "The Spirit Medium" by Stuart Hirschberg, and some memories of Yeats at his father's occult bookshop in Cecil Court by Geoffrey N. Watkins.

IRELAND AND YEATS'S POLITICS

The subtitle of the English edition of Herbert Howarth's *The Irish Writers, 1880–1940* (1958) is *Literature under Parnell's Star*, and thus the treatment of Yeats centers on his attitudes toward Ireland and especially Parnell. Howarth stresses Yeats's "Messianism" (which he sees as characteristic of the six writers included) and suggests that *A Vision* was Yeats's substitute for the "Sacred Book" he once thought of writing for Ireland. Howarth emphasizes the importance of the 1896 vision of the Archer (described in *Autobiographies*): surprisingly, he says little about the poems on Parnell or the long commentary to "Parnell's Funeral." The study is acceptable as an introductory sketch but is better on the political milieu than on the literature. The curious will find the most detailed description available of Yeats's Steinach operation in 1934.

Donald Davie's chapter "The Young Yeats" (in *The Shaping of Modern Ireland*, ed. Conor Cruise O'Brien, 1960) is a brief and general account of Yeats's attempts to create an ideal Ireland and his later abandonment of those hopes. The examination of Yeats in Richard J. Loftus' *Nationalism in Modern Anglo-Irish Poetry* (1964) is likewise somewhat elementary. Loftus outlines Yeats's three ideals of peasant, hero, and aristocrat and then shows the application to them of Yeats's "mythopoeic art." He concludes that Yeats is the only writer of his time to be totally successful in treating his national heritage.

Edward Malins' *Yeats and the Easter Rising* (1965) provides a useful sketch of the activities connected with the 1916 rebellion; however, the monograph is not especially perceptive when dealing with Yeats's political poems. A more important study is found in *The Imagination of an Insurrection: Dublin, Easter 1916: A Study of an Ideological Movement* (1967) by William Irwin Thompson. The first three chapters give an account of the background to the Rebellion and comment extensively on Yeats's early nationalistic activities. The chapter on Yeats himself includes a survey of his changing attitudes toward the event. Although Thompson overestimates "Easter 1916" as a "turning point" in Yeats's career, he rightly sees the poem not as "ambiguous" but as illustrative of Yeats's "double consciousness."

Peter Faulkner's monograph *Yeats and The Irish Eighteenth Century* (1965) is too brief to be of much interest and has been quickly superseded by Donald Torchiana's important *W. B. Yeats and Georgian Ireland* (1966). The value of this careful study is increased by extensive references to some unfamiliar sources, including newspaper interviews with Yeats and reports of his speeches. Torchiana goes well beyond the implications of his title: the chapter on Swift, for example, also treats Yeats's Senate speeches on censorship and divorce and gives a detailed account of the Blueshirt movement of the 1930's. The reading of *Purgatory* as a political play is interesting although partial.

Adele M. Dalsimer's "Yeats's Unchanging Swift" (*Éire*, 1974) is an effective if tedious demonstration of the importance of Richard Ashe King's *Swift in Ireland* (1895) to Yeats's conception of Swift. More interesting is Douglas N. Archibald's "*The Words upon the Windowpane* and Yeats's Encounter with Jonathan Swift," in *Yeats and the Theatre* (ed. O'Driscoll and Reynolds), which shows the influence of Swift not only on the play but also on Yeats's poetry, especially the Crazy Jane poems.

The attack on Yeats's political activities by Conor Cruise O'Brien (in *In Excited Reverie*) is continued, though much less effectively, by John R. Harrison in *The Reactionaries: A Study of the Anti-Democratic Intelligentsia* (1966). Harrison concentrates on Yeats's anti-democratic feelings and his admiration for violence; he says little directly on the question of fascism. The book draws too heavily on V. K. N. Menon's dated study and often quotes poems and remarks with little awareness of their context. Harrison tries without much success to connect Yeats's stylistic changes with his changes in political thought. The comments on Yeats in Michael Sheehy's *Is Ireland Dying? Culture and the Church in Modern Ireland* (1968) are interesting but too undeveloped to justify his view that Yeats's "synthesis of paganism and ascetical Christianity" is "the best of the vital interpretations which has come out of modern Ireland." The study of Yeats's poems on political and historical topics in J. A. V. Chapple's *Documentary and Imaginative Literature 1880–1920* (1970) is of little interest or originality. Much more significant is the section on Yeats in F. S. L. Lyons' *Ireland since the Famine* (1971; rev. 1973), which provides an authoritative context for Yeats's early nationalistic activities. Lyons suggests that 1903 marks the point when Yeats began to turn away from direct political involvement.

In "Yeats, Johnson, and Ireland's Heroic Dead" (*Éire*, 1972), Barton R. Friedman notes some borrowings from Lionel Johnson in Yeats's political poems but overstresses Yeats's pessimism toward Irish politics. Poorly written and researched, Ian C. Small's "Yeats and Johnson on the Limitations of Patriotic Art" (*Studies*, 1974) attempts to argue that Johnson anticipated some of Yeats's views on the proper relationship between nationalism and art.

Malcolm Brown's *The Politics of Irish Literature: From Thomas Davis to W. B. Yeats* (1972) presents a useful sketch of nineteenth-century Irish history and is salutary in showing the distortions involved when history is transformed into literature. But the commentary on Yeats is seriously marred by Brown's hostility toward Yeats's attitudes. The lack of sympathy for Yeats leads Brown to make numerous inaccurate statements and to invent for Yeats the absurd device of "forensic masking"—"public and private meanings that contradict one another." Brown's ability to interpret symbolic poetry is clearly deficient. A more precise study is David Fitzpatrick's "W. B. Yeats in Seanad Éireann," in *Yeats and the Theatre*, which presents a survey of Yeats's activities in the Irish Senate and shows his essential alignment with the "Independents." A defense of Yeats on the grounds that his politics are fundamentally spiritual, Fahmy Farag's "W. B. Yeats and the Politics of *A Vision*" (*Canadian Jour. of Irish Studies*, June 1975) neither adds much new information nor concentrates on *A Vision*. "Ideological Factors in Yeats' Early Drama" by David Blake Knox (*Anglo-Irish Studies*, 1975) is of no value. William C. Barnwell's "Utopias and the 'New Ill-Breeding': Yeats and the Politics of Perfection" (*Éire*, 1975) traces Yeats's growing disillusionment with Irish politics through four poems but adds little to previous commentaries.

POETIC STYLE

In a valuable chapter in *Eras and Modes in English Poetry* (1957; 2nd ed., 1964), Josephine Miles distinguishes three stages in Yeats's stylistic development: from an early balanced mode to a predicative mode (ca. 1900–15) and then back to a "balanced and classical mode." Miles effectively shows Yeats's awareness of these shifts as evidenced in his correspondence and *Autobiographies* but regrettably does not allow for the stylistic changes after *The Tower*.

Sarah Youngblood's "The Structure of Yeats's Long Poems" (*Criticism*, 1963) and Marjorie Perloff's "Spatial Form in the Poetry of Yeats: The Two Lissadell Poems" (*PMLA*, 1967) provide interesting comments on selected poems but fail to demonstrate that Yeats's later poems fuse "two structural modes, the discursive and the imagistic" (Youngblood) or "shift from sequential to spatial form" (Perloff). In attempting to show Yeats's techniques as a precursor of the long poems of Eliot and others, both essays find more ambiguity in Yeats than obtains. Perloff unfortunately overlooks Ian Fletcher's lucid commentary on the Lissadell elegy in *W. B. Yeats: Centenary Essays*. Perloff's "Yeats and the Occasional Poem" (*PLL*, 1968) hardly supports her claim that the "Yeatsian occasional poem" is a fusion of "the

Jonsonian verse epistle and the Coleridgean conversation poem";
Yeats is now seen as the main influence on the confessional poetry of
Robert Lowell and others. Of even less interest is Stuart Hirschberg's
"Yeats and the Meditative Poem" (*Éire,* 1974).

The chapter on "Hopkins and Yeats" in William E. Baker's *Syntax
in English Poetry 1870–1930* (1967) makes the rather obvious contrast between the irregularity of Hopkins' syntax and the "predominant conventionality" of Yeats's. In *W. B. Yeats: The Rhetoric of
Repetition* (1968), William R. Veeder defines his key term so broadly
that he includes such devices as ambiguity and syntactic patterns.
The discussion of the various uses of repetition is dependent on the
readings of the poems, which range from perceptive to strained; thus
this monograph must be used with some caution. The constant comparisons of a poem to a bridge and Veeder's belief that poets are
concerned with their readers being too "tired" to finish their poems
are not helpful.

Though sometimes repetitive, Robert Beum's *The Poetic Art of
William Butler Yeats* (1969) is a sensible volume, in many ways an
ideal corrective for those students who see no value in the "technical"
analysis of poetry. Beum's brief study argues that prosody expresses
the "mind and heart" of the writer. He provides a list of seventeen
prosodic features of Yeats's verse and includes chapters on meter,
rhyme, and stanzaic patterns. Especially good is the study of Yeats's
use of *ottava rima.* The remarks on the prosody of the plays concentrate on the "carry-all form" of *The Herne's Egg* and *Purgatory* but
strangely make no reference to D. R. Clark's *The Theatre of Desolate
Reality.* Beum attempts to refute the position of Thomas Parkinson
that Yeats is not an iambic poet.

If Beum's volume is in the nature of a handbook, Marjorie Perloff's
Rhyme and Meaning in the Poetry of Yeats (1970) is a highly complex and technical study that will appeal only to the most dedicated
specialist of prosody. About half the volume is given over to tables
and graphs dealing with the kinds of rhyme Yeats uses and the relationship between rhyme and meaning in the several collections of
poetry. After showing the percentages of rhyme and approximate
rhyme, Perloff classifies approximate rhyme in three "broad categories" with subdivisions: phonemic variation (six types), stress
variation (four types), and "combinations" (seven types). The discussion of the relationship between rhyme and meaning draws heavily on Russian Formalist criticism. Perloff finds three kinds of
relationship: semantically neutral, semantically congruent (five subclasses), and semantically disparate (three subclasses). The reader
who is able to make sense of these classifications, graphs, and tables
will find still other problems. Not only are the classifications arbitrary
(as Perloff admits), but the analysis of the function of the rhymes
depends on whether one accepts Perloff's explications, which are
often debatable. Perloff's book is an example of a study in which the
critical methodology appears to have overwhelmed the critic; it will
surely overwhelm most readers.

Unfortunately similar is Adelyn Dougherty's *A Study of the
Rhythmic Structure in the Verse of William Butler Yeats* (1973),
which is impossible to follow by any except linguistic specialists. Over

half the book is composed of appendices, including nineteen charts. Her main conclusions, based on an analysis of approximately 25 percent of the *Collected Poems*, are: (1) contra Parkinson, "Yeats is clearly to be located, as metrist, in the mainstream of the English tradition" (that is, accentual-syllabic verse); (2) the stylistic changes in "early" versus "late" Yeats, insofar as meter is concerned, do not begin until after *Responsibilities* and are not fully evident until *The Tower*. The dedicated student will also find numerous minor points, of various degrees of comprehensibility. However, the statistical apparatus should not be allowed to obscure the necessarily subjective scansions of the poems.

Neither Perloff nor Dougherty mentions Beum's volume, which can still be recommended as sufficient for most students.

OTHER TOPICS

In *The Metamorphic Tradition in Modern Poetry* (1955), M. Bernetta Quinn provides little more than a sketch of Yeats's various images of transformation and some unintended humor in her reference to the "Hermits of the Golden Dawn."

A much more important study is Frank Kermode's *Romantic Image* (1957). Kermode traces the development of and influences on the image of the Dancer and Tree in symbolist esthetic, with particular reference to Yeats. He sees the images as receiving their seminal presentation in "Among School Children." He begins by showing the influence of Pater and Arnold on the artist's sense of isolation. He reads "In Memory of Major Robert Gregory" as equating Gregory's death with the escape of the artist; this chapter also provides the full text of Yeats's *Observer* notice of Gregory. Kermode then argues that the "Dancer is one of Yeats's great reconciling images, containing life in death, death in life, movement and stillness, action and contemplation, body and soul." The related image of the Tree is discussed more briefly. The second part of the book includes chapters on Symons, Hulme, and "dissociation of sensibility," the last useful for giving a context for Yeats's "Unity of Being." Kermode exaggerates the extent to which the Dancer is the "central icon" in Yeats, but *Romantic Image* is essential reading.

Two important related studies are Ian Fletcher's "Symons, Yeats and the Demonic Dance" (*LonM*, June 1960) and Kermode's "Poet and Dancer before Diaghilev" (*PR*, 1961). Fletcher shows the influence of Symons' poetry on Yeats's conception of the Dancer and also provides a valuable sketch of Symons' career. Kermode's essay shows the "liturgical, poetic, and music-hall aspects of this renaissance of dancing" and discusses the work of Jane Avril and Loie Fuller, both of whom are relevant to Yeats's poetry.

The chapter on "Yeats and Transition" in Barbara Seward's *The Symbolic Rose* (1960) adds little to previous accounts (particularly that in *The Identity of Yeats*). Her claim that Yeats's Rose "embodies the first successful attempt since Blake to create in British literature a full-scale symbolic method . . . and the first successful attempt since Dante to express traditional as well as personal meanings in a single symbol" seems a bit excessive. She also puts too much emphasis on Yeats's "self-projected death-wish." Mary Ballard Duryee's *Words Alone Are Certain Good: William Butler Yeats: Himself, The Poet, His Ghost* (1961) contains some poems addressed to Yeats and some introductory comments of little value.

In *Yeats and Innisfree* (1965) Russell K. Alspach traces the background of the poem and discusses (mainly through quotation) the use of the fountain and tree images. The monograph is of only passing interest. Giles W. L. Telfer's *Yeats's Idea of the Gael* (1965) is also too brief to be an adequate treatment. Telfer does, however, make the interesting suggestion that we should be aware of the influence of the contemporary reception of Yeats's works on his changing esthetic.

Yeats and the Heroic Ideal (1965) by Alex Zwerdling has occasional insights but too often betrays its origins as a dissertation. After tracing the decline of the concept of the hero from ancient to modern times and Yeats's search for a national hero, he examines three kinds of heroes in Yeats: "The Aristocrat," "The Public Hero," and "The Visionary." The book is basically sound but could have been significantly shorter. Zwerdling is also often guilty of a too literal acceptance of some of the poems. Few will agree that "*The Resurrection* is a highly orthodox play."

George Mills Harper's *Yeats's Quest for Eden* (1966) is a cogent study of Yeats's continuing search for "radical innocence" and of the varieties of Edenic myth in his work. Harper's monograph shows the increasing sophistication of Yeats's use of the pastoral mode and centers on "A Prayer for my Daughter." Of much less interest are the few pages devoted to Yeats in Martin Green's *Yeats's Blessings on von Hügel: Essays on Literature and Religion* (1967), not the only recent book whose title is designed more for the market than for accuracy. Green argues that von Hügel is inappropriately used in "Vacillation" because he represented not "'miraculous' religion" but a "religious-rationalist position." Green is impatient with Yeats's philosophy.

Aside from the comments in Engelberg's *The Vast Design* and a useful introductory survey by Peter Faulkner (*Criticism*, 1962), Yeats's critical writings have received little serious attention. Cleanth Brooks' "William Butler Yeats as a Literary Critic," in *The Disciplines of Criticism: Essays in Literary Theory, Interpretation, and History* (ed. Peter Demetz, Thomas Greene, and Lowry Nelson, Jr., 1968) is not especially helpful. Brooks does little more than summarize Yeats's comments on his "basic conception of poetry and the role of the poet." Brooks scarcely demonstrates his claim that Yeats "was obviously a brilliant literary critic." More provocative is Hazard Adams' "Yeats, Dialectic and Criticism" (*Criticism*, 1968), which argues (but is too brief to demonstrate effectively) that Yeats "synthesizes the neo-Kantian tradition of speculation about art with a Blakean dialectic."

Joseph Ronsley's *Yeats's Autobiography: Life as Symbolic Pattern* (1968) is a disappointing study. Ronsley is unconvincing in his attempt to show the overall unity of the work and indeed often loses sight of his thesis. Although some of the remarks on the individual sections of *Autobiographies* are perceptive, his study will not endure a comparison with Ian Fletcher's much shorter examination of the work in *An Honoured Guest* (which Ronsley cites but once, in a note). Fletcher's article can be supplemented by his "The 1890's: A Lost Decade" (*VS*, 1960), an essay-review that mentions *Autobiographies* in the course of a lucid commentary on the period. Gerald Levin's "The Yeats of the *Autobiographies*: A Man of Phase 17" (*TSLL*, 1964) is not effective in suggesting that Yeats's early life progressed through the first sixteen phases of *A Vision* and that he sees himself at Phase 17 in the *Autobiographies*. Vincent Buckley's "Yeats: The Great Comedian" (*MHRev*, 1968) discusses the humor in the later sections of the *Autobiographies*; he covers much the same ground as Hazard Adams' essay in *In Excited Reverie*, meanwhile claiming "I have searched through one collection of critical essays after another, and have not found a single essay on his prose comedy." Dillon Johnston's "The Perpetual Self of Yeats's *Autobiographies*" (*Éire*, 1974) is an acceptable but unenlightening study of the 1926 edition, which contains only "Reveries over Childhood and Youth" and "The Trembling of the Veil."

The Development of William Butler Yeats: 1885–1900 (1968) by Harold Orel is of little note. Although Orel correctly argues that Yeats's retrospective accounts of his early career are not always accurate, his monograph contains more plot summary than analysis and is acceptable only on an introductory level. His examination almost avoids Yeats's occult activities, which were of undoubted importance in his early career.

Edward Malins' *Yeats and Music* (1968) may be somewhat confusing to a reader without a musical background, but it presents a useful account of Yeats's interest in music, with particular attention to the psaltery experiments with Florence Farr. The monograph reprints six examples of scores for Yeats's poems and plays, by Farr, George Antheil, Edmund Dulac, and Walter Rummel. Malins strangely does not refer to the chapter "W. B. Yeats and the Art of Song" in V. C. Clinton-Baddeley's *Words for Music* (1941), which argues that "he was not so much interested in the art of song as in the art of the public presentation of poetry." A more important supplement is Michael B. Yeats's "W. B. Yeats and Irish Folk Song" (*SFQ*, 1966), an authoritative survey which identifies the sources of both the words and music for many of Yeats's songs. More general is Patrick Holland's "Yeats and the Musician's Art in 'Last Poems'" (*ArielE*, 1971), which concentrates on the refrains but pays little attention to previous criticism.

The comments on Yeats's plays and poems by Austin Clarke in *The Celtic Twilight and the Nineties* (1969) contain little more than plot summary and quotation. This printing of some 1965 lectures is useful mainly for the occasional anecdote and for Clarke's recalling of a host of forgotten writers, especially in the chapter on "Victorian Verse Drama."

More important is *Yeats and the Beginning of the Irish Renaissance* (1970) by Phillip L. Marcus, an account of Yeats's activities in the 1890's with special attention to his organizational abilities. Marcus begins by showing the problems Yeats faced in avoiding propaganda and including non-Irish materials in his work. A discussion of the early prose fiction is followed by a detailed if sometimes tedious examination of various public controversies, such as that over the "New Irish Library." Marcus then treats Yeats's relationship to a number of contemporary Irish writers. The chapter "Old Irish Myth and Modern Irish Literature" is unstimulating in concluding that Yeats used the "personal method" in handling mythic materials. Although Marcus only partially re-creates the milieu of Yeats's early years, his study provides a useful corrective to Yeats's own version of the beginning of his career.

W. B. Yeats and the Designing of Ireland's Coinage (ed. Brian Cleeve, 1972) contains the full text of "What we did or tried to do" from *Coinage of Saorstát Éireann* (1928), related documents by Thomas Bodkin and others, a brief introduction and afterword by the editor, and valuable illustrations of the designs submitted. This monograph gives an interesting picture of one of Yeats's happiest activities as an Irish Senator.

The only separate study of the prose fiction is Richard J. Finneran's *The Prose Fiction of W. B. Yeats: The Search for "Those Simple Forms"* (1973). This monograph traces Yeats's use of different genres in his early fiction; of some value is the bibliographical appendix on the various editions of the fiction. There are also some brief remarks on this topic in Maurice Beebe's *Ivory Towers and Sacred Founts: the Artist as Hero in Fiction from Goethe to Joyce* (1964) and Wendell V. Harris' "English Short Fiction in the Nineteenth Century" (*SSF*, 1968), the latter of which indicates that Pater's "influence is certainly there . . . but, to the extent that Pater is a successor to Morris and Rossetti, not only the style but the intent has a longer history." Augustine Martin's "Apocalyptic Structures in Yeats's *Secret Rose*" (*Studies*, 1975) ignores all previous scholarship while discussing the order and themes of the stories in the collection.

George Mills Harper's *"Go Back to Where You Belong": Yeats's Return from Exile* (1973) is an interesting discussion of the influence on and Yeats's belief in the mythology of exile and return. Harper's monograph notes the continual comparisons Yeats made between London/Dublin and Sligo, the last of which he always considered his true home. Liam Miller's *The Dun Emer Press, Later the Cuala Press* (1973) is a careful account of the history of the presses Yeats's sisters ran and with which both Yeats and his wife were intimately associated. This monograph, which contains numerous illustrations, supersedes Miller's *A Brief Account of the Cuala Press* . . . (1971; rev. 1972) and *A List of Books Published by the Dun Emer Press and the Cuala Press* . . . (1972).

Robert O'Driscoll's monograph *Symbolism and Some Implications of the Symbolic Approach: W. B. Yeats during the Eighteen-Nineties* (1975) begins with an explanation of Yeats's theory of symbolism, stressing the influence of Blake and denying the importance of the French Symbolists; little is said of the occult background of his thinking. O'Driscoll then discusses some of the early poems, plays, and stories, noting the shifting balance between the material and the spiritual worlds; the epilogue argues for the influence of Synge in Yeats's rejection of symbolism in favor of his theory of personality. Containing an excess of summary and quotation, the study is less an advancement of knowledge of the period than a consolidation of current critical thought. More significant is Edward O'Shea's *Yeats as Editor* (1975), a well-written examination of a neglected topic. This monograph draws on unpublished materials to show Yeats's aims as an editor and the alterations he frequently made in his selections. Although O'Shea might have referred to the Yeats/Turner correspondence and the extant manuscript of the Yeats/Ellis edition of Blake, his study conclusively demonstrates the importance of Yeats's editorial activities.

XIV. *Sources, Parallels, and Literary Contacts*

Given both his long life and the eclectic nature of his reading, it is doubtless possible to write a study of "Yeats and" almost anyone or anything. Indeed, such studies have always formed a significant portion of the scholarship. Not all of them have been successful in avoiding the dangers of source studies: exaggerating the extent of Yeats's indebtedness and/or reading the Yeats work as simply a restatement of the source. A representative example of the first error is Marjorie Perloff's "Yeats and Goethe" (*CL*, 1971). Though an intelligent and well-written essay, it concludes by inflating minor sources into exclusive influences. For instance, even though Perloff admits that there is at best one (muddled) reference in the Yeats canon to Goethe's *Dichtung und Wahrheit* (in the *Senate Speeches*), she nonetheless concludes that "it may well have been the model for his own autobiography"—because "for both poet-autobiographers, tension is viewed as existing on three levels: the personal, the artistic, and the religious." In any event, this section will concentrate on areas where there is firmer evidence for significant influence or contact.

NINETEENTH CENTURY WRITERS (GENERAL STUDIES)

The chapter on Yeats in John Bayley's *The Romantic Survival: A Study in Poetic Evolution* (1957) has only moderate value. Bayley argues that Yeats "brings Romanticism back to earth, but he pays the price of making himself and his poetry the measure of all things" and proceeds to discuss Yeats's attempts to "attain a wide and intense poetic vision" by means of the Mask, the Conversation, and the Symbol. More interesting are the comparisons drawn with Auden. Donald Pearce's "Yeats and the Romantics" (*Shenandoah*, Spring 1957) tries to argue that "Supernatural Byzantium, Art's intellectual city" was "the true objective of the romantic movement in English poetry" but suffers rather badly from its prose style. Much of the article discusses the relationship between Keats and the Byzantium poems.

The correct title for Harold Bloom's *Yeats* (1970) should be, as he admits, "a study of Yeats in relation to Romantic doctrine," with the subtitle of "a kind of case history testing a theory of poetic influence." The theory, the subject of the first quarter of the book and developed further in Bloom's *The Ringers in the Tower: Studies of Romantic Tradition* (1971), *The Anxiety of Influence: A Theory of Poetry*

(1973), and *A Map of Misreading* (1975), is one of "creative misinterpretation": the new poet deliberately misreads his precursors (whether consciously or unconsciously is not always clear) in order to free himself from "creative anxieties." Much of the rest of the volume attempts to show how individual *clinamen*, or "swerves," are apparent in Yeats's works. Bloom's thesis is extremely interesting but highly suspect. Indeed, before accepting it the careful student might ponder the two implicit assumptions on which it is based: (1) Bloom's understanding of the Romantic tradition, especially as manifested in Blake and Shelley, is "right," whereas Yeats's is "wrong"; (2) although the "right" doctrine did not begin to be promulgated until the late 1950's, Yeats should have been able to find it in the 1890's but chose not to. An alternative theory of some interest can also be found in Douglas N. Archibald's "Yeats's Encounters: Observations on Literary Influence and Literary History" (*NLH*, 1970), which attempts to distinguish between five varieties of interaction: "confrontation," "encounter," "sanction," "resonance," and "mediation."

The bulk of *Yeats* is Bloom's "Guide" to the works. He is overtly polemical about Yeats's reputation in general and the regard given certain works. He suggests that "current criticism has been unfair to the early Yeats, too kind to the middle Yeats, and most uncritically worshipful of the later Yeats." Bloom locates Yeats's lasting achievement in *The Wind Among the Reeds, The Tower*, and *The Winding Stair*; he comments on almost all the poems and plays, *Per Amica Silentia Lunae*, and *A Vision*. Since he so admires the early Yeats, his omission of the prose fiction is difficult to understand. It must be stressed that Bloom's selection and explication of individual works is determined by his thesis—thus "Easter 1916" is given only a paragraph because it is an "eighteenth-century poem," and *Purgatory* is quickly dismissed as an example of "eugenic tendentiousness." Although it must be used with caution, *Yeats* offers some brilliant explications. Also valuable is the examination of Yeats's internalization of the "quest-romance" within the context of the Romantic tradition; and there are seminal comments on Yeats's relationship to the major influences of Blake and Shelley and also to some relatively minor ones, such as Browning and Pater. Bloom's position on Yeats versus Blake and Shelley is summarized in his "Yeats and the Romantics," in *Modern Poetry: Essays in Criticism* (ed. John Hollander, 1968).

Bloom's attitude toward previous criticism demands an aside, for it is typical of a current and regrettable trend in Yeats studies. Although Bloom indicates his "hope" to record his "debts to the scholarly criticism devoted to Yeats," he finds it necessary to cite only perhaps a half dozen articles and two dozen books. Other critics of Yeats are anonymously grouped together as "pseudo-scholars," "literary Rosicrucians," or, more usually, "doctrinal exegetes." This group includes such scholars as B. L. Reid (*The Lyric of Tragedy*) and Peter Ure (*Towards a Mythology*); even more inexplicable omissions include Margaret Rudd (*Divided Image*) and Kathleen Raine ("Yeats's Debt to William Blake"). When Bloom, in an atypical remark, writes of "Under Ben Bulben" that "I do not recall, in my reading of available criticism of Yeats, anyone stating what is perhaps too palpable to be worth the stating, how bad and distressing the poem is," the careful student may well be perplexed. B. L. Reid, for instance, had commented that "Yeats makes a formal and on the whole deplorable return upon his own self-conscious Celticism in 'Under Ben Bulben,' and that had always been really the phoniest side of him"; or, in language even closer to Bloom's, Frank Kermode had remarked in "The New Apocalyptists" (*PR*, 1966; as "The Modern Apocalypse" in his *The Sense of an Ending: Studies in the Theory of Fiction*, 1967) that "we are surely losing the power to be charmed by the dry paradigmatic rant of such poems as 'Under Ben Bulben.' " The work of both writers was surely "available" and worthy of "recall."

Such examples could be easily multiplied. A full survey of previous criticism is doubtless an impossible demand; but a student has the right to expect that the major studies have been taken into account. Bloom's cavalier attitude toward his precursors is best symbolized in a single comment: "As I think Frye remarks somewhere, God occupies the place of death in the Yeatsian system" (the "somewhere" is Frye's less-than-obscure essay in *An Honoured Guest*). It is surely unfortunate if not disturbing that a distinguished scholar would write such a sentence and that an equally distinguished press would publish it. Even more unfortunate is the possibility that less distinguished members of the scholarly community will adopt Bloom's attitude toward previous criticism—a possibility more real than remote, as several recent studies have shown.

Dwight Eddins' *Yeats: The Nineteenth Century Matrix* (1971) concentrates on Shelley, Keats, Allingham, Ferguson, Tennyson, the Rhymers, and the French Symbolists. The study offers little that has not been said elsewhere and is not always accurate in details, especially its quotations. The book is a classic example of a study published with excessive haste: too soon after major studies to assimilate their insights (i.e., Bloom and George Bornstein); and too soon after its origins as a dissertation to eliminate the immaturity and verbosity of its style or the continual asides to bicker with previous critics over minor points while almost ignoring important relevant studies (Eddins gives more attention to Patty Gurd's 1916 study than to Engelberg's *The Vast Design*).

Also incompletely researched is the chapter "W. B. Yeats and the Wisdom of Daimonic Images" in Brian John's *Supreme Fictions: Studies in the Work of William Blake, Thomas Carlyle, W. B. Yeats, and D. H. Lawrence* (1974). John tries to show Yeats's relationship to the Romantic vitalist tradition, though he agrees with Bloom that Yeats is often guilty of a "Urizenic perversion" of the true tradition. John begins with a general sketch of Yeats's Romanticism, suggesting that "the Romantic concern with the nature and fulfilment of the self is the supreme theme out of which Yeats's entire work comes." Too much is made of Yeats's "supremely subjectivist faith in the individual self," but this part of the chapter contains some interesting comments. However, the application of the thesis to the poems in *The Tower* and *The Winding Stair* produces a number of strained explications.

WILLIAM BLAKE

That Blake was a major influence on Yeats has long been acknowl-edged. In a satiric attack on Yeats in *The Wild Irishman* (1905), for instance, T. W. H. Crosland remarked with more spite than accuracy that "Mr Yeats's Poetry and Mr Yeats's Literary Theatre are Blake's poetry and Blake's Literary Theatre." The first full-length examina-tion was Margaret Rudd's *Divided Image: A Study of William Blake and W. B. Yeats* (1953), which attempts to develop a contrast be-tween Blake as "mystic" and Yeats as "magician." Anticipating Har-old Bloom, Rudd emphasizes that Yeats misread Blake to make him "magical," though she notes that he had partial justification for so doing. Unfortunately, Rudd often misunderstands both writers and has little sympathy for Yeats's position. Although she provides some acute comments, such as the relevance of *Urizen* to "The Second Coming," the imprecision of her use of the terms "mysticism" and "magic" prevents the study from being satisfactory.

Much more significant is Hazard Adams' *Blake and Yeats: The Contrary Vision* (1955; rpt. 1968 with an added preface), a compara-tive study of their symbolism and esthetics. Adams suggests that the "important relationship" is in "the modes or forms of experiencing and creating poetic worlds." His first chapter outlines the major com-parisons and the central contrast: "Yeats focused upon the frustra-tions of this world from within this world, and Blake focused upon the possibilities of this world from a position extremely difficult to pinpoint anywhere in the delusion we call space." The section on Blake includes some important comments on Yeats, including those on the 1893 Yeats-Ellis edition with its errors of interpretation and the parallels between Byzantium and Golgonooza. The chapters on Yeats begin with a discussion of the weaknesses of the early poetry and of Yeats's need to find a system. Adams approaches *A Vision* through some of the early fiction and the introductory sections of the book itself. He treats Yeats's views of history and personality through analyses of selected poems. Particularly lucid are his remarks on the bird symbol and on the Byzantium poems. He concludes by printing the "Seven Propositions" but questioning the extent to which Yeats believed in them. A valuable appendix publishes "Michael Robartes Foretells," a rejected conclusion for *A Vision*. Adams at times seems more in sympathy with, and a better critic of, Blake than Yeats; and his study provides a more nearly complete view of Blake than it does of Yeats. But *Blake and Yeats* is an intelligent and carefully written study, essential for any serious student.

In *Beulah to Byzantium: A Study of Parallels in the Works of W. B. Yeats, William Blake, Samuel Palmer and Edward Calvert* (1965), Raymond Lister notes some visual parallels. The monograph is a useful gloss on some lines from "Under Ben Bulben" but has little general interest. Lister overlooks the extended remarks on Palmer and Calvert in Marion Witt's "The Making of an Elegy: Yeats's 'In Memory of Major Robert Gregory'" (*MP*, 1950). Kathleen Raine's chapter "Yeats's Debt to William Blake" in her *Defending Ancient Springs* (1967) argues that "the common characteristic of Yeats's thought and Blake's is neither image nor mythology, but precisely its diagrammatic character." She is perhaps overly sympathetic to Yeats in the claim that "Ellis' and Yeats's work comes near to the underlying principle and intention of Blake's symbolic thought." The essay is valuable for stressing the importance to Yeats of "The Mental Traveller."

Raymond Lister's "W. B. Yeats as an Editor of William Blake" (*Blake Studies*, 1969) adds little new information while concluding that the Yeats-Ellis edition "is a sad sequence of misquotation, deliberate alteration and faulty arrangement." Of more value is Deborah Dorfman's *Blake in the Nineteenth Century: His Reputation as a Poet from Gilchrist to Yeats* (1969), which gives a useful context for the edition and shows both the advances and the errors the editors made. Dorfman suggests that their most important contribution to Blake studies was the explanation of the Four Zoas. Dorfman's attempt to establish the extent of Ellis' and Yeats's individual efforts through an examination of their other writings on Blake has been essentially superseded by Ian Fletcher's discovery of the extant manuscript of the edition, described in his "The Ellis-Yeats-Blake Manuscript Cluster" (*BC*, 1972). Drawing on both the manuscript (discovered in Germany and now at the University of Reading) and an unpublished letter to Lady Gregory, Fletcher suggests that most of the edition was "collaboration in the deepest sense." Fletcher also provides the fullest sketch available of Edwin Ellis (correcting his dates to 1848–1916) and some interesting quotations from John Todhunter's lectures on Blake. An edition of the manuscript is in progress by Fletcher and Robert O'Driscoll.

PERCY BYSSHE SHELLEY

The other central influence on Yeats's career is of course Shelley. H. W. Häusermann's pioneering "W. B. Yeats's Idea of Shelley," in *The Mint: A Miscellany of Literature, Art and Criticism* (ed. Geoffrey Grigson, 1946) is undeserving of the neglect it has received from later critics. This essay concentrates not on influences but on Yeats's picture of Shelley, which changed from admiration in youth to ambivalence in old age. Häusermann argues that Yeats had two conceptions of Shelley: one "a great popular poet who expresses, as it were, the age-old wisdom of humanity" and the other a "man who was denied the power of deep and constructive thought."

George Bornstein's *Yeats and Shelley* (1970) is an overly schematic but valuable account of the relationship. Bornstein suggests that "the impact of Shelley upon Yeats shaped his art before 1903" and that "Yeats's later development can be understood convincingly as a reaction against Shelley"; a parallel simplification is found in his contrast between "Intellectual Vision" and "Antinomial Vision" in the early and late Yeats. The first half of the study includes a careful tracing of Yeats's various attitudes towards Shelley, an examination of the early imitative verse, and comments on Yeats's adoption of the roles of the poet of *Alastor*, Athanase, and Ahasuerus. The second section compares and contrasts the Epipsyche with the Mask and Athens with

Byzantium; it also tries to explain Yeats's idiosyncratic statement that Shelley lacked the "Vision of Evil." As does Bloom, Bornstein recognizes that Yeats often misread Shelley. But he notes that in many instances Yeats was simply following the lead of Mary Shelley, and for the other points he is not compelled to develop a theory of *clinamen*: "Like most original modern artists Shelley and Yeats read past literature in the light of their own preoccupations and created there a tradition within which they could place their own work." Though its origins as a dissertation are sometimes too apparent (as in the long discussion of whether Shelley or Blake had ever met Thomas Taylor), *Yeats and Shelley* remains a well-written and intelligent study.

Bornstein's work and Bloom's *Yeats* were published in the same year. Both should be studied, with Bornstein's modest and documented claims being balanced against Bloom's brilliant but unproved assertions. In any case, there seems little justification for an essay like H. C. Merritt's (*YES*, 1971), which makes no reference at all to the previous criticism. Somewhat better in that respect is Adele M. Dalsimer's "My Chief of Men: Yeats' Juvenilia and Shelley's *Alastor*" (*Éire*, 1973), which adopts the position of Bloom.

OTHER NINETEENTH-CENTURY WRITERS

Paul de Man's chapter "Symbolic Landscape in Wordsworth and Yeats" (in *In Defense of Reading: A Reader's Approach to Literary Criticism*, ed. Reuben A. Brower and Richard Poirier, 1962) includes only a few comparisons while providing a misreading of "Coole Park and Ballylee." Much more significant is the chapter on "Flute Song Yesterday: W. B. Yeats" in Abbie Findlay Potts's *The Elegiac Mode: Poetic Form in Wordsworth and Other Elegists* (1967), which includes numerous comparisons and suggests some possible influences, of which that of the *Excursion* on *A Vision* is the most interesting. Potts also notes the presence of classical devices in the poems and plays.

In "Yeats and Keats: The Poetics of Romanticism" (*BuR*, 1965) Malcolm Magaw draws some over-rigid contrasts, arguing that "Keats intuits; Yeats wills" and that Keats uses "natural symbols," Yeats "unnatural artificial symbols." James Land Jones's *Adam's Dream: Mythic Consciousness in Keats and Yeats* (1975) suggests a few parallels and sources (many of the latter tenuous at best) but is primarily a comparative study. The treatment of Yeats is interesting but fundamentally unsatisfactory. Jones pays little attention to either previous criticism (ignoring, for instance, Lillian Feder's *Ancient Myth in Modern Poetry*) or *A Vision* and Yeats's occultism. He tries to argue that Yeats's mythic vision is evident by the presence in the poems of metamorphosis, a sense of reciprocity in the cosmos, a double sense of time, and the denial of death; and he suggests that Yeats strove toward "the Great Moment, an experience of timelessness and reconciled contraries that reveals, often through apprehension of process, the solidarity of all life." The conclusion that Keats's and Yeats's "myth is their quest for the mystery of being through mythic apprehension" is more redundant than provocative. Throughout

Jones pays more attention to, and is perhaps a better critic of, Keats than Yeats.

Although not always precise in explicating Yeats's poems, Marvel Shmiefsky's "Yeats and Browning: The Shock of Recognition" (*SEL*, 1970) suggests some interesting parallels and sources and is a useful supplement to the comments on Browning and Yeats by Bloom. Peter Faulkner's brief *William Morris and W. B. Yeats* (1962) considers the influence of Morris "as poet, as generous personality" and "as social critic." Faulkner does not credit sufficiently the influence of Morris' writings but instead emphasizes Yeats's interest in his social criticism. Though on only one aspect of the relationship, a more precise study is T. McAlindon's (*MP*, 1967), a seminal discussion of Morris' view of Byzantium and its effect on Yeats.

The relationship with Pater is more often assumed than demonstrated. An important exception is Leonard E. Nathan's "W. B. Yeats's Experiments with an Influence" (*VS*, 1962), which suggests that Pater gave Yeats "a thoughtful and authoritative rationale for the lyrical drama" and that the failure of the hero in "Rosa Alchemica" is Yeats's commentary on the limitations of Pater's position. Nathan concludes that "Pater affirmed for Yeats that human experience has greatest value when it is most pure and intense and that art should be made to approach the purity and elevation of religious ritual. . . . But Yeats was compelled by his own convictions to go beyond what Pater offered." Lorna Sage's interesting "Hardy, Yeats and Tradition," in *Victorian Poetry* (Stratford-upon-Avon Studies, 15, 1972), makes some comparisons with Hardy but centers on Yeats's conception of "renaissance," suggesting that "Yeats needed his notion of renaissance in order to get contemporary Ireland into his poetry." John Adlard's mistitled *Stenbock, Yeats and the Nineties* (1969) contains exactly six passing references to Yeats; Adlard admits that he was unable to examine Yeats's unpublished account of his meeting with Count Eric Stenbock.

A much more significant relationship is that with Nietzsche. The fullest account is the chapter on Yeats in David S. Thatcher's *Nietzsche in England, 1890–1914: The Growth of a Reputation* (1970), which carefully traces Yeats's reading of Nietzsche and publishes all of his annotations to Thomas Common's *Nietzsche as Critic, Philosopher, Poet and Prophet* (1901). Thatcher concentrates on Yeats's interest in the concepts of "self-conquest" and the Superman. He concludes that Yeats is "the chief beneficiary of the Nietzsche movement in England" and that he is "very close to the predominant spirit" of Nietzsche's thought. Erich Heller's "Yeats and Nietzsche: Reflections on a Poet's Marginal Notes" (*Encounter*, Dec. 1969) says little on the marginalia but is still an interesting essay, arguing that Yeats's "vestigially sustained anachronism" that "the Day of Judgment will be the Day of Art" is indebted to Nietzsche. The chapter on Yeats in Patrick Bridgwater's *Nietzsche in Anglosaxony: A Study of Nietzsche's Impact on English and American Literature* (1972) ignores Thatcher while presenting an unoriginal survey of Yeats's reading of Nietzsche and his influence on various works. The chapter "Burke, Nietzsche and Yeats" in Conor Cruise O'Brien's *The Suspecting Glance* (1972) does little to advance the discussion, arguing that

"Yeats remains a Nietzschean, behind a façade of late Burke." Lorna Reynolds' "Collective Intellect: Yeats, Synge and Nietzsche" (*E&S*, 1973) makes no reference to the previous scholarship while suggesting that Yeats saw in Synge "an embodiment of Nietzschean values."

IRISH MYTHOLOGY

Since the sources have been more conclusively identified, Dorothy M. Hoare's *The Works of Morris and of Yeats in Relation to Early Saga Literature* (1937) is of little value. Hoare discusses Yeats's interest in a remembered ideal past and the connection of that past with the peasantry. She is critical of Yeats's handling of his sources, arguing that it shows his "tendency to withdraw from reality." She concludes that both Morris and Yeats use the saga material as a false escape from and simplification of life: "Their escape was therefore twofold: first, from life to the sagas; and secondly, from the actuality which the sagas reveal to the dreaming and stilled refuge, with all harshness eliminated, which they made of them."

Russell K. Alspach's "Some Sources of Yeats's *The Wanderings of Oisin*" (*PMLA*, 1943) remains the standard treatment of its subject, as does the section on sources in his "Yeats's 'The Grey Rock'" (*JAF*, 1950). Essentially in the mode of Hoare's work, though more interesting, is Birgit Bjersby's *The Interpretation of the Cuchulain Legend in the Works of W. B. Yeats* (1950), a somewhat discontinuous study. The first chapter gives plot summaries and a partially muddled discussion of the sources for the Cuchulain poems and plays. After providing biographical readings of the plays, Bjersby presents "A Survey of Yeats' Outlook upon Life." This last chapter centers on *A Vision* but also touches on many other areas, including the Leo Africanus correspondence. The study is more valuable for the unpublished material it includes than for Bjersby's explanations.

Edward Callan's "Huddon and Duddon in Yeats's *A Vision*: The Folk Tale as Gateway to the Universal Mind" (*Michigan Academician*, 1973) locates the source for one of the poems in *A Vision* in *Celtic Fairy Tales* (ed. Joseph Jacobs, 1892). In "Yeats and the Image of the Singing Head" (*Éire*, 1974), P. L. Marcus identifies the major sources for "The Binding of the Hair" and notes a later version of the story, revised with the assistance of Lady Gregory. Two essays on sources are found in *Hereditas: Essays and Studies presented to Professor Séamus Ó Duilearga* (ed. Bo Almqvist, Breandán Mac Aodha, and Gearóid Mac Eoin, 1975). Birgit Bramsbäck's "William Butler Yeats and Folklore Material" does little more than list some possible sources. More significant is Sheila O'Sullivan's "W. B. Yeats's Use of Irish Tradition," a scholarly examination of the sources of various poems and the last line of *Cathleen ni Houlihan*.

NEOPLATONIC TRADITION

Though they provide a close examination of many of Yeats's sources, including the Cabala, alchemy, Indian thought, and Irish mythology and folklore, F. A. C. Wilson's *W. B. Yeats and Tradition* (1958, with a brief reply to his reviewers added in the American ed.) and *Yeats's Iconography* (1960) focus on Yeats's indebtedness to the Neoplatonic tradition. Between them, Wilson's studies discuss ten of the late plays and a substantial number of poems. It is hard not to agree that Yeats had read or at least knew about the source material Wilson cites; thus for the identification of these sources the books are essential reading. But Wilson too often allows the sources to replace Yeats's work itself and misreads the work to make it accord with the sources. For instance, although Wilson brilliantly locates the sources for *The Only Jealousy of Emer* in the Noh drama, Renaissance Platonism, Indian and Irish myth, and *A Vision*, few readers will be satisfied with his assertion that Fand is the most tragic character in the play. The tone of Wilson's writing is also not helpful, as when he describes himself as "the first student of Yeats's ultimate symbolic intentions." Wilson's work cannot be ignored but must be approached with caution.

The other important critic in this area is Kathleen Raine. In "Yeats and Platonism" (*TQ*, 1967), Raine defends Yeats's use of both the Neoplatonic and the "unwritten" traditions and suggests that the exact source for any individual symbol is usually impossible to locate because of the universality of symbols. She concludes with a commentary on two late poems. The material in this article is essentially repeated and only slightly expanded in her "Life in Death and Death in Life: Yeats's 'Cuchulain Comforted' and 'News for the Delphic Oracle'" (*SoR*, 1973). The study has perhaps reached its final form as *Death-in-Life and Life-in-Death: 'Cuchulain Comforted' and 'News for the Delphic Oracle'* (1974), a monograph with twenty illustrations and a note on *The Death of Cuchulain*.

VISUAL SOURCES

The line of study initiated by T. R. Henn received its fullest development in Giorgio Melchiori's important *The Whole Mystery of Art: Pattern into Poetry in the Work of W. B. Yeats* (1960). Melchiori does for certain of Yeats's images and poems what J. L. Lowes did for "Kubla Khan"—traces in an exhaustive and scholarly manner the literary and especially the pictorial sources and suggests the reasons why they coalesced in Yeats's mind. Melchiori begins by discussing Yeats's emphasis on "pattern" or form in his poetry and the essential basis in magic of his theory of symbolism. After tracing the genesis of the unicorn symbol, he devotes three chapters to the sources of "Leda and the Swan." Other symbols traced include the egg, the sphere, and the gyre. His commentary on the Byzantium poems stresses the importance of Yeats's 1923 visit to Stockholm. Melchiori includes six appendices of varying interest. Typical of Melchiori's conclusions is the following: "It is reasonable to advance the opinion that, in some dim recess of Yeats's consciousness, the two Spenserian contexts (Leda and the Swan, and Chrysogone raped by the sun beam) became fused together, alongside Blake's Leda-Swan in *Jerusalem* and the woman raped by fire in *The Marriage of Heaven and Hell*; and with the help of Madame Blavatsky's teachings, of hints from Pater and from the *Hypnerotomachia*, and of the poet's other theosophic and occult notions, they formed a unique intellectual accretion from which *his* conception of the Leda myth was to spring." Although this type of investigation obviously will not appeal to everyone, those with an interest in the "mental pattern upon which Yeats's poetry is built" will find *The Whole Mystery of Art* full of fascinating detail.

That the identification of sources is an unending process was well illustrated by some essays and letters in *TLS* in 1962. Though Melchiori's investigations of the subject might have seemed final, in "Leda and the Swan" (*TLS*, 20 July 1962) Charles Madge pointed out a central source in a relief formerly exhibited in the British Museum (conveniently reproduced, though not identified, in the second edition of Henn's *The Lonely Tower*, opposite p. 329). In a letter (*TLS*, 3 Aug. 1962) Melchiori accepted this relief as the major source and argued that it confirmed his belief in "the priority of visual over intellectual stimuli for Yeats." Finally, in "Leda and the Swan" (*TLS*, 9 Nov. 1962) Charles B. Gullans suggested a woodcut by T. Sturge Moore and also his poem "To Leda." The enthusiasm of some source scholars is seen in Gullans' remark that the two Moore items and the relief "explain every feature of all the versions of 'Leda and the Swan.'"

In "Raphael: The Dead Child on a Dolphin" (*TLS*, 25 Oct. 1963), Edgar Wind indicated two statues (one of which was in Ireland) which answer to Yeats's description in a letter to T. Sturge Moore of "Raphael's statue of the Dolphin carrying one of the Holy Innocents to Heaven." In letters Margaret Whinney (*TLS*, 7 Nov. 1963) noted a copy in England, and James Tudor-Craig (*TLS*, 21 Nov. 1963) pointed out other replicas. The most recent identification of a visual source is Rosemary Franklin Tully's "A Pictorial Source for Yeats's 'The Magi'" (*Éire*, 1973), which is not especially convincing in suggesting Benozzo Gozzoli's *The Journey of the Magi*, a fresco in the Medici-Riccardi Chapel in Florence. Margaret Stanley's "Yeats and French Painting," in *France-Ireland: Literary Relations* (ed. Patrick Rafroidi, Guy Fehlmann, and Maitiu Mac Conmara, Paris, 1974) is an elementary sketch which ignores most previous studies.

MEDIEVAL AND RENAISSANCE LITERATURE

In "Dante, Yeats, and Unity of Being" (*Shenandoah*, Winter 1966) Thomas Vance notes some interesting comparisons but concludes with the exaggerated claim that Dante was Yeats's "spiritual hero and guide" in his later career. Giorgio Melchiori (*EM*, 1968) carefully traces Yeats's interest in and knowledge of Dante, stressing the influence of Rossetti and Blake. Both Vance and Melchiori note that the phrase "Unity of Being" does not appear in Dante. Brian John's "'To Hunger Fiercely after Truth': Daimonic Man and Yeats's Insatiable Appetite" (*Éire*, 1974) is more interesting for suggesting some sources for Yeats's image of Dante in Rossetti, Carlyle, and Morris than for the overextended study of the imagery of appetite in the poems.

T. McAlindon's "Yeats and the English Renaissance" (*PMLA*, 1967) is a cogent general survey, stressing the influence of Shakespeare, Spenser, and Jonson in the development of Yeats's aristocratic attitudes. McAlindon is particularly effective in showing Yeats's interest in Jonson and its effect on his style; his account should now be supplemented by Daniel A. Harris' *Yeats: Coole Park and Ballylee*. Also of some value is B. Rajan's "Yeats and the Renaissance" (*Mosaic*, 1972), though it concentrates more on the concept of "Unity of Being" than on the Renaissance.

Corinna Salvadori's *Yeats and Castiglione: Poet and Courtier* (1965) is brief but still belabors some of the obvious connections between Yeats's works and *The Book of the Courtier*. Salvadori develops the parallels between the poet and the courtier, Coole Park and Urbino, and Lady Gregory and the Duchess of Urbino. Her examination of the relationship of the concept of *sprezzatura* to Yeats's style does not equal Arnold Stein's early "Yeats: A Study in Recklessness" (*SR*, 1949).

Peter Ure's *The Shakespearian Moment: On W. B. Yeats's Attitude towards Shakespeare as Revealed in His Criticism and in His Work for the Theatre* (1969) is hardly longer than its title but does provide a good summary of Yeats's attitudes and their effect on his work. Ure stresses the importance to Yeats of *Richard* II and suggests that Yeats uses Shakespeare "as a stick with which to beat the naturalists." He also treats the moment of "reverie" which Yeats found in Shakespeare and aimed at in his own work.

Rupin W. Desai's uneven *Yeats's Shakespeare* (1971) begins by tracing Yeats's basic attitudes toward Shakespeare and the influence on them of John Butler Yeats. Desai discusses the productions Yeats saw but overlooks the comments on Poel's staging of *Measure for Measure* in "Discoveries: Second Series." The second chapter concerns Yeats's knowledge of Shakespeare criticism. Desai then examines Yeats's views in more detail and concludes that his final attitude toward Shakespeare was one of "ambivalence." The fourth chapter explains why Shakespeare was placed in Phase 20 in *A Vision*. Up to this point the study is fairly effective. Desai then suggests, however, that Yeats considered Shakespeare his "Daimon" and finds parallels between their plays; these parallels are often more ingenious than convincing. More to the point are the discussions of the place of Shakespeare in Yeats's personality/character distinction and of the differences between the Fools of the two writers. The book concludes with three appendices: direct references to Shakespeare, references to his works, and "echoes." The lack of any reference by Desai to Engelberg's *The Vast Design* is unfortunate. A minor addition is made by A. M. Gibbs in "The 'Rough Beasts' of Yeats and Shakespeare" (*N&Q*, 1970), which suggests *The Rape of Lucrece* as a source for "The Second Coming."

JAPANESE TRADITION

A few studies of Yeats and the Noh have already been cited, particularly in Section XII. In addition, a valuable early study is Anthony

Thwaite's "Yeats and the Noh" (*TC*, 1957), which concludes that "Yeats, like Pound, was fascinated more by the ideas he read into the Noh than in its actual tradition and performance." Another good general survey is Earl Miner's *The Japanese Tradition in British and American Literature* (1958). Miner deals not only with the Noh but also with Yeats's use of Japan as an image of "aristocratic culture." He makes the interesting suggestion that the Japanese poetic technique of "super-position" can be observed in "Veronica's Napkin," "Byzantium," and elsewhere. *W. B. Yeats and Japan* (Tokyo, 1965) by Shotaro Oshima is a lavishly produced volume, replete with numerous illustrations including facsimiles of Yeats letters. The book is perhaps most valuable for the fifteen unpublished letters to Oshima and others. Also of interest are Oshima's account of a 1938 interview with Yeats and of a 1964 interview with Junzo Sato, the latter giving a full report on the sword "Montashigi" (correctly "Motoshige"). The study also contains an annotated bibliography of Yeats studies in Japan, 1887–1964. Oshima's introduction to this material (which is not listed by Cross and Dunlop or Jochum) stresses the influence of Yeats on Japanese drama. The essays by Oshima on the Noh, Yeats and Zen, the elements, "Meru," and "The Statues" are of minor interest.

Akhtar Qamber's *Yeats and the Noh* (1974), which includes the texts of two Yeats plays and the Pound/Fenollosa translations of *Hagoromo* and *Nishikigi*, is rambling, anecdotal, poorly researched, and unillustrated.

INDIAN THOUGHT

The work of H. R. Bachchan and Shankar Mokashi-Punekar noted in Section XIII is relevant to this topic. But the most useful examination is Naresh Guha's *W. B. Yeats: An Indian Approach* (Calcutta, 1968), a relatively careful study with only mild overemphasis. Guha begins with a lucid account of the rise of Indian studies in the eighteenth and nineteenth centuries and the use before Yeats of Indian matter in literature. He also notes Yeats's awareness of the parallels between India and Ireland. The chapter on Mohini Chatterjee and Theosophy includes a study of "The Wanderings of Oisin" in terms of the three gunas. The analysis of Yeats's interest in Yoga and Puranic Hinduism centers on *The Shadowy Waters*. Chapter iv recounts Yeats's relationship with Tagore, essentially one of early admiration followed by disillusionment; Guha notes the similarity in their views on nationalism and the differences in their attitudes toward abstractions, sex, and the supernatural. Guha concludes by tracing Yeats's interest in Patanjali's Yogic system, the Tantras, and Purohit Swami; his argument that *The Herne's Egg* is a conscious adaptation of Tagore's *King of the Dark Chamber* is interesting but urged too strongly. Guha provides a useful chronology, which draws on Thomas L. Dume's "William Butler Yeats: A Survey of His Reading" (Diss. Temple 1950). The study prints a single letter to Chatterjee and fifteen letters to Tagore, the latter reprinted from *VQ* (1964–65). Also of note is the preface by Richard Ellmann.

Overlooked by Guha and still of value is Harold H. Hurwitz' "Yeats and Tagore" (*CL*, 1964), a competent sketch of the relationship. Hurwitz notes some similarities in their works but refrains from pressing them. *Rabindranath Tagore and William Butler Yeats: The Story of a Literary Friendship* (ed. R. K. DasGupta, Delhi, 1965) is most important for printing Yeats's speech at the dinner given Tagore in 1912. Sushil Kumar Jain's "Indian Elements in the Poetry of Yeats: On Chatterji [sic] and Tagore" (*CLS*, 1970) fails to mention any of the earlier studies and exaggerates Yeats's indebtedness to Chatterjee. The same lack of attention to previous scholarship is found in Shamsul Islam's "The Influence of Eastern Philosophy on Yeats's Later Poetry" (*TCL*, 1973), a brief survey which concentrates on some sections of "Supernatural Songs."

P. Lal's edition of *The Isa Upanisad* (Calcutta, 1968) includes an "Essay on The Difficulties of Translation (based on a study of the Yeats-Purohit version of the Īśa-Upaniṣad)." This interesting essay provides a line-by-line literal rendering and notes both the accuracies and inaccuracies of Yeats's version. More hostile toward Yeats and his collaborator is J. Masson, who in "Yeats's *The Ten Principal Upanishads*" (*Jadavpur Jour. of Comp. Lit.*, 9, 1971?) charges that "opening the book at random nearly every passage is inaccurate, and what is more important, the inaccuracies are never on the side of poetry." Masson blames Purohit Swami for not telling Yeats enough about the originals.

FRENCH SYMBOLISM

In retrospect, Arthur Symons' dedication of *The Symbolist Movement in Literature* (1899) to Yeats as "the chief representative of that movement in our country" seems a mistake, for it has resulted in an overstatement of Yeats's indebtedness to the French tradition. Used early in his career to attack his Irish nationalism, the relationship was given authority by the studies of Edmund Wilson and C. M. Bowra (noted above). A. M. Killen's "Some French Influences in the Works of W. B. Yeats at the End of the Nineteenth Century" (*CLS*, 1942) is unusual in not pressing the claims of influence while recognizing some parallels. In general, few critics have paid much attention to, or been deterred by, Eileen Souffrin-Le Breton's "W. B. Yeats to Mallarmé" (*TLS*, 26 Nov. 1954), which prints a letter from Yeats to Mallarmé and demonstrates that the fabled meeting between them in Paris could not have occurred. Thomas L. Watson's conclusion in "The French Reputation of W. B. Yeats" (*CL*, 1960) that "Yeats remains relatively unknown in France" is perhaps a fitting irony.

Of the work that follows Wilson and Bowra, the chapter in Enid Starkie's *From Gautier to Eliot: The Influence of France on English Literature* (1960) is representative in continuing the overemphasis—though Yeats is not the only one to suffer. E. Davis' *Yeats's Early Contacts with French Poetry* (Pretoria, 1961) consists of a series of short essays on the influence of a host of figures in Yeats's developing knowledge of French literature. It is an unconvincing study, which works mainly through parallel passages and credits Yeats with a greater knowledge of French than he possessed.

Studies that concentrate on parallels rather than sources are more likely to be successful. Somewhat midway is Daphne Fullwood's "The Influence on W. B. Yeats of Some French Poets (Mallarmé, Verlaine, Claudel)" (*SoR*, 1970). Despite her title, Fullwood states that she does not mean to "suggest any direct borrowing"; in fact, the essay varies between suggesting sources and discussing parallels. Of the most interest is her attention to the later French writers such as Claudel. In "Yeats's Use of *Axël*" (*CompD*, 1970–71) Marilyn Gaddis Rose studies with some effectiveness the relationship of *Axël* with *The Countess Cathleen* and the "Rosa Alchemica" stories, showing that Yeats modified rather than accepted the philosophy of the French work. More clearly a study of parallels is Stella Revard's "Yeats, Mallarmé, and the Archetypal Feminine" (*PLL*, 1972), which notes some similarities in their treatment of the feminine beauty/Muse image but argues that Yeats is fundamentally different from Mallarmé in accepting the necessity of descent into the real world. Although incompletely researched, Gayatri C. Spivak's "A Stylistic Contrast between Yeats and Mallarmé, (*Lang&S*, 1972) is useful in demonstrating the differences in their approaches to the symbol: Mallarmé moves "towards the autotelic sign . . . Yeats towards a solidification of referentiality." Also related to this general topic is the chapter on "Discovering Symbolism" in Richard Ellmann's *Golden Codgers*, which carefully traces the interaction between Arthur Symons and Yeats in their developing attitudes toward Symbolism.

SOME LITERARY CONTACTS

Yeats's relationship with J. M. Synge has been commented on at length, though it is not yet the subject of a separate monograph. Two of the better accounts are T. R. Henn's chapter in *The Lonely Tower* and D. Gerstenberger's "Yeats and Synge: 'A Young Man's Ghost,'" in *W. B. Yeats: Centenary Essays* (ed. D. E. S. Maxwell and S. B. Bushrui). Although it contains too much quotation, the chapter on the relationship in Alan Price's *Synge and Anglo-Irish Drama* (1961) makes the interesting suggestion that "Synge embodied in his plays, better than Yeats or anyone could, Yeats's vision of drama." Balachandra Rajan (*YeatsS*, 1972) presents one of the most effective of the innumerable comparisons between the Deirdre plays of Yeats and Synge. *Sunshine and the Moon's Delight: A Centenary Tribute to John Millington Synge 1871–1909* (ed. S. B. Bushrui, 1972) includes two essays on the relationship. Robert O'Driscoll's "Yeats's Conception of Synge" overemphasizes the importance of Synge in Yeats's developing esthetic theory. Bushrui's "Synge and Yeats" repeats much of the material from his *Yeats's Verse Plays* and thus takes a moderate position on Synge's influence. More significant is Jon Stallworthy's "The Poetry of Synge and Yeats," in *J. M. Synge: Centenary Essays* (ed. Maurice Harmon, 1972), a sensitive commentary which notes some biographical similarities and concludes that "when Synge the poet showed Yeats the way forward into his later style, he was but redirecting him along a road he had already taken under guidance from Synge the playwright. Yeats profited from Synge's example, because he understood the nature of the man and his achievement." For additional studies of Yeats and Synge, see the chapter on Synge in the present volume.

In "An Exile Returned: Yeats and Moore in Ireland" (*Éire*, 1968) Jack Wayne Weaver presents a general sketch of the relationship, with emphasis on the collaboration on *Diarmuid and Grania* and *Where There Is Nothing*. More detail on the composition of the later play is given by David S. Thatcher (*MD*, 1971), who argues that Yeats rejected the play partly because of guilt feelings over his treatment of Moore. Patricia Ann McFate and William E. Doherty (*IUR*, 1972) present a few more details on the process of collaboration and suggest that the character of Paul Ruttledge is partially modeled on Moore. Meredith Cary's "Yeats and Moore—An Autobiographical Conflict" (*Éire*, 1969) provides a useful summary of *Hail and Farewell* and *Dramatis Personae* but is heavily weighted in favor of Moore; Cary overlooks both T. R. Henn's article (*DM*, 1965) and Yeats's humor.

In "Yeats, Shaw and Unity of Being" (*SoRA*, 1973), A. M. Gibbs suggests that the two writers are "alike in some essentials" but concentrates on the more patent contrasts. Gibbs is critical of Yeats's "conception of life as tragedy" and his lack of "a particularly broad range of human sympathies." Of the numerous accounts of the Yeats-O'Casey entanglement over *The Silver Tassie*, the fullest is the chapter "The Playwright's Not For Burning" in David Krause's *Sean O'Casey: The Man and His Work* (1960; 2nd ed., 1975), which can be supplemented by Krause's "O'Casey and Yeats and the Druid" (*MD*, 1968). William A. Armstrong's "Sean O'Casey, W. B. Yeats and the Dance of Life" (in *Sean O'Casey: Modern Judgments*, ed. Ronald Ayling, 1969) is a brief but interesting comparative study.

Most of the remaining important relationships are treated in Richard Ellmann's *Eminent Domain: Yeats among Wilde, Joyce, Pound, Eliot, and Auden* (1967). Brief and somewhat casual, though, this study can be usefully supplemented. The chapter on Wilde centers on the influence of his esthetic theory and is reasonably complete, although Ellmann does not mention Yeats's gathering of letters of support during Wilde's trial. An interesting addition is W. Schrickx's "On Giordano Bruno, Wilde and Yeats" (*ES*, supp., 1964), which traces the interest in Bruno by several writers in the 1890's and also suggests Yeats's indebtedness to *The Picture of Dorian Gray*. A less important addition is made by George Bornstein in "A Borrowing from Wilde in Yeats's 'The King's Threshold'" (*N&Q*, 1971), which shows Yeats's use of the nature/art concept from *The Decay of Lying*.

Ellmann's chapter on Joyce, revised and with notes added from his *Yeats and Joyce* (1967), is of course a cogent essay. Although some notes by Joyce on Yeats are published for the first time, one must refer to *The Identity of Yeats* for the full text of the rejected preface to *Ideas of Good and Evil*, which recounts Yeats's first meeting with Joyce. Other useful supplements include Hugh Kenner's *Dublin's Joyce* (1956), which offers brief comments on Joyce's poetry in relation to Yeats's and on Joyce's use of *The Tables of the Law*; John

Rees Moore's "Artifices for Eternity: Joyce and Yeats" (*Éire*, 1968), a general essay showing the basic contrasts; George L. Geckle's "Stephen Dedalus and W. B. Yeats: The Making of the Villanelle" (*MFS*, 1969), which somewhat exaggerates the influence of Yeats on the hero of *Portrait*; John A. Lester's "Joyce, Yeats, and the Short Story" (*ELT*, 1972), which draws some rather obvious contrasts between their short fiction; and Adaline Glasheen's brief "The Yeats Letters and FW" (*WN*, 1973), which uses the Wade *Letters* to note some allusions in *Finnegans Wake*. The most provocative addition is M. J. Sidnell's "A Daintical pair of accomplasses: Joyce and Yeats," in *Litters from Aloft* (ed. Ronald Bates and Harry J. Pollock, 1971). Sidnell discusses some parallels and allusions on both sides, giving special attention to the relationship between "The Wanderings of Oisin" and *Finnegans Wake*; he also reasserts that Joyce was parodying *A Vision* in his last work.

Ellmann's chapter on Pound offers some interesting comparisons and provides full details on the changes Pound made in several of Yeats's poems (not always to the latter's liking). In "W. B. Yeats's Criticism of Ezra Pound" (*ES*, 1948; *SR*, 1949), H. W. Häusermann presents a useful if somewhat dated analysis of Yeats's comments on Pound, arguing that Yeats gives "an astonishingly penetrating and coherent evolution of Pound the man and the poet." More important is Thomas Parkinson's seminal "Yeats and Pound: The Illusion of Influence" (*CL*, 1954), which demonstrates that "if Pound had any effect on Yeats's lyrics during the Sussex winters, it is not visible." Parkinson also rightly concludes that the Noh "encouraged and strengthened; it did not shape and change." In all, Pound's influence was "minor and adventitious." Essentially the same conclusions are reached by K. L. Goodwin (*The Influence of Ezra Pound*, 1966), though some further details are provided. Parkinson's ideas are also accepted by Herbert N. Schneidau (*ELH*, 1965), but Schneidau suggests that during the early part of the relationship Pound was drawn into "esoteric Yeatsism" and that the effects of the Symbolist tradition are evident in his poetry even after he had rejected it. K. K. Ruthven has identified (*N&Q*, 1968) an allusion to "The Withering of the Boughs" in Pound's *Homage to Sextus Propertius*.

The chapter on Eliot in *Eminent Domain* is far too brief and does not mention Yeats's selection of poems for the *Oxford Book of Modern Verse*. Though not essentially a comparative study, A. Alvarez' *The Shaping Spirit: Studies in Modern English and American Poets* (1958; as *Stewards of Excellence* in the United States) contains some interesting comments, such as "you go to Eliot for the controlled allusive subtlety of mind and feeling, for whatever is not obvious or easily stated; to Yeats for the central, living subtlety, the tension between rage and generosity, impotence and desire, between, often, an attitude and truthfulness." G. S. Fraser's lucid "W. B. Yeats and T. S. Eliot" (in *T. S. Eliot: A Symposium for His Seventieth Birthday*, ed. Neville Braybrooke, 1958) effectively contrasts Yeats's "*accepting attitude*" with Eliot's "*rejecting attitude*," particularly in their approaches to sexual matters. Ellmann's chapter on Auden is more complete but should be supplemented by Samuel Hynes's essay in *Modern Irish Literature*, cited in Section VIII. Also of some interest is

Joost Daalder's "Yeats and Auden: Some Verbal Parallels" (*N&Q*, 1973).

Another relationship to receive attention is Yeats's influence on the plays of Samuel Beckett. Ruby Cohn's article has been noted in Section VII. A more complete study is Katharine J. Worth's "Yeats and the French Drama" (*MD*, 1966). Andrew Parkin's "Similarities in the Plays of Yeats and Beckett" (*ArielE*, 1970) is well written but ignores previous criticism.

Conclusion

One of the earliest of Yeats's writings to be preserved is a draft of a letter and poem sent to one Mary Cronan (about whom, I am happy to say, we know nothing). Probably eighteen or nineteen years old and without a single publication to his credit, Yeats nevertheless predicted, "my peculiaritys . . . will never be done justice to until they have become classics and are set for examinations." Concerning his "classic" stature and his appearance on examinations at all levels, none of his many prophecies has proved more accurate; but we may yet wonder to what extent he has been done "justice."

Certainly the student must not be misled by the sheer quantity of Yeats criticism. Too many studies have been published which either repeat or ignore previous scholarship; which substitute paraphrase and quotation for analysis; which are partial, over-ingenious, or merely inaccurate; which betray an ignorance of even the broad outlines of his career; or which show no awareness of the contexts in which he lived and wrote. In particular, too many books have appeared, a fact which can be explained—though not justified—by Yeats's steadily increasing reputation and the conditions of academic publishing, especially in America, in the 1950's and 1960's. That this last situation has fundamentally changed and that fewer books are likely to be published in the next several years will perhaps be more of a blessing than a curse. A list of essential studies of Yeats would be relatively short.

Nor is Mary Cronan the only gap in our knowledge. The very bulk of the scholarship on Yeats obscures our ignorance, of which a few examples may suffice. Of, say, Yeats and Maud Gonne we know the broad outlines, but the destruction or unavailability of their correspondence has so far frustrated a detailed study. Of Yeats and his wife we know far less. His lecture tours in America have never been traced in a significant way. Only a handful of scholars have a clear understanding of his almost lifelong occult activities and their relationship to his achievement. His contemporary reputation has been more often asserted than documented. If perhaps not endless, a list of lacunae is more extensive than the approximately 6,000 items of criticism might have implied. Nor should it be forgotten that we are less than four decades from Yeats's death and that a significant portion of his work remains either unedited, uncollected, or unpublished.

Although examinations of special topics will certainly continue to appear, it seems clear that any important major studies will necessarily await the completion of various projects now under way—most obviously the authorized biography and the *Collected Letters*. Once past this brief interregnum, and with new materials at hand, we can profitably continue our always doomed attempt to do Yeats "justice," or, to draw on the conclusion to *A Vision*, to replace that partial "image of Heracles that walks through the darkness" with "that other Heracles, man, not image, he that has for his bride Hebe, 'The daughter of Zeus, the mighty, and Hera, shod with gold.'"

As always, Yeats will doubtless anticipate us: as he did not only by providing the lines which began this chapter but also by furnishing its conclusion, in a remark he is reported to have made to his wife—"I don't want them to know all about everything."

J. M. SYNGE

Weldon Thornton

I. Editions

The standard edition of Synge's works is the *Collected Works*, published by Oxford University Press in four volumes, 1962–68, under the general editorship of Robin Skelton. *Poems* (I, 1962) was edited by Skelton; *Prose* (II, 1966), by Alan Price; *Plays* (III, IV, 1968), by Ann Saddlemyer. These volumes include, in addition to the standard edition of each of Synge's works, some previously unpublished material in all three genres and a considerable amount of material from Synge's notes and drafts. The aim of the *Collected Works*, to provide a definitive edition of Synge's works, is only partially realized.

Each of the editors faced problems, produced by Synge's habits of composition, his often difficult handwriting, and the considerable number of surviving manuscripts. These problems, discussed in the introductory matter of Volumes I and II, stem mainly from Synge's habit of writing several drafts of a work, often on facing pages of a

The following special abbreviations and acronyms are used in this chapter:

Bushrui, Sunshine S. B. Bushrui, ed. *Sunshine and the Moon's Delight: A Centenary Tribute to John Millington Synge 1871–1909*. Gerrards Cross, Eng.: Colin Smythe, 1972.

CW *J. M. Synge: Collected Works*. 4 vols. London: Oxford Univ. Press, 1962–68.

Greene/Stephens David H. Greene and Edward M. Stephens. *J. M. Synge 1871–1909*. New York: Macmillan, 1959.

Harmon, Centenary Maurice Harmon, ed. *J. M. Synge Centenary Papers 1971*. Dublin: Dolmen, 1972.

JMS Donna Gerstenberger. *John Millington Synge*. New York: Twayne, 1964.

JMSCS P. P. Howe. *J. M. Synge: A Critical Study*. London: Martin Secker, 1912.

JMS&IT Maurice Bourgeois. *John Millington Synge and the Irish Theatre*. London: Constable, 1913.

S&A-ID Alan Price. *Synge and Anglo-Irish Drama*. London: Methuen, 1961.

S&A-IL Daniel Corkery. *Synge and Anglo-Irish Literature*. Dublin and Cork: Cork Univ. Press, 1931.

WJMS Robin Skelton. *The Writings of J. M. Synge*. London: Thames & Hudson, 1971.

notebook, without indication of the sequence of the drafts. For the plays the manuscript material is sometimes more coherent than for the verse or prose, by virtue of Synge's indicating successive drafts by letters of the alphabet and because much of the material is typewritten. But the sheer volume of manuscript material for some of the plays presented Saddlemyer with an appalling task.

In the *Poems*, Skelton offers 58 poems, 34 previously unpublished; Synge's translations from Villon, Leopardi, Petrarch, and others; excerpts from three fragmentary verse plays; and appendices presenting typical worksheets and draft material for some of the poems. In his introduction Skelton says, "It is high time that as complete a collection of Synge's poems as is reasonable should be published in order both to document his 'poetic progress' and to bring into the light many good poems which have not previously been available for consideration. This edition is, therefore, not only an attempt at providing a definitive canon of Synge's work as a poet, but also an attempt to show something of his methods of composition and of the gradual development of his work over the years." But this claim to definitiveness must be questioned, for, as Skelton's statement suggests and examination of the Notebooks confirms, he does not give us all of Synge's verse. Further, nowhere does he describe the amount, nature, or date of the portion of the verse that remains unprinted. And some of this verse, while admittedly too poor to enhance Synge's reputation as a poet, is of interest for the light it sheds on Synge's psychology and development: much of Synge's "juvenilia" was written not when he was fourteen or fifteen, but when he was in his early twenties, already graduated from Trinity and traveling on the Continent.

Price's edition of the *Prose* consists largely of previously published material. It contains *The Aran Islands*; *In Wicklow, West Kerry, and Connemara*; and Synge's essays and reviews, which were scattered in journals and newspapers. The volume also contains Synge's early autobiographical sketches, some previously published in part, others unpublished; a gleaning of "Various Notes" on literature from Synge's Notebooks; and previously unpublished drafts for the longer essays.

Several features of Price's editorial practice should be noted. First and most important, he does not print all of Synge's dicta, drafts of essays, and the like, nor does he describe the shape of what remains unpublished, so that considerable manuscript material of interest to Synge scholars remains unmined, even uncharted. Second, Price does not always give the full text of the reviews he prints. For example, he gives only about one fourth of Synge's article on Le Braz (*CW*, II, 394), saying, "The rest of the article is little more than quotation from Le Braz." But the reader may wish to know what Synge chose to quote, and the omitted section does contain some noteworthy comments by Synge.

Third, when faced with several drafts of a work, Price produces a conglomerate text, rather than attempting to determine any priority among the drafts. This procedure results in quite different versions of Synge's "Autobiography" in *CW* II and in the typescript biography of Synge by his nephew, Edward M. Stephens (Stephens builds his around the version in Notebook Fifteen). The reader can see Price's approach in his editing of "On a Train to Paris" (*CW*, II, 37–38), since he provides a photocopy of most of the manuscript. Price's comment on these versions is "Two versions, neither quite complete, exist on opposite pages in Notebook 15. Both versions seem to have been drafted hurriedly and are scrawled across the pages in almost illegible handwriting much altered and crossed-out, as the photograph (between pp. 40–41) indicates. Only a conflation of them would make sense, and this is here provided." But this procedure is questionable, for the right-hand version is crossed out, and it breaks off in midsentence (on the following page of manuscript, not shown), while the left-hand version is not crossed out, seems more concise and finished, and does come to an ending. Price's conflation has the advantage of giving us all that Synge wrote, but it sidesteps the problem of priority and results in something structurally different from anything Synge wrote. And while Price's readings are generally accurate, his reading "frank obscenity" (which neither draft supports) for "rank obscenity" perturbs the logic and alters the tone of the piece.

Saddlemyer gives standard versions of Synge's six plays, buttressed by voluminous but convenient editorial apparatus, plus some sixteen plays, scenarios, drafts, and fragments, most previously unpublished. Her choice of a facing-page format for plays with considerable draft material enables her to present clearly and conveniently a large amount of material accessory to the main text. The various sources and draft manuscripts are discussed in appendices, which also print related passages from Synge's essays and Notebooks. Saddlemyer's care and accuracy, and her choice of format, make this edition of the plays admirable for its scope and clarity. Perhaps someone wishing to pursue in Lowesian depth the origin and evolution of a given play may need to go beyond this material; but even in that event, Saddlemyer's editorial apparatus and description of the material will be indispensable. In lieu of a primary bibliography on Synge, the editorial information in these two volumes is the fullest and best description we have both of earlier editions and of typescripts and manuscripts.

In addition to the *Collected Works*, note should be taken of Robin Skelton's edition of the Houghton Library (Harvard) typescript of *Riders to the Sea* (1969). This attractive volume, with color linocuts by Tate Adams, is No. 8 in the Dolmen Editions series.

Robin Skelton's *J. M. Synge: Some Sonnets from "Laura in Death" after the Italian of Francesco Petrarch* (1971) provides facing Italian and English texts of Synge's translations of seventeen of Petrarch's sonnets. There is a new introduction by Skelton, but the text is that of the 1962 *CW* edition, which contained all of the sonnets printed here.

Stanley Sultan has published an edition of *Playboy* (1970) based upon the original production copy from the Abbey Theatre, registered by the Lord Chamberlain's office on 27 April 1907. In his introduction Sultan acknowledges the problems in using a production text as copy for an edition, but argues that his "chief purpose is to provide a version of one of the great works of drama in English alternative to the versions whose line of descent is that of the printed editions." He further contends that attention to this text clears up discrepancies that persist in all editions of the play.

My Wallet of Photographs (1971) presents the collected photographs of Synge, arranged and introduced by Lilo Stephens. This quarto volume contains 53 photographs by Synge, mostly of Dublin and Wicklow, Galway and the Aran Islands, and the Blaskets. Stephens' introduction provides background information.

II. Correspondence

There is no collected edition of Synge's correspondence. One is in progress, by Ann Saddlemyer, to be published by Oxford University Press. This edition will include all of Synge's correspondence, including that published in the items listed below.

At present, Synge's letters are available only in scattered sources. The largest and most fully annotated collection is Ann Saddlemyer's *Letters to Molly: John Millington Synge to Maire O'Neill* (1971). These letters from Synge to his fiancée span the period 1906–09 and are an indispensable biographical source. They are buttressed by full editorial apparatus, including introduction, annotations, index (marred by occasional incorrect page references), a chronology, photographs, and a map. Other important sources are Max Meyerfeld, "Letters of John Millington Synge: From Material Supplied by Max Meyerfeld" (*YR*, 1924), 23 letters from Synge about Meyerfeld's translation of *The Well of the Saints* into German. *John Millington Synge: Some Unpublished Letters and Documents of J. M. Synge* (1959) contains nine notes or letters from Synge, plus a publishing agreement and drafts of some poems. The letters are from 1906–09, and correspondents include Pan Karel Musek, M. J. Nolan, and Elkin Mathews. Another gathering is "Synge to MacKenna: The Mature Years" (*MR*, 1964), nine letters from Synge to Stephen MacKenna, introduced and annotated by Ann Saddlemyer.

An important collection of letters is *Some Letters of John M. Synge to Lady Gregory and W. B. Yeats* (1971), containing 56 letters and notes from Synge to Lady Gregory or Yeats, dating from 1898 to 1909 and relating mainly to the business of the Abbey Theatre. There are an introduction and postscript by Ann Saddlemyer.

Another collection of letters that has been announced but has not yet appeared (though erroneously listed in some bibliographies) is Saddlemyer's edition of some of the correspondence among Yeats, Synge, and Lady Gregory, from the New York Public Library Collection. Entitled *Theatre Business, Management of Men: The Letters of the First Abbey Directors*, the book will be published in late 1976 or early 1977.

Other letters of Synge are printed passim in the Greene/Stephens biography, and still others are quoted in the introductions to Volumes III and IV of *CW*.

III. Bibliography

PRIMARY BIBLIOGRAPHY

There is at present no full-length primary bibliography for Synge, so that those interested in Synge's publications and manuscripts must consult the scattered sources listed here.* *John Millington Synge 1871–1909: A Catalogue of an Exhibition Held at Trinity College Library Dublin on the Occasion of the Fiftieth Anniversary of His Death* (1959), though primarily a catalog of an exhibition, lists items beyond those exhibited. Of the 146 items listed, 83 are books, 13 are contributions to periodicals, 20 are manuscripts or letters, and 29 are miscellaneous items (mostly programs, playbills, and photographs). Technical bibliographic descriptions are provided for many of the books, and the listing is extensive in translations of Synge's works.

By far the largest collection of Synge manuscripts and letters is that in Trinity College, Dublin. *The Synge Manuscripts in the Library of Trinity College Dublin* (1971) provides the fullest published description of this collection, listing the manuscripts both by the number Trinity has assigned to them and by the earlier numberings used by Stephens and Greene. Ann Saddlemyer's " 'Infinite Riches in a Little Room'—The Manuscripts of John Millington Synge" (*Long Room*, 1971) describes some of the highlights of the collection. (A more detailed typescript description is available in the Rare Book Room of Trinity College. And some items have been added to the collection since the 1971 pamphlet was published—most notably the lengthy typescript biography by Edward M. Stephens and letters and diaries relating to Synge's mother and brothers.) Other noteworthy holdings of Synge manuscript material are in the Berg Collection and the Manuscript Collection of the New York Public Library; the Houghton Library of Harvard University; the Lilly Library of Indiana University; and the Humanities Research Center of the University of Texas. The National Library of Ireland also holds microfilm of much of the manuscript material at Trinity, as well as many related manuscripts. Some material is in private hands, most notably those of Lilo Stephens and Ann Saddlemyer.

Another valuable source of information about Synge's publications and manuscripts is the editorial apparatus in *CW* (esp. Vols. III and IV, *Plays*). In the appendices relating to each of the plays, Saddlemyer provides a "Description of Textual Sources," describing both editions and manuscripts; these appendices constitute one of the fullest and most reliable sources of bibliographic information.

Other less extensive but noteworthy sources for primary bibliography include: the appendices to Maurice Bourgeois's *JMS&IT* (1913), quite complete up to its date of publication; M. J. MacManus, "Bibliographies of Irish Authors, No. 4: John Millington Synge" (*DM*, 1930), later issued as a pamphlet; P. S. O'Hegarty, supplemental to Bourgeois and MacManus (*DM*, 1942); P. S. O'Hegarty, "Biblio-

* I have been told, but have been unable to confirm, that a primary bibliography has been undertaken by Frances-Jane French of Dublin.

graphical Notes: The Abbey Theatre (Wolfhound) Series of Plays" (*DM*, 1947); O. F. Babler, on Czech translations (*N&Q*, 1946); David H. Greene, "An Adequate Text of J. M. Synge" (*MLN*, 1946); "A Check-List of First Editions of Works by John Millington Synge" (*T.C.D. Annual Bulletin*, 1956); Ian MacPhail (*IB*, 1959); and Manfred Triesch, "Some Unpublished J. M. Synge Papers" (*ELN*, 1966), which describes some items in the University of Texas collection. Some additional items are listed in Paul Levitt's *Bibliography* (pp. 11–12), cited in the next section.

SECONDARY BIBLIOGRAPHY

Two book-length bibliographies of material about Synge have appeared in the last two years. The first is Paul Levitt's *John Millington Synge: A Bibliography of Published Criticism* (1974). A relatively complete listing of material, it is organized partly around various subject headings such as "General Literary Criticism," "Biography," titles of individual plays; in addition, there is a "Newspaper" section, which is more than half the list. Levitt's citations are accurate, he avoids several errors fallen into by earlier bibliographers, and he appears to have examined most of the material first hand. However, that this bibliography, which appeared in 1974, includes only a few items later than December 1969 is particularly unfortunate, since 1971 and 1972 were productive years for Synge criticism. Moreover, while the organization of the book does facilitate locating material on individual plays, it also involves some problems. First, the plan of organization necessitates complete duplication of many items, so that the list becomes much longer than need be. Levitt's organization requires that a general book on Synge such as Daniel Corkery's *Synge and Anglo-Irish Literature* be fully listed in eleven sections of the bibliography. Further, the six reviews of Corkery's book that Levitt lists are scattered through four sections. Since Levitt's entries are not numbered, his index is of limited use. In short, Levitt's *Bibliography* is impressively complete and accurate, but loosely organized and difficult to use.

E. H. Mikhail's *J. M. Synge: A Bibliography of Criticism* (1975) is also a very complete listing, and it has the advantage of a 1971 termination date (plus some later items). Mikhail is not as consistently accurate as Levitt and does not appear to have examined all the material at first hand. Mikhail's organization is weak: it makes no attempt to group material by topic or by play. It does list reviews of Synge's books and plays under individual works, but there is no attempt to group the books or essays themselves in any such way. Nor does Mikhail's index correct the problem since, like Levitt, he does not number items individually. His "Index of Works" is brief and reflects only explicit references to the plays in the titles of articles (e.g., H. Orel's "Synge's Last Plays 'And a Story Will Be Told for Ever'" is not indexed under *Deirdre* since Orel's title does not mention the play by name).

Both Levitt's and Mikhail's bibliographies attempt to be exhaustive, and both are impressive in the fullness of their listings. Precise comparison of their scope is made difficult by their different organizational plans, but scrutiny shows that there are differences in emphasis. Levitt is more extensive in his listing of newspaper articles, especially for provincial newspapers, while Mikhail zealously lists anthologies, general literary histories, and general reference works, including the *New Funk and Wagnall's Encyclopedia*, the *World Book Encyclopedia* (2 different eds. are cited separately), and even *Webster's Biographical Dictionary*. Levitt's method at least leads to material which, however slight, could not be found otherwise; Mikhail's often causes him to list material so general no user of his *Bibliography* would need it.

Other secondary bibliographies that deserve notice are the one in the *NCBEL, 1800–1900* (ed. George Watson, 1969) and the "Select Bibliography" in Bushrui, *Sunshine*. The Bushrui list, while much shorter than Levitt's and Mikhail's and marred by several errors, enables one to see at a glance the books and monographs dealing mainly with Synge, something Levitt's and Mikhail's organization prohibits. For listings of material about Synge since the Levitt and Mikhail lists, the reader must turn to annual bibliographies, such as the *MLA International Bibliography* and those in *IUR*.

Noteworthy too are the review-discussions of Synge criticism by Alan Price in his *Synge and Anglo-Irish Drama* (1961) and his updating in Bushrui, *Sunshine*. In these essays, Price provides a historical overview of Synge criticism, as well as summary and evaluation of many books and essays. Donald M. Michie's brief "Synge and His Critics" (*MD*, 1973) attempts a bird's-eye view of critical response to Synge from his death to the present.

IV. Biography

The standard biography of Synge is David H. Greene and Edward M. Stephens, *J. M. Synge 1871–1909* (1959; the 1961 paperback ed. is riddled with typographical errors and should be avoided). This biography, as Greene explains in his introduction, was a joint project of Greene and of Synge's nephew, Edward M. Stephens, who had worked on a biography of his uncle for several years. Stephens' manuscript had grown to some 3,300 pages and had been declined by several publishers, and he asked Greene's help in shaping it. When Stephens died in 1955, Greene continued to work with the material, publishing the biography in 1959.

Though Greene says in his introduction that "the chief thing a biography can do is to record the deeds of a man's lifetime," he does present an interpretation of his subject: Synge emerges as a taciturn man who early discovered his inability to accept his family's religion and politics and who remained distanced, even alienated, from them throughout his life. He is viewed as a rationalist whose first intellectual crisis was his discovery of Darwin and his consequent disavowal of Christianity. His visits to the Aran Islands from 1898 to 1902 are the source of his coming into his own as a writer. While Greene gives some attention to the composition and reception of each of the plays, the period that gets greatest scrutiny—nearly one fourth of the

biography—is from June 1906 to June 1907, the year of the completion, production, and reception of *Playboy*, and of much of his tumul-
tuous courtship of Molly Allgood.

In writing the biography, Greene had access to a great deal of
personal material—letters, manuscripts, diaries—as well as to the
typescript Stephens had composed from that material and from his
own recollections. Faced with a large volume of primary material and
an unwieldy manuscript, Greene necessarily had to select and prune.
But we may wonder whether that process was not carried too far and
whether Synge's readers do not need a more detailed, more fully
documented account of his life. In 1959, when no full-length book on
Synge had appeared in nearly thirty years, it may have appeared
that the moderate interest in Synge would be satisfied by a moder-
ately detailed biography. In the past fifteen years, however, interest
in Synge has grown impressively (partly as a result of the biography), with some dozen books and monographs, a full edition of his
works, and an impending edition of the letters. In the wake of this
interest, a larger and more detailed biography may well be called
for.

Since the Synge material was in the hands of the family and carefully controlled, there were few biographical publications of any importance prior to the Greene/Stephens biography. Even as energetic
a scholar as Maurice Bourgeois (whose *JMS&IT* has wrongly been
called a biography) could get little accurate biographical information,
so that what he does tell us about Synge's life contains several errors.

The most important sources of biographical information prior to
Greene/Stephens were the essays, memoirs, and introductions written
by those who knew Synge. W. B. Yeats wrote frequently and perceptively about him, especially in the "Preface to the First Edition of
The Well of the Saints" (in *Essays and Introductions*, 1961); in "J. M.
Synge and the Ireland of his Time (*Essays and Introductions*); and
throughout the *Autobiographies* (for a fuller listing see Levitt's *Bib-
liography*). These articles contain a strong admixture of interpreta-
tion and often reveal more about Yeats than about Synge. Lady
Gregory's *Our Irish Theatre* (1913) contains chapters dealing with
Synge and with *Playboy*. John Masefield wrote a reminiscence (*John
M. Synge: A Few Personal Recollections*, 1915) and the *DNB* article
on him; there was, however, little contact between the two men, and
Masefield's impressions rest upon a narrow base.

Other contemporary accounts, though less important, deserve notice. George Moore's *Vale* (1914) contains a brief, impressionistic
sketch. Padraic Colum discusses Synge in *The Road round Ireland*
(1926), though most of his biographical information is not firsthand.
The Journals and Letters of Stephen MacKenna (ed. E. R. Dodds,
1936) contains only passing references to Synge (see, however, the
article listed above in the Letters section). *The Fays of the Abbey
Theatre: An Autobiographical Record*, by W. G. Fay and Catherine
Carswell (1935), contains a few brief comments on Synge, mainly in
relation to the production of his plays. Fuller and more interesting
accounts appear in Maire Nic Shiubhlaigh's *The Splendid Years*
(1955), as well as in Gerard Fay, *The Abbey Theatre: Cradle of
Genius* (1958). James Stephens' "Reminiscences of J. M. Synge," in

James, Seumas & Jacques (1964), while interesting, is not a firsthand recollection. Joseph Holloway, the Dublin playgoer, knew Synge and disliked him; consequently, *Joseph Holloway's Abbey Theatre* (ed. Robert Hogan and Michael J. O.'Neill, 1967) contains many observations about Synge, few of them complimentary, though he does give an interesting account of the last days of Synge's life. Walter Starkie also reminisces about Synge in his "Memories of John Synge and Jack Yeats" (*YeatsS*, 1972) but had only the briefest contact with Synge.

One other firsthand response that deserves notice is that by Cherrie Matheson, whom Synge loved and proposed to. Her reminiscence appeared over the initials "C. H. H." in the *Irish Statesman* for 5 July 1924. While her comments are inherently interesting and cast some light on the young Synge, she makes no reference to their love or to Synge's proposals.

Synge's brother Samuel has combined three types of material in *Letters to My Daughter: Memories of John Millington Synge* (1931): letters from Samuel to his daughter, 1914–28, dealing mainly with Samuel's memories of John and their experiences together; excerpts from Mrs. Synge's letters to Samuel, 1896–1902, dealing with John; and excerpts from Mrs. Synge's diaries, 1887–1907, dealing with John. Though of some interest for establishing the facts or chronology of Synge's life, the book contains few passages that give any feeling of the person. There is no index.

A recent important biographical source is Andrew Carpenter's edition of a portion of Stephens' typescript biography. *My Uncle John* (1974) prints about one tenth of the original 3,300 pages of the typescript. While this seems drastic surgery indeed, much of the typescript was devoted to detailed descriptions of the Dublin-Wicklow vicinity and to the texts of essays, reviews, and letters that are now available elsewhere. Carpenter has selected those portions relating most directly to Synge himself and to his family relationships. Readers will be interested to see that in several important respects Stephens' sense of Synge's relationship with his family—especially his mother—differs from that of David Greene in the biography. The full typescript is now a part of the Trinity College Synge collection.

Discussions of Synge's relationships with others and interpretations of aspects of his biography have become more frequent since the appearance of *CW* and the beginning of public access to the Synge collection at Trinity College. The important relationship between Synge and Yeats, however, has long been a topic of critical discussion. One recurrent idea in this discussion has been that Yeats was influenced by Synge both in his theories of personality and in his drama and poetry and that the main effects of this influence were to encourage realism in Yeats, to redeem him from ethereality and spirituality, and to enable him to blend body and soul. While these ideas are not new—Maurice Bourgeois proposed this general thesis in 1913 —they have been developed and reiterated by several critics in the last fifteen years. Alan Price stresses how incisive Yeats's opinions of Synge were, how well Synge's plays embodied Yeats's own ideas on drama, and how the minds of the two cross-fertilized (*S&A-ID*). T. R. Henn, in an appendix to his edition of *Plays and Poems of J. M.*

Synge (1963), concurs, calling Yeats the most sensitive critic of Synge's works and suggesting that Yeats took more from Synge than is commonly recognized (Henn had broached these ideas earlier in *The Lonely Tower*, 1950). Donna Gerstenberger, in "Yeats and Synge: 'A Young Man's Ghost'" (in *W. B. Yeats Centenary Essays*, ed. D. E. S. Maxwell and S. B. Bushrui, Ibadan, 1965), acknowledging that the influence of Synge on Yeats's diction, subject matter, images, and attitude has already been discussed, adds that Crazy Jane probably traces her ancestry to Mary Byrne of *The Tinker's Wedding*.

Robin Skelton has also pursued the question of Synge's influence on Yeats, first in an essay on Synge's poetry in *Poetry Ireland* in 1962 and more fully in *The Writings of J. M. Synge* (1971), where the ideas about the poetry are repeated and reciprocal influences among the dramas of the two writers are several times suggested. Robert O'Driscoll contends that Yeats's concept of the mask and his theory of tragic ecstasy developed about the figure of Synge and that Synge "restored for Yeats the proper relation between art and life" (in Bushrui, *Sunshine*). O'Driscoll also, however, refers to Synge as a symbol in Yeats's mind, suggesting what Balachandra Rajan says explicitly—namely, that what Yeats saw in Synge "was what the profession of being William Butler Yeats allowed or equipped him to see" ("Yeats, Synge, and the Tragic Understanding," *YeatsS*, 1972). S. B. Bushrui's "Synge and Yeats" (in Bushrui, *Sunshine*), calls special attention to Synge's influence during the early years of the theater movement.

Synge's relationship with Lady Gregory has been discussed by Elizabeth Coxhead in *Lady Gregory: A Literary Portrait* (1961; rev. 1966) and in "Synge and Lady Gregory" (in Bushrui, *Sunshine*). Coxhead posits little influence between the two beyond the influence of *Cuchulain of Muirthemne* on Synge's language, and she stresses Lady Gregory's efforts to win a hearing for Synge, efforts he seems not to have appreciated. She concludes that theirs was a "fine and generous literary friendship." A somewhat different impression is created by Ann Saddlemyer's "Synge and Some Companions, with a Note concerning a Walk through Connemara with Jack Yeats" (*YeatsS*, 1972). She quotes from Lady Gregory's correspondence the opinion that Synge was thankless and ingracious, and she contends that the "mythologizing" process Synge underwent at their hands required that Lady Gregory and Yeats not publicize Synge's human weaknesses. Saddlemyer's essay also discusses Synge's relationship with several other persons: she argues that Masefield did not know Synge well, that MacKenna was a friend with whom Synge could be completely himself, and that Synge and Jack Yeats became fast friends and had much in common.

K. P. S. Jochum (*Éire*, 1971), casts some light on Maud Gonne's attitude toward Synge by printing an article by Maud Gonne that appeared in *Les Entretiens Idéalistes* in January 1914, occasioned by a French production of *Playboy*. Maud Gonne says, "Synge has successfully managed to imitate [the Irish peasants'] dialect, but he never understood their soul."

Ronald Ayling has discussed Synge's relationship with Cherrie

Matheson in his "Synge's First Love: Some South African Aspects" (*MD*, 1964). Drawing on information from Cherrie's children, Ayling contends that Cherrie may not even have known of Synge's love for her until he proposed and concludes that her refusal was caused both by her lack of love for him and by their religious differences. Ayling also says that Cherrie seems to have sent Synge's letters to her to Synge's nephew, Edward Hutchinson Synge, who apparently destroyed them.

W. R. Rodgers' "J. M. Synge" is a script of Rodgers' BBC broadcast on Synge, compiled from interviews with various persons who knew Synge (in *Irish Literary Portraits*, 1972). Those participating include Seamus O'Sullivan, Edward Stephens, Richard Best, Oliver St. John Gogarty, George Roberts, Dossy Wright, and Fred O'Donovan.

Robin Skelton's *J. M. Synge and His World* (1971) contains no new biographical information of note, since, as Skelton explains, it is based largely on the Greene/Stephens biography and on *CW*. This well-written summary is interesting, however, for its 130 photographs relating to Synge (though several of the captions contain errors).

One aspect of Synge's personality that has occasioned discussion is his purported morbidity. Sean McMahon's "Clay and Worms" (*Éire*, 1970) argues that Synge was not morbid, but he does not present his thesis convincingly. He acknowledges that the poems are morbid and sees an apparent "unbridgeable gap between the man half-perceived in the plays and the wraith near-coffined in the poems." Briefly scanning the prose, he quotes a selected passage from the "Autobiography" to show that there is no morbidity there and implies that there is none anywhere in the "Autobiography." McMahon argues that Synge sees that "death is a part of life and preferable to the death-in-life of a soul without spirit." He does not deny that death plays a large part in Synge's work, but he does deny that this role is morbid. In closing he says, "Is all this morbidity? It depends on your definition." This is true, and McMahon never clarifies his own.

Roger Stillings, on the other hand, finds morbidity, or at least the reaction to death, the primary motive force behind Synge's work (*DM*, 1973). Stillings says, "Basically two broad categories of reaction [to death] can be determined, and they correspond roughly with the dominant mood of Synge's two major dramatic modes: first, the Dionysian rebellion against death that is the basis of life and the impetus for the comedies; second, the various ways of succumbing to death or the death motive—from timidity and conventionality to overwhelming grief or anger." Stillings discusses briefly each of the major plays except *Well of the Saints* in terms of this idea. The pervasiveness of morbidity in the plays for Stillings is shown by the range of characters he applies the term to: Nora and Dan Burke; Sarah Casey (even Mary Casey grapples with and overcomes it); Maurya; Deirdre; and Owen.

Alan Warner, in his "Astringent Joy: The Sanity of Synge" (*WascanaR*, 1971) rejects the charges of morbidity and the macabre brought against Synge. He contrasts Beckett's *All That Fall* with Synge's *Playboy* to argue that "although Synge had a deep vein of melancholy, his plays affirm a basic joy in life."

V. General Books and Essays

This section deals with books and monographs on Synge, listing them in chronological order. Comment here is directed toward giving an overview of each book, with attention to its scope, its emphases, its underlying theses. No attempt is made to summarize ideas about works or topics that are treated in the other sections of the chapter.

Three books on Synge appeared within four years of his death— Francis Bickley's *J. M. Synge and the Irish Dramatic Movement* (1912); P. P. Howe's *J. M. Synge: A Critical Study* (1912); and Maurice Bourgeois's *John Millington Synge and the Irish Theatre* (1913). All three writers were hampered by the inaccessibility of Synge's manuscripts and letters and the Synge family material. Bourgeois, by dint of impressive energy, meticulous care, and some degree of critical acumen, overcame the difficulties and produced a book that critics of Synge still need to consult. The two other books have worn less well.

Bickley's small book devotes four of its seven chapters to Synge, the rest dealing with other figures or aspects of the literary movement. He consistently praises Synge's plays and poetry, deeming *Riders* his greatest work—comparable to *Hamlet* or *Agamemnon*—and *Well of the Saints* his least interesting. He praises Synge's poems for "a good smell of earth" but values them primarily as "the personal confessions of an artist whose real art was objective," enabling us to see how Synge was "satisfied neither with modern romance, nor with modern symbolism, nor with modern realism." Bickley's biographical comments are now worthless, and his "discussions" of the individual plays are largely summary and quotation.

Howe's book deals more specifically with Synge, but its value too is vitiated by the large proportion of summary and of general, unremarkable comment. The chapter of most interest is that on "Design and Composition," where he emphasizes Synge's working from the concrete and particular outward, and his delight in sharp contrasts. Howe also points out Synge's linguistic debt to Lady Gregory and Douglas Hyde (citing specific examples in *Playboy*) and says that it is irrelevant whether any Irish people ever spoke in this fashion, for Synge developed "a speech that is apt for every demand put upon it for character and beauty."

Bourgeois's longer and fuller work discusses many aspects of Synge in detail. Bourgeois's biographical information is scant and unreliable, deriving mainly from statements by Yeats, Lady Gregory, and Masefield and from Synge's own works. Various literary influences on Synge are discussed, especially the French. He argues that Synge knew a considerable amount of modern Continental literature; he singles out Loti and Anatole France as important influences, but concludes that Synge remained fundamentally Irish. In discussing Synge's works, Bourgeois devotes most of his time to the plays, for he regards the prose as embryonic of the plays and the poetry as a by-product. He stresses Synge's opposition to the mystical lyricism of Yeatsian drama, his reaction against didacticism, and several themes that later critics have developed more fully: the influence of Synge on

Yeats; the "perpetual antagonism of Dream *versus* Reality," which
Bourgeois says is "the theme of all his dramatic writings"; Synge's
insensitivity to religion, especially to the Roman Catholicism of the
peasants; and his sensitivity to nature. Bourgeois's discussions of the
plays deal usually with their sources, their reception, and their critical
strengths and weaknesses. He considers *Riders* Synge's best play, *The
Tinker's Wedding* his least successful, and *Playboy*, though not
Synge's masterpiece, his most important contribution to the stage.
Synge's dialect, he acknowledges, is not a veridical presentation of
peasant speech, but it possesses great literary value. Bourgeois's book
is valuable too for its appendices, in which he lists all publications by
and about Synge to 1913; all known portraits; many of the versions of
the Deirdre story; and the dates, places, and casts of the first performances of Synge's plays. In short, while his biographical information is now valueless and he underestimates the prose and poetry (we
should remember that he had no access to unpublished material),
Bourgeois's discussions of the influences on Synge, of Synge's Irishness and of his language, and of recurrent themes in the plays are
substantial and have influenced many critics.

Daniel Corkery's *Synge and Anglo-Irish Literature* (1931), written
in a style sometimes vigorous and colorful, sometimes long-winded,
deals almost as much with the literary relations between the "two
Irelands" as with Synge. Corkery's approach to Synge and his evaluation of his works are dominated by the question of how fully Synge
managed to elude the Anglo-Irish ascendancy and discover and articulate Gaelic Ireland. While this makes for some provocative and
interesting observations, it also becomes a simplistic criterion of judgment. Corkery's discussion of "The Man," for example, turns almost
solely on Synge's "conversion" to nationalism and the quality of that
nationalism. *Riders to the Sea* is judged Synge's best play, because
there he came closest to full empathy with and expression of the true
Ireland. While Corkery's comments about individual works are sometimes surprising and shrewd, his persistent thesis gives a predictable
color to most of his discussions.

Samuel Synge's *Letters to My Daughter* is discussed above in the
section on biography.

Herbert Frenzel's *John Millington Synge's Work as a Contribution
to Irish Folk-Lore and to the Psychology of Primitive Tribes* (Duren,
1932) is a gathering of Synge's statements about various folklore
topics under appropriate headings (e.g., "Names and Surnames,"
"Dresses and Clothes," "Sports"). Frenzel collects statements primarily from *The Aran Islands*, to a lesser extent from the Wicklow,
Kerry, and Connemara essays, and still less from the plays. Though
he occasionally relates Synge's statements to those of scholars such as
Lévy-Bruhl, Frenzel provides no interpretation of Synge's ideas.
Some of the points Frenzel makes are elementary, and his own ideas
about primitive people and their language seem naïve.

Adelaide Duncan Estill's *The Sources of Synge* is discussed in the
section on sources, as is Jan Setterquist's *Ibsen and the Beginnings of
Anglo-Irish Drama*.

David H. Greene and Edward M. Stephens' *J. M. Synge 1871–*

1909 is the standard biography and is discussed above in the biography section.

Alan Price's *Synge and Anglo-Irish Drama* (1961) is a full-scale discussion of Synge's works. It has a chapter or section on each of the six plays, on the poems and translations, and on the prose works. It also discusses such general topics as "Synge's Idiom," "Yeats and Synge," and "Synge's Notions about Literature." With his helpful survey of Synge criticism, Price goes a long way toward placing Synge in the context of the Anglo-Irish dramatic movement. The book is avowedly an attempt to trace a theme through Synge's work: "The theme may be called the tension between dream and actuality. It occurs in various shapes, but they are all aspects of a basic tension between life and death, between an intuitive, imaginative outlook and a materialistic, mercenary outlook, between grace and physical progress, between loveliness and desolation. Mingled with this tension is an ever present and deep awareness both of close links between Man and the natural world and also of the mutability of life and beauty." In practice, this "theme" is broad enough and Price's analyses flexible enough, so that the approach is not as procrustean as one might fear, and the result is detailed and helpful analysis of Synge's works.

Donna Gerstenberger's *John Millington Synge* (1964) is a general, introductory work but is nevertheless interesting and perceptive. Its opening chapter deals mainly with *The Aran Islands* and the Wicklow and Kerry essays, approaching them in terms of what they reveal about Synge's mind and his views of art. This is followed by a chapter on each of the plays; one on the poems, verse plays, and translations; and a brief concluding chapter on the Synge-Yeats relationship and on Synge's influence, reputation, and achievement. Other general topics are discussed in relation to various plays. Discussions of the plays are intelligent and never purely laudatory. While Gerstenberger is interested in Synge's recurrent themes, she tries to avoid approaching the works in terms of preset ideas.

Denis Johnston's pamphlet *John Millington Synge* (1965) is a sympathetic and intelligent account of the man and the plays. In his biographical presentation, drawn from Greene/Stephens, he emphasizes (perhaps overemphasizes) the rationalist and anticlerical strains in Synge's temperament. He also praises Synge as an interpreter of the people of Ireland and his use of an admittedly stylized Anglo-Irish dialect. In his discussions of the plays, he frequently points out how Synge's technique or attitude foreshadows more recent tendencies in later drama. The brief discussions of the plays are shrewd and provocative, though his suggestion that the Douls prefer to remain blind because "they are each unfortunate in a particular spouse" is an atypical lapse. *Shadow of the Glen* he sees as a play that "offends against all the canons of good melodrama, while looking like a melodrama"; *Riders* is an Oresteian tragedy in which there is no choice available, only a protest against the law of life. *The Tinker's Wedding* Johnston finds to be infected in its ending by Synge's animus against Roman clergy; *Playboy* is filled with appropriate and skillful psychological ambiguities; *Deirdre* presents another quintessentially Irish femme fatale.

Ann Saddlemyer's pamphlet *J. M. Synge and Modern Comedy* (1968) approaches the plays in terms of three varieties of conflict that permeate them. The first of these involves awareness of nature's beauty, sensuality, and richness on the one hand; and its ugliness, darkness, and decay on the other. The second involves "the conflict within his characters between the life surrounding them and the dream of escape into a world of beauty and joy which cannot wither"; the third, explored mainly through *Well of the Saints* and *Playboy*, involves the power of the imagination.

Robin Skelton's brief illustrated biography is noted above in the biography section. His *The Writings of J. M. Synge* (1971), the first critical work to appear after *CW*, includes critical discussion of every facet of Synge's canon, including the early autobiographical writings, *When the Moon Has Set*, the fragmentary verse plays, and the *Manchester Guardian* essays, as well as the usual works. The book eschews annotation and caters to the needs of general readers and students by attempting to make each chapter a separate entity. Among the themes that nevertheless reoccur are the idea that several of Synge's works were reactions against certain of Yeats's works, presenting a hard, unsentimental foil to Yeats's dreaminess; and that Synge was a major influence on Yeats's poetry. Skelton also presents Synge as a champion of individual liberty and a forerunner of certain contemporary attitudes, such as black humor and the "hippies." Skelton's presentation occasionally takes on political overtones, as when *Well of the Saints* is presented in terms of the "inalienable right" of the Douls to their dream, or when we are told that Martin "unwittingly epitomizes heroically one aspect of the Protestant ethic and the principle of dissent." Other recurrent ideas are Synge's "anti-clericalism" and the grouping of *Riders to the Sea, Shadow of the Glen, The Tinker's Wedding*, and *Playboy* as "shanachie plays," the first three of these forming a trilogy with some progression among its parts. But Skelton fails to define precisely either anticlericalism or shanachie play, forcing the reader to infer their meanings from his occasional uses of the terms. It is unclear whether anticlericalism implies Synge's opposition to one denomination of Christianity, to institutionalized Christianity, or to the entire religious sensibility. The shanachie plays apparently derive from stories told by shanachies; they have a "conglomerate quality" and a "mythic element," but these are vague and general characteristics. Skelton's views on the plays (summarized elsewhere) are usually interesting and distinctive. About the poetry, he stresses two ideas: first, the influence of Synge's poetry on that of Yeats; second, Synge's success in producing in his poetry a persona that is his greatest contribution to the poetry of our time and an important formative influence on Yeats after 1908. These points are more fully discussed elsewhere but are mentioned here for sake of contrast with Skelton's *J. M. Synge* (1972). While in some respects predictably a précis of the longer 1971 book, it is in other ways puzzlingly different. For example, the anticlericalism theme is more lightly handled; there is no suggestion of the shanachie plays as a genre; and the discussion of the poetry lacks the idea of the persona and of the influence on Yeats. Skelton seems even to contradict his earlier view of the persona when he says that the poems "are often filled with the vitality of his love for Molly," that the translations were "just as personal to him as his own poems," that one translation was "made as a direct rebuke to Molly," and that the poems "carry a great deal of his own emotional situation." The student who reads both of these books is puzzled to know whether the later one is an incomplete version of the former, presents a pruning away of inessentials, or represents a change of mind.

Paul M. Levitt's and E. H. Mikhail's bibliographies are discussed above in the section on secondary bibliography. Edward Stephens' *My Uncle John* is discussed above in the section on biography.

In addition to the books and monographs described above, several *Festschriften* and special issues of periodicals relating to Synge have appeared. The December 1961 issue of *Modern Drama*, a Synge and O'Casey number, contained five essays on Synge. The March–April 1971 issue of *Ireland of the Welcomes* was a special Synge issue. Four essays on Synge are to be found in the Fall 1971 issue of *Mosaic*. Six essays on various aspects of Synge's life and work are included in *Yeats Studies* (No. 2, 1972).

J. M. Synge Centenary Papers 1971 (ed. Maurice Harmon, 1972) contains eleven essays on various aspects of Synge's life and work, most of them focusing not on an individual work but on a topic (e.g., the prose, the poetry). There is an index and a list of contributors.

S. B. Bushrui's *Sunshine and the Moon's Delight: A Centenary Tribute to John Millington Synge 1871–1909* (1972) contains twenty-three essays on a wide range of topics. There are essays on each of the plays, on *The Aran Islands*, on the "Autobiography," and on the poems as well as discussions of Synge's relationships with Yeats and Lady Gregory and a series of essays discussing his influence on modern Irish drama, the Arab world, Japan, France, and Germany. There is also a select bibliography, an updating of A. Price's survey of Synge criticism, a glossary of Synge's works, and an index.

Three books provide gatherings of previously published essays on one of Synge's works. Henry Popkin's edition of *Playboy* (1967) provides a text of the play, some relevant excerpts from Synge's other works, and parts or all of various essays by W. B. Yeats, David H. Greene, Ronald Peacock, Norman Podhoretz, Ronald Gaskell, and Ann Saddlemyer. Thomas R. Whitaker's *Twentieth Century Interpretation of* The Playboy of the Western World (1969) collects part or all of eleven essays, with an introduction by Whitaker.

David R. Clark's casebook on *Riders to the Sea* (1970) provides a text of the play, plus part or all of twelve discussions of it.

The following are some of the more important or representative general essays or chapters on Synge.

Cornelius Weygandt's laudatory essay in *Irish Plays and Playwrights* (1913) focuses mostly on the tonal qualities in Synge's work, saying that "incongruity . . . is of the very texture of Synge's art, which has reconciled qualities . . . never before reconciled in English literature." Weygandt begins by emphasizing the omnipresent joy and exultation in Synge's writing. Having set this keynote, he turns to the extravagance, grotesquerie, and irony blended into the works. He acknowledges a sardonic quality in Synge's humor, but says, "the more I read him, the less cruel and sardonic that humor seems." He particularly praises Synge's style and characterization as his main claims to greatness. Weygandt praises all of the plays but has a relatively low opinion of *Riders*, criticizing its crowding of events and calling it unrepresentative in its single tone, its lack of humor, and its relative lack of originality. He treats the verse and "travel sketches" as interesting revelations of Synge himself and as background to his plays.

Ernest Boyd, in *Ireland's Literary Renaissance* (1916; rev. 1922), is interested in Synge's influence in bringing Irish peasant drama into being but is aware that Synge's work transcends that category. While Boyd sees Synge as a "realist" only in a sense that would encompass Cervantes, he says that later playwrights "followed him only where he was most easily imitated" and "adopted his external procedure, ignoring the attitude of mind which brought him to the peasantry." Boyd calls Synge "one of the great dramatists of European literature" and praises all the plays except *The Tinker's Wedding*. While acknowledging the importance of French literature to Synge, he stresses that his roots and sources are native Irish. Boyd's generally perceptive comments about the plays have been echoed and expanded by later critics.

L. A. G. Strong's monograph *John Millington Synge* (1941; mainly an expansion of the *Bookman* and *Dublin Review* essay) consists largely of secondhand judgments and of quotations. He does devote a large proportion of his essay to Synge's poems and translations, and he notes the influence of Synge's poetry on "almost all his successors in Ireland, including Yeats." He says, "The outstanding quality of Synge's work is its intensity."

Una Ellis-Fermor, in *The Irish Dramatic Movement* (1939; rev. 1954), sees as the "peculiar characteristic of Synge that he is at once a nature-mystic and a dramatist, that the two things are one in him, as perhaps in no other poet before him. Stressing that Synge seems "to carry on unbroken the tradition of ancient Irish nature poetry," she says "it was no less than a miracle that he found . . . the race of people who were themselves the inheritors of the original Irish worship of nature." She examines the plays to reveal the various facets of nature they emphasize. *Playboy* is seen as the work that "shows his dramatic power at its ripest," but *Deirdre* is the "consummation of his dual power, that of dramatist and of nature mystic." Noting the "curious absence of metaphysical or religious implication in the tragedies," Ellis-Fermor speculates that the "synthesis of Synge's mind is not so complete as we had at first supposed."

Herbert Howarth, in *The Irish Writers 1880–1940: Literature under Parnell's Star* (1958), discusses several aspects of Synge's work and responses to it. He stresses first of all the new element Synge brought to the dramatic movement—his amorality, his unwillingness to impose doctrine on his material, and his energy. He praises Synge's realism, which, however "doubled reality into surreality, giving Ireland what she lacked as well as what she showed him"; and Synge's intuitive control of the dramatic medium, already present in *Shadow* but particularly evident in *Playboy*. He discusses the effect of *Playboy* on the dramatic movement, and describes Synge's "free-minded-ness," an "offense" that "did away with the accepted scale of values and postulated a new scale graded according to energy." He discusses Synge's rapid fame in Europe and England, and the later cooling of British response, especially among the Bloomsbury group; and, finally, he speculates on Synge's effects on the young James Joyce.

F. L. Lucas' long chapter on Synge in his *The Drama of Synge, Yeats, and Pirandello* (1963) draws its biographical information mainly from Greene/Stephens, and his discussions of the plays often consist largely of summary and quotation. He admires the language of *Shadow* but feels uneasy about the ending, concluding grudgingly that "under the spell of that entrancing style I have no difficulty in suspending any scepticism I might incline to feel." *Riders* is judged a little thin and hurried, the characters a little dim, the language less colored, vivid, and exciting than in the other plays. *The Tinker's Wedding* is passed over quickly as a slighter work than the others. In *Well of the Saints*, Lucas discusses the theme of "the blessing of illusion" and Synge's possible sources. His section on *Playboy* consists largely of summary and quotation from the play and a description of its reception and speculation as to the causes. While he admires *Deirdre*, he stresses its unfinished state and calls it "a play with first-rate passages rather than a first-rate play." In conclusion he suggests that "Perhaps Synge's greatest achievements were that he found a new corner of the world to write of; took the trouble to know thoroughly what he wrote of; and worded his writing in a style both new and bewitching."

Elizabeth Coxhead's pamphlet *J. M. Synge and Lady Gregory* (1969) is a general survey that brings no new facts or interpretations to light.

Raymond Williams' chapter "J. M. Synge" in his *Drama from Ibsen to Eliot* (1952; rev. 1969) classifies each of Synge's plays except *Deirdre* under some species of Naturalism and is most concerned with how the dramatic language relates to other aspects of the dramas. Language is all that distinguishes *Shadow of the Glen* from other Naturalist comedy, he says, and the paradox of *Riders to the Sea* resides in "the depth of its language and the starved, almost passive experience." Only in *Playboy* does he think Synge succeeds in "integrating the range of language with an action to which the range is relevant."

Emil Roy's chapter "J. M. Synge" (in his *British Drama since Shaw*, 1972) continues the depiction of Synge as aloof, objective, and antididactic. Roy deals briefly with each of the plays and calls attention to several recurrent motifs and themes, including "Synge's refusal to disguise, even in his endings, a deep anxiety that talk, homoerotic competition and affection, or stereotyped diversions may be inadequate defenses against engulfment by a threatening matrix, whether it be aggressive women, paranoid social groups, or a beautiful but indifferent nature."

Clifford Leech's "John Synge and the Drama of His Time" (*MD*, 1973) compares Synge with several of his contemporaries, discusses his language, and deals briefly with each of the plays. Leech stresses Synge's affinities with such writers as Ibsen, Zola, and Conrad—affinities Synge himself seems not to have recognized. Synge's Anglo-Irish background, says Leech, enabled him to overcome the general erosion of the dramatic potentialities of English in his day.

VI. *Studies of the Drama*

THE SHADOW OF THE GLEN

The Shadow of the Glen, Synge's first play to be performed, has received only a moderate amount of critical attention. The main topics of discussion have been its source and Synge's adaptation of it, whether the play degrades the Irish peasantry, and the appropriateness or realism of the ending.

Discussion of the play got off to a rocky start with the generally hostile reactions of the early reviewers, who accused the play of distorting, even libeling, the image of Irish woman. The charge was led by Arthur Griffith, who declared the play no more Irish than the *Decameron*, called it "a corrupt version of that old-world libel on womankind—the 'Widow of Ephesus,'" and said that Synge's Irish woman "never existed in the flesh in Wicklow nor in any other of the thirty-two counties" (*UI*, 17 Oct. 1903; for other responses and details of the play's reception, see Ch. ix of Greene/Stephens).

M. Bourgeois (*JMS&IT*), however, affirms the play to be Irish and describes it as "a bitter sketch of the loveless marriages of Irish country-folk." He talks most about the tramps and the primitiveness and poetic revolt against settled existence that they represent for Synge and for Anglo-Irish writers generally. He sees Nora as the most vitally arresting figure, with her poetic desire for something new and exciting, a desire she satisfies through the tramp. Nevertheless, Bourgeois still admits that he is puzzled as to why Nora goes off with the tramp.

Daniel Corkery (*S&A-IL*) acknowledges that the plot derives from the story Synge heard on the Aran Islands, and he approaches the play in terms of the changes Synge made—most of them, Corkery believes, mistaken. He objects that while the original story was comedy with a dash of the illicit, we cannot tell whether Synge's play is comic or tragic, nor could Synge. The play, he charges, swings incongruously back and forth between comedy and tragedy, is too small for the various changes of mood that occur in it, and involves "uncertain psychology." Nora, for example, exhibits a "disparate" character, at times "wearing her lusts upon her sleeve, a being all appetite and no faculty," and then showing an incongruous melancholy.

David H. Greene is concerned to show both that the story behind the play is authentically Irish and that the ending of the play combines realism and symbolism (*PMLA*, 1947). While he sees the play as "essentially the tragedy of a young girl condemned to a life of loneliness with her crusty old husband," he stresses that we must not see Nora as a woman of the world seeking sexual fulfillment, nor the tramp as a mere opportunist, for to do so would destroy the symbolism the play moves into at its conclusion. Just how literally Greene means us to take his claim that the play becomes symbolic at its ending remains unclear, as does his attitude toward whether Synge justifies or wins assent to the supposed shift of mode. He concludes that "the tramp is not flesh and blood: he is a password to happiness." In the second half of his article, Greene traces the play to *The Aran Islands* and several versions of the story in Irish folklore.

Alan Price stresses how Synge has individualized and humanized the type figures he derived from Pat Dirane's story (*S&A-ID*). Nora embodies the tension between emotional fulfillment and material security which is at the heart of Synge's work—opposites represented by her husband, Dan, and the old Tramp. Price also emphasizes the role of setting or environment, calling it one of the most active forces in the play. He specifically counters several of Corkery's criticisms, finding in the play a subtlety, complexity, and mastery of dramatic technique that fuses disparate elements into a whole.

Donna Gerstenberger regards the play as only partially successful (*JMS*). She makes two specific criticisms. First, Synge does not adequately dramatize the conflicts of the play, especially the conflict between the worlds of Dan Burke and Patch Darcy. Second, the ending "seems highly romanticized and unjustified by the action of the play." Gerstenberger quotes with approval Frank O'Connor's judgment (in *The Irish Theatre*, ed. Lennox Robinson, 1939) that Nora's leaving with the Tramp "is arbitrary and comes not out of life but literature—middle class literature."

Though every commentator on the play touches on Synge's adaptation of it from Pat Dirane's folktale, Robin Skelton argues that in modifying the story for the stage Synge "deliberately brought it closer in both mood and plot to the classical folk-tale" (*WJMS*) and that Synge's letter to Griffith about the source was disingenuous. Skelton proposes that *Riders to the Sea, Shadow of the Glen,* and *The Tinker's Wedding* form a kind of trilogy, involving a progression, for as we move in the trilogy of "Shanachie plays" (discussed in the previous section) from *Riders* through *Shadow* to *Tinker's Wedding,* "the age of the central female character diminishes and the psychological complexity of the drama increases." Skelton calls *Shadow of the Glen* a transitional play, where "the main themes of Synge's drama are first effectively, though perhaps summarily, displayed, and the main varieties of his characterization suggested." He sees the play as dominated by Nora, the most "trapped and bitter" of Synge's heroines, and dwells more on her sexual hunger and frustration than have previous critics. The "lyricism and bitterness" of the play reveal it as "the precursor of much black comedy, and the true forerunner of *Juno and the Paycock* and *Waiting for Godot.*"

Jean Alexander sees in the play a tension between the external action and the action of imagination (in Bushrui, *Sunshine*). The external action is presented mainly through a stock, comic plot, while the countering imaginative action is necessarily verbal. The first represents "nature," the second "imagination," and Eros is the power in nature and man that enables the reconciliation of the two. Alexander concludes, "The proposition of *The Shadow of the Glen* is that the tragic recognition of the nature of mortality leads to a choice of total, if brief, experience in which the fruition of life is in exposure and sensuous vulnerability."

Paul N. Robinson (*CEA*, 1974) finds beneath the surface of the play "a medieval allegory on spirit *vs.* matter and time." In Robinson's unlikely schema, old Dan represents Time, Michael is Worldly Goods or matter, the tramp is *res spirituales* or the soul, Patch stands for faith, and Nora becomes Everyman.

Nicholas Grene (*MD*, 1974) explores certain uses of repetition and allusion to show how Synge achieves depth and subtlety. Grene discusses the use of Dan's repetitions of overheard conversation to show his obsessions, the association of the repeated references to sheep with death, the dark connotations of the repeated allusions to shadows, and the references to offstage characters to reveal Nora's plight. He concludes that Synge's use of these techniques enables him to achieve a level of dramatic response that varies from "situation comedy through 'problem play' and 'peasant naturalism' to a drama of poetic symbolism."

RIDERS TO THE SEA

While there have been a few dissenting voices, *Riders* has been the most consistently, if not the most highly, praised of all Synge's plays, and the volume of criticism devoted to it has been second only to that given to *Playboy*. The most persistent issue has been the question of the play's status as tragedy—whether or not it is a tragedy and how its mode of tragedy relates to traditional definitions of the genre. Several critics have argued in different veins that the play stands apart from Synge's other plays, and several have praised and attempted to account for its intensity.

P. P. Howe (*JMSCS*) certainly expressed a minority opinion when he contrasted *Riders* unfavorably with *Shadow*, calling it "not so perfect a masterpiece in one act as . . . *In the Shadow of the Glen*." His criticism, which has been echoed by some later critics, is that the great rapidity of presentation of events involves a necessary unreality and constitutes a structural flaw in the play. M. Bourgeois (*JMS&IT*) thinks highly of the play, laying stress on the certainty of its development, a certainty so great that it removes all suspense. He says that Synge's fatalism in the play is "a distinctly Pagan, hence artistic, fatalism" and compares the play to Aeschylean tragedy. The one flaw in the play for Bourgeois is the bringing of the drowned body onto the stage, though this is redeemed by the august solemnity of the ending.

Hugh I'A. Fausset is one of those whose appreciation of the play is muted by its failure to achieve tragedy ("Synge and Tragedy," *FortR*, 1924). He calls *Riders* "perhaps the most relentlessly melancholy and yet the least tragic of his plays" and says, "Such a one-sided conflict is pitiful beyond words, but humanity is too dwarfed a participator in the contest, the idea is too slenderly opposed to the natural for tragedy of a high significance."

Daniel Corkery (*S&A-IL*) calls Synge particularly fortunate in his choice of theme in this play—it brought out the best and even more than the best in him. Given Synge's Anglo-Irish background, says Corkery, he succeeded surprisingly well in evoking Gaelic culture: "It was Synge's thorough immersion in the matter he dealt with, his feeling for it, the surrender of himself to its genius, that in this case enabled him to create a piece of art that is at once local and universal in its appeal."

R. L. Collins approaches the play in terms of its uniqueness in Synge's canon (*UKCR*, 1947). Arguing that "one side of Synge's nature finds expression in *Riders to the Sea*; the other side, in all the other plays," Collins explains that in this play alone Synge deliberately dehumanizes his characters, denying "all personality and individuality in favor of depicting the forces that governed the lives of these people." While Collins overstates the uniqueness of the play, the point about the impersonality of the characters has been echoed by several other critics.

Denis Donoghue begins "Synge: 'Riders to the Sea': A Study" (*UnivR*, 1955) by arguing that the "relationship between 'Catholic' and 'Pagan' becomes one of the most significant of the dramatic tensions established within the context of 'Riders to the Sea': the tension between orthodox, institutional religion and the implacable power of the Sea." While Maurya does achieve "Acceptance," he contends, the scales are so heavily weighted against her that no action on her part is possible, no purpose can be formulated, and that for such reasons the play cannot be called a tragedy.

Alan Price typically defends the play in every respect (*S&A-ID*). In a detailed analysis he illustrates the progression and the variety and contrast of texture, pace, and mood of the play by discussing its four movements, which, he contends, are "parts of a seamless whole." He regards the play as a tragedy, calls Maurya "the true tragic protagonist," and contends that "at the end one feels that remarkable exultation which is at the heart of real tragedy." Maurya, having supped pain, horror, and agony, goes on to achieve calm and compassion, humility and charity, reconciliation and a new concern for others.

Thomas F. Van Laan, in a long, detailed analysis of the play (*DramaS*, 1964), deals with two questions: the precise identity of Maurya's antagonist and Synge's means of establishing it; and the several ways that the formal elements of the play work to achieve its intense and unique effect. Noting that most critics have identified the protagonist as the sea, Van Laan says that he prefers Una Ellis-Fermor's more general term Nature; but he then argues that the identity of the protagonist is inseparable from the problem of form in the play—that finally the formal elements *define* the protagonist. He sees the play as tragic and Synge as the "tragic hero": "Through form, through the total movement of the piece and all its parts, Synge has achieved perception, and in the fulness of that perception, no matter how frightening the prospect discovered, lies the resolution of tragedy."

Donna Gerstenberger (*JMS*) notes that the play is atypical of Synge's work in its lack of social concern and the absence of conflict between the individual and society. She praises its inevitability and economy, which she attributes largely to Synge's subtle use of certain images or analogies, to a sense of repetition derived from recurrent patterns of events, and to the poetic language. Specific examples of these techniques that she cites are Synge's use of an implicit analogy between the three women of the play and the three fates; the horses, which echo the horses of the Apocalypse; the loaf and holy water; and the colors of the play, especially red, white, and black.

William W. Combs (*Papers of the Michigan Acad. of Science, Arts, and Letters*, 1965) stresses Maurya's centrality and argues that, partly through the merging of all her lost men in her mind, she becomes "almost a high priestess of sorrow." In the same vein, "All Maurya's praying, sorrow, and loss can be viewed as part of a ritual of propitiation for what she has done—her having brought into the world children who have no future except to go out on the cruel sea and die, or to become old and broken." The world of the play is "an elemental, pagan world, over which only a veneer of civilization and religion exists," and the sea has a dual nature as "a source of both life and death." He concludes that while Synge's "deep and despairing pessimism" did not permit the play to follow the conventional form of tragedy to any resolution ending in hopefulness and reconciliation, the drama does enable us to feel, in Nietzsche's phrase, the "'metaphysical comfort . . . that, in spite of the flux of phenomena, life at bottom is indestructibly powerful and pleasurable.'"

Ryder Hector Currie and Martin Bryan's "*Riders to the Sea*: Reappraised" (*TQ*, 1968) is a freewheeling approach to the play, more suggestive than substantial. They call the play "an archetypal mystery, a mystery of the duality infusing all, of the mystic union of opposites, the *coincidentia oppositorum* of the alchemists and mystics." They view Maurya as related to the Morrigan in Celtic myth and to the Icelandic nightmare hag the *mara*. They also attribute to Synge a letter of doubtful provenance.

Malcolm Pittock (*ES*, 1968), in one of the few negative essays on the play, opposes the many critics who feel an unsatisfactoriness in the play's lack of tragic conflict; he locates the trouble elsewhere, mainly in Synge's ambiguous presentation of the beliefs of the island community: "though Synge enables us to appreciate the function of the islanders' pattern of belief, he cheats us, for the sake of effect, into actively assenting to some of its least acceptable elements." Specifically, Pittock is disturbed by the justification of Maurya's "subjective misgivings," her implicit belief in fate. It is, he says "one thing for Maurya to see a vision and to believe that vision fulfilled, but quite another for a modern audience, formed in a different cultural pattern, to believe in such superstition with any real seriousness." For Pittock the play "offers two incompatible attitudes to the experience it presents: one that takes it seriously and one that exploits it sensationally," and the result is that "the play is a mixture of tragedy and melodrama."

Paul M. Levitt (*Éire*, 1969) also attempts to explain the "extraordinary compactness and intensity" of the play. Levitt attributes these virtues to two factors: the biblical imagery of the play and its careful organization. The imagery he traces to the fatal ride of the Pharaoh's horsemen in Exodus (the title deriving specifically from Exodus xv.1), and from the Four Horsemen of the Apocalypse in

Revelation vi.1–8. About the organization, he says, "Synge captures the pattern of death by focussing on a point shortly before the end of the cycle, dramatizing only the last two deaths in the family—those of Michael and Bartley. In this way, and by careful exposition, he compresses past and present action into the closing moments of a tragedy long unfolding." Levitt's chapter "The Whole Analysis: *Riders to the Sea*," in his *A Structural Approach to the Analysis of Drama* (1971), expands these ideas, with emphasis on how the structural aspects of the play contribute to its overall effect.

Robin Skelton's discussion (*WJMS*) ranges over several aspects of the play. Skelton compares and contrasts it with Yeats's *Cathleen Ni Houlihan*, pointing to some "mathematically precise contrasts" and arguing that *Riders* is in some ways "a counterblast to Yeats." He spends most of his time, however, discussing the mythic parallels and archetypal symbolism of the play: he compares Bartley's death with that of Hippolytus and comments on Synge's use of number (especially nine), birds, and horses in the play, contending that Synge "filled *Riders to the Sea* with mythic intimations." He also briefly and generally compares and contrasts the play with Greek tragedy. He discounts the role of Christianity in the world of the play, contending even that the "Holy Water" Maurya sprinkles on Bartley is water she collects from the Spring Well in the nights after Samhain.

Errol Durbach, in "Synge's Tragic Vision of the Old Mother and the Sea" (*MD*, 1972), reads the play as "a delicately wrought, perfectly constructed tragedy," built around Maurya's growing awareness and acceptance of her own "implication in the death of her sons which converts pathos into a tragic vision of existence." Comparing Maurya with other mothers—Mrs. Alving, Mother Courage, and the Mother in *Blood Wedding*—as instances of the Pietà, he notes that "in each case the tragedy derives from this collision within the protagonist of intense maternal love and her own firmly held moral values." He considers Maurya "her own antagonist, embodying within her maternal function that universal principle of destruction suggested through the pervasive symbolism of the sea." Further comparing Maurya and the sea, Durbach stresses the scene in which her "white, tossed hair" is revealed, and says, "If, like the sea she is the womb of life, she is also, like the sea, the natural source of her children's death as well." He concludes that "the splendour of Maurya's growth towards a confrontation of this Necessity" (that death comes to all) makes *Riders to the Sea* "a perfectly conceived and exquisitely wrought tragedy of the Sorrowing Mother and her fated sons."

T. R. Henn (in Bushrui, *Sunshine*) draws heavily on his comments in his introduction to his edition of Synge's *Plays and Poems* (1963). He evokes briefly some of the features of the world of the Aran Islands of Synge's day, notes some of the archetypal or "depth-images" of the play, compares and contrasts the play with Greek tragedy, and praises it as perhaps the only one-act tragedy in literature.

David R. Clark's "Synge's 'Perpetual "Last Day" '": Remarks on *Riders to the Sea*" (in Bushrui, *Sunshine*; essentially the same as Clark's introd. to his 1970 casebook on *Riders to the Sea*) makes two main points. The first stresses the apocalyptic imagery and the importance of Michael (who bears an archangel's name); the second argues against Yeats's view that the play is too passive in suffering. Clark contends that the play does have an "action" and even a "tragic rhythm," these being centered in Maurya's suffering and the "sense of heightened life" that results from it: "If there is too much passive suffering, not enough positive will in Maurya and her play—that is because Synge chose an action which is suffering, the action of enduring. The fault, then, if any, is in the aim and not the execution." But Clark feels that there is no fault and that this play is, in the Aristotelian sense, "one of the great modern tragedies."

Daniel Casey (*AntigR*, 1972) takes off from Synge's fascination with the primitive, exotic world of the Gael, especially with its blending of pagan and Christian, and emphasizes the importance of setting to what Synge achieves in the play: " 'Riders to the Sea' succeeds largely because it realized an Aran-consciousness and has a subtle awareness that character and situation are somehow subordinated to setting." Casey quotes the relevant passages from *The Aran Islands*, echoing T. R. Henn's observations about the archetypal quality of much of the imagery. While he does refer to the "final cathartic realization of man's tenuous existence in the cosmos," he talks of the play more as elegy than tragedy and says that it "reaches Greek-perfection not because it is Aristotelian, but because it translates a primitive Gaelic experience which is also universal."

THE TINKER'S WEDDING

The Tinker's Wedding has received less critical attention than any other of Synge's plays, and what it has received has been variable. Those who dislike the play think that Synge's animus against the clergy got out of hand; those who like it feel that the comic, farcical presentation sublimates any bad spirit. Almost all critics remark upon the foiling of two cultures, that of the tinkers and that of settled society.

Maurice Bourgeois sees two purposes in the play—to depict the life of the tinkers; and to present the two types of Irish civilization, heathen and Christian (*JMS&IT*). But he regards it as an immature comedy upon a slender theme, in which the depiction of a tinker woman as an "earnest Catholic," the "malignant portraiture of a covetous priest," and the "grotesque blasphemousness of its language" cause it to offend against esthetic decency and good taste. What humor it has involves a fierce, scorching, and sinister irony that leaves one on the borderland between joy and sadness, and Bourgeois concludes that the comedy is illustrative of Synge's peculiarly nonreligious attitude.

Daniel Corkery too is severe on the play, finding the "true Synge" only in the depiction of Mary Byrne and in her monologue ending Act I (*S&A-IL*). For the rest, he finds hardly a note of poetry in the play, and he is bothered by the contrivance of the tin-can device. Finally, he sees Synge's depiction of the priest less as an attack than as a depiction of an extreme variation from type that no Irish audience could accept.

David H. Greene briefly reviews the process of composition through six successive manuscript versions, in the course of which the play evolved from one act to two (*PMLA*, 1947). This expansion, in Greene's view, reveals the main value of the play—it is a connecting link between the one-act plays of Synge's apprenticeship and the three-act plays of his maturity. As for its quality, Greene calls the play an artistic failure and the publication of it a mistake: "it contains a crude farcical element which is typical of Synge, little or no deftness of characterization, perhaps one good scene at the end where the tinkers rush off in confusion with the priest's curses ringing in their ears, and a few passages of lyric vigor such as one associates with Synge's best writing." As an example of this vigor, Greene quotes the same passage spoken by Mary at the end of Act 1 that Corkery praised.

Denis Donoghue tries to redeem the play, suggesting that significant aspects of it have escaped notice (*IW*, 1955). Seeing the play as a successful comic farce, he argues that, though the characters may not be delineated in detail, "Synge has contrived his comic effects from the sheer interplay of attitudes on certain questions of morality and social living." The whole action of the play derives from Sarah's "unnatural" hankering after marriage (an institution not of her own society, but of orthodox religious society). Donoghue examines several passages to show that the comedy "depends on the mock-conflict between certain attitudes in the tinkers themselves and all those other conventions which are covered by the word 'orthodoxy.'"

Alan Price's discussion is the first to treat the characters as fully rounded and worthy of analysis (*S&A-ID*). Predictably, he sees the play as another variation on the theme of dream versus actuality and as embodying a tension between a cautious, respectable, settled way of life and an unrestrained, materially insecure way allowing scope for passion and imagination. He compares Sarah's situation with that of Nora in *Shadow*, seeing Sarah's environment as wholesome for her and her dream of respectable marriage as a chimera. While he acknowledges some contrast between Christian and pagan in the play, he points out that the two worlds have filtered into each other. Price praises Synge's characterization of Mary which contrasts her generosity and candor with the priest's avarice and hypocrisy. Consistently laudatory, Price regards the play as a successful presentation, in terms of exhilarating comedy, of recurrent themes and characters in Synge's works.

Most of Donna Gerstenberger's chapter on this play (*JMS*) deals with the large, general issues growing out of it—Synge's attitudes toward the Church and toward comedy—rather than with the play itself, which she clearly does not regard as successful drama. She specifically criticizes Synge's failure to clarify the motivation behind Sarah's desire for marriage; she regards the whole play as an "inflated incident" and inferior drama hardly worth staging; and she shares David Greene's opinion that the play is primarily illustrative of Synge's transition from the one-act to the three-act form.

Robin Skelton approaches the play as the third of Synge's "shanachie plays" (*WJMS*). He discusses earlier drafts of the play, especially Synge's use of tinker children, whose talk of a "green man" imports into the play the idea that pre-Christian customs co-exist with Christianity as part of the tinkers' inheritance. While Synge later eliminated the children from the play, they reveal themes he presented more subtly in the final version. For Skelton, Sarah Casey, in the wildness of her imagination and her excited language, represents this cultural heritage. Her yearning for marriage is a yearning for the greatest novelty she could experience, that of becoming part of an established moral and social order. Mary combines in her outlook the pagan and the ostensibly Christian. The priest is a reasonably friendly man, and we are to admire the resourcefulness and cunning he shows at the end of the play. Skelton concludes that in this play, "Synge chose by means of rollicking farce to present a conflict that has become in the ensuing years ever more central to our Western society."

For Vivian Mercier (in Bushrui, *Sunshine*) the weakest point in the play is the ambiguous treatment of the priest. We are shocked by the rough treatment he receives from the tinkers, a violence that seems forced, melodramatic, esthetically out of place in a comedy, and lacking in credibility. Mercier would have preferred the violence against the priest to have been left as mere threat, for by enacting it the tinkers forfeit our sympathy and force us to see the priest as a martyr. Mercier points out that Synge's comedies are essentially "mock-pastoral," in that the values of an "antisociety" are contrasted with those of established society and shown to be equally valid. In the other three comedies our hearts go with the antiheroes as they depart, but in *Tinker's*, Mercier says, it is doubtful that they do, although Synge probably intended that they should. Mercier then raises the broader question of how much of the apparently pastoral drama of the Irish Literary Revival was really closer to mock-pastoral: "Here lies the crux: in what sense were the early Abbey Theatre plays 'their own' for the Irish country people?" Mercier concludes that while we cannot accuse Synge of malice, and he is closer to the Irish tradition than most of his critics would admit, he does show a lack of empathy or of tact: *The Tinker's Wedding* ends too savagely, because the savagery is "wreaked on one who is essentially kindly and muddleheaded, for all the awesome power that stands behind his priestly office."

THE WELL OF THE SAINTS

The Well of the Saints has produced more variable evaluations than any other of Synge's plays. Irish reviewers and critics were from the first harsh on the play (though for a variety of reasons), but the actors who performed it generally praised it. As elsewhere, chauvinistic critics detected slander of the Irish and of their religion. More recent critical debate has turned mainly on the implications of the Douls's refusal to have their sight restored a second time.

P. P. Howe (*JMSCS*) praises the stagecraft, "Synge's astonishingly certain sense of the theatre," and "the excellence and economy of the stage directions." Discussing the ending, he compares the wedding of Timmy and Molly and the departure of Martin and Mary, calling these two ways "an equal triumph; and all sorts, normal and abnormal, have an equal right to live."

Most of M. Bourgeois's discussion (*JMS&IT*) deals with sources, but Bourgeois does find time for some strictures, judging the plot a "little jejune for the three-act form" and declaring Martin's striking the can from the priest's hand to be "utterly untrue to the Irish nature." He also calls the play "perhaps of all Synge's dramatic works the one in which we find embodied the truest expression of his pessimistic view, if not philosophy, of life."

Daniel Corkery's generally affirmative discussion (*S&A-IL*) centers on the characters and the tone of the play, concluding, "The abundance in Martin's character, the mellowness of the medium through which we are given that character: these are the two main features in the play which account for its flavor." He sees in this abundance in Martin's character (rather than in the retreat from fact into dreams) the truly Celtic element in the play. Criticizing the "want of carry-over between act and act," each of the three acts being too self-contained, he also calls the ending of the play weak, especially in its "effort at pointing the moral."

Alan Price, pursuing the main thesis of his book (*S&A-ID*), finds in this play, combining four complementary versions of the theme of tension between dream and reality, Synge's fullest and most direct treatment of that theme. "The theme is considered in relation to Mary Doul, to Martin Doul, to the villagers, and to the Saint," for all have the same problem and need "to construct something upon which to rejoice." Presenting Martin as having the "temperament and the imagination of the artist," Price contrasts the way he and the Saint, both of whom "know actuality," respond to what they see. Comparing Synge and Martin, Price says that "as a man he was in exactly the same position as Martin—he found life meaningless—but as an artist he behaved quite differently from Martin. He did not turn away, he embraced actuality in his writings." "Martin, the artist, used his imagination in the end to create merely private fancies. Synge, the artist, used his imagination to grapple with the horror of actuality and formed from it a *new* actuality that is good—his writings."

Donna Gerstenberger (*JMS*) focuses on themes, arguing that the conclusion seems inconsistent with what Synge himself believed. She sees here the same basic theme as in *Playboy*—the relation between dream and reality—but finds the conclusion that *The Well of the Saints* suggests unacceptable, "for the play ends with a preference for the lie, an insistence upon illusion in place of reality." This conclusion runs counter to the preferable solution in *Playboy*, and to what Synge himself believed, Gerstenberger says, and Synge fails to bring these questions to a meaningful conclusion in this play: "The choice the Douls finally make is not one between illusion and reality, but between illusions. The quality of the illusions provides the criterion for choice. Their gains in blindness are greater than their losses; their blindness is more honest than that of the self-deceiving sighted world. Nevertheless, their choice is one that denies the wholeness of the world, the totality of experience; it also denies what Synge himself had learned about reality."

Robin Skelton (*WJMS*), while acknowledging that "the dream of perfection which is possible to the blind cannot be sustained in the world of reality," disagrees that we or Synge should judge against the Douls's choice to remain blind. Rather, he argues, Synge took "what we would now label an existentialist view": "Their dream may not be as profound or glorious as that of the dedicated Christian, but it is the only one they have been able to create. . . . In every play he completed, with the possible exception of the first, he shows individuals asserting their 'right' to be 'blind' to realities that torment them and to protect and defend the vision that sustains their belief in their own human dignity, and in the perfectibility of their world." This play "expresses more distinctly than any other of Synge's plays his belief in individualism."

In a brief, dense essay, M. J. Sidnell (in Bushrui, *Sunshine*) argues against any simple metaphorical reading of sight or blindness: "the issue is not between reality and delusion (or actuality and imagination) but between various ways of understanding the world. There is reality and delusion in both sight and blindness." What Sidnell proposes in place of what he rejects is less clear. It involves a foiling of Martin's response to reality against those of the Saint and of Timmy and Molly, so that the Saint and Martin become Blakean opposites (Irish *doul,* "devil," Sidnell suggests). But beyond that Sidnell's argument is hard to follow, and the concluding sentence is typically opaque: "What we make of Martin's choice is the way out of the play's action into reflection; the reconstruction, if we want it, of metaphor and metaphysic from an unaccommodated man's fragments of reality."

Vincent Nash (*LWU*, 1972) touches on several facets of the play. Acknowledging that the apparent message is that "a beneficent illusion is preferable to a harsh reality," Nash warns that this is a total simplification and promises to show that it is. But his sporadic approach does not pursue any of the issues clearly. For example, in discussing the affinity Synge felt between the artist and the vagabond, he says we need to consider the "strange link" Synge establishes between Martin and that "equivocal figure" the Saint. He then proposes that Martin and the Saint are "engaged in a similar activity, using similar means and exerting themselves to a similar degree," and that "Martin, in sustaining his vision, has to call on the same resources of willpower and tenacity which the Saint displays in his service of God."

Grace Eckley (*MD*, 1973) cultivates the archetypal overtones in the images of well, water, and seasons to see something positive in the Douls's choice and departure at the end of the play. Martin's refusing the cure is "self-assertion in Lucifer-like rebellion."

THE PLAYBOY OF THE WESTERN WORLD

The best point of departure for anyone interested in the story of the *Playboy* riots is the lengthy chapter on the subject in the Greene/ Stephens biography. Also pertinent are Lady Gregory's accounts in *Our Irish Theatre* (1913) and Yeats's various pronouncements and discussions (see Levitt's *Bibliography* for detailed references).

James Kilroy's *The Playboy Riots* (1971) reprints most of the relevant contemporary newspaper accounts, with a running commentary. A similar, briefer, account is Richard M. Kain's (*EUQ*, 1966) description of his own scrapbook of news clippings on the events of the week of *Playboy*'s opening. Kain gives a running account of the week, quoting from the clippings.

Daniel J. Murphy's "The Reception of Synge's *Playboy* in Ireland and America: 1907–1912" (*BNYPL*, 1960) gives some background to the Irish response to the play and a fairly detailed account of the reception of the play on both sides of the Atlantic, quoting from contemporary Irish and American reactions. Hilary Berrow describes the first week of the *Playboy*'s staging in some detail in "Eight Nights in the Abbey" (in Harmon, *Centenary*). Richard M. Kain (in Bushrui, *Sunshine*), drawing again on his scrapbook and other contemporary sources, gives a more detailed account than his article cited above. Ida G. Everson's "Lennox Robinson and Synge's *Playboy* (1911–1930): Two Decades of American Cultural Growth" (*NEQ*, 1971) deals with Robinson more than with Synge. Its main interest for Synge scholars is in its account of a 1930 production of *Playboy* at Amherst, directed by Robinson, and of the circuitous route by which the Quinn manuscript of *Playboy* arrived at the library of Indiana University.

Irving D. Suss (*IW*, 1952) explores the psychological sources behind the stormy reception of *Playboy*. Acknowledging the importance of the political considerations the play raised, Suss proposes the depth-psychology explanation that Christy "remains for Irishmen a symbol of a deep-felt need, an unsocietal wish." Suss sees Christy, under the heavy hand of patriarchy in Ireland, as "the new god that destroys the old: Saturn, the conqueror of Uranus; Zeus, Saturn's death" and concludes, "In this social context the self-liberation of the Playboy by violence—especially by violence—was a picture of the hidden dream of the Irishman brought into the light of day."

After the tumult of its presentation in Dublin and in America began to fade (and in some cases even before), it became evident that *Playboy* was one of Synge's finest achievements, perhaps his best play. Since then, few voices have been raised against it, and some of those have later been ameliorated (e.g., George Moore and Frank O'Connor). Recurrent strands in the critical discussion include the question of whether the play is fair to Ireland (in earlier discussions), the question of the consistency or clarity of the play's psychology (especially in regard to Christy), and the related question of genre. Critics have also praised the language of the play, especially that of the love scenes. The theme is generally acknowledged to be the relation of imagination to reality, and Christy is usually seen as the poet whose language and imagination bring a new mode of reality into being. In recent years several critics have explored the mythic roots or analogues of the play in Christianity, in early Irish literature, and in folklore, especially the idea of Christy as a Christ-figure.

P. P. Howe's comments on the play, though general, contain the seeds of much that has been said subsequently (*JMSCS*). He praises the play as being "rich and copious in speech and character," notes its blending of tragedy and comedy, and observes Synge's delight in sharp contrasts. Howe lauds the subtlety of characterization, especially that of Christy, the "only practicising poet" in all the plays, whose "speech is wonderful; the touches by which we are made to perceive the birth and growth of his confidence in it, not the less so." Howe especially praises the language of the love passages in the play. In a separate essay (*OCR*, 1912), he deals with the various censorships, deletions, interpolations, and stage business that developed in early Irish and British productions.

M. Bourgeois's discussion consists largely of paraphrase of earlier comments on the play, summary of it, and a brief account of its reception (*JMS&IT*). He obviously agrees in some respects with what he calls the two "principal and ever-recurring objections" to the play —the first being to its coarse language and events; the second the "dramatic verisimilitude of certain scenes." He puzzlingly complains of an "incidental underplot"; criticizes the conclusion of Act II as technically weak; sees Pegeen's psychology as inconsistent; and is doubtful that real Irish peasants would have admired such a man as Christy. He sees Christy as a poet and liar and points to the embellishments of his successive accounts of his father's death; but he notes with disapproval that Christy believes his own lie and in the end "falls a victim to it." While he acknowledges that *Playboy* is Synge's "most important and representative contribution to the modern stage," he still "positively refuse[s] to regard [it] as his masterpiece."

Daniel Corkery (*S&A-IL*) talks around the play rather than about it and clearly has a low opinion of it. He calls the play "Dionysiac," meaning it serves the "irresponsible spirit of the natural man." Of Christy he says: "Christy Mahon himself is the only character that changes and grows; once it is seen for what it is, the graph of his progress is so direct as not to be interesting." The language of the play offends Corkery both by its blasphemy and its floridness. His only praise for the play is that compared with Synge's earlier work, "it is more obviously the work of a playwright. . . . *The Playboy* has more of the feel of legitimate drama in it."

David H. Greene's "The *Playboy* and Irish Nationalism" (*JEGP*, 1947) deals rather generally with the psychology of the reception of the play and with manuscript drafts of certain passages that show Synge's meticulous care with his language.

Norman Podhoretz' brief but complex analysis of the play (*EIC*, 1953) focuses on the depiction of an evolving moral consciousness on the part of both Christy and the Mayo society, reflected in their attitudes toward Christy's successive "murders" of his father. On Christy's part, these reflect an increasing awareness of the implications of his act, first committed spontaneously, then more deliberately. The first act is symbolic and beyond morality to the people; the second is concrete, immoral, and offensive to them. Podhoretz suggests that both Christy and the Mayo society change and profit from what has happened, and that Synge's "sympathy is patently divided between those two extremes."

Hugh H. MacLean, in his "The Hero as Playboy" (*UKCR*, 1954), sees the play as an archetypal "rendering into Christian terminology of the scapegoat-theme, a clever parody of the orthodox Christian story." In Synge's parody, MacLean argues, Christy is a Christ who is

weak and complacent and who nearly disposes of his birthright before he realizes what is required of him. This is a Christ who can save
only himself, not the world, and whose mission is to show men the
fatuity of seeking salvation through an external agency. Synge's "central message in the play" is that "the individual can and must transcend the tragedy of lost mankind to reach the level of true divine
comedy; to do this, however, he must tap his own resources to the
fullest extent." MacLean's approach almost parodies itself, however,
when he worries that Christy claims to have killed his father on a
Tuesday, the day of Mars, "rather than on a Friday, as one would
expect of a true Christ," or when he explains the Widow Quin's
antagonism to Christy, and her name, as deriving from the Tarot
pack, in which "the Pope's card is five, and the Devil's fifteen."

Patricia Meyer Spacks's interesting "The Making of the *Playboy*"
(*MD*, 1961) acknowledges the perennial dilemma of the play—
whether it is realistic or fantastic—and the curious tone in which
Synge treats the usually dreadful theme of parricide; Spacks proposes
to deal with these peculiarities and to account for the power of the
play by revealing its similarity with the folk and fairy tale. Like these
tales, she points out, *Playboy* has violence that is somehow unreal; in
both, ritual murders represent successive stages of development; in
both, language seems to have power in the real world. Developing
this last idea in more detail, she points out that while Christy's progress is reflected in his language, that progress is not uniform: Christy's too quick assumption of independence is reflected in extravagant
metaphor, which is ameliorated as he truly comes to independence.

T. R. Henn acknowledges what many other critics have noticed—
that "*The Playboy* does not lend itself readily to classification"—and,
to illustrate, he speculates on the various genres that the play might be
thought to belong to, including sheer extravagant comedy with elements of farce, "free" comedy, Dionysiac comedy, satire, mock heroic,
and tragicomedy (Introd. to *Plays and Poems of J. M. Synge*, 1963).

Donna Gerstenberger's discussion of the play (*JMS*) has two parts.
In the first she argues that "the real scene of the play is, finally,
Christy's imagination, just as the real action of the play is, finally, the
growth of his conception of self," and she discusses briefly Christy's
murders of his father in terms of the Oedipal pattern and of primitive
ritual. In the second section, she discusses Synge's intentional questioning of the assumptions and conventions of comedy and even of
"the assumptions on which society and its conventions are founded."
In doing this he presents the kind of truth "which not only avoids
stereotypes but also turns against the stereotyped mode of creating
reality," and offends audiences, in Yeats's phrase, by "its way of seeing."

M. J. Sidnell (*DR*, 1965) explores *Playboy* in relation to the early
Irish "Championship of Ulster," contending that "in its essence *The
Playboy* is the same story as 'The Championship of Ulster,' and though
there is no exact correspondence in all details yet there is more than
enough to suggest that Synge was aware of the essential similarity."
But Sidnell sees an ironic aspect in Synge's use of the myth: "That
Christy, unlike the 'Cuchulanoid' hero, does not appear in some lights
to be the stuff that Champions are made of, may be seen as Synge's

ironic comment on the concept of the hero and heroic virtues, denigrating the past rather than the present." Sidnell's point is weakened by his drawing his parallels partly with Cuchulain and partly with Uath, and by his slightly supported claim that the sword of irony cuts against the myth as well as against the present.

Howard D. Pearce (*MD*, 1965) notes several analogies between Christy and Christ but is concerned "to show Christy as a mock-Christ, a mock-hero." Atypically, he sees Christy as making no substantial progress toward self-realization in the play.

P. L. Henry (*PP*, 1965) discusses the play generally and then turns to the rhythms of its prose. He proposes that the play is understandable "only in terms of the heroic concept of life on which it is immediately based," for this is what "knits it into an organic whole, suggests the criteria on which it is to be assessed and classified as a dramatic and literary work, and offers the vital cue to its presentation." But this section of the essay consists largely of summary and quotation, and Henry does not illustrate his thesis. He then turns to Synge's prose, saying that its rhythmic structure "appears most clearly in the long, balanced periods drawn out by parataxis and marked by parallelism." He illustrates several recurring rhythms, especially the cadence ‿ ‿′ ‿′ ("At the fall of night"), and points out how often this cadence occurs in temporal or spatial references, or in use of the cardinal points of the compass to indicate position and direction. While he cites many passages illustrating various cadences, the point Henry is illustrating remains vague.

Ronald G. Rollins' "Huckleberry Finn and Christy Mahon: The Playboy of the Western World" (*MTJ*, 1966) fails in its attempt to draw meaningful parallels between Huck and Christy, mainly because the parallels are too general and the dissimilarities too basic. Rollins' "O'Casey and Synge: The Irish Hero as Playboy and Gunman" (*ArQ*, 1966), which compares Christy with Donal Davoren, suffers from the same difficulties but is slightly more successful because of the greater similarity of cultural and imaginative milieu between the two works involved.

Wallace H. Johnson's "The Pagan Setting of Synge's *Playboy*" (*Renascence*, 1967) is a thin article contending that "*The Playboy* takes its tone of veiled bleakness from the Aran Islands as Synge experienced them, and that he shifted the setting of the play to Mayo merely to facilitate the plot."

Reed Sanderlin (*SoQ*, 1968) feels that Christy is a fully ironic hero who does not in the least attain self-realization. Arguing that the people admire him at the outset because the police have not arrested him and that Christy is in reality no more of a poet than some of the villagers, Sanderlin denies any true development on Christy's part; he even proposes that old Mahon submits himself to his son at the end not because Christy has become a new man but because there is "a chance to exploit his son as a raconteur." The theme, according to Sanderlin, is not the poet's ability to synthesize dream and reality but "the foolishness of the Irish people who like to indulge in romantic illusions about their rascals, and the foolishness of the rascals who delude themselves into believing that the romantic illusions are the truth."

James F. Kilroy's "The Playboy as Poet" (*PMLA*, 1968) charts more carefully than before the idea that Synge "is portraying the gradual growth of a poet; Christy Mahon passes from an apprenticeship, in which are evident the immature poet's errors and failings—strained similes, exaggerated emotional display, and weak language—to maturity in which he achieves Synge's ideal poetry—rich and earthy, humorous but profound." As a part of this process he contends (as Spacks did earlier) that just as Christy's progress wavers, so does the poetic quality of his language—a point more asserted than shown.

Stanley Sultan's "The Gospel According to Synge" (*PLL*, 1968) is among the best of the several essays discussing Christ parallels in *Playboy*. Sultan approaches the play in terms of the Messiah theme in Anglo-Irish literature (which Herbert Howarth develops, but excepts Synge from), calling it "perhaps the most subtly developed example of the Anglo-Irish motif of the betrayed and rejected messiah." Sultan argues that the Christ analogue has "its functional significance, principally in terms of Jesus' *relationship to* ordinary men: not the character of Christy but the whole action is its subject"; consequently Sultan lays great emphasis on "The good people of Mayo" and the analogy between their response to Christy and the Jews' response to Jesus, especially in explaining the apparent twist at the play's end: "Like Jesus, when Christy confronts with the true significance of his message those who have followed and praised him, they prepare to have him executed by the standard method used for common criminals."

Diane E. Bessai, in "Little Hound in Mayo: Synge's *Playboy* and the Comic Tradition in Irish Literature" (*DR*, 1968), takes M. Sidnell's 1965 essay as point of departure and suggests other parallels between the play and stories or personages of the Ulster cycle (e.g., Pegeen: Emer; Michael James: Forgall; Widow Quin: Scathach). The proposed parallels are often loose or general, and any differences among the characters are regarded as "parodic" rather than as evidence against the thesis. Synge is said to handle the mythic material in consistently mock-heroic vein. Bessai challenges Mercier's statement that Synge is "almost entirely outside the Gaelic literary tradition," stressing the qualities of satire, fantasy, and the macabre and grotesque in *Playboy*, qualities that Mercier himself points to as Irish.

Harry T. Smith (*QJS*, 1969) stresses the propensity for violence in Christy and in the Mayo community and suggests that the "psychic state of the locality" Synge spoke of is a propensity to violence that is visible in the very form and texture of the play. "The action pattern of the play is the creation of a hero in a violent archetype," but it is "perversely unconscious" in the people; thus they can admire the violence when it is "romantically distant" but must reject it when it occurs near at hand, which Smith find analogous to the situation in America in the 1960's.

Mary Rose Sullivan begins "Synge, Sophocles, and the Un-Making of Myth" (*MD*, 1969) with the assumption that Synge wrote *Playboy* with *Oedipus Rex* clearly in mind, calling Synge's comedy a "deliberate re-working" of Sophocles' tragedy. The basic link between the two is their protagonists, both of whom find their identity in their society's eyes through a mythologizing process, and then undergo a demythologizing that results in their finding a truer identity but being cast out from the community. Both plays show that "although man needs myth to discover his heroic potential, it is only in unmaking the myth that he can realize that potential."

D. J. Conacher's "Some Profane Variations on a Tragic Theme" (*Phoenix*, Univ. of Toronto, 1969) explores more tentatively the parallels between *Playboy* and *Oedipus*. For Conacher it is an open question whether Synge wrote with Sophocles in mind; but he concludes that he did, for "the reminiscences of Sophocles *Oedipus* . . . are too precise and too numerous to be accidental." He notes especially the analogies between the Widow Quin and Jocasta and calls attention to various similarities in phraseology.

Eric Salmon (*MD*, 1970) contends that most discussions of the play isolate aspects of it and fail to do justice to its wonderful unity. He then focuses on six *leitmotifs* which are intertwined throughout the play: (1) the blend of reality and illusion; (2) the sense that violence and gentleness spring from the same source; (3) the apprehension of a single moment which creates a reality and conditions all subsequent life; (4) isolation as a basic part of the soul's experience; (5) the moral conflict between the individual and the community; and (6) that nobility contains within itself banal elements that diminish it. Salmon also discusses the language, stressing that its special quality is what binds the play together and that an important part of this is its "self-satirizing quality."

Donna Gerstenberger's "Bonnie and Clyde and Christy Mahon: Playboys All" (*MD*, 1971) compares *Playboy* and the film *Bonnie and Clyde*. After pointing briefly to analogies of subject matter and situation, she emphasizes the way both work to achieve similar effects. Both, she contends, intentionally question the comic mode, drawing the audience in and then violating the comic proprieties, so as to make the audience "an accomplice to the deed."

Robin Skelton (*WJMS*) notes earlier attempts to approach Christy as a Christ figure; he warns that the Christian analogue is intermittent but tends to dominate the play once it is proposed. Approaching the drama as another example of the "shanachie play," he stresses its "extraordinary richness of echo," its conglomerate character, and its mythic element. He also stresses the importance of character in generating meaning. He believes that Christy does achieve a transfiguration at the end, that "Words have created the reality they pictured," and that Christy "becomes an orphic figure whose music survives his destruction." Skelton then proposes how the Christ analogue should be seen: "Societies get the leaders they deserve and Christy Mahon is more fitted for Mayo than Christ Messiah, but even Christy is betrayed."

Two aspects of *Playboy* discussed by E. H. Mikhail (*CLQ*, 1971) are Synge's deliberate workmanship and various parallels with *Peer Gynt*. To illustrate the first, Mikhail briefly reviews information available in Greene/Stephens and in *CW*, III. His comparison with *Peer Gynt* pursues similarities of situation and character and touches vaguely on the question of influence.

Augustine Martin, in "Christy Mahon and the Apotheosis of Loneliness" (in Bushrui, *Sunshine*), approaches the play in terms of a

Dionysiac/Apollonian contrast and distinguishes three groups of characters: the Dionysiac (old Mahon, and Christy at play's end); the Apollonian (Shawn Keogh, Father Reilly); and the pseudo-Apollonian (Michael James, Philly, Jimmy). (It is not clear, however, whether Pegeen is in this last category or is wavering between Dionysian and Apollonian.) Martin then traces Christy's development through the play, mainly in terms of his loneliness and his response to it, concluding that at play's end, "He has at last discovered his true Dionysiac nature, and in discovering it he has shaken off all domination and transfigured his lonesomeness into a posture of gay, predatory adventure."

Leslie D. Foster (*Éire*, 1973) proposes to trace certain "heroic overtones" in *Playboy* deriving mainly from qualities associated in the play with the points of the compass. The play is scrutinized for references to north, south, east, and west, and certain qualities are related to each. The result is contrived and unconvincing (lack of characterization of east and north in the play is regarded not as evidence against the thesis, but as a "strong element of irony"). Foster's underlying point in unearthing this heroic dimension of the play is that Christy is *not* a Christ figure, but that "in order to make *that* point, the play must also emphasize the extent to which he might have been."

Donald Gutierrez' "Coming of Age in Mayo: Synge's *The Playboy of the Western World* as a Rite of Passage" (*Hartford Studies in Lit.*, 1974) is another mythic approach to the play, discussing it as a "puberty rite of passage," but one in which "the relationships traditional in the puberty initiation ceremony between initiand, initiator, and community are complexly reversed." Contrary to the usual pattern where the "initiand" is led into the community, Christy's rite of passage makes him realize that "life as an ethical adult might well include standing apart from the collective will," with the result that "adult status is in part acquired despite, rather than because of, society, and the initiand moves beyond the circle of the community to elaborate his new estate in solitude."

Bernard Laurie Edwards (*ELT*, 1974) develops the dubious thesis that the special significance of the play lies in Christy's being "implicitly able to assess the myth of his personality and ultimately, forced by actuality, to discard the myth and all its trappings in an assertion of selfhood." Laying emphasis on Christy's self-understanding, Edwards contends that he is "finally, no ironic creation for he understands his own significance." Further, he contends that "Christy finally casts off his need for the myth which has, in a measure, liberated him. By this act he creates of himself a true Syngean hero; he draws together in one co-ordinated being a valid relationship with nature, a sense of meaningfulness in simple things . . . and an heroic acceptance of the essential aloneness of man's life."

DEIRDRE OF THE SORROWS

Because it remained unfinished at Synge's death, *Deirdre* received relatively little critical attention from early scholars, and those who discussed it tended to dwell on its roots in Synge's imminent death and his love for Molly Allgood. It has consistently been seen as a new departure for Synge, both in subject matter and in tone. Many critics discuss Synge's adaptation of the legend, generally arguing that he "humanizes" it, brings it down to earth. In the inevitable comparisons with the versions of Yeats and A. E., Synge's is usually judged more realistic and more successful as drama.

P. P. Howe (*JMSCS*) praises *Deirdre* highly, saying "never was [Synge's] sense of the dramatic so clear and so unfailing." In the use of "tragic inevitability," Howe says, "Synge has secured a background . . . of curious orderliness and serenity, by sending all through the play a feeling that whatever happens is foretold, a feeling of inevitability almost Greek." He also praises Synge's powerful sense of contrast, and the fact that each act, even each passage, has its own separate atmosphere.

Francis Bickley (*IrishR*, 1912) contrasts Synge's play with those of A. E. and Yeats, finding that Synge's alone succeeds as drama. He calls Synge "Elizabethan," and "our one great imaginative dramatist since the theatres were closed in 1642."

M. Bourgeois (*JMS&IT*) declines lengthy criticism of the play on the basis of its being unfinished. He notes that many critics regret this play "as a contradiction in Synge's literary career"; but he says that the contradiction is only apparent, since the oldtime Gael and the Irish country-folk had become identical in his mind. Like other critics, he says that Synge has brought Deirdre out of the mystical lands where A. E. and Yeats had held her and into the world of flesh and blood reality.

Daniel Corkery (*S&A-IL*) praises the dramaturgy of the play, calling it well proportioned and well laid out, but he is concerned mostly with its intensity. Characterizing Synge's other plays as lyric, he calls this one lyrical, and says that "intensity should be the chief note in tragedy." He also sees Synge's mastery of this note of intensity as the end of his first phase and argues that *Deirdre* "would have been the first of a number of plays more serious than those he had previously written."

David H. Greene (*PMLA*, 1948) draws on Synge's notes to show that the version of the story Synge most used was one by the eighteenth-century poet "Audrey MacCurten" [i.e., Andrew MacCurtin] first published in 1898. He suggests that Owen, who is unique to Synge's version, may derive from a minor character in MacCurtin's version, named Strongfist. Greene also argues that the play was essentially completed at Synge's death and that "there is no evidence that anyone else touched a pen to a single line of the play." (Ann Saddlemyer, *CW*, IV, alters this conclusion only slightly.) In discussing Synge's modification of his source, Greene says, "The realization of the passing beauty and the presentiment of death endow the entire action with a motivation distinctly different from that found in the original legend." He says that "The Deirdre of the original legend is too lacking in self-assertion to be the central character of a tragedy"; and he argues that in place of Deirdre's helplessness and Naisi's being duped into returning, Synge "added a far stronger motive which became the mainspring of the action, the fear of old age and the passing of beauty."

Edward M. Stephens' "Synge's Last Play" (*ContempR*, 1954) complements Greene's discussion, in that it stresses the sources of the play in Synge's personal experiences. Arguing that Synge's "writings were always inspired by his personal experience," Stephens traces many of Synge's interests in the play to his developing relationship with Molly Allgood. Specifically, he contends that Synge's joyful experiences with Molly in Glen Cree in July, 1907, "inspired the dramatization of Naisi in the woods with Deirdre" and that this experience provided Synge with "the best opportunity that he ever knew for fulfilling a longing he had to unite, as if in one emotion, his love for places of inspiration and his love for a woman." Though occasionally too specific ("Lavarcham was inspired by his appreciation of his mother and Ainnle and Ardan by his devotion to his brothers"), Stephens does say that none of Synge's characters simply represents a real person.

Roger McHugh's "Literary Treatment of the Deirdre Legend" (*Threshold*, 1957) compares the versions of A. E., Yeats, Synge, and Stephens. In discussing Synge's, he points to Synge's approaching death and his knowledge of the people of the Aran Islands as shaping influences in the "humanizing" of Deirdre, making her less heroic and more human. He also says that in no previous version does Deirdre *urge* Naisi to return to Ireland, and he points to Owen's important role in this, claiming that he "provides the big change in motive in Deirdre's wish to return to Ireland."

Alan Price (*S&A-ID*), in his lengthy and laudatory analysis of the play, pursues his general themes of tension between two inimical ways of life and between dream and reality, but he also points to Synge's felicitous revisions of the received story, his broadening and deepening the theme by "shifting the emphasis from the destructiveness of an individual ruler to the destructiveness of Time." He contrasts the play favorably with the versions of Yeats and A. E., especially in Synge's two unexpected turns at the conclusion— "Deirdre's almost successful attempt to make peace between Conchubar and Naisi" and "the sudden and unexpected quarrel of Deirdre and Naisi." Price calls the ending of the play "perhaps the finest thing Synge ever wrote." He goes on to praise Synge's handling of Conchubar and Lavarcham, his making the former a "credible and human figure of some complexity," his using the latter as a foil to Deirdre— "a living example of the pass to which Deirdre will come if she elects to survive Naisi," so that "seeing her we know that Deirdre made the right choice."

Harold Orel, in "Synge's Last Play: 'And a Story Will Be Told for Ever'" (*MD*, 1961) says that the special qualities of Synge's *Deirdre* (following Synge's own words) are its stoicism, asceticism, and ecstasy, though he gives unusual meanings to these terms. The stoicism manifests itself in Synge's depicting, without condemnation, the limitations of his fellow human beings and in the compassion that is found here uniquely among Synge's works. Asceticism, understood in its Irish context, involves the artist's treasuring the relatively few materials available to him. Of the third element, Orel says, "Ecstasy, for Synge, came at the moment when meaning separated from the emotion, usually toward the end of the work of literature."

Donna Gerstenberger begins her discussion (*JMS*) by noting the factors that have caused the play to be neglected—the biographical context, its being unfinished, and its apparent departure from other plays of Synge. She then focuses the distinctiveness of Synge's handling of the material on his having "accomplished a dramatic tension by creating a vision of human reality at variance with the usual emphasis of the heroic material." Through this emphasis upon the human rather than the traditional, Synge achieves a turn against the audience's expectations similar to that achieved in *Playboy*, so that they react with surprise, but without anger, to what they are made to learn.

Herbert V. Fackler (*MD*, 1969) stresses three facets of the play: the "reciprocal sympathy between characters and nature, a surprising reversal of the treatment of death, and a heightened sense of the tragic essence of the old legend that is very nearly Greek in spirit." The unusual handling of death, perhaps a result of Synge's own illness, involves his presenting it as a victory, as a means of escaping old age and the loss of love. Fackler also contends that "the tragedy of *Deirdre of the Sorrows* is one in which all of Synge's characters share, through a common flaw—surrender to the will."

Robin Skelton (*WJMS*) praises the language of the play, saying that it approximates verse more than that of Synge's other plays. But he sees the work as a comparative failure as drama—too close to mere narrative and lacking in dramatic tension. He criticizes Deirdre as "an egotistical young woman full of her own destiny and given to luxuriating in self-adoration, and self-pity," and he feels that she "does not have the emotional complexity of Synge's other heroines."

Jon R. Farris (*MD*, 1971) criticizes earlier commentators for imprecision in discussing the nature of the tragedy. Arguing that any reading of the play as a triumph of love over death would undercut the possibility of tragedy, Farris says that "The hardness of death does not unite them forever and affirm the beauty of their life; it produces their first quarrel, shatters their magnificent joy, and leaves them unreconciled in death. The romantic Deirdre would close with a smiling death in act II; it is the tragic Deirdre which progresses to the realization that 'We've had a dream, but this night has waked us surely.'"

Balachandra Rajan (*YeatsS*, 1972) deals with Yeats's tragic understanding and the role Synge played in forming it, and to a lesser extent with Synge's own mode of tragic response and its expression in *Deirdre*. Saying that Yeats's tragic understanding comes in "great creative defiances," Rajan finds Synge's harder to pinpoint, involving acceptance, resignation, aloofness, dignity, and desolation.

Ann Saddlemyer, in "*Deirdre of the Sorrows*: Literature First . . . Drama Afterwards" (in Harmon, *Centenary*), discusses the backgrounds of Synge's turning to this mythic subject, emphasizing the challenge he found in bending the traditional, established material of the myth to his own evolving esthetic. She says that "Synge's greatest originality remains the blending of theme and character, the shifting of emphasis and climax, in keeping with his developed theory of art and drama. He would not be satisfied until all was strengthened, 'made personal,' simple, intense, charged with his own vision of the world." Her discussion of the play turns largely on the nature of the characters and on Synge's "simplification of character and emphasis upon individual ruling passions," which she traces to his earlier study of music and his reading of Racine. In Deirdre, Synge sought to convey "imperious freedom, strength of will, and maturity of passion." Discussing Owen, she suggests that he derives from a type Synge saw on the Aran Islands and quotes a supporting passage from *The Aran Islands*.

John Rees Moore's "Synge's *Deirdre* and the Sorrows of Mortality" (in Bushrui, *Sunshine*) says that only in *Deirdre* did Synge attempt "to combine the breadth of comedy with the intensity of tragedy" and that "Deirdre alone among Synge's characters gives full resonance to the mingled sweetness and sorrow of true ecstasy." He sees the play as unique in modern drama in being a "heroical-lyrical-pastoral-mythical-realistic play" and says, "if it fails from trying to do too much . . . it also succeeds to some extent in all its compartments."

Brenda Murphy (*MD*, 1974) begins by focusing on two clichés she says have encumbered criticism of *Deirdre*: first, "that the play is preeminently a 'peasant drama,' and therefore a strikingly new treatment of the Deirdre legend," and second, "that its theme is chiefly autobiographical." Then, drawing on Saddlemyer and Orel, Murphy proposes that Synge, using his earlier training in harmony and counterpoint, makes this play a blend of the three qualities he told Yeats should be united: stoicism, asceticism, and ecstasy. Murphy's development of this idea, however, does little to justify the invocation of the musical techniques, and she succeeds no better than Orel in giving these three terms meanings appropriate to this drama. She concludes, "It is through the stoic acceptance of the inevitability of her death . . . and the ascetic rejection of both the beauty of life in nature and the luxury of life in Emain Macha that Deirdre reaches a final ecstasy in her realization of the imminence of her death."

VII. Poetry

Synge's poetry has received relatively little critical attention. Early critics, who knew only the slim gathering of poems in the *Works* (1910), generally dismissed the poetry and translations as a by-product of only biographical interest or expatiated on some of Synge's quotable comments in the Preface.

Bourgeois is typical of these early attitudes, saying that the greatest merit of the poems is "that they are principally a self-revelation of Synge" (*JMS&IT*), that nature is the main source of Synge's inspiration, and that a folk-inspiration is shown in his choice of subject matter and form; and he points to the strong current of melancholy and pessimism in the verse.

Daniel Corkery too dismisses the poems and translations quickly, seeing them as exercises rather than final achievements and stressing the relaxed temper, the weakness of grip, the want of skill in poetic form, and Synge's failure to take the same pains here that he took with the texture of his prose. Corkery says that Synge always selected items for translation on the basis of their subject matter rather than their craftsmanship, and the subject matter is always "the profound and common interests of life" (*S&A-IL*).

Robert Farren discusses Synge's poetry briefly in *The Course of Irish Verse in English* (1947). He quotes, as do so many, the statement in the Preface that "before verse can be human again it must learn to be brutal" and stresses the crudeness and violence of Synge's subject matter, much more akin to Gaelic verse than to what was being written by Synge's Anglo-Irish contemporaries. He suggests too that Synge's work influenced Yeats's poetry and perhaps Jack B. Yeats's painting.

The idea of Synge's influence on Yeats was pursued by Vivian de Sola Pinto in his chapter "Yeats and Synge" in his *Crisis in English Poetry 1880–1940* (1951; rev. 1961). Though de Sola Pinto gives only a few paragraphs to Synge, he makes the perceptive points that "The younger writer's 'harsh, heroical, clean, windswept view of things' was exactly the stimulant that was needed by a poet who was growing weary of romantic idealism and the inhumanity of symbolist doctrine" and that Synge's "handful of short poems must be reckoned as an important contribution to the poetry of the modern crisis."

Donald Davie (*DM*, 1952) makes the unsurprising point that "Synge is not, as he seems to think, avoiding poetic diction altogether, but only substituting one sort of diction for another. He is still refusing to use certain words, the words of romantic glamour; he has only chosen to exclude a different set of words." Working from the questionable assumption that a poet's choice of diction always reflects his sense of what lends "dignity" to man, Davie says that Synge's diction proceeds from his "novel idea of seeing human dignity not in what distinguished man from the brute, but in what he and the brute had in common, in a word, in man's brutality."

Denis Donoghue qualifies Davie's point, saying that Synge's poems reveal two distinct dictions, the "romantic" and the "earthy," and arguing that Synge's "characteristic poetic method is the deliberate confrontation of these two distinct kinds of speech" ("Flowers and Timber: A Note on Synge's Poems," *Threshold*, 1957). While he says that these poems are not very important, comments on a curious unevenness among them, and accuses them of much more morbid self-pity than irony, Donoghue does find "Queens" and "In Kerry" to be successful examples of Synge's poetic method.

Alan Price's discussion of the poetry follows the same lines—he points to the tension between the "romantic" and the "realistic" and stresses how different it was from nearly all the other poetry written between 1890 and 1908 (*S&A-ID*). What individuality the verse has comes from "the glint of irony or humor," and Price suggests that the ballad "Danny" is perhaps Synge's best poem. In the translations, Price sees reflections of Synge's own recurrent themes and finds the language frequently no more than singular and charming.

For T. R. Henn, some of the poems contain rhythms that are authentic and words that are alive, but most of them show a breakdown attributable to "sheer failure of technique; a lack of desire or ability to shape and re-shape until a poem becomes a unity," and he quotes several examples of slack rhymes and pseudo-poeticisms to exemplify his point (*Plays and Poems of J. M. Synge*, 1963).

Donna Gerstenberger, working with the fuller canon of poems available in *CW*, gives a more detailed discussion of the poetry (*JMS*). She posits an important difference between Synge's early, apprentice poems and his later ones, the difference being mainly that in the early poems Synge has found neither a voice of his own nor a controlling attitude.

Robin Skelton has written more fully and more warmly of Synge's poetry than has any other critic, claiming that Synge "left behind him a couple of dozen poems that will always keep his name in mind as one of the great renewers of tradition" (*WJMS*). His main points about the poetry are that Synge created a persona, inimitable by other poets, which was his chief gift to modern poetry and to Yeats's poetry after 1908. In his development of these ideas—of the persona and of the great influence on Yeats—however, Skelton does not clarify his bases for claiming some of the poems which seem direct and personal to involve a persona; and he seems to exaggerate Synge's influence on Yeats by implying that Yeats's turn away from dreamy estheticism began in 1908 and that Synge was its sole source.

Francis Warner notes at the outset of "A Note on the Poems of Synge" (in Bushrui, *Sunshine*) the wide divergence of critical evaluation of Synge's poetry, from Henn's low estimate to Skelton's praise. In an attempt to resolve the issue, Warner scrutinizes the techniques of several poems. While he finds some poems that succeed, for the most part he finds forced rhymes, syntactic awkwardness, and sentimental and insincere emotion. Warner concludes that Synge was a fine dramatist but not a good poet.

Jon Stallworthy, in "The Poetry of Synge and Yeats" (in Harmon, *Centenary*), traces Synge's poetic development more carefully than has anyone heretofore, bringing into his discussion the "Vita Vecchia" cycle and even some poems not published in *CW*. In doing this, Stallworthy suggests several parallels between the development of Synge and that of Yeats. While some of these are interesting, others are very general ("Yeats's poems, early and late alike, also show a marked concern with time"). Stallworthy believes Synge's indebtedness to French literature to be greater than the Greene/Stephens biography suggests, and he counters Skelton's suggestion that Synge's persona derives from the Cavalier poets with the suggestion that the native Celtic tradition can account for many of these qualities. He also qualifies Skelton's ideas about Synge's influence on Yeats by pointing out that some of the brusque hardness of tone supposedly derived from Synge was already present in "Adam's Curse" in 1902 and that Synge's poems simply furthered an influence the plays had already begun.

VIII. The Aran Islands, the Essays

Early critics of Synge regarded his prose works as of value either for the scanty biographical information they provided or as the source material of the plays. Bourgeois provides no separate discussion of the prose, and P. P. Howe uses the term "Notebooks" to describe these writings.

Daniel Corkery took a new tack in speaking of the prose as the result of long and anxious toil, "elaborated into simplicity, directness, and unity," and suggesting that the essays would be valuable if the plays had never been written (*S&A-IL*). He praises the "essays" for their ability to capture the spirit of the place and people they describe and calls attention to Synge's sensitivity to color, to highly charged emotions, and to dramatic incident; but he faults Synge for his lack of feeling for the people's religious sentiments. Corkery does not discuss the style or structure of the prose; and, though he values these essays as descriptive of the consciousness of the people, he feels they are even more important for the insight they give us into Synge's own consciousness.

While his discussion of *The Aran Islands* dwells almost entirely on its reflection of Synge's personality and interest in the things he wrote about, Alan Price says that he hopes "Some cause has been shown for saying that *The Aran Islands* is a piece of writing of distinctive merit not only because it embodies so admirably the main theme of Synge's writings: the tension between dream and actuality, between two inimical ways of life; the interaction between Man and the natural world; the awareness of mutability" (*S&A-ID*).

Donna Gerstenberger makes more specific claims for the artistry of *The Aran Islands*, distinguishing it from the rest of the prose as "a unified and carefully completed whole" (*JMS*). Saying that the book is best viewed as a "documentary," she stresses Synge's use of universal patterns and rhythms to give the book structure. Gerstenberger fails, however, to demonstrate any carefully controlled patterns of development in the book.

Jeanne Flood's "The Pre-Aran Writings of J. M. Synge" (*Éire*, 1970) examines Synge's "Autobiography," "Vita Vecchia," and "Étude Morbide" in terms of the light they cast on Synge's conception of the relationship between art and external reality. While the "Autobiography" is treated as autobiography, the other two works are regarded as literary translations of Synge's inner life. Flood contends that there was a close, even causal, relationship between Synge's discovery of Darwinism and his turning from natural science to art. She argues that reading Darwin caused in Synge a "powerful revulsion at the idea of human inclusion in nature" and that this produced his unwillingness to continue in natural science. The "Autobiography," according to Flood, shows that at this time Synge saw art as the expression of the emotions constituting the inner life, the essence of the personality, which implies that the artist has no esthetically significant relation to the physical world: art is a means of transcending physicality. The incoherence of "Vita Vecchia" and "Étude Morbide" arises from a disparity between Synge's emotive needs and the techniques that this view of art committed him to. The musical failure depicted in the works reflects the performer's (and Synge's) inability to achieve a life truly exalted and freed from the brutal. The physical world, which art should be able to transcend, impinges and causes failure. At the end of "Étude Morbide," however, Flood sees a change of theory, so that art is conceived not as expressing sheer subjectivity, sheer soul, but as expressing the emotions the artist has felt from a rapport with the external world. This art is created not by a mere self but by, in Synge's words, "a soul in harmony with some mood of the earth." But while the figure in "Etude Morbide" has come to conceive of art this way, he cannot adequately express these emotions and so concedes defeat.

T. R. Henn's "The Prose of John Millington Synge" (in Harmon, *Centenary*; a briefer version appeared in *Hibernia*, 30 Apr. 1971) ranges widely over Synge's prose, dealing mostly with style. Stressing the role of Synge's personality and his choice of subjects in giving form to his prose, Henn says, "It is informed, given shape, by the interweaving of compassion and irony with a delicacy and integrity that is the reflection of his own complex personality." He also calls attention to the laconic structure and tone, to the spare, frequently monosyllabic vocabulary, and to the sentences lightly punctuated to the point of ambiguity—in general to the simplicity and precision of the prose.

Lanto M. Synge, in his "The Autobiography of J. M. Synge" (in Bushrui, *Sunshine*), proposes to show the importance of the "Autobiography" as literature, as a document of social history, and as a biographical essay of first-rate importance. His chief concern is its biographical importance, and he allows whatever historical implications it has to emerge by inference, saying almost nothing about the work as literature. The essay discusses the importance of nature, religion, and music in forming the sensibilities of the young John Synge. Lanto Synge's attitude toward the "Autobiography" as an integrated work seems uneven: on the one hand he refers to Alan Price's editions of the work (disregarding the differences between them) as being "constructed from a number of different and disjointed MSS" and acknowledges that it was never completed, while on the other hand he describes the work as a whole and says that it is constructed in "a musical form in which various contrasting themes are harmoniously resolved." Certainly we are given no demonstration of artistic form or integrity in the work.

Ann Saddlemyer's "Art, Nature, and 'The Prepared Personality': A Reading of *The Aran Islands* and Related Writings" (in Bushrui, *Sunshine*) suggests that a closer reading of Synge's prose works provides a deeper understanding of the man himself. In *The Aran Islands*, the adventures Synge records "reflect the contours, emotions and temperament of the author's personality, for this journey to the western world was also an exploration and revaluation of his own consciousness." She suggests that *The Aran Islands* is organized around a cyclic pattern, and that "with each cycle of events he reports, the exhilaration reaches a higher peak, the author's reserve before the forces of nature is further dissipated, the barrier between the islander and the natural and supernatural forces around him loosens." Saddlemyer suggests, without demonstrating, that this cyclic pattern proceeds to the end of the work. She also contends that "the rest of Synge's prose, though incomplete and unpolished, indicates the same intentional patterning and engrossing ambition," a reflection of Synge's "concept of the harmonic progression of existence, the cycle of experience in man which reflects the cycle of experience in nature."

Keith Hull's "Nature's Storms and Stormy Natures in Synge's *Aran Islands*" (*Éire*, 1972) argues that Synge depicts the "tragic" situation of the Aran people and shows their life against nature to have the unity of tragic art. But Hull's thesis is weakened by his loose use of "tragic" and by the absence of that term from any of the passages he quotes from *The Aran Islands*. Hull also suggests, but does not develop, the idea that *The Aran Islands* presents a progression of Synge's understanding of the people, from his seeing their relationship to nature as simple to seeing it as complex.

IX. *Sources, Language, Esthetics, and Other Themes and Techniques*

The question of the influences and sources behind Synge's dramatic works has been a persistent strain in Synge criticism. The discussion was set in motion by the response of reviewers to *The Shadow of the Glen*, which Arthur Griffith and others charged with springing from a foreign model and slandering Irish womanhood. From the first, then, the question of the influences working on Synge was cast in terms of whether Synge was a loyal Irishman or had been seduced by such Continental models as Petronius, Boccaccio, and the French decadent writers.

The debate was pursued by D. J. O'Donoghue (*Irish Independent*, 21 Aug. 1911). O'Donoghue (who had written a sympathetic "Appreciation" upon Synge's death) attacks Synge's Irishness, saying, "The ideas underlying the plays are so obviously foreign that it is hardly necessary to dwell upon the fact," and that "not only are Synge's method and outlook foreign, but even his main ideas are traceable to foreign sources." Synge "was more indebted to Baudelaire than to any other single writer," his morbid outlook matched the French poet's, and from him he learned "épater les bourgeois."

The earliest full-scale discussion of the influences on Synge was by M. Bourgeois (*JMS&IT*); and while some other specific sources have come to light since 1913, Bourgeois's conclusions are still basically sound. Bourgeois disagrees with Yeats that Synge had read few contemporary writers. He contends that Synge had read Balzac, Flaubert, Maupassant, Huysmans, Zola, Le Braz, and Baudelaire, as well as the seventeenth-century French dramatists (Synge's diaries and notebooks bear this out), and that Pierre Loti and Anatole France were of special interest to him. He says too that Synge knew the German playwrights and was familiar with the intellectual movement begun by Maeterlinck and Ibsen. But Bourgeois concludes that while these writers and currents influenced Synge, they did not determine him. He traces Synge's morbidity not to Baudelaire but to Synge's own constitution (as Masefield had earlier suggested) and argues that "in spite of all, he remained fundamentally Irish."

Bourgeois acknowledges the Continental and Oriental parallels to the plot of *The Shadow of the Glen*, but he accepts Synge's assertion that the story derived from one he heard on the Aran Islands. Of

Riders to the Sea, he notes that scattered germs of the play are found in *The Aran Islands* but that there seems to be no central source, though he sees Pierre Loti's *The Iceland Fisherman* and Hermann Heijerman's *Meerspeil, On Hoop van Vegen* as "external sources." *The Tinker's Wedding* Bourgeois believes to stem from stories Synge heard in Wicklow and perhaps from a song in Hyde's *Religious Songs of Connacht*. The source of *The Well of the Saints* is more problematic, since there is no definite source in Synge's nondramatic writings. Bourgeois acknowledges O'Donoghue's suggestion that it stems from a Clemenceau play, *Le Voile du Bonheur*, but says that similar stories occur in most folklores. Synge himself acknowledged a source in a pre-Molière French farce, says Bourgeois, then proposing a source previously undetected—a short story by Lord Lytton entitled "The Maid of Malines." Bourgeois touches briefly on the origin of *Playboy*; he acknowledges O'Donoghue's opinion that it derives from Baudelaire's having opened a conversation with the words "after having assassinated my poor father" but then points to the anecdote recorded by Synge and to the case of Lynchehaun. For *Deirdre*, Bourgeois mentions several adaptations of the story but does not speculate on which most influenced Synge. (Appendix C of Bourgeois's book provides a list of editions and adaptations of the Deirdre story.)

Most subsequent discussions have come to conclusions similar to those of Bourgeois—that Synge did know Continental literature and was influenced by it, but that he absorbed the influences and that they did not render him un-Irish. In addition, few likely sources have been found to add to those Bourgeois proposes.

Adelaide Duncan Estill's *The Sources of Synge* (1939) is simply a review of earlier suggestions about Synge's sources (including several not noted here), with no attempt to find new sources. Estill concludes that for most of the plays, Synge's source is to be found in his "journals" (i.e., *The Aran Islands* and the Wicklow, Kerry, and Connemara-Mayo essays). In two cases—*Well of the Saints* and *Deirdre* —Estill acknowledges outside sources, but says that Synge's use of the material involves a distinctive transformation.

Jan Setterquist's *Ibsen and the Beginnings of Anglo-Irish Drama: John Millington Synge* (Upsala, 1951) deals with the "influence" of Ibsen on Synge. Each of Synge's plays is compared and contrasted with certain plays of Ibsen: *The Shadow of the Glen* with *A Doll's House* and *The Lady from the Sea*; *Riders to the Sea* with *The Lady from the Sea* and *Rosmersholm*; *The Tinker's Wedding* with *The League of Youth* (very briefly); *The Well of the Saints* with *The Wild Duck*; *The Playboy of the Western World* with *Peer Gynt, The Wild Duck*, and *The Master Builder*; *Deirdre* with *Love's Comedy*. While some of the parallels are interesting, they all remain general— parallels of theme or situation—and can be accounted for more readily as ideas whose time had come than through the influence of Ibsen on Synge. There is no analysis of Synge's plays, so that the book has no value beyond its thesis. Setterquist suggests that Synge's plays involve several technical characteristics usually regarded as peculiar to the Ibsen drama, but he discusses only Ibsen's use of parallel scenes to evoke the past, something certainly not unique to the Norwegian. Setterquist acknowledges the great differences in tone and social setting between Ibsen's plays and Synge's, but concludes rather questionably that "The Ibsenite trends in Synge's plays are indeed so many and so heterogenous that, in my opinion, they must be regarded as evidence of ubiquitous influence exercised upon him by the Norwegian dramatist."

Synge's language has been a recurrent topic of discussion. The main issues relate to the realism or authenticity of the language and its sources. Several critics have pointed out how unordinary, almost unique, the language is, and some have questioned whether it is too special to carry much dramatic weight. Others have discussed the poetic quality of the prose and have attempted to explain how it is achieved.

A. G. van Hamel (*EngS*, 1912) finds in Synge's work authentic examples of how strongly Gaelic syntax, idiom, and vocabulary survive in Anglo-Irish. (He also uses Yeats as an equally authentic source.)

M. Bourgeois declares that Synge's dialect cannot be regarded as a mere notebook transcript, that it is a bold re-creation from Gaelic, too Irish to be the actual Anglo-Irish dialect but of inestimable literary value (*JMS&IT*). He acknowledges Lady Gregory's *Cuchulain* as one of Synge's sources and cites examples of the influence of Hyde's *Love Songs of Connacht*.

Helen Cascy's brief "Synge's Use of the Anglo-Irish Idiom" (*EJ*, 1938), while it draws its examples from *Deirdre*, deals more with how certain Celtic constructions exemplify the "dramatizing instinct of the race" than with Synge's use of the language. She does say that while other playwrights have tried to give us the language of the Irish people, "no one of them has caught into words the blue fire of their spirit as Synge has done."

After discussing Synge's language generally, Daniel Corkery (in *S&A-IL*) complains about the omnipresence of an "almost riotous lyricism" that interferes with the dramatic presentation. Corkery acknowledges occasional blunders in Synge's Anglo-Irish; but he compares Synge favorably with others who have tried the dialect, saying that "Synge's speech is more unified than theirs, has been more thoroughly kneaded by a more strongly creative spirit." He also suggests that this is Synge's "folk period style," not really his own, and that he would have outgrown it.

T. R. Henn discusses Synge's language in the Introduction to *Plays and Poems of J. M. Synge* (1963). Henn acknowledges the limitations of Synge's diction and then discusses idiom, imagery, and rhythm. He notes that Synge's two main classes of imagery are the "literary" and the "folk," "the latter by far the more successful." He criticizes Synge for his occasional straining after rhetorical effects and says that his "fondness for violently colliding images often leads to failure." Henn notes four components in Synge's rhythms: the speech of the peasantry; Gaelic; echoes of Tudor or Jacobean prose; and "Synge's own preferences for certain rhythmic combinations, certain tastes and

flavours of words." Henn wonders whether "it was the individuality
of Synge's style that [it] could combine the outrageous and the lyric,
realism and irony and pity, in a manner beyond imitation."

Pat Barnett, in "The Nature of Synge's Dialogue" (*ELT*, 1967),
begins by citing several earlier opinions about Synge's language and
then counters Corkery's charge that lyricism undermines the dramatic
elements in Synge's plays. Barnett argues that, on the contrary, the
lyricism contributes to establishing the atmosphere and tone of the
plays and even builds theme and conveys character. Barnett also
discusses the strong rhythms of Synge's plays, rhythms which "fall
easily and frequently into blank verse meter," and briefly considers
his use of simile and hyperbole.

Jiro Taniguchi's *A Grammatical Analysis of Artistic Representation
of Irish English* (1955; rev. Tokyo, 1972), in addition to using
Synge's works as one source of its illustrations of Anglo-Irish diction
and syntax, has sections on the language of each of the plays and
detailed tables depicting various linguistic features of Synge's works
—e.g., "Statistical Table of Percentage of Anapests to Iambuses." The
statistics are based on the dubious foundations of Taniguchi's scan-
sion of Synge's prose, and the book tells us little of value about
Synge's language.

Seamus Deane (in Harmon, *Centenary*; also in *Mosaic*, 1971) argues that Synge's language involves basic oppositions between language as joy and richness and language dealing with the reality of
life in joyless and pallid words; and between the energy of paganism
and the restraint of Christianity. Deane notes that Synge owes both
his joy in language and his sense of the inseparability of truth and
language to the Gaelic heritage. Building on this, he argues that
Synge's characteristic use of language involves both an incarnation of
his themes in his language and a use of linguistic oppositions that
become resolved and transformed as the works develop. He illustrates this by discussing the opposition between the morphemes
"lone" and "fear" and the morphemes "decent" and "sainted" in *Playboy*, saying that "The play's theme is incarnate in its language.
Christy's emergence from the unreal opposition between lonesomeness and decency to the new world of wonder . . . is the emergence of
a Gaelic pagan myth hero from a Christianized, anglicized and
therefore impoverished community."

Lorna Reynolds' "The Rhythms of Synge's Dramatic Prose" (*YeatsS*,
1972) proposes that Synge's alterations of native Irish speech are
most distinctive in the rhythms he selects and heightens; and that by
his use of cadence with almost the same regularity that rhyme would
be used in verse, he solved the problem of how to preserve the
illusion of prose speech while creating the heightened effect of verse.
Most of Reynolds' essay is devoted to illustrating the various cadences of Synge's prose.

Alan Bliss's "The Language of Synge" (in Harmon, *Centenary*)
devotes several pages to the background of Anglo-Irish and to Douglas Hyde's use of it; says that none of the purported resemblances
between Synge's language and Hyde's are very striking and that
Synge's debt to Hyde is subtle and hard to formalize. Synge's language, Bliss points out, is not homogenous among the plays. He also

argues rather strangely that we must regard the dialogue of some of the plays as a *translation* from the Irish which the characters would have been speaking (true, he says, of *Riders* and *Deirdre*, probably of *Well*, perhaps of *Playboy*). As to the realism of Synge's language, Bliss contends that had it been truly representative of Irish speech, the Abbey players should not have had the trouble with it they did. He points to several inaccuracies in Synge's Anglo-Irish and concludes that "His dialogue is not, and was not intended to be, an accurate representation of peasant speech: it is rather a 'distillation' or 'selection' from that speech."

Nicholas Grene (*Long Room*, 1974) discusses what he calls the "creative development" observable when we compare Synge's notebooks and manuscripts with the published version of *The Aran Islands*. What Grene actually traces, in rather predictable terms, is the change in Synge's language, especially his growing skill in the use of dialect. He points to Synge's transition from a reported to a dramatic form of presentation, and to his increasing self-effacement, but he deals most with Synge's increasingly skillful use of Gaelic-based dialect, which he says "involved both the cultivation of favorite forms, and the exclusion of those found to be unsuitable."

Two sources of annotations of Synge's language are T. R. Henn's "Notes on the Plays, Poems and Translations," in *Plays and Poems of J. M. Synge* (1963); and Alan Bliss's "A Synge Glossary" (in Bushrui, *Sunshine*, 1972).

In recent years, with the availability of the early prose and the accessibility of Synge's manuscripts, several essays have appeared discussing Synge's esthetics. One of these, Jeanne Flood's "The Pre-Aran Writings of J. M. Synge," is discussed in the section on Synge's prose writings; two others are dealt with here.

Ann Saddlemyer, in "'A Share in the Dignity of the World': J. M. Synge's Aesthetic Theory" (in *The World of W. B. Yeats*, ed. R. Skelton and A. Saddlemyer, 1965; rev. 1967), argues that Synge gave considerable thought to his esthetic credo, which had much to do with Synge's musical training in harmony and counterpoint. She sees that training resulting in the "rhythmical balance and formal intricate structure of his plays" and in his "conscious effort to build up 'currents' of tension through crescendos and contrasts, juxtaposing tragedy and comedy through exposition and poetry." She also emphasizes Synge's wish to achieve a "union of the realist qualities of naturalism with the symbolism of aestheticism" or a "balance" that would "escape both the extremes of aestheticism and naturalism." This is achieved by discarding all ideas of didacticism and by the artist's accepting life in the mixture in which it comes. The result was to be an art that dealt with the whole of life, by its very nature encompassing both tragedy and comedy.

William Hart (*YeatsS*, 1972) argues that "the formal design of the *Playboy* derives ultimately from a general philosophy of life and art which shaped Synge's theory of poetry and drama." The design of the *Playboy* "has two formal characteristics: an essential dualism and a cyclical movement." Synge's view of life "is emotive, pantheistic, evolutionary and tragically joyous. It is also fundamentally dualistic and cyclical." Synge views art as essentially the expression of mood; it also involves some juxtaposition of disparate elements—the grotesque and the lyric—and some humor or irony that are the signs of a healthy imagination.

David Krause, in " 'The Rageous Ossean': Patron Hero of Synge and O'Casey" (*MD*, 1961), argues that in modern Irish writing, the works of Synge and O'Casey best reflect that spirit and literary tradition of anticlericalism and comic irreverence symbolically projected by Ossian. He points to evidence of Synge's awareness of Ossian and his dialogues and also to traits in Synge's plays—wildness, paganism, satire, anticlericalism—that are Ossianic in spirit.

Abdalla A. Metwally's "Synge's *When the Moon Has Set*" (*Studies in Modern Drama*, Beirut, 1971) is a not very enlightening discussion of Synge's first play. Metwally touches on its Irish background, its universal themes, the intimacy between man and nature, and a preoccupation with death. He calls for giving the play its rightful place in Synge's dramatic oeuvre.

David Greene's "Synge in the West of Ireland" (*Mosaic*, 1971) argues that Synge did not go to the Aran Islands to study Irish or to elaborate his own Anglo-Irish dialect. On the contrary, Synge "had nothing to learn from the people, any more than Gauguin had in Tahiti. Both the painter and the writer had brought their European attitudes with them, and the plays which Synge brought out of Aran are as European as the paintings which Gauguin sent home from Tahiti." What Synge did find on the Aran Islands was "a solitude which enabled him for the first time to deepen his thoughts and perceptions and to find that purpose in life that had up to then eluded him."

In "Synge the Dramatist" (*Mosaic*, 1971) Thomas Kilroy, after reviewing the program of the early Irish Dramatic Movement as expressed by Yeats and Lady Gregory with its aims of rejecting contemporary Naturalism and restoring poetic language to drama, proposes that Synge's peasant plays, while in keeping with the formula, also involved distinctly Continental and Modernist traits. "Synge's work is informed by a radical, anarchic spirit unlike anything in Lady Gregory or Yeats at this time, whose only counterpart is to be found outside Ireland, in the main tradition of modern drama." Kilroy then discusses how Synge's stagecraft and dramatic modes reflect earlier Continental drama.

J. F. Lydon's "John Millington Synge: The Man and His Background" (*Mosaic*, 1971) addresses the question, "How could a man with Synge's background succeed in entering that world of the hidden Ireland, as Daniel Corkery so aptly called it?" His answer is built on the assumption that "for Synge to succeed as he did, he had first to free himself from the restrictions of his domestic environment." The main factors in this escape, Lydon believes, were his dislike for the land-grabbing mentality, his loss of religious faith, his interest in science, and most of all his Continental sojourns. These prepared him to respond to what he found on the Aran Islands, but they also determined that his response would take forms unacceptable to orthodox Irish nationalists.

Robert H. Orr's "The Surprising Ending: One Aspect of J. M. Synge's Dramatic Technique" (*ELT*, 1972) discusses *Well of the Saints, Tinker's Wedding, Shadow of the Glen,* and *Playboy* mainly in terms of Synge's surprise endings in his plays. Orr contends that the device is not a gimmick, but a device to focus on "the permanent struggle which results from the inevitable confrontation of the expansive, inquiring, affirming temperament and the timid, restrictive, complacent one."

Gérard Leblanc's "Ironic Reversal as Theme and Technique in Synge's Shorter Comedies" (in *Aspects of the Irish Theatre*, ed. Patrick Rafroidi et al., Paris, 1972) discusses the variety and importance of reversals and inversions in *Shadow of the Glen* and *Tinker's Wedding.*

Jeanne A. Flood's "Thematic Variation in Synge's Early Peasant Plays" (*Éire,* 1972) is a comparison/contrast of *Riders, Tinker's Wedding,* and *Shadow of the Glen* in terms of the themes of shelter versus physical nature and of female versus male sexual power. Her intricate thesis draws her into several questionable assumptions and judgments. For example, she regards *Riders* and *Tinker's Wedding* as "reversed treatments of the same situation," a mother presiding over her son's death in one and over his marriage in the other. Because she believes that the "fertilisable female chaos" generally destroys the "male ordering principle," she finds the males that survive to be asexual: the priest in *Tinker's Wedding* "possesses as the end of the play shows considerable power—considerable because not genital." She also sees Dan Burke at the end of *Shadow of the Glen* as remaining "safe and powerful inside the shelter," since he has never consummated his marriage with Nora.

Harold Orel (*Éire,* 1972) puts Synge's interest in tramps in the context of a general nineteenth-century interest in vagrants, expressed by many writers, Continental, British, and American. He compares Synge and Borrow in some detail. Orel finds Synge's vagrants interesting because "they possess vibrantly alive temperaments," "because they remain true to themselves rather than to any conventional expectation of what they should be doing," and "because they have not been stained by the world's contagion."

C. S. Faulk's "John Millington Synge and the Rebirth of Comedy" (*SHR,* 1974) deals with the origins and modes of Synge's comedy. Pointing out that Synge's richly cultivated sensibility enabled him to draw on a wide range of past literature, she praises his success in recovering the dynamics of a genuinely dramatic art. The first segment of the essay traces Synge's "movement from theory to original dramatic image." She then says that his romantic themes were enhanced by the primitive and archaic element he derived from Gaelic literature and culture, reflected most in *Riders to the Sea* and *Deirdre.* Between these dramas lie Synge's plays that enraged audiences by their willful mixture of perspectives. Faulk characterizes Synge's mode of comedy as akin to Greek Old Comedy, antisocial but not revolutionary; unlike Yeats and Nietzsche, he did not idealize conflict, but he did understand that elimination of conflict is a questionable goal.

JAMES JOYCE

Thomas F. Staley

I. Bibliography

Compared with the work of other major literary figures of this
century, James Joyce's canon is not a large one. His reputation as a
dominant figure in twentieth-century literature rests upon four major
works, *Dubliners* (1914), *A Portrait of the Artist as a Young Man*
(1916), *Ulysses* (1922), and *Finnegans Wake* (1939). He also wrote
a play, *Exiles* (1918), and a small quantity of poetry (a suite, *Chamber Music*, 1907; and *Pomes Penyeach*, 1927, as well as several occasional poems). Some of his critical essays, reviews, and notes have
been published as *The Critical Writings* (1959); and an earlier version of *A Portrait*, *Stephen Hero* (1944), came out posthumously.
Other minor works have also been published as well as three volumes
of Joyce's *Letters* (1957, 1966).

PRIMARY BIBLIOGRAPHY

With the possible exception of P. S. O'Hegarty's preliminary work
(*DM*, 1946), the first full-scale bibliography of Joyce's works was
Alan Parker, *James Joyce: A Bibliography of His Writings, Critical
Material and Miscellanea* (1948). A number of other primary bibliographical articles or catalogs of a more specialized nature also appeared prior to 1953. John J. Slocum and Herbert Cahoon's *A
Bibliography of James Joyce* (1953; rpt. 1971) superseded Parker and
has remained a distinguished primary bibliography. Given the curious and complex history of Joyce's published work, this bibliography
is an important document in modern literary history besides being a
valuable scholarly tool. Although Joyce's canon appears to be fairly
small, the circumstances surrounding the publication of his work,
such as the appearance in book form of sections of *Finnegans Wake*,
account for the fact that Slocum and Cahoon list fifty-two publications by Joyce in the first section of the *Bibliography*.

Slocum and Cahoon extend the primary material to 1950, "with occasional subsequent additions." In spite of its comprehensiveness, the book omits several publications prior to 1950. Besides omissions, further variants have also been discovered in several editions, but it remains to be determined whether these are merely freak copies or true variants. Because of the relatively large number of primary works published after 1950, there is also a serious need for a new primary bibliography accounting for later posthumous publications and editions. At this writing there are tentative plans by Fred H. Higginson to undertake a new bibliography. Merely supplying addenda and corrigenda to the old edition, however, will not do. The new bibliography should reproduce title pages of all the important editions described and employ the latest bibliographical techniques.

SECONDARY BIBLIOGRAPHY AND SURVEYS OF CRITICISM

In contrast to the rather modest canon of Joyce, there has been a massive outpouring of criticism and scholarship. Only William Faulkner and Henry James, among writers of English prose of this century, have attracted such wide and voluminous scholarly attention. Because of the sheer mass of material, Joyce scholarship has acquired the epithet, whether pejorative or simply amazed, the "Joyce Industry" (see Thomas F. Staley, "James Joyce and the Dilemma of American Academic Criticism," *DM*, 1967).

Prior to 1960 a number of secondary bibliographies and checklists appeared. Alan Cohn's "Joyce Bibliographies: A Survey" (*ABC*, 1965) is an attempt to sort them all out and show their relations to one another. Cohn also includes primary bibliographies. In his primary bibliography Alan Parker included a chapter on the secondary material, which was first supplemented by William White (*PBSA*, 1949, *JJR*, 1957), later by Richard M. Kain (*JJR*, 1957) and Cohn (*JJR*, 1958), and again by Cohn with H. K. Croessmann (*JJR*, 1959). The most comprehensive checklist to appear prior to 1960 was by Maurice Beebe and A. Walton Litz (*MFS*, 1958), especially useful for providing sections devoted to studies of separate works. During the fifties a number of general secondary bibliographies and checklists appeared, but none was as comprehensive as the Beebe and Litz checklist.

In 1964, following the advent of the publication of the *James Joyce Quarterly* (1963), Cohn and Richard M. Kain published the "Supplemental James Joyce Checklist, 1962," which added to the Joyce listings for 1962 in the "Annual Bibliography" of *PMLA*. In subsequent issues of *JJQ*, Cohn has supplemented the annual *MLA International Bibliography* listings that have appeared since the Beebe and Litz checklist. His bibliographies are far more extensive than the MLA annuals, for he not only corrects omissions of secondary materials but also lists book reviews and new primary material, new translations, recordings, tapes, musical settings, films, dissertations, and so forth. His work has become the most accurate and complete bibliographical tool for all Joyce studies.

Robert H. Deming's *A Bibliography of James Joyce Studies* (1964) contains over 1,400 numbered entries which cover Joyce studies through December 1961. He has classified the entries, annotated each item, and provided a thorough author index. This bibliography lists at least one hundred items that had not been accounted for in previous bibliographies, but all bibliographies are provisional, and Deming has many omissions. Too, Deming's annotations are not reliable and his summaries frequently miss the point. Kain and Cohn have supplemented Deming, mainly for the most recent years up to 1961 (*JJQ*, 1966).

In 1969, in a special Joyce number of *MFS*, Beebe, Phillip F. Herring, and Litz published a selected checklist. This secondary bibliography developed out of the 1958 *MFS* checklist and follows the same general outline. The 1958 checklist had been updated by Beebe and Litz and was reprinted in *RLM* (1959/1960) and later still supplemented for 1959 to early 1964 by Cohn and Herring (*RLM*, 1965). These supplements were re-edited, updated, and pulled together for the 1969 *MFS* checklist. In spite of its length (over 75 pages), the compilers note that their checklist "is a selection from the vast amount of material that might have been included." As of this writing, however, the 1969 *MFS* checklist remains the best single bibliography of secondary material for Joyce scholars. The most complete and up-to-date bibliographical source is, of course, the *MLA International Bibliography* listings together with Cohn's continuing supplements in *JJQ*. Deming is preparing a new edition of his 1965 bibliography, which will make corrections, extend his coverage through 1972, and add previously omitted material. William White compiled the Joyce section of *NCBEL* (Vol. IV, 1972), which presents a thorough coverage of both primary and secondary material through 1969. The most recent bibliographical survey is A. Walton Litz's chapter on Joyce in *The English Novel: Select Bibliographical Guides* (ed. A. E. Dyson, 1974). Although not exhaustive, it surveys the best studies and places them in the perspective of Joyce's changing reputation.

Besides the bibliographical material mentioned above, there have been a number of articles that have attempted to evaluate portions of Joyce criticism by either periods or individual works. A survey of Joyce criticism through the 1940's is provided by Herbert M. McLuhan (now better known as Marshall McLuhan) in *Renascence* (1951). A lengthy early survey of Joyce criticism is provided in Marvin Magalaner and Richard M. Kain's *Joyce: The Man, the Work, the Reputation* (1956), which is based on about 2,500 items. Staley's "Joyce Scholarship in the 1960's" (*Papers on Eng. Lang. and Lit.*, 1965; now *PLL*) discusses general developments in Joyce criticism through 1965; Cohn's "Haveth Critics Everywhere" (*Mad River Rev.*, 1966) reviews almost two dozen books published 1965–66 dealing with Joyce; Bernard Benstock offers an evaluation of general trends in Joyce scholarship in his "The James Joyce Industry: An Assessment in the Sixties" (*SoR*, 1966); and his essay "The James Joyce Industry: A Reassessment," in a forthcoming *Festschrift* for William York Tindall, is a general survey of developments in Joyce criticism through 1970. In this context Robert Martin Adams' "The Bent Knife Blade: Joyce in the 1960's" (*PR*, 1962) should be mentioned. Though not a bibliographical essay, it does provide a broad critical perspective from which the scholar can view Joyce's art in light of the modern critical and cultural climate.

Several specialized bibliographies or surveys of criticism on particular works by Joyce have appeared. T. H. Gibbons, for example, has published a broad but incomplete survey of *Dubliners* criticism (*CritQ*, 1967). The most complete bibliography on *Dubliners* is Fritz Senn's, which appears in *Materialien zu James Joyces* Dubliners (Frankfurt-am-Main, 1969). The most complete bibliography of *A Portrait* has also been published in Germany in a volume that includes a number of essays by German scholars (*James Joyces* Portrait: *Das Jugenbildnis im dichte neuerer deutscher Forschung*, ed. Wilhelm Füger, Munich, 1972). The bibliography lists 455 secondary items and offers as well a special section listing translations of *A Portrait*. Two valuable bibliographical items are Thomas Connolly, *The Personal Library of James Joyce: A Descriptive Bibliography* (1955); and Bernard Gheerbrant, ed., *James Joyce: Sa vie, son oeuvre, son rayonnement* (Paris, 1949), a catalog describing an exhibition of Joyce material later acquired by the Lockwood Memorial Library, State University of New York, Buffalo (see Peter Spielberg's *James Joyce's Manuscripts and Letters at the University of Buffalo: A Catalogue*, 1962).

An extremely important collection of materials, both critical and biographical, appeared in the Critical Heritage Series with *James Joyce: The Critical Heritage* (2 vols., ed. Robert Deming, 1970). Perhaps this collection should more properly be cited in the section under general criticism, but because of its breadth it is mentioned here. The collection presents critical commentary on Joyce's work from 1902 to 1941. The purpose is to provide "as complete as possible a spectrum of the contemporary response" to Joyce's work. Although much of the material is ineptly excerpted, the essays offer a thorough picture of Joyce's critical reputation during his lifetime. The collection is especially valuable because it reprints material inaccessible in many libraries, including foreign items in (if not always the best) English translations. Deming also provides in his introduction a brief general survey of the criticism on individual works. Taken as a whole, these two volumes form a good survey of contemporary reaction to Joyce's work.

Although limited or partial assessments have been made of the reception of Joyce's writing, few systematic studies have been undertaken. Studies of Joyce's critical reception in various Western European countries are also lacking, with the notable exception of Breon Mitchell's Oxford dissertation on *Ulysses* and the German novel (1968) and Rosemarie Franke's *James Joyce und der deutsche Sprachbereich*, a dissertation for the Freie Universität Berlin (1970). One article that reveals the curious fluctuation of Joyce's reputation in the USSR through the translation of various editions of Soviet encyclopedias is William B. Edgerton's "Dzhoising with the Soviet Encyclopedias" (*JJQ*, 1968). In the same issue of *JJQ*, Sigfrid Hoefort has published "James Joyce in East Germany." See also Gleb Struve's chapter "Socialist Realism versus James Joyce" in his *Russian Literature under Lenin and Stalin 1917–1953* (1971). However, thorough studies of Joyce's reputation based upon critical reception of translations and literary influence remain for the most part a lacuna in Joyce scholarship.

II. *Manuscript Holdings and Catalogs*

Manuscripts and papers of Joyce are widely scattered, though most of the materials are in various libraries in the United States. The major exceptions are the final holograph manuscript of *A Portrait* ("a fair copy in ink written in very clear handwriting and with no corrections") which was given by Harriett Shaw Weaver in July 1951 to the National Library of Ireland, Dublin; almost all of the *Finnegans Wake* manuscript in the British Museum; and the surviving *Ulysses* notesheets, "Cyclops" through "Penelope," also in the British Museum (Add. MS. 49975), both of these likewise the generous gift of Harriett Shaw Weaver. The manuscript holdings in various libraries in the United States and abroad were initially described by Slocum and Cahoon, and in several cases their pioneer work has been greatly supplemented.

The two greatest collections of Joyce manuscripts are held by Cornell and Buffalo; full descriptive catalogs of both collections have been published. The Buffalo collection as described by Peter Spielberg in his *James Joyce's Manuscripts and Letters at the University of Buffalo: A Catalogue* contains nearly 450 items, or 20,000 written pages. A major portion of the Buffalo Joyce collection consists of manuscripts, letters, and books acquired in 1959 from Sylvia Beach. In 1961 Robert Scholes published *The Cornell Joyce Collection: A Catalogue*. The Cornell holdings are strong in materials related to Joyce's life and work prior to 1920; it is a collection of private papers that were in the possession of Joyce's younger brother Stanislaus.

Yale and the University of Texas also have rich holdings in primary materials. The Texas collection has been described by Weldon Thornton in "Books and Manuscripts by James Joyce" (*LCUT*, 1961). Yale was the recipient of John J. Slocum's extensive collection. Neither of these collections is as large or as important as those at Cornell and Buffalo. Southern Illinois University has a strong collection, portions of which have been briefly and selectively described by Alan Cohn in *James Joyce: An Exhibition from the Collection of Dr. H. K. Croessmann* (1957). The famous fair-copy manuscript of *Ulysses* (see Slocum and Cahoon, pp. 138–40), a facsimile of which was published in 1975, is held by the Rosenbach Foundation in Philadelphia, and Harvard holds the galleys of *Ulysses*. The University of Kansas acquired an excellent Joyce collection, which is especially rich in Irish background material, from J. F. Spoerri.

III. *Editions, Concordances, and Textual Studies*

A definitive collected edition of Joyce's work does not exist, nor are there any prospects for such until the copyrights expire. The complex publication history of Joyce's canon accounts in part for the deplorable condition of the texts of *Ulysses* and *Finnegans Wake*, but it is difficult to imagine that the major texts of any other modern author of Joyce's stature exist in such a corrupt state. When one considers the great body of critical study done on *Ulysses*, for example, and the extremely close textual analysis devoted to it, it is all the more frustrating that the text remains filled with egregious errors. Recently, however, Joyce's entire canon has come under much closer textual scrutiny, and scholarly work on the earlier texts has produced more reliable editions. The problems related to Joyce's manuscripts are also receiving considerable attention. In spite of Joyce's herculean struggles with the publication of his work, one underlying irony, suggested by Fred H. Higginson, should be kept in mind as one attempts to unravel the textual problems: even though his later work poses complex linguistic and printing problems of greater magnitude than that of any writer before him, Joyce did not himself understand editing. He was quite willing, for example, to turn the "authoritative" edition of *Ulysses* (Odyssey Press, 1932) over to Stuart Gilbert. The critic of Joyce's work, when dealing with delicate interpretative matters that rely on close textual evidence, must indeed be cautious; and this is most true of *Ulysses*.

It has been previously noted that Joyce's poetry forms a very small part of his canon, but his first book was a collection of 36 interrelated poems published by Elkin Mathews in 1907 (London). In 1926 Sylvia Beach's Shakespeare and Company published thirteen of Joyce's later poems under the title *Pomes Penyeach*; a baker's dozen sold for twelve francs. These two collections with the addition of the poem "Ecce Puer" (1932) were later published by the Viking Press under the title *Collected Poems* (1937), still in print. In 1954 William York Tindall completed with a thorough introduction and extensive notes an edition of *Chamber Music*. Tindall's effort reflects his collation of all previous editions and the manuscripts. He reprints the Elkin Mathews text and supplies notes immediately following each poem that list the variants from nine previous editions as well as from earlier magazine publications of the poems. At present, this edition is out of print. Tindall's peculiar reading of the poems themselves will be treated later. The most comprehensive collection of Joyce's poetry is the Mondadori edition, *James Joyce Poesie* (Milan, 1961), a bilingual edition which includes Joyce's occasional pieces as well as the better known poems.

The myriad problems Joyce experienced in his attempts to have *Dubliners* published, which brought him near to despair, have been well documented by Robert Scholes's "Grant Richards to James Joyce" (*SB*, 1963). As early as 1905 Joyce offered the manuscript to Grant Richards, but it was not published until 1914 (London). A definitive text, which restores many of Joyce's manuscript entries and later corrections, was published in 1967 by Viking Press and edited by Scholes. Most of the corrections were based upon his earlier studies, "Some Observations on the Text of *Dubliners*: 'The Dead' " and "Further Observations on the Text of *Dubliners*" (*SB*, 1962, 1964). Scholes's 1967 text was also used in the Viking Critical Library edition of *Dubliners* (ed. Litz and Scholes), which includes criticism, detailed notes, and bibliography.

The Viking Press has also published a "definitive text" of *A Portrait* (1964) corrected from the Dublin holograph by Chester G. Anderson with editorial assistance by Richard Ellmann. This text is based upon a comparison of Joyce's final fair-copy holograph manuscript with all the texts published in England and the United States and with lists of corrections and changes noted by Joyce, some of which were never made in any of the published versions. It is important to note, however, that Anderson has disclaimed the definitiveness of his Viking edition in a long essay describing in detail the textual problems in *A Portrait* (*NM*, 1964). Anderson did not have, for example, the typescript from which the printer set the book. A recent essay ("Zur Textgeschichte und Textkritik des *Portrait*," in *James Joyces Portrait*, ed. Wilhelm Füger, Munich, 1972) and "Towards a Critical Text of James Joyce's *A Portrait* . . ." (*SB*, 1974) by Hans Walter Gabler substantiate Anderson's work and reveal further textual corruptions and problems. Robert M. Adams has also discussed the *Portrait* text (*James Joyce: Common Sense and Beyond*, 1966) and offered reasons for preferring the 1924 Jonathan Cape edition. Nevertheless, grateful for any progress where Joyce texts are concerned, we can generally agree that the 1964 Viking edition represents a considerably better text than all previous *Portrait* editions. The 1964 Viking edition of *Portrait* has also been issued in the Viking Critical Library series which includes selections of criticism, detailed explanatory notes, and selected bibliography (ed. Chester Anderson). In England, Heinemann has also published an edition of *A Portrait* (1964), with an introduction and notes by James S. Atherton.

Joyce's single published dramatic work was *Exiles* (1918); the critical reception (or rather, lack thereof) given to it disappointed him for years. The play was republished by Viking in 1951 with an introduction by Joyce's friend Padraic Colum. This edition included the previously unpublished and revealing notes that Joyce had written to the play. Subsequent reprints, including the Viking Compass Edition, have included Colum's introduction together with the notes.

The Portable James Joyce (ed. with introd. and notes by Harry Levin, 1946) includes the full texts of *Dubliners*, *A Portrait*, *Exiles*, the *Collected Poems* (as well as "Gas from a Burner," "The Holy Office," and "Ecce Puer"), and selected episodes from *Ulysses* and *Finnegans Wake*. Recent printings include the Scholes text of *Dubliners* and the Anderson text of *A Portrait*. Because of its comprehensiveness, *The Portable* (in England, mistitled *The Essential James Joyce*) has remained a popular text in schools and colleges.

The textual problems surrounding Joyce's earlier work (and perhaps those of any other major work of fiction of this century) dim when compared with those of *Ulysses*. As noted earlier, the circumstances of its publication account in part for many of the corruptions in the various editions (see R. F. Roberts, *Colophon*, 1936), and the difficulties Joyce had with his eyes is another complicating factor, to say nothing of the palimpsest nature of the manuscripts themselves. The Shakespeare and Company editions present a number of textual problems. As Roberts points out, the compositors in Dijon were confronted with setting type in another language and recomposing from proof sheets that can only be described as a printer's nightmare. This situation, coupled with Joyce's failing eyesight, accounts for the many errors in the first edition. The first English edition was struck from the original plates because no English printer would set up the type; thus no textual corrections were made in this edition, although eight errata pages listing 200 typographical errors were laid in. These errors were corrected by the fourth edition, but an additional list of errors was laid in through the seventh edition. For the eighth edition, printed in May 1926, the type was entirely reset, but, as Roberts has pointed out, in spite of the numerous editions, progress on the text is at best partial.

Before *Ulysses* was published in book form by Shakespeare and Company in Paris in 1922, portions of it appeared serially in *The Little Review*; in all, 23 installments appeared between March 1918 and December 1920. Thirteen complete episodes and part of the fourteenth (of a total of 18) were published before the courts ordered publication to stop as a result of an action filed in New York by the Society for the Suppression of Vice. Both before and during this action, several issues of *The Little Review* containing episodes of *Ulysses* were banned by the United States Post Office. It should be noted that the chapters of *Ulysses* that appeared in *The Little Review* were in a different state from those that appeared in the first edition of 1922.

Following the famous decision handed down by the Honorable John M. Woolsey on 6 December 1933 (*United States of America* v. *One Book called* Ulysses), *Ulysses* was published on 25 January 1934. Thus began the book publication of *Ulysses* in the United States and shortly thereafter the many reprints with, in the famous phrase of Fredson Bowers, their "remorseless corrupting influence." Ironically, the Random House edition of 1934 was set from a copy of the 1929 pirated edition, laden with errors. After nearly thirty years and over a half million copies sold, in 1961 Random House published a "new edition, corrected and reset," and used the corrupt 1960 English resetting (Bodley Head). Even before a careful examination of this new edition, an outcry was raised by the scholarly community for the failure to follow the old pagination. No work of fiction published in this century has had such close annotation and explication with scrupulous reference to page and line number; this lack of concern only deepened the bitter reception that the text received. The publisher later partially corrected this serious defect in the 1961 edition by printing the old page numbers at appropriate lines in the margin.

The far more serious problem was, of course, the disastrous text which evolved in the 1961 edition based on the 1960 Bodley Head and the "corrections" which were made independently by the publisher; these must be considered proofreading and not editing—and poor proofreading at that. The gruesome story of this edition and its ancestors is told with fervor by Jack P. Dalton in "The Text of *Ulysses*," *New Light on Joyce from the Dublin Symposium* (ed. Fritz Senn, 1972). In short, a definitive text of *Ulysses* does not exist; and although the Hamburg edition (Odyssey Press, 1932, 1933, 1935) may be the most accurate, it can under no circumstances be considered a replacement for a desperately needed reliable, far less "definitive," edition. The Odyssey edition is, of course, not accessible, having long been out of print, and the plates were destroyed during World War II.

The British text is not a reliable one. The Bodley Head edition, referred to earlier, was published in a limited edition in 1936; the first unlimited edition was published in 1937; it was reset in 1960, ran through nine impressions, and was revised in 1969 with an appendix for corresponding pages between the old and new editions. The first Penguin edition (paperback) was published in 1968 for sale outside the United Kingdom and in 1969 for sale within the United Kingdom; it was reprinted with corrections in 1971. Though based upon the Bodley Head edition, it introduces new inaccuracies.

At the Fourth International James Joyce Symposium held in Dublin in June 1973, a special meeting was held in which three Joyce textual scholars explained in detail the intricate problems associated with the establishment of a corrected text of *Ulysses*, after which a committee of Joyce scholars was established to oversee articles and lists of errata to be published in the *James Joyce Quarterly* as a means of preparing for a corrected text of *Ulysses* that will eventually contribute to a "scholar's edition." This committee will act as a clearing-house and be responsible for printing specimen varia, but the establishment of a text remains the responsibility of the publishers since they still hold the copyright.

Finnegans Wake was first published simultaneously by Faber & Faber in England and the Viking Press in the United States on 4 May 1939. As with *Ulysses*, earlier episodes appeared prior to publication of the work in its entirety. In 1945 Faber & Faber published a list of "Corrections of Misprints in *Finnegans Wake*," subtitled "As Prepared by the Author after Publication of the First Edition." In printings after 1945 (each version itself seriously misprinted), the list was bound into the book, and by the eighth printing, in 1958, the author's corrections were incorporated in the text itself. There are still errors in the present edition, many of which involve complex textual considerations, such as the author's intention and like matters. Fred H. Higginson has discussed a number of the general editorial problems associated with the book in "The Text of *Finnegans Wake*" (*New Light* . . . , 1972). James Blish has speculated that the present edition may contain as many as 7,000 errors, ranging from the omission of a full stop at the end of page 161 to the dropping of whole phrases and even whole lines of type (*JJQ*, 1971). Originally Faber & Faber had proposed that the more serious omissions and corrections be printed and bound into the back of subsequent printings. The listings would not include the scholarly arguments for or against each new reading, but only the readings themselves. More recently (1975), Faber published a new edition of *Finnegans Wake*, in both paperback and hardcover. This edition includes the incorporation of corrections compiled by Joyce and Paul Léon, misprints in previous editions, and thirty-one corrections introduced into the Viking text from which the new Faber edition was offset.

A number of Joyce's works have been published posthumously. For example, Joyce wrote two earlier versions of *A Portrait*. The first "A Portrait of the Artist" (1904) was a prose work of nearly 2,000 words; this was published (introd. Kain and Scholes, *YR*, 1960; rpt. in their

The Workshop of Daedalus, 1965) from the original holograph manuscript. *Stephen Hero*, the second version of what was to become *A Portrait*, was first published by New Directions in 1944 and reprinted in 1955 with the incorporation of additional manuscript pages, and with further material in 1963. Background information on this manuscript and its close and interesting relationship to *A Portrait* are discussed in the introduction to the editions by Theodore Spencer. At approximately the same period of composition (1903–06) as *Stephen Hero*, Joyce also wrote a series of very short pieces that he called "epiphanies." Twenty-two of these, carefully written on separate sheets of ruled paper, are in the Lockwood Memorial Library at Buffalo. They were published in a limited edition (*James Joyce Epiphanies*, 1956) with an introduction and notes by O. A. Silverman. Kain and Scholes later (*The Workshop of Daedalus*) republished the twenty-two epiphanies with the addition of eighteen others found in the Cornell Library.

Beyond the occasional review in the early stages of his career, Joyce wrote little literary criticism. His book reviews were edited with an introduction by his brother Stanislaus and Ellsworth Mason and published as *The Early Joyce: The Book Reviews, 1902–1903* (1955). This book, limited to 500 copies, is out of print, but pirated copies are easy to come by. In 1956 Viking Press published *The Critical Writings of James Joyce* (ed. Ellsworth Mason and Richard Ellmann), incorporating the reviews in *The Early Joyce*. Except for material that exists in manuscript, this volume is virtually complete and remains in print. A lecture Joyce delivered on Daniel Defoe in Trieste has been edited and translated by Joseph Prescott and published as a monograph in the Buffalo Studies series (*Daniel Defoe by James Joyce*, 1964).

In 1967 *Giacomo Joyce* was published in an elaborate limited edition in slipcase, including complete facsimiles of the work, with an introduction by Richard Ellmann. Most of this short piece had appeared earlier in Ellmann's biography. A less elaborate edition without the facsimiles has subsequently been published by Viking and remains in print. This curious little piece is an autobiographical love story about a young girl and her English tutor which Joyce probably wrote in 1914. Set in Trieste, it recalls in its delicacy Joyce's earlier poetry, but it is also a wry if ambivalent glance at the passing of youth into middle age.

A single volume of Joyce's letters (ed. Stuart Gilbert, 1957) was reissued with corrections in 1966 in conjunction with the publication by Viking Press of two further volumes (ed. Richard Ellmann). The three volumes together include over 1,100 letters by Joyce and 197 letters of importance written to Joyce. Gilbert's volume covers the span of Joyce's life from struggling young writer to famous author but leaves much of his life unaccounted for. Ellmann's volumes include 226 valuable family letters to Joyce's father, mother, and brother Stanislaus, and 62 letters written to his wife, Nora.

This three-volume edition of letters presents one problem of inconvenience. The Gilbert volume should have been incorporated into the two new ones, thus providing three volumes with all the letters arranged in chronological order. Moreover, the first volume is far inferior to the later two volumes; it is neither so carefully edited nor so carefully indexed, and it does not provide sufficient documentation. Ellmann's introductions in the second and third volumes are thorough and illuminating, and his chronology of Joyce's addresses is extremely useful. An edition of the *Selected Letters* (1975) is also edited by Ellmann. This prints selections from the three-volume set and includes previously suppressed letters and portions of letters, as well as newly discovered ones. It should be noted that the German edition of the letters offers a liberal selection and the letters are in chronological order. An important specialized volume is *Pound/Joyce* (ed. Forrest Read, 1967), which includes Ezra Pound's letters to Joyce as well as Pound's essays on Joyce and other material. Read provides detailed commentary on the letters and other material.

Additional letters by Joyce have been published since 1967. Philip R. Yannella published "James Joyce to *The Little Review*: Ten Letters" (*JML*, 1971). Other letters to and by Joyce are forthcoming in various journals. For anyone interested in Joyce's letters, Lionel Trilling's "James Joyce in His Letters" (*Commentary*, 1968) is a valuable essay.

Foreign language translations of Joyce's works are far too numerous to discuss here. For example, there are three different translations of *Dubliners* into Italian. A fascinating study of some translations of *Ulysses* which also probes the inherent and almost insurmountable difficulties which confront the translator is Fritz Senn's "*Ulysses* in Translation" (in *Approaches to Ulysses*, ed. Staley and Benstock, 1970). An earlier version of this essay by Senn is aptly entitled "Seven against *Ulysses*" (*JJQ*, 1967). The Spring 1967 issue of *JJQ* is devoted to various aspects of translating Joyce.

Although it was stated at the beginning of this section that a definitive, collected edition of Joyce's work does not exist, one should note that the five-volume Mondadori edition in Italy and the seven-volume Suhrkamp edition (not yet completed) in Germany aim at reasonable completeness and are carefully edited and translated.

As the previous discussion of the textual and manuscript difficulties with Joyce's work would suggest, a number of attempts have been made to determine and clarify the stages of Joyce's composition. A. Walton Litz's *The Art of James Joyce* (1961), subtitled *Method and Design in* Ulysses *and* Finnegans Wake, offers a detailed and systematic account of the genesis and growth of the two works through a careful study of the stages of composition from rough drafts through proof sheets. His work is especially valuable for its insights into the overall design and creative process in Joyce's work. Litz concludes that there is not "one controlling design," but rather an evolving process through the various stages of composition. Consistently, however, Joyce's compositional process is one of accretion. Litz's revelations are invaluable for the student of *Ulysses* and *Finnegans Wake*.

Another important and illuminating textual study of *Ulysses* is Phillip F. Herring's *Joyce's* Ulysses Notesheets *in the British Museum* (1972). Herring has transcribed the entire ninety pages of manuscript. The notesheets are for the last seven episodes of *Ulysses*, and Herring has provided lucid descriptive essays on each as well as accurate notes to his transcriptions. Elsewhere Herring has published his textual studies of other Joyce manuscripts related to *Ulysses*, such as his "*Ulysses* Notebook VIII. A. 5 at Buffalo" (*SB*, 1969). Further textual scholarship by Herring has been announced for publication, and his thorough examinations and accurate transcriptions will be most welcome.

Five doctoral dissertations have studied the textual development of individual episodes of *Ulysses*: Norman Silverstein, "Joyce's 'Circe' Episode: Approaches to *Ulysses* through a Textual and Interpretative Study of Joyce's Fifteenth Chapter" (1960); Richard E. Madtes, "A Textual and Critical Study of the 'Ithaca' Episode of James Joyce's *Ulysses*" (1961); Robert E. Hurley, "The 'Proteus' Episode of James Joyce's *Ulysses*" (1963); James V. D. Card, "A Textual and Critical Study of the 'Penelope' Episode of James Joyce's *Ulysses*" (1964); and Robert Janusko, "The Sources and Structure of the 'Oxen of the Sun' Episode . . ." (1967). The first four were done at Columbia University under the direction of William York Tindall, the last at Kent State University with Bernard Benstock.

No significant manuscript study of *Finnegans Wake* appeared until 1960 with the publication of Fred H. Higginson's distinguished *Anna Livia Plurabelle: The Making of a Chapter*. Higginson has collated all the extant versions of the "Anna Livia Plurabelle" chapter and established six texts, and he provides, through an ingenious system of brackets, a method that enables scholars to reconstruct the various drafts and note the revisions and additions.

Two other works devoted to *Finnegans Wake* are Thomas E. Connolly's *James Joyce's Scribbledehobble* (1961) and David Hayman's *A First-Draft Version of* Finnegans Wake (1963). Connolly edited a notebook which Joyce used as a sourcebook for *Finnegans Wake*; *Scribbledehobble* has created a great deal of controversy from the time of its initial reviews in the popular press to later reviews and corrections in scholarly journals. (See, e.g., Vivian Mercier, *New York Times Book Rev.* 19 Mar. 1961, and subsequent correspondence; and David Hayman's "A List of Corrections for the *Scribbledehobble*," *JJQ*, 1964.) The controversy centers around Connolly's ability to read Joyce's difficult handwriting. Hayman's *Wake* book is a construction of a "liberally defined" first draft version based upon Joyce's notebook, fair copies, typescripts, and proof sheets, as well as notes and changes in galley and page proof. It would be a mistake to consider Hayman's volume an authentic first draft version, for his compendium raises as many questions concerning the composition of *Finnegans Wake* as it answers.

Concordances have been published to virtually all of Joyce's works except *Exiles*; the earliest was Miles L. Hanley's *Word Index to . . . Ulysses* (1937), based on the 1934 Random House edition. Besides the errata, the *Index* omits all but the last four lines of page 470 of *Ulysses* and excludes words occurring more than 25 times. When a definitive edition of *Ulysses* is published there will be a need for a new concordance, for there are errors in the *Index*, but the Hanley volume has been an important and invaluable scholarly tool for over thirty years; it is lamentable that it is out of print.

Other concordances include Clive Hart's *A Concordance to* Finnegans Wake (1963; rpt. with corrections, 1974) which includes syllabifications and overtones and is a much handier tool than a mechanical list; and Chester Anderson's *World Index to . . .* Stephen Hero (1958; rpt. 1974). Paul A. Doyle has compiled *A Concordance to the* Collected Poems (1966). His concordance is a word index to the *Collected Poems* (1937), and he has wisely included the two poems not in this volume but included in *The Portable*, "The Holy Office" (1904) and "Gas from a Burner" (1912). Neurine W. LaPorte's "A Word Index to *Giacomo Joyce*" constitutes issue 26 of *The Analyst* (1971).

Two computerized volumes have been published: Leslie Hancock's *Word Index to . . .* Portrait of the Artist (1967) and Gary Lane's *A Word Index to . . .* Dubliners (1972).

IV. *Biography*

BIOGRAPHICAL STUDIES

Biographical and background studies of Joyce abound; and many memoirs, discussions, and studies of Joyce's life were published before the appearance of Richard Ellmann's masterful, definitive biography, *James Joyce* (1959). Ellmann's biography, which won the National Book Award and several other literary prizes, made an enormous contribution not only to Joyce studies but also to modern literary biography. Its thoroughness, general accuracy, method of presentation, insight, sophistication, style, and comprehensive understanding of its subject as writer and man have brought fame and recognition to both the book and the biographer. It is fair to say that Ellmann's biography advanced Joyce scholarship in all of its aspects and widened the interest in Joyce far beyond the academic community. Little need be added to the general public praise this book has already received, nor can its contribution to Joyce studies be overemphasized. So much of what had been tentative, unestablished, or speculative became fixed and certain after Ellmann's biography. At this writing, over fifteen years after its publication, there have been a number of minor inaccuracies exposed; many questions regarding tone and emphasis have been raised and various interpretations questioned, but the reception of the work among Joyce scholars has remained extremely favorable. Ellmann's biography is the most important work to be written on Joyce and is the book with which students and scholars must begin their secondary reading.

Herbert Gorman had been authorized by Joyce to be his "official" biographer and had been given controlled access to those materials which he and Joyce thought would be helpful. His *James Joyce: His First Forty Years* (1924) was followed by *James Joyce* (1939; rev. 1948). On the dust jacket of its 1949 reprint, Bodley Head claimed Gorman's book to be a "definitive biography." It was in no sense "definitive" but was the only biography available prior to 1959. Gorman's work is not to be discounted, though it remains a biography written by one loyal to the subject and dependent upon him for access to nearly all material; Gorman, therefore, had the advantages and disadvantages of such a relationship, and his book clearly reveals this. As Ellmann's biography indicates, his own access to letters and material as well as the candor offered by Joyce's friends and relatives after his death far outweighed Gorman's advantage of having known Joyce personally. In fact, Gorman's relationship with Joyce on occasion was a detriment, for Joyce actively interfered and at least once exercised a veto.

Two important essays that appeared prior to Ellmann's biography were Richard M. Kain's "The Joyce Enigma" and Marvin Magalaner's "The Problem of Biography" in their *Joyce: The Man, the Work, the Reputation* (1956). These chapters were quite valuable and strove to offer "points of departure for further investigation."

Many aspects of Joyce's life have been treated in critical books and articles, but several exclusively biographical studies that deal with a specific aspect of Joyce's life (exclusive of memoirs by friends or acquaintances, which will be dealt with in the following section) have been published in book or pamphlet form. Leon Edel has provided a sensitive sketch of Joyce's last days in Zurich, *James Joyce: The Last Journey* (1947); and Lucie Noel has traced Joyce's relationship with his friend Paul Léon in *James Joyce and Paul L. Léon: The Story of a Friendship* (1948).

Throughout his life Joyce had severe health problems, the most formidable of which was eye disease. Joseph Collins touches on this latter topic in a chapter entitled "Ireland's Latest Literary Antinomian: James Joyce," in his *The Doctor Looks at Literature* (1923), and Noah D. Fabricant devotes a chapter to Joyce's eye disease in *Thirteen Famous Patients* (1960). The most thorough study of Joyce's medical and psychological history together with its influence on his work is J. B. Lyons' *James Joyce and Medicine* (1973), a book more notable for its medical than its literary speculations.

Shorter biographical sketches and studies of Joyce covering various aspects of his life are far too numerous to mention here. A thorough listing of these appears in Section C (Biographies, Reminiscences, Interviews and other primary material dealing with Joyce the man) of the Beebe, Herring, and Litz checklist (*MFS*, 1969).

Memoirs by Contemporaries

Unlike his fellow countryman Yeats, who led a wide public life, or his contemporary T. S. Eliot, who was actively engaged in the profession of letters, Joyce had neither prominence in public life nor wide literary associations. Through the years, however, he had a number of good friends (and a few not so good ones) as well as acquaintances, professional and personal, who have published memoirs or reminiscences of him.

The most important firsthand account of Joyce's life is given by his brother Stanislaus in *My Brother's Keeper* (ed. with introd. & notes by Richard Ellmann; preface T. S. Eliot, 1958). This work offers a thorough, if slightly biased, account of Joyce's early years in Dublin and is especially valuable for the information it provides on Joyce's immediate family background and his early struggles to become a writer. Together with the rich collection of correspondence, this volume forms an excellent record of the close if frequently strained relationship between the two brothers. As Eliot suggests in his preface, it would be a mistake to dismiss this work as "merely a unique piece of documentation on the early life of one of the great writers of the century." In its candor and depth, it is a remarkable study of the relationship between brothers. An equally revealing document, and an important source book for Joyce study, is *The Complete Dublin Diary of Stanislaus Joyce* (ed. George H. Healey, 1971; an abridged ed. had appeared as *Dublin Diary* in 1962). A later lecture by Stanislaus given in May 1955 in Trieste was published as a pamphlet by the University of Trieste, *The Meeting of Svevo and Joyce* (1965).

Four books by early Dublin friends of Joyce recall associations with him; together they form an interesting account of his college years. J. F. Byrne's *Silent Years: An Autobiography with Memoirs of James Joyce and Our Ireland* (1953) is especially rich in providing contemporary Dublin background. In 1909, Joyce visited Byrne at No. 7 Eccles Street, an address later immortalized as the Blooms' house in *Ulysses*. More important, Byrne was the model for the character of Cranly in *A Portrait*, and his book recalls many experiences shared with Joyce that found their way into Joyce's books.

Padraic Colum, the Irish poet, and his wife Mary, a perceptive critic and writer, knew Joyce throughout nearly his entire life, including his Dublin years at the turn of the century and his later life in Paris. They have recorded their friendship in *Our Friend James Joyce* (1958). Although largely anecdotal, the book offers a witty portrait of their extended encounters with Joyce. Eugene Sheehy, in his humorous autobiography, *May It Please the Court* (1951), recalls Joyce in his university days with Thomas Kettle and Francis Sheehy-Skeffington, with the latter of whom Joyce collaborated in the publication of the *Two Essays* (1901) pamphlet. The most recent book to be published by a Dublin contemporary of Joyce's is Arthur Power's *Conversations with James Joyce* (1974), edited with an introduction by Clive Hart. Power records a number of interesting passages on Joyce's attitudes to Western and Russian literature.

The best single account by a friend of Joyce's Dublin years is Constantine Curran's *James Joyce Remembered* (1968). Curran and Joyce met as fellow students at University College and remained friends throughout Joyce's life. Of particular interest is the full description of the intellectual and cultural background of Dublin and University College. Curran's depiction of this ambience forms an interesting contrast with that offered in *A Portrait*. His description reveals the dangers of seeing Joyce and Dublin life as they appear in his work as an authentic historical and autobiographical account rather than as a world seen through an artistic vision rendered into fiction.

Three volumes offer collections of memoirs by Joyce's Dublin contemporaries: a substantial section of *The Workshop of Daedalus*, cited above; *The Joyce We Knew* (ed. Ulick O'Connor, 1967); and *A Bash in the Tunnel* (ed. John Ryan, 1970). This last reprints an earlier essay by Samuel Beckett as well as extracts from other memoirs, but it is especially interesting for its inclusion of a number of essays by a younger generation of Irish writers who lived and wrote under Joyce's shadow. Here they tell how they encountered his legend and his work and record the intellectual and emotional impact of these on their own artistic formations. Joyce studies have so often and quite properly focused on Joyce as a Continental writer that the Irish background frequently has become submerged, but biographical works such as these reinforce the importance of Ireland as a shaping and controlling element in Joyce's development. In this context one should mention W. R. Rodgers' *Irish Literary Portraits* (1972), which includes edited transcriptions of BBC interviews with several of Joyce's contemporaries recorded in 1950.

Of course, many other Irish memoirs discuss Joyce more or less fully in passing, but especially noteworthy are the autobiographical works of Oliver St. John Gogarty who, forever piqued at having been cast as Buck Mulligan, is less respectful than most; see especially *As I Was Going down Sackville Street* (1937).

Joyce moved from Trieste to Paris in 1920, a move that brought him to the artistic and intellectual center of modern art in all of its forms. Literary memoirs of Paris during the 1920's are rich and varied, and most of them include chapters or accounts of short meetings with Joyce. Literary reminiscences of Paris during this period are far too many to mention here; this subject has been well treated in a lecture by Maurice Beebe. Three volumes of special importance should, however, be mentioned. Louis Gillet's *Claybook for James Joyce* (1958) provides a good account of Joyce's literary associations and activities in Paris and also the French reaction to and acceptance of his work. A curious little book, Philippe Soupault's *Souvenirs de James Joyce* (Algiers, 1943; Paris, 1945), provides additional personal background. Soupault also includes fragments from *Finnegans Wake*, of which he was one of the translators. Sylvia Beach, the original publisher of *Ulysses*, has written *Shakespeare and Company* (1959). Although it is a general account of her bookshop and many of the writers with whom she came into contact, a large section of the book is devoted to Joyce and the publication of *Ulysses*. She also discusses the complexities and difficulties of being Joyce's publisher and offers an account of his family circumstances.

A number of primarily biographical essays on Joyce by his Paris contemporaries have been published in periodicals. A thorough listing of these appears in the *MFS* Checklist. Essays by Eugene and Maria Jolas and Jacques Mercanton are important. *A James Joyce Yearbook* (ed. Maria Jolas, Paris, 1949) is best known for its inclusion of Hermann Broch's essay on Joyce, but it also contains biographical material by several other writers and critics who knew Joyce.

An important creative period in Joyce's life was spent in Trieste, and a number of articles and monographs by Joyce's friends there have appeared. His most famous friendship was, of course, with the Italian writer Italo Svevo (Ettore Schmitz). A lecture Svevo delivered in Milan in 1927 was translated by Stanislaus Joyce and published as *James Joyce* (Milan, 1950) under the auspices of New Directions as a Christmas gift. This little booklet has since been reprinted by City Lights Books (n.d.). The title of this work is often confused because the lettering on the spine of both editions reads "Svevo on Joyce." Svevo's wife, Livia, treats the Joyce-Svevo relationship in her *Vita di mio marito* (Trieste, 1950). A pamphlet entitled *Ricordi di James Joyce e Italo Svevo* (Trieste, 1965) by Svevo's daughter, Letizia Fonda Savio, also recalls her firsthand knowledge of the relationship. Another close friend of Joyce's was the critic and publisher Silvio Benco, who has written of Joyce's Trieste years in "James Joyce in Trieste" (*Bookman*, 1930). The Trieste painter and writer Dario de Tuoni kept notes of his friendship with Joyce, published posthumously as *Ricordo di Joyce a Trieste* (Milan, 1960). Alessandro Francini Bruni, a fellow Berlitz teacher with Joyce, has recorded his memories of their association in *Joyce intimo spogliato in piazza* (Trieste, 1922) and in "Ricordi personali su James Joyce" (*Nuova anthologia*, 1947). Several short remembrances of Joyce are included in *JJQ*'s Joyce and Trieste issue (1972).

The English painter Frank Budgen first met Joyce in Zurich, where they both lived during World War I, and he remained one of Joyce's closest lifelong friends. His chapter on Joyce in his autobiography, *Myselves When Young* (1970), offers a brief but penetrating portrait of Joyce during his years in Switzerland. The latest edition of Budgen's *James Joyce and the Making of Ulysses* (1934; reissued with additional material, introd. Clive Hart, 1972) includes three new essays that provide further recollections of Joyce as well as critical material. The critical content of this book will be dealt with in a later section of this essay.

The last few weeks in Joyce's life were spent in Zurich, where he died on 13 January 1941. Later that year Joyce's close friend Carola Giedion-Welcker published a handsome memorial volume, *In Memoriam James Joyce* (Zurich, 1941). The volume includes a number of essays of biographical interest as well as Professor Heinrich Straumann's burial speech for Joyce. Giedion-Welcker has also provided a general account of Joyce's years in Zurich in *The Golden Horizon* (ed. Cyril Connolly, 1955). Straumann has also written a biographical memoir based on a visit with Joyce in Zurich in 1940, "Litzte Begegnung mit Joyce," *James Joyce Yearbook* (Paris, 1949).

BACKGROUND AND MILIEU STUDIES

A number of works obviously test the categories established in this chapter. Inclusion of a work within a category was based upon the balance of the work's emphasis. Many primarily critical works which emphasize intellectual and cultural background will be dealt with in Section v.

Book-length background and milieu studies have been confined largely to Joyce's Dublin experience and his Catholic education and religious influence. A number of studies related to Joyce and Trieste have also been published. Gisèle Freund and V. B. Carleton's *James Joyce in Paris: His Final Years* (1965) is a volume of photographs, many of which (handsome as they are) have little to do with Joyce. A full-length study of Joyce and Paris does not exist. A volume which offers a general topographical background to Joyce is Patricia Hutchins' *James Joyce's World* (1957). This book has been superseded by Ellmann's biography and later works, but it provides a good general literary and biographical background in its emphasis on geographical location and literary activity contemporaneous with Joyce's writing. A more thorough and precise work is Chester Anderson's *James Joyce and His World* (1968). Anderson's profuse use of photographs is accompanied by a well-written and carefully drawn biographical account of Joyce. Hutchins also wrote *James Joyce's Dublin* (1950), an illustrated volume that attempts to capture Joyce's Dublin life. As with her aforementioned work, this volume, with its emphasis on the physical detail of places such as houses in which Joyce lived; statues he passed; seascapes, buildings, and parks he strolled by, attempts to reveal the living world Joyce saw in Dublin. An excellent collection of Dublin photographs related to Joyce's works has been published by William York Tindall, *The Joyce Country* (1960; enl. ed., 1970). Tindall's book includes 83 pictures, and with each scene depicted is an appropriate description of it from Joyce's work. As more of Joyce's Dublin is razed each year, volumes such as Tindall's become increasingly valuable for student and scholar alike. Another book of this type is Cyril Pearl's *Dublin in Bloomtime* (1969). In spite of several blatant errors, it provides, in addition to turn-of-the-century photographs, a kind of popular culture background of Dublin during Joyce's early years. It reproduces newspaper headlines, advertisements, want ads, cartoons, and musical programs in an attempt to capture the everyday life of Dublin during this period. Pearl's text is informative if not exact on this background. The most recent photographic work on Joyce is Edward Quinn's *James Joyce's Dublin* (1974), which is interspersed with excerpts from the canon. A more thorough and formal study on this subject is Deirdre Henchy's "Dublin 80 Years Ago" (*Dublin Hist. Record*, 1972). The Irish Eastern Regional Tourism Organization has published an attractive 24-page volume, *James Joyce's Tower* (1969), which includes many of the legal papers related to the tower as well as photographs, appropriate letters associated with Joyce's stay there, and a text by Richard Ellmann.

The most valuable background study of Joyce's contemporary Dublin is Richard M. Kain's *Dublin in the Age of William Butler Yeats and James Joyce* (1962), which provides important chapters on the political and cultural ambience of Dublin as well as Joyce's relationship to the writers of the Irish Revival. Kain's book is more than an introduction to the subject, but as an introduction it is superb. Herbert Howarth's chapter on Joyce in his *The Irish Writers* (1958), the English edition of which carried the subtitle *Literature under Parnell's Star*, offers an excellent discussion of Joyce's work in relation to political life, Irish nationalism, and the mythic elements that developed in Anglo-Irish literature after Parnell's fall.

Two works which treat Joyce's Catholic heritage and its influence on his work are Kevin Sullivan, *Joyce among the Jesuits* (1958), and J. Mitchell Morse, *The Sympathetic Alien* (1959). While treating of the same general subject, these volumes are quite different. Sullivan makes extremely close comparison of factual and primary materials, such as class records, grade reports, school catalogs, contemporary sketches of faculty members with whom Joyce came into contact, retreat manuals, textbooks, student themes, and the like, all of which help to provide a meticulous account of Joyce's academic career. Sullivan's study was one of the important works that shifted critical opinion away from the loose biographical assumptions made about Joyce from *A Portrait* and *Stephen Hero*. His work clearly revealed the essential separation between Joyce and his character Stephen Dedalus. Morse's book, more than Sullivan's, is an intellectual-historical account of Joyce's artistic confrontation with the Church fathers, such as Scotus, Aquinas, William of Occam, and Ignatius Loyola. The general tone as well as certain theses (perhaps more than the content itself) of Morse's book produced some rather sharp replies. Specifically, Morse's view of the Jesuits came under attack when a section of his book was earlier published in *PMLA*. For example, his mistranslation from the Latin of the Jesuit Constitution occasioned a demand from a number of dissenting Jesuits that his error be acknowledged. He did so; nevertheless, the overall view he presents of the Jesuits remains harsh and unconvincing.

Works on the Trieste background are sparse, and no thorough study of this period exists. Several studies which treat various aspects of this area have, however, been published. Gianni Pinguentini's *James Joyce in Italia* (Verona, 1963) recounts interesting biographical incidents of Joyce's life in Trieste and makes intriguing speculations regarding Joyce's links with Italian Futurism and his contact with other literary and cultural movements to which he was in one way or another exposed during his Trieste years. Stelio Crise's idiosyncratic *Epiphanies and Phadographs: Joyce e Trieste* (Milan, 1967) tries to recreate, through a biographical narrative partially seen through Joyce's consciousness, the author's experiences in Trieste. Crise also prepared an excellent pictorial source book for the Third International James Joyce Symposium held in Trieste, *And Trieste, Ah Trieste* (Milan, 1971), which includes an "album" of photographs related to Joyce and Trieste. Mario Nordio's "Gli anni triestini di James Joyce" (*Ateneo veneto*, 1968) also covers this period. A number of biographical and background studies have dealt jointly with Svevo and Joyce; in fact, a great deal of Svevo criticism in English is devoted to his relationship with Joyce and the Trieste background (e.g., see the special Svevo number of *MFS*, 1972). P. N. Furbank's *Italo Svevo: The Man and the Writer* (1966) devotes a chapter to Svevo's perceptions of Joyce. A brief topographical study of Joyce's relationship to Trieste landmarks is Niny Rocco-Bergera's *Itinerary of Joyce and Svevo through Artistic Trieste* (Trieste, 1971). Finally, the Spring 1972 issue of *JJQ* is devoted to Joyce and Trieste.

Two recent volumes that focus on Joyce in Italy are Edvige Schulte's *L'eroe all'antipodo* (Naples, 1973) and Giovanni Cianci's *La fortuna di Joyce in Italia* (Bari, 1974). The latter is a thorough study of Joyce's reputation in Italy and provides a complete chronological bibliography of Joyce's work published in Italian and also criticism published on Joyce in Italy. The Schulte study is highly derivative, and although it treats Joyce's debt to the Futurists and other Italian writers, it provides very little in the way of new insights.

V. *Criticism*

The first sentence from the introduction of Ellmann's biography sets the context for this section of the essay; he writes: "We are still learning to be James Joyce's contemporaries, to understand our interpreter." Ellmann's sentence is cited here not to offer a tone of solemnity (although much in Joyce criticism is flat and solemn), but rather to suggest the broader cultural context from which Joyce criticism has grown and perhaps to describe in a peripheral way its early confusion, its vicissitudes, and, at times, even its seeming madness. An account of Joyce criticism from the reception of his first works to the middle seventies follows a complex and at times a serpentine route— one, however, which reflects the struggles of three generations of scholars to understand much that is embodied in what we call the modern movement of this century.

GENERAL STUDIES

What with the early charges of obscurity and the modern publisher's propensity for the introductory critical series, Joyce has been "introduced" to redundancy. It is perhaps worthwhile to mention this phenomenon in the beginning before moving on to the more central critical studies. Over twenty general, introductory books or pamphlets have been written, many of these in foreign languages. Among the more competent foreign introductions are *James Joyce* by Joseph Majault (Paris, 1963); *Joyce* by Jean-Jacques Mayoux (Paris, 1965), which also includes excerpts from Joyce's works; *Vita e opere de James Joyce* by Francesca Romana Paci (Bari, 1968); *Joyce par lui-même* by Jean Paris (Paris, 1957), which has also been translated into German and Italian, *James Joyce—Chronik von Leben und Werk* by Damel von Recklinghausen (Frankfurt-am-Main, 1968), an extremely accurate and informative study which is a reference book as much as an introduction; *Joyce* by Joris Duytschaever (Bruges, 1970); *James Joyce* by Hideoki Oketani (Tokyo, 1970); *James Joyce* by Armin Arnold (Berlin, 1963); and *James Joyce* by Manuel Arturo Vargas (Madrid, 1972), which includes excerpts from the works translated into Spanish. Majault's very elementary introduction was translated into English and published in London in 1971. Aneirin Talfan Davies has written an introductory study on Joyce in Welsh which was published in London, *Yr Alltud James Joyce* (1944). These works, with the exception of von Recklinghausen's, are critically derivative but serve the purpose to introduce Joyce to general audiences in their native countries. The most recent addition to this large body of introductions is a volume in the Twentieth Century Views series, *Joyce* (ed. William H. Chace, 1974). The collection reprints many excellent essays, but because of space limitations lacks the broad coverage that an introduction requires. The student is better served by A. Walton Litz's and John Gross's introductions, which will be discussed later, for they provide a more systematic approach to the subject.

The best early commentary on Joyce in England and elsewhere is found in essays, diaries, and letters by his fellow writers who shared, at least partially, an understanding of what he was attempting to do. The first generation of critical introductions had as their purpose to "explain" Joyce's work to the general reader; there was little or no critical evaluation of Joyce's work. Charles Duff's *James Joyce and the Plain Reader* (1932) and Louis Golding's *James Joyce* (1933) are of little value other than in assessing the symptoms of the very limited and mundane critical understanding of Joyce at this time in England, ten years after the publication of *Ulysses*. By contrast, one may still profit from the brilliant critical acumen and understanding of Joyce demonstrated in Edmund Wilson's *Axel's Castle* (1931), of which neither of the above authors demonstrated awareness. Wilson's chapter on Joyce is, of course, far more than an introduction; he places Joyce in the context of European literature and its modern development and, while stressing Joyce's originality and imagination, illustrates how his methods and techniques are a part of a larger "modern" imagination that grew out of French Symbolism as well as Flaubert. *Axel's Castle* was the first important assessment of Joyce's achievement and remains a seminal contribution to the criticism of modern literature as well as to Joyce studies.

The first thorough and critically astute general book-length study was Harry Levin's *James Joyce: A Critical Introduction* (1941; rev. and augmented, 1960). In the light of thirty years of Joyce scholarship, there is much in the book which now seems inadequate, but it remains a largely reliable study filled with intelligent understanding and sound critical judgment. It is difficult to gauge the influence of Levin's book in the United States, but one may accurately state that the work widened Joyce's appeal among sophisticated readers and helped to make Joyce "respectable" within the academic community, thus encouraging further scholarship. Levin's book also placed Joyce in the tradition of modern European literature and viewed him as a major figure in this tradition. The augmented and revised edition adds a chapter entitled "Revisiting Joyce."

Several general works that followed Levin's were attempts to introduce Joyce to a yet wider audience. L. A. G. Strong's *The Sacred River* (1949), William Powell Jones's *James Joyce and the Common Reader* (1955), and J. I. M. Stewart's National Book League pamphlet *James Joyce* (1957) perhaps succeeded in their authors' purposes, but at the risk of oversimplification. Stewart's later work on Joyce is an uncomfortable 62-page chapter in *Eight Modern Authors* (1963), Volume XII of the *Oxford History of English Literature*, which is appallingly narrow in its appraisal of Joyce's work and so constricted in its critical vision of *Finnegans Wake* that Stewart must frequently rely on Edmund Wilson's critical judgments written prior to 1931.

S. L. Goldberg's *James Joyce* (1962) is a sound introduction, though with one qualification. Goldberg dismisses *Finnegans Wake* in a brief final chapter and peevishly rejects all criticism on the work as "a happy hunting-ground for what passes as 'scholarship' and 'research.'" Goldberg's case against *Finnegans Wake* can be sympathetically heard, but his contentiousness does not strengthen his points.

Armin Arnold's introduction, mentioned earlier, was published in New York in 1969 with an updated bibliography (and many of the errors in the original edition corrected) in Modern Literature Monographs series. In yet another series, Profiles in Literature, Arnold Goldman has provided *James Joyce* (1968), a student's basic introduction to Joyce that includes excerpts, with good analyses, from Joyce's works.

Two excellent introductions alluded to earlier which do more than complement Levin's are A. Walton Litz's *James Joyce* (1966) in the Twayne English Authors Series and John Gross's *James Joyce* (1970) in the Modern Masters Series. Litz's study is a fresh and complete introduction to Joyce's life and work and takes into account the enormous critical development in Joyce studies throughout the fifties and early sixties. The precision and clarity of this work, together with Litz's uncanny ability to devote time to the complex problems Joyce presents to his readers, give the book special value to those who are beginning Joyce studies. Gross's little book is of a different kind, also distinguished by its style; it assumes a broader literary background and is enjoyed by one who has read most of Joyce thoroughly. It is a book with many wise statements about Joyce's works and literature in general. Its graceful style well submerges but does not hide the author's awareness of the more specialized aspects of Joyce scholarship.

Anthony Burgess' *Re Joyce* (1965), published in England as *Here Comes Everybody*, is an idiosyncratic work that takes many critical short cuts and makes far too many generalizations. Surprisingly, for Burgess at least, the work often reflects a narrow, parochial view of Joyce. Much of what Burgess writes has been written more thoroughly before him, but it goes unacknowledged. Most interesting in his study are his observations on Joyce's use of language and rhythm. Burgess has no eye for scholarship and often an easy generalization suffices for critical rigor, but he has an ear for Joyce's language and a writer's appreciation for his achievement. Burgess' more recent *Joysprick* (1973) is devoted almost exclusively to the author's use of language and is superior to his earlier work, for in the latter Burgess' instincts are more compatible with the subject. *Joysprick* is in no sense, as Burgess admits in his preface, a systematic linguistic study, but rather an inquiry into Joyce's esthetic disposition of language. His treatment of Joyce's use of dialect and the implication engendered in his use of names is especially interesting.

The critical work of William York Tindall exerted a strong influence on Joyce studies in the 1950s, beginning with his *James Joyce* (1950) followed by *A Reader's Guide to James Joyce* (1959). He wrote many other studies which included Joyce. Tindall's work stresses the symbolic and archetypal patterns that run through Joyce's canon and lays heavy emphasis on the meaning of Joyce's "symbols." His studies have been more popular with students than scholars, for his interpretations, while often clever and interesting, lack evaluative quality, placing nearly equal stress on both minor and major points— the stress being determined by the richness of symbolic dimensions rather than by their immediate importance within the fabric and structure of Joyce's work itself. Tindall's studies, of course, reflect the emphasis on a facile Freudian criticism generally and the development of the explication of fiction that emerged from the New Criticism as it was applied to poetry. His criticism reflects the strengths as well as the limitations of this approach. His analytical rigor is not sustained in his larger analysis of the work's totality; his suggestions are frequently provocative, but the vital connection between the array of symbolic allusions and thematic meaning is often absent, and this leads to superficial interpretation. On the other hand, perhaps Tindall's greatest contribution to Joyce studies is his example of close scrutiny of the text and careful attention to detail which is demanded by Joyce's art. His influence on Joyce studies has been large.

The work of Hugh Kenner in Joyce criticism is more difficult to assess. Kenner's studies, by their very nature, raise some of the most persistent esthetic questions that reflect comprehensive judgments related to Joyce's canon and his contribution to modern art. His *Dublin's Joyce* (1955) became a springboard from which several controversies arose; these were debated extensively but not conclusively. The first chapter of his book is entitled "Double Writing," and here Kenner discusses Joyce's use of parody and its thematic effects. From this basis he establishes a thesis that the "controlling ideas" in Joyce's work are developed from his analogical vision which emanates from an essentially ironic conception; thus the fictional world of *Ulysses* (this also applies to *Dubliners* and *A Portrait*), for example, suffused with Joyce's irony, does not directly reveal the author's spiritual or—perhaps a better word—moral values. Rather, those values lie outside the work, drawn by the ironic implications in the work itself. Kenner's assessment of Stephen Dedalus offers a focus for our discussion. Kenner writes: "Joyce's irony goes deep indeed. . . . Stephen . . . is aware that he is Hamlet, but his awareness is put to the wrong uses. It provides him with no insight." Kenner further argues that Joyce has accomplished by the quality of his irony an abstraction that implies a clear moral connective. This moral vision grows out of the ironic treatment of his creation. The detached artist reveals the nature of his antipathy through technique, but a technique which forces interpretation outside of the world of the novel. Kenner's concentration on Stephen Dedalus has been debated, and frequently not very well, by a number of critics. S. L. Goldberg and L. A. Murillo, in studies which will be treated later, have come to grips with Kenner's contentions. Wayne C. Booth in *The Rhetoric of Fiction* (1961) devotes considerable space to the implications of this argument. Little that has subsequently been written on Stephen Dedalus fails to take into account some aspect of Kenner's arguments.

Kenner's explications and unraveling of complicated Joyce passages are frequently brilliant, but his penetrating insights have only recently been scrutinized in an atmosphere free from heated polemic. More recently, Kenner's criticism has stressed different elements; in his essay "Molly's Masterstroke," in *Ulysses: Fifty Years* (1974), through a Sherlock Holmesian method of deduction he has drawn us back to the narrative line in *Ulysses* to reveal how much there is still to be learned from an even closer scrutiny of the narrative events themselves. Kenner's *The Pound Era* (1971) offers a rich, kaleidoscopic portrait of the modern period, which in turn provides further insights into Joyce's art.

An important collection of essays which brought together many of the major early writings on Joyce, *James Joyce: Two Decades of Criticism* (ed. Seon Givens, 1948; augmented, 1963) included essays by a number of Joyce's friends, Budgen, Eugene Jolas, and Stuart Gilbert; and Eliot's seminal essay "*Ulysses*, Order and Myth" (to be discussed later). This collection, in a sense, marked the emergence of the great American interest in Joyce and, in retrospect, it can be seen to signal the American domination of Joyce studies for a number of years. Among the Americans who contributed to the book and who were later to become important critics of their generation were Hugh Kenner, S. Foster Damon, William Troy, Joseph Campbell, and Frederick J. Hoffman. Nearly all of the essays published in the volume had appeared elsewhere (with the exception of those by Vivian Mercier and Hugh Kenner and one of James T. Farrell's two contributions), but the volume itself as a collection gave focus to Joyce's increasingly higher stature in modern literature.

Marvin Magalaner and Richard M. Kain's *Joyce: The Man, the Work, the Reputation* (1956) offered a thorough appraisal of Joyce's position in modern literature and stressed the many facets of his personality as revealed through his work—those of Dubliner, Catholic, cynic, and others. The first extended treatment of Joyce's critical reputation, the study provided a systematic survey of important aspects of Joyce's life and art. In a sense, the Magalaner and Kain volume represented the culmination of Joyce studies through the mid-fifties, and it also pointed to directions that Joyce scholarship needed to take. The volume not only gives an excellent synthesis and evaluation of Joyce studies but also makes its own distinct contribution to the field. It rightly dismissed much of what was errant, arrant, and wild in Joyce criticism, for the authors focused on the central and meaningful and on those areas that needed further exploration.

In the fifties and early sixties some of the very good Joyce criticism was contained in three volumes entitled *A James Joyce Miscellany* (1957, 1959, 1962). The first volume was published by the James Joyce Society in New York, which holds regular meetings at the Gotham Book Mart and continues to flourish under the patronage of Frances Steloff and the presidency of William York Tindall. The initial volume featured essays by Thornton Wilder, Maria Jolas, and Leon Edel. With the exception of Julian Kaye's essay, "Simony, the Three Simons, and Joycean Myth," which treats the continually perplexing problem of Joyce's attitude toward the Catholic Church, the essays are general, appreciative, or biographical. The second and third volumes in the series (ed. Marvin Magalaner, published by Southern Illinois Univ. Press) reflect the increasingly scholarly drift in Joyce criticism that began in the fifties. The general quality of the twenty-nine essays in these two volumes is high; most of them take up narrow and specialized interpretative problems or source investigations. Magalaner's introduction to the third volume offers a brief but solid overview of Joyce criticism as it had developed through the end of 1962.

Two general works of far less value than the *Miscellanies* and removed from the mainstream of Joyce criticism are Kristian Smidt's *James Joyce and the Cultic Use of Fiction* (Oslo, 1955) and Sisir

Chatterjee's *James Joyce: A Study in Technique* (Calcutta, 1957). Smidt's study, a biographical interpretation of Joyce's work, concludes that Joyce's books are informed by important elements of public ritual and private cult and that these two aspects bring about a "sacral" attachment to Dublin that no amount of ridicule on Joyce's part can obscure. Smidt's work, a rigidly conceived and narrow academic study, takes little risk and offers little illumination. Chatterjee's, an amateurish, enthusiastic study of Joyce's fictional technique, is both highly derivative and ill informed.

Another important collection of essays, all previously published and widely translated, is Joseph Prescott's *Exploring James Joyce* (1964). Of the seven essays, five focus on *Ulysses* and one on *Stephen Hero*, and the remaining essay is concerned with Joyce's "word-technique" throughout his canon. All but one of the essays were first published in the forties and fifties. Prescott's work, noted for its precision and care, represents some of the best early scholarship on Joyce. His essays address themselves to several fundamental issues at the heart of Joyce's work; those on the characterizations of Stephen Dedalus and Molly Bloom have frequently been used as starting points by later critics who have dealt with these questions. His essay on *Stephen Hero* remains a sound introduction to that work today, and the suggestiveness of his remarks no doubt enhanced the detailed studies of *Stephen Hero* that followed.

Two collections of essays, the major portions of which are devoted to Joyce, are Clement Semmler's *For the Uncanny Man* (Sydney, 1963) and Anthony Cronin's *A Question of Modernity* (1966). Semmler's book is devoted largely to general essays on Joyce, but his "James Joyce in Australia" is an especially interesting discussion of Joyce's reception there—not dissimilar to the initial censorship problems in other English-speaking countries. Cronin's essays are largely taken up with the distinctive contribution of the "moderns." These two volumes are not noteworthy for their contribution to Joyce scholarship, but their publication suggests the wider range of interest in Joyce that developed through the sixties.

Through the work of a number of scholars and teachers in Europe during the sixties, a great deal of interest in Joyce was rekindled. This interest has produced a number of new translations and editions as well as important critical work. In 1967 the first International James Joyce Symposium was held in Dublin; on a biennial basis meetings have subsequently been held in Trieste, Dublin, and Paris. After the first meeting, co-chaired by Fritz Senn, Bernard Benstock, and Thomas F. Staley, an average of over two hundred scholars have attended the week-long meetings. From these symposia two volumes of essays have emerged, and a third, the Trieste proceedings of 1971, was published in 1975. A selection of papers from the first meeting was edited by Maurice Harmon under the title *The Celtic Master* (1969). The five essays, with the possible exception of Norman Silverstein's "Evolution of the Nighttown Setting," are not of importance, but the contributions by two Dubliners, Niall Montgomery and the late Donagh MacDonagh, are not without charm. The far better volume is *New Light on Joyce from the Dublin Symposium* (ed. Fritz Senn, 1972). This collection includes thirteen papers presented at the 1969

Symposium (two of which have been referred to earlier in this chapter). As a volume its subject matter offers a good representation of the shifting scholarly interests being pursued at that time in Joyce studies. Four essays are concerned with textual and stylistic matters, one with Joyce's politics, another with his view of "Love and Sex." Ihab Hassan's contribution is a "scenario" in eight scenes and introduces this critic's increasing interest in Joyce as the fulcrum between Modernism and post-Modernism, a subject Hassan has developed more thoroughly since. Leslie Fiedler's contribution is based upon his Bloomsday Dinner speech, and offers a highly personal and sympathetic account of Leopold Bloom, the modern Jew in Dublin. As a single volume the book tends to lack focus, but this is more than made up for in the quality of several of the essays.

Another collection of essays occasioned by a Joyce meeting is *Litters from Aloft* (ed. Ronald Bates and Harry J. Pollock, 1971). These papers were delivered at the Second Canadian James Joyce Seminar. Again, the essays are all competent; Michael H. Begnal's "Who Speaks When I Dream? Who Dreams When I Speak? A Narrational Approach to *Finnegans Wake*" insists that HCE is not alone in his dreaming. This is the freshest essay in the collection. Maurice Beebe's essay is of interest because it offers further development, with special emphasis on Joyce, of his theories related to the characteristics of Modernism. A collection which deserves mention in passing is an issue of *Studies in the Literary Imagination* (Vol. 3, No. 2, 1970), published at Georgia State University: "James Joyce in the Seventies: The Expanding Dimension of His Art" (ed. Ted R. Spivey). Among the eight essays are contributions by Joseph Campbell and Richard M. Kain. If there are fears that the literary radical James Joyce has fallen into the establishment, "the latter day perpetuators of the nineteenth-century middle-class system," Potter Woodbery's contribution (which I am quoting) does not allay them ("The Irrelevance of Stephen Dedalus: Some Reflections on Joyce and the Student Activist Movement"). The essay reveals far more of the student activist mentality than it does of Stephen Dedalus, but certain thrusts in his argument, although poorly cast, are revealing.

Perhaps it is appropriate at this point to emphasize that Joyce criticism has been marked by a great deal of controversy; the most shrill has appeared in scholarly journals and literary periodicals, but much of the debate has been carried over into the longer, book-length studies. A good deal of the controversy was the result of a clear shift in emphasis in Joyce studies during the sixties from explication to extended interpretation. One scholar has remarked that potential serious readers of Joyce are "doubtless frightened away by the scholarly brawl which surrounds and obscures him, and there seems to be little possibility of reconciling these opposites" (Darcy O'Brien, *The Conscience of James Joyce*, 1968). As Joyce criticism developed during this period more widely divergent and seemingly irreconcilable views did emerge, many of which can be treated only in the interpretative context in which they arose, for they focus, on the whole, on particular works. However, the critical assumptions underlying them have prompted a number of scholars to face head-on—if not to synthesize —these conflicting critical viewpoints in order to move beyond them.

Two works written in the mid-sixties illustrate in part this attempt. Arnold Goldman's *The Joyce Paradox* (1966) is an attempt to "reconcile major critical approaches," while Robert M. Adams' *James Joyce: Common Sense and Beyond* (1966) offers a provocative discussion of various critical viewpoints, although much of its emphasis is on explication.

Goldman's study follows a group of related themes through Joyce's fiction up to *Finnegans Wake*. In the last analysis, he observes, the major issues in Joyce criticism are "questions of the mode of existence of 'symbols' in the fiction and of the quality of Joyce's feeling, the extent of his human sympathies." Goldman, however, is far more open in his appraisal of Joyce criticism than Adams; for Goldman, in large part, sees the apparent paradoxical positions taken with regard to Joyce's work as reflecting the inherent paradoxes in the work itself, even as early as the first *Dubliners* stories. *The Joyce Paradox* is more successful in its analysis of Joycean paradox than of the paradoxical critical positions the works spawned. Out of his study, however, a number of critical positions are reconciled and balanced, but these in light of the duality in Joyce's own work. In short, *The Joyce Paradox* insists that paradox is capable of defining itself. For example, Goldman's analysis of the "symbolist" elements in Joyce and how critical emphasis on these has led to a less appreciative reading of the character of Stephen Dedalus is especially well drawn, and it confronts a real crux in Joyce studies. There are useful parallels drawn with Freud and Kierkegaard. Kierkegaard's ideas are used to provide analogues for Goldman's "balancing." Joycean "epiphany," according to Goldman, has certain similarities to the epistomological and ontological assumptions of certain of Freud's explanations of the methods of the psychoanalyst. His point is more than a *rapprochement* between psychoanalysis and literary criticism, for psychoanalysis has expanded the dimensions of symbolic interpretation in literary criticism, especially as it relates to dream. This very expansion, however, creates a more divergent analysis of a character, more closely scrutinized questioning of his motives. Nowhere has this been apparent than in the interpretations of Stephen Dedalus and Leopold Bloom, to say nothing of Molly and her last utterance in *Ulysses*. In the end, however, perhaps Goldman is too generous regarding his fellow critics, for he suggests that the wide critical diversity in *Ulysses* is a projection of thematic conflicts within the work; but his critical argument is finely drawn, and summary statements hardly do it justice. Regarding his own use of Kierkegaard, Goldman's discussion is informative, but even for the purposes of analogy it is difficult to draw comparisons between philosophical speculation and the realized creativity of an author.

Adams' book, on the other hand, offers a general study of Joyce's life and work and provides a good chapter on the Irish background and influence on Joyce. Beyond this, though, Adams is especially interesting in his comments concerning a number of critical issues widely argued earlier by other Joyce critics, including himself (*Surface and Symbol*, 1962). Adams, for example, debunks much of the importance attributed to the "epiphany" by critics, especially the more sustained arguments that attach central significance to it in Joyce's esthetic. He dismisses the importance of the term itself; he argues that "epiphany" as Joyce used it implies no transcendent reality, and we see this with particular clarity in the *Dubliners* stories. The term, if I interpret Adams correctly, has had far too much made of it; epiphanies as they reveal themselves in *Dubliners* are not unlike those points of revelation in the works of Meredith or Stendhal. The last chapter of the book is a brief but convincing essay on the importance of *Finnegans Wake*, and, in the long run, of its larger contribution to modern literature. *James Joyce: Common Sense and Beyond* is well titled, because much of Adams' book offers a balanced interpretation of Joyce's life and work, a "common sense" approach. "Beyond" this, however, are occasions when Adams ventures to assail certain critical interpretations or arguments with which he disagrees and to venture his own, often controversial extrapolations.

Commemorating the twenty-fifth anniversary of Joyce's death, a volume of essays, *James Joyce Today* (ed. Thomas F. Staley, 1966), was published. Of special note in this volume is William Blissett's essay "James Joyce in the Smithy of His Soul," which traces the persistent Wagnerian influence on Joyce throughout his literary career and especially the embodiment of the Wagnerian elements in Stephen's character. Clive Hart's "*Finnegans Wake* in Perspective" remains perhaps the best and most illuminating introductory essay on the work.

A number of studies of Joyce have laid stress on psychology and psychoanalysis, both as a critical approach to his work and as an attempt to understand the man more fully. Darcy O'Brien's *The Conscience of James Joyce* (1968) deals with the moral judgments embodied in Joyce's writings, an area which has undergone considerable debate. O'Brien sees Joyce's sense of comedy intricately interwoven into the moral judgment that imbues his work. Out of Joyce's guilt-ridden, puritanical, Dublin Catholic background there emerged a comic view of man's folly that overrode but left essentially unchanged his fundamental moral outlook. This view of Joyce, in its broadest contours, is not dissimilar to Helmut Bonheim's in his *Joyce's Benefictions* (1964). O'Brien, however, focuses a great deal more attention on the sexual element of Irish Catholic morality and the "indelible mark" it left on Joyce's thinking. More specifically, O'Brien contends that Joyce's early education and family upbringing left him with a moral disgust for the world and that his early works reflect this bitterness; it was only later, when he developed a comic view of man, that his work was able to reconcile this opposition. Joyce himself, argues O'Brien, was obsessed with the "duplicity" of experience, the polarity between the ideal and the actual. In fact, the unity of theme in Joyce's work is engendered by this constant but never resolved attempt at reconciliation within Joyce's own conscience. O'Brien's argument that Joyce was not, as so many writers of the Modern movement were, a moral relativist is a point well taken, and it explains certain differing aspects of his work. On the other hand, interpretations that bring into close focus the conscience of the artist are not without pitfalls, from which O'Brien does not escape. I am uncomfortable with certain conclusions O'Brien draws when he extends his argument into character analysis, for he takes too little account of Joyce's fictive art and, more important, narrows the rich and discriminating process Joyce used in the creation of his characters. O'Brien's methods and powers of analysis are effective, and his subsequent work along these lines of inquiry (to be discussed below) has offered a more penetrating interpretation. A more directly psychoanalytical approach is Sheldon R. Brivic's "James Joyce: From Stephen to Bloom" in *Psychoanalysis and Literary Process* (ed. Frederick Crews, 1970).

Two later studies that approach Joyce's work from a more exclusively psychoanalytical perspective are Edward Brandabur's *A Scrupulous Meanness* (1971), which focuses mainly on *Dubliners* and *Exiles* but also offers commentary on *A Portrait* and *Ulysses*; and Mark Shechner's *Joyce in Nighttown* (1974), subtitled *A Psychoanalytic Inquiry into Ulysses*. Shechner's book is the most extended psychoanalytic study of Joyce's work to date.

Hélène Cixous's treatment of Joyce has certain affinities with psychological approaches but is conceived very differently. An evaluation of *The Exile of James Joyce* (1972; first pub. in French, 1968) presents a number of difficulties, for many of the problems and concerns it raises emanate from its context within French criticism— concerns which, with the advent of Structuralism in Anglo-American literary criticism, are only now coming to closer attention. In one sense her treatment is not new, for it reflects an aspect of a French tradition that has its roots in Lanson and Mornet, but more immediately, one sees reflections of the work of Roland Barthes. The Structuralist influence has until recently been restricted, in the United States at least, to linguistics. An exception to this is the Structuralist treatment of Joyce's work by Robert Scholes in *Ulysses: Fifty Years* (1974).

Despite many interesting incursions on the Joycean landscape, Cixous' book is marked by inaccurate and often preposterous generalities. To mention the first one, which occurs in the second paragraph: "from a reading of *Dubliners* and *Ulysses* one can discover *all* urban Ireland and Dublin society" (italics mine). One may contemplate this possibility only if one is unaware of Dublin society in Joyce's time. Some have found this study fresh and challenging, but the book's very diffusiveness undermines Cixous's attempt to describe the totality of Joyce's art.

Two studies of more limited scope are Virginia Moseley's *Joyce and the Bible* (1967) and Maria Elizabeth Kronegger's *James Joyce and Associated Image Makers* (1968), the latter a discussion of Joyce's imagery that insists on its kinship with Edgar Allan Poe. The thesis traces Joyce's affinity as an image maker with Poe as Poe's theories are adumbrated and protracted by the French Symbolists, a relationship observed by Edmund Wilson (sans Poe) more broadly many years before. The theory as posed by Kronegger seems curiously wrongheaded, especially in the singularity of vision it attributes to Joyce, but there are in her book some interesting comparisons between the esthetic theories of the Impressionist painters and Joyce's own early concepts of art. Moseley's study traces the biblical elements throughout Joyce's canon, devoting a chapter to each work, but she insists in her generalizations on far too great a reliance upon the Bible in his work.

Throughout his life Joyce was deeply interested in music, especially opera and vocal music. Many of the themes and techniques in his work derived from this interest. Matthew J. C. Hodgart and Mabel Worthington have provided an excellent starting point for the study of this aspect of his work in their *Song in the Works of James Joyce* (1959). They have traced the song references and noted the sources in Joyce's work and have also included an essay on the function of songs in *Finnegans Wake*. Zack Bowen's *Musical Allusions in the Works of James Joyce: Early Works through* Ulysses (1974) is an outgrowth of Hodgart and Worthington. Whereas they identify and list song allusions, Bowen's book is an annotation of musical allusions and a study of Joyce's use of music in terms of style, characterization, structure, and theme.

Many broad studies have been devoted to Joyce's esthetic theories, or, in most cases, those theories that appear in Joyce's fiction and are formulated by Stephen Dedalus; in fact, there are few studies of any length which do not include extensive discussion of the philosophical and religious elements related to the artistic theories as they are embodied in Joyce's notebooks and the fiction. The subject has generated considerable scholarly interest and wide divergence of opinion. Extensive examination has been made of Joyce's sources, such as Aquinas, Aristotle, Boehme, and Bruno, among others.

One area of concentration and subsequent debate has been Joyce's use of the word "epiphany" and its meaning in his fiction. The term occurs in *Stephen Hero* in the mind of Stephen Daedalus (as his name is spelled in *Stephen Hero*): "By an epiphany he meant a sudden spiritual manifestation, whether in the vulgarity of speech or of gesture or in a memorable phase of the mind itself. He believed that it was for the man of letters to record these epiphanies with extreme care, seeing that they themselves are the most delicate and evanescent of moments." William Noon in writing of the prominence that the term has been given by critics has referred to it ironically as the "quasi-rubrical imperative of Joycean aesthetics." Early importance was given to the "epiphany" as a literary technique by Irene Hendry in her essay, "Joyce's Epiphanies" (*Two Decades . . .*), in which she pointed out that the theory of epiphanies was central to Stephen Dedalus' entire literary theory and was applied far more extensively by Joyce himself in his work. Tindall (*Reader's Guide to James Joyce*) extended this analysis to include a symbolic function: "Plainly Stephen's epiphany or radiance, a shining out or showing forth, is what we call symbolism and his radiant object a symbol." Dorothy Van Ghent in *The English Novel, Form and Function* (1953) extended this position further by showing the epiphany's central relevance to the dialectical movements and structural elements in *A Portrait*. Florence L. Walzl in "The Liturgy of the Epiphany Season and the Epiphanies of Joyce" (*PMLA*, 1965) insists on an even greater centrality of the epiphany in Joyce's work. She and Robert Scholes engaged in a debate on the matter in a later issue of *PMLA* (1967). Scholes had earlier debunked the claims of the epiphany's importance in his essay,

"Joyce and the Epiphany: The Key to the Labyrinth?" (*SR*, 1964).
For a particular example of the disagreement on Joyce's esthetic theory and his use of source material, see the Scholes/Shawcross controversy in the *James Joyce Quarterly*. It stems from Robert Scholes's
"James Joyce, Irish Poet," (*JJQ*, 1965) and John T. Shawcross' " 'Tilly'
and Dante," (*JJQ*, 1969). See also Scholes's letter to the editor and
Shawcross' reply in *JJQ* (1970) and Scholes's later reply in *JJQ*
(1971).

Besides the critical attention given to the epiphany and its various
mutations, considerable emphasis has been placed on larger questions
concerning Joyce's sources in the formulation of Stephen's entire
esthetic theory and its relationship to all of the author's work. Beginning with Harry Levin, much scholarship has concluded that the
theory is derivative of Aquinas and is, in fact, "Applied Aquinas."
Tindall, Kenner, Beebe, Noon, and other critics have refuted this
conclusion, pointing out a great deal of distortion by Joyce in his
borrowing from Aquinas. An extensive discussion on this point by
David E. Jones, "The Essence of Beauty in James Joyce's Aesthetics"
(*JJQ*, 1973), traces the various opinions and insists that a more fruitful, less partial, and indeed more conclusive understanding of the
theory is dependent upon closer scrutiny of Aristotle's *De Anima* and
Metaphysics, as well as a far closer comparison of Joyce's critical
writings with *Stephen Hero* and *A Portrait*. Other significant essays
which treat this subject are: A. D. Hope, "The Esthetic Theory of
James Joyce" (*Australasian Jour. of Psychology and Philosophy*,
1943); Maurice Beebe, "Joyce and Aquinas: The Theory of Aesthetics"
(*PQ*, 1957); Frederick M. Link ("The Aesthetics of Stephen Dedalus,"
PLL, 1966). Extensive discussions on the subject are also taken up in
many of the book-length studies of *Ulysses*, which will come to our
attention later.

William T. Noon's *Joyce and Aquinas* (1957), while devoting considerable attention to Joyce's esthetic theory, is concerned with an
analysis of the entire framework of religious elements in Joyce's
canon and how they emerged from Joyce's religious training and
educational background. As mentioned above, Noon, in isolating the
Thomistic aspects of Joyce's work, finds those elements frequently
distorted by Joyce for his own artistic purposes and theoretical for-
mulations. Thomism in Joyce, Noon concludes, "is for the most part a
matter of thematic correspondence and general categories or affinities
of outlook." Noon's point here qualifies the rather easy assumptions
made before him that related Joyce's theories directly to Aquinas,
although he does insist, at certain points perhaps too strongly, upon
Joyce's debt to Aquinas. Of considerable importance in this study are
the careful considerations of the Trinitarian theme in *Ulysses* and its
relationship with the Sabellian heresy. Underlying Noon's excellent
study is his inquiry into the vast resourcefulness Joyce possessed as he
transmuted divergent theories, both philosophical and theological,
and organized them by way of theme or image into the structure of
his own work.

Jacques Aubert's *Introduction à l'esthétique de James Joyce* (Paris,
1973) is the broadest and most sustained study of the development of
Joyce's esthetic. Paying careful attention to Joyce's own critical essays

on such writers as James Clarence Mangan, and to key entries from
the notebooks, Aubert ably traces its germination and elaboration. He
suggests a much wider possibility of European sources than has been
previously recognized and argues convincingly that there is a much
greater evolution in Joyce's theory than has been grasped before.
Umberto Eco, the Italian writer and critic, has devoted a long section
of his *Opera Aperta* (Milan, 1962) to Joyce. A slightly revised version
appeared in a single volume as *Le poetiche di Joyce* (Milan, 1966). A
translation in English is soon to appear as *James Joyce and the
Aesthetics of Chaosmos.* Eco's study treats all of Joyce's major work,
but concentrates on theoretical problems. He points out Joyce's affinity through his Catholic training with the medieval mind and his
proximity to many of the characteristics of medieval art.

A substantial amount of analysis has focused on illuminating Joyce's
works and techniques by comparing them with those of other writers.
There have been innumerable comparative articles linking Joyce with
such a diverse range of writers as George Moore, Swift, Beckett,
Sterne, Virginia Woolf, Meredith, Pater, d'Annunzio, Dante, Blake,
Defoe, Rabelais, Fitzgerald, Balzac, and Flaubert. These articles
range greatly in value, some being substantial contributions and others being merely lists of superficial similarities. In 1969, Joyce was the
subject of the annual Comparative Literature Symposium at Texas
Technological College. *James Joyce: His Place in World Literature*
publishes the proceedings of this symposium and includes essays by
William T. Noon, S.J., Dounia Christiani, Thomas F. Staley, and
William J. Handy. It focuses on assessing Joyce's reputation in world
and contemporary world literature. Another comparative monograph
is the special "Joyce et le roman moderne" number of *L'ARC* (No. 36,
n.d.). This collection, entirely in French, includes essays on Joyce and
Svevo, d'Annunzio, Beckett, Pound, and Flaubert.

There have been a number of book-length comparative studies as
well. One of the earliest is David Hayman's *Joyce et Mallarmé: Sty-
listique de la suggestion* (Paris, 1956) which deals principally with
Mallarmé's influence on *Ulysses* and *Finnegans Wake.* Hugh Kenner's *Flaubert, Joyce, and Beckett: The Stoic Comedians* (1963), in a
unique approach, studies how these writers employ "the language of
the printed word." L. A. Murillo's *The Cyclical Night* (1968), which
has been mentioned in an earlier section, treats the ironic dimension
in Joyce from *Stephen Hero* through *Finnegans Wake* and compares
it with Jorge Luis Borges' use of irony. Published in the same year, B. J
Tysdahl's *Joyce and Ibsen* is a valuable study examining and tracing
Ibsen's influence from Joyce's youthful enthusiasm through *Finnegans Wake.* Richard K. Cross's thorough examination of Flaubert—
Flaubert and Joyce: The Rite of Fiction (1971)—deals principally
with *Ulysses*, though it includes chapters on *Dubliners* and *A Portrait.*
Peter Egri's *Avantgardism and Modernity* (1972) compares *Ulysses*
with Thomas Mann's *Der Zauberberg* and *Lotte in Weimar* and examines the Joyce/Mann relationship.

Frequently, comparative studies are complicated by the difficulty
of determining the extent of Joyce's knowledge of an author or group
of authors. Joyce himself pointed to this problem when he wrote
Harriet Weaver in 1927, "I never read Rabelais either though nobody

will believe this. . . . I read a few chapters of a book called *La langue de Rabelais.*" In light of this, Claude Jacquet's *Joyce et Rabelais: Aspects de la creation verbale dans* Finnegans Wake (Paris, 1972) is a valuable study. It collates Joyce's Buffalo notebook VI.B.42 with Sainéan's *La Langue de Rabelais* and shows how this work contributed to Joyce's verbal construction in the *Wake*.

One of the most recent and ambitious comparative studies is John B. Vickery's *The Literary Impact of* The Golden Bough (1973) which includes five chapters on Joyce from the early works through *Finnegans Wake*. Vickery compiles an impressive number of correspondences and parallels between *The Golden Bough* and Joyce's works, especially *Ulysses*, and these parallels do add to our knowledge of Joyce. Vickery's case for Frazer's influence on Joyce, however, is severely weakened by the fact that there is no direct evidence that Joyce was acquainted with any of Frazer's works.

THE EARLIER WORKS

Although it is now generally recognized that Joyce's earlier work assumes an integral place in his canon, the development of scholarship proceeded far more slowly and differently from that on *Ulysses*. Overshadowed from the beginning by the wide, if often hysterical commentary devoted to *Ulysses, A Portrait* and *Dubliners* were relatively late in receiving the serious attention they deserved.

Joyce's poetry—by and large very early work—represents such a minor place in the canon that little has been written about it. Several of the general studies devote chapters or sections to the poems: Magalaner and Kain discuss them in *Joyce: The Man* . . . , and so do A. Walton Litz in *James Joyce* and Harry Levin in *James Joyce: A Critical Introduction*. Hugh Kenner explicates some of the poems in *Dublin's Joyce*. There are also a number of articles published on individual poems. Zack Bowen's "Goldenhair: Joyce's Archetypal Female" (*Lit. and Psychology*, 1967) traces Joyce's paradoxical feminine figure throughout the poems and relates it to the women in the later works. To date, the only full-length study of the poems is Francesco Gozzi's *La poesia di James Joyce* (Bari, 1974).

Most of the longer studies center on *Chamber Music*. Herbert Howarth places it in perspective (*James Joyce Today*, 1966). William York Tindall (*Poetry*, 1952) looks at these poems in terms of verbal and thematic echoes in the later works. In a more recent study, Ruth von Phul also attempts to illuminate the earlier writings with the later. Her "*Chamber Music* at the *Wake*" (*JJQ*, 1974) is a Freudian analysis of the poems through the looking-glass of *Finnegans Wake*. The most extended commentary on them is William York Tindall's introduction and notes to his variorum edition of *Chamber Music* (1954), currently out of print. Although Tindall gives much useful biographical and source material, his scatological interpretations of the poems have been rejected by most Joyce critics.

In the case of *Dubliners* early discussions centered around the publication and censorship difficulties rather than upon the stories themselves. The recognition of the importance of *A Portrait* both as a work of art and as an integral part of the canon came also relatively late, but scholars for the past twenty years have become increasingly impressed with its importance. At present *A Portrait* is considered so central to our interpretation of Joyce's art that nearly every extended study that has been undertaken, even those concentrating on the later work, has treated some aspect of its meaning or design. The compelling richness of the work itself and its technical accomplishments have also prompted a wide critical discussion in a broader and more general context; for example, many studies of the modern novel have devoted entire chapters or significant portions of discussion to *A Portrait*.* Extensive treatment of the novel within the context of Joyce's work, however, may be attributed in large measure to two other factors: the first has been mentioned earlier, the inherent unity of Joyce's work along with its recognizable development; the second is the fact that the important figure of Stephen Dedalus appears in *Stephen Hero, A Portrait, Ulysses,* and, if only as a blurred or philosophical extension or embodiment, as Shem, the penman, the artist figure in *Finnegans Wake.*

Even as he began writing the initial stories, Joyce conceived of *Dubliners* as an integrated whole. As early as 15 October 1905, he wrote to Grant Richards that he had a book ready for publication entitled *Dubliners,* and that there were twelve stories in the collection. In 1906 he added "Two Gallants" and "A Little Cloud," and in 1907 he finished "The Dead." The difficulties associated with the publication of *Dubliners* have been mentioned in an earlier section. As a result of Joyce's own reluctance to compromise but mainly the fear, real or imagined, of printers and publishers, *Dubliners* was not published until 1914. The early reviews pointed out the drab and "mean" atmosphere of the stories and noted their affinities with the literary Naturalism of French and Russian short stories. In spite of its relatively favorable reception, the work was long neglected by critics, who saw it as merely an effective achievement of Joyce's apprenticeship. It was not until the late fifties that *Dubliners* began to receive closer scrutiny. From that period until recently, studies of varying quality and approach have poured out. Many interpretations of *Dubliners* stories have been absolutely outrageous, having no basis in context or logic.

It is difficult to do justice to the great volume of criticism on *Dubliners,* for the majority is concentrated on the individual stories and has appeared in essays in nearly all the journals that publish studies on modern literature. Criticism of *Dubliners* can, however, be divided roughly into two categories: (1) studies that focus on the unity of the entire work through an examination of the themes, the structure, or other elements which define the centrality of the collection, or its place in the Joyce canon; (2) studies, far greater in num-

---

* A sampling of such books which devote a chapter or extensive discussion to *A Portrait* around various themes: William R. Mueller, *The Prophetic Voice* (1951); Margaret Church, *Time and Reality* (1962); John Edward Hardy, *Man in the Modern Novel* (1964); Harold Kaplan, *The Passive Voice* (1966); Frederick J. Hoffman, *The Imagination's New Beginning* (1967); Louis D. Rubin, Jr., *The Teller in the Tale* (1967); Morris Beja, *Epiphany in the Modern Novel* (1971).

ber, devoted to individual stories. In this latter group there are well over a hundred that attempt to interpret the stories from every possible perspective, employing all types of critical methods. "The Sisters," "Araby," "Clay," and "The Dead" have attracted the most attention. Examples of the comprehensive and exhaustive treatment of individual stories can be seen in Harry Stone, " 'Araby' and the Writing of James Joyce" (*AR*, 1965), and Florence Walzl, " 'The Sisters': A Development" (*JJQ*, 1973).

"The Dead," the longest and most complex story, has been exhaustively analyzed; it has inspired more than thirty critical essays. Most of the early criticism offered symbolic interpretation. Allen Tate ("Three Commentaries," *SR*, 1950) first pointed out Joyce's use of naturalistic detail to achieve symbolic meaning, a subject that has received a great deal of subsequent attention in relation to all of the stories. Thomas F. Smith's "Color and Light in 'The Dead,' " (*JJQ*, 1965), Florence L. Walzl's "Ambiguity in the Structural Symbols of Gabriel's Vision in Joyce's 'The Dead,' " (*Wisconsin Studies in Literature*, 1965) offer examples of symbolic interpretations. Bernard Benstock's "The Dead" in *James Joyce's Dubliners: Critical Essays* (ed. Clive Hart, 1969) summarizes the symbolic aspects of the story most completely. John V. Kelleher's "Irish History and Mythology in James Joyce's 'The Dead' " (*Rev. of Politics*, 1965) is an illuminating source study, which also suggests the way in which Joyce used Irish myth and history for dramatic and ironic effect. The conclusion of "The Dead" draws together the symbolic naturalistic elements of the story in Gabriel's final epiphany, and it is this climax which has provoked the widest divergence of critical opinion. Many early critics have pointed out the ambiguity of the ending. Florence Walzl's "Gabriel and Michael: The Conclusion of 'The Dead' " (*JJQ*, 1966) summarizes earlier interpretation and concludes that the ambiguity is deliberate, for the story gathers all of the earlier themes of *Dubliners* into a deeper and more profound meaning. Lionel Trilling, from a different point of view, also argues that the story ends on an ambiguous note resulting from Joyce's own rising sympathy, a sympathy which overcomes his earlier ironic tone in the story (*The Experience of Literature*, 1967).

There are many aspects of *Dubliners* that reveal its progressions and unity—a unity at the same time so obvious and so varied—and much study has been given over to this subject. Joyce himself outlined the four stages of life he attempted to depict in his "moral history": childhood, adolescence, maturity, and public life. At the center of the stories is, of course, the city itself, Joyce's great subject, Dublin. Many of the Dubliners of the stories reappear in *Ulysses*, and a great deal of attention has also been given to this aspect of the work. General studies of *Dubliners* have also laid stress on its place in the Joyce canon. In the preface to their Viking Critical Library edition of *Dubliners* Litz and Scholes summarize this latter view. Noting the life stages in the structure, they emphasize that "the real hero of the stories is not an individual but the city itself, a city whose geography and history and inhabitants are all part of a coherent vision; and in this aspect *Dubliners* anticipates the anatomy of the modern city made by Joyce in *Ulysses*. Even *Finnegans Wake*, with its fabric of rumor and 'popular' culture, may be seen as a grotesque extension of the world of *Dubliners*."

Attention, too, has been given to literary antecedents. Magalaner and Kain (*Joyce: The Man* . . .) have pointed out the influences on the work, especially that of Chekhov. Many later studies have examined the influences on individual stories.

Brewster Ghiselin has written the most extensive analysis of structure (*Accent*, Spring and Summer 1956). He argues that the collection is not loose and episodic, but "really unitary," asserting that a symbolic structure is given to *Dubliners* through significantly disposed controlling images and metaphors, which function throughout to make *Dubliners* a sustained and unified work of art. An earlier essay by Richard Levin and Charles Shattuck, "First Flight to Ithaca: A New Reading of Joyce's *Dubliners*" (*Two Decades* . . .), sees the unity established by Odyssean parallels. This is an oversimplified and procrustean reading, but it did focus attention on the unity of the work and prompted later critics to look more carefully at this aspect.

Four later studies focus on basic themes. James R. Baker (*A James Joyce Miscellany, Third Series*, 1962) points out Joyce's debt to Ibsen in which he adopted Ibsen's basic metaphor of the paralyzed life to describe those who are living but spiritually dead. Gerhard Friedrich (*CE*, 1965) also treats the unity of the work through the theme of paralysis. Anthony Ostroff (*Western Speech*, 1965) argues that the essential unity is an esthetic, not a thematic, design, that this unity is afforded by a consistency of vision, that the "moral vision is the reality behind the stories." A more recent study by Monroe Engel (*"Dubliners* and Erotic Expectations," *Twentieth Century Literature in Retrospect*, ed. Reuben A. Brower, 1971) argues that the "conflict between high erotic aspiration and a low estimate of the possibility of erotic fulfillment is very near the dynamic center of Joyce's literary production." This conflict is pervasive, according to Engel, and is revealed in erosive irony.

Several volumes of reprinted essays on *Dubliners* are available. The best is the previously mentioned Viking Critical Library edition of *Dubliners*, which includes a number of essays and some background materials as well as a selected bibliography and notes on the stories. *James Joyce's* Dubliners: *A Critical Handbook* (ed. Baker and Staley, 1969) offers a great deal of material and an extensive bibliography. Peter K. Garrett has edited *Twentieth Century Interpretations* of Dubliners (1968). A German collection *Materialien zu James Joyces* Dubliners (ed. Klaus Reichert, Fritz Senn, and Dieter F. Zimmer, Frankfurt-am-Main, 1969) is an excellent volume which provides charted maps of Dublin tracing the journeys of the characters in the various stories. Several casebooks on individual stories have also been published in the United States and Europe.

As popular as *Dubliners* has been among critics, there have been only three book-length studies published thus far. Two are by individual authors—Epifanio San Juan, Jr., *James Joyce and the Craft of Fiction: An Interpretation of Dubliners* (1972); and Warren Beck, *Joyce's* Dubliners: *Substance, Vision, and Art* (1969). Neither is distinguished. San Juan spends a great deal of time attacking earlier interpretations and then renders rather narrow moral readings of the characters and offers some untenable conclusions which attempt to find humble virtues in nearly all the characters. Beck, on the other hand, reveals a blissful ignorance of all previous interpretations and at the same time assumes a rather dogmatic and lofty posture in his own analysis. Nevertheless, Beck's book is not without insight. He frequently renders a careful and sensitive reading of individual stories, but his is a work that is lacking in the necessary dialogue of scholarship.

The third volume is *James Joyce's* Dubliners (ed. Clive Hart, 1969), a collection of original critical essays. The fifteen different contributors, with two or three exceptions, have provided sound readings of the stories that collectively illustrate their richness and the wide variety of approaches they elicit from imaginative critics. As this volume evidences, scholarship on *Dubliners* has borne out the book's intricate and seminal relationship to Joyce's mature art, as well as its own esthetic importance, and the trend in criticism of *Dubliners* and *A Portrait* is to look even more closely at their pivotal position in the development of Joyce's canon.

Edward Garnett, a reader for the British publishing house of Duckworth and Company, upon reading the manuscript of *A Portrait* commented that it was not "a book that would make a young man's reputation." In his report Garnett went on to note that *A Portrait* was "too discursive, formless, unrestrained." When it was published the early reviews belied Garnett's opinions, as has most of the criticism devoted to it over the past sixty years. As Marvin Magalaner has observed, "From its first appearance, the *Portrait* was recognized as a work of genius."

A Portrait first appeared in book form in 1916, when the American publisher B. W. Huebsch brought it out. It was published in England in 1917 with the American sheets; English printers refused to accept the responsibility of printing the manuscript. It ran serially in *The Egoist* from 2 February 1914 to 1 September 1915 in 25 installments. The text, as Slocum and Cahoon point out in their 1953 bibliography, is substantially the same as the text of the first edition, with the exception of some corrected misprints and the opening pages of chapter iii, p. 115, line 9, to p. 116, line 5, which are omitted from *The Egoist* serialization.

The earliest commentary on *A Portrait*, beginning with Ezra Pound's various laudatory comments as it was being published serially and upon its book publication, placed the novel in the tradition of European realism, specifically French. Virginia Woolf, who was later to have her problems with *Ulysses*, also saw it as a work which "attempts to come closer to life," and H. G. Wells noted that the "interest of the book depends upon its quintessential and unfailing reality." But another distinguishing element, its deliberate artistry, was also recognized and commented upon—both favorably and unfavorably. Wyndham Lewis, for example, who rarely liked anything he read, felt it to possess far too tenuous an elegance for his taste. On the whole, however, initial reception of *A Portrait* was favorable. It is important to recognize the various shades of response to the novel, for a number of these colorings influenced or were followed by the later interpretations. Because the novel seemed so "real" to early

readers, a light but persistent assumption arose that the work was solely autobiographical with many interesting technical embellishments added—an assumption that has died hard. The subtleties of Joyce's art, which established an extremely complex relationship between art and life, were not quickly understood and became evident only through the careful study and perception of a number of scholars.

The early impact of *A Portrait* was rapidly submerged by the far more startling appearance of the installments of *Ulysses*, which began in *The Little Review* in March 1918. Critical studies of *Ulysses*, later joined with those of *Finnegans Wake*, dominated Joyce studies to the exclusion of the earlier work until the later fifties. At that time *A Portrait* came to the increasing attention of students and scholars alike, and became more and more a part of college curriculum offerings. The novel has over the years achieved the critical importance and central place in Joyce scholarship that it so obviously deserves. The quality and volume of scholarship devoted to the work over the past twenty years clearly reveals its individual significance in Joyce's canon.

Scholarly attention to *A Portrait* is initially reflected in the easy availability of useful materials for the scholar and helpful tools for the beginner, such as the concordance and the raw materials, the sources, the influences, and the Dublin background provided in Kain and Scholes's *The Workshop of Daedalus*. As noted earlier, certain textual problems remain.

A number of volumes have been designed to provide help for the student or to make basic secondary material easily accessible. Don Gifford's *Notes for Joyce* (1967), which extensively annotates allusions and nuances of vocabulary, especially late nineteenth-century Dublin slang in both *A Portrait* and *Dubliners*, is a helpful little book; James S. Atherton's good introduction and sound notes provided in the Heinemann Educational Books edition of *A Portrait* (1964) are worthwhile; the Viking Critical Library edition (ed. Chester G. Anderson) includes a valuable selection of critical and background material, notes, and Anderson's corrected text. Thomas F. Staley's *Critical Study Guide to Joyce's* A Portrait . . . (1968) and Harvey Peter Sucksmith's *James Joyce:* A Portrait . . . (1973) are designed as starting points of critical exploration for the beginner. Two collections of essays, *Portraits of an Artist* (ed. William E. Morris and Clifford A. Nault, Jr., 1962) and *Joyce's Portrait, Criticisms and Critiques* (ed. Thomas E. Connolly, 1962) provide representative selections of studies on the work, but they are now dated. A later volume in the Twentieth Century Interpretations series (ed. William Schutte, 1968) provides several later essays but is more abbreviated and limited and less satisfactory than either of the other two. Wilhelm Füger's volume, mentioned earlier, although in German, is a valuable addition to works of this type and includes an essay on the text by H. W. Gabler as well as Rosemarie Franke's article on the critical reception of *A Portrait* and its German translation in the German speaking countries. The valuable bibliography the Füger book provides was discussed previously. Nathan Halper's recent *The Early James Joyce* (1973), in the Columbia Essays on Modern Writers series, is an idiosyncratic introduction to Joyce but offers a concise analysis of his early accomplishments in the context of the later work and cautions the reader about various interpretative pitfalls. A new "casebook," well arranged and clearly presented, is Dubliners *and* A Portrait . . . (ed. Morris Beja, 1973). It provides a good index and a selected annotated bibliography. A collection of original essays by various hands, aimed primarily at students but also dated, is *Dedalus on Crete* (1956), perhaps its most distinguishing feature being one of Sister M. Corita's first book cover designs.

The most valuable source other than the novel itself for the serious study of *A Portrait* are two of Joyce's earlier works. In January of 1904 Joyce wrote a narrative essay, "A Portrait of the Artist," in which he stated his early intentions as a writer—intentions that remained constant throughout the composition of the novel. Joyce concludes the first paragraph of the essay by stating that "a portrait is not an identificative paper but rather the curve of an emotion," a point cited again and again by critics. This essay led to the long autobiographical novel, in the Naturalist tradition, which he called *Stephen Hero*. Only one fourth of the manuscript survives, and it was published posthumously. Whatever its own merits, it is an invaluable source for the study of *A Portrait*.

Biographical and background studies are also of special value. For example, much of what we know of Joyce's structural plans for the novel is revealed through biographical sources, most notably in Ellmann's biography.

Because *A Portrait* is central to all of Joyce's work, much of the best criticism can be found in general book-length studies of Joyce's entire canon. Levin's *James Joyce . . .*, cited earlier, includes a chapter on the novel that remains an excellent starting point. Levin places the novel in the European tradition of the Bildungsroman, or, more specifically, the Kunstleroman, and also establishes its centrality in Joyce's canon. Later studies have also viewed the novel in the tradition of the Bildungsroman. Jerome Buckley in his *Season of Youth* (1974) sees Joyce as summing up, even as he transforms, the traditions of the nineteenth-century Bildungsroman in *A Portrait*. Although many critics disagree with him, Buckley concludes that the ending of the novel, "like that of many another Bildungsroman, presents problems of indecision and inconclusiveness."

An important but not well-known essay which examines the symbolic struture of *A Portrait* is Kenneth Burke's "Fact, Inference, and Proof in the Analysis of Literary Symbolism" (in Burke's *Terms for Order*, ed. Stanley Edgar Hyman, 1964). He treats the individual words of *A Portrait* as the basic "facts," and "the essay asks how to operate with these 'facts,' how to use them as a means of keeping one's inferences under control, yet how to go beyond them, for purposes of inference when seeking to characterize the motives and 'salient' traits of the work, in its nature as a total symbolic structure." Primarily theoretical, Burke's essay uses *A Portrait* as a test case for establishing a modus operandi for the analysis of literary symbolism, but in so doing illuminates the symbolic network of the novel.

The major topics of critical interest have been the character of Stephen Dedalus, especially his relationship to the author; Stephen's esthetic theories as propounded in the novel and their comparison or contrast with Joyce's own art; structure, problems of irony, and point of view; symbolic elements; mythic framework; psychological elements; and the influences and traditions from which the novel emerged. These categories, of course, overlap, but they represent workable divisions in organizing and describing the criticism devoted to the novel. Besides these specific areas of focus a number of broad studies have been devoted to the work which have concentrated on the early development of Joyce's fiction, discussing *A Portrait* in relationship to *Dubliners* and more closely to *Stephen Hero*.

By implication nearly all the studies of *A Portrait* insist on or at the very least admit to its centrality in Joyce's art. Robert Ryf's *A New Approach to Joyce* (1962) is the most insistent on this point. He sees the themes and techniques of the novel as embodying, in their expanded forms, all of Joyce's work. His theory that Joyce uses Stephen's esthetic theories in his later work has, of course, been largely and correctly discounted. However, Ryf's observations on certain cinematic techniques employed in *A Portrait* are revealing. His study of *A Portrait* attempted to correct or, better, redirect certain critical assumptions which had minimized the work, but his claims are far too strong and ignore the growing esthetic subtleties and larger dimensions of the later work. Joyce's development required much sifting and sorting, much changing after false starts; there was more than mere sophisticated assimilation and a clean line of evolving esthetic unity, a point many later critics have established clearly.

The earlier work of Marvin Magalaner and Joseph Prescott is far more valuable on this point, especially in accounting for the technical development that led to the achievement of *A Portrait*. Magalaner's *Time of Apprenticeship* (1959) devotes more attention to *Dubliners*, but it is a valuable study of Joyce's growing craftsmanship, of the painstaking care he took to achieve desired effects, and of how he assimilated influences from his reading and allowed them to shape his imagination.

The way in which Joyce traversed the differences between art and reality through form and technique are Magalaner's central concern, and he produces abundant evidence from the early drafts of *Dubliners* and *Stephen Hero* to study Joyce's craftsmanship and growing accomplishments. Magalaner and Joseph Prescott (*Exploring James Joyce*, 1964) have made important observations on the nature of the relationship between *Stephen Hero* and *A Portrait*, especially on form and craft, which others have expanded upon; but Magalaner and Prescott have concentrated their discussions more on the esthetic concepts and their refinements.

One problem that has persisted is the difficulty in accounting for the success of *Dubliners* and Joyce's growing recognition of the artistic failure of *Stephen Hero*, since he was engaged in the composition of both simultaneously—a question which involves a number of formal narrative considerations: point of view, structure, and style. A recent study by Homer Obed Brown, *James Joyce's Early Fiction* (1972), subtitled *The Biography of a Form*, treats this problem in detail. Brown argues that changes in the formal development of the early work make possible the later evolutions in style; Joyce's changing concept of the nature of reality accounts for the shift from the early realism of the first stories of *Dubliners* and *Stephen Hero* to "The Dead" and *A Portrait*. "The Dead" signals a crucial stage of Joyce's development, Brown argues, for with it he was able for the first time to harmonize disparate visions of reality, fusing the cold and distant observer of a dead world and the Symbolist poet who sought spiritual transcendence. The fixed outside world which the Stephen of *Stephen Hero* sees shifts in "The Dead" to the union we see with Gabriel Conroy, where the outer world dissolves as he recognizes his oneness with it; in this integration the end of "The Dead" looks forward to the world of *A Portrait* with its organic unity "held together by a narrator who represents both sides of this dualism." As Hugh Staples has noted, many Joyce critics would agree with Brown's points, but most have explored this critical question from a biographical point of view rather than through the careful and logical analysis Brown has brought to bear.

The character of Stephen Dedalus is, of course, an interesting and provocative topic itself. Hugh Kenner's extensive treatment of this subject has been discussed earlier, and his analysis has raised several compelling issues that have created constant controversy and debate in Joyce studies; namely, Joyce's relationship to and attitude toward his young hero and the attendant questions of esthetic distance and point of view and the proximity of Stephen's esthetics to Joyce's. Critical arguments have tied interpretations of Stephen to the nature of Joyce's irony. Besides Kenner, Tindall, Kenneth Burke, John V. Kelleher, and Denis Donoghue, among others, have considered this subject and reached varying conclusions. Chester Anderson has summarized this controversy in his critical edition of *A Portrait*, and he includes in his edition two essays by Wayne Booth and Robert Scholes that present summary views and offer representative opposing conclusions. The selection from Booth appeared originally in his *The Rhetoric of Fiction* (1961). Booth concludes that the critical uncertainty surrounding Joyce's attitude toward Stephen's vocation, his esthetics, and his villanelle reflects Joyce's own uncertainty; the text itself combines "irony and admiration in unpredictable mixtures." Scholes offers ample evidence that the text can yield a predictable mixture. Using both external and internal evidence, he concentrates on an analysis of the villanelle, refutes Booth's position, and challenges the early position of Kenner (in *Dublin's Joyce*) which ascribes to Joyce an ironic vision of Stephen. Another thorough and convincing challenge to Booth's allegations is offered by James Naremore in "Style as Meaning in *A Portrait of the Artist*" (*JJQ*, 1967). The topic is still treated frequently. In the same issue, Thomas W. Grayson suggests that the novel itself "serves to exorcise Stephen from the personality of Joyce, thereby permitting the emergence of the artist." One is tempted to suggest that the entire argument of Stephen's relationship to Joyce, the problem of point of view, and the ironic dimension of Joyce's art has gone through a Viconian cycle, that is, back to where it began but with a difference. In light of Grayson's, Scholes's, and Booth's arguments, one should recall Mark Schorer's seminal essay "Technique as Discovery," (*HudR*, 1948) to which Booth objects so strongly. Schorer described the esthetic achievement of *A Portrait* in terms of technique. He argues that *A Portrait* "analyzes its material rigorously, and it defines the value and the quality of its experience not by appended comment or moral epithet, but by the texture of the style." Joyce's success, Schorer points out, was achieved by refining himself out of existence (a point Booth cannot accept, but which Grayson from a different perspective argues for fully); that is, by refusing any overt commentary on the content of the novel. By the texture of the style Joyce defines the value and quality of experience in the novel.

Essays dealing with the subject of Stephen's esthetic theory are abundant; a selection of the most helpful, although several are dated, are those by A. D. Hope, Irene Hendry Chays, Geddes MacGregor, Haskell M. Block, Marshall McLuhan, Thomas E. Connolly, Maurice Beebe, and J. Mitchell Morse that appear in a special section of Connolly's casebook referred to earlier. William T. Noon's *Joyce and Aquinas* is the most valuable source study on this subject.

The fullest treatment on this range of subjects related to Stephen Dedalus is Edmund L. Epstein's extensive study, *The Ordeal of Stephen Dedalus* (1971). Especially valuable in this study is the description of the way themes introduced in *A Portrait* are developed, refined, and expanded in *Ulysses* and *Finnegans Wake*. Epstein's close and careful reading of the novel offers the best account thus far on the nature and source of Joyce's irony in the first section of chapter iv of *A Portrait*, but this delineation is not sustained for the later portions of the novel. Epstein also offers an extended analysis of Stephen's lecture on esthetics in chapter v in light of the King David figure, the mature artist in the *Wake*. He sketches the historical meaning of David as it may have come to Joyce and how he embodied this historical and mythical figure in Stephen, especially the messianic aspects, and how Joyce contributed facets of his own concept of King David as visionary. Epstein reads the book with an essentially optimistic ending—Stephen is confirmed in his vocation as artist and is reaching for maturity as a man. He is careful to point out, however, the clear limitations in Stephen's character at the conclusion of the novel, seeing Stephen as being too confident of his own powers and not aware of how confused some of his ideas are.

Contrary to Booth's view, ambiguity remains a central aspect of life as well as art, and Joyce's character, like Hamlet, reflects this. Kenner's early contention that Stephen's weaknesses were not unintentional but, rather, poignant examples of Joyce's irony enriched by a moral vision of the world is not easily tenable today, and Kenner's own view has been modified (see *Windsor Rev.*, 1965, and "The Cubist Portrait" in the forthcoming *Approaches to* A Portrait . . . , ed. Staley and Benstock). Later criticism has moved away from the simple dichotomies and thus closer to the complex reality that Joyce attempts to reveal in *A Portrait*. Sympathy and irony are somehow joined and it is toward the discernment of this balance that the more recent distinguished criticism has turned. S. L. Goldberg's *The Classical Temper: A Study of James Joyce's Ulysses* (1961), although it deals primarily with *Ulysses*, examines closely and well Joyce's engagement in and distance from his characters; and L. A. Murillo's *The Cyclical Night: Irony in James Joyce and Jorge Luis Borges*

(1968) deals fully with the ironic dimension in Joyce's work and its major function in his art. Further examination of the ironic dimension can be found in F. Darvin Sharpless' excellent "Irony in Joyce's *Portrait*: The Stasis of Pity" (*JJQ*, 1967).

Although this controversy is specifically related to Joyce's poetry, the opposing arguments are related to the esthetic concerns of *A Portrait*. Morris Beja's *Epiphany in the Modern Novel* (1971) treats the conception and function of the epiphany in a number of modern writers, and his discussion of Joyce's use of the epiphany is a valuable analysis.

During his recovery period from rheumatic fever Joyce decided to rewrite *Stephen Hero* completely, and he told Stanislaus in September of 1907 that he would write the book in five chapters. As Ellmann points out, it was at this time that Joyce discovered a "principle of structure." The drastic changes in organizational principle which Joyce employed in the later version which became *A Portrait* have been the subject of much critical speculation, and structural studies of the novel abound. The early works of Hugh Kenner and Dorothy Van Ghent have been the most influential and still stand as essential reference points on the subject.

All of the studies agree that the central structural principle in the novel is informed and even controlled by Stephen's own spiritual growth and development. Thomas F. Van Lann (*JJQ*, 1964); Robert J. Andreach, *Studies in Structure* (1964); and Sidney Feshback (*JJQ*, 1967) all recognize Stephen's development as the central ordering device Joyce used, but each points to different external ordering principles that inform the structure. Van Lann argues that an analogous correspondence exists between the novel and Ignatius Loyola's *Spiritual Exercises* and that Joyce employs Loyola's pattern of meditation and spiritual exercise. This offered a system of introspective focus in a design that integrated miscellaneous units into a meaningful whole. Andreach contends that the structure of *A Portrait* is built upon the stages of the five-fold Christian division of the spiritual life, "with a difference—the order of the stages is reversed and the individual stages are inverted." Even with Joyce's obvious delight in reversing religious symbols, Andreach's pattern seems too neat and forces him to conclude his judgment of Stephen on a far too simplistic basis. Feshback notes clearly in his intriguing essay that he does not account for what appears to him to be the implicit irony in the Joyce-Stephen relationship, but he sees the source for the organization of the novel emanating out of the traditional progression of the character called "the ladder of perfection" and that Joyce had made Stephen's soul the soul and form of the novel.

Three additional structural studies with different approaches are Evert Sprinchorn's "A Portrait of the Artist as Achilles," in *Approaches to the Twentieth-Century Novel* (1965); Lee T. Lemon's (*MFS*, 1967–68); and Grant Redford's (*MFS*, 1958). Redford's essay is the most similar to the three above in that he suggests that the themes of search and rebellion in the book are made meaningful through structure, and "structure is the embodiment of an artistic proposition proclaimed by the central character himself as being basic to a work of art." Lemon bases his methodology on the work of the Russian

Formalists and thus argues that it is Joyce's adroit handling of the various motifs that reveals Stephen's development and subsequently unifies the novel. Sprinchorn, however, attempts to account for what he sees as Joyce's loss of sympathy for Stephen in Chapter v, but it is not convincing. His study offers an elaborate if somewhat pretentious explication of the chapter and further attempts to show its integration with the other four chapters and its consistency with the overall structural and symbolic pattern of the novel as a whole. Bernard Benstock's "A Light from Some Other World" in the forthcoming *Approaches to* A Portrait . . . (ed. Staley and Benstock) is the most extensive treatment thus far of the way in which the various levels of symbolism accent and extend meaning to develop the entire symbolic structure of the novel.

These structural studies afford an excellent example of the general evolution of criticism of *A Portrait,* in their move to a more qualified but more acute understanding of the relationship of character to author, technique to form, and design to content.

The epigraph of the novel, from Ovid; the obviousness of the hero's surname; and the frequent mythological allusions in the text itself make abundantly clear the mythic framework of *A Portrait.* This aspect of the work has been discussed by a number of critics. The most extensive treatment has been Diane Fortuna's long essay entitled "The Labyrinth as Controlling Image in Joyce's *A Portrait*" (*BNYPL,* 1972), in which she traces with careful attention to archeological detail and mythic artifact the Daedalus myth together with its ritualistic associations. David Hayman's "Daedalian Imagery in *A Portrait,*" *Hereditas* (ed. Frederick Will, 1964), a thorough study of the mythic framework of the novel, suggests the way myth gives dimension and force to Stephen's character. Perhaps it is a testament to the novel's originality that relatively little scholarship has been devoted to the literary influences on *A Portrait.* As any number of critics have pointed out, when Joyce abandoned the largely naturalistic framework of *Stephen Hero* for more formally controlled symbolic realism of *A Portrait,* he seemed to have left many of his literary debts behind. There have been, however, a number of comparative studies which have treated the similarities of *A Portrait* and other works such as Hayman's "*A Portrait* . . . and *L'Education sentimentale*: The Structural Affinities" (*OL,* 1964); Ilse Dusoir Lind, "*The Way of All Flesh* and *A Portrait* . . ." (*VN,* 1956); and Joyce W. Warren, "Faulkner's *Portrait of the Artist*" (*MissQ,* 1966). Far more scholarship has been devoted to the influence of *A Portrait* on later works.

Source studies on *A Portrait* have been most revealing on the subject of the retreat sermon of Chapter iii. Both James R. Thrane (*MP,* 1960) and Elizabeth Boyd (*MLN,* 1960) have shown conclusively that the sermons Father Arnall gives were borrowed by Joyce from Giovanni Pietro Pinomonti's *L'inferno aperto,* or *Hell Opened to Christians* in its nineteenth-century English translation. The two essays were published independently of each other, but Thrane's, which appeared first, is by far the better. James Doherty has dealt further with this source (*MP,* 1963), and Eugene August has analyzed Arnall's use of scripture in his sermons (*JJQ,* 1967).

The more specifically technical problems posed by *A Portrait* with regard to irony and point of view have been well treated by James Naremore in "Style as Meaning in *A Portrait*" (*JJQ*, 1967) and F. Parvin Sharpless in "Irony in Joyce's *Portrait*: The Stasis of Pity" (*JJQ*, 1967).

In the history of literary criticism sixty years is a very short time, but it is a large enough span to estimate the permanent place that *A Portrait* has established in modern fiction. While neither so monumental as *Ulysses* nor so spectacular as *Finnegans Wake*, its achievement lies in the brilliant ordering and fulfillment of its art, the universal depth of its themes, and, as so much of the criticism devoted to it attests, the full realization of its purpose. Its artistic achievement is confirmed in the creation of the character of the artist-hero who possesses in various degrees the strengths and weaknesses of modern man, which we are able to see and understand, to mock or praise. But in either mood he touches us; and if he did not, however perfect the novel's symmetry, *A Portrait* would be far less an achievement.

EXILES

There has been a great deal of critical and biographical speculation surrounding Joyce's single completed play, *Exiles*; but specific study of the work has been relatively limited. The failure of the play, even as a *succès d'estime*, troubled Joyce throughout his life. As Harry Levin points out in the preface to the play in the Viking Portable edition of Joyce, it was "written during his most fruitful year, 1914, immediately after completing *Portrait*, and before undertaking *Ulysses*." But even Joyce's most ardent supporters refrained from high praise when it was published in 1918. Although *Exiles* has been played a number of times, and recently in a heralded production in London by Harold Pinter, it has never been a critical success; however, Pinter's version, which excised a great deal of material, was a theatrical success. Ezra Pound's statement in 1933 summarizes much of the critical commentary: "*Exiles* is a bad play with a serious content . . . the play's many excellencies are those of a novelist and not of a dramatist." A later edition, first published in 1951, incorporates the valuable notes Joyce made to the work. These have enhanced critical speculation insofar as they reveal Joyce's expanding esthetic and thematic concerns and anticipate the themes of *Ulysses*. Further speculation on the play stems from the discovery of manuscript pages containing dialogue for *Exiles* that was never incorporated into the text. See Robert Martin Adams' "Light on Joyce's *Exiles*? . . ." (*SB*, 1964).

In summarizing the criticism on the play through the middle fifties, Magalaner and Kain, in their *Joyce: The Man . . .* , note Joyce's indebtedness to Ibsen as well as the superficial autobiographical elements and point out that the play has suppressed personal undertones and that the Ibsenesque style inhibits the symbolic associations that color Joyce's conceptions. Their point was later echoed in the *Reader's Guide to James Joyce* by Tindall, who ponders the questions of theme, motive, and meaning, concluding that in spite of Joyce's ability to handle increasingly complex material he had not as yet achieved the esthetic distance needed, especially in the drama.

The most extended early study of *Exiles* was Hugh Kenner's chapter in his *Dublin's Joyce*, in which he set down the major critical concerns *Exiles* scholarship has followed to date—the influence of Ibsen's naturalism; the establishment of its place in Joyce's canon both in theme and subject matter; the treatment of the themes of betrayal and exile which obsessed Joyce.

Ibsen's influence on *Exiles* has been taken up by a number of critics. James T. Farrell (in *Two Decades* . . .) shows how Joyce attempted to capture the mood of Ibsen; Frances Ferguson (in *Hound and Horn*, 1932) offers a more formal analysis of the play's affinities with Ibsen's drama and praises it for its dramatic substance. On the other hand, B. J. Tysdahl in his *Joyce and Ibsen: A Study in Literary Influence* (Oslo, 1968) points out how unsystematic and incomplete Joyce's understanding of Ibsen was. Benstock's essay, "*Exiles*: 'Paradox Lust' and Lost Paladays" (*ELH*, 1969) argues that the great interest of the play is in what it reveals of Joyce's developing art. John MacNicholas (*JJQ*, 1973) takes issue with those whom he believes have done a disservice to the play by studying it primarily as a commentary on Joyce's fiction. He maintains that the treatment of the play presents an elaborately crafted surface which is necessary to the complex themes developed in the work and that although Joyce's refusal to disclose to the audience certain knowledge of Robert and Bertha's actions has made the play more static, this uncertainty is not simply a vagueness of mood but a dramatization of Richard's own crippling doubt.

Earl John Clark (*JJQ*, 1968) has traced several autobiographical elements as they develop into human relationships within the play and circumscribe thematic development. An earlier article which stresses the dramatic function of the characters is D. J. F. Aitken's (*MFS*, 1958). Aitken argues that two "archetypal dramas" are played out by the four main characters in *Exiles* and that the play has its general meanings on two different thematic levels. On one of these, each of the protagonists has an archetypal personality: Richard is spirit, Robert is body, Bertha is fecundity, Beatrice is intellect; each struggles both toward union with the others and to retain his or her integrity. On the other level, Richard is the archetype of the conscience-forging artist, pitted against all the others, who represent different aspects of unregenerate Ireland. These schemes, while not totally convincing, give Aitken opportunities for commentary on the symbols and motifs that Joyce employed to illuminate his characters and their relationships with each other.

One consistent point in nearly all the studies of *Exiles* is that the themes and characterizations look forward to Joyce's future work and that drama was simply not the genre most suitable for Joyce's growing artistic ambitions and powers; recognizing this, he wisely turned to pursue the course that resulted in *Ulysses*.

ULYSSES

No novel written in English in this century has been studied more widely or more deeply over so impressive a range of topics as Ulysses —studied not only because of its own intrinsic complexity, depth, and worth but also because of its impact on the whole of modern literature. Janet Flanner has succinctly described the stature that Ulysses has achieved in its first fifty years: "that masterpiece . . . which slowly turned into what it immediately remains today: a literary classic and the guidebook marking the new territory of the twentieth century English language novel" (NY, 3 June 1974). No longer able to shock, having itself taken much of the shock out of modern literature, Ulysses continues to attract a wide and seemingly endless critical response as nearly every aspect of the work is examined and reexamined by critics who have applied countless approaches and points of view in trying to yield up at least part of its meaning. There is, of course, no single reason a work of art achieves great stature and compelling critical and cultural interest. Ulysses is that rare work of art which in a remarkable number of ways, not all of them esthetic, encapsulates, defines, and reflects the concerns and dilemmas of an age.

The publishing history along with textual matters have been discussed in an earlier section of this essay, and many of the general studies treated in the previous section focus significant attention on Ulysses; in fact, as pointed out earlier, frequently those works devoted to Joyce's complete canon are the most influential, and their specific impact on Ulysses criticism will be briefly assessed in this section. The sheer volume of commentary devoted to Ulysses is in itself intimidating. Richard M. Kain has provided an excellent outline of the early reception of the book and has deftly sketched the major critical issues and debates that preoccupied the early critics (Joyce, The Man . . .). Clive Hart has also provided a solid narrative of the highlights of the major critical issues which evolved through the mid-sixties in his James Joyce's Ulysses (Sydney, 1968).

Amid so many of the outrageous comments (e.g., "the maddest, muddiest, most loathsome book") and the cries of obscenity in the popular press which greeted the publication of Ulysses, were a number of astute and far-reaching evaluations that judged the work on its own terms and attempted to estimate its future impact on modern literature. Several intelligent readers, such as E. M. Forster and Virginia Woolf, also voiced reservations about the novel. Pound and Eliot, on the other hand, responded with more important and influential judgments. The earliest and one of the most perceptive critics was Valery Larbaud, the Frenchman and friend of Joyce who delivered a lecture on Ulysses in December, 1921, when only half of the book had appeared serially. A fuller study by Larbaud was published in Nouvelle Revue Française (1922); it was translated as "The Ulysses of James Joyce" (Criterion, 1922). Armed with Joyce's schema, Larbaud emphasized the Homeric parallels, the symbolic patterns, and concentrated on the central themes in the book.

Of greater importance, however, were the critical statements of

Pound and Eliot, whose essays not only established the critical acceptance of *Ulysses* but profoundly influenced the direction of the critical arguments. A. Walton Litz has carefully argued ("Pound and Eliot on *Ulysses*: The Critical Tradition" [*Ulysses: Fifty Years*, 1974]) that their initital arguments have become large critical touchstones, and that "*Ulysses* criticism can be viewed . . . as an extended conversation . . . between the spiritual descendants of Pound and Eliot."

Pound's essay, "James Joyce et Pécuchet" (*Mercure de France*, 1922; trans. Fred Bornhauser, *Shenandoah*, 1952) stressed Joyce's uncompromising realism, which emanated out of the tradition of Flaubert but went beyond; Pound also insisted on the unity of the work and compared it in form to the sonata. Although Pound placed *Ulysses* in the tradition of Flaubert and Realism, he used the term "realism," as Litz points out, in his own special way. He praised the "luminous detail" that created the universal in the sharp and clearly focused particular, which in turn yielded a resonance beyond itself. He dismissed the Homeric structure as mere scaffolding and glossed over the more elaborate labyrinthian designs of the later chapters to concentrate on the "realism," the style, the counterpoint, the rhythm —those aspects of the work that emphasized its precision of detail.

Eliot's essay ("*Ulysses*, Order and Myth," *The Dial*, 1923) reflects not only his appreciation and understanding of *Ulysses* but also Eliot's own critical and creative preoccupations. As with *The Waste Land*, he saw *Ulysses* as an attempt to come to terms with and create a synthesis out of what he regarded as the chaos of the fragmented modern experience. He concentrated on what he saw as the central unifying method, the parallel to the *Odyssey*, which gave the book its shape and significance as it delicately balanced "contemporaneity and antiquity." While Pound stressed the work's inclusive realism Eliot pointed out the classical dimensions, the deft parallels between the past and present, as well as the symbolist techniques and Joyce's use of myth, which provided a new method for giving shape to the "immense panorama of futility which is contemporary history." It is more than a convenient polarity to draw attention to the contrasting emphasis given to two major dimensions of *Ulysses* by Pound and Eliot, for Litz's observation is an accurate one—the major critical studies that have followed have run the course between Pound's concentration on the naturalistic impulse and Eliot's on the mythic dimension, between the realistic and symbolic. *Ulysses* criticism from the 1920's through the mid-1970's seems to flow between these two positions, poles between which the novel as a genre has always glided, both of which are uniquely embraced in *Ulysses*.

The years immediately following the first flurry of critical attention produced little in the way of a significant response to *Ulysses*; however, Wyndham Lewis in *Time and Western Man* (1927) launched an attack on the formlessness of the book and called it a "night-mare of the naturalistic method"; whether in spite of or because of his bombastic rhetoric and petulant imagery, he scored many points, accusing Joyce, among other things, of having "unorganized susceptibility to influences." A few years later, Joyce set out to answer this charge through the good auspices of Stuart Gilbert. The most ambitious study of the book during the twenties was S. Foster Damon's "The Odyssey in Dublin" (*The Hound and Horn*, 1924; rpt. in *Two Decades . . .*) which offered the broadest assessment of the total meaning of the work thus far. The novel, according to Damon, operated on three levels: the symbolic (*Odyssey*), the spiritual (*The Divine Comedy*), and the psychological (*Hamlet*). Homer offered the plot, Dante the setting, and Shakespeare the motivation; the three major characters play out symbolic roles all of which culminate in the frustration and degradation of the modern world. It is difficult to assess the influence of Damon's allegorical reading, but the depth of his treatment of the major themes and literary influences obviously opened up further considerations for subsequent investigation.

The remainder of the 1920's produced little of critical importance. The first book-length study of *Ulysses* to be published was Paul Jordan Smith's *A Key to the* Ulysses *of James Joyce* (1927), a slight volume that provided a narrative sketch of the novel and stressed the influence of the *Odyssey* and its importance to an understanding of *Ulysses*. There were, of course, further essays written by Joyce's Paris coterie. For example, Eugene Jolas, who was later to figure so prominently in the serial publication of *Finnegans Wake*, translated an essay by Ernst Curtius, "Technique and Thematic Development in James Joyce," and published it in his magazine, *transition* (1929). Curtius' essay foreshadows in part the argument that was to be developed by Stuart Gilbert a few years later. Partly because of Wyndham Lewis' attack on the book, Joyce felt compelled to have its purposes and design better explained. But he recognized that Lewis' charges were symptomatic of a larger hostility and disdain brought about as a reaction to the extravagances in the arts created by the Dadaists and Surrealists. By showing the precision, the deliberate artfulness, and the classical background of the novel, he believed he could clearly distinguish it from the literary excesses with which it was being compared. In this context Joyce authorized Stuart Gilbert to write *James Joyce's* Ulysses (1930; rev. 1952).

Gilbert's study, he assured us, carried the endorsement of Joyce, and, in fact, it did, Joyce having aided and directed Gilbert in its composition from the beginning. The book answers the charge of the formlessness of *Ulysses* to the extent that one has the impression that the novel is too rigid, too formalized, overly structured, and far too schematic. In Gilbert's study the human experience of the book is submerged by his concentration on the formal trappings, the esoteric influences and allusions, and especially his relentless depiction of the Homeric parallels which create, in his view, the formal relationship between *Ulysses* and the *Odyssey*. Gilbert first concentrates on the various sources upon which Joyce drew (including the esoteric doctrine of metempsychosis) and follows with a chapter-by-chapter commentary emphasizing the Homeric parallels. He also traces the motifs and notes their complex expansion as they appear and reappear through the novel. Gilbert defends the elaborate stylistic variations as justified by Joyce's adaptation of form to content to create an organic unity. Gilbert's study, of course, suffers from the defensive context in which it was written and from the weak appeal to authority (Joyce himself); it does not demonstrate his arguments through

JAMES JOYCE / *Thomas F. Staley*   415

critical rigor. The book did, however, exert a large influence on *Ulysses* studies—an influence that was frequently negative through its imbalanced emphasis.

Another important book by a friend of Joyce's is Frank Budgen's *James Joyce and the Making of* Ulysses (1934; enl. ed., 1972). Called by Hugh Kenner "the best possible introduction to the Joyce world" and by Clive Hart "the best ever written about Joyce," the book remains one of the most enduring studies of Joyce. Free from the dogmatic critical positions that dominated early *Ulysses* criticism, it is a sensitive combination of relevant biographical detail and critical commentary that describes the genesis of the novel and reveals a sympathetic awareness of Joyce's art. Budgen's study is in no sense systematic, but through revelations in Joyce's letters, remembrances of conversations with Joyce, and his own perceptive observations of the novel itself, he illuminates Joyce's conscious craft and the human dimensions of the novel.

The importance of Edmund Wilson's *Axel's Castle* (1931) has been noted in an earlier section; it is worth mentioning, however, that his discussion of *Ulysses* brought together the two positions that Pound and Eliot had chosen to emphasize. Wilson pointed out the affinities of *Ulysses* with both the French Naturalism of Flaubert and the French Symbolists and showed how *Ulysses* joined the two. Carl Jung, a year later, wrote an essay on *Ulysses* ("Ein Monolog," *Europäische Rev.*, 1932), describing *Ulysses* as a Cubistic work which, through its hidden rational control, depicted a world of seeming madness that revealed a new consciousness, "the epitome of being and not being." Jung's essay, although it frequently misses Joyce's point, is representative of the growing awareness and consensus among European intellectuals of the achievement of *Ulysses*. (An English translation appeared in *Nimbus*, 1953.)

In spite of this recognized achievement, *Ulysses* could still not be published in either England or the United States. From the 1920's until the Woolsey Decision in 1933, and the subsequent publications of *Ulysses* in 1934, much of the discussion surrounding the novel was related to censorship and obscenity—important issues, of course, but these arguments contributed little to the understanding of the work itself. There were, however, from the late 1920's through the late 1930's, a number of more scholarly commentaries. The following are representative of a highly diverse and useful cross section of views on *Ulysses* during this period: Cyril Connolly (*Life and Letters*, 1929) and Joseph Warren Beach, *The Twentieth Century Novel* (1932) attempt to assess the place of *Ulysses* in the modern novel, and Beach discusses the technical accomplishments. Alick West in his *Crisis and Criticism* (1937) offers a perceptive social reading of the novel. Paul Elmer More, the noted humanist critic, admired Joyce's linguistic and technical mastery but felt his achievement was limited by his rejection of an elevating philosophy (*Amer. Rev.*, 1935). Henry Miller in an essay on *Ulysses* noted that Joyce revealed his "perpetual frantic search for God" (*The Phoenix*, 1938). Alec Brown offered a belated Irish attack on *Ulysses* (*DM*, 1934).

The general critical contribution and influence of Harry Levin, William York Tindall, and Hugh Kenner have been discussed previously, but brief attention needs be given to their work on *Ulysses*. Each has a significantly different approach to the novel that has influenced subsequent criticism. Levin described *Ulysses* as a "modern" novel, a work that revealed a synthesis between Naturalism and Symbolism, observing that Joyce when he wrote *Ulysses* was armed with the map and the myth to create the epic symbolism and the naturalistic atmosphere. Levin's careful analysis of the novel, and especially his close attention to the text, marked the way for later critics and brought into *Ulysses* criticism modern exegetical methods that could more systematically yield the novel's complex richness. Tindall's *James Joyce* (1950) placed great value on the multidimensional qualities of *Ulysses* achieved through symbolism. His great emphasis on the symbolic was perhaps excessive, for from his readings it would appear that nothing was accidental or insignificant and thus the merely clever assumed equal importance to the more pressing major themes of the book. Whatever the limitations and excesses of Tindall's methods, his explications and his analysis of the rich associative fabric of the novel were both illuminating and important for later critics. Kenner's work (*Dublin's Joyce*), always marked by its originality and independence, placed great emphasis on the ironic dimension in Joyce's work and on precision in reading the text.

Richard M. Kain's *Fabulous Voyager* was the most thorough and detailed reading of *Ulysses* to date (1947). An outgrowth of one of the earliest courses on Joyce, the book emphasized the naturalistic details of the novel, showing how intricately they were interwoven to provide a rich, resonant, and poetic tone. Kain's appendices offer lists of over 530 references to Leopold Bloom, a list of over 150 characters, a directory of Dublin addresses, and an index of verbal motifs. Beyond setting the novel brilliantly within its own world and in Dublin, Kain emphasized the human nature of the characters and the themes of alienation and of modern man's search for community. Kain's study was extremely influential; besides its eloquent arguments for the novel's human portrayal and modern themes, it also revealed the order and purpose of Joyce's awesome use of naturalistic detail. The immediate effect of Kain's study was to balance the influence of Gilbert's work with its stress on the epic and esoteric. Kain put *Ulysses* back in Dublin; but at the same time, his study revealed in new ways Joyce's essentially modern vision of how man was locked in history and bounded by geography, within the cosmic expanse of the universe.

From the late 1940's through the early 1950's the criticism was erratic and uneven. R. P. Blackmur's brilliant essay on the paternity theme in *Ulysses*, "The Jew in Search of a Son" (*VQR*, 1958), depicted the moral and cultural breakdown as the seminal theme in the novel, exemplified by the son's unfulfilled quest for the father; Rolf Loehrich's *The Secret of Ulysses* (1953) pointed out the extremes of the worst aspect of Joyce criticism with its chaotic associative method leading to fantasy. William Empson's enigmatic "The Theme of *Ulysses*" (*KR*, 1956) put forth another strange theory in which he saw the book as an autobiography of Joyce's hypothetical affair with a married woman. D. S. Savage in a chapter of his book *The Withered Branch* (1950) echoed Blackmur's view in that he saw no stability of values in the novel, no solidity of focus in a world of flux. On the other hand, a number of essays by Joseph Prescott written in the early 1950's and later published in his *Exploring James Joyce* carefully studied Joyce's style and technique by examining the earlier drafts of the book and noting the development of the characters. Philip Toynbee (in *Two Decades . . .*) is exuberant in his support of the novel and points out the growing difference in method and purpose between the first half of the book and the second, taking into account the function of the imitative style in the later chapters. An excellent study of the Odysseus figure throughout history, from Homer to Kazantzakis, is W. B. Stanford's *The Ulysses Theme* (1954; rev. 1963).

While the longer and more general treatments of *Ulysses* illuminated its broader themes, purposes, methods, and sources and assessed its contribution to modern literature, an enormous body of narrowly focused criticism treating nearly every conceivable aspect of the novel has developed over the past twenty-five years. These include such topics as: Who was M'Intosh?; Was Bloom a Freemason?; Who was Lizzie Twigg?; the meaning of parallax; Who moved the furniture at 7 Eccles Street?; astronomical allusions; Why does Stephen pick his nose?; and Why does Molly menstruate? Exclusive of all the hundreds of general studies, well over 100 articles have been written on individual themes or sources in the novel and 100 others have been devoted to single episodes. A. M. Klein's essays on the first two episodes ("The Black Panther, a Study in Technique," *Accent*, 1950; "A Shout in the Street: An Analysis of the Second Chapter . . . ," *New Directions*, 1951), and, more especially, his elaborate exegesis of the fourteenth episode of *Ulysses* ("The Oxen of the Sun," *Here and Now*, 1949) were extremely detailed analyses of those chapters. Klein's analysis of "Oxen" remains the fullest commentary on that episode to date. Leonard Albert's "Ulysses, Cannibals and Freemasons" (*A.D.*, 1951) offers an extensive study of the "Lestrygonians" episode but also deals with the Masonic codes and rituals throughout the book. There have been a number of studies devoted to the "Sirens" episode, the most extensive being Zack Bowen's informative and thorough monograph-length essay, "The Bronzegold Sirensong: A Musical Analysis of the Sirens Episode . . . ," in *Literary Monographs* 1 (1967, ed. Eric Rothstein and Thomas K. Dunseath). Much of this study has been incorporated into Bowen's recent *Musical Allusions in the Works of James Joyce* (1974). The "Circe" episode has been the subject of over a dozen essays, besides one book-length study by Frances Boldereff, *A Blakean Translation of Joyce's "Circe"* (1965), a strange reading of the episode which attributes nearly every aspect of the work to Blake's influence and even spiritual presence. Richard E. Madtes has written a detailed analysis of the development of the "Ithaca" episode (*ELH*, 1964). The "Penelope" episode, Molly Bloom's soliloquy, has perhaps attracted more critical attention than any other single episode. An outline of the interpretation of Molly will be treated presently.

William Schutte's *Joyce and Shakespeare* (1957) is an extended study of the nature and use of Shakespeare's life and work in *Ulysses*. Besides examining carefully the complex network of Shakespearean allusions and themes, Schutte also delineates the way in which these references illuminate and reinforce the meanings of the major themes, such as Stephen's concept of art and its relationship to life. Schutte's extended treatment of the "Scylla and Charybdis" episode is valuable for its analysis of the Shakespearean material, whether one agrees with his interpretative conclusions or not. He concludes that Stephen's theory of Shakespeare's life and work is woven in Stephen's own image and reveals the essential limitations of Stephen's artistic vision rather than his comprehension of Shakespeare's richly human vision. In short, Stephen's convoluted and limited vision of Shakespeare, both as man and as artist, reveals his own limited human dimension. Schutte's conclusions are not arbitrary, but they perhaps push too far toward a larger interpretation than the evidence supports. A number of earlier studies had dealt with the Shakespearean elements in *Ulysses*, such as Edward Duncan's "Unsubstantial Father: A Study of the 'Hamlet' Symbolism in Joyce's *Ulysses*" (*UTQ*, 1950) and Arthur Heine's "Shakespeare in James Joyce" (*Shakespeare Assoc. Bull.*, 1949), among others, but no one has so exhaustively covered the full range of Shakespeare material as Schutte.

Two influential studies of *Ulysses* were published in the early 1960's: Robert Martin Adams' *Surface and Symbol* (1962) and S. L. Goldberg's *The Classical Temper* (1961). These two studies represent a trend begun in the 1960's. By this time the definitive biography had been written by Ellmann; Walton Litz and other critics had begun systematic studies of the manuscripts; and students of *Ulysses* had begun to look more closely and rigorously at the text and its genesis and—having achieved some distance—at the novel in a broader historical context. The two studies mentioned follow these two lines.

Surface and Symbol, winner of the *Explicator* award for the best book of explication de texte in 1962, offers a necessarily selective but penetrating investigation into the raw materials that went into the making of *Ulysses*. Adams examines these materials in order to clarify "the texture" (the consistency) and thus "define some of the ways in which the novel was put together." Adams stresses Joyce's own consistency in using factual materials, and, while acknowledging his essential accuracy, discovers that Joyce frequently deliberately confused or blurred certain factual details to create or emphasize patterns or relationships, or to break down relationships and leave a deliberately grainy texture. Adams has made a few factual errors of his own which have been pointed out by reviewers and later commentators (e.g., see Robert Boyle's "A Note on Reuben J. Dodd as 'a dirty Jew,'" *JJQ*, 1965; also Hart in *James Joyce's* Ulysses, 1968). Though Adams has a rather low opinion of *Ulysses*, his book points to an important shift in the textual criticism; it marked the presence of more critical rigor and less elaborate suggestive and associative readings which characterized much of the criticism of the 1950's. The work of critics such as Adams who probed with care the texture of the novel revealed the technical skill of Joyce that enabled him to blend surface and symbol in a careful balance rather than lay on, as some critics suggest, a supra-naturalism and neo-symbolism in an unstable mixture that placed them at war with each other.

The dual epigraph of Goldberg's book reflects his fundamental view of *Ulysses*; he quotes Stephen's remarks on the classical temper from *Stephen Hero* and a line from D. H. Lawrence: "Most books that live, live in spite of the author's laying it on thick." Goldberg's book is frequently brilliant; for example, his discussion of Stephen's growing esthetic from *A Portrait* through its articulation in "Scylla and Charybdis" may well be the best written on the subject, although it does not supersede Noon's carefully researched study of the sources. One argues outside rather than inside Goldberg's book; he states clearly in his introduction the limitations of his study—he will not emphasize the mechanical intricacies, the symbolic elements, or the "psychological subtleties" in order "to focus attention on the meanings . . . [Joyce] creatively revealed in his material, upon themes realized dramatically." It is not the Leavisite turn toward "moral enactment" that is disturbing, but rather the suggestion that an evaluation of a novel such as *Ulysses* can be made without emphasizing those elements which give the work its complexity and significance, for they reflect, together with the dramatized material, that "constant state of mind" in which Joyce says the Romantic and Classical tempers must rise. It is frustrating in the limited space available to raise broad objections to a work which is in many ways so admirable. A recent essay that treats in more detail the specific points raised here is Litz's "The Genre of *Ulysses*," in *Theory of the Novel: New Essays* (ed. John Halperin, 1974). Litz's essay is, of course, important beyond its argument with Goldberg, for he reviews theoretical attempts to define the genre of *Ulysses*, a problem with which many critics have attempted to come to terms. The work stands, as Litz points out, "at the confluence of so many literary traditions and genres . . . that it has become the supreme challenge for the theoretical critic of fiction."

Stanley Sultan's *The Argument of Ulysses* (1964) is a thorough rendering of the narrative detail, cogently tracing the relationship among the narrative, the symbolic, and the thematic. He is especially illuminating when he brings into sharp focus the interplay between the dramatic events and the symbolic patterns. The book follows a chapter-by-chapter analysis, giving an excellent account of the full growth and import of the novel. On the other hand, Sultan's view of Stephen's ultimate destiny seems almost arbitrary, his too loosely drawn thesis on the source of Bloom's conflict is disappointing in its limitations, and his rigid moral bias leads to a far too narrow and restricted interpretation of the major characters. Sultan's study remains valuable, however, for its close examination of the text.

Also published in the early 1960's was Mary Parr's *James Joyce: The Poetry of Conscience* (1961), a weak book in which the author attempts to reveal Charlie Chaplin as the real-life model for Leopold Bloom and maintains that both blend into the archetype of the common man. Besides the extremely dubious reading, Parr's is a discursive, wandering work. The fullest and most interesting discussion of the comic elements in *Ulysses* is David Hayman, "Form of Folly in Joyce: A Study of Clowning in *Ulysses*" (*ELH*, 1967). An earlier, less extensive, and more theoretical treatment of the comic is Lawrance Thompson's monograph *A Comic Principle in Sterne, Meredith, and*

Joyce (Oslo, 1954). Vivian Mercier also treats this subject in *The Irish Comic Tradition* (1962), especially in his chapter on parody. Finally, Hugh Kenner treats the subtleties of Joyce's "comic" verbal technique in *Flaubert, Joyce, and Beckett: The Stoic Comedians* (1962).

Recent years have produced several excellent introductory studies. The two best are Clive Hart's *James Joyce's* Ulysses (1968) and David Hayman's Ulysses: *The Mechanics of Meaning* (1970). Michael Mason's *James Joyce:* Ulysses (1972) is very slight in comparison to the Hart and Hayman volumes. Hayman's study is designed primarily to serve the general reader as a descriptive introduction, and it fulfills its purpose admirably. To call Hayman's book an introduction is not to demean it, for even the most advanced student of *Ulysses* can profit from reading it. Hayman's opening chapter is especially valuable for its succinct discussion of the literary traditions out of which Joyce's ideas and work grew. Hart's book assumes less background than Hayman's and provides brief introductions to various aspects of Joyce's art. His second chapter offers a clear reading of the narrative line, comments on the developing themes, and concludes by pointing to the limited degree of reconciliation achieved between Bloom and Molly and Stephen's limited recognition of common humanity. Hart's final chapter, mentioned earlier, provides an excellent review of the major developments and positions in *Ulysses* scholarship through the mid-1960's. The Hayman and Hart volumes complement each other, and together they provide the best critical introduction to the novel available.

A different type of introduction is Harry Blamires' *The Bloomsday Book: A Guide through Joyce's* Ulysses (1966). Designed primarily for students, the book provides a line-by-line commentary. Although there are a substantial number of misreadings of fact and interpretation, it is a detailed guide. Giulio D'Angelis has also written an introductory guide: *Ulysses Guida alla lettura dell'* Ulisse *di James Joyce* (Milan, 1961). Also published in Italy was Francesco Flora's introductory study *Poesia i empoesia nell'* Ulisse *di Joyce* (Milan, 1962). Besides the books designed primarily for students, one book was written by students, *The Celtic Bull: Essays on James Joyce's* Ulysses (ed. Judy-Lynn Benjamin, 1966), a collection that grew out of a seminar on *Ulysses*.

As noted earlier, some of the most concentrated studies of *Ulysses* have appeared in journals, and of these the majority has been devoted to single episodes. An example of the extensive criticism can be seen in the many studies of "Oxen of the Sun," the episode Joyce considered the most difficult to write. Sultan, Goldberg, Toynbee, Wilson, Levin, Burgess, Tindall, and Williams considered the episode overworked and lacking in artistic discretion; while Kenner, Ellmann, Klein, Ruth Bauerle ("A Sober Drunken Speech: Stephen's Parodies in the . . . ," *JJQ*, 1967), and Joseph Campbell ("Contransmagnificandjewbangtantiality," *SLitI*, 1970) do not question the methods employed but rather focus on interpretation. The structural elements as well as the parodies themselves have interested most of the critics, Klein's work being the most elaborate. Bauerle discusses Stephen's parodies of liturgical and religious documents and services, while

Thomas Whitaker ("The Drinkers and History: Rabelais, Balzac and Joyce," *CL*, 1959) finds remarkable parallels with Rabelais's work. The most significant critical argument involves the ending or "tail-piece" of the episode after the ninth month and after the parodies of English prose stylists cease. Klein calls this section the afterbirth, and Ellsworth Mason ("Commentary: The End of 'Oxen of the Sun,'" *The Analyst*, 1955) agrees, replying to Daniel Weiss's article in an earlier issue of *The Analyst* (1955). Weiss considers the ending the fertilization in the womb of possible linguistic forms (a future language), and Ellmann (*Ulysses on the Liffey*, 1972) interprets it to be the ejaculative spray following coitus interruptus. Kenner, Hayman, Hart, Ellmann, and Sultan comment on the sterility theme as well as the reasons Joyce might have had for using this particular method of parody. Thomas M. Lorch ("The Relationship between *Ulysses* and *The Waste Land*," *TSLL*, 1964), Campbell, and Kenner discover many parallels with *The Waste Land*, especially with regard to the thunder, drought, and rain. Many critics agree that the main importance of the episode is that Bloom and Stephen finally meet in the hospital, arguing that both are perhaps sterile, but not so sterile as the students whom they accompany. James Atherton ("The 'Oxen of the Sun,'" in *James Joyce's* Ulysses: *Critical Essays*, ed. Hart and Hayman, 1974) offers the most extensive study of the parodies thus far, calling the episode "an exercise in imitative form." He concludes, however, that the "chapter appeals, admittedly, only to readers concerned with the technique of writing," though Joyce's achievement here is "one we cannot afford to ignore or undervalue."

While there has been extensive study of the individual episodes such as "Oxen of the Sun," more general essays continue to appear. Weldon Thornton's *Allusions in* Ulysses: *An Annotated List* (1968; rpt. 1973) is an indispensable reference tool, listing the literary, historical, philosophical, and theological allusions in the book. Although some corrections and additions to this list have been published in *JJQ*, it remains a valuable, well-documented work for scholar and student alike.

Approaches to Ulysses: *Ten Essays* (ed. Staley and Benstock, 1970), a collection of original essays by various hands, represents the broad range of interest as well as the persistent questions the novel continues to evoke. Five of the essays examine the three major characters of the novel, four deal with technique and method, and the last, by Fritz Senn, examines and frequently compares seven translations of *Ulysses* into European languages. His study is an excellent commentary on the general problems of translation as well as a fascinating excursion into the myriad problems that the translator encounters when tackling *Ulysses*. Weldon Thornton's essay points out that Joyce's major device in achieving an effective blend of naturalism and symbolism was his mythical, allusive method. Thornton goes on to suggest, perhaps too easily, that the method itself is its own theme, revealing the solipsism and depletion of modern life.

Throughout the 1960's critical emphasis shifted from explication to extended interpretation, but a number of technical aspects of the work remained neglected. For example, the stream-of-consciousness technique in *Ulysses* had been taken up in part by Robert Humphrey,

Stream of Consciousness in the Modern Novel (1954); Melvin Fried-man, *Stream of Consciousness: A Study in Literary Method* (1955); and Shiv K. Kumar, *Bergson and the Stream of Consciousness Novel* (1962); but Erwin R. Steinberg's *The Stream of Consciousness and Beyond in* Ulysses (1973) is the first full-scale treatment of this important aspect. Drawing heavily upon psychology and on developments in the other arts, he traces the historical development of the technique in literature and analyzes in systematic detail Joyce's particular use of it. After describing, generally, Joyce's version, Steinberg compares the streams of consciousness of Molly, Bloom, and Stephen, analyzing sentence structure, word usage, and intellectual content. His study is based on the earlier drafts as well as the final ones and reveals the careful and elaborate way in which Joyce developed his character through technique. It is on the basis of this close analysis that Steinberg reaches assessments of the three characters. He differs from Ellmann and a host of other critics by concluding that Molly's monologue is essentially negative, that it does not affirm life as so many previous critics have argued. Steinberg's conclusion on this point is, of course, a highly debatable one, but is inevitable given his method. His careful analysis of so many technical aspects of the novel poses challenges to the speculative, easy interpretations that many critics have fallen prey to. Perhaps more importantly, his study brings to light an area in Joyce's development that heretofore had not been adequately taken into account. But this study also raises questions concerning methodology of analysis and the need for clearer premises.

Two systematic studies using clear methodological principles have appeared in Germany, originally as doctoral dissertations at the University of Bonn. Eberhard Kreutzer's *Sprache und Spiel in "Ulysses" von James Joyce* (Bonn, 1969) deals with Joyce's play on words in the widest possible sense, emphasizing its multiple functions and the literary traditions of word play. His careful study, together with its long (150-page) index of word play and puns, manages to convey a sense of the intricate texture of *Ulysses*. Ulrich Schneider's *Die Funktion der Zitate in "Ulysses" von James Joyce* (Bonn, 1970) is a detailed inquiry into the functions of quotation (documentation, parody, composition). His treatment of the Moses configuration remains the most comprehensive thus far. Both Schneider and Kreutzer are careful readers of the text, wary of the more extravagant symbolic readings.

A later study published in Germany is Therese Fischer's, *Bewusstseinsdarstellung in Werk von James Joyce: Von "Dubliners" zu "Ulysses"* (Frankfort-am-Main, 1973), a perceptive examination of how consciousness is actually presented and of the complex narrative devices employed in Joyce's work through *Ulysses*. Its tendency toward scientifically precise abstractions makes it difficult to read even for its German audience, but its precise terminology and its conceptual exactness represent an advance in Joyce scholarship, for no study in English, including Steinberg's, offers such a sophisticated and thorough methodology in the analysis of Joyce's presentation of consciousness.

The second of February 1972 marked the fiftieth anniversary of the book publication of *Ulysses*; celebrations such as this have a way of stimulating publishers and critics alike. The event provides, too, an interesting focal point for the observer of the critical fortunes of the book. Of all the evocations in books, scholarly journals, and in the popular press, the one to draw the most attention was Richard Ellmann's *Ulysses on the Liffey* (1972). One's first impressions on reading this study is that *Ulysses* criticism is going through Viconian cycles, and we are back exploring with Stuart Gilbert schema, Homeric themes, and the like. This feeling is enhanced by the fact that the author acknowledges little of the criticism since Gilbert. This omission gives the book a certain freedom and freshness, which is, of course, Ellmann's avowed purpose, but many of his insights have been yielded up by earlier scholars. Ellmann's study attempts to show the precise way in which Joyce has drawn elements from both the classical and medieval mind "into modern experience so that they have a present rather than an atavistic life." Ellmann perceives the structural form of *Ulysses* as moving in groups of three episodes— three being the determining element of structure—and each group embracing thesis, antithesis, and synthesis. He also proposes "that in every group of three chapters the first defers to space, the second has time in the ascendant, and the third blends (or expunges) the two." Ellmann has created a new schema out of the Gorman-Gilbert and Linati schemata, one he believes reflects more completely the esthetic and moral dimensions of the novel.

Ellmann's book generated a number of strong reactions, recalling the debates of the 1950's. Kenner's reaction was perhaps the most negative (although many other critics deplored Ellmann's factual misreadings, among other things), arguing that Ellmann has aligned himself "with the old tradition that general ideas will do, and that the meaning of *Ulysses* is to be sought on some plane where large generalities intersect" (*JJQ*, 1973). Kenner, in short, felt the book to be an anachronism, going back to the broad symbolic readings of the 1950's and ignoring the interpretative "novelistic" readings of the 1960's and the direction of literary criticism generally. But this opposition itself echoes, as Walton Litz has suggested ("Pound and Eliot on *Ulysses*"), "the debate which Pound and Eliot initiated while *Ulysses* was still a work in progress."

Another work that, in a different way, seemed appropriate to mark the anniversary of *Ulysses* was *Bloomsday* (1972); published by the New York Graphic Society, it offers the engravings of Saul Field and a series of interpretative vignettes by Morton P. Levitt. Field's color engravings, created by a unique process, attempt to capture visually the themes and characters of *Ulysses*, with signal emphasis given to Leopold Bloom. Levitt's essay is a competent contribution to the book, but it lacks focus. He seems unsure whether he is writing merely an accompanying text for Field's art, an introductory essay, or one with more specialized focus.

Three journals devoted special issues to the commemoration of the fiftieth anniversary of the book publication of *Ulysses*, and collectively they provide a view of the diversity and range of *Ulysses* scholarship. "*Ulysses* and *The Waste Land*, Fifty Years After" is the title given to the number of *Mosaic* (1972). The essays on *Ulysses* are fairly general; Kain and Staley discuss the present stature of *Ulysses* and the evolution of the critical opinion respectively. Marvin Magalaner attempts to balance the negative interpretation of Stephen that has been rendered by many critics. Chester Anderson argues that Joyce had close knowledge of Freud's *The Psychopathology of Everyday Life* and demonstrates this knowledge through the internal evidence found in the "Lestrygonians" episode. His essay is carefully documented and thoroughly investigated, and the most significant of the *Ulysses* essays in the volume. Besides the obvious mutual publication year, it is appropriate that the *Mosaic* volume include essays on *The Waste Land*, because the two works have been frequently compared over the years. The most exhaustive study is Robert Adams Day's "Joyce's Waste Land and Eliot's Unknown God" (in *Literary Monographs*, Vol. IV, ed. Eric Rothstein, 1971). Mario Praz's *James Joyce, Thomas Stearns Eliot, due maestri dei moderni* (Turin, 1967) offers a broader study of the two writers, but is not a comparative examination. *Ulysses Cinquante Ans Après* is a special volume of *Études Anglaises*, No. 53, edited by the late Louis Bonnerot. The book brings together twenty-five essays covering a wide range of subjects on or closely related to *Ulysses* by well-known critics from America and Europe. Also included are the Gilbert, Gorman, and Linati schemata. Several of the essays are in French, but most are in English and, in the main, they deal with more specialized subjects than the *Mosaic* articles.

The commemorative *Ulysses* issue of *JJQ* (1972) published the papers from a colloquium held at the University of Tulsa in July of 1972. This volume has subsequently been published in book form with a preface added by the editor (*Ulysses: Fifty Years*, ed. Thomas F. Staley, 1974). It is the most unified of the anniversary volumes, for each author concentrates on a particular critical problem in *Ulysses* and attempts to view it from the perspective of fifty years. The essays synthesize a good deal of previous scholarship and frequently place emphasis on certain aspects of the work which have received less attention. It is significant that a number of the essays in this fiftieth-anniversary volume stress close textual reading rather than broad interpretative or thematic studies, with the exception of Maurice Beebe's "*Ulysses* and the Age of Modernism," which offers a view of the novel in the broad context of Modernism and argues for its centrality within the movement. Also published in this year was Louis Hyman's *The Jews of Ireland from the Earliest Times to the Year 1910* (Shannon, 1972). It includes a valuable chapter entitled "Some Aspects of the Jewish Background of *Ulysses*," which gives important factual information about the real-life counterparts for such minor characters in the novel as Dlugacz, Dr. Hy Franks, and Julius Mastiansky.

In 1974 Joyce criticism continued at a prolific rate, and several book-length studies of *Ulysses* appeared. Mark Shechner's *Joyce in Nighttown: A Psychoanalytic Inquiry into* Ulysses, a Freudian analysis of the book, is the most thorough psychoanalytic study of Joyce to date. Don Gifford with Robert Seidman published *Notes for Joyce: An Annotation of James Joyce's* Ulysses. This compilation includes allusions, Dublin addresses, translations of foreign words, definitions of slang terms, and maps of Dublin and Gibraltar. Although the book has many shortcomings, it is useful for the beginning student. The documentation is frequently too sketchy to be helpful to the specialist, and some material of marginal value is included. Also, most of the material from Thornton's *Allusions in Ulysses* is repeated, but the authors overlook many of the subsequent discoveries and corrections that have appeared as brief notes in journals. An English version of Wolfgang Iser's *Der Implizite Leser* (Munich, 1972) was published in 1974 under the title *The Implied Reader: Patterns of Communication in Prose Fiction from Bunyan to Beckett*. Though it deals with the reader's role in reading novels in general, it devotes two chapters to the experimental style of *Ulysses*. Also published in this year was Zack Bowen's *Musical Allusions in the Works of James Joyce*, which deals principally with *Ulysses*.

The most significant critical book on *Ulysses* in 1974 was *James Joyce's* Ulysses: *Critical Essays*, (ed. Clive Hart and David Hayman). Each of the eighteen contributors discusses one of the episodes; some of these essays have been referred to above. The contributors include Bernard Benstock on "Telemachus," Phillip F. Herring on "Lotus Eaters," Fritz Senn on "Nausicaa," Hugh Kenner on "Circe," and Robert Boyle, S.J., on "Penelope." Although the essays are somewhat uneven in quality, they are filled with new ideas and information and show that new approaches can still be taken to the novel. One of the best and most important is Clive Hart's essay on "Wandering Rocks," which includes a discussion of the interpolations in the episode and a chart of the times and places mentioned, demonstrating Joyce's realistic precision.

Hart's approach in this essay is continued in his monograph, co-authored with Leo Knuth, *A Topographical Guide to James Joyce's Ulysses* (Colchester, Eng., 1975). It includes an address list of the Dublin places mentioned in *Ulysses*, a discussion of Joyce's use of *Thom's Directory* and eighteen detailed maps for the various episodes. It is an extremely useful work and represents a current emphasis on factual inquiry.

Another area of current emphasis is manuscript materials. This interest is reflected in *JJQ*'s recent Textual Studies issue (1974/1975), which transcribes the notes in the Cornell Collection for Joyce's *Hamlet* lectures delivered in Trieste (1912–13) and of Buffalo copybook V.A.8, an early draft of the "Cyclops" episode. This stress on pre-publication materials is continued with the publication of *Ulysses: A Facsimile of the Manuscript* (1975). This is a facsimile reproduction of the 810-page holograph manuscript that is now owned by the Rosenbach Foundation.

Up to this point we have traced the development of *Ulysses* scholarship largely along chronological lines, while occasionally tracing developments related by subject or theme. Such a course provides continuity but risks neglecting several of the most discriminating as well as controversial aspects of the critical dialogue. The major critical polarity has, of course, been emphasized from the early positions of Pound and Eliot through Ellmann, but the chief themes of the book, especially those of paternity, adultery, guilt, paralysis, responsibility, and exile have been expounded in countless critical contexts. The most rigorous and continuous discussion concerning the dominant themes has, of course, focused on the three major characters, Stephen, Bloom, and Molly, their relationship to each other and the way in which their destinies relate to the meaning of the book as a whole.

Earlier discussion has pointed out the frequent divergence of opinion on Stephen Dedalus. Throughout the later 1950's and the 1960's the most persistent critical attitude toward him was the one expressed by Hugh Kenner, which views him as an imprisoned, somewhat morbid, self-pitying, if brilliant, would-be poet. This position was challenged by S. L. Goldberg, who insisted that Stephen's potentialities as an artist should not "be dismissed because he is very immature and clearly portrayed as such" (*The Classical Temper*). Sultan, E. M. W. Tillyard (*The Epic Strain in the English Novel*, 1967), Goldman (defining Stephen in terms of his attitude as the "ironic" man and Bloom as the "comic" man), Staley ("Stephen Dedalus and the Temper of the Modern Hero," *Approaches to Ulysses*), Hart, and Steinberg see potential for growth in Stephen, but none makes large claims for his development. Nearly every critic who has treated the broad themes of the novel has focused attention on Stephen, beginning with Prescott's early studies on the consistency in the development of his character from *A Portrait* through *Ulysses*, to Steinberg's analysis of his stream-of-consciousness. At first, Levin, Kain, and Tindall identified Stephen with Joyce, but Levin rejected the theory that the meeting of Bloom and Stephen had a substantial effect on either. Stephen has been viewed largely as the modern artist figure in quest, and this quest is represented archetypally in the search by the son, the Telemachus figure, for the lost father. As William Schutte points out in summarizing the earlier critical views of Stephen and his union with Bloom, a number of critics seem to agree that the tragedy of the novel is the inability of Bloom and Stephen to achieve any substantial union (*Joyce and Shakespeare*). Tindall, on the other hand, has argued that a union is achieved at least on the symbolic or representational level. Earlier, Stuart Gilbert insisted on this union enforced through the analogies to the *Odyssey*. Kain's "The Significance of Stephen's Meeting Bloom" (*Ulysses: Fifty Years*) offers an extensive summary of the full development of criticism on this subject and concludes that the ambiguity of the union "reflects the richness and mystery of life" that the novel itself reveals.

Interpretations of Leopold Bloom are far more varied, numerous, and specific. From his ancestral characteristics (Robert Tracy, "Leopold Bloom Fourfold: A Hungarian-Hebraic-Hellenic-Hibernian Hero," *MR*, 1965) to his performance of the Corporal Works of Mercy (Richard Gill, *TCL*, 1963), nearly every aspect of Bloom's heritage, character, and activities has been discussed. Odysseus, the wanderer, the outsider, the cuckold, the failed father, the Everyman, the comic hero, the urban man, the sensual man—all of these facets of Bloom have been the universal dimensions which interpreters see embodied in him. Through all of this analysis, opinions of Bloom still vary widely. Leslie Fiedler has praised him extravagantly: "Bloom is not merely mythic, much less an ironic commentary on a dying myth. He is a true, a full myth, a new and living myth" ("Bloom on Joyce: Or, Jokey for Jacob," *JML*, 1970). J. Mitchell Morse's more balanced comments offer a central position when he asserts that Bloom is among other things "neurotic," "naive," and "foolish," but also "kind," "good," "brave" and "magnanimous." (See his "Karl Gutzkow and the Novel of Simultaneity," *JJQ*, 1964.) Interpretation of Bloom in the 1960's moved away from the mythic and representational to focus on the more human and personal elements of his character (see Sultan, Goldberg, and Goldman), and this trend has continued into the 1970's. From the beginning, however, critics such as Levin and Kain elaborated upon the richness of Bloom's character, and R. P. Blackmur's valuable essay "The Jew in Search of a Son: Joyce's *Ulysses*" (*VQR*, 1948) acknowledged Kain and Levin and went on to explore Bloom's character in light of the individual's relativity to society and the broad esthetic question of the accessibility of *Ulysses* itself to the modern reader. Twenty-five years after Blackmur's study, critical attention has tended to focus on narrower interpretative problems to determine Bloom's nature within the novel rather than the universal implications of his character. For example, William M. Schutte in "Leopold Bloom: A Touch of the Artist" (*Ulysses: Fifty Years*) has noted that "much of what has been said about the early Bloom episodes has been hurried and inconclusive," but Schutte also summarizes the large majority of critical opinion when he concludes that "as the day wears on, the wit, the perception, the compassion, the justness and reasonableness of Bloom prevail." An opposing view of Bloom has recently been offered by Adaline Glasheen in an interesting essay, "Calypso" (*James Joyce's* Ulysses: *Critical Essays*). She balances with a great deal of wit Bloom's ten years of "roaming" against Molly's recent relationship and discusses his marital failures and his quest for other "goddesses." It is generally agreed upon by critics, however, that the achievement of *Ulysses* is embodied to a large extent in the creation of Leopold Bloom. As Miriam Abbott concludes in her "James Joyce: The Hedgehog and the Fox" (*On the Novel*, ed. B. S. Benedikz, 1971), "the true and strong things in *Ulysses* derive from the qualities celebrated in Leopold Bloom, the man who watches 'kindly and curiously' everything from his cat to his Penelope; who reflects on everything, feels something for all he sees, is sensuous, observant and weak, rarely impatient, and always generous."

While critics have been nearly unanimous in their praise of Bloom, opinions of Molly vary widely and run to extremes. From bitch-goddess and whore to earth mother and source of life, whether seen as a symbolic and allegorical figure or on a realistic level, critical judgment ranges from hostility to lavish praise. In an essay that draws much evidence from Joyce's letters to Nora and other biographical evidence and upon the Homeric figure of Penelope, Phillip F. Herring ("The Bedsteadfastness of Molly Bloom," *MFS*, 1969) suggests that a more balanced reading can be obtained by looking at her characterization in the broader terms of Joyce's artistic aims. His essay also provides a sound summary of previous criticism, noting that Budgen, Gilbert, Ellmann, Kain, Prescott, and Tindall find Molly "in varying degrees attractive"; while Kenner's early view (*Dublin's Joyce*) is negative; Goldberg scores the "emotional falsity"; and other critics find her gross, repulsive, lascivious. Herring's essay points out the polarity of critical opinion and the nature of its divergence. Herring, however, seems to accept as fact that Molly has had a number of lovers. Two later essays in *Approaches to* Ulysses exemplify the critical dichotomy on this subject. David Hayman in "The Empirical Molly" argues that Molly is having her first affair, while Darcy O'Brien, "Some Determinants of Molly Bloom," admits that the list of twenty-five lovers is obviously exaggerated but sees her as a frequent adulteress. More recently, Hugh Kenner ("Molly's Masterstroke," *Ulysses: Fifty Years*) agrees with Hayman that Boylan is Molly's first lover and suggests that Molly even tries to avoid sexual intercourse with Boylan while inviting it.

Source studies by James Van Dyck Card ("A Gibraltar Sourcebook for 'Penelope,'" *JJQ*, 1971), Herring's transcription of the *Ulysses Notesheets* (1972), and Robert M. Adams in *Surface and Symbol* have shown not only Joyce's sources for the chapter and the changes and additions at different stages of composition, but also reveal, in Card's words, "a chapter made cunningly by a calculating mind."

The most attention has, of course, been given to Molly as a symbolic figure. In *Ulysses on the Liffey*, Ellmann contends that by the Penelope episode the narrative level of *Ulysses* is less important (a contention Kenner's essay directly opposes) and that Joyce has negotiated the characters' symbolic reconciliation. Robert Boyle ("Penelope," *James Joyce's* Ulysses: *Critical Essays*) combines a symbolic reading with a moral one, affirming the positive attitude of Tindall and Sultan, and disagreeing with the evaluation of Morse and Steinberg. Boyle views her as an essentially good person who affirms life but who is also a part of that complex Joycean vision of the universe who remains shrouded in mystery.

The wide variety of opinion surrounding Stephen and Bloom and more especially Molly not only reflects their complex role in *Ulysses*, but just as surely attests to the density and richness of the work itself.

FINNEGANS WAKE

In reading through even the more important of the five hundred or so studies published on *Finnegans Wake*, one has difficulty recognizing the directions and developments of criticism that surround this remarkable work; because of the nature of *Finnegans Wake*, it has not been easy to discern the clear contours of critical dialogue until recently; the work has presented and, in fact, demanded so many avenues of approach that the critical response has frequently been highly speculative and confusing. Even today the question still looms among many whether it is Joyce's madness or our own that we pursue in trying to unravel its mysteries and make it yield up its meaning. It is inevitable that a work so obscure as *Finnegans Wake* would lead some to believe that the entire work is written in code. Maciej Slomczynski is only the most recent of many claimants who believe they have at last broken the code ("Upon First Decoding *FW*," *Polish Perspectives*, 1973). On the whole, however, the élan of such large claims has disappeared and two approaches, although frequently widely divergent in their individual interpretations, have been dominant: the thematic and structural analyses, on the one hand, and the sequential readings or explications of particular passages or sections, on the other.

Only in the last dozen or so years, however, has *Finnegans Wake* attracted sustained critical and scholarly attention. Until the middle fifties, prior to and following its publication in 1939, most of the critical response, with several outstanding exceptions, was highly speculative and frequently cultish; study after study claimed to unlock the work's secret, or, perhaps influenced by World War II, break its code. From our perspective it is possible to draw general outlines of critical progression, but they must be seen broadly. Clive Hart in the best introductory essay on *Finnegans Wake* (in *James Joyce Today*, 1966) has divided the studies into three major periods, the first running "from 1923 when 'Work in Progress' was just beginning, to 1939, when the completed *FW* was published"; the second from 1939 to 1955, prior to Adaline Glasheen's *A Census of* Finnegans Wake, 1956; the third continuing from 1956 to 1966, when his own essay was published. One may now add a fourth period, when a heavy emphasis on lexicographical aspects developed along with new attempts to penetrate the work's meaning by close, textual reading and examination of more specific themes. Hart's essay is invaluable for its discussion of the first forty years of scholarship, its clarification of Joyce's working methods and attitudes toward *Finnegans Wake*, its evaluation of the consistency of the text, and its survey of the possibilities of explication.

While *Finnegans Wake* was still "Work in Progress" (several sections appeared serially in *transition*, *transatlantic review*, and *Navire d'Argent* between 1924 and 1938; these were extensively revised prior to book publication), a collection of twelve essays with the now famous title appeared; *Our Exagmination round His Factification for Incamination of "Work in Progress"* (Paris, 1929; rpt. 1974). In one sense it revealed the collective confusion the work aroused, but it did offer a preliminary understanding of Joyce's purposes. The book, orchestrated by Joyce himself, has a bit of the publicity release about it, or so it seems in retrospect. Although Beckett's essay "Dante . . . Bruno.— Vico.– Joyce" has been given the most attention, I believe Frank Budgen's "James Joyce's 'Work in Progress' and Old Norse Poetry" to be the best in the volume. Also, Robert McAlmon offers several good observations on the language ("Mr. Joyce Directs an Irish Word Ballet"), and William Carlos Williams provides a sharp view of the "modernist" literary background ("A Point for American Criticism"). Edmund Wilson devoted a section of his chapter on Joyce in *Axel's Castle* (1931) to "Work in Progress," in which he wrote an appreciative response, and, considering the date, an exceptionally astute one. His later essay "The Dream of H. C. Earwicker" (in *The Wound and the Bow*, 1947; rpt. in *Two Decades* . . .), based upon his *New Republic* reviews of 28 June and 12 July 1939, is the most important of the early reviews.

Having had some preparation for *Finnegans Wake* through the publication of "Work in Progress," the early reviewers, on the whole, paid tribute to its verbal achievements while admitting general puzzlement; there were a few reviewers, however, such as Richard Aldington in *Atlantic Monthly* (June 1939) who suggested that the work might be an "elaborate hoax." One of the most perceptive reviews was William Troy's (*PR*, 1939, rpt. in *Two Decades. . .*). During the war years little of significance was published, with two large exceptions. Harry Levin's section "The Fabulous Artificer" in his *James Joyce: A Critical Introduction* gave an excellent appraisal of *Finnegans Wake* and suggested the range of its accomplishments and the general pattern of its structure; his is an important initial statement on the book and one that remains salient today. The first book-length study after the publication of *Finnegans Wake* was Joseph Campbell and Henry Morton Robinson's *A Skeleton Key to* Finnegans Wake (1944), a real breakthrough and a highly influential work, but one which hardly unlocked the secrets of the book. The authors' accomplishment cannot be undervalued in spite of the many errors in the book and its undue emphasis on the mythic aspects of the *Finnegans Wake*, which led them to see the work as largely allegorical. The authors of the *Key* attempted to offer a translation of the book, or to provide a summary, but their resulting emphasis on the mythic level, the cycles of human development, and the racial unconscious presented a severely unbalanced reading, which left out the intensely human aspects of the work—the human dimensions that one found in *Ulysses* and which are very much in the *Wake*. A partial corrective to the *Skeleton Key* has been provided by Bernard Benstock in his *Joyce-again's Wake*, which will be discussed below. William York Tindall's studies (*James Joyce*, 1950; *A Reader's Guide to James Joyce*, 1959) frequently provided more accurate interpretation of individual sections of the book than Campbell and Robinson's, but his overall concern is with the major symbolic and archetypal themes; and as Clive Hart has pointed out, although his analysis is "more sophisticated than that of the *Skeleton Key*," "the meaning of *Finnegans Wake*, as far as detail is concerned, is hardly discussed at all" (*James Joyce Today*). Tindall's later study, *A Reader's Guide to* Finnegans Wake (1969), although frequently informative, is limited in scope, presenting, as Hart states, "a bare outline which is sane, amusing, common-sensical, and often illuminating, but of insufficient weight to oust the *Key* from its position in the mind of the average graduate student."

Besides the textual studies (discussed earlier) by Higginson, Hayman, Connolly, and Litz, as well as Hart's invaluable concordance, all of which began to emerge in the later fifties and early sixties, different approaches have appeared, as seen in the work of Adaline Glasheen and James S. Atherton. Glasheen's *A Census of* Finnegans Wake (1956) and *A Second Census of* Finnegans Wake (1963) represented a new direction in *Wake* studies—away from the broad interpretations to closer analysis of content and an application of empirical methods. Glasheen's first book provided a short synopsis and then catalogued the personages in the *Wake*, those created by Joyce and those preexisting in fiction, myth, or history. The *Second Census* offered an extended and revised synopsis, nearly doubled the number of entries, and greatly amplified many of the earlier entries. Glasheen is more interpretative in the entries in her later edition, suggesting, moreover, that *Finnegans Wake* is largely about Shakespeare. In a large and pioneering undertaking such as Glasheen's it is inevitable that omissions and inaccuracies should occur, but it is difficult to overestimate the importance of her work, for it provided a solid base for closer textual scrutiny and established new, penetrating critical directions such as source studies and closer attention to the characters. (A *Third Census* is forthcoming that may clarify some of the obscurities in the earlier versions.) Between the publication of Glasheen's two works, James Atherton's *The Books at the Wake* (1960; rpt. 1974) appeared, a work of exemplary scholarship, thorough understanding, and discriminating taste. His study is primarily on the use and function of literary allusions in *Finnegans Wake*. Divided into three parts—the structural books, the literary sources, and the sacred books—Atherton's work offers a careful scrutiny of the multilevel structures and patterns of *Finnegans Wake* and a penetrating analysis of Joyce's richly allusive method. Atherton's study has encouraged further source investigation by other scholars, largely in the form of essays in *A Wake Newslitter* and *James Joyce Quarterly*, and Atherton himself has written "A Few More Books at the *Wake*" (*JJQ*, 1965). In the recent reprinting of *Books at the Wake*, Atherton has revised and enlarged the appendix of literary allusions, including new discoveries and deleting several entries from the first edition. Discussed earlier, Hodgart and Worthington's *Song in the Works of James Joyce* is extremely valuable as a source study for *Finnegans Wake*.

Through the sixties closer exegetical work continued, and Clive Hart's *Structure and Motif in* Finnegans Wake (1962) reflected in its comprehensive view of the internal organization and formal structure that the book was, indeed, written by James Joyce, an expression of the last phase of his career and consistent with his theory of "imitative form," his central and most consistent literary principle. Hart's book offers an analysis of the broad architectonics of *Finnegans Wake* and describes in careful detail the correspondences and the complex formal patterns, the major ordering principles. He concentrates on the spatial configurations he believes Joyce had in mind as he conceptualized and wrote the book, and which provide the structural tensions for it. Hart's study may appear overly schematic, but, nevertheless, he acutely explores the organic structure of *Finnegans Wake* and the way the formal beauty enriches, expands, and deepens the individual sections and passages and provides a richly textured meaning. In this balanced study the characters are never lost but are better understood and their roles as well as their individuality are made more clear. No study of *Finnegans Wake* at this writing can, in any sense of the imagination, be considered definitive, but Hart's work will remain an important and pivotal study in *Wake* scholarship.

A group of books which appeared in the sixties reflect the major lexicographical problems associated with *Finnegans Wake*. Dounia Bunis Christiani's *Scandinavian Elements of* Finnegans Wake (1965), Helmut Bonheim's *A Lexicon of the German in* Finnegans Wake (1967), and Brendon O Hehir's *A Gaelic Lexicon for* Finnegans Wake (1967) collectively provide basic linguistic background. Christiani's work offers detailed comment as well as translations, but it lacks a coherent methodology and reflects a number of serious misreadings. Bonheim's and O Hehir's volumes reveal a much more thorough understanding of the book as a whole. A large number of foreign word lists have appeared in the pages of *WN* and *JJQ*, but a comprehensive study of Joyce's complex word building and use of so many languages remains to be written, for with all of the word lists we still do not have a very clear idea of the significance of the language in *Finnegans Wake*. We do not know why a word with a Dutch root is used in one place and an Italian in another, nor, when a cluster of foreign roots appears in a word, what, if any, principle of selection Joyce was using. Along with many others, the question remains whether there is any formal method in Joyce's polyglot wordhoard.

In charting the major developments in *Wake* scholarship, it should be noted, at least in passing, that many blatant excesses and even imbecilic interpretations have appeared. With a work such as *Finnegans Wake* this is, of course, not surprising, and most of them are fortunately forgotten. Two book-length studies are Frances Boldereff's *Reading* Finnegans Wake (1959) and *Hermes to His Son Thoth: Joyce's Use of Giordano Bruno in* Finnegans Wake (1968). Although the first is of some value for its noting of Irish allusions and certain curious and arcane observations, these two works represent several of the worst aspects of literary criticism; whatever intelligent comment is present is wholly lost by excessive, fallacious, and extravagant claims pulled wildly from the imagination without critical principle or analysis. These works deserve mention because they represent a small but persistent fringe that has existed in the response to the *Wake*. It cannot be denied that the book has attracted its share of this sort of commentary, nor is it unexpected.

Bernard Benstock's *Joyce-again's Wake* (1965) is firmly set on the track of sanity and reason. Benstock's study is an attempt to bridge the specialized works that appeared previously in order to reach "middle-range" readers—"those with enough patience to be willing to participate in the work necessary for an understanding of Joyce's masterpiece, but without that ideal insomnia being simulated by Joycean scholars." He begins with a working outline of the book and then offers an excellent discussion of Joyce's religious and political background. In subsequent chapters he discusses the narrative, comic, and epic elements in *Finnegans Wake*. Animated by a lucid and enthusiastic style, with an eye for excellent textual examples to clarify points, this work more than any other does narrow the gap between specialist and nonspecialist. For the nonspecialist it opens up doors to understanding because he deals with the *Wake* as a work of literature, and Benstock's critical method is easily discernible and amply fulfilled in his analysis; but for the specialist his intentions would be better served had he worked more closely with the draft versions of the book. The specialist is, however, well aided by Benstock's clear interpretative principles and lucid textual examinations of the themes of the book.

Some of the most important work on the *Wake* has appeared in essays in various journals. Clive Hart's "The Elephant in the Belly: Exegesis of *Finnegans Wake*," *A Wake Digest* (Sydney, 1968), sets out six propositions or guidelines concerning the reading and exegesis of *Finnegans Wake*—principles of explication which would avoid speculative excesses, yet, at the same time, not be bound by an all-too-rigorous rational and logical method that would lead to an expulsion of the poetry of the work. This carefully reasoned essay, though frequently debated among *Wake* scholars, has been an important influence. In fact, the great bulk of criticism on *Finnegans Wake* has appeared in the form of articles, notes, and annotations, rather than in book-length studies. The work's density, complexity, and very nature have, of course, spawned this form of response.

Three excellent essays which deal with particular aspects or sections of the *Wake* are Adaline Glasheen's "*Finnegans Wake* and the Girls from Boston, Mass." (*HudR*, 1954), James S. Atherton's "*Finnegans Wake*: The Gist of Pantomime" (*Accent*, 1955), and Thornton Wilder's "Giordano Bruno's Last Meal in *Finnegans Wake*" (*WN*, 1962; with emendations, *HudR*, 1963). A later essay by Bernard Benstock, "Every Telling Has a Taling: A Reading of the Narrative of *Finnegans Wake*" (*MFS*, 1969), is an excellent consideration of the narrative problems in *Wake* in which he traces with care the narrative line. In another direction there have been a number of equally fine long essays which deal with only a sentence or a page of the work, among them David Hayman's (*PMLA*, 1958) and Robert Boyle's (*JJQ*, 1966). Two important Joyce critics who have written widely on the *Wake* are Fritz Senn and Nathan Halper; each has published nearly a dozen essays on the book, most of them appearing in *WN*. A. Walton Litz's significant work on the manuscripts in his *The Art of James Joyce* was discussed earlier.

A Wake Newslitter is the most important forum for *Wake* studies. Edited by Clive Hart and Fritz Senn, it began publication in March 1962 and continues to date, published now at the University of Essex in England. In 1968 Hart and Senn edited *A Wake Digest*, referred to above, which reprinted some of the most important essays that appeared in *WN*, first series (1962–63). Divided into three sections, source studies and general explications, linguistic studies, and notes, the volume is one of the most valuable works on *Finnegans Wake*. The *James Joyce Quarterly*, though far broader in scope than *WN*, has also published a great number of essays on *Finnegans Wake* and has devoted two special numbers to it (Spring 1965 and Summer 1974). A few titles in the later issue will perhaps indicate some of the broader contexts in which the book is currently being studied: Leo Knuth, "*Finnegans Wake*: A Product of the Twenties"; David Hayman, "Farcical Themes and Form in *Finnegans Wake*"; Margot C. Norris, "The Function of Mythic Repetition in *Finnegans Wake*" (essentially a structuralist-based study); and Eric McLuhan, "The Rhetorical Structure of *Finnegans Wake*." *The Analyst* also printed a number of articles on the book during its years of publication (1953–65).

In attempting to grasp the meaning of *Finnegans Wake*, writers of book-length studies to date have offered general interpretations of the entire work, have concerned themselves with extended explications of the entire text, or have presented source studies or lexicographical material. Margaret C. Solomon's *Eternal Geomater: The Sexual Universe of* Finnegans Wake (1969) is the first extended study to deal with one thematic aspect of the book. Solomon deals with sexual themes and representations in a number of sections, especially as they relate to geometric forms. Her study no doubt represents the inevitable trend to more sustained specialized aspects of *Wake*. It is clearly aimed at the specialist, for it assumes a close familiarity with the text. Although difficult to follow at times, it is an illuminating study and is especially valuable for its treatment of a number of geometrical forms such as the circle. The thesis evolved regarding Joyce's geometrics, however, is perhaps more remote from Joyce's vision of the universe than the author concludes.

Two volumes of essays by diverse hands have appeared. Jack P. Dalton and Clive Hart's *Twelve and a Tilly* (1965) is a collection which celebrates the twenty-fifth anniversary of the publication of *Finnegans Wake*. It includes essays by well-known Joyce scholars. Frank Budgen, Richard M. Kain, Frederick J. Hoffman, and Vivian Mercier offer general essays, A. Walton Litz suggests the uses to be made of the *Wake* manuscripts, and Dalton discusses the text; the remaining essays are of a more specialized nature, dealing with narrower aspects of the book. *A Conceptual Guide to* Finnegans Wake (ed. Michael H. Begnal and Fritz Senn, 1974) suggests a systematic approach. Although the book does attempt to cover all the books and chapters of *Finnegans Wake*, the unity and coverage for which the editors aimed are not offered. Begnal notes in his introduction that it is not the purpose of the volume to provide a new collective paraphrase, but to offer "entry into a section at something deeper than a surface level." Frequently insightful as they are, very few of the essays offer sufficiently broad coverage of the books or chapters of the *Wake* that they deal with. For example, Morse's essay is largely a treatment of Vico and does not pretend to cover section one as a whole. Roland McHugh does cover Chapters ii–iv of Book i and discusses the attacks on Earwicker, his trial and entombment. Benstock and Epstein follow with good coverage of Chapters v and vi. Boyle's essay on Chapters vii and viii of Book i is far more narrow in its coverage and broader in its implications. Concentrating largely on pages 185–86 in Chapter vii, Boyle discusses Joyce's emerging artistic vision, culminating in the controlling metaphor in this passage and Joyce's debt to Oscar Wilde. As the essays continue they do reveal the multiplicity of approach Begnal suggests, but collectively they do not offer the unity at which the editors aimed—the kind of unity needed for a "conceptual guide." This criticism should not, however, detract from the individual essays in the book, many of which offer richly suggestive insights into *Finnegans Wake*. The parts, however, are greater than the whole.

Thirty-five years after its publication, *Finnegans Wake* is obviously less remote from us, but it still cannot be considered accessible except to the most dedicated readers and critics. The development of the scholarship when treated in an outline such as this tends to make it appear more unified than it is. In the body of criticism there are still many incompatible readings and seemingly irreconcilable interpretations. But as this outline also suggests, the critical development in *Finnegans Wake* studies is anything but static.

Despite the large body of biographical, critical, and scholarly work that has been written on Joyce so far, the subject has not been exhausted and there is still much that needs to be done. For example, there are still aspects of the biography that are hazy, such as the Trieste years. There are also a number of significant reminisences about Joyce that need to be translated and made accessible. The focus of Joyce studies in the future seems likely to be on such prepublication materials as copybooks and manuscript versions of all the major works, especially *Ulysses* and *Finnegans Wake*. This direction is evident in the recent publication of the Buffalo copybooks and the *Ulysses* notesheets, and the publication of the *Ulysses* manuscript. In the 1950's and 1960's, there was a proliferation of "a critical reading of . . ." articles. Now the trend is toward more substantial scholarly work concentrating on the text itself and Joyce's sources. This will result in a greater knowledge of Joyce's creative methods and his artistic development and will also contribute toward the establishment of a scholar's text of *Ulysses* and an appendix of variant readings of *Finnegans Wake*.

FOUR REVIVAL FIGURES:

Lady Gregory, A. E. (George W. Russell),

Oliver St. John Gogarty, and James Stephens

James F. Carens

Though Lady Gregory (née Isabella Augusta Persse, 1852–1932), A. E. (George W. Russell, 1867–1935), Oliver St. John Gogarty (1878–1957), and James Stephens (1880?–1950) were all part of the movement we speak of as the Irish Literary Revival, they must seem an ill-assorted group to jostle one another in a chapter. The playwriting widow of an Anglo-Irish aristocrat; a visionary poet who was a newspaper editor and agricultural economist; the son of a member of the small Roman Catholic professional class, who went to Trinity and Oxford and became a nose and throat specialist famous for his ribaldry *and* lyricism; a semi-orphan who concealed his early history, who trained as a gymnast though only slightly more than five feet tall and became a celebrity on the publication of his second novel: an extraordinary literary gathering. Yet each of these gifted persons was infused with the same atmosphere of national aspiration, torment, triumph, and disaster; and each contributed something important to the yeasty atmosphere of the Revival. Lady Gregory, patroness of Yeats, whose genius she recognized and nurtured, played a central role in the development of the Abbey Theatre—so central and practical a role that George Bernard Shaw once described her as "charwoman of the Abbey." She managed also, in the course of a career begun in middle age, to produce a substantial oeuvre in prose and drama that satirized, reflected, and celebrated the national spirit of Ireland. A. E., Yeats's lifetime friend and rival, was the center of a literary and artistic circle and the encourager of younger talents—including both Gogarty and Stephens. For decades A. E.'s mystical paintings and poems, his prose fables, his editorials and reviews, even his public letters, however seemingly diverse, were all part of a single creative impulse: to spiritualize the ideals of the Nation. Gogarty, depicted by Joyce as a mocker of the National Literary Revival and certainly no admirer of its sentimental aspects, began his literary career, as did James Stephens, writing for Arthur Griffith's *Sinn Féin*. Closely associated with Yeats throughout his most productive years, he sought, in poetry and prose, images of beauty and heroic action that would link ordinary Ireland to the eternal values he evoked. And Stephens, who eschewed the violence and narrowness of doctrinaire nationalism, devoted himself, after early successes like *The Charwoman's Daughter* and *The Crock of Gold*, which he might have sought to repeat, to modern retellings of the heroic legends of Ireland at a time when the liberated nation was experiencing disillusionment. The individual literary reputations of all four writers have been subject to fluctuations. Only now does the position of each in the literary history of the age they helped to shape seem to be coming into proper focus.

I. Lady Gregory

More than a decade ago, in " 'Charwoman of the Abbey' " (*ShawR*, 1961; also "That Laurelled Head," *ESA*, 1961), a long review of Elizabeth Coxhead's study of Lady Gregory, Ronald Ayling applauded the biographer's belief "that Lady Gregory's plays form the natural complement to those of Synge." He observed that "we rob his plays of a dimension, if we ignore hers," and agreed with Elizabeth Coxhead that Lady Gregory's Kiltartan dialect had provided Synge with a precedent for his own dramatic language. A year later, in a review of Synge's *Collected Works* and a selection of Lady Gregory's plays (*NewS*, 19 Oct. 1962), Geoffrey Grigson dismissed Augusta Gregory as "mawkish" and implied that only the genius of Synge had given life to the monotonous "Gregorian chant." There one has, in essence, the extreme poles of approbation—to see her as the near equal of Synge—and disdain—to see her as a shallow imitator—that have persisted in critical responses to the work of Lady Gregory. Indeed, nothing could demonstrate better the persistence of critical disparagement or neglect than the defensiveness of those writers who have most admired her. For instance, Elizabeth Coxhead lamented that "except for the inevitable *Rising of the Moon*," Lady Gregory's plays had almost disappeared even from the repertory of the Abbey Theatre. There are already, however, definite indications of a quickening of critical and scholarly interest in the works of Lady Gregory. There is a possibility, too, that, following on substantial scholarly enterprises and publications now under way, we may be witness to an even more extensive revival of interest. Should a thorough revaluation of Lady Gregory's character, career, and artistry take place, it might end in freeing us from the terms that have hitherto governed critical discussion of her work.

MANUSCRIPTS, LETTERS

Lady Gregory's Archives, preserved intact for decades, were acquired by the Berg Collection of the New York Public Library. Not the least extraordinary trait of an extraordinary woman was Lady Gregory's apparent tendency to preserve everything of literary or historical interest. In consequence, the collection at the Berg is rich and massive, containing the manuscripts of her principal works and her Journals; and also personal records, letters, first editions, and presentation copies. Financial accounts running from 1900 to 1930; a publishing history of her own work, dated by her in 1929; her Journals, Books 1–44, in typescript with her own corrections and with marginal comments by W. B. Yeats and others; holograph records and other documents pertaining to key moments in the history of the Abbey Theatre; *Cuchulain of Muirthemne* in six holograph notebooks and a typescript of the same, including Yeats's Preface in typescript with his and Lady Gregory's autograph corrections: these are characteristic of the riches of the collection that may suggest its importance to students of Yeats, Lady Gregory, the Abbey Theatre, and the Literary Revival. With the exception of the Lady Gregory–Wilfrid Scawen Blunt correspondence, which is at the Fitzwilliam Museum, Cambridge, letters to Lady Gregory from her contemporaries—in particular from the leading figures of the Revival—will be found at the Berg, as well as Lady Gregory's copies of her letters to such figures as Yeats, John Quinn, Lennox Robinson, and Lord Dunsany.

Groups of letters to or from Lady Gregory have already been published. Glenn O'Malley and Donald Torchiana, in "Some New Letters from W. B. Yeats to Lady Gregory" (*REL*, 1963), edited a correspondence held by the Deering Library, Northwestern University; these touch on the Lane Gallery controversy and affairs of the Abbey Theatre, among other matters. The same editors' "John Butler Yeats to Lady Gregory: New Letters" (*MR*, 1964) included eight letters, also from the Deering Library; more revealing of Yeats's father than of Lady Gregory, they do suggest her interest in portraits of W. B. Yeats, Standish O'Grady, and others prominent in the Revival. "The Lady Gregory Letters to Sean O'Casey" (ed. A. C. Edwards, *MD*, 1965), sad to read, record her dignified, tactful, and always rebuffed efforts to see O'Casey after the Abbey's rejection of *The Silver Tassie*. From the Berg Collection were the nearly 200 letters Lady Gregory sent her financial adviser, published as "Letters from Lady Gregory: A Record of Her Friendship with T. J. Kiernan" (ed. Daniel Murphy, *BNYPL*, 1967–68). This extensive correspondence deals not only with Lady Gregory's financial affairs but also with the Lane pictures controversy with England, with events in the Dublin literary world, and other subjects. Finally, the same editor's "Lady Gregory's Letters to G. B. Shaw" (*MD*, 1968) deals with such matters as the Abbey's defiance of the attempted censorship of *The Shewing-up of Blanco Posnet*, with Shaw's advice to Lady Gregory on Abbey issues, and with the troublesome Lane bequest.

EDITIONS, BIBLIOGRAPHY

An indication of the extent of scholarly interest in the works of Lady Gregory is the number of recent editions and reprints of her works. Chosen and introduced by Elizabeth Coxhead and with a foreword by Sean O'Casey, *Selected Plays* appeared in England in 1962 and in the United States in 1963; the selection, a balanced and useful one, ranged from early farces such as *Spreading the News* to folk history (e.g., *The White Cockade*) and tragedy (e.g., *Grania*). Among recent Cuala Press volumes are three facsimiles (1971) of Lady Gregory's *A Book of Saints and Wonders* (1906); *The Kiltartan Poetry Book* (1918); and *Coole* (1931), which also appeared, with additional chapters written in 1927 and 1928, in a Dolmen Press edition (ed. Colin Smythe, 1972). Reprints of other works have followed with increasing rapidity: *Seven Short Plays* (1970); *Three Last Plays* (1971); *The Kiltartan Molière* (1971); *Gods and Fighting Men* (1971); *Irish Folk History Plays* (2 vols., 1971); *Poets and Dreamers* (1973); and *Ideals in Ireland*, to which she was a contributor (1973).

A major undertaking has been that of Colin Smythe, bibliophile, bibliographer, and publisher, who is responsible for *The Coole Edition of the Collected Works of Lady Gregory* (1970–   ), and whose own account of this venture may be found in "Collecting Yeats and Publishing Lady Gregory" (*Private Library*, 1971). The Coole Edition should run to twenty-one volumes. Though it is, regrettably, not an annotated critical edition, it does include original prefaces, such as those by Yeats, and, in some instances, useful appendices. Each volume has a brief foreword; these last have been generally sound, and one, Daniel Murphy's foreword to *Gods and Fighting Men*, is particularly useful for its economic account of the inspiration and composition of the work. To date, thirteen volumes have been published. *Visions and Beliefs in the West of Ireland* (1970), foreword by Elizabeth Coxhead; *Cuchulain of Muirthemne* (1970), foreword by Daniel Murphy; *Gods and Fighting Men* (1970), foreword by Daniel Murphy; *The Collected Plays* (4 vols., 1970), edited and with foreword by Ann Saddlemyer; *The Kiltartan Books* (1971), foreword by Padraic Colum; *A Book of Saints and Wonders* (1971), foreword by Edward Malins; *Our Irish Theatre* (1972), foreword by Roger McHugh; *Sir Hugh Lane* (1973), foreword by James White; *Poets and Dreamers* (1974), foreword by T. R. Henn; and *Seventy Years* (1974), edited and with foreword by Colin Smythe. It proved necessary to modify the original numbering of the Coole Edition to allow for the inclusion of the last of these, Lady Gregory's hitherto unpublished memoir, a recent manuscript discovery. Though it is possible to defend Colin Smythe's decision to publish the manuscript just as it came to him, *Seventy Years* reflects, particularly in its later sections, Lady Gregory's reluctance to give final and polished form to her "life." A store of riches, *Seventy Years* is, nevertheless, often more journal or commonplace book than autobiography; probably more than any other volume in the series it deserved much fuller editorial annotation than it has been given. Lady Gregory's *Journals*, now available only in Lennox Robinson's inadequate selection, *Lady Gregory's Journals, 1916–1931* (1947), will constitute two volumes in the Coole Edition (ed. Daniel Murphy). Even in the unsatisfactory and chronologically confusing arrangement Robinson gave his selection, the Journals are filled with social, historical, and literary detail and with moments of great emotional force. It seems likely that, together with *Seventy Years* and the publication of important correspondence, they will play a central role in any reappraisal of Lady Gregory. Among anticipated volumes of letters are the correspondence of Lady Gregory and John Quinn, the New York lawyer, bibliophile, patron, and art collector (ed. Daniel Murphy) and the selected correspondence of Lady Gregory and William Butler Yeats (ed. Daniel Murphy).

Lady Gregory was an even more prolific writer than she is customarily thought to have been, publishing both anonymously and pseudonymously. New publications, according to Murphy, are still being discovered—recent discoveries include an early defense of the Abbey Theatre, a three-part article on tree planting, a group of sonnets. The extent of the undertaking of Colin Smythe and Daniel Murphy, who hope to produce a Gregory bibliography, is as great as the need for their effort. "The Theatre of Lady Gregory," a bibliography of secondary works (*BB*, 1970) by Edward Hakim Mikhail, runs to sixty items; but being neither sufficiently inclusive nor very selective, it has limited usefulness.

BIOGRAPHY

Elizabeth Coxhead's *Lady Gregory: A Literary Portrait* (1961; rev. and enl., 1966) is the only "life" now available. The biographer herself observed, in the preface to the first edition, "This book does not pretend to be the documented biography that must be written one day when all the materials are available." A novelist herself, Coxhead writes of Lady Gregory with some skill and considerable sympathy. Yet the book suffers not only from the limitations of which the author was conscious, but from a superficial view of the character of its protagonist and even from touches of sentimentality. In addition, Coxhead's feminism, though in advance of its time, was overstated; and her portrait of Yeats as a male chauvinist who thwarted Lady Gregory's talent was too hostile to be convincing. Though dwelling at length on the relationship of Yeats and Lady Gregory, a relationship both literary and emotional, this biographer failed to understand or explain the psychic energies the friendship released in both Augusta Gregory and W. B. Yeats. Coxhead returned to the subject of Lady Gregory once again in relation to another dominant male figure in *J. M. Synge and Lady Gregory* (1962). Better on Synge than on Lady Gregory, simply because he is given more space than she, this pamphlet in the series published by the British Council and the National Book League was editorially misconceived, for each of the writers treated surely should have had a separate essay. Coxhead's conclusion that Synge and Lady Gregory "ally Irish charm and a rich flow of language to a universal applicability" suggests the inadequacy of the essay to its subjects: "Irish charm" is a cliché that suits neither Augusta Gregory nor John Synge.

Probably the finest piece of biographical criticism is "Isabella Augusta Gregory, 1852–1932," Chapter iii of Herbert Howarth's admirable *The Irish Writers: Literature and Nationalism, 1880–1940* (1958). As acute in his critical perceptions as in his psychological insights, Howarth here gives an accomplished account not only of Lady Gregory's limitations as folklorist, translator, and dramatist but also of her strengths in each, her commitment to the national cause, her energetic character, and her selfless imagination. By contrast, Mary Colum's "Lady Gregory of the Abbey Theatre," *Life and the Dream* (1947; with additional material, 1966), though based on some degree of personal association, is of questionable value and unpleasant in tone. Colum concludes the chapter with conventional words of praise, but she mostly amuses herself with the purveying of self-revealing gossip designed to prove Lady Gregory a "snob."

Important materials, soon to be accessible to all, should encourage a definitive "life": Lady Gregory's complete *Journals*, revealing the full extent of her involvement in the literary Revival; her own autobiography; the letters to and from Quinn, revealing the depth of her attachment to him (tactfully implied by Quinn's biographer, B. L. Reid); the correspondence with Yeats, revealing even more influence on his life than has been assumed.

Me and Nu: Childhood at Coole (1970) by Lady Gregory's granddaughter, Anne Gregory (de Winton), with its account of visits from Shaw, Yeats, O'Casey, and Gogarty, gives a special and private perspective on public men; if, as an attempt to render a child's view of experience, it is not entirely accurate, the memoir nevertheless gives some sense of the quality of life at Coole. George Moore's account of his visit to Coole with Yeats in *Ave* (1911) gives us a vivid picture of Lady Gregory's appearance, her protectiveness of Yeats, and her distancing of Moore himself. Moore returned to her for his revenge in *Vale* (1914), where he accuses her of having plagiarized from a translation by Kuno Meyer. For Moore, "Lady Gregory had never been . . . a very real person," which is to say that she never regarded him as an intimate or as the equal of Yeats; yet he has to grant that if no play of hers "compares with the *Playboy*, . . . all are meritorious." Wilfrid Scawen Blunt's journal, *The Land War in Ireland* (1912), gives an account of Lady Gregory's early political views and an insight into the class attitudes she managed to overcome. Lady Gregory's visits to London, often with Yeats, and the stories that crossed the luncheon table of Blunt, his impressions of his visitors and of Lady Gregory's theater, make Blunt's *My Diaries, Being a Personal Narrative of Events, 1888–1914* (1919–20) an even more valuable source. Yeats's tribute to Lady Gregory, *Dramatis Personae* (1935, 1936), focusing on their early association and the growth of the theater, seems to Coxhead to belittle his patroness, because Yeats published other autobiographical memoirs along with it. Apparently Coxhead did not know that "Dramatis Personae" first appeared alone as a Cuala Press book and only subsequently with "Estrangement," "The Death of Synge," and "The Bounty of Sweden." Nor can one escape the emotional force of the quotation from Lady Gregory with which Yeats concludes "Dramatis Personae": "the sound of her clear voice is sweet; she is not sleeping between the streams." The Cuala Press also published another tribute to Lady Gregory, Mario Rossi's *Pilgrimage to the West* (trans. Joseph Hone, 1938), which the Italian scholar closes with a beautiful and moving address to Lady Gregory. Yeats's Journal, in the only recently published *Memoirs* (1972), contains his most explicit and passionate account of her importance to him: "She has been to me mother, friend, sister and brother. I cannot realize the world without her." And the *Letters of W. B. Yeats* (ed. Allan Wade, 1954) are so pervaded by his allusions to her that the index by itself reveals her centrality in his life. The memories of Thomas J. Kiernan, Lady Gregory's financial adviser, in "Lady Gregory and William Butler Yeats" (*Southerly*, 1953; *DR*, 1958), have very little to offer despite his long association with the two writers. Sean O'Casey's tribute to Lady Gregory and to Coole, *Inishfallen, Fare Thee Well* (1949), is not without sharp touches of criticism, even satire; and *Rose and Crown* (1952) recounts his break with her, when the Abbey refused *The Silver Tassie*. But O'Casey's final word on Lady Gregory may be found in his foreword to the *Selected Plays*, which closes with a litany of devotion to her, as Roger McHugh points out in his account of the friendship and estrangement (*JJQ*, 1970).

Among biographies of the men of genius associated with her, the following are essential: Joseph Hone, *W. B. Yeats, 1865–1939* (1943; 2nd ed. 1962); David H. Greene and Edward M. Stephens, *J. M. Synge, 1871–1909* (1959); David Krause, *Sean O'Casey* (1960); B. L. Reid, *The Man from New York: John Quinn and His Friends* (1968); and Stanley Weintraub, *Journey to Heartbreak: The Crucible Years of Bernard Shaw, 1914–1918* (1971). Bernard Shaw's *Collected Letters, 1898–1910* (ed. Dan H. Laurence, 1972) are important, too, recording another friendship, and particularly the Abbey's defiant performance of *The Shewing-up of Blanco Posnet*. *Images and Memories: A Pictorial Record of the Life and Works of W. B. Yeats* (1970), selected and edited by S. B. Bushrui and J. M. Munro, includes a number of photographs of Lady Gregory and Coole; more important is Colin Smythe's *A Guide to Coole Park, Co. Galway, Home of Lady Gregory* (1973), foreword Maurice Craig.

LITERARY HISTORY AND CRITICISM

Among general studies of the modern drama, there is little that particularly illuminates the dramatic career of Lady Gregory. F. W. Chandler, *Aspects of Modern Drama* (1923), included the folk history plays in his praise but regarded her contribution to the development of the theater in Ireland as more substantial than her plays; Anna Miller in "The National Theatre of Ireland," *The Independent Theatre in Europe 1887 to the Present* (1931; rpt. 1966) makes some reference to Lady Gregory and a feeble effort to relate the Abbey to the wider European scene; Camillo Pelizzi's *English Drama: The Last Great Phase* (1935) contains a chapter, "In Ireland," that is superficial and inaccurate in its treatment of Lady Gregory.

Among studies of the Irish theater, there is more substantial material. Lady Gregory's own *Our Irish Theatre* (1913) is essential, though distinctly an account of *her* Irish theater and the crises it surmounted. (That among her papers was found a holograph draft of chapter headings for a history of the Abbey suggests she knew that something more was also needed.) Joseph Holloway's *Diary*, at the National Library of Ireland, is invaluable, not necessarily in providing accurate information or objective judgments but in reporting public response, newspaper articles, overheard comments, conversations in which Holloway participated, and glimpses of public gatherings and of Lady Gregory at the theater. Representative selections of the *Diary* are provided in *Joseph Holloway's Abbey Theatre* (1967) and *Joseph Holloway's Irish Theatre* (3 vols., 1968–70), both edited by Robert Hogan and M. J. O'Neill. Ernest Boyd, whose *Contemporary Drama in Ireland* (1917) was the first full-scale treatment of developments in the Irish theater, was considerably less than enthusiastic about Lady Gregory's work. Under the influence of Yeats's Prefaces to *Cuchulain of Muirthemne* (1902) and *Gods and Fighting Men* (1904), both essential reading, he praises her for giving form and dialect to the epic material; but the plays, excepting the folk comedies, he regards as unsuccessful. Moreover, Boyd was among the first to complain of too frequent performances of those short comedies. By contrast, in *The Irish Drama* (1929; rpt. 1965) Andrew Malone gives a forceful and sympathetic account of Lady Gregory's role and achievement, arguing that had she "never become interested in the verse plays of Mr. Yeats the Irish Theatre and Irish Drama might never have been." In *The Gaol Gate* (1906), which he describes as "one of the great tragic experiences," he finds all the tragic intensity of Synge's *Riders to the Sea*. Lady Gregory's *Grania* (1912) he finds superior to Ibsen's *The Vikings of Helgeland* and comparable to Synge's *Deirdra*. In a later but scarcely less enthusiastic appraisal (*DM*, 1933), Malone argues that the unperformed *Grania* refutes the notion that she could write only one-act plays and finds thirteen of her forty works "of surpassing merit and interest." More restrained but markedly favorable in judgment was Una Ellis-Fermor's *The Irish Dramatic Movement* (1939; 2nd ed., 1954; rpt. 1964), where one reads that "there is one unforgettable brief peasant tragedy, *The Gaol Gate*, where she shows a sudden surprising kinship with the tragic side of Synge." Developing the paradoxical notion that a combination of dramatic inexperience and intuitive craftsmanship was responsible for Lady Gregory's success, Ellis-Fermor also argued that in her bold later treatment of history "Lady Gregory found her way to a new kind of playwriting, one which had a fruitful succession in English drama." More concerned with the development and survival of the theater than with the quality of individual plays, Peter Kavanagh, *The Story of the Abbey Theatre* (1950), blames most of the theater's difficulties on Lady Gregory's interference with the management, in particular with Lennox Robinson; and he argues that she was responsible for turning it, between 1912 and 1914, from a poetic theater to a peasant theater. More sympathetic to Lady Gregory was Lennox Robinson himself. In "Lady Gregory," *The Irish Theatre* (ed. Lennox Robinson, 1939), he praises her spartan character, and, while admitting that she tended to employ "over-rich dialogue" in her later works, hails the Wonder Plays as revealing "the imagination of a genius." Robinson's later work, *Ireland's Abbey Theatre 1899–1951* (1951; rpt. 1968) is mostly concerned with the history of production and views Lady Gregory as those involved in production saw her, while Gerard Fay's *The Abbey Theatre: Cradle of Genius* (1958) views her from the standpoint of the actors' relations with the three directors.

Among longer monographs on Lady Gregory, Hilda von Klenze's *Lady Gregorys Leben und Werk* (Kolnes Anglische Arbeiten 37, 1940) is little more than a mechanical listing and cataloguing of the principal works. Ann Saddlemyer's *In Defense of Lady Gregory, Playwright* (1966), by no means so contentious or defensive as the title suggests, does implicitly make a case for Lady Gregory's craft and imaginative range. Emphasizing the variety of her language, the psychological insight of her characterization, the dominant element of fantasy in the work, and her celebration of the rebellious individual, Saddlemyer found in those works she regards as the dramatist's best—*The Rising of the Moon, The Image, The Jester, Spreading the News, Grania, Dave*—"a highly skilled fusion of . . . theatrical qualties." Anne Dedio's *Das Dramatische Werk von Lady Gregory* (Cooper Monographs 13, Bern, 1967), while characteristically systematic and perfunctory, is somewhat more imaginative in its concluding section, where it suggests the irrational sources of Lady Gregory's art. The appendices to the work, containing Gregory letters and American newspaper interviews, all from the Harvard Theatre Collection, are useful. Like Ann Saddlemyer's book, Hazard Adams' *Lady Gregory* (Bucknell Univ. Press Irish Writers Series, 1973) takes us where we need to go, into the plays themselves; but Adams sees those plays as the product of personal and cultural concerns. Lucid and succinct, Adams' monograph explores Lady Gregory's economy of form, her mythmaking capacity, and her ability to universalize the provincial world she depicts. In the plays he sees "a humanized mythology that grew from the life around her, but that gave something too—the vision of great things happening among a simple and long-oppressed people."

Of those studies dealing with special aspects of Lady Gregory's career, Anne Bower's "Lady Gregory's Use of Proverbs in Her Plays" (*SFQ*, 1939), though mechanical and unimaginative, contains some useful information about the universal currency of the proverbs found in the plays. On a higher level of critical sophistication, Ann Saddlemyer's "Image-Maker for Ireland: Augusta, Lady Gregory," *The World of William Butler Yeats* (ed. Robin Skelton and Ann Saddlemyer, 1965; rev. ed. 1967), relates her maturing nationalism to the image-making of the plays. In "A Scrapbook of the *Playboy* Riots" (*EUQ*, 1966), Richard Kain describes a contemporary scrapbook that preserved newspaper accounts of the riots occasioned by the performance of Synge's *Playboy*, and, evaluating the episode, concludes that Yeats and Lady Gregory made tactical mistakes in their utterances and actions. Two 1973 dissertations, Mary Margaret Fitz-Gerald's "The Dominant Partnership: William Butler Yeats and Lady Gregory in the Early Irish Theatre" (Princeton) and Olive S. Mullet's

"The War with Women and Words: Lady Gregory's Destructive Folklore Woman" (Univ. of Washington), confirm an assumption of increasing interest in the work of Lady Gregory.

The subject of literary collaboration almost always comes up in studies of the Irish Theatre Movement, the first crisis in the history of which was really precipitated by the quarrel of George Moore and Yeats over their *Diarmuid and Grania*. Estella Ruth Taylor's *The Modern Irish Writers* (1954) surveyed this subject, and a whole series of special studies have dealt with various aspects of the collaborative efforts and with the issue of "influences." William Chislett, in "On the Influence of Lady Gregory," *Moderns and Near Moderns* (1928), argued that Lady Gregory had influenced Yeats to realism, to the abandonment of his early style, with unfortunate consequences for his poetry. Insisting that *Where There Is Nothing* (1903) showed the influence of Synge, Chislett argues that in *The Unicorn from the Stars* (1908), a reworking of the former and a collaboration with Lady Gregory, Yeats "surrendered his peculiar genius to a lesser talent." On the collaboration of Lady Gregory and Douglas Hyde, Patrick Henchy's "The Origin of *The Workhouse Ward*" (IB, 1959) established, in face of persistent Dublin rumors crediting Hyde with *The Workhouse Ward*, that Hyde wrote *Tigh na mBocht* from a scenario by Lady Gregory in 1905. In her translation, the latter play was performed at the Abbey under both names. Dissatisfied, Lady Gregory then rewrote the play, with Hyde's permission, as *The Workhouse Ward* (1908). J. A. Byars' "The Heroic Type in the Irish Legendary Drama of William Butler Yeats, Lady Gregory, and J. M. Synge" (diss. North Carolina 1963), found that the three writers shared a common heroic type, rooted in the pagan and the primitive, and that Yeats broke with his earlier values in committing himself to the type. Daniel J. Murphy resumed discussion of Lady Gregory's influence and collaboration (MD, 1964); in its revised form, "Lady Gregory, Co-Author and Sometimes Author of the Plays of W. B. Yeats," *Modern Irish Literature* (ed. R. J. Porter and J. D. Brophy, 1972), he makes a persuasive and documented case for Augusta Gregory's share in at least thirteen of Yeats's works and offers circumstantial evidence for her sole authorship of *Cathleen Ni Houlihan*, the Berg manuscript of which is entirely in her hand and in the kind of copy book she ordinarily used for her own plays. Vivian Mercier entered the discussion of this vexing topic with "Douglas Hyde's Share in *The Unicorn from the Stars*" (MD, 1965), arguing that Hyde had a share in both *Where There Is Nothing* and *The Unicorn from the Stars*, his part in an unorthodox work being concealed out of political necessity. Mercier also argued that *Where There Is Nothing* was a far better work than Yeats believed and one so different from the later version as to deserve separate publication, an argument that returns us to William Chislett's attack on Lady Gregory's influence. Frank O'Connor, standing above the quagmires of particular collaborations, in the superbly written "All the Olympians" (SatR, 10 Dec. 1966) asserts that Yeats, Synge, and Lady Gregory cannot be dealt with in isolation and that for all three association was a "conversion." Admitting Lady Gregory's "Victorian" side, he nevertheless claimed for her a genuine, if limited, tragic sense, and celebrated *The Gaol*

Gate as "haunted by the triumph of life." Phillip Marcus, whose method in *Yeats and the Beginning of the Irish Renaissance* (1970) does not lead him into the disputed territories either, points to the positive results of the association between Yeats and Lady Gregory. Not only the extent of this discussion of collaboration and influence but its duration indicate a real need for a comprehensive study of the subject that will bridge the gap between general assumptions and controversies over specific works.

II. A. E. (*George W. Russell*)

When Yeats reviewed A. E.'s *Song and Its Fountains* (1932) his task was no easy one. He had to grace the occasion with something appropriate and yet offer an appraisal of the book, in which A. E. describes the visionary origin of his poetic faculty. "My Friend's Book," which may be found in *Essays and Introductions* (1961), manages, extraordinarily enough, to do both, and manages by the bold stroke of a devastating honesty. Yeats admits forthwith that there is hatred in friendship, claims his "hatred has won the right to call itself friendship," and proceeds to declare one of the grounds of his hatred in his criticism of the work. It is not only that he finds the language of the book—left over from the last century—a dead language, but that he is offended, as always, by A. E.'s willingness to rest with the sensuous surfaces of his visions and his unwillingness to ask any serious questions about the visionary images that had come to him. What Yeats does find that he can admire in the book is A. E.'s honest admission that he had to confine himself to "a seemingly sensuous external panorama," that to have probed into his experience would have been more than he could endure. The paradox of A. E.'s life was that the visionary poet and painter who refused to ask any of the difficult questions of himself or his art was also, as Yeats put it, "that influential journalist and economist Dublin knows so well." The judgment of history and of criticism seems long since to have been given and to have confirmed Yeats's perception. It is A. E. the dedicated agricultural reformer, the patron of younger writers, the forceful editorial writer, the moral spokesman for the Irish nation, we admire. A. E., as nearly a saint as any figure of the Revival could be—except to Sean O'Casey, who lampooned him as "Dublin's Glittering Guy" in *Irishfallen, Fare Thee Well* (1949)—will continue to figure in history. But the visionary artist is not apt to be seen again as other than a man of considerable talent who produced nothing in prose or poetry comparable to the best imaginative work of the secondary figures of his day.

MANUSCRIPTS, LETTERS, BIBLIOGRAPHY

Alan Denson's *Printed Writings by George W. Russell (A.E.): A Bibliography* (1961), a scrupulous work, is essential. While two earlier bibliographies had appeared among the *Bibliographies of Irish Authors* (DM, 1930, 1935) and three German dissertations had included bibliographies, Denson's work was not only descriptive but very nearly exhaustive. It includes, in addition to a detailed chronology and a list of books, symposia, prefaces, and articles by A. E., a catalog of letters and manuscripts, public sales, books known by A. E., and allusions to A. E. in the works of others. There is also a list of public exhibitions of paintings and one of present owners. Denson was able to include a list of letters to and from A. E. and of manuscripts at Lilly Library, University of Indiana, which has the largest holdings of A. E. letters and manuscripts; and he chose to include a list of probable letters he had not seen. To the list of sixteen institutional collections of letters, manuscripts, and association copies, one would want to add the small collection of A. E.–Gogarty items at Bucknell University and the substantial collection of A. E. letters to Yeats, Stephens, Colum, and others and the A. E.–Lady Gregory items at the New York Public Library, both of which postdate Denson's work.

A useful supplement to Denson's bibliography is Edward Doyle Smith's "A Survey and Index of 'The Irish Statesman' (1923–1930)" (diss. Univ. of Washington 1966), which, following an account of A. E.'s editorship, provides an author, title, and subject index that gives access to contributions by such figures as Lady Gregory, Gogarty, O'Casey, Frank O'Connor, Sean O'Faolain, and Liam O'Flaherty. "The George Russell Collection at Colby College: A Checklist" by Carlin T. Kindilien (*CLQ*, 1955) includes a convenient list of A. E. letters to Yeats, Moore, Gogarty, Ernest Boyd, and others in the collection.

Alan Denson's edition of *Letters from AE* (1961) manifests the same careful scholarship as his bibliography. Reviewing the *Letters*, René Frechet (*EA*, 1962) complained of the absence of various groups of letters, those published elsewhere, those not available, those lost the letters to Simone Téry, for instance and, finally, those simply not included. To be sure, *Letters from AE* is a selection and a limited one, as Denson makes clear in his preface and in the *Bibliography*. In the latter he wrote, "The published *Letters* comprises approximately one-third only of the edited typescript selection from the manuscripts of AE's letters seen and transcribed by the editor." Regrettable as it is that Denson was not able to publish his entire typescript—itself a selection from a vast correspondence—the present selection is judicious and representative; and both Denson's notes to the letters and his biographical notes are helpful.

AE's Letters to Mínanlábain (1937) consists of letters to the Americans A. Kingsley and Lucy Porter, written during the last years of his life; these are filled with allusions to various Irish writers, including Yeats and Gogarty, to his disillusionment with the De Valera regime, and to his interest in American affairs. "'AE' to E. H. W. Meyerstein" (ed. Vera Watson, *English*, 1959) is a collection of A. E.'s letters to an ill-fated young writer in whom he saw a transcendental impulse. In these there is a running commentary on modern literature, with comments on Joyce and others, and psychological advice to Meyerstein. Reflecting a more extended correspondence than this brief one, Reid's *The Man from New York* (1968) contains numerous quotations from A. E.'s letters to John Quinn. Henry Summerfield (*MHRev*,

1970) has edited a group of "Unpublished Letters from AE to John Eglinton," filled with A. E.'s enthusiasm for the Irish landscape, news of mutual friends, comments on the emergence of Sean O'Casey, and reflections on the Irish political scene. These several groups of letters, in fact, suggest that while it seems futile to regret the absence in Denson's edition of letters that no longer exist or cannot be obtained, it would be desirable to have a fuller selection, including all the available letters to Yeats.

One other item that reflects the range of A. E.'s interests and his political thinking is "The Rural Exodus in America: Unpublished Notes by AE" (ed. Henry Summerfield, *CLQ*, 1968), a set of notes A. E. prepared during his American tour for a speech on the American situation and its possibilities.

EDITIONS

Very little of A. E.'s work is now in print. *The Candle of Vision* (1918), a spiritual autobiography and an account of A. E.'s private religion, is available in reprint (1965), as is the 1917 *Collected Poems* (1970). An important document of the nationalist movement and the literary Revival, the 1901 *Ideals in Ireland*, edited by Lady Gregory and with contributions by A. E., Yeats, and others, is a more recent reprint (1973). The posthumous anthology of A. E.'s prose, *The Living Torch* (1937; rpt. 1970), edited and with an excellent introduction by Monk Gibbon, includes too many snippets but gives a real sense of A. E.'s versatility. A. E.'s contributions to the Dun Emer and Cuala Presses—*The Nuts of Knowledge* (1903), *By Still Waters* (1906), *Some Passages from the Letters of AE to W. B. Yeats* (1936) —are available in facsimile editions (1971). Volume v of the De Paul Irish Drama Series is A. E.'s *Deirdre* (ed. Herbert V. Fackler, 1970); based on the text found in *Imaginations and Reveries* (1915) and collated with three other texts, this edition has been carefully produced. Colin Smythe has scheduled for publication a six-volume edition of the collected works of A. E., edited by Henry Summerfield and others. Alan Denson will edit the *Collected Poems* and produce a new A. E. *Bibliography and Iconography* for the edition.

BIOGRAPHY

That section of Denson's bibliography entitled "Biographical and Critical Allusions to AE and to Some among His Associates and Contemporaries" is a list of nearly all significant biographical, memorial, and critical studies of A. E. up to 1961. Among the few items Denson missed were Lord Dunsany's "Four Poets: AE, Kipling, Yeats, Stephens" (*Atlantic Monthly*, Apr. 1958), negligible except for an anecdote of A. E.'s visionary experience involving transmigration of the soul; and H. T. Hunt Grubb's "AE, Poet, Painter and Mystic" (*PoetryR*, 1938), the informative recollections of an old friend, who, as a former member of the Hermetic Society of Dublin, had also reviewed *Selected Poems of AE* (*PoetryR*, 1936). Unmentioned also, except for the listing of the volume and editor, was J. J. Byrne's "AE and Sir Horace Plunkett," *The Shaping of Modern Ireland* (ed. Conor Cruise O'Brien, 1960), a very good account of A. E.'s role as editor, agricultural reformer, and political leader in relation to the man who drew him into these national activities. Denson included his own additions and revisions to his bibliography in another work, *James H. Cousins (1873–1956) and Margaret E. Cousins (1878–1954), a Bio-Bibliographical Survey* (1967).

Among later biographical or memorial studies there is little that is essential. Two broadcasts on A. E. by James Stephens, found in *James, Seumas and Jacques* (ed. Lloyd Frankenberg, 1964), are anecdotal, but the first develops some useful contrasts between Yeats and A. E., and the second illuminates the quality of A. E.'s visions and the limitations Stephens discerns in his prose and poetry. Frank O'Connor's "The Scholar" (*KR*, 1965) relates some comic reminiscences about A. E. and the Gaelic scholar Osborn Bergin, but these are negligible, as is Raynor C. Johnson's attempt to define A. E.'s "spiritual greatness" in *The Light and the Gate* (1964).

Essential, however, are "AE," in W. R. Rodgers' *Irish Literary Portrait* (1972) and William Butler Yeats's *Memoirs* (ed. Denis Donoghue, 1972). In the first of these, one of W. R. Rodgers' excellent BBC broadcasts, a group of A. E.'s protégés, friends, and associates —among them Monk Gibbon, Lady Glenavy, Frank O'Connor, Austin Clarke, and Cecil Salkeld—record their remembrances, in particular of A. E.'s complex association with Yeats. In the hitherto unpublished texts of his Memoirs and Journal, Yeats is far more detailed and direct in the account of his attempt to influence A. E. than he is in either *The Trembling of the Veil* or the review of 1932, "My Friend's Book." Here Yeats records most fully his view that A. E. has religious genius but neither the will nor the analytic intellect to express himself in art as well as in personal association.

Among the early biographical works listed by Denson, Darrel Figgis' *AE (George William Russell): A Study of a Man and a Nation* (1916; rpt. 1970) and John Eglinton's *A Memoir of AE, George William Russell* (1937) are the only significant book-length studies. The Figgis book, overblown and excited in rhetoric, is really an essay on A. E.'s and the author's sense of nationhood. Eglinton's *Memoir*, on the other hand, has sufficient merit of its own to be classified among the minor works of the literary Revival. Excellent on A. E.'s response as a painter to certain of the paintings brought to Dublin by Hugh Lane, on his idealistic nationalism, on his association with Horace Plunkett, on the cordiality which allowed him, despite his mysticism, to enjoy Moore and Gogarty, the book also reveals a subtle grasp of A. E.'s asexual nature. Also cited in Denson's bibliography are three German life-and-works produced between 1934 and 1940 and an American dissertation, in the German manner, that became a book, Francis Merchant's *A.E.: An Irish Promethean* (1954). Though A. E. and his works are carved up into appropriate segments in all four, none is satisfactory as a study of the thought and works.

The publication of what may be the definitive "life" of A. E. is expected shortly: Henry Summerfield's *A Myriad-Minded Man: The Life and Work of AE (George William Russell)*. Summerfield's "A

Mystic in the Modern World" (*Iliff Rev.*, 1969), an account of A. E.'s grounding in orthodox Theosophy, its impact on the color symbolism of his poetry, and his fundamental criticisms of institutional Christianity, leaves no doubt of Summerfield's control of the essential materials needed for a "life."

LITERARY HISTORY AND CRITICISM

Almost never has a work of A. E.'s been given the kind of close exegetical reading so typical of modern criticism. An anonymous explication, "AE's 'Self-Discpline' " (*Explicator*, 1943) is thus an exception, though, not surprisingly, the analysis concentrates on showing the doctrinal basis of the poetry rather than upon the language and structure of the poem. Hoxie Neale Fairchild's section on A. E. in *Religious Trends in English Poetry* (Vol. v, 1962) questions even the coherence of that doctrinal basis, arguing that there was a radical confusion in A. E. between immanence and transcendence, so that he could look only *through* the phenomenal, not *into* it. Not even in A. E.'s imagery does Fairchild find a principle of order, for he regards neither the Celtic myths nor the Indian wisdom as organic forces. (See, though, Syed Amanuddin's diss. Bowling Green 1970, "AE: A Mystical Poet," where it is argued that the structure of A. E.'s vision does inform the poems of vision.) No more favorable in his judgment of A. E.'s short stories was George Brandon Saul, whose "Minor Irish Miscellany" (*BNYPL*, 1964) dismisses A. E.'s 1904 collection, *The Mask of Apollo and Other Stories*, as "hardly consequential." Indeed, most of the criticism subsequent to that listed in Denson's bibliography has tended to neglect individual works and to emphasize A. E.'s themes or his role in the intellectual history of his time, taking for granted that his verbal texture is weak. Criticism devoted to A. E. has thus been dominantly biographical or historical.

Richard M. Kain's *Dublin in the Age of William Butler Yeats and James Joyce* (1962) is particularly good in suggesting the role A. E. played in the cultural life of the city and in the imagination of the major Irish writers. Kain points out that the lighter and comic side of A. E.'s personality was not allowed to appear in his writings; and Weldon Thornton's recent note, "A. E.'s 'Ideal Poems, J(ame)s St(ephen)s' " (*Éire*, 1973), concerning an unpublished parody of James Stephens and other parodies by A. E. in *Secret Springs of Dublin Song*, provides some evidence for that other side. A number of other studies have treated A. E. by detailed or occasional contrast with Yeats. Richard J. Loftus, whose *Nationalism in Modern Anglo-Irish Poetry* (1964) includes a chapter "A. E.: The Land of Promise," seems to have been influenced by Yeats's belief that A. E. lacked a sense of evil and the discipline to create from inner tensions; Loftus seems influenced, too, by O'Casey's notion of A. E.'s pomposity. Tracing the course of A. E.'s entirely subjective nationalism to its end in post–Civil War disillusion, he concludes that even in his major efforts, such as "The House of Titans," "the pomposity of AE's vision— the hyperbolic abstractions, the unrestrained diction— . . . renders it unconvincing." Making Loftus' contrast between Yeats and A. E.

central in his essay "Division and Unity: AE and W.B. Yeats," *The World of William Butler Yeats*, Robin Skelton shows how close the two were to each other in religious and political assumptions, how different in the way they expressed these assumptions. Skelton offers striking verbal and conceptual parallels between A. E.'s *The Interpreters* (1922) and Yeats's *A Vision* (1925) and indicates that one of A. E.'s achievements was his provocation of Yeats. Philip Marcus also deals with the Yeats–A. E. relationship in *Yeats and the Beginning of the Irish Renaissance* (1970), emphasizing its productiveness during the early years of the Revival.

Considering A. E. the man and candidly admitting his artistic inadequacies, James O'Brien (*AQ*, 1966) develops parallels between A. E.'s thought and that of Jung; O'Brien concludes that although A. E.'s psychology and cosmology were too loose, he can serve as a model of the contemplative life. William Daniels, in a centenary tribute to A. E. (*UnivR*, 1967), quotes extensively from unpublished letters, many derived from Denson's microfilm of his uncut typescript, attempting to show as many facets of A. E. as possible. (Certain of the letters, in fact, indicate that A. E. was not as placid or sure of his talent as he has seemed.) Daniels' essay also stresses that A. E. was more of a craftsman than has been assumed and traces the various revisions of "Carrowmore" and "Illusion." Really in rebuttal to the Daniels argument, Philip Marcus' study, described above, discusses the revisions of "The Gates of Dreamland," later "Carrowmore," and A. E.'s correspondence with Yeats concerning it; he concludes that, despite the revisions, A. E. had not Yeats's commitment to his craft and regarded beauty of language as separate from or secondary to poetic thought.

Another book treating Irish nationalism in relation to literature, *The Imagination of an Insurrection* (1967) by William Irwin Thompson, includes a chapter "The Mystic Image: A. E." Less convincing on A. E.'s last years than Loftus, Thompson offers an interesting reading of *The Interpreters*, A. E.'s attempt to come to terms with the Easter Rising and the violence he had always abhorred. Thompson identifies the central figures of A. E.'s symposium with A. E. and certain of his contemporaries—Pearse, Collins, and possibly Yeats—and concludes that A. E. managed to fuse his esoteric faith and his nationalism in an ending that implies war may be a necessary rejection of attachment to the material order. In a study of A. E.'s only other major fiction, "AE's Portraits of the Artist: A Study of *The Avatars*" (*Éire*, 1971), Patricia McFate finds an even more striking complexity and also relates the main characters to A. E. associates—Yeats, Maud Gonne, Moore, and others; she argues that the book has a double time scheme, that two moments of rebirth—the turn of the century and the period of the Easter Rising—and two sets of people known to A. E. are simultaneously implicit in the fable. Some attention has also been given to A. E.'s single dramatic effort, another product of nationalist concern. Gordon Wickstrom's "The Deirdre Plays of AE, Yeats, and Synge: Patterns of Irish Exile" (diss. Stanford 1968) finds in the three works a conflict between Ireland and the heroic individual that leads each protagonist to a tragic defeat—an interesting thesis in view of A. E.'s later disillusionment with nationalism. Herbert V. Fackler's informative introduction to *Deirdre*, in the DePaul Irish Drama Series cited earlier, indicates the importance of the play in the history of the Irish National Theatre and reveals its thematic complexity.

Recently published (1976) is *George Russell* (*A. E.*), a joint effort by Richard Kain and James O'Brien in the Bucknell Irish Writers Series. In this productive collaboration Kain treats the public life, the painting, and the prose; O'Brien, Theosophy and the poetry. Their concerns and their judgments reflect what now seems to be the critical consensus: that A. E. survives not as painter and poet but as an exemplar of his age.

III. Oliver St. John Gogarty

When Cornelius Weygandt turned to the poetry of Oliver St. John Gogarty in *The Time of Yeats: English Poetry of Today against an American Background* (1937; rpt. 1969), he did so with an uncertainty as undisguised as his excitement. Weygandt, one of the first American scholars to devote himself to the study of modern Anglo-Irish literature, wrote of Gogarty's lyric "Golden Stockings" that it is "as winning a poem about a child as we have in English literature." But Weygandt confessed that he feared his own appreciation might have unsettled his judgment and that he was "not quite sure my enthusiasm for his verse is justified." Weygandt's enthusiasm and his uncertainty, expressed at the very close of the literary Revival, serve to illustrate the peculiar history and state of Gogarty's literary reputation. For the first three decades of the century, Gogarty was actively engaged in medical practice and made his poetic excursions into print with diffidence. In consequence, Gogarty has often been seen as a medical man who amateurishly strayed into print rather than as a professional writer or committed artist, who gradually abandoned medicine for his real life's work. Both as a doctor and a Senator of the Irish Free State and as a visitor in England, Gogarty cut such an extravagant figure that he had become legendary by the end of the 1920's. Moreover, even before the publication of *Ulysses*, it was widely known that Joyce planned an unflattering portrait of Gogarty in his Irish Inferno; and from the publication of *Ulysses* to the present, Gogarty has frequently been confused—even by those who should know better—with Buck Mulligan. In short, the nature of his career, the myth he himself created, the portrait Joyce painted in *Ulysses*, and the animosity to Gogarty that it has evoked—all these have stood in the way of adequate critical attention to Gogarty's substantial canon and to an assured "placing" of him in literary history.

MANUSCRIPTS, LETTERS

The largest collection of Gogarty material, at Bertrand Library, Bucknell University, is composed of manuscripts, letters, autograph and presentation copies from Gogarty's library, and memorabilia. In-

cluded in the collection are two notebooks containing holograph
poems and notes, one dating ca. 1903–07, another ca. 1926–36;
among the manuscripts are typescripts, with autograph revisions, of
Going Native (1940) and *Mr. Petunia* (1945), and drafts and typescripts with autograph revisions of many of the essays that formed
three late collections, *Mourning Becomes Mrs. Spendlove* (1948),
Intimations (1950), and *A Week End in the Middle of the Week*
(1958). There are also numerous poems, published and unpublished,
in various stages of composition. In addition to letters from Gogarty
to various people, there are approximately 1,000 letters to Gogarty,
including a substantial number from such figures at A. E. (George
Russell), Witter Bynner, Padriac Colum, W. T. Cosgrave, Lord
Dunsany, Robert Flaherty, Lady Gregory, Hugh McDiarmid, Joseph
Hone, Augustus John, Compton MacKenzie, George Moore, Sean
O'Casey, Sir Horace Plunkett, Seumas O'Sullivan (James Starkey),
James Stephens, and William Butler Yeats and his wife. Among re-
cent acquisitions are Gogarty's correspondence with Lady Leonie, Sir
Shane, and Seymour Leslie, and approximately 200 letters from
Gogarty to editor and publisher Mary Owings Miller, with manu-
scripts of poems written during his American years. An annotated
bibliography of the collection is available at Bertrand Library.

Houghton Library, Harvard University, has a small but choice
Gogarty collection, an offshoot of the Horace Reynolds Collection.
Among the Gogarty materials are his letters to Reynolds (whose
complementary letters are at Bucknell); a collection, regrettably incomplete, of his unpublished bawdry put together by Reynolds; and
galley proofs of *As I Was Going down Sackville Street* (1937) with
autograph revisions. The Humanities Research Center, University of
Texas, Austin, has a varied Gogarty collection, including some letters
and miscellaneous manuscript materials, some of the raw materials
for W. R. Rodgers' BBC broadcast on Gogarty, many copies and photo-
copies of Gogarty letters and related correspondence, and, most important, a typescript of *Sackville Street* with autograph revisions and
printer's notes. At Cornell, the Joyce collection also includes important Gogarty items, his letters and notes to Joyce written over
the brief course of their friendship (ca. 1904–14); these letters are
items 521–40 in Robert Scholes's *The Cornell Joyce Collection: A
Catalogue* (1961). In the private collection of James A. Healy, a
patron of Irish letters, is a substantial collection of Gogartiana, including Gogarty's extensive correspondence during the 1920's and
1930's with Ernest Boyd and Judge Richard Campbell. Among
Healy's benefactions to the library at Colby College, Waterville,
Maine, are a typescript with revisions of the novel *Mad Grandeur*
(1941) and another typescript of *Mr. Petunia*. The National Library
of Ireland has, among its Seumas O'Sullivan Papers, letters, notes,
and occasional poems from Gogarty to O'Sullivan, many from the
first two decades of the century, and among the O'Sullivan materials
at Trinity College, Dublin, are other notes and poems, as well as
manuscript and typescript fragments of Gogarty's *Blight* (1917). The
Robert Hillyer Papers at the George Arents Research Library, Syra-
cuse University, include letters written over the last decade of
Gogarty's life to Jeanne and Robert Hillyer. In the Gregory Archives

of the Berg Collection, New York Public Library, are a number of Gogarty letters, 1917–30, to Lady Gregory. Complementary to Gogarty's letters to Judge Campbell, Lady Gregory, and the Hillyers are their own letters at the Bucknell University Library.

EDITIONS, BIBLIOGRAPHY

Very little of the substantial Gogarty canon now remains in print. The American edition of the *Collected Poems* (1954) is still available, though the English edition (1946) has gone out of print. Of the major prose works, only the "unpremeditated" autobiography *It Isn't This Time of Year at All!* (1954) is available, in a reprint (1970), though there currently is an American paperback edition (1967) of *Sackville Street*. Fortunately, Gogarty's Cuala Press volumes, *An Offering of Swans* (1923), *Wild Apples* (1928), *Wild Apples* (1930) —not the same as the 1928 edition but a selection from earlier volumes—and *Elbow Room* (1939), have been issued in facsimile editions (1971). The three plays Gogarty wrote for the Abbey Theatre, *Blight: The Tragedy of Dublin* (1917), *A Serious Thing* (1919), and *The Enchanted Trousers* (1919), have been published as *The Plays of Oliver St. John Gogarty* (ed. James F. Carens, 1972). *Many Lines to Thee: Letters of Oliver St. John Gogarty to G. K. A. Bell* (1971), edited and with a commentary by James F. Carens, contained a group of letters to G. K. A. Bell, some from the famed Martello Tower at Sandycove, written between 1904 and 1907; these provide rich details concerning the period and notable Dublin figures —in particular James Joyce, W. B. Yeats, and George Moore—and give insights into Gogarty's own personality and poetic interests. They point as well to the need for a more comprehensive edition of his letters. Indeed, standard critical editions of the best prose works, not only *Sackville Street* but *I Follow St. Patrick* (1938), *Tumbling in the Hay* (1939), and *Rolling down the Lea* (1949), are much needed. So also are selections from the poetry and the essays and a comprehensive bibliography.

BIOGRAPHY

It is not surprising that so colorful a person as Oliver Gogarty should appear in a considerable number of memoirs and autobiographical works; the variety of these attests to the number of worlds in which he moved. It was *Salve* (1912), the second of George Moore's volumes of *Hail and Farewell*, that gave fictive reality for the first time to the legendary Gogarty. Other works contribute a multitude of details, anecdotes, and perspectives, which are, in differing degrees, real or fictive. Various facets of a complex and volatile nature are revealed by generally sympathetic observers in Simone Téry's *En Irlande: De la guerre d'indépendance à la guerre civile, 1914–1923* (Paris, 1923); in John Eglinton's *Irish Literary Portraits* (1935); in Lord Dunsany's *My Ireland* (1937); in Mario Rossi's *Pilgrimage in the West* (1938); in Sir William Rothenstein's *Since Fifty*

(1939), the third volume of the artist's memoirs; in Augustus John's *Chiaroscuro* (1952); in Lady Glenavy's *'Today We Will Only Gossip'* (1964); in Sean O'Faolain's *Vive Moi* (1964); in Compton Mackenzie's *Octave Two* (1964) and *Octave Six* (1967), second and sixth volumes of *My Life and Times*; and in Hugh McDiarmid's *The Company I've Kept* (1967). Simone Téry's phrase "cet homme d'esprit" might well characterize the image of Gogarty in these works. Padriac Colum's section of *Our Friend James Joyce* (with Mary Colum, 1958), though more critical of Gogarty, is able to suggest the atmosphere Joyce and Gogarty could create and gives a generally sympathetic portrait. Indispensable to a real understanding and filled with biographical detail is "Oliver St. John Gogarty," in *Irish Literary Portraits* (1972), a collection of the BBC broadcasts arranged by the late poet W. R. Rodgers. Participating in this broadcast, in addition to Gogarty's elder son and his daughter, were a skillfully chosen and interviewed group of friends, contemporaries, and associates, including, among others, Lady Glenavy, Padraic Colum, Msgr. Patrick Browne, Denis Johnston, Austin Clark, Brinsley MacNamara, Compton Mackenzie, Major Dermot Freyer, William Cosgrave, and Brian Aherne. Rodgers' own assessment of Gogarty and his account of friendship with him may be found in a conversation recorded by Darcy O'Brien in his *W. R. Rodgers* (1970). Quite another, and altogether hostile, view of Gogarty may be found in Monk Gibbon's *The Masterpiece and the Man: Yeats As I Knew Him* (1959). The nasty and malevolent Gogarty appears in even fuller flower in the memories Stanislaus Joyce summons up in *My Brother's Keeper: James Joyce as I Knew Him* (1963), as in his earlier "Open Letter to Dr. Oliver Gogarty" (*Interim*, 1954), the latter a reply to Gogarty's "They Think They Know Joyce" (*SatR*, 18 Mar. 1950). *The Complete Dublin Diary of Stanislaus Joyce* (ed. George H. Healey, 1971) gives, with all the intensity of immediate response, Stanislaus' unlimited account of the Joyce-Gogarty friendship and break and the grounds for Stanislaus' detestation of Gogarty. Each of these three works makes apparent more, perhaps, than Stanislaus Joyce understood, not only the psychological basis for his enmity but also his own role in the Joyce-Gogarty conflict. Indeed, speaking from personal acquaintance with all involved, C. P. Curran in *James Joyce Remembered* (1968) found no truth in the charges Stanislaus made against Gogarty. The first two volumes of *Joseph Holloway's Irish Theatre* (ed. Robert Hogan and M. J. O'Neill, 1968, 1969) present selections from another diary that gives a whole series of Gogarty entries, nearly always unfriendly, frequently shocked, and maybe sometimes accurate. Still, the rumors, reactions, records of conversation, and encounters that Holloway sets down must be read in the light of his startling conclusion, after reading "some 42 pages" of *Sackville Street*, that the doctor "must be sex mad" and that "his coarseness of expression is unbounded." *The Letters of James Joyce* (Vols. II and III, ed. Richard Ellmann, 1966) essential to an understanding of what Gogarty meant to Joyce throughout the latter's life, give Joyce's account of details of the association. Yeats's Gogarty, manifest in *The Letters of W. B. Yeats* (ed. Allan Wade, 1954) and in *Letters on Poetry from W. B. Yeats to Dorothy Wellesley* (1940; introd. Kathleen Raine, 1964) is randy but always appreciated. Once established, this friendship was unswerving, but Yeats's view of his friend was no more static than anything could be for him. Thus his references in these letters show us how Gogarty's importance grew for Yeats as he aged; they also give evidence of how Gogarty grew as poet and writer.

A central document in perpetuating Joyce's notion of a conventional and commercial Gogarty's insensitivity and cruelty is Richard Ellmann's massive *James Joyce* (1959). Probably the most distinguished scholarly biography of the age, Ellmann's *Joyce* is, nevertheless, so committed to its subject that it seems to cast Gogarty in the role of villain. Ellmann's illustrated pamphlet, *James Joyce's Tower* (1969), is even more explicitly hostile to Gogarty in its account of Joyce's "expulsion" from Gogarty's Tower and less persuasive in its interpretation of key episodes in Joyce's brief residence. In the Tower pamphlet, what might or might not have been the psychological and moral forces unleashed between Joyce and Gogarty is subordinated to the biographer's assurance that he knew every motive of Gogarty, always base and finally reckless, and of Joyce, always high-minded, even if slightly absurd. An effort to demonstrate that the relationship of the two men was more complex and ambiguous and that something could be said in Gogarty's defense, James F. Carens' "Joyce and Gogarty," *New Light on James Joyce* (ed. Fritz Senn, 1972), also argued that a distinction must be made between Gogarty the man and Mulligan the character and that one could believe in Joyce's genius without denying Gogarty's talents. Profoundly indebted to Ellmann's *James Joyce*, Hélène Cixous's *L'Exil de James Joyce* (Paris, 1968; trans, 1972), nevertheless argued that Joyce sought to gain psychological power over his associates by letting them know that he would portray them in his books. Yet, influenced by Ellmann, Cixous observes that Gogarty responded to Joyce's psychological ploy by fluctuating between "flatterie" and a "brutalité grinçante"—the latter expression rendered in the translation, absurdly enough, as "threats of violence." Probably the most extreme view of the Joyce-Gogarty relationship, however, is that advanced by Ruth von Phul, who says in " 'Chamber Music' at the 'Wake' " (*JJQ*, 1974) that in 1903, "Gogarty so far Hellenized Joyce as to seduce him." On the track of something in Joyce's psyche and literary method, von Phul certainly is. But were the article in question to offer either substantiating or convincing evidence for its startling assertion, it might not raise such questions of critical judgment as it does. "Buck Mulligan," the fourth chapter of Dr. J. B. Lyons' *James Joyce and Medicine* (1973), offers a measured view of the Joyce-Gogarty relationship that helps to correct Ellmann, adds to our knowledge of the Dublin turn-of-the-century medical world, and quotes many of Gogarty's letters to Joyce from the Cornell Joyce Collection. Mark Amory's recent *Biography of Lord Dunsany* (1972) gives an account of Gogarty's far happier association with another Irish writer, an association that lasted more than forty years, and contributes some additional details to our knowledge of Gogarty's life, as does, to some slight extent, the earlier *The Man from New York: John Quinn and His Friends* (1968) by B. L. Reid.

Ulick O'Connor's *Oliver St. John Gogarty: A Poet and His Times* (1964)—entitled in the United States *The Times I've Seen*—the only full-scale biography, is not a definitive one. Written with gusto, enthusiasm, and pronounced admiration and drawing upon some degree of personal association with its subject, more substantially upon unpublished *facetiae*, interviews with surviving friends, and some of the available primary source materials, this biography does give a real sense of Gogarty's crowded life and vigorous personality. Like so much else that has been written about Gogarty, it allows the personal legend to usurp interest in the books its subject produced; more seriously, it seems to have been written with near indifference not only to such scholarship as distinguishes books like Ellmann's on Joyce or Reid's on Quinn but also to matters of chronology and even to vast areas of its subject's life—most notably to his long stay in America.

LITERARY HISTORY AND CRITICISM

The most pressing need now is that more attention be given to Gogarty's poetry and prose, inasmuch as the themes that inform his works and the craft with which he composed them have scarcely been explored. Fortunately there is some indication of a quickening of interest in the works themselves.

The brief prefaces Yeats contributed to *An Offering of Swans* (1923) and *Wild Apples* (1930), both of which he selected; his praise of Gogarty in the Preface to the *Oxford Book of Modern Verse* (1936) and the generosity of his selection in it; the BBC broadcast "Modern Poetry" (1936): all of these had an opposite effect on the critical reception of Gogarty than that intended. Though in each of these critical statements Yeats gave every possible indication that his judgment was a personal preference and not the utterance of a universal truth, many readers have taken him to be advancing the latter. For Yeats, the statements at issue reveal, Gogarty had something of the quality of the Renaissance men of action who were also makers of song: he was an impersonal lyricist rather than a subjective explorer of the self, who, though uneven, could achieve at his best truly noble effects. Most of what Yeats says about Gogarty is discerning, but a particular phrase—"one of the great lyric poets of our age"—has provoked rather futile discussion of whether Gogarty was an amateur poet, a minor writer, or a major figure. Yeats's attribution of heroic traits to his friend has led to overemphasis upon what Yeats would call "character" at the expense of the work; and another phrase of his, "confused exuberance," has led to critical uncertainty about Gogarty's craft. It was the legendary Gogarty that Horace Reynolds dwelt upon in the preface he contributed to *Selected Poems* (1933), included also in the *Collected Poems*. A. E.'s preface to the American *Wild Apples* (1929) and its expanded version, found in both *Selected Poems* and *Collected Poems*, on the other hand, demonstrate that A. E. could be a better critic of his own and others' poetry than he was a poet, for he stresses the effects of delicacy and precision found in Gogarty's poetry, so different from his own diffuseness.

Among general critical studies, David Morton, in *The Renaissance of Irish Poetry* (1929), emphasizes Gogarty's satiric verse, alluding to the anonymously edited *Secret Springs of Dublin Song* (1918), a group effort but mostly Gogarty's work; yet Morton also recognizes in him "two bardic strands of reprimand and compliment." Stephen Gwynn's *Irish Literature and Drama in the English Language: A Short History* (1936) deals with Gogarty's lyrics as "high poetry . . . not specifically marked with the impress of any period," and notes that, while the poetry betrayed no traces of the Irish literary movement, it could have been written only by an Irishman. Estella Ruth Taylor's *The Modern Irish Writers* (1954) quotes James Stephens' contrasting view that Gogarty's verse was "not breathed in the Irish manner" and his belief that the "Celt in Dr. Gogarty," forgetting classical scholarship, would soon burst into song and soar. Arguing the historical importance of Gogarty's novel *Going Native* (1940), Taylor concludes that, however incoherent the work, future students of Yeats would be grateful for Gogarty's portrait of him in it. A sheer pleasure to read, Richard Kain's *Dublin in the Age of William Butler Yeats and James Joyce* (1962), though cultural history rather than literary criticism, manages not only to reveal Gogarty as the characteristic product of an extraordinary epoch but also to suggest the comic quality of his imagination. Vivian Mercier's *The Irish Comic Tradition* (1962) dismisses Gogarty's prose works, preferring the historical and literary survivals of his famous conversation; but Mercier points rightly to the element of purely verbal play in the poetry, in which he finds "the witty *amour courtois* of the Elizabethans and Dánta Grádha"; the poet himself he terms "one of the few successful modern explorers of this vein."

No more than the offshoot of a luxuriant talent given sustenance by the rich soil of the epoch, Gogarty's plays, excepting *Blight*, have almost escaped notice. Joseph Holloway was, of course, present at performances; and his voluminous Diary at the National Library of Ireland records his, the audiences', and the newspapers' reactions to *Blight* and to the two political farces, *A Serious Thing* and *The Enchanted Trousers*. Andrew Malone, in *The Irish Drama* (1929), was the first to note Sean O'Casey's indebtedness to *Blight* and the historic importance of the play as "the best . . . yet produced by an Irish dramatist dealing with a specifically Irish social problem." Not until Michael Hewson published "Gogarty's Authorship of *Blight*" (*IB*, 1959) was the pseudonymous work definitely attributed to its author. Further evidence for sole authorship and for attribution of the two farces was added by James Carens' introduction to *The Plays of Oliver St. John Gogarty*.

Though a "pen portrait" of an Irish exile and under the influence of Yeats's remarks, Gerald Griffin's essay on Gogarty in *The Wild Geese* (1938) is a lively appreciation of the Horatian and classical elements in the verse; in *Sackville Street*, Griffin finds not only wit but Dublin social history, and he praises its "wealth of detail about all levels of society . . . for over a quarter of a century." Among later and recent essays in literary criticism, more detailed scrutiny has been given to Gogarty's poetry. Vivian Mercier's important review of *The Collected Poems* (*Commonweal*, 1954) and his appraisal of the career (*Poetry*,

1958) show a sensitivity not only to defects but to strengths, in particular to the poetry's true wit, classical affinities, and mock-heroic triumphs; these essays are essential. Another landmark in Gogarty criticism is A. Norman Jeffares' Chatterton Lecture, *Oliver St. John Gogarty* (1960), also found in *The Circus Animals* (1970), for Jeffares traces the poetic career and explores the governing impulses in it. Analyzing the rhetoric of Yeats in the collection *In Excited Reverie* (ed. A. Norman Jeffares and K. G. W. Cross, 1965), T. R. Henn contrasts Gogarty's "Non Dolet" with Yeats's "New Faces" and finds it to be "superficially attractive" but "shallow" and "pretentious." James F. Carens' "Gogarty and Yeats" (*Modern Irish Literature*, ed. R. J. Porter and J. D. Brophy, 1972) describes a fruitful relationship between the two poets, explores the influences they exerted on each other's poetry, and identifies the Malachi Stilt Jack of "High Talk" as Gogarty; D. J. Huxley's valuable "Yeats and Dr Gogarty" (*ArielE*, 1972) sets forth Yeats's persistent and substantial indebtedness to classical motifs and details he found in Gogarty's poetry. Mary Regan (Diss., New York Univ. 1974) sought to relate the classical elements to the ethos of early modern Dublin. The continuing, perhaps distorting, impact of Yeats's generous praise of Gogarty lingers in David Ridgley Clark's "Oliver Gogarty's 'The Crab Tree,'" *Lyric Resonance* (1972), but Clark's analysis demonstrates that contemporary exegetical methods can be applied to Gogarty's poetry with interesting results. Grover Smith's "Yeats, Gogarty, and the Leap Castle Ghost" (*Modern Irish Literature*) contrasts the different manner in which the two poets used a ghost story they discussed, Gogarty in a skillful essay, "The Most Haunted House of Them All" (*A Week End in the Middle of the Week and Other Essays on the Bias*, 1958), and Yeats in the second version of *A Vision* (1937); Smith's analysis of the structure of this minor piece by Gogarty suggests, like Clark's treatment of some of the poems, that exegetical analysis of Gogarty's major prose works should prove rewarding.

Oliver St. John Gogarty (1976), the monograph of a Dublin neurologist, Dr. J. B. Lyons, in the Bucknell University Press Irish Writers Series, is a succinct critical life, particularly good in relating the literary and medical careers of its subject. James Carens has completed a critical study of Gogarty's prose and poetry; this study will include a descriptive bibliography.

IV. James Stephens

More than any other writer of the Irish Literary Renaissance, James Stephens has been the victim of literary journalists and literary critics. A gentle, whimsical, and engaging wit, Stephens achieved fame suddenly with the publication of *The Crock of Gold* (1912) and was fated thereafter to be nearly overwhelmed by a succession of sentimental tributes and bad critical essays, saccharine in their effect and eventually disastrous to his literary reputation. The earliest reviewers of his work tended to be badly confused in their attempts to pigeonhole him. W. A. Bradley (*Bookman*, 1915) looked for parallels in Dostoevsky, Anatole France, and Maeterlinck; A. L. Salmon (*Book*

News Monthly, 1917) looked closer to home, to Seumas O'Sullivan and Padraic Colum, but, rather confused on matters of biography, finally concluded that the earliest novels were typical "tramp books." Ernest Boyd, writing in the revised edition of *Ireland's Literary Renaissance* (1922), perhaps saw what might happen to Stephens, for he took pains to say of *Irish Fairy Tales*, "These are not the hackneyed fairy tales which usually serve, as this book has unfortunately done, as an excuse for a 'gift-book' with illustrations by some artist in vogue." But Stephens' publication history was to be one of bad and voguish illustrations and a critical response very nearly as cloying. In the portrait by Arthur Moss (*Bookman*, 1922), the tradition of literary treacle came into its own, but Moss was more than excelled shortly by A. Brulé (*RAA*, 1924), who, comparing Stephens to Synge, Yeats, and Joyce, ran on: "Mais, après tout, il y a dans cette œuvre une telle richesse de suggestion et une telle puissance de sincérité que voici paraître, à l'incantation des mots, l'admirable contrée dont le charme libre et fier se glise dans l'âme avec le douceur d'une petite pluie mélancolique et tiède." Less purple was E. L. Davison, who was content in "Three Irish Poets," *Some Modern Poets* (1928), to describe Stephens as an "elf" among the moderns. Cornelius Weygandt's lecture notes, "The Riddling of James Stephens," *Tuesdays at Ten* (1928); Frank Swinnerton's "Barrie, Milne, James Stephens," *Fancy Fair* (1934) and "Three Rogue Poets," *Figures in the Foreground* (1964); Lloyd Frankenberg's "James Stephens–Touchstone," (*SatR*, 22 Mar. 1947), his introductions to *A James Stephens Reader* (1962) and to *James, Seumas and Jacques* (1967), and his "James Stephens Himself," *Pleasure Dome* (1949; rpt. 1968): all these dealt, to one degree or another, in the same exhausted currency —associating Stephens with his own leprechauns, praising his whimsicality, his sensitivity, his fancifulness, or even, the sharper of them, making an occasional allusion to his satiric fierceness. Not surprisingly, a reaction to these excesses set in; and just as crude as the sentimental adulation was the hostility that emerged. For instance, Hoxie Neal Fairchild, in *Religious Trends in English Poetry* (Vol. v, 1962), says that if Stephens was more of a craftsman than A. E., "that advantage is outweighed by the triviality of his mind." Dismissing Stephens with the observation that "mystic is too formidable a noun for him," Fairchild concluded his discussion by offering instead "brainless cheerfulness" as a phrase appropriate to a poet whose "favorites are drunkards and idiots." In this context one can understand why Randall Jarrell felt the need, when reviewing the *Collected Poems* (*YR*, 1955), to observe, "No one calls James Stephens great, and he long ago stopped being fashionable, but at his best he is a fine poet." In this context, one can understand the present concerns of Stephens scholarship.

MANUSCRIPTS, LETTERS

Birgit Bramsbäck's Stephens bibliography, to be discussed in the section following this, gives an account of the major library holdings of Stephens manuscripts. The Berg Collection, New York Public Library, has the most substantial collection: manuscripts of four of the major prose works, *A Charwoman's Daughter, The Crock of Gold, Here Are Ladies, Irish Fairy Tales*, and, in addition to a large number of individual poems or groups of poems, a holograph notebook of the preliminary work on *Reincarnations*. The Rare Book Room, Boston Public Library, has a typescript with holograph revisions of *Theme and Variations*; while the Beinecke Rare Book Room, Yale University, has *The Demi-Gods* in manuscript. In addition to its holograph manuscript of *Deirdre*, the Library of Congress, as a result of the recent Halsted Vander Poel donation, has a substantial collection including typescripts with holograph corrections of *Etched in Moonlight, Strict Joy, Theme and Variations*, "Hunger," and many other individual pieces, both poetry and prose. The Berg Collection of the New York Public Library and Houghton Library, Harvard University, have the greatest number of Stephens letters; smaller holdings are in the private collection of James A. Healy, in the Healy Collection at Colby College, in the University of Buffalo Poetry Collection, and at the Library of Kent State University. The Stephens manuscript materials and letters (to Ernest Boyd and from A. E.) at Colby are described by Richard Cary (*CLQ*, 1961). "The James Stephens Papers: A Catalogue" (*Serif*, 1965) lists 58 letters, more than half from Stephen MacKenna and several from A. E. to Stephens, and 29 additional items of a recent acquisition at Kent State. Richard J. Finneran edited "Three Unpublished Letters from James Stephens" (*PLL*, 1970) not included in the Bramsbäck bibliography. Of real interest, these were written to Lewis Chase of the University of Wisconsin in 1917; they describe, in great detail, Stephens' method of composition and the periods of greatest productivity that he experienced. One of the three, alluding to the poetic scene in Dublin, mentions Seumas O'Sullivan as "far better than Joyce," and then adds, "but they are both bankrupt." Such letters as these, hitherto unnoticed but important to an understanding of Stephens, were a harbinger of Finneran's later collection of Stephens' letters. It is not that *Letters of James Stephens* (1974) includes any correspondence that will startle or much that is particularly intimate, but that the 376 letters Finneran selected, most published for the first time, give the best account of the artistic development and imaginative concerns of this writer. Finneran made a laudable decision to define the term "letter" broadly and thus to include various public letters to such newspapers and magazines as *Sinn Féin*, the *Irish Homestead*, the *New Age*, and the *Dial*. Among the later "Dublin Letters" to the *Dial*—reviews of Moore, Gogarty, and O'Casey—there are sharp insights and appreciations; and among the earlier forensic letters to editors, there are passages of ironic waggery and comic outrage that can be described only as verbal genius. Among those included in this edition with whom Stephens carried on sustained correspondence were Thomas Bodkin, Stephen MacKenna, Edward Marsh, A. E., John Quinn, Sir Frederick Macmillan, W. T. H. Howe, and S. S. Koteliansky; there are also significant groups of letters to Lord Dunsany, James Joyce, George Moore, and others. The greatest number of letters Finneran has included are from Stephens' first two creative periods, 1907–15 and 1915–24; fewer letters are included for the period 1925–38, as Stephens' creative energies waned, and the smallest number from the period 1939–46, a time of depression and, except for his BBC broadcasts, creative sterility. Among the letters of the last period, that of 15 December 1940, to "Dear Kot," S. S. Koteliansky, reveals in a few fanciful and painful lines far more than Hilary Pyle's critical biography is able to recount about Stephens' last decade and his sense of isolation. Finneran's headnotes and introductions establish both continuity and context but are not intrusive in providing explanations of allusions and references.

EDITIONS, BIBLIOGRAPHY

Though more of the works of Stephens are available than of Oliver Gogarty, he is almost as badly in need of a Colin Smythe as his old friend. To be sure, two posthumous collections were published early in the 1960's. The first of these appeared in the United States as *A James Stephens Reader* (1962; in England as *James Stephens: A Selection*), selected and with an introduction by Lloyd Frankenberg, preface by Padraic Colum. A useful collection, designed, according to Frankenberg, to bring out-of-print Stephens to a new generation, this collection included the complete *A Charwoman's Daughter* and selections from the poetry and the other major prose works, excepting *The Crock of Gold*. *James, Seumas and Jacques* (1964), edited with an introduction by Lloyd Frankenberg, was composed, for the most part, of unpublished BBC broadcasts on various subjects, including Yeats, A. E., and his own poetry. These two volumes indicated continuing interest in Stephens, as did the publication, during the 1960's, of six paperback editions of his works in England and the United States. *The Collected Poems*, New, Revised and Enlarged Edition (1954), which contains Stephens' quirky preface, stating that the lyric may be about to join other outmoded forms such as epic, tragedy, and romance, has been reprinted (1965) in England but not in the United States. Among more recent American editions are a new *Crock of Gold* (1960); a selection from the poetry, *The Singing Wind* (ed. Quail Hawkins, 1968); a 1968 reprint of *Irish Fairy Tales* (1920); a 1970 reprint of *Mary, Mary* (1912), the American title of *The Charwoman's Daughter*; and a new edition, 1970, of *Deirdre* (1923). Still, excluding various paperback editions, the two story collections, *Here Are Ladies* (1918) and *Etched in Moonlight* (1928), and the two longer prose works, *The Demi-Gods* (1914) and *In the Land of Youth* (1924), are out of print. In the light of this history of publication, it would seem that a modest standard critical edition of Stephens' prose might be viable. Furthermore, since Stephens chose to arrange *The Collected Poems* thematically and to exclude many of the poems from earlier collections, a new critical edition of the poetry would certainly facilitate its study.

A special James Stephens number of *JIL* (ed. Richard J. Finneran and Patricia McFate, 1975) includes Finneran's edition of the unpublished dramatic version of *The Demi-Gods* and McFate's edition of early writings from the *United Irishman*, *Sinn Féin*, and *Sinn Féin Daily*.

In contrast to Lady Gregory and Gogarty, Stephens has been given considerable attention by bibliographers. The first brief descriptive bibliography was by I. A. Williams (*London Mercury*, 1921; *Bibliographies of Modern Authors*, 1921–22); this was followed by Hilde Poepping's bibliography in her *James Stephens* (Halle, 1940). George Brandon Saul produced two very useful bibliographies dealing with aspects of Stephens' career, "James Stephens' Contributions to the *Irish Review*" (*PBSA*, 1952) and "James Stephens' Contributions to *Sinn Féin*: A Descriptive Record" (*BNYPL*, 1953). Saul followed these with a more comprehensive work, "Crutches towards Stephens: A Tentative Checklist" (*BNYPL*, 1954), which he correctly described as more accurate than any preceding bibliography. (These three bibliographical pieces by Saul may be found in the collection *Stephens, Yeats, and Other Irish Concerns*, 1954.) Hilary Pyle's *James Stephens* (1965) contains a useful selective bibliography, but this had been preceded by the principal bibliographical work on Stephens, Birgit Bramsbäck's *James Stephens, A Literary and Bibliographical Study* (Upsala Irish Studies, 1959; rpt. 1973), a descriptive list of more than 800 items—manuscripts, unpublished letters, separate publications; contributions to books, periodicals, and newspapers; secondary materials, biographical and critical; and BBC recordings. A substantial "Introductory Chapter," hampered by lack of biographical information, offers an account of Stephens' life and a history of his publications. Two notes by Patricia McFate have made significant corrections of items in this bibliography. In "A Holograph Notebook and the Publication of Its Contents" (*PBSA*, 1963), McFate offered a more accurate account of the publication history of the four stories in the Notebook; and in "The Publication of James Stephens' Stories in 'The Nation'" (*PBSA*, 1964) she corrected the Bramsbäck account of the periodical publication of individual stories in *Here Are Ladies*. Finneran's edition of Stephens' letters has a substantial bibliographic appendix that includes numerous items not listed in previous bibliographies and corrections of many other entries. In the Stephens number of *JIL*, Mary T. Reynolds explains how the title of an unpublished Stephens poem made its way into the bibliographies as the title of a volume, and Geoffrey Blum adds a number of hitherto unrecorded editions.

Biography

James Stephens, His Work and an Account of His Life (1965) by Hilary Pyle is the only biographical account of Stephens. A restrained critical biography, this study avoids the sentimentalism that pervades so much of the writing about Stephens, though the quality of his comedy and irony evade Pyle and she leaves everything to be done in giving an account of Stephens' marriage and pathetic later years. Pyle drew extensively on Stephens' letters to Thomas Bodkin and S. S. Koteliansky and somewhat less on those to Stephen MacKenna, but scarcely at all on the other correspondence.

Picking up suggestions from Oliver St. John Gogarty's "James Stephens (1880–1950)" (*DNB*, 1951), to which she makes only very

oblique reference, though it was the first attempt to dispel some of
the confusion about Stephens' parentage and birth, Pyle gives an
account of Stephens' origin and argues, like Gogarty, for 9 February
1880 as the birthdate. In an appendix to the *Letters of James Stephens*, Finneran has argued that the case Gogarty and Pyle make for
that date has not been proved; and Finneran argues that, whether
accurately or not, Stephens insisted upon 2 February 1882 long before he was friendly with Joyce, who shared that birthdate. Pyle's
account of Stephens' early years, difficult to give because of the
paucity of detail and accretions of legend, is very sparse but very
deliberate. No less deliberate is Pyle's treatment of the poetry, in
which she traces the diverse impulses of Blakean mysticism and
Browningesque metrical experimentation, separate strains of influence, as she sees them, that merge in such a poem as "Goat Paths." In
establishing these oppositions, Pyle ignores the many early poems
that are formally as well as thematically indebted to Blake. In Stephens' last two volumes of poetry, Pyle notes, there is a radical alteration of his characteristic expression; but, though she admits that there
is "philosophical" aridity, she finds "much of excellence."

While she explores Stephens' metrical notions and effects in greater
detail than the prose, Pyle does indicate the influence of Blake's
"system" and of Theosophy on the novels; and she discerns the influences of D. T. Suzuki, Buddhism in general, Yoga, and Brahmanism
on the later works.

"Merely the opening volume in Stephens criticism" was Hilary
Pyle's own assessment of her work.

Alan Denson (*Irish Times*, 20 Jan. 1965) vehemently attacked
Pyle's biography on its publication, calling into question Pyle's scholarly probity, critical faculty, and factual accuracy. Though Denson's
case against Pyle was overstated, the book suffers from inadequate
documentation; it would have been strengthened by more extensive
use of letters and manuscripts, and it would certainly benefit from
some more adequate and complete system of footnotes.

Certain of the earlier brief portraits do convey Stephens' unique
personal qualities. Ernest Boyd depicts Stephens in *Portraits* (1924)
with more emphasis on his gnomish qualities than one might desire;
yet Boyd already perceived the possible consequence of Stephens'
exile and did communicate the quality of his wit and conversation.
Boyd reports, too, on Stephens' early disapproval of Joyce. Simone
Téry, *L'Île des bardes* (Paris, 1925), is fresher in her perceptions,
describing how Stephens "fait onduler de joie l'assemblie la plus
morose," depicting him as "un petit enfant très sage qui regarde le
monde" and discerning in the poetry an innocent paganism. Mostly
impressionistic are the pieces in *James Stephens* (ed. Padraic Colum,
1928; rpt. 1973 as *On James Stephens*) to which Boyd, Colum, Francis Hackett, and J. C. Powys contributed essays. Gerald Griffin,
whose *The Wild Geese* (1938) includes a portrait of Stephens, curiously has nothing to say about his departure from Ireland. Griffin is
most effective when he turns from the gentle personality to the work
and draws attention to a strain of realism in the prose and a strain of
bardic "truculent vituperation" in the poetry. Novelist Norah Hoult's

sketch (*IW*, 1954) is a touching but unsentimental account of friend-ship and gives some hint of the melancholy of Stephens' last years. Oliver Gogarty's tribute to Stephens (*CLQ*, 1961), like his *DNB* article, stresses the lyrical and supernal genius of Stephens' personal pres-ence.

In the same Stephens special issue of the *CLQ*, Birgit Bramsbäck offered not a portrait but an account of the main creative stages of Stephens' career. "James Stephens: Dublin—Paris—Return" demon-strates that, if Stephens was able to write about Dublin on one so-journ in Paris, it was in Dublin that he found his material; thus Bramsbäck brings us to the threshold of an unanswered crucial ques-tion: Was the creative failure of his later career due to ill health or denationalization? "James Stephens: The Nation of Love," a chapter in Richard J. Loftus' *Nationalism in Modern Anglo-Irish Poetry* (1964), is a treatment of Stephens in relation to the nationalist move-ment that no future biographer can afford to ignore. Taking issue with the argument of Dorothy Hoare, *The Works of Morris and Yeats in Relation to Early Saga Literature* (1937), that Stephens had a historical imagination that permitted him to treat the saga material without romanticizing it, Loftus insists that Stephens always saw his material in terms of the present. Loftus points out that, despite Ste-phens' close ties to Arthur Griffith and *Sinn Féin*, his delicate irony liberated his early works from the narrow and restricted nationalism of those who could regard Yeats as an enemy; that Stephens grew increasingly critical of violent nationalism; and that his essential commitment always was to an anarchic vision of love. One of the few really distinguished critical essays on Stephens, this one nevertheless does not explain how so vague a notion as universal love could inform the fiction and early poetry with vitality but not the later poetry. Did Stephens need the tension created by his early tie to Griffith?

Useful in addition to Hilary Pyle's work and these biographical portraits or essays in biographical criticism are George Moore's *Vale* (1914) for Dublin's legendary version of Stephens' early life and his discovery by A. E.; *The Journal and Letters of Stephen MacKenna* (ed. E. R. Dodds, 1937), for details of an important friendship; Sir William Rothenstein's *Since Fifty* (Vol. III of *Men and Memories*, 1940), for an account of Stephens' life at Wembley and other anec-dotes; *Letters from AE* (ed. Alan Denson, 1961), for A. E.'s account of his protégé; *Letters of James Joyce* (ed. Richard Ellmann, 1966), for a record of the Stephens-Joyce friendship and Joyce's proposal that Stephens finish *Finnegans Wake*; Beatrice, Lady Glenavy's *'Today We Will Only Gossip'* (1964) for a description of the friend-ship of Stephens and S. S. Koteliansky and of an illuminating encoun-ter with Stephens' widow; and B. L. Reid's *The Man from New York* (1968) for its account of Stephens' letters to John Quinn, a man he never met. Richard J. Finneran's "James Joyce and James Stephens: The Record of a Friendship with Unpublished Letters from Joyce to Stephens" (*JJQ*, 1974) gives an account of Stephens' gradual accep-tance of Joyce and recognition of his talent and of Joyce's growing conviction—a seriously held one, Finneran contends—that Stephens should finish the *Wake* in the event that Joyce was unable to do so.

LITERARY HISTORY AND CRITICISM

The earliest studies of the literary Revival were uncertain in their handling of Stephens. Lloyd Morris was inclined to take Stephens more seriously as a novelist than as a poet; and, in *The Celtic Dawn* (1917), insists upon the realism of Stephens' fiction because it was "the fruit of experience and reflection upon it." Though Ernest Boyd, in *Ireland's Literary Renaissance* (1916; rev. 1922), treats Stephens as one of the poetic disciples of A. E. and is far more assured in handling the fiction, he also indicates he is not quite sure of Stephens' direction. Boyd was, however, convinced—wrongly, it turned out— that Stephens was at the very outset of his career; and he guessed that poetry might become his central activity. Hugh Law's *Anglo-Irish Literature* (1926) relegates Stephens to a paragraph of empty generalization. Stephen Gwynn's *Irish Literature and Drama in the English Language: A Short History* (1936) hails Stephens as "a genius less crabbed" than Synge—"happier, luckier, destined to larger fulfillment." Wise enough to see that Stephens must be "judged by the whole, not in relation to some exceptional felicity" and shrewd enough to see that he was "not a pioneer but a profiteer of the Irish literary revival," even Gwynn was forced by the scope of his work to rest the high claim he made for Stephens on generalization. Robert Farren, *The Course of Irish Verse in English* (1947), points out that it was Stephens' *Insurrections* that had introduced, in 1909, a new note of harshness into Irish poetry, Synge's poems not yet having been published; but Farren then seems unable to go beyond the observation that Stephens, as he developed, "sloughed off rawness but kept his strength."

A. E., who can always startle by his critical acumen, may have been scoring a few points on Yeats, when, in 1912, he wrote "The Poetry of James Stephens," *Imaginations and Reveries* (1915); but the man who introduced Stephens to Theosophy commends the physicality of Stephens' early verse by contrast to the shadowy qualities of Celtic Twilight poetry. Turning to Stephens' second volume, *The Hill of Vision*, he offers some hardheaded advice, all the more telling for his own admission of poetic vagueness: "I find myself going back to his men and women; and I hope he will not be angry with me when I say I prefer his tinker drunken to his Deity sober. None of our Irish poets has found God." In one of the early attempts to offer a critical estimate of the entire body of Stephens' work, H. P. Marshall (*London Mercury*, 1925), while admiring the work, was puzzled that the prose seemed to hint at a comprehensive vision it never quite achieved, while the poetry seemed "explanatory rather than inspired." Cornelius Weygandt, in "The Art of Mr. James Stephens" (*General Mag. and Hist. Chron.*, 1928), was appreciative of Stephens' epigrammatic qualities, certain that the prose was superior to the poetry, and conscious of a fabulous element in the prose works; but not assured enough to probe below the surface. Hilda Poepping, *James Stephens: Eine Untersuchung uber die Irische Erneuerungs-bewegung in der Zeit von 1900–1930* (Halle, 1940) had read everything and understood nothing.

So, with the exception of A. E.'s perspicacious essay, only in later and recent treatments of particular aspects of Stephens' works does one find valuable or, at least, provocative criticism. Benedict Kiely's pages on Stephens in *Modern Irish Fiction—A Critique* (1950) are excellent; Kiely finds that Stephens was able to join reality and fantasy without incongruity in his later works. By contrast, in "Re-Reading *The Crock of Gold*" (*IW*, 1953), G. E. Hatvary failed to see that the work is not really a novel but a modern instance of an older form, the Menippean satire; thus Hatvary has difficulty reconciling satire and "philosophy" in it, despite his "enchantment" with the book. Whereas Vivian Mercier's seminal *The Irish Comic Tradition* nearly dismisses Stephens, his sympathetic earlier essay (*IW*, 1951) demonstrates the pervasiveness of pastoralism in both prose and poetry and implies that in his later years Stephens could no longer achieve his vision of a golden age. Going further in the direction of myth criticism, Clarice Short (*WHR*, 1956) ascribes primitivism to Stephens' vision, particularly in his identification of woman with earth and intuitive wisdom. In effect, she discovers that Stephens' women are aspects of the archetypal triple-goddess and points out that woman as wife is generally destructive in his work. Augustine Martin's "The Poet and the Policeman: A Note on *The Charwoman's Daughter*" (*UnivR*, 1964) points to a fundamental ambivalence of Stephens' imagination that permitted him to render the actual Dublin slum world in terms of the familiar and archetypal pattern of the fairy tale. Martin also describes each of the subsequent novels as dealing with the same set of archetypal characters and relationships no matter how the idiosyncratic traits by which Stephens characterizes may appear to alter them.

Arguing that Theosophy gave Stephens a foundation, among other things, in comparative mythology, James O'Brien produced a useful history of Theosophy in Dublin and a sound study of its use in literary works in "Theosophy and the Poetry of George Russell (AE), William Butler Yeats, and James Stephens" (diss. Univ. of Washington 1956). O'Brien demonstrates that Stephens was indebted not only to Blake and Emerson but to the Theosophical notions he absorbed from A. E. and to the knowledge of Plotinus he gained from Stephen MacKenna. Other writers have since pursued the Blakean and Theosophical strains in particular works. Augustine Martin, in "*The Crock of Gold*: Fifty Years After" (*CLQ*, 1962), was the first to discern an underlying theosophical fable, though he did not regard the work as a fixed allegory, seeing instead "the major personages as different aspects of man." Barton R. Friedman (*Éire*, 1966) demonstrates persuasively the influence of Blake on both the vision and the form of the early poetry, and the influence of Theosophical evolutionary notions and, more pervasively, of Blake's Prophetic works on *The Crock of Gold*, which derives its fable and characters from Blake's myth of the Fall and reintegration of the Soul. Patricia McFate's "James Stephens' Verso Additions to the Manuscripts of *The Crock of Gold*" (*BNYPL*, 1969) confirms the Blakean fable, the unique value of her study being that she shows how Stephens' revisions and additions to the manuscript were designed to articulate aspects of the fable.

These last three writers, who have, along with Richard J. Loftus, done the best recent critical work on Stephens, have also opened up the subject of Stephens and nationalism. Of related interest is an earlier essay by Hilary Pyle, "James Stephens and the Irish Language" (*DM*, 1964), some portions of which were adopted for the critical biography. This essay gives a useful account of how Stephens' study of Irish influenced both his style and the direction of his literary career. More information on one aspect of this topic can be found in Richard J. Finneran's "The Sources of James Stephens's *Reincarnations*" (*TSE*, 1976). More directly on the question of nationalism, Augustine Martin (*UnivR*, 1962) draws attention to the ironic fact that *In the Land of Youth* and *Deirdre* appeared at a time of nationalist disillusionment. Drawing upon Roger McHugh's earlier "Some Treatments of the Deirdre Legend" (*Threshold*, 1957) and examining the structure of *Deirdre*, Martin shows that it was designed as the prolegomena to a version of the *Tain* that Stephens never completed; Martin regards the nationalist vision of *Deirdre* as close to the idealized nationalism of the early Revival. Barton Friedman (*ArQ*, 1966) analyzes the original structure of *Green Branches* (Stephens' poetic response to the Rising of 1916), its Edenic motif, and the later dismantling of the poem. Arguing the persistence throughout Stephens' career of a cultural rather than a political nationalism, Friedman both confirms the thesis of Loftus and disputes it, believing that, in exile, Stephens lost his subject. Writing on the same novel in "James Stephens' *Deirdre*" (Éire, 1969), Patricia McFate disputes the claim of Dorothy Hoare that Deirdre is not a romanticized figure and Hilary Pyle's contention that Stephens ignored the rest of the *Tain* in writing his *Deirdre*. McFate convincingly analyzes the comic effects Stephens achieved by introducing material from other parts of the saga and the modifications he introduced to render Deirdre more in the romantic tradition of the Revival. Richard J. Finneran (*SAB*, 1975) draws on the correspondence to trace Stephens' changing attitudes toward Ireland.

On the subject of Stephens' lesser prose works, well worth reading is another essay by Augustine Martin, "The Short Stories of James Stephens" (*CLQ*, 1963), which locates Stephens as a transitional figure between the early Yeats and A. E., on the one hand, and the later sophisticated masters of the Irish short story, on the other; in the stories, he finds a typical sparseness of characterization, an obsessive theme of marital conflict, and a lyrical strain characteristic of the later short story writers. Concentrating on a single story from *Irish Fairy Tales* and examining the manuscript revisions, Patricia McFate shows in "*Deirdre* and 'The Wooing of Becfola'" (*PLL*, 1972) that Stephens consciously reshaped his source material for the Becfola story in order to achieve a comic effect that would contrast with his novel of the tragic Deirdre.

George Brandon Saul has, almost alone, scrutinized Stephens as a literary critic. His "On Mercury and Reason: The Criticism of James Stephens" (*BNYPL*, 1953), later included in *Stephens, Yeats, and Other Irish Concerns* (1954), concludes of the small quantity of criticism that, at its worst, it is watered down Yeats or sheer idiosyncrasy; at its best, notable for its "self assured tone, vigor, and occasional vexatiousness."

On the subject of Stephens' poetry, David Morton's *The Renaissance of Irish Poetry* (1929) gives a restrained but sympathetic description of Stephens' range and his relation to dominant traits of the Revival. There is a relatively early piece by Groff Conklin (*EJ*, 1936) that treats Stephens in greater depth. Though badly dated by Conklin's hostility to Modernism, the piece is valuable in demonstrating how Stephens' revisions of his poems indicate that he has learned something valuable from "vers librists and their followers." What Conklin shows is that by rearrangement of lines on the page and by new uses of ellipses, exclamations, and such, Stephens intensified his effects. Roibeard O'Farachain (*IM*, 1939) also seems rather foolishly hostile to Modernist verse; but, analyzing certain of the later poems, O'Farachain, who vigorously defends *Kings and the Moon*, does demonstrate the presence of subtle musical effects. By way of contrast with these enthusiasts, George Brandon Saul has argued in "Withdrawn in Gold" (*ArQ*, 1953, revised in *Withdrawn in Gold*, The Hague, 1970) that the best of Stephens' poetry was in his prose. To Augustine Martin we are indebted for the most detailed and perceptive commentary on the poetry. His "James Stephens: Lyric Poet" (*Studies*, 1960) and "*Reincarnations* and Remaining Works" (*Studies*, 1961) are part of a sustained examination of the entire poetic career. Rejecting the vulgar notion of Stephens as a poet of whimsicality, Martin argues that at the start of his career Stephens had gone further than Yeats in introducing vigorous and earthy elements into his poetry; he argues too that from the beginning Stephens was concerned with metaphysical issues, though by going back to Blake and the Elizabethans, he was able to achieve "pure song." Overstating his case at this point, Martin describes "The Pit of Bliss" as the "best poetic statement of poetic theory in the language, for it is itself the supreme exemplar of what it says by the very manner in which it says it." But, though he finds Stephens' talent as a translator of Raftery, O'Bruadair, and O Rathaille a true one, he sees an essential weakness in the late poetry: as esoteric doctrines requiring the "shedding of matter" became more important to Stephens, the poetry "by an analagous process, discards its concreteness and much of its imagery."

Both Patricia McFate and Augustine Martin promise critical studies of Stephens' work in the future.

SEAN O'CASEY

David Krause

I. Bibliographies

There is no complete bibliography of works by O'Casey, but Ronald
Ayling and Michael Durkan are now in the process of compiling one,
a descriptive catalog of all his known writings: books; articles in
books, magazines, and newspapers; translations and manuscripts. It is
expected that this valuable work will be ready for publication in
1976. The first attempt at a fairly comprehensive but understandably
incomplete bibliography of works about O'Casey has recently been
published by E. H. Mikhail (1972). This important volume provides
a checklist of some 2,500 entries, including plays and books by
O'Casey and some reviews of them, critical books on O'Casey and
some reviews of them, critical articles and some news items about
O'Casey, and a list of unpublished dissertations—all this material
covering the period up to 1970. As might have been expected in an
initial and such a vast undertaking, there are some factual errors; for
example, four of O'Casey's early works were published by Fergus
O'Connor, not Maunsel; "P. O'Cathasaigh" was not his pseudonym,
for he had gaelicized his name from John Casey to Sean O'Cathasaigh, and the P was a printer's error; and the correct subtitle of Oak
Leaves and Lavender is A World on Wallpaper, an allusion to Yeats's
rejection of The Silver Tassie. It is also questionable whether the
Jesuit priest who attacked O'Casey as "A Tired Oul' Blatherer" in
1959, the Reverend John McLaughlin, is the same person as the
Professor John McLaughlin who wrote favorably about political allegory in Purple Dust in 1970. There are also a number of curious
omissions, but one misses particularly the significant denigrations of
O'Casey in Daniel Corkery's Synge and Anglo-Irish Literature
(1931), Robert Brustein's The Theatre of Revolt (1964), and William Irwin Thompson's The Imagination of an Insurrection: Dublin,
Easter 1916 (1967). No doubt Mikhail will want to cope with some
of these matters in a subsequent edition. See also Mikhail's A Bibliog-

raphy of Modern Irish Drama, 1899–1970 (1972), which lists some works that deal with O'Casey.

For further bibliographical material, some of which is reprinted by Mikhail, see Charles A. Carpenter's "Sean O'Casey Studies through 1964" (MD, 1967; rpt. in The Sean O'Casey Reader, ed. Brooks Atkinson, 1968); select bibliographies in Sean O'Casey (ed. Ronald Ayling, 1969) and in William A. Armstrong's Sean O'Casey (1967); I. M. Levidova and B. M. Parchevskaya's Shon O'Keisi bibliograficheskii ukazatel (Moscow, 1964); bibliography in Saros Cowasjee's Sean O'Casey: The Man behind the Plays (1963); notes in David Krause's Sean O'Casey: The Man and His Work (1960, enl. ed., 1975); Otto Brandstädter's "Eine O'Casey-Bibliographie" (Zeitschrift für Anglistik und Amerikanistik, 1954).

Some of these bibliographies contain errors of fact or wrong dates, as well as considerable gaps and omissions, and therefore the entries should be cross-checked carefully.

II. Editions, Letters, and Manuscripts

PLAYS

The Shadow of a Gunman and Juno and the Paycock, in Two Plays (1925); The Plough and the Stars (1926); The Silver Tassie (1928); Within the Gates (1933); The End of the Beginning and A Pound on Demand, in Windfalls (1934); Five Irish Plays (1935): The Shadow of a Gunman, Juno and the Paycock, The Plough and the Stars, The End of the Beginning, A Pound on Demand; The Star Turns Red (1940); Purple Dust (1940); Red Roses for Me (1942); Oak Leaves and Lavender (1946); Cock-a-Doodle Dandy (1949); Collected Plays (Vol. I, 1949): Juno and the Paycock, The Shadow of a Gunman, The Plough and the Stars, The End of the Beginning, A Pound on Demand; Collected Plays (Vol. II, 1949): The Silver Tassie, Within the Gates, The Star Turns Red; Collected Plays (Vol. III, 1951): Purple Dust, Red Roses for Me, Hall of Healing; Collected Plays (Vol. IV, 1951): Oak Leaves and Lavender, Cock-a-Doodle Dandy, Bedtime Story, Time to Go; Selected Plays (1954), selected with a foreword by Sean O'Casey and introduction by John Gassner: The Shadow of a Gunman, Juno and the Paycock, the Plough and the Stars, The Silver Tassie, Within the Gates, Purple Dust, Red Roses for Me, Bedtime Story, Time to Go; The Bishop's Bonfire (1955); Three Plays (1957): The Shadow of a Gunman, Juno and the Paycock, The Plough and the Stars; Five One-Act Plays (1958): The End of the Beginning, A Pound on Demand, Hall of Healing, Bedtime Story, Time to Go; The Drums of Father Ned (1960); Behind the Green Curtains, Figuro in the Night, The Moon Shines on Kylenamoe (1961); Kathleen Listens In, Nannie's Night Out, in Feathers from the Green Crow (ed. Robert Hogan, 1962); Three More Plays (1965): The Silver Tassie, Purple Dust, Red Roses for Me; The Sean O'Casey Reader (ed. Brooks Atkinson, 1968): Juno and the Paycock, The Plough and the Stars, The Silver Tassie, Within the Gates, Purple Dust, Cock-a-Doodle Dandy, Bedtime Story, The Drums of Father

Ned (also contains selections from the essays and autobiographies, and one short story).

Collected Plays, Volume II, contains O'Casey's revised text of *The Silver Tassie* and *Within the Gates*, which are now described as the "Stage Versions." The revised text of *Purple Dust* was published in the Dramatists Play Service edition in 1957 (rpt. in *The Genius of the Irish Theatre*, ed. Sylvan Barnet, Morton Berman, and William Burto, 1960). The revised text of *Red Roses for Me* was published in the Dramatists Play Service edition in 1956 (rpt. in *Three More Plays*). There are various typographical errors in all editions of the plays, which await a definitive edition.

AUTOBIOGRAPHIES

I Knock at the Door (1939); *Pictures in the Hallway* (1942); *Drums under the Windows* (1945); *Inishfallen, Fare Thee Well* (1949); *Rose and Crown* (1952); and *Sunset and Evening Star* (1954) are reprinted in three editions: *Mirror in My House* (2 vols., New York, 1956); *Autobiographies* (2 vols., London, 1963); and *Autobiography* (6 vols., London, 1971–73).

SONGS, STORIES, HISTORIES, POEMS, ESSAYS

Songs of the Wren, 1st and 2nd Series (1918); *More Wren Songs* (1918); *The Story of Thomas Ashe* (1918); *The Sacrifice of Thomas Ashe* (1918); *The Story of the Irish Citizen Army* (1919); *Windfalls* (1934); *The Flying Wasp* (1937); *The Green Crow* (1956); *Feathers from the Green Crow: Sean O'Casey, 1905–1925* (ed. Robert Hogan, 1962); *Under a Colored Cap* (1963); *Blasts and Benedictions*, selected and introduced by Ronald Ayling (1967).

LETTERS

The Letters of Sean O'Casey, Volume I, 1910–41 (ed. David Krause, 1975). Volumes II and III will follow by the same editor: 1942–54 (1977); 1955–64 (1978).

MANUSCRIPTS

In 1969 the Berg Collection of the New York Public Library acquired the O'Casey Papers, an important collection of manuscript material that had been in the possession of Eileen O'Casey. "O'Casey Papers Acquired" (*BNYPL*, 1969) describes the contents of the acquisition: "Twenty-five manuscript notebooks in O'Casey's hand, twenty-seven packages of typescripts, some typed by O'Casey and some professionally typed although corrected and altered by him, and a large amount of corrected page and galley proofs comprises the new acquisition. The manuscript notebooks—many are books of ruled paper such as used for school exercises—date from 1918 to as late as 1962—almost the entire period of O'Casey's long career." Among this material of early sketches, partial drafts of plays, fragments of dialogue, songs and poems, there is a 56-page manuscript of "The Harvest Festival," an early play that was rejected by the Abbey Theatre in 1920. In the same issue of the *BNYPL*, see Ronald Ayling's note for a very useful discussion of O'Casey's writing habits, some sources of his inspiration, and his textual revisions.

III. Biographical, Critical, and Historical Studies

There is no definitive biography of O'Casey, and a good deal of the basic information about his life, much of it impressionistic and most of it undated, can be found in the six volumes of his autobiography; also in some of his personal essays in *The Flying Wasp* (1937), *The Green Crow* (1956), *Under a Colored Cap* (1963), *Feathers from the Green Crow: Sean O'Casey, 1905–1925* (1963); in his letters; in articles and news items on his life; in published interviews; and in the following works.

Most recently published, *The Sting and the Twinkle, Conversations with Sean O'Casey* (ed. John O'Riordan and E. H. Mikhail, 1974) contains a collection of interviews and personal recollections, covering the years 1923 to 1964, written with varying degrees of reliability and significance by many people who knew or thought they knew O'Casey. His widow, Eileen O'Casey, in *Sean* (1971), offers the best account of the second half of his life, a moving and forthright portrait that covers many of the private and public events of his career 1926–64. Gabriel Fallon's *Sean O'Casey, the Man I Knew* (1965) provides some important information in its early chapters on the Abbey Theatre and on his personal relationship with O'Casey during the 1920's and 1930's when the men were on very friendly terms; but Fallon is somewhat less than candid and sometimes misleading or inaccurate in his interpretation of the events of O'Casey's later years, especially the controversial incidents following the break in their friendship in the 1940's. For a sharp and reliable corrective, see Ronald Ayling's review of Fallon's book (*DM*, 1965); and in the same issue, see Fallon's reply and Ulick O'Connor's injudicious puff for Fallon.

Martin B. Margulies' *The Early Life of Sean O'Casey* (1970) contributes some enlightening information about O'Casey's youth and early manhood in Dublin, his family and friends, though occasionally the material in this monograph is based on hearsay or slender evidence supplied by biased witnesses, or by O'Casey's too-proud Protestant relatives, who were apparently embarrassed by his years of poverty and tried to improve the family image by minimizing or denying some of the facts. Sean McCann edited a collection of largely biographical essays, *The World of Sean O'Casey* (1966), in which some people who knew O'Casey in Dublin and Devon, some who knew people who said they knew him, and some who never knew him offer a pastiche of amusing and dubious recollections and judgments on his life and art. Rising above this general level of semifiction and cheerful malice, however, are Tim Pat Coogan's "The Exile," one of the most illuminating and convincing accounts of the necessity of O'Casey's self-exile from Ireland in 1926, and the less ambitious but nevertheless astute appraisals by Kevin Casey, Donal Dorcey, and John O'Donovan.

Saros Cowasjee's *Sean O'Casey, The Man behind the Plays* (1963) examines O'Casey's work in relation to the known and unknown events of his life, but this "biographical approach" is undermined by numerous factual errors and questionable evidence. The attempt to use this information as an insight into the plays raises biographical and critical fallacies, and it is no surprise that the conclusions are often misleading or imprecise. For a comprehensive review of Cowasjee's problems, see Ronald Ayling (*KM*, 1964; rpt. *DramaS*, 1965); see also the reply by Cowasjee (*DramaS*, 1966). Several years later Cowasjee wrote a shortened and more controlled version of his book, *O'Casey* (1966), in which he omits or corrects some of the earlier errors and speculations, but his biographical-critical method remains less than convincing.

The following studies touch lightly upon some aspects of O'Casey's life, but they are mainly critical assessments of his work. Bernard Benstock's monograph *Sean O'Casey* (1970) and William A. Armstrong's pamphlet *Sean O'Casey* (1967) are very useful as brief and intelligent introductions to the plays. David Krause's chap-book, *A Self-Portrait of the Artist as a Man* (1968), examines briefly some of O'Casey's traits and attitudes as they are revealed in his letters. Maureen Malone's *The Plays of Sean O'Casey* (1969) concentrates on "the political and sociological material from which he shaped his plays." While this may be a valid exercise for a dissertation, it means that the sociopolitical background upstages the dramatic art, and the result is a myopic view of the playwright as sociologist. For a corrective to the Malone book and this approach to drama, see David Krause's review, "The Playwright as Entertainer" (*MD*, 1970).

Robert Hogan's *The Experiments of Sean O'Casey* (1960) is a refreshing synthesis of dramatic theory and theatrical technique. Though he may tend to force the early plays into a somewhat rigid Chekhovian mold and is reluctant to grant O'Casey the freedom to pursue unorthodox experiments with realism and symbolism in the expressionistic plays, especially *The Silver Tassie*, Hogan is consistently wise and creative in his treatment of the later comedies. David Krause's *Sean O'Casey: The Man and His Work* (1960) begins with a biography of O'Casey's Dublin and the seeds of his Swiftian discontent in that world, but the book is mainly a critical study that concentrates on the tragicomic and comic techniques in the plays and autobiography; see also the enlarged edition, published in 1975, with a new chapter that reappraises O'Casey's life, his work, and his critics. First in the field, Jules Koslow's *The Green and the Red, Sean O'Casey—The Man and His Plays* (1950) is a well-meaning but naïve effort, a brief and impressionistic commentary on "the social and political aspects of his plays." Three recently published works are Heinz Kosok's *Sean O'Casey: Das dramatische Werk* (Berlin, 1972); Herbert Goldstone's *In Search of Community: The Achievement of Sean O'Casey* (1973); *Sean O'Casey, A Collection of Critical Essays*

(1975) ed. Thomas Kilroy, in the Twentieth Century Views series. See also *MD* (Dec. 1961), a Synge-O'Casey issue; *JJQ* (Fall 1970), an O'Casey issue; and the *Sean O'Casey Review*, edited by Robert G. Lowery, which began publication in 1975.

Works in progress: Desmond Greaves is writing a study of the political and social aspects of O'Casey's life and work for Lawrence and Wishart. Ronald Ayling is writing a biography of O'Casey. David Krause is writing the text for a pictorial biography, *Sean O'Casey and His World*, for the Thames & Hudson series on outstanding figures; and he is writing a book on Irish Comedy, which will deal in part with O'Casey. Eileen O'Casey is writing a sequel to her *Sean* (1971), to be called, appropriately enough, *Eileen*. Gabriel Fallon is writing a history of the Abbey Theatre.

Selective reference works of literary and historical background are Paul Blanchard, *The Irish and Catholic Power* (1954); Malcolm Brown, *The Politics of Irish Literature* (1972); Timothy Patrick Coogan, *Ireland since the Rising* (1966); Giovanni Costigan, *History of Modern Ireland* (1969); Elizabeth Coxhead, *Lady Gregory: A Literary Portrait* (1961; rev. 1966); Earnán De Blaghd (Ernest Blythe), *Trasna Na Boinne* (Across the Boyne) (1957); Una Ellis-Fermor, *The Irish Dramatic Movement* (1939; rev. 1954); Robert Hogan, *After the Irish Renaissance: A Critical History of the Irish Drama since* The Plough and the Stars (1967); *Joseph Holloway's Abbey Theatre: A Selection from His Unpublished Journal, "Impressions of a Dublin Playgoer"* (ed. Robert Hogan and Michael J. O'Neill, 1967); *Joseph Holloway's Irish Theatre* (ed. Robert Hogan and Michael J. O'Neill, 3 vols., 1968–70); Patrick Kavanagh, *Collected Prose* (1967); Peter Kavanagh, *The Story of the Abbey Theatre* (1950); Emmet Larkin, *James Larkin* (1965); Andrew E. Malone, *The Irish Drama* (1929); Vivian Mercier, *The Irish Comic Tradition* (1962); Dr. Walter McDonald, *Reminiscences of a Maynooth Professor* (1925); Frank O'Connor, *A Short History of Irish Literature* (1968); Sean O'Faolain, *The Irish* (1947; rev. 1969); Patrick C. Power, *A Literary History of Ireland* (1969); Lennox Robinson, *Curtain Up: An Autobiography* (1942); Lennox Robinson, *Ireland's Abbey Theatre: A History, 1899–1951* (1951); W. P. Ryan, *The Pope's Green Island* (1912); William Irwin Thompson, *The Imagination of an Insurrection, Dublin, Easter 1916* (1967); Arland Ussher, *The Face and Mind of Ireland* (1950); *The Irish Theatre* (1939) and *Lady Gregory's Journals, 1916–1930* (1946), both edited by Lennox Robinson; *1913, Jim Larkin and the Dublin Lock-Out* (ed. Donal Nevin, 1964); *The Shaping of Modern Ireland* (ed. Conor Cruise O'Brien, 1960); *Theatre and Nationalism in 20th Century Ireland* (ed. Robert O'Driscoll, 1971); *The Vanishing Ireland* (ed. John A. O'Brien, 1954). For the literary and historical background see also the following Irish magazines: *The Bell*, *DM* (as *The Dubliner*, 1961–64), *Dublin Opinion*, *Envoy*, *Hibernia*, *IW*, *KR*, *The Leader*.

IV. General Criticism

The best selective guide to the state of O'Casey criticism is Ronald Ayling's introduction to *Sean O'Casey* (ed. Ronald Ayling, 1969).* What follows is an attempt to offer a representative but by no means complete survey and appraisal of the main critical literature.

James Agate, in his reviews of the original London productions of *Juno* and *Plough* in the *Sunday Times* (16 Nov. 1925, 16 May 1926; rpt. in *O'Casey*), shrewdly pointed out some Shakespearean parallels in both plays: "*Juno and the Paycock* is as much a tragedy as *Macbeth*, but it is a tragedy taking place in the porter's family." And on *Plough* he wrote with equal wisdom: "It moves to its tragic close through scenes of high humour and rich, racy fooling, about which there is something of Elizabethan gusto. Young Covey roars his gospel of economic regeneration with the emphasis of Pistol; there is a Falstaffian ring about Fluther, mercurial excitability taking the place of the lethargic sweep; old Flynn is Shallow all over again; and Rosie is pure Doll." All of this is Agate at his best critical insight, though he and O'Casey were to quarrel bitterly over his harsh judgment of *Within the Gates* some years later.

But if Agate was able to see how the comedy heightens the tragedy with Shakespearean contrasts, Irish critics have often been embarrassed by the comedy in O'Casey's early plays, which they feel should have been outright tragedies. Andrew E. Malone, in *The Irish Drama* (1929), partly blamed the playwright for pandering to the low taste of his audience—but he also blamed the Irish audiences and actors for laughing instead of being harrowed by the plays: "Life is a rollicking farce to the audiences, and a harrowing tragedy to the dramatist; but it was not entirely the fault of the audiences that they failed to be harrowed by O'Casey's tragedies. As they were played at the Abbey Theatre it was the comic rather than the tragic aspects of the plays that were emphasised." Aside from the obvious fact that actors like F. J. McCormick and Barry Fitzgerald, for example, were essentially comic artists of the first rank who interpreted their rich roles as they knew O'Casey had created them, apparently it did not occur to Malone, and many other critics, that the plays were in no sense traditional tragedies or comedies but tragicomedies, and therefore audiences might be deeply harrowed *and* wildly amused by them, which is the prevailing view of the more enlightened critics.

Joseph Holloway, in *Joseph Holloway's Abbey Theatre, A Selection from His Unpublished Journal, "Impressions of a Dublin Playgoer"* (ed. Robert Hogan and Michael J. O'Neill, 1967), records some interesting and quaint impressions of the younger O'Casey. He tells us that the rough dramatist from the slums was "a strange, odd fish, but a genius in his way," though we soon realize that Holloway himself was quite another kind of a pedestrian fish when, for example, he describes his playgoing habit of galloping from cowboys to O'Casey: "I saw a film picture, Zane Grey's *Roaring U. P. Trail* at the Grand

---

* This collection, which reprints most of the significant criticism on O'Casey, will be cited throughout this chapter simply as *O'Casey*.

Central before going on to the Abbey and slipping into a front seat in the stalls just as *The Shadow of a Gunman* was beginning." Daniel Corkery, however, in *Synge and Anglo-Irish Literature* (1931), cannot mention O'Casey's name without a sense of outrage and invariably accuses him of the same "moral irresponsibility" and "wasteful and ridiculous excesses" that he attributes to Synge, though they are even more dangerous in O'Casey—corruptive "pagan" elements which he traces to the alien Protestant Ascendancy mind. Measuring all Irish writers by his provincial standard of Catholic nationalism, Corkery predictably rejects the works of O'Casey as a betrayal of holy Ireland. In his defense of the "national virtue," Corkery condones the riots in the Abbey against the *Playboy* and the *Plough* because these plays—particularly the works of O'Casey—were a libel against the Irish people: "To sit among the audience in the Abbey Theatre when one of, say, Sean O'Casey's plays is on the stage, is to learn how true it is that the single blot is, *with great gaiety*, attributed to the whole people. To remain silent in the midst of that noisy gaiety, even to fling brickbats about, protesting against it, is, one thinks, to avoid the deeper vulgarity."

Peter Kavanagh, in *The Story of the Abbey Theatre* (1950), believes that Yeats's "blunder with respect to *The Silver Tassie* was one of tactics, not of judgment"; but of the early plays he says: "Sean O'Casey was the first and only great playwright who wrote for the Abbey Theatre about the real Ireland. Yeats wrote about the Ireland of his imagination, and Synge imposed his genius on the peasants. But O'Casey was of the people and sang of their sorrows and joys— less to entertain an audience than for his own inner satisfaction." Kavanagh insists that the Abbey Theatre began its artistic collapse with the exile of O'Casey in 1926 and completed the demolition with the death of Yeats in 1939. Ulick O'Connor, in *Oliver St. John Gogarty* (1964), traces O'Casey's early plays back to Gogarty's *Blight*, a tragicomedy about Dublin tenement life, written with the help of Joseph O'Connor, which O'Casey saw performed at the Abbey in 1917. Ulick O'Connor says that one of Gogarty's comic characters, Tully, "is a forerunner of the personality that was to form the basis of O'Casey's three famous characters: Joxer Daly, Fluther Good and Captain Boyle . . . Tully affects imaginary pains in his back as Captain Boyle does in *Juno and the Paycock*, and for the same reason, a disinclination to do any hard work. In both *Juno and the Paycock* and *Blight* the plot turns on the reaction of a tenement family to the prospect of a large sum of money coming to them. The opening scenes of *Blight* and O'Casey's *The Shadow of a Gunman* are similar . . . Agate thought O'Casey was the greatest master of tragi-comedy since Shakespeare. But it was Gogarty who first saw the possibilities for stage purposes of what Joyce called the 'sacred eloquence of Dublin.' " Perhaps Gogarty was first in the field, but with a second-rate play; and the argument over its possible influence on O'Casey may well raise a question of coincidental geography more than one of artistic debt.

Lennox Robinson, in *Curtain Up* (1942), records some interesting comments on the early rejected manuscripts that O'Casey submitted to the Abbey in 1921–22; and then, in a subsequent remark on Brinsley MacNamara, Robinson makes the right judgment of the wrong man in defining what may be the quintessential approach to tragicomedy: "To write a tragedy in terms of comedy is to write the perfect play and I feel that some day Brinsley MacNamara may achieve this difficult thing." MacNamara never achieved it, but O'Casey did; and so did Synge and Fitzmaurice, Beckett and Behan. In *The Irish Dramatic Movement* (1939; rev., 1954), Una Ellis-Fermor arrives at something like Robinson's concept of tragicomedy from another direction when she relates O'Casey's early plays to the tradition of satire and says that "he seems to belong most nearly to a class of writers rare in all literature, and very rare in drama, the tragic satirists in whom the comedy of satire points directly to tragic implications."

Perhaps the rarely expressed views of Samuel Beckett should be invoked at this point, on the comic aspects of tragicomedy in O'Casey's plays. In a little known review of *Windfalls*, "The Essential and the Incidental" (*Bookman*, 1934), Beckett not only praises O'Casey but prophetically anticipates the wild and dark comic techniques he was to use himself twenty years later in a play like *Waiting For Godot*:

> Mr. O'Casey is a master of knockabout in this very serious and honourable sense—that he discerns the principle of disintegration in even the most complacent solidities, and activates it to their explosion. This is the energy of his theatre, the triumph of the principle of knockabout in situation, in all its elements and on all its planes, from the furniture to the higher centres. If "Juno and the Paycock," as seems likely, is his best work so far, it is because it communicates most fully this dramatic dehiscence, mind and the world come asunder in irreparable dissociation— "chassis" (the credit of having readapted Aguecheek and Belch in Joxer and the Captain being incidental to the larger credit of having dramatised the slump in the human solid).

For an analysis of these knockabout "dehiscences" and "dissociations" in the comic art of O'Casey and Beckett, see David Krause (*JJQ*, 1970).

Some critics prefer to approach O'Casey through his life rather than his art, and this method usually produces some incredible speculations. For example, Alan Simpson, in *Beckett and Behan and a Theatre in Dublin* (1962), argues that O'Casey never overcame a Protestant bias and even attributes to him a "slight case" of subconscious Orangeism (or Protestant bigotry), a view shared by many of the playwright's opponents in Dublin. One could argue with Simpson's reasoning, but it might be enough simply to point out that O'Casey aimed some very conscious and deliberate attacks at the bigotry of Orangeism in *Red Roses for Me* and his autobiography. One might also refer to a letter Brendan Behan wrote in 1942, quoted in *Brendan Behan's Island, An Irish Sketch-Book* (1962), in which he liberates O'Casey from his Protestant roots, disconnecting him from the Anglo-Irish tradition by the basic facts of his life: "Sean O'Casey is not claimed as an Anglo-Irish writer, because he had no land except what a window-box would hold on the sill of a Northside tenement." And according to Patrick C. Power, in *A Literary History of Ireland* (1969), the later O'Casey living in exile sounds more like a Joycean failed Catholic than the failed Protestant he was.

Perhaps few critics have followed more misleading biographical scents than Frank O'Connor and Saros Cowasjee, and the two of them combine to produce the following bit of divertissement. Commenting on the early plays, O'Connor says, in *A Short History of Irish Literature* (1967): "A good many years ago I suggested that what made the plays remarkable was that in them O'Casey was castigating an aspect of his own character about which he felt particularly guilty. His biographer, Saros Cowasjee, quotes this suggestion, and then goes on to prove it (as I think) from *The Shadow of a Gunman.*" It is the O'Connor-Cowasjee thesis that "Davoren is more or less a picture of O'Casey himself, or rather 'that part of his own character that every great writer chooses to castigate.'" Although there is no way to prove this theory about the artist's compulsion toward self-castigation, O'Connor then goes on to double his bet by adding that O'Casey also castigates himself through the character of Seumas Shields. After quoting one of Shields's ironic speeches, O'Connor remarks: "This is not only Seumas—or Micheál O Maoláin, who kindly posed for the part—it is Sean O'Casey, thinking unhappily and guiltily about his own days in the Gaelic League and the Irish Republican Brotherhood, the rifle levy and the kilts and the bagpipes and the hurleys he could afford while his poor mother fretted over rent and food." And then this psychoanalytical image of the guilty and unhappy O'Casey leads O'Connor to his grand conclusion—unhappy writers produce great work, happy writers produce inferior work. One can only conclude that O'Connor must have been a very happy critic.

For those who are intrigued by this sort of analysis, John Jordan, in "A World of Chassis" (*UnivR*, 1955), toys with another version of the happy Sean versus unhappy Sean syndrome but comes out with a complete reversal of the O'Connor theory, for he finds happiness in the early Sean of Dublin and unhappiness in the later Sean of Devon. Jordan creates his split portrait by dividing O'Casey into equal parts of sweet Sean and sour Sean, the warm Dickensian genius versus the anticlerical covey:

> For us then there are two Seans. They may be described as Our Sean, and, if I may borrow a phrase from the Bishop of Meath, Poor Old Sean. They would appear to be different men. Our Sean portrayed a gallery of Zanies and grotesques without rival since the death of Charles Dickens. Our Sean recorded passionately and sympathetically the slum world of the nineteen twenties, and in so doing came upon the mystery of tragic suffering. Our Sean, in fact, was a man we could all be proud of, a feather in Ireland's cap. Poor Old Sean, on the other hand, is an affront to Faith and Fatherland, an elderly corner boy who does not care for priests or nuns, and who seems forever to be holding his thumb to his nose. So far as I can make out, the most expected from Poor Old Sean is that he will be reborn as Our Sean. But if we really hope for that, we are crying for the moon.

For a more jaundiced view of "Poor Old Sean" as a thorn in Ireland's soul, see John McLaughlin's "A Tired-Out Oul' Blatherer," *America* (7 Mar. 1959).

For a refreshing change, Tim Pat Coogan's "The Exile," in *The World of Sean O'Casey* (ed. Sean McCann, 1966), offers one of the most convincing defenses of O'Casey's self-exile. Coogan carefully documents and justifies O'Casey's lifelong quarrel with his countrymen in perhaps the wisest essay on the dramatist written by an Irishman. He believes, for example, that Irish critics of O'Casey have consistently assumed a pious attitude of outraged nationalism, "an attitude of 'How dare you hit me now with Cathleen ni Houlihan in my arms.' " One can find variations of this pious attitude in some of the essays in Sean McCann's book, with a few notable exceptions, for one, Kevin Casey's "The Excitements and Disappointments." And for a typical view of the pious and petulant Irish critic with Cathleen ni Houlihan in his arms, see Alec Reid's "The Legend of the Green Crow: Observations on Recent Work by and about Sean O'Casey" (*DramaS*, 1963).

Further on the subject of O'Casey and Cathleen ni Houlihan, Thomas MacAnna, in "Nationalism from the Abbey Stage," *Theatre and Nationalism in 20th Century Ireland* (ed. Robert O'Driscoll, 1971), recognizes that O'Casey outraged the nationalists but believes that the playwright took a neutral or even detached view of the national struggle for independence in his first three plays: "O'Casey takes no sides. He writes as he sees, his gifts are language and character; he deals with people he knew during his Dublin days, the poor of the rotting slums. He stands aside, he does not get involved; like Synge he has his circle of truth. And like Synge he aroused the wrath of the nationalists who waited for the *Plough*, in the words of Yeats, to disgrace themselves again and rock the cradle of genius." In the same book on theater and nationalism, however, David Krause, in "Sean O'Casey and the Higher Nationalism: The Desecration of Ireland's Household Gods," argues that the big four—Yeats, Joyce, Synge, O'Casey—did not stand aside but got involved through their works by questioning and even desecrating the sanctity of the national idealism: "Synge and O'Casey, like Joyce and Yeats, carried on the fight for the artist's right to present his own vision of Ireland . . . the higher nationalism . . . for they were fiercely subjective men who provoked an atmosphere of intense hostility because they went against the grain of the national and patriotic sentiments." Yeats's comment on Synge covers all these writers and "exposes the gap that exists between the artist and the nation: 'When a country produces a man of genius he is never what it wants or believes it wants; he is always unlike its idea of itself.' "

Some critics, like Joseph Wood Krutch, who come to the drama with formalistic concepts of what a play should be and say, are predictably confounded by the tragicomic ironies in O'Casey's works. His reaction to the original New York productions of *Juno* and *Plough*, in "Poet Laureate," *The Nation* (21 Dec. 1927), probably tells us more about Krutch than about O'Casey: "No one can deny that O'Casey has an extraordinary gift for racy dialogue or that he can hit off the foibles of the Irish character with malicious wit, but his plays lack form, lack movement, and in the final analysis lack any informing purpose. . . . To this day I do not know where the author's sympathies lie, and I defy anyone, after six months have passed, to recall the play [*Plough*] in any form except that embodied in a jumbled memory of rather confused events." And a quarter of a century later in *Modernism in Modern Drama* (1953), Krutch was still bewildered: "O'Casey offers no solution; he proposes no remedy; he suggests no hope."

Unlike Krutch, Raymond Williams changed his mind about O'Casey. In his first response to O'Casey's plays, in *Drama from Ibsen to Eliot* (1952), Williams commented acidly, in a brief note at the end of a chapter on Synge, that O'Casey's excesses of language and misplaced comedy add up to "Naturalistic caricature . . . a particularly degenerate art." Many years later, in *Drama from Ibsen to Brecht* (1968), Williams had second thoughts, devoted a chapter to O'Casey, and conceded that he had misunderstood O'Casey's rhetorical and comical excesses: "I remember reacting very bitterly against them, and against the repeated tricks of colour—the naming of colours—which O'Casey carried to the point of parody. But the real point is more complex. Through all the early plays, it is the fact of evasion, and the verbal inflation that covers it, that O'Casey at once creates and criticizes: Boyle and Joxer, or again Fluther, are in the same movement engaging and despicable; talking to hold the attention from the fact that they have nothing to say." Actually, the real point is even more complex than this—they do have something ironic to say, about idealism and survival, among many other things—but perhaps one should be satisfied that after sixteen years Williams began to make sense about O'Casey.

But fortunately many critics who make good sense about O'Casey are not blind to some of his shortcomings as a dramatist. John Gasner, in "The Prodigality of Sean O'Casey" (*TA*, 1951; rpt. in *O'Casey*), mixes high praise with the recognition of what he feels are O'Casey's excesses and oversimplifications: "He is the natural man, who is apt to run to excess. He is sometimes too intoxicated with the gush of words and mastered by sentiment, though not by sentimentality. He is apt to see things only in terms of right and wrong, black and white. He is apt, like Dickens, to rely on caricature rather than portraiture, as in *Purple Dust*. He is sometimes hortatory rather than suggestive in simplified situations of plays such as *Within the Gates* and *The Star Turns Red*."

Even George Jean Nathan, one of O'Casey's closest friends and an ardent champion of his works, was completely honest in his praise and censure. In his foreword to *Five Great Modern Irish Plays* (1941), Nathan weighed O'Casey's plays:

> If *The Plough and the Stars* is not one of the finest dramas in the modern theatre, if *Juno and the Paycock* is not one of the richest human comedies, if *The Silver Tassie* with all its admitted deficiencies is not one of the most honorable experiments, if *Within the Gates*, for all its lapses, is not beautiful, brave and thrilling song, if *Purple Dust* is not a ringing, moving melody orchestrated with a resounding slapstick, and if even the incontroverti-

bly poor *The Star Turns Red*, the feeblest play O'Casey has written, is not oddly invested with what may conceivably turn out to be a poet's prophetic vision—if these plays are not these things, then I am not the man to have been engaged to write this foreword.

And in his *Encyclopaedia of the Theatre* (1940), Nathan bluntly pointed out what he felt were the two greatest dangers for modern playwrights in general, and Carroll and O'Casey in particular: "The two worst influences on present-day playwrights are, very often, Strindberg and Communism. Strindberg, for example, did all kinds of things to Paul Vincent Carroll before he reformed, as his *Things That Are Caesar's* sufficiently attested. And Communism, one fears, has now adversely affected Sean O'Casey as a dramatic artist, as a perusal of his latest play, *The Star Turns Red*, disturbingly hints."

Strindbergian expressionism and Marxist communism are often simplistically identified as the chief sources of the later O'Casey's problems as a playwright. Yet some critics, like Allardyce Nicoll, in *World Drama* (1949), consider the experimental plays a significant breakthrough in dramatic form, and Nicoll has only unqualified praise for the expressionism in O'Casey's works. Referring to the plays from *Tassie* (1928) to *Red Roses* (1943), Nicoll writes, "From this time on the expressionistic has been O'Casey's chosen form of dramatic composition, his torrential outpouring of words finding fitting channel in those freer and unhibited realms which Toller and Kaiser had substituted for the tight and economical Ibsenian structure." Then there are critics like Vincent C. De Baun (*MD*, 1961), who claims "that O'Casey's application of expressionistic techniques actually began not with *The Silver Tassie*, but with *The Plough and the Stars* (1926)." In the same issue of *MD*, Katharine J. Worth carries De Baun's argument much further by illustrating the variety of symbolic and/or expressionistic techniques in the early as well as the later plays. Further to this point, Joan Templeton (*MD*, 1971) makes a very sound investigation into the possible sources and techniques of O'Casey's expressionism and corrects some misconceptions along the way. For example, she rejects the notion that Eugene O'Neill's works were the initial inspiration for O'Casey's experiments with expressionism, a view held by Ronald G. Rollins in "O'Casey, O'Neill and Expressionism in *The Silver Tassie*" (*BUR*, 1962). Templeton tells us:

Rollins argues that it was O'Casey's chance acquaintance with *The Hairy Ape* that caused him to discard Realism for the Expressionism of *The Silver Tassie*. Since *Rose and Crown* and *The Flying Wasp*, and other prose volumes by O'Casey plainly show that his decision to experiment with dramatic form grew out of his personal conviction that Realism no longer answered the needs of the modern theatre, it is doubtful that one play, even by an author whom he admired, led him to change his methods. Actually, O'Casey was introduced to Expressionism through the Dublin Drama League's presentation of *Masses and Man* in 1922.

Above all it is probably O'Casey's unorthodox but very red brand of communism that has puzzled and angered many critics. Representative of this distressed opinion is Molly Day Thacher's judgment, in "Bentley on Theatre" (*NL*, 10 Jan. 1955), that it was not Expressionism but Communism that undermined O'Casey's later plays. "The deep and serious issue with O'Casey is not: Has a certain senator [Senator Joseph McCarthy] prevented production of his plays throughout the world? It is, rather: How has the Communist doctrine, which is so alien to the nature of his talent, affected a playwright of great endowment and previous achievement? Is it an accident that the power and spontaneity of his writing deteriorated after his 'political awakening'?" But Eric Bentley, in "A Funny Sort of Red," *What Is Theatre*, (1956), attempting to avoid precisely the intolerant liberalism of a Thacher as well as the more obviously intolerant conservatism of a McCarthy, reminds us that "one should not be jockeyed into assuming that there is a simple and direct relation between talent and political rectitude. . . . I propose to let Mr. O'Casey have not only his Communism but also the possibility of greatness as a Communist writer—or, which is not the same thing, of greatness as a writer who, incidentally, supports Communism." Looking at the early plays, in "Heroic Wantonness," *In Search of Theatre* (1953), Bentley asks: "In what other realistic plays does the imagination play so freely, does the primitive heart of man sing so spontaneously, as in those of O'Casey?" Then he goes on to state that O'Casey's original and many-sided dramatic methods extend beyond realism: they are "naturalistic, Elizabethan, epic."

Not so enlightened or fair as Bentley, Robert Brustein, in *The Theatre of Revolt* (1964), quickly dismisses the early plays as inferior efforts, and then he confronts the issue of O'Casey's communism or revolt by avoiding it. O'Casey, one of the most likely modern playwrights of revolt, in his original themes and techniques, whether or not one approves of his tragicomic and expressionistic methods or his red and rhetorical madness, simply does not fit conveniently into Brustein's type of apolitical rebellion, and he must therefore be drummed out of the theater of neat and tidy revolt: "There are those who may regret the omission of Sean O'Casey; but he has always struck me as an extremely overrated writer with two or three competent Naturalistic plays to his credit, followed by a lot of ideological bloat and embarrassing bombast."

Brustein is by no means alone in his rejection of O'Casey, for Richard Findlater, in *The Unholy Trade* (1952), also comes down hard on the unholy playwright, whom he calls a "poet *manqué*" whose "failures illustrate the failure of prose" and the failure of religious faith, due to communism and anticlericalism: "Just as the drama of Eliot and Fry springs from the soil of English Christianity, so the plays of Sean O'Casey derive from the ethos of Irish Communism. As Mr. Eliot is concerned with the relationship of man to God, Mr. O'Casey is preoccupied with man's relationship to society. Like Mr. Eliot, the Irish dramatist has experimented in new forms outside the naturalistic convention, but unlike Mr. Eliot, his recent plays have not found a place on the contemporary London stage and are rarely performed outside it. Both men write from a deeply religious sense of life, for Mr. O'Casey's militant rationalism conceals a passionate ambivalence of feeling towards the Christian Church. His anti-clericalism, indeed, is the unresolved personal problem whose intrusion has helped to thwart the development of his later style." In accord with this notion that O'Casey was thwarted by his religious and political apostasies, Vivian Mercier provides his own psychoanalytic version of the problem in "The Riddle of Sean O'Casey: Decline of a Playwright" (*Commonweal*, 13 July 1956). Promptly and neatly he solves the riddle by relating O'Casey's decline as a playwright to his double sense of guilt as a man. First, according to Mercier's Freudian analysis, O'Casey must have carried a heavy burden of guilt because of his conscious or unconscious cowardice in failing to take part in the 1916 Easter Rising. Second, according to Mercier's Marxian analysis, O'Casey must have carried a heavy burden of guilt because he had consciously or unconsciously betrayed his economic and religious class background in falling as a poor Protestant into that state of destitution usually reserved for the Catholics in Ireland. It would be unfair even to attempt to solve the riddle of the critic's decline, but perhaps the record should indicate the following facts: that O'Casey had deliberately chosen to reject the nationalistic fervor that led to the Rising because he had previously committed himself to what he considered the higher cause of labor in the 1913 General Strike; that no Irish Protestant, indigent or otherwise, had liberated himself from his Christian faith with less pain and more exuberance than the free-thinking O'Casey.

It is somewhat refreshing to turn to William A. Armstrong who, in "The Irish Point of View: The Plays of Sean O'Casey, Brendan Behan, and Thomas Murphy," *Experimental Drama* (ed. William A. Armstrong, 1963), finds the prevailing motifs in O'Casey's later plays much more Dionysiac than Marxist, and maybe even compatible with if distinct from Christianity: "His Marxist ideas have not disappeared, but they are subordinate to what I would call a Dionysiac religion of beauty, fertility, and the free expression of the senses and the imagination in song, dance, painting, and poetry. It finds its ritual and symbolism in colours, in Irish mythology, and sometimes in images and ideas deriving from the poetry of W. B. Yeats. Though it has primitive and pagan associations, O'Casey does not feel that it is a religion irreconcilable with Christianity."

Brooks Atkinson, a friend of O'Casey since the 1930's, is one of the American critics who is skeptical about the source and nature of the dramatist's communism, which he feels is more poetic than political. In his introduction to *The Sean O'Casey Reader* (1968), Atkinson refers to O'Casey's eclectic belief that Jesus, Keats, Shelley, Dickens, and Whitman were all communists, and then he goes on to say:

> O'Casey was never a member of the Communist Party. I think his non-membership in a party he actively supported was significant. It indicated not only his fundamental independence, but also his congenital distrust of any organization that required so much discipline, whether it was a political party or the Roman Catholic Church. He was incapable of accepting discipline from any external source. There is not much about Lenin or Stalin in

his comments on Communism. . . . O'Casey's Communism had a flamboyant style. But it must have perplexed orthodox Communists.

On the other hand, Ronald Ayling, in the preface to *Blasts and Benedictions* (1967), says that many of O'Casey's critics have been confused or embarrassed by his communism and have therefore distorted or softened it. "These impressions have been given by his friends and admirers as well as by detractors. Several American critics who were friendly with him were obviously embarrassed by his avowed political standpoint and seemed unwilling to believe that a man of such humane and compassionate vision could *really* be a socialist of any kind, or an agnostic either. Certain of their criticisms, therefore, have tended to portray him as a half-hearted communist, or a naïve idealist fallen among Marxists." Clearly, O'Casey's unique and unpredictable communism remains a genuine credo and a genuine enigma.

Jack Lindsay, in "Sean O'Casey as a Socialist Artist" (*O'Casey*) looks at another aspect of the religious and revolutionary themes in the plays. He considers the fact that many critics have pointed out O'Casey's apparent "obsession with religion," but he insists they have misunderstood the function of religious references in the context of the plays: "there is the simple fact that his people do use the religious point of reference and at the moments of most deeply stirred emotion turn to religion for their answers—or at least for the way in which to frame their questions. We come back to the peculiar stage reached by the Irish working-class in the earlier years of this century, which marks them out as unlike any fully urbanised group of workers. (The only analogy is to be found in Tolstoy and Dostoevsky, who, also dealing with a peasant-type of workers, turned to the Orthodox religion which dominated their minds, both in order to define them and to express social crisis.) On the other hand, O'Casey himself welcomes the choice of the religious idiom for the definition of the conflicts of his society and the way they are fought out in people's minds. Here again he is like Tolstoy and Dostoevsky, though less personally involved in the Christian creed and looking directly toward political revolution."

Lindsay raises some important issues in his fine essay, especially in an analogy he draws between the nonurbanized peasant workers of Russia and Ireland and their inclination to hold fast to their religious orthodoxies; nevertheless, he does not resolve the paradoxical context of religious and revolutionary motifs in O'Casey's works. Why, for example, if O'Casey is supposed to be less involved in the Christian creed and more in political revolution, is the pervasive tone of the early plays as skeptical about political revolution as it is about religious orthodoxies; and why, when O'Casey is supposed to be closest to communism, do the Celtic rituals of celebration in many of the later plays often combine revolutionary and religious impulses in what almost amounts to a fusion of communism and Christianity— the Red Star united with the Star of Bethlehem, the creed of Father Ned united with Michael Binnington's joyous shout for revolutionary freedom?

Hugh MacDiarmid, in "Slàinte Chùramach, Seán" (*O'Casey*), calls these paradoxical fusions a return to the tradition of Gaelic literature, and he believes that O'Casey's flamboyant style and immoderate rage are uniquely Gaelic characteristics. In an impassioned defense of O'Casey, MacDiarmid proclaims that his Irish friend's mighty Gaelic spirit was not diluted by the tradition of English gentility. "Two features of O'Casey's writing that have been severely criticised— namely, his immoderate expressions of rage and of *argumentum ad hominis*—so distasteful to English gentility—manifest his Gaelic background and have their virtues, no matter how they may go against the grain of the English tradition (and, indeed, the 'flytings' are one of the great features of Scottish poetry and the English dislike them)." His convincing attempt to link the rhetoric of the plays to the uninhibited tradition of Gaelic literature is a relatively unexplored area of O'Casey criticism, though David Krause, in "The Hidden Oisín" (*SH*, 1966) and " 'The Rageous Ossean: Patron-Hero of Synge and O'Casey" (*MD*, 1961), has attempted to connect O'Casey's works with the tragicomic tradition of Gaelic myth, particularly the medieval Celtic dialogues between Oisín and St. Patrick.

Perhaps finding the right tradition and structure for O'Casey's dramatic extravagances is an essential part of the critical problem. It should therefore come as no surprise that the Aristotelian tradition of tragedy is not the right one for O'Casey, that it must create difficulties for those academic critics who try to force his plays into a classical mold. For example, T. R. Henn, in *The Harvest of Tragedy* (1956), as might be predicted, looks in vain for a Greek catharsis of pity and fear in the three early Dublin plays. "It is clear that O'Casey is a writer of limited experience and still more limited negative capability, with a certain rough skill in counterpoint. The moral values are clear; 'patriotism is not enough,' the deadly power in Ireland of the dream embodied in rhetoric; the inchoate character of popular 'war' emotions; the suffering of the women for the arrogance and stupidity and vanity of the men. It fails to become great or moving tragedy because it possesses no inner core, because it seeks to achieve depth by mere counterpointing of emotions, and because the speech cannot encompass the emotions which it seeks to express. There is a deliberate forcing of O'Casey's characters into a language which is admirable for low comedy, provided the actors can achieve its peculiar intonations, but which has no flexibility to cope with pity and fear." What is not clear here is why the "inner core" and mock-heroic language of tragicomedy should conform to the "inner core" and exalted language of Aristotelian catharsis.

Another critic who begins with Aristotle is Robert Bechtold Heilman, who, in *The Iceman, the Arsonist, and the Troubled Agent: Tragedy and Melodrama on the Modern Stage* (1973), insists that O'Casey did not write tragedies but melodramatic "drama of disaster"; and in a discussion of some ironic "excellences" in *Juno* cannot extricate himself from his preconceptions of irony in classical tragedy: "It is a melodrama of disaster that gains a special character from a large infusion of Falstaffian and satiric comedy. . . . The joining of diverse elements is O'Casey's great talent. But the irony is not that of tragedy." Again, why should it be? Arguing from a similar position,

Ronald Peacock, in *The Poet in the Theatre* (1946), is a critic with a built-in concept of traditional tragedy, and in lamenting the disappearance of the tragic hero in modern drama he doesn't know how to cope with O'Casey's tragicomic antiheroes: "The tragic plays of O'Casey are symptomatic of this situation. His characters, vivid as some of them are, are not as important as the larger political tragedy of which they are fortuitous victims. In themselves they are not in the least inevitable and unique tragic persons, like those of tradition; any set of Dublin people will do." Emil Roy, in *British Drama since Shaw* (1972), is willing to grant O'Casey his departure from "outworn tradition" but objects that the characters are too commonplace: "His later plays are supposed to be imaginative, experimental dramas with no concessions to outworn tradition. But his casts increasingly fill with stage Irishmen, stock English villains, and excited crowd choruses worthy of Dion Boucicault."

For a more favorable approach to the influence of Boucicault and a different view of O'Casey's ironic treatment of the stage Irishman, see Robert Hogan's *Dion Boucicault* (1969) and David Krause's "The Theatre of Dion Boucicault," *The Dolmen Boucicault* (ed. David Krause, 1963). See also Bernard Benstock, in "Kelly, Burke and Shea" (*JJQ*, 1970), for a brief but lively treatment of what he calls O'Casey's favorite literary sport, "*épater les irlandais.*"

Kenneth Muir, in "Verse and Prose," *Contemporary Theatre* (Stratford-upon-Avon Studies 4, 1962), recognizes the uneven quality of the later plays but makes the important point that they have been attacked more for their merits than their defects, merits that involve the attempt to discover new sources of poetic and symbolic value in prose drama. "O'Casey has tried deliberately to write poetic drama in prose. If his early model was Synge, his later models were Strindberg and O'Neill. He surpasses O'Neill in eloquence, but in nearly all his later plays he seems to be eloquent in a vacuum. But one may be tempted to suspect that it was the merits rather than the defects of his plays that banished them from the professional stage."

With considerable insight, Robert Hogan and Ronald Ayling connect the merits to the innovative techniques of Chekhov and Brecht. Hogan, in *The Experiments of Sean O'Casey* (1960), says that O'Casey, like Chekhov before him, had created "a third major genre, tragi-comedy." As the basis of this genre he describes a "second structure," as distinct from the traditional single-action structure ("*Protasis, Epitasis, Catastasis,* and *Catastrophe*"), a tragicomic form of ironic counterpoint and indirection, after the method of Chekhov in *The Three Sisters* and *The Cherry Orchard*, which O'Casey used unevenly in *Gunman* and *Juno* but perfected in *Plough*:

> From the beginning, then, O'Casey was straining against the confines of realism and by the poorly understood success of *The Plough and the Stars* reasserting the vitality of this second structure with its unique utilization of tragic irony and its broadness of scope that the conventional, four-point, single-action plays of his contemporaries denied. Perhaps the chief device of the second structure is the ironic juxtaposition of the comic and the

pathetic or the grotesque and the sublime, a juxtaposition prac-
tised also by Jonson, Chekhov, Congreve, Charlie Chaplin, and
Clifford Odets.

For another treatment of O'Casey's plays in Chekhovian terms, see
Ronald G. Rollins' "Form and Content in Sean O'Casey's Dublin
Trilogy" (*MD*, 1966).

Ronald Ayling, in "Character Control and 'Alienation' in *The
Plough and the Stars*" (*JJQ*, 1970), makes a strong case for some
flexible variations of Brecht's theory of alienation in the plays of
O'Casey, confronting the paradoxical issue of alienation and empathy:

> O'Casey's playwriting allows for a considerable degree of *rap-
> port* between spectators and certain of his *dramatis personae*,
> yet the empathy thus engendered does not impede a *Verfrem-
> dungseffekt*. On the contrary, the alienation that O'Casey
> achieves for critical purposes is reinforced, and not undermined,
> by the creation of conventional empathy for particular individ-
> uals, from whom the audience's sympathies are subsequently
> estranged by shock tactics of one kind or another. The depth and
> quality of the spectator's emotional attachment to a particular
> stage creation necessarily conditions the impact of the eventual
> alienation. If the character is initially well liked the disillusion-
> ment will be the more unexpected and painful. . . . The shock
> may thus produce a more critical scrutiny of the spectator's val-
> ues and judgments, fresh recognition of the unpredictability of
> human nature, and of the uncertain conditions of life.

But since Ayling tends to minimize the comedy in these "tragic"
plays, he is faced with the problem of accounting for the fact that
those ironic and alienating shocks are more often reserved for the
more complex comic characters rather than for the straight or tragic
characters.

In an attempt to associate O'Casey with the modern theater of the
grotesque, in spite of his protestations to the contrary, Robert P.
Murphy, in "Sean O'Casey and 'The Bald Primaqueera'" (*JJQ*,
1970), assesses O'Casey's lampoon of the modern theater of absurdity
and cruelty as a "mixture of great perceptiveness and great wrong-
headedness." He stresses O'Casey's ironic failure to understand how
often his own later plays reflect some of the mock-heroic principles
and techniques of Artaud and Ionesco. This is a convincing argument, except that Murphy might have indicated the extent to which
the vitalistic O'Casey, in his art and life, rejected the themes of frustration and despair that predominate in the theater of absurdity and
cruelty, a theater which nevertheless he does anticipate and participate in, with regard to nonrealistic and extravagant dramatic techniques, in his experimental plays. On subject matter, as distinct from
technique, this view is reinforced by B. L. Smith (*JJQ*, 1970), who
points out the affirmative aspects of O'Casey's satiric motifs. He
maintains that O'Casey is not a cynical or destructive satirist, that he,
"unlike many of his predecessors, is almost consistently optimistic: he

is a reformer who knows that personal involvement and personal action are the only real avenues toward personal wholeness." Smith examines the satiric elements in many of the plays and concludes that these exposures of human folly illustrate O'Casey's affirmative view that "laughter is a weapon against evil."

Bernard Benstock (*JJQ*, 1964) compares the satiric treatment of the Irish clergy in the works of Joyce and O'Casey, and after an extensive catalog of various clerical characters he concludes: "The effect of the cleric to Joyce is essentially pernicious merely because it makes demands upon the soul of the individual, while for O'Casey the effect varies with the perspective of the particular clergyman, the majority of whom, however, at least in Ireland, are spokesmen for conformity, narrowmindedness and a fear of the future." One might add, however, that the later O'Casey began to see the possibility of such open-minded and visionary priests as Father Boheroe in *The Bishop's Bonfire* and Father Ned in *The Drums of Father Ned*.

To move from satire to comedy, one should not overlook Enid Welsford's *The Fool* (1935), for although she never mentions O'Casey in her classical and historical work, she makes many observations that might illuminate our understanding of his comic characters. For example, she writes: "The Fool is an unabashed glutton and coward and knave, he is—as we say—a *natural*; we laugh at him and enjoy a pleasant sense of superiority; he looks at us oddly and we suspect that he is our *alter ego*; he winks at us and we are delighted at the discovery that we also are gluttons and cowards and knaves. The rogue has freed us from shame." It would be difficult to deny that O'Casey's rich variety of comic rogues, male and female, help us to achieve precisely this state of compensatory freedom, which may well lie at the heart of the comic experience.

Robert Hogan, in "In Sean O'Casey's Golden Days" (*DM*, 1966; rpt. in *O'Casey*), suggests that O'Casey's later comedies were written in the pastoral tradition and its quest for a Golden Age, with some significant variations: "Unlike earlier writers of Pastoral, O'Casey never brings his Golden Age entirely onstage. It is either in the process of dying or of being born. The O'Caseyan Golden Age is a vision of Ireland filled with golden lads and lasses full of vigour and love and life. The Golden Age comes in conflict with the debased age of the real world, the world of business, of hypocrisy, of narrow religiosity." This important article opens up new ground for O'Casey criticism, though it should be added that Hogan might have pointed out the degree to which the comic mode of the early as well as the later plays often follows the mock-pastoral tradition. For a discussion of the mock-pastoral as it might apply to O'Casey, see William Empson's *Some Versions of Pastoral* (1950).

On the pastoral mode in the early and later plays, Jack Lindsay, in "Sean O'Casey as a Socialist Artist" (*O'Casey*), writing in 1966, also makes an important contribution:

A few more words must yet be said about the four pastoral plays [*Purple Dust, Cock-a-Doodle Dandy, The Bishop's Bonfire, The Drums of Father Ned*], in which peasants of the village take the place which the tenement-dwellers held in the Abbey plays. In the ritual-elements of his last works O'Casey goes deep back to the origins of drama; but he does not do this by an abstract exercise of his intellect. Rather, he does it by a steady deepening of the traditional and folk elements present in his work from the start. Much nonsense has been written about the stage-Irishman in his plays, and about the melodramatic aspects—though his link with Boucicault (and with Carleton, Lever, and others of their kind) has been correctly enough stressed. The stage-Irishman of Boucicault is in fact a traditional type of character, with roots both in native folk-humour and in the immemorial line that runs back through the Commedia dell'Arte to the ancient world. By purging the sentimentalities and falsities that had gathered round such types in the nineteenth century, O'Casey reached back to origins and achieved what may be called the only true recreation of Aristophanic comedy ever made; for he found the links, not in literature, but in life itself and in a folk-tradition from which he had himself emerged.

There is a deep and rich vein of critical ore to be mined in this extraordinary passage, this challenging attempt to establish a sense of folk continuity, through the pastoral and comic traditions, in all the plays.

Equally bold but with less enlightening results, R. B. Parker (QQ, 1966) illustrates a number of valid comic parallels in the plays of Shaw and O'Casey, and then in his central thesis fashions a critical melodrama for O'Casey's sources of influence, in which Shaw is the hero and Yeats and Synge the villains. Parker proposes that the early O'Casey was influenced fortunately by Shaw, which accounts for the ironic treatment of Irish nationalism and myth in *Gunman, Juno*, and *Plough*; whereas the later O'Casey was influenced unfortunately by Yeats and Synge, which accounts for the romantic treatment of Irish myth and blarney in plays like *Purple Dust, Cock-a-Doodle Dandy*, and *The Drums of Father Ned*. Parker unfolds his plot in the following manner: "The tendency to blarney and to refer to Ireland's mythical past is treated comically, or at least ironically, in all the early O'Casey plays; but in the later ones he swings away from Shaw back towards Yeats and Synge, and begins to treat romanticism seriously—a bias foreshadowed from the first perhaps in his attraction to Father Keegan in *John Bull's Other Island*. The heroes now begin to use elaborate speeches about the mythical heroes of old, and their blarney is presented as practically effective instead of, as formerly, an excuse for inaction." Shaw may be all right here, but Yeats and Synge are miscast, and O'Casey is misunderstood.

Shaw and O'Casey, yes, but what is one to make of a critic who insists on comparing Oscar Wilde with O'Casey, as Morris Freedman does in "The Modern Tragicomedy of Wilde and O'Casey," *The Moral Impulse, Modern Drama from Ibsen to the Present* (1967). In full solemnity Freedman tells us that Wilde and O'Casey were both very Irish "in their love of the well-turned phrase"; and then he presumes to treat *The Importance of Being Earnest*, one of the most brilliant and sophisticated high comedies ever written, as a tragicomedy in the low comic manner of *Juno* and *Plough*:

Certainly family politics, the arrangements involved in making and breaking marriages, stand in relation to the larger politics of society as municipal affairs stand in relation to national ones, the smaller politics effected by the larger politics. And this is exactly what we see in Wilde and in O'Casey. Lady Bracknell's handling of the marriage of her daughter to Jack Worthing is carried on in the context of the demands of the larger society (the criteria she applies to Jack and the list of eligible young men she has made up are shared by other mothers in her set); the marriages of the Boyles and of the Clitheroes break up slowly under the variety of pressures of the Irish revolution. But what connects Wilde and O'Casey most meaningfully is their tone of tragicomedy.

In an unusual but stimulating comparison, William A. Armstrong, in "Sean O'Casey, W. B. Yeats and the Dance of Life" (*O'Casey*), assesses the symbolic function of the dance in O'Casey's plays in contrast to parallel motifs in the plays of Yeats. In another very significant comparison, Elizabeth Coxhead, in "Sean O'Casey," *Lady Gregory: A Literary Portrait* (1961; rev. 1966), and Roger McHugh, in "Sean O'Casey and Lady Gregory" (*JJQ*, 1970), explore important aspects of the personal and literary friendship between the aristocratic lady and the proletarian Dubliner. And Lady Gregory herself makes a number of shrewd insights into the personality and early dramatic methods of the younger O'Casey in *Lady Gregory's Journals, 1916–1930* (ed. Lennox Robinson, 1946)—one must say younger rather than young because he was already in his early forties at the start of his writing career. The formative years are also the concern of Herbert Coston who (*TDR*, 1960; rpt. in *O'Casey*) examines some of O'Casey's early nondramatic writing in the decade prior to his first plays. Robert Hethmon, in "Great Hatred, Little Room" (*TDR*, 1961), analyzes the far-ranging satiric aspects of *Kathleen Listens In*, one of O'Casey's earliest experimental and symbolic plays (printed for the first time in this issue of *TDR*), which he says was probably a failure in its first and only production at the Abbey Theatre in 1923 because O'Casey had managed to mock everything sacred in Irish life.

The dramatic language of the early plays is treated effectively by Roger McHugh, who (*TQ*, 1965) concentrates on the comic dialogue that captures the authentic Dublin "tradition of racy idiomatic speech, often alliterative and rhythmically phrased." McHugh also offers some striking illustrations of the rich Dublin idiom, as it appears in the life of the city and in the works of O'Casey and Joyce. By pale comparison, J. A. Snowden's "Dialect in the Plays of Sean O'Casey" (*MD*, 1972), a rather superficial catalog of the obvious, sets out to prove that O'Casey used "authentic Dublin speech" for his dialogue. Unlike McHugh, who like most Irish critics takes a dim view of the later plays, Robert Hogan, in "The Haunted Inkbottle: A Preliminary Study of Rhetorical Devices in the Later Plays of Sean O'Casey" (*JJQ*, 1970), launches an interesting investigation into the linguistic variety in the later comedies, such devices as "parody, pastiche and mis-allusion," alliteration, word-play, derogatory epithets, and comic allusions. For some further studies of O'Casey's language, see Hogan's "The State o' Chassis: A Study of Style," *The Experiments of Sean O'Casey* (1960), and David Krause's "The Playwright as Poet," *Sean O'Casey: The Man and His Work* (1960).

As happens too seldom, Gordon Rogoff, in "Sean O'Casey's Legacy" (*Commonweal*, 23 Oct. 1964), makes a theatrical approach to the later plays, concluding that the real problem is that the right director and the right theater have not yet been found to produce them properly. "Published and frozen before ever reaching the stage the most intriguing of them—'Red Roses for Me,' 'Purple Dust,' 'Time To Go,' and most of all 'Cock-a-Doodle Dandy'—never found *their* director . . . What may well be missing is some gloriously dotty Irish Berlin Ensemble led by an equally improbable Bertolt Littlewood." O'Casey himself didn't approve of the excessive liberties that a director like Joan Littlewood took with playscripts, but Rogoff's prescription for an O'Casey Theatre is clear and urgent.

V. *Criticism of Specific Works*

THE SHADOW OF A GUNMAN (1923)

While Lennox Robinson in *Curtain Up* (1942) insists that *Gunman* is "one of O'Casey's finest plays," Andrew E. Malone, in *The Irish Drama* (1929), is unimpressed by this first play: "Because of its superficiality, and because of its close resemblance to an Irish weekly newspaper in the year 1921, *The Shadow of a Gunman* is merely melodrama . . . that parody of tragedy . . . which must inevitably lose its significance with the passage of time." Many critics have answered the charges of superficiality and melodrama, and furthermore, the resurgence of the gunmen in the stricken Ireland of the 1970's, and their counterparts in countries throughout the world, has intensified the present-day significance of this prophetic play.

Frank O'Connor, in *A Short History of Irish Literature* (1967), points out one of the structural anachronisms in the play, but then he goes on to defend its considerable quality: "This is generally regarded as lightweight O'Casey, which it is not. It has a shocking bit of construction in the first act in which a man called Maguire appears, leaves for a place called Knocksedan, thirty miles away, joins some other Republicans there in an attack on a British column, is killed, identified and reported dead in a Stop Press edition which is on sale in the Dublin streets ten minutes after his departure. Apart from this—the neatest trick in theatrical history—there is nothing in the least immature about the play. Its title, *The Shadow of a Gunman*, might be the title of the whole trilogy."

Since O'Connor also believes that a "guilty" O'Casey was "castigating an aspect of his own character" through Davoren and Shields (see above, under "General Criticism"), it might be relevant to point out here that some critics insist rather that he was castigating or mocking some shadowy aspects of the national excesses in religious, patriotic, and romantic idealism. Michael W. Kaufman, in "The Position of *The Plough and the Stars* in O'Casey's Dublin Trilogy" (*JJQ*, 1970), presents this view as becoming the pervasive theme of the plays that followed:

In O'Casey's sharp contrast between Shields and the artist, Donal Davoren, is the beginning of his examination of the religious, patriotic, and poetic excesses of the Irish imagination, and the way these romantic idealisms distort the characters' practical acceptance of actuality. In its emphasis on individual vanity and collective fantasies of heroic idealism *The Shadow of a Gunman* sets the tone and establishes the theme of the plays to follow where the resulting comical self-delusions and poignant defeat of such fantastic dreamers is given scope.

Then there are some critics like John Jordan who, in "The Irish Theatre—Retrospect and Premonition," *Contemporary Theatre* (Stratford-upon-Avon Studies 4, 1962), say that too much stress has been placed on the comedy, especially on the scene-stealing role of Shields in productions, with the result that the tragic tone and theme have been minimized. Jordan therefore protests that "little attention was paid to the poet Donal Davoren, who is a key-figure not only in this play, but to the whole O'Casey canon." On the other hand, there are those critics who would argue that O'Casey was not at the top of his form with his noncomic characters; that Seumas Shields, in his comic foibles and protective ironies a forerunner of Captain Boyle and Fluther Good and The Prodigal, is an even more persistent and representative "key-figure" for the whole O'Casey canon; that to minimize the organic comedy of this play, of any of the plays, would be to undermine the essential Dickensian power of O'Casey.

Perhaps Kenneth Tynan very effectively brings this problem of how to read and play *Gunman* into sharp focus. In his review of the 1958 revival of the play in New York by the Actors' Studio, in *Curtains* (1961), Tynan insists that it should be performed as volatile comedy rather than contemplative tragedy, and he raises some important questions about precisely how an O'Casey play should and should not be staged:

> O'Casey belongs to the boisterous gallery of Irish satirists, comedians, ironists, and mock-heroic wits who, since the death of Shakespeare, have written nearly everything of lasting importance in what is sardonically known as the English drama. He means us to laugh at the plight of two men trapped in a lie, and he expects of his small-part players the pace and timing of vaudeville. And this is where the Actors' Studio lets him down. Instead of expedition, they give us exploration. Where O'Casey prescribes panic, they offer rational concern . . . they present a number of thoughtful investigations into character, entirely ignoring the element of volatile caricature that is the glory of the play, its essence and its life.

JUNO AND THE PAYCOCK (1924)

It should be no surprise that some conventional critics try to apply the so-called principles of Aristotelian tragedy to Juno Boyle and promptly conclude that while she may be a courageous woman she is not a tragic heroine on the grand scale, even though it must be obvious that O'Casey never intended his tenement mother with the ironically classical name to be cast in a Greek mold. So Curtis Canfield, in "Plays of the Modern Movement," *Plays of the Irish Renaissance* (1929), predictably denies Juno the status of tragic Greek heroine; but then he bestows upon her the vague yet presumably honorific status of pathetic Christian heroine:

> Like Maurya, in the one criterion for all Irish tragedy, *Riders to the Sea*, Juno is a pitiful rather than a truly tragic figure. A chain of unfortunate events bears her spirit heavily down and she cries aloud her grief. That is all. The greatest fault she has, and the one which finally proves her undoing, is her long indulgence of the wretched "Captain." She behaves in too negative a fashion to be described as a tragic heroine, whose true function, if we follow Aristotle, lies in positively breasting the waves of disaster, but, then, she is like all Irish tragic heroines—of the Christian, not the Greek Pagan, type, and we seek and find in her some last vestige of nobility and genuineness remaining in this drunken, chaotic world.

Well, that is not all. It would not be difficult to prove that Maurya and Juno are neither pitiful nor like a Medea; that the "Captain" is much more than "wretched" in his drunken culpability, clever cowardice, and comic complexities; that if Juno has her frailties she is anything but negative and certainly raises her spirit at the end, even if she is fortunately spared the spectacle of "breasting the waves of disaster" in that Victorian sentimentalization of Aristotle. Andrew E. Malone, in *The Irish Drama* (1929), mercifully avoids Aristotle, but he finds some "superficial qualities" in the play, mostly in the comic scenes, especially the antics of Boyle and Joxer, which he finds distasteful in a work that he claims should be "tragic." Therefore he stresses the suffering of Juno and makes her a paragon of motherly nobility. Gerard Fay, in *The Abbey Theatre, Cradle of Genius* (1958), also holds that the comedy should be restrained because "the play is crystal clearly a tragedy in which the principal theme is expressed in the words 'Sacred Heart of Jesus, take away our hearts o' stone, and give us hearts o' flesh! Take away this murdherin' hate, an' give us Thine own eternal love!'"

Even a normally shrewd critic like John Jordan, in "The Irish Theatre—Retrospect and Premonition," *Contemporary Theatre* (Stratford-upon-Avon Studies 4, 1962), worries so much about the farcical elements in the play that he suspects O'Casey's comic genius almost submerges the main element of tragedy in the work: " 'Jackie' Boyle and 'Joxer' Daly cajole and whine and preen and jack-act and inevitably convulse complacent and aware alike. But O'Casey was not concerned with the provision of high farce and lovable clowns. He was scalded at heart by the experience, over forty years, of hunger and disease and brutality, and above all of what they may do to the human spirit." Of course it would be sheer folly to diminish the heart-scalding experience, to diminish the power of Juno's tragic prayer; but it would be equally absurd to diminish the "high farce" (shouldn't it be *low* farce?), to sacrifice the magnificently irresponsible clowns, who, one would like to believe, are something more than "superficially agreeable gargoyles." What may be at issue here is the fact that some critics are apparently still reluctant to accept tragedy *and* comedy in the same play.

George Jean Nathan, in his foreword to *Five Great Modern Irish Plays* (1941), had no such inhibitions and defended the comic vitality of the play in a spirited manner:

> The derogation of O'Casey by certain critics, first among them his fellow countryman and fellow playwright, [St. John] Ervine, as—in the instance of *Juno and the Paycock*—mere superb music-hall seems to me not only obvious critical snobbery, for superb music-hall remains nonetheless still superb, but equally obvious critical superficiality, inasmuch as it overlooks the play's rare comedy scenes' deep roots in dramatic character, the deep penetration into human eccentricity, and withal their beautiful, drunken dramatic literature. They are Molière full of Irish whiskey, now and again Shaw off dietetic spinach and full of red meat, Flanagan and Allen (if such critics insist) in the classical garb of Falstaff and Dogberry.

Another writer who was quick to expose critical snobbery, the Irish poet Patrick Kavanagh, in "Self Portrait," *Collected Pruse* (1967), had an instinctive suspicion of the solemn and elevated style of tragedy, and he aimed a telltale comment that hit some Irish as well as English reviewers: "Anybody can write tragedy. The English reviewers went crazy about the poetry of O'Casey's *Juno*, whereas in fact we only endure that embarrassment for the laughs in Captain Boyle." No doubt he hit an aspect of O'Casey too.

Nathan's Shakespearean allusions are developed by Alice Fox Blitch, who (*MD*, 1972) argues convincingly that O'Casey "was decidedly influenced by Shakespeare's ways of creating character." She illustrates many parallels between the comic characters in the two parts of *Henry IV* and *Juno* and insists that there are structural parallels: "There is a remarkable correspondence between the position of comic scenes in the historical matter of *Henry IV* and their position in the tragical matter of *Juno*. In the first five scenes or episodes of the three plays, for example, scenes two, four, and five are comic. The section of *Juno* in which the wastrels carouse after the tragedy has reached its conclusion, like Act v, scene v of *2 Henry IV*, in which Falstaff is rejected after a great deal of merriment, allows the audience a last glimpse of its 'favorites.'" And literary detectives who may wish to pursue the possibility of some Joycean allusions to *Juno* in *Finnegans Wake* should examine pp. 87.5, 203.20, 245.12, 538.1, 551.4–5.

In what might be an ingenious attempt to resolve the tragic Juno versus comic Paycock issue, William G. McCollom, in *Tragedy* (1957), tries to unite the two characters in an allegorical representation of Ireland: "Juno and her drunken husband constitute a single hero, for the Paycock is Juno's flaw . . . Mr. and Mrs. Boyle are one. . . . Both are Ireland. If Juno's devotion is the glory of her people,

Boyle's irresponsibility is the curse, the Ate, of Ireland. So at last the play builds itself in our minds as the drama not of an individual but of a nation."

Perhaps it is in stage production that a play like *Juno* irresistibly expresses its broadly comic or tragicomic values. When the National Theatre revived the play in London in April 1966, the Director of the Theatre, Sir Laurence Olivier, in an article, "Meditations on *Juno*," printed in the theater program, related O'Casey's tragicomic technique to the performance of counterpoint one experiences in the popular tradition of Irish ballad singing:

> Its switchback ride between hilarity and extreme pathos puts me in mind of a definition by Miss Rose Brennan, the Irish singer, of an Irish "hooley" ("If you're Irish, come into the parlour" is the record O'Casey requires Boyle to put on, so it's all splendidly relevant): "In the middle of the fun somebody will get up and sing a nostalgic song and before you can say Ballaghaderreen we're all crying in our beer. The whole essence of a hooley is this sudden switch from hilarity to sadness and the equally sudden explosion back to noise, song and laughter." . . . I think just possibly O'Casey might have described *Juno* as a "hooley."

THE PLOUGH AND THE STARS (1926)

By more or less common critical agreement, *Plough* is considered to be O'Casey's best play. For Irish nationalists who had rioted against it in the Abbey Theatre, however, and for the present-day patriots who have never forgiven this outrageous insult to the national honor, O'Casey had committed the unforgivable sin of desecrating the heroes of the 1916 Easter Rising. Fortunately, intense patriotism is not a reliable source of literary criticism. For an incisive understanding of the historical and dramatic conflicts in the play, one should turn to Eric Bentley, one of the most perceptive drama critics, who, in "Heroic Wantonness," *In Search of Theatre* (1953), made some shrewd comments that offer perhaps the soundest justification for O'Casey's anti-heroic theme: "In 1916 Yeats felt that a terrible beauty was born, but O'Casey belonged to a class that was the victim rather than the agent of the heroism, and to a generation that saw the heroes degenerate into bureaucrats. 'A terrible beauty is borneo. . . .' " He went on to say that O'Casey was "in reaction against the heroics of the second-rate men. He does not scorn their ideals. He observes that they use these ideals for the deception of others and, sometimes, themselves. Amid the unheroic facts the heroic words are incongruous. From this incongruity springs the tears and laughter of O'Casey's realistic plays." And finally the incisive Bentley concludes: "In *The Plough and the Stars* we see the Easter Rising itself, yet O'Casey shows us, not Pearse and Connolly in the Post Office, but Bessy [sic] Burgess and Fluther Good looting the shops. O'Casey takes no side in the struggle, or rather he takes both sides: he is for the people and against the war. The people's cynicism seems justified, in that, Catholic or Protestant, Republican or Loyal, they have everything to lose by the war. O'Casey nowhere suggests that they have anything to gain." This prophetic passage reflects the timelessness of the play, in relation to the merciless warfare between Catholic and Protestant gunmen in Northern Ireland in the 1970's.

While the patriots were rioting in the Abbey, a group of writers were objecting to O'Casey's literary credentials in the letter columns of the *Irish Statesman* (Feb.–Mar. 1926), led by Liam O'Flaherty, Austin Clarke, and F. R. Higgins. Richard J. Loftus, in *Nationalism in Modern Anglo-Irish Poetry* (1964), examines the literary side of the controversy and identifies O'Casey's "sin" against the nation as his artistic integrity in using ironic truth rather than sentimental idealism: "In these three letters one may perceive the underlying objection to *The Plough and the Stars*. O'Flaherty and Clarke are indignant at what they regard as an insult directed at the Irish people; and Higgins defines the nature of that insult when he accuses O'Casey of wanting sincerity ["Mr. Sean O'Casey, in his new play, entirely lacks the sincerity of an artist."]; for the word 'sincerity,' as it is commonly used by Irish writers and by Irishmen in general, is synonymous with the word 'sentimentality.' O'Casey's sin, like that of Synge in writing another play, was that he failed to sweeten the Irish character with sentiment."

Denis Johnston, another Irish dramatist who refused to sweeten the Irish character, in "Up the Rebels!" *Collected Plays* (Vol. 1, 1960), the ironic introduction to his *The Scythe and the Sunset*, which Johnston calls a parody of *The Plough and the Stars*, sees O'Casey's play as a pacifist work, adding: "also, it may be noticed that the mouthpiece for most of O'Casey's pacificism is provided by his women; whereas in actual fact the women of Ireland, ever since the Maud Gonne era, have been the most vocal part of its militancy." But perhaps Johnston's irony overlooks the stubborn fact that O'Casey's earthy tenement women could not afford Maud Gonne's idealistic luxury of trying to play the role of an Irish Joan of Arc. Michael W. Kaufman (*JJQ*, 1970) draws two very effective analogies for the play. First he reminds us of Denis Johnston's deflating comment, "The birth of a nation is never an immaculate conception" and insists that this remark "captures with remarkable clarity the peculiar entanglements of religious and political attitudes that enmeshed an unwitting Ireland on that fateful Easter Monday in 1916." And in his second analogy, Kaufman says that the *Plough* is "a dramatized embodiment of Yeats's 'Easter 1916,' where casual comedy is transferred utterly, giving birth to terrible tragic beauty of 'needless death.' Like Yeats, O'Casey questions the unforseen results of the 'excess of love'—the bewilderment, the stony-heartedness, the unpredictable changes it elicits—and like the poet, the dramatist explores the abysmal gulf between word and deed, ideal and fact, expressed succinctly in Yeats's awful alliteration, 'they dreamed and are dead.' "

John Jordan, in "The Irish Theatre—Retrospect and Premonition," *Contemporary Theatre* (Stratford-upon-Avon Studies 4, 1962), brings us round again to the problem of tragicomedy; though he has some doubts about this unorthodox mixture of genres in the first two plays, he is convinced that in *Plough* O'Casey successfully links his comic characters to the tragic theme:

The Plough and the Stars remains, I believe, a magnificent play, and unique in the canon for its resolution of a problem which O'Casey had not tried to and would not solve elsewhere. There is again the dual grouping of the redeemable and the unsalvageable, but here for once the unsalvageable catch some of the light that surrounds the good stock and some of the reflected lustre of a revolution in which O'Casey was emotionally deeply involved. The clowns and blatherers participate in the newly born terrible beauty.

In the category of critical disaster, one comes sooner or later to a William Irwin Thompson. Thompson, in "The Naturalistic Image: O'Casey," *The Imagination of an Insurrection: Dublin, Easter 1916* (1967), reveals little understanding of the terrible beauty and less of O'Casey's play; and he goes about his pseudo-Aristotelian ordeal of proving that *Plough* is an unsuccessful play because Nora Clitheroe is an unsuccessful tragic heroine: "O'Casey is trying to lift Nora's laments into the realm of tragedy, but Nora is incapable of understanding her situation, and therefore she is incapable, as a dramatic figure, of generalizing her situation into anything resembling a tragic predicament. . . . Medea, Clytemnestra, Lady Macbeth: these are tragic heroines, but poor Nora is only an object of pity." Of course Nora, like little Mollser, is an object of pity since she is one of the victims of the pervasive tragedy, not its heroine. If there is in fact any heroine in the play it could only be the powerful Bessie Burgess, who, though she is clearly no Clytemnestra, certainly comes to understand her situation in the war-torn tenement and acts decisively and tragically upon that painful knowledge. But the undaunted Thompson presses on to prove that O'Casey's play is also a failure as a political tragedy: he reasons that since "tragedy is not a Marxist genre," according to Trotsky, and O'Casey was a Marxist, according to Thompson, therefore *Plough* cannot be a tragedy. So much for the Covey of literary criticism.

J. L. Styan, in *The Elements of Drama* (1960), calls *Plough* more successful than *Juno* "because the tragic implications flow more smoothly from a source itself potentially comic. In *Juno and the Paycock* the author tries to conjure comedy out of tragedy; in *The Plough and the Stars* he conjures tragedy out of comedy." But perhaps this neat aphorism overlooks the fact that the flexible O'Casey can play his conjuring game with equal dexterity both ways. And Styan doesn't inspire confidence by comparing the comic Rosie Redmond with the offstage Voice of Pearse and concluding that they are "talking of the same thing, the urge to rise above the frustration of the human spirit." In an example of very sound critical research, W. A. Armstrong (*MD*, 1961) traces all the original sources of the offstage Voice in Act II to the actual speeches and writings of the 1916 martyr Padraic Pearse. For an excellent research text, see Bernard F. Dukore's *Documents for Drama and Revolution* (1971), in which he provides some original historical documents as a background for *Plough*: a selection of revolutionary statements by Wolfe Tone, Robert Emmet, Padraic Pearse; and comments on the Easter Rising by Shaw and O'Casey.

In spite of all this revolutionary relevance, there is no room for O'Casey in Robert Brustein's *The Theatre of Revolt* (1964); however, in the midst of a discussion of Brecht's *Mother Courage*, Brustein briefly alludes to *Plough*, only in order to denigrate poor Nora Clitheroe again: "The responses evoked by Brecht's heroine are a good deal more complicated than those evoked, say, by the pathetic Nora Clitheroe, the heroine of another antiwar play, O'Casey's *Plough and the Stars*: Courage is not just a passive sufferer, playing on the sentiment of the audience, but also an active source of suffering." It is incomprehensible why Brustein should have ignored Bessie Burgess, who might more accurately be called O'Casey's heroine, insofar as O'Casey or Brecht is concerned about a heroine here; the brazen and indomitable Bessie, who in her mock-heroic and heroic actions could certainly be compared favorably with Courage.

In a more meaningful comparison between the dramatic techniques of O'Casey and Brecht, Ronald Ayling (*JJQ*, 1970) argues convincingly that O'Casey used his own version of Brecht's theory of "alienation" in *Plough* (see above, under "General Criticism").

This O'Casey-Brecht comparison contains many interesting possibilities, and Herbert Blau, in *The Impossible Theatre* (1964), rings some striking changes on the two playwrights. Having produced *Plough* and *Courage* at his Actor's Workshop theater in San Francisco, Blau is in a formidable position to speak about theatrical as well as literary parallels and contrasts:

> Though O'Casey encourages all the Brechtian vices of empathy and illusion, the principal ironies [in *Plough*] resemble those of *Mother Courage*. The heroic event is undermined by the routine activities of common men; great things are shown up by small. . . . To the American actor, if I can judge from our experience, O'Casey is more immediately appealing than Brecht. He requires gusto and comic ability, but no special technique of feeling, no intellectual wit, beyond knowing how to play and breathe naturally through the racing curiosities of the language. . . . Brecht is not above pathos, but pathos is more strategically deployed and surrounded by an iron curtain for conceptual purposes. A sob can be costly. Pity is ground out of the tough logic of plot. In O'Casey it is always just under the skin and on the tip of the tongue. Brecht is mordantly witty, O'Casey unregenerately humorous, breaking into harshness. He reminds us of Hals; Brecht of Hogarth—at his darkest, of Goya. But O'Casey sings in a register that is rare in Brecht. And when he is aroused, he boils and soars and rages. If he can be appallingly sentimental, he can also shock.

THE SILVER TASSIE (1928)

W. B. Yeats struck the blow that broke O'Casey's vital link with the Abbey Theatre when he rejected *The Silver Tassie*; and in his letter to O'Casey on 20 April 1928, in *The Letters of W. B. Yeats* (ed. Allan Wade, 1954), Yeats stated some of his reasons for the rejection:

The mere greatness of the world war has thwarted you; it has refused to become mere background, and obtrudes itself upon the stage as so much dead wood that will not burn with the dramatic fire. Dramatic action is a fire that must burn up everything but itself; there should be no room in a play for anything that does not belong to it; the whole history of the world must be reduced to wallpaper in front of which the characters must pose and speak.

Yeats had thwarted O'Casey much more than the war had, and in his withering reply, a copy of which he sent to the *Irish Statement* (9 June 1928), along with all the letters from the Abbey directors, O'Casey shot back his uncompromising stand:

I have pondered in my heart your expression that "the history of the world must be reduced to wallpaper," and I find in it only the pretentious bigness of a pretentious phrase. I thank you out of mere politeness, but I must refuse even to try to do it. That is exactly, in my opinion (there goes a cursed opinion again), what most of the Abbey dramatists are trying to do—building up, building up little worlds of wallpaper, and hiding striding life behind it all. . . . It is all very well and very easy to say that "the dramatic action must burn up the author's opinions." The best way, and the only way, to do that is to burn up the author himself.

For some discussion on this crucial controversy, see O'Casey's "The Silver Tassie" and "The Friggin Frogs," *Rose and Crown* (1952); Robert Hogan's " 'The Silver Tassie' Controversy," *The Experiments of Sean O'Casey* (1960); David Krause's "The Playwright's Not for Burning," *Sean O'Casey: The Man and His Work* (1960). The extensive correspondence related to the controversy appears in *The Letters of Sean O'Casey* I, 1910–41 (ed. David Krause, 1975).

The play itself remains an enigmatic challenge to literary and theatrical interpreters, a visionary work of symbolic stagecraft far ahead of its time, and it may turn out paradoxically to be one of the most daring and unsuccessful plays of unmistakable genius in modern drama. Charles Morgan, in his review of the London premiere, in *The Times* (12 Oct. 1929; rpt. in *O'Casey*), called it "a brilliant failure": "But the method and not the drawing of character is the central interest of this play. It is rash; it fails sometimes with a great tumbling failure. But it is a method with a future." A more cautious critic like Curtis Canfield, in "Plays of the Modern Movement," *Plays of the Irish Renaissance* (1929), did not see much of a future for symbolic expressionism in modern drama, and like most of the Irish critics he warned O'Casey to be satisfied with conventional storytelling in the theater: "*The Silver Tassie* opens in the familiar Dublin tenement but the last acts move away from realism into the realm of philosophic expressionism, and the result is an awkward and indecisive play. It may be that O'Casey is in grave danger of making the mistake Eugene O'Neill is guilty of in his last play, the mistake of thinking himself a better philosopher than he is a dramatist and storyteller (the two terms are, of course, synonymous)." And Richard Findlater, in *The Unholy Trade* (1952), while granting O'Casey his powerful pacifist vision, has some doubts about the second act and ends up by echoing Yeats: "Although this is a scene of remarkable power, one can see several flaws fused by the white heat of the dramatist's imagination. There is a weakness of vocabulary, of poetic diction, shown both in the stage Cockney of the soldiers' colloquial speech and in the rhetoric of their choral chants. The images of O'Casey's poetry are ready-made: they do not hold his experience, but someone else's."

Eric Bentley, in "The Case of O'Casey," *The Dramatic Event* (1956), looks at the controversy from another direction and suspects that O'Casey had offended many critics who preferred the sentimental storytelling one finds in a war play like the popular *Journey's End*, in which British gentlemen play at soldiering and die bravely and beautifully: "*The Silver Tassie* gave offence for not being *Journey's End*—that is, for exposing wounds instead of filming them over with gentility." Then Bentley goes on to tackle Yeats: "Yeats was under no obligation to make a success story of Mr. O'Casey's career; he was under no obligation to like *The Silver Tassie*. But, all other questions aside, we may judge his famous rejection of it in terms of the consequences. Yeats did more than any other man to deflect from the theatre one of its two or three best playwrights." And perhaps no one took Yeats's measure more shrewdly than Bernard Shaw. In a letter to O'Casey, written at the time of the controversy and quoted in "The Silver Tassie," *Rose and Crown* (1952), Shaw stated: "If Yeats had said 'It's too savage; I can't stand it,' he would have been in order. . . . Yeats himself, with all his extraordinary cleverness and subtlety, which comes out when you give him up as a hopeless fool, and (in this case) deserts him when you expect him to be equal to the occasion, is not a man of this world; and when you hurl an enormous chunk of it at him, he dodges it, small blame to him."

Many critics have mixed feelings about the play. J. L. Styan, in *The Dark Comedy* (1968), praises "the daring structure of this play . . . which impresses in its attempt to enlarge the audience's vision by effects of calculated irony"; but he finds the ironic edge of the anti-war anguish sometimes too bitter. John Gassner, in "The Prodigality of Sean O'Casey" (*TA*, 1951, rpt. in *O'Casey*), can be eloquent in his praise of O'Casey's genius: "The manifest fact is that O'Casey is a baroque poet in a largely trivial and constricted theatre given over to neat construction and small-beer feeling. He is as baroque, as lavish and prodigal, as were Marlowe, Shakespeare, Jonson, and John Webster. He belongs to the spacious days of the theatre." Nevertheless, when O'Casey tried to be spacious and expanded his baroque and prodigal genius, even Gassner had some reservations: "Beginning with *The Silver Tassie*, his structural sense, so sure in the early days, leaves him at times when the surge of passion or fancy overpowers him in stylized drama."

On the other hand, G. W. Brandt, in "Realism and Parables: From Brecht to Arden," *Contemporary Theatre* (Stratford-upon-Avon Studies 4, 1962), places the *Tassie* in the stylized tradition of Brecht and calls it the best anti-war play in the English language (leaving *Troilus and Cressida* out of consideration for the moment). . . . Perhaps more than any other playwright, O'Casey has managed to cram the essence of modern war into the limits of one single play. But whereas Yeats cherished the notion of a drama "remote, spiritual, and ideal," *The Silver Tassie* assailed the spectator with a long, silent scream of protest, like Helene Weigel's Mother Courage; it protested against man's inhumanity to man; more specifically and more dangerously, it protested against the remediable idiocy of war.

And Ronald Ayling, in "Character Control and 'Alienation' in *The Plough and the Stars*" (*JJQ*, 1970), continues the Brechtian parallel for this play in relation to the technique of "alienation" or "distancing" the audience's emotional responses: "The audience's fluctuating attitude towards Harry Heegan in the course of *The Silver Tassie* is a case in point. . . . While never wholly estranging our sympathies from Harry Heegan, O'Casey makes us view him as self-absorbed and impossibly possessive (an understandable result of his physical incapacity, of course) at significant moments during the last two acts of *The Silver Tassie*, when his selfishness threatens the future welfare or happiness of other people like Jessie, Barney, and even Susie."

Some critics object to the religious symbolism in the play on the grounds that it is anti-Christian, although others feel that it is actually a deeply religious work which mocks the cruel hypocrisy of war, not divine faith; and that it employs the symbolic rituals of the Mass to stress the ironic gap between God's will and man's deeds. Relevant to this issue, Jacqueline Doyle, in "Religious Structure and Imagery in *The Silver Tassie*" (unpublished graduate seminar essay, Brown 1973), says:

> the entire play participates loosely in the structure of the Mass. . . . The first act is the "Mass of the Catechumens," the portion of the Mass open to the uninitiated—O'Casey's "faithful." . . . The second act corresponds to the Offertory of the Mass—offering the soldiers as the sacrificial victims of the "faithful." . . . The third act traces the Consecration, and the reluctant bathing of Simon and Sylvester represents a sort of mock-purification, and certainly the breaking of the Host (Christ's body) is tragically present in Harry Heegan's crippled body. And this leads to the failed Communion of the fourth act.

As an extension of Doyle's strikingly original approach to the four-act structure as "Public Mass—Offertory—Consecration—Eucharist," another member of the seminar, Michael Cervas, was inspired to suggest that the four acts also correspond to the last four days of Christ: "thus Act I includes the Last Supper and Holy Thursday (Gethsemane and the vision of the chalice), Act II is Holy Friday and the Crucifixion (and certainly the crucifix plays a prominent part in the act), Act III is Holy Saturday (with the body interred in the hospital rather than the tomb), and Act IV is Easter Sunday." Doyle includes these comments by Cervas in her paper, and she concludes with the final irony: "Both Acts III and IV contain denials of miracle; the women came to Christ's tomb but Jessie refuses, and, of course, the Resurrection in Act IV is a failed one." Perhaps this unique interpretation brings a whole new dimension to the play.

WITHIN THE GATES (1933)

In their contrasting reviews of the London premiere of *Within the Gates*, Charles Morgan and James Agate reflect some of the varying degrees of praise and scorn that have been associated with this play. Morgan, in *The Times* (8 Feb. 1934), wrote: "Mr. O'Casey's fierce play is that very rare thing—a modern morality play that is not a pamphlet but a work of art. . . . Except in Strindberg and the early O'Neill, there are no precedents for Mr. O'Casey. He is opening up a new country of the imagination from which, by its rigid photography, the fashionable theatre has hitherto been shut out." Agate, in the *Sunday Times* (11 Feb. 1934), called the play "pretentious rubbish," and then went on to explain his phrase in a pretentious qualification: "But first we must do a little ground clearing and explain that 'pretentious rubbish' is not nearly so offensive as it sounds. Grandeur of form may well go with vacuity of content, and it is the latter which makes the thing rubbish and the combination of the two which makes that rubbish pretentious. See Swinburne." See also O'Casey's unpretentious reply to Agate's "rubbish" in his letter to the *Sunday Times* (18 Feb. 1934). The stinging letter (O'Casey was already in the process of becoming "the flying wasp") was reduced to half its length by the editor, but the original version appears in *The Letters of Sean O'Casey* I, 1910–41 (ed. David Krause, 1975).

John Mason Brown, in "Without Mr. O'Casey's Gates," *Two on the Aisle* (1938), his review of the 1934 American premiere, agreed with Agate when he wrote that the characters were puppets, the language pretentious, the satire flat, the humor dull, so that: "as Mr. O'Casey's allegory of post-war disillusionment becomes more and more choked in its condemnation of almost everything from Genesis to Winston Churchill; and as one realizes how flat and tiresome such a muddy attempt at symbolism can prove, one begins to feel a little more friendly to the most trivial examples of realism." On the other hand, Jack Lindsay, in "Sean O'Casey as a Socialist Artist" (*O'Casey*), following in the sympathetic path of Morgan, sees this park allegory as a dramatization of modern man's Fall from Eden, in peace as well as in war: "Here, using Hyde Park as a setting of garden-nature, a pastoral contrast with the city in which it lay, he devised a pageant-allegory in which he sought further to link the inner Christian conflict with the patterns of a class-world in decay. He wanted to show that in the last resort the issues were the same in peace as in war. The play was thus a complement to *The Silver Tassie*, and once again he sought to find a ritual basis. Indeed, this time the correlations were even more thorough. He turned to the Breviary and the Missal." Lindsay supports his interpretation with Saros Cowasjee's *Sean O'Casey: The Man behind the Plays* (1963): "The four seasons, which were further reduced to the component parts of a single day—

Morning, Noon, Evening and Night—are parallel at the religious level to the Canonical Hours of the Breviary. The Spring and Summer choruses are a variation of the psalms of the morning hours, Matins and Lauds. The Winter scene, set in violet, purple and black, symbolises the traditional liturgical colours for penitence and death."

Richard Findlater, in *The Unholy Trade* (1952), finds the failure of *Within the Gates* in O'Casey's inability to control the overindulgent theme and the non-Irish idiom:

> The essence of the play's message, thrust home at every turn, is that life must be lived and enjoyed to the utmost, but that it is thwarted by the hypocrites, the pious and the Puritans. It is a somewhat self-conscious apotheosis of sexual indulgence and youth, the invalid's glorification of health. The language is curiously unexpressive and impersonal, both in the comic Cockney dialogues about evolution and space time, and in the poetry of the Dreamer's songs. Only in the words of the Old Woman, Jannice's mother, is there the real beat and glow and fire of O'Casey's poetry.

R. Mary Todd, in "The Two Published Versions of Sean O'Casey's *Within the Gates*" (*MD*, 1968), makes a careful study of the revisions O'Casey made in the play and discovers a stronger mood of affirmation in the later "Stage Version," a strengthening of the life-force motif in spite of Jannice's death, and a significant humanizing of the "villainous" Bishop:

> The added stress on the Young Woman's courage has something to do with this, but the new treatment of the Bishop has more. Despite the Dreamer's scorn of him as a "poor, purple-button'd dead-man, whose name is absent from the book of life," there is hope that life will claim him as well as Jannice, for he has begun to condemn his own fears and negations and those of the evangelists, and despite his relegation of the Young Woman to the ranks of the Down-and-Outs he reaches the point of praying for the acceptance of her dance by a God who "takes pleasure in his people."

THE STAR TURNS RED (1940)

Perhaps the wasp-shy James Agate was determined to avoid a public quarrel with O'Casey this time, for he hailed the premiere performance of *The Star Turns Red* as "A Masterpiece!" in his review in the *Sunday Times* (17 Mar. 1940). Whatever the psychological or critical reasons for this burst of enthusiasm for one of O'Casey's lesser efforts, Agate's rave notice declared the arrival of a "great" play: "I find the piece to be a *magnum opus* of compassion *and* a revolutionary work. I see in it a flame of propaganda tempered to the condition of dramatic art, as an Elizabethan understood that art." But in contrast to the exuberance of England's foremost critic, George Jean

Nathan, his counterpart in America and a very close friend of O'Casey, was distressed by the political theme, though he admired O'Casey's humanistic intentions. Nathan, in his *Encyclopaedia of the Theatre* (1940), now saw "Communism" as a very dangerous element in O'Casey's art, and he provided a detailed synopsis of *The Star Turns Red* so that the reader might judge how the melodramatic struggle between good Communists and evil Fascists had oversimplified life and drama. John Gassner, in "The Prodigality of Sean O'Casey" (*TA*, 1951; rpt. in *O'Casey*), was not overly impressed by the play, which he felt had "polarized the world into revolutionary and counter-revolutionary factions"; but he also believed that it had appeared at the wrong historical moment, when it was difficult to find sympathetic audiences: "*The Star Turns Red* came out in 1940 during the Soviet-Nazi pact when communism's stock had dropped sharply in the Western world."

Trying to find a politically unbiased audience, John Jordan, in "Illusion and Actuality in the Later O'Casey" (*O'Casey*), treats the play favorably and says that "if we can persuade ourselves to ignore the emotive power of 'Fascists' and 'Communists,' we are confronted with a powerful allegory of the struggle between the powers of darkness, the old order regimented into authoritarianism, and the powers of light, that will usher in the new order of O'Casey's dream." Jack Lindsay, in "Sean O'Casey as a Socialist Artist" (*O'Casey*), examines the political climate and theme of the play in positive terms, though he also recognizes some dramatic problems:

> Behind *The Star Turns Red*, published in 1940, lay the political turmoil caused by the rise of Hitlerism and by the Spanish Civil War. O'Casey sought to bring the whole conflict into the open, dealing with the overt political issues instead of concentrating on the Christian-bourgeois contradictions as in the two previous plays. Indeed he attempted to bring into a single focus his ideas and feelings on three great events, the 1913 Dublin strike, the 1917 Russian Revolution, and the Spanish Civil War. The result is not the simple piece of misguided and misfiring propaganda which it is often described as; but the effort to link the two sides of the political struggle with the two aspects of Christianity only succeeds at moments. Such force as the play owns is largely derived from O'Casey's thinking back to 1913; and yet the world-issues that he raises can hardly be contained in Larkin's Dublin. There is thus a continued chafing between what is concrete and what is abstract or over-generalised in the conception. However, O'Casey was regaining his power to translate what he felt of the world's deep conflicts into dramatic terms rooted in his early vital experiences in Ireland.

Some critics contend that it was precisely because O'Casey felt so deeply about these political conflicts that he was not sufficiently able to establish the esthetic objectivity necessary for drama. For example, Pat M. Esslinger, in "Sean O'Casey and the Lockout of 1913: Materia Poetica of the Two Red Plays" (*MD*, 1963), claims that he was too emotionally involved in the 1913 strike and lockout to be able to write a successful play on the subject: "He fails in these two last plays [*The Star Turns Red* and *Red Roses for Me*], not because he was not interested in the subject, as Yeats said of his *Silver Tassie* failure, but because he is too immersed in it. The subject, the Dublin strike of 1913 with its inherent Communism, is too ingrained to be rewoven into successful drama." Nevertheless, Esslinger blurs or avoids a series of key questions here: First, wasn't it only the prosperous Dublin employers and the Roman Catholic hierarchy who tried to discredit Jim Larkin and the 1913 strikers by calling them part of a "communist" attempt to undermine Irish life and faith, rather than recognizing the strike as the first attempt to organize the unskilled workers in a bona fide union? Second, if the "Red" in *The Star Turns Red* is clearly a communist symbol, what reason is there not to believe the same about the "Red" in *Red Roses for Me*? And last, is it O'Casey's excessive immersion in the subject of the strike or is it the fact that the theme deals with communism that defeated him in *The Star Turns Red*? Is Esslinger, like some politically inhibited critics, trying to say that it is not possible to write a play about communism that is also successful as drama?

Eric Bentley deplores the scare-tactic of using an expression like "communist playwright," and in "The Case of O'Casey," *The Dramatic Event* (1956), he voices his suspicion that O'Casey had apparently broken some unwritten genteel rule simply by writing a political play: "*The Star Turns Red* gave offence for turning red—when the palette of a Cecil Beaton or an Oliver Messel had so many other colors to offer. It was opposed in England not for its brand of politics but for being political at all."

PURPLE DUST (1940)

It is probably accurate to say that every play O'Casey wrote was political in some sense, although it would be misleading to describe him as a political playwright. The politics of *Purple Dust*, for example, must be one of the lesser aspects of the play, certainly not as important as the mock-pastoral framework that controls the whole work, the overall satiric theme with its broadly comic innovations, and the visionary Celtic motifs and resolution. John J. McLaughlin, in "Political Allegory in O'Casey's *Purple Dust*" (*MD*, 1970), calls O'Casey a "romantic Marxist" who fortunately had the saving grace of comedy.

So while some critics worry about O'Casey's political themes, others argue over the sources of his comedy. R. B. Parker (*QQ*, 1966) stresses the Shavian influence and tells us that "*Purple Dust* is the O'Casey play closest in structure to *John Bull's Other Island*." But Ronald G. Rollins (*ShawR*, 1967), after pointing out some minor similarities of theme in the two plays, concludes that the dramatic techniques and characterizations are quite different: "Hence *John Bull's Other Island* is essentially a Shavian discussion drama, a long, sustained cerebral orchestration, while *Purple Dust* frequently approaches farce, repeatedly relying on cardboard characters who romp through stock situations merely for the sake of the action itself." No doubt some critics will in turn object to that curiously phrased "merely" and insist that of course the farcical romping is carried out for the very specific sake of the satiric and mock-pastoral rituals. And Walter C. Daniel (*BNYPL*, 1962) considers the characters and situations neither cardboard nor stock, for he traces their origins back to the dramatic types and structures of Aristophanic comedy. He illustrates how O'Casey's play follows the "ritual patterns of Old Greek Comedy and the comic resolution to New Greek Comedy": the conventions of the *agon*, the *parados*, the Dionysian revelry, the sexual raillery, and the victorious resolution—all these Aristophanic elements of ritual comedy, according to Daniel, can be found in *Purple Dust*. From another point of view, B. L. Smith, in "O'Casey's Satiric Vision" (*JJQ*, 1970), traces the comic characters back to Synge: "The Irishmen in *Purple Dust* are close kinsmen to Synge's tramps and tinkers: existence and the necessities of life are not their prime concerns; nor are they conspicuously nationalistic. They revel in freedom and joy and life."

The strategies of language are the main concern of Robert Hogan (*JJQ*, 1970). He indicates how some of the rhetorical devices in *Purple Dust* are based upon a variety of exaggerations and extravagances: "The language of the play is similarly extravagant, and its most notable devices are parody, pastiche and mis-allusion." The parody covers "stage-Irish dialogue," "philosophical discourse," "art criticism," and "stock patriotism." Next Hogan sees an ironic debt to Synge. Finally, the conversation of Poges is full of "erronious allusions . . . so drolly unexpected in their details that the play is lifted up into the realm of lyrical nonsense."

Jack Lindsay, in "Sean O'Casey as a Socialist Artist" (*O'Casey*), makes two important observations about the use of mythic and Christian rituals in *Purple Dust* that expand the artistic range of his socialist credo. First, Lindsay points out: "O'Casey . . . draws on Irish mythology for imagery of heroic liberation and renewal, and, in so doing, brings it vigorously to life; he, whom Yeats rejected, here achieves the very things Yeats long wanted to do—to vivify the mythic images by linking them effectively with modern life and its issues." Secondly, Lindsay underscores the fact that in *Purple Dust* O'Casey "dispenses with the elaborate symbolic structures such as he used in *The Silver Tassie, Within the Gates*, and even *The Star*, and trusts to his imaginative verve as he opposes the deathly elements in established Christianity to a sort of fertility creed. This creed is wholeheartedly pagan, and yet is linked with the aspects of revolt and life-assertion that have kept on reappearing in Christianity at the popular levels, where they revived the spirit of the Magnificat and the hope of earth as a paradise regained."

RED ROSES FOR ME (1942)

On several occasions Eric Bentley has pointed out what he believes to be the major strengths and weaknesses of *Red Roses for Me*. Commenting on the printed text of the play, in "Drama Now" (*PR*, 1945; rpt. in *What Is Theatre?, Incorporating The Dramatic Event and Other Reviews, 1945–1967,* 1968), he wrote: "Its strength lies in familiar O'Casey virtues—rich dialogue, strong situation, deeply-felt characters, stark contrasts of mood and texture. The weakness of the piece is its failure to exist in its own right: it is made up of pieces of the O'Casey we already know." Reviewing the 1955 New York production of *Red Roses,* in "A Funny Sort of Red," *What Is Theatre?* (1956), Bentley wrote: "Mr. O'Casey is neither anti-protestant nor anti-catholic, and is able to play one faction off against the other in a riot of loving fun. It is the capitalists he hates; and is unable to portray; instead, the ruling class is 'symbolized' by a police inspector —a cartoon, as it were, by one of *The Daily Worker*'s less gifted collaborators." He concludes, "For Communism will pass, but Mr. O'Casey's clowns will endure forever."

Although it is probably difficult to object to this assessment of the strengths and weaknesses of the play, Harold Clurman, reviewing the 1955 New York production, in *Lies like Truth* (1958), called it "one of the more successful of O'Casey's later plays. Better balanced than most of the other plays in his 'second manner,' it combines the earthy folk realism of his first work and the later attempt to invest that quality with a more conscious, stylized and exalted lyricism." And Allardyce Nicoll, in *World Drama* (1949), sees mainly the poetic or visionary strengths of the play:

> *Red Roses For Me* is a magnificent colourful fantasy, with a poetic dialogue that soars and sears, with a fine distillation of that tragic sense, that irony, and that comedy he is so skilful in intermingling into an impressive whole. There is a central figure here in Ayamonn, but again the vision goes beyond the individual. What is memorable in the play is the mass effect of the whole, the miseries and the splendours of the unemployed and the flower-girls, the quiet searching of the uttermost reaches in the ironic graveyard scene, the philosophical atmosphere which enwraps the entirety of the action. O'Casey has no need to prate about an epic theatre: by his genius, whatever its failures, he has succeeded in creating a theatrical impression of the epic sweep which goes far beyond anything achieved by any of his contemporaries.

In a parallel expression of unqualified praise, but with a different emphasis, A. G. Stock, in "The Heroic Image: *Red Roses For Me*" (*O'Casey*), maintains that the heroic characters, Ayamonn and his mother, are more significant than the epic impression of the play. After comparing Mrs. Breydon to Juno Boyle, Bessie Burgess, and O'Casey's own mother, Stock tells us that although O'Casey had often created heroic women,

> Ayamonn Breydon is his only full-length study of a heroic man in action. He is conceived somewhat in the spirit of epic, at once mythical and authentic; an ideal image, but shapely by real experience of workers' life. He is not the creature of a doctrine, and is a long way from the fanatical politician abominated by Yeats, whose heart has been made a stone by too long a sacrifice.

He is pictured as a whole man, whose capacity to use the riches
of the world to the full gives him a natural right to possess them.
In sheer excess of life he takes death in his stride, and the con-
tinuance of the world is his immortality.

The essence of this play must lie somewhere between the qualifica-
tions of Bentley and the exaltations of Stock.

OAK LEAVES AND LAVENDER (1946)

This play, together with *The Star Turns Red*, is usually considered
to be O'Casey's least successful work, mainly because the dramatic
action is often overwhelmed by the blatantly stated political views. In
his review of the 1947 London production of the play, in *Theatre*
(1948), Harold Hobson offered some limited praise of O'Casey's original use of fantasy, but he concluded that "on the whole the play does
not succeed in its intention of showing that fustian and tweeds may
be as brave as fine linen. Why not? Partly, I think, because too much
of Mr. O'Casey's eloquence is just eloquence and nothing more; it is
big words used bigly without regard to characters or circumstance;
and though it tickles the ears, it does not always, or even often, move
the heart." Jules Koslow, in *The Green and the Red: Sean O'Casey,
the Man and His Plays* (1950), strains in his attempt to admire the
"heroism" of the play, calling it "an elaborate picture of heroism
under the most difficult circumstances. There is no despair and no
shirking. Danger is met full-face, and impending death does not scar
the full-flush of vibrant life vigorously lived." But even he cannot fail
to point out, for example, that Drishogue's "speeches defending the
Soviet Union very often sound like an editorial from a Communist
newspaper or an order of the day from the Soviet High Command."
Richard Findlater, in *The Unholy Trade* (1952), is uneasy about
the mixture of pro-British and pro-Soviet sympathies in *Oak Leaves*,
but he locates the main weakness of the play in the characterizations:
"None of these characters are credible human beings, except for Free-
lim, the Irish butler, who has the best lines in the play, none have any
symbolic reality, and all have a curious confusion of stilted speech."
Jack Lindsay, in "Sean O'Casey as a Socialist Artist" (*O'Casey*), who
agrees with the play's politics, attributes its failure to the fact that the
British background was alien to O'Casey's experience and imagination. He contends that *Oak Leaves* "reverses the symbolism of *Purple
Dust*. As the British get down to the anti-fascist war, the backward-
looking elements fade out and the past is valuably drawn into the
present. But, despite Feelim, the English setting held O'Casey back
from the full release of his imaginative realism."

Some of the theatrical techniques in the play are daring and even
exciting in their conception, like the masque-like Prelude and Epilogue. Robert P. Murphy, in "Sean O'Casey and 'The Bald Primaqueera'" (*JJQ*, 1970), makes this observation: "Through various uses
of music and lights in *Oak Leaves and Lavender* Nazism is made all
the more threatening because of the vagueness of its particular evil."

COCK-A-DOODLE DANDY (1949)

Although *Cock* is generally considered to be the most successful of the later plays, some critics remain singularly unamused by its ingenious comedy. For example, J. L. Stylan, in *The Dark Comedy* (1968), is convinced that this play illustrates "the sad demise of the later O'Casey." He feels that the didacticism undermines the comedy, that the theme of vitality versus repression is handled too mechanically. Herbert Blau, in *The Impossible Theatre* (1964), who is willing to grant O'Casey the seemingly simple terms of his good versus evil conflict in the later plays because it is an inherent condition of the morality play structure, goes on to raise the unavoidable issue that O'Casey may have had problems with his noncomic or heroic characters, particularly in *Cock*:

> If the sides are more clearly drawn in the later plays—the golden lads and girls against the forces of darkness—it is not because drama has turned into morality (there is nothing simplistic about morality), but because O'Casey had never been able to do very well with the prime sources of light. In *Cock-a-Doodle Dandy*, Lorna and Loreleen are very inconsiderable characters, the maid Marion has a stereotyped bounce, and the Messenger Robin Adair has a major function in a minor key. The early plays are scarcely free of this naïveté, but they are also more urgent.

Those critics who insist on making a strong case for the heroic affirmations in the later plays will surely have to find a way to reply to Blau's objection to "the prime sources of light." Perhaps Ronald G. Rollins and Jack Lindsay make an important if only partial reply when they argue with considerable persuasion for an approach based on ritualistic or folk traditions. Rollins, in "Clerical Blackness in the Green Garden: Heroine as Scapegoat in *Cock-a-Doodle Dandy*" (*JJQ*, 1970), treats the play as a ritualistically dark comedy of "purification by sacrifice." He relates the play to the myth of the dying god in Frazer and Jung, but adds that O'Casey ironically discarded "the motifs of redemption and resurrection central to scapegoat-fertility procedures. . . . So O'Casey modifies the myth to accentuate the trauma and tyranny of a sin-sick society intent on preserving its old, confining traditions, especially religious ones. Tragically, the black world defeats the green one." Jack Lindsay, in "Sean O'Casey as a Socialist Artist" (*O'Casey*), believes that in his four pastoral plays— *Purple Dust, Cock-a-Doodle Dandy, The Bishop's Bonfire, The Drums of Father Ned*—O'Casey "achieved what may be called the only true recreation of Aristophanic comedy ever made," an achievement, he adds, which is most successfully rendered in *Cock*: "Above all in *Cock-a-Doodle Dandy* he produced a remarkable work: in it wild fantasy has the earthy reality which it has in Aristophanes and which seems to owe nothing to literary invention, but to spring directly, with absolute and ecstatic relevance, from folk-experience." The ritualistic structure of the play may be more sustained than the rhetorical texture, for Robert Hogan, in "The Haunted Inkbottle: A Preliminary Study of Rhetorical Devices in the Late Plays of Sean O'Casey" (*JJQ*, 1970), finds a limited scope of rhetorical devices to explore here: "*Cock-a-Doodle Dandy* is usually considered among the best—indeed, perhaps the best—of the late plays. It is somewhat curious, then, that the play is not rhetorically too interesting. There is some humor in Sailor Mahon's nautical diction, but this is a quite stereotyped device of comic rhetoric and handled with no great flair by O'Casey. There is a good deal of alliteration. . . . Perhaps the most engaging device is the 'Latin-lusthrous' language. This would include the playful dog-Latin which O'Casey often used also in the auto-biographies as a device of genial satire . . . and the incongruous use and misuse of polysyllables derived from the Latin, and juxtaposed against the ordinary monosyllabic diction of colloquial discourse."

On a matter that probably still remains an open argument, Robert P. Murphy, who in "Sean O'Casey and 'The Bald Primaqueera' " (*JJQ*, 1970), sets out to prove that O'Casey's later theater has a closer affinity to Artaud's theater of cruelty and violence than O'Casey was willing to admit, refers to a violent incident in *Cock* to support his case: "Jack, the lorry driver in *Cock-a-Doodle Dandy*, is killed when he is 'accidentally' struck too hard by Father Domineer, a death that goes apparently unpunished and almost unnoticed, but is nonetheless there in true Artaudian fashion." There is less argument, however, about the sense of theatrical freedom and technical innovation in this play; and people working in the theater are generally more receptive to these liberating qualities than some tradition-bound critics. For example, Philip Burton, who directed *Cock* and many other O'Casey plays in America, in "Something to Crow About: An Approach to *Cock-a-Doodle Dandy*" (*TA*, 1958), illustrates how O'Casey success-fully breaks all the so-called "rules" of theater and drama in this uninhibited work, cheerfully mixing the realistic and the surrealistic, the music-hall and the pulpit, the farcical and the profound.

THE BISHOP'S BONFIRE (1955)

This play created a mild furor when it was first performed in Dublin in 1955, and two of the visiting British critics, Kenneth Tynan and Harold Hobson, reviewed the Irish audience as well as the play. Tynan's review, in *The Observer* (6 Mar. 1955; rpt. in *Curtains*, 1961), began with this rebuke to the Irish:

> Truly, the Irish never forgive those they have insulted. Back from long exile came Sean to Dublin, and his compatriots hissed his play at the curtain fall. At the first night of Mr. O'Casey's *The Bishop's Bonfire* there were more stage Irishmen in the house than in the cast, and by the first interval venomous tongues were already lamenting the play's failure. Those who had uprooted the author now charged him with having forgotten his roots; those who had expelled him from the parish charged him with being too parochial.

Tynan continued with a rebuke for O'Casey too, as well as some considerable praise, for he found the playwright at his best in the scenes of broad comedy, heavy-handed with his serious theme of religious repression. The play was written in what Tynan called a "manic-depressive" mood, not one but "two plays, one ghastly, one gorgeous, in unhappy juxtaposition. The depressive (or serious) theme is youth's subservience to authority. What matters is the manic half of the play. Here, dealing with the wild inconsequent rustics who are redecorating Ballyoonagh for the Bishop's impending visit, Mr. O'Casey hits his full stride as the old mocker and fantastic ironist, ever happier with tongue in cheek than hand on heart."

Harold Hobson, in a special review for the *Christian Science Monitor* (12 Mar. 1955), more or less in agreement with Tynan, called the play "clumsy" with "flashes" of the O'Casey genius for comedy, and he too felt he had to assess the audience as well: "The protests of much of the audience and of influential parts of Irish opinion were not aesthetic, but political and religious. Mr. O'Casey is a rebel socially and philosophically; he is essentially a Protestant in the sense that he protests; and he protests with passion, with eloquence, with perversity, and with fire. This does not go down well in Ireland, where orthodoxy is more highly regarded than it is, for example, in England or France."

If the British critics had reviewed the Irish audience as well as the play, the Irish critics reviewed the anticlerical exile as well as his play. As the defenders of Irish orthodoxy, all the Dublin reviewers said no, both to the "blasphemous" man and to his "incendiary" play. The editors of the ultra-montaine *Standard* even pre-reviewed the play (18 Feb. 1955) two weeks before it opened, condemning it in advance without having read or seen it; the fact that an "enemy" of Ireland had written it was evidence enough. For a fairly representative justification of an Irish critic's rejection of the play, see Gabriel Fallon's *Sean O'Casey, The Man I Knew* (1965), Chapter xii, where Fallon calls the work doomed from the start by the playwright's "excessive hatred" of Ireland and Roman Catholicism.

Robert Hogan sees the imperfections in the play—its excesses of sadness, melodrama, and didacticism, rather than any calculated hatred—in "In Sean O'Casey's Golden Days" (*DM*, 1966; rpt. in *O'Casey*), but he argues very convincingly that the work was written in the comic spirit and structure of the pastoral tradition:

> *The Bishop's Bonfire* is subtitled "A Sad Play within the Tune of a Polka," and might best be described as a lament for the passing of the Golden Age, for in it the Pastoral world is almost extinguished. . . . In this play the Pastoral figures are either beaten or exiled, leaving the blighted wasteland to the priest and the Papal count. The old sage Codger is the most indomitable figure, but he is almost ninety. . . . The play contains many other qualities of the Pastoral—the complicated love plots, the swains and nymphs, the old shepherd and the satyrs, and a delightful assembly of clowns, buffoons, and rustics.

Moving from Pastoral to Punch and Judy, Katharine Worth, in "O'Casey's Dramatic Symbolism" (*MD*, 1961, rpt. in *O'Casey*), tries to account for and justify the dark themes and symbols in the later comedies:

> The grim or ugly ideas challenged in his plays often find expression through comical symbols like the 'bookaneeno boyo' in *The Bishop's Bonfire*, just as his profound feeling for the sanctity of life is so often symbolised by a high-spirited dance. Father Boheroe, in *The Bishop's Bonfire*, tells Daniel and Keelin that God is laughing at the 'punch and judy show of Ballyoonagh.' It is on the pattern of a Punch and Judy show that much of O'Casey's comic symbolism is built. . . . The Harlequins and Columbines of the Commedia del Arte [*sic*] are reflected in O'Casey's figures in fancy dress, top hats, black robes, and mayoral chains engaged in an unending combat with Pierrettes, gipsies, and scarlet Cocks.

THE DRUMS OF FATHER NED (1959)

Clearly Katharine Worth's stress on the influence of the Punch and Judy symbolism and Robert Hogan's evidence of pastoral sources have an even greater relevance to O'Casey's last full-length play, the festive *Drums of Father Ned*. Hogan, who co-directed and acted in the world premiere performance of the play at Lafayette, Indiana, in 1959, in "In Sean O'Casey's Golden Days" (*DM*, 1966; rpt. in *O'Casey*), sees it as an excellent example of the pastoral mode:

> *The Drums of Father Ned* is a triumph. Its dominant mood is as gay as *The Bishop's Bonfire* was sad. It is as if some of O'Casey's own indomitability, muted in *The Bishop's Bonfire*, suddenly blazed out to make what is in every sense a brilliant play. The story again concerns the clash between the loveless world of today and the vital Pastoral past. The modern world is represented again by elderly businessmen and a priest, and the Pastoral world by a large group of golden lads and lasses. . . . The basic ingredients of the Pastoral are present. There are two pairs of young lovers, a delicious comic satyr and coy nymph scene in Act II, and clowns and rustics aplenty.

It is important to take note of this nice paradox, the extent to which a rebellious and innovative playwright like O'Casey was apparently following some of the traditional modes and conventions of drama in his later plays. Another aspect of this point is picked up by G. Wilson Knight and William A. Armstrong in their exploration of classical analogues in *The Drums of Father Ned*. Knight, in "Ever a Fighter: *The Drums of Father Ned*," *The Christian Renaissance* (1962; rpt. in *O'Casey*), discusses the two dominating symbols of the play, Father Ned and Angus the Young, in terms of the Nietzschean dualism of Dionysus and Apollo, "the one aural and mysterious, the other visual and seraphic." Knight also sees Father Ned "as covering the best of both Catholicism and Protestantism, the traditional authority of the one and the critical impetus of the other." And he associates Angus with "the Platonic Eros, with all its multi-directional potentialities; he is also Apollo, god of art, with his harp; and a bird, for aspiration to higher spheres." This is a very illuminating essay on O'Casey's last major play.

William A. Armstrong, in "The Irish Point of View: The Plays of Sean O'Casey, Brendan Behan, and Thomas Murphy," *Experimental Drama* (ed. William A. Armstrong, 1963), draws some significant parallels between Greek and Irish myth:

> *The Drums of Father Ned* is the most joyous expression of the Dionysiac spirit of O'Casey's later plays. . . . O'Casey's Tostal also resembles the *komos*, the vintage festival of ancient Greece, in which a procession of revellers carried the emblem of Dionysus, the fertility god, sang songs in his praise, and ridiculed those bystanders who were not participating in their celebrations. . . . Correspondingly, O'Casey's youthful revellers mock and bewilder their elders, follow a banner with a harp on it, and speak the praises of Angus, the god of youth and beauty, with his harp and his brilliant birds.

Phillip L. Marcus, in "Addendum on Joyce and O'Casey" (*JJQ*, 1965), comments on the link between the two writers in Michael Binnington's echoing of Stephen Dedalus' phrase that God is "but a shout in the street"—a parallel that several critics have identified. But then Marcus goes on to suggest a direct connection between God and the mysterious and all-powerful Father Ned, who is described in the play as "the burnin' bush," and who, Marcus insists, "is meant to be a portrait of the Deity Himself (modified, of course, to conform with peculiarly O'Caseyan standards). . . . A few pages later, Father Fillifogue's henchmen the Town Clerk and the Mace Bearer mysteriously drop dead. The cause? A shout in the street. Who made the shout? Father Ned."

John Jordan, in "Illusion and Actuality in the Later O'Casey" (*O'Casey*), points out some of the ironies that accompanied the background and banning of the play:

> For *The Drums of Father Ned*, O'Casey drew on the materials for satire and for celebration provided by the second Tóstal of 1954, a kind of National Festival which was abandoned after a few years. . . . This is the most joyous of all O'Casey's plays, written in a mood of optimism, and comparatively mild in its satiric railing. . . . It was the first play since 1928 and *The Silver Tassie* that O'Casey had sent, admittedly by request, to a Dublin-based management. Thirty years after the obtuseness of Yeats came the obtuseness of the directors of the Globe Theatre Company, who wanted "changes" in the play. O'Casey of course withdrew it, and imposed a ban on all professional performances of his plays in Ireland.

In making his catalog of the obtuse, Jordan has not completed his list, for he fails to mention the "obuseness" of the Archbishop of Dublin, whose disapproval of the works of O'Casey and Joyce (a dramatization of *Ulysses*, along with *The Drums of Father Ned*, had been scheduled for the 1958 Dublin International Theatre Festival) was a significant factor in the unfortunate controversy that provoked O'Casey to ban his plays. For a discussion of the whole controversy, see David Krause, "Bonfires and Drums," *Sean O'Casey: The Man and His Work* (1960).

THE AUTOBIOGRAPHY (1939–54)

Using many of the open techniques of drama and fiction, with a third person narrative point of view, O'Casey tells the impressionistic story of his life in six volumes: *I Knock at the Door* (1939); *Pictures in the Hallway* (1942); *Drums under the Windows* (1945); *Inishfallen, Fare Thee Well* (1949); *Rose and Crown* (1952); *Sunset and Evening Star* (1954). It was later issued in a two-volume edition under the title *Mirror in My House* (1956). Like everything he wrote, this monumental justification of his life and art divided the critics. Padraic Colum, in "The Narrative Writings of Sean O'Casey" (*IW*, 1948; rpt. in *O'Casey*), appropriately compares O'Casey's ironic point of view in the autobiography with the technique in George Moore's *Hail and Farewell* and with the satiric brilliance of *The Vision of MacConglinne*. But then Colum objects to what he calls the excessive "Joycean" aspects of O'Casey's stream-of-consciousness style: "The author is a great writer who has a great fault. That fault is wilfulness—an abandonment to his own issues and his own idiom. There is in *Pictures in the Hallway* a description of the end of Parnell as it effects Johnny's family: it begins magnificently, goes on memorably. But we come to lose patience when he turns Joycean on us and keeps on with anything that comes into his head."

Some critics try to deal with O'Casey's "Joycean" manner in more organic and constructive ways. Hubert Nicholson, in "The O'Casey Horn of Plenty," *A Voyage to Wonderland and Other Essays* (1947; rpt. in *O'Casey*), confronts the comparison with a refreshing point of view:

He has been accused lately of imitating (I suppose "imitating badly" is meant) James Joyce. He is certainly no Daedalus, no maze-maker, as Joyce is; but to me he seems the one completely natural inheritor of some of the Joyce techniques: some of the methods of word-minting, the punning and portmanteauing into multiple meanings, and that melting from place to place, as the emotion roused by a scene seems to dissolve the outer appearances and show something else underneath. Joyce did not patent his methods; when they were invented they were available at once, for all: "my sword I give to him that shall succeed me in my pilgrimage, and my courage and skill to him that can get it." That is the law; and O'Casey is the man, for all the tremendous differences between him and Joyce. (Personally, I like his neologisms, his "soulos" and "insectarianism" and "chasubulleros bullen a laws.")

In a somewhat similar vein, Marvin Magalaner, in "O'Casey's Autobiography" (*SR*, 1957; rpt. in *O'Casey*), draws a number of apt comparisons between Joyce's treatment of Stephen Dedalus and O'Casey's treatment of Johnny Casside; and he shrewdly illustrates how O'Casey uses the traditional techniques of *Stephen Hero* as well as the experimental techniques of *A Portrait of the Artist as a Young Man*.

Some critics see only the flaws, and for a view of the autobiography as a "second-rate" work, see Ulick O'Connor's "The Autobiographies of Sean O'Casey," *The World of Sean O'Casey* (ed. Sean McCann, 1966). Even the usually reliable Eric Bentley nods over the autobiography, but mainly with the motivation of an admirer of O'Casey's drama who is pained to think of all the unwritten plays in those six volumes. In "The Case of O'Casey," *The Dramatic Event* (1956), Bentley writes: "Though diffuse, and blemished by self-pity and proletarian snobbery, the autobiography, half of the time, is as good as the blurbs say it is; one shakes one's head, not over what O'Casey has written, but over what he has been side-tracked from writing; the autobiography is *ersatz*; the best passages are scenes from plays that will never be written; scenes by a playwright without a theatre." If further proof were needed to support this notion that there are many excellent dramatic scenes in the autobiography, perhaps it has been supplied by the adaptation of several of the early volumes for stage presentation; by Paul Shyre in New York: *I Knock at the Door* (1956), *Pictures in the Hallway* (1956), *Drums under the Windows* (1960); and by Patrick Funge and David Krause in Dublin: *Pictures in the Hallway* (1965), *Drums under the Windows* (1968), *Inishfallen, Fare Thee Well* (1972).

Then there are the critics who think that O'Casey's "reputation may ultimately rest more on the autobiographies than the plays," as David H. Greene suggests in "A Great Dramatist's Approach to Autobiography" (*Commonweal*, 25 Jan. 1957). Greene states that the autobiographies "became the stage where his genius has found more congenial surroundings. Certainly few of his plays can compete with the variegated farce of 'Cat 'n Cage,' the melodramatic violence passing quickly into sex and farce in 'The Raid,' the tragedy of a small boy bewildered by the comedy attendant upon his father's funeral in 'His Father's Funeral,' or the many people who pass briefly through the pages of *Mirror in My House*." Without in any way belittling the brilliance of these examples, some critics can probably find early and late O'Casey plays to compete favorably with them.

Perhaps the tentative last word should be given to Brooks Atkinson, the drama critic and nonidolatrous friend of O'Casey, who, in the introduction to his *The Sean O'Casey Reader* (1968), described the autobiography as "a conscious work of art," a mythic, not a literal, record of life: "O'Casey tells the story of his life in terms of a grand myth, like Joyce's 'Ulysses,' and, in some elusive manner, the Old Testament, as if his own life were a footnote to the mythology of mankind, part of the 'sad, sweet silent music of humanity.' . . . The

point of view is detached, as if the volumes were fiction, but the style
is overwhelmingly personal. Some of it is fantastically comic; some of
it is fiercely proud; some of it explodes with anger. It is also, I think, a
lonely book by a man separated from the centers of activity and
recalling with nostalgia things that happened long ago."

THE MODERN DRAMA*

Robert Hogan, Bonnie K. Scott, and Gordon Henderson**

Until the 1960's, little critical attention was given to aspects of the Irish theater other than the Abbey and a handful of its playwrights, chiefly Yeats, Synge, and O'Casey. The great growth of Irish studies in the last decade has, however, directed critical attention to other theaters and other playwrights. Some basic documents have been reprinted or, indeed, printed for the first time. Some major figures, notably Synge and Lady Gregory, have appeared in collected editions, as have some hitherto neglected figures, such as George Fitzmaurice, Oliver Gogarty, Jack B. Yeats, and Austin Clarke.

There remains, nevertheless, much important work to be done. No satisfactory one-volume history of the entire period is available; there is no adequate bibliography; there is no full and judicious anthology; many significant plays are long out of print or have never reached print at all; and, as Section IV of this essay indicates, many important figures remain almost totally unevaluated.

A multivolume documentary history by Robert Hogan and James Kilroy, *The Modern Irish Drama*, which began appearing in 1975, should make available much basic information, such as authoritative cast lists of important first productions; the history of the Abbey Theatre should be more factually documented in a forthcoming book by

---

* In addition to the abbreviations used throughout this volume, the titles of several books frequently mentioned in this chapter have also been abbreviated, as follows. *AIR*: Robert Hogan, *After the Irish Renaissance*; *CDI*: Ernest Boyd, *The Contemporary Drama of Ireland*; *FCT*: *Flight from the Celtic Twilight*, ed. Des Hickey and Gus Smith; *HAT*: *Joseph Holloway's Abbey Theatre* (ed. Hogan and Michael J. O'Neill); *ID*: Andrew E. Malone, *The Irish Drama*; *IT*: *The Irish Theatre* (ed. Lennox Robinson); *LPIR*: *Lost Plays of the Irish Renaissance* (ed. Hogan and James Kilroy); *PCI*: *Plays of Changing Ireland* (ed. Curtis Canfield); and *SIP*: *Seven Irish Plays* (ed. Hogan).

** Sections I–IV of this essay are primarily the responsibility of Hogan, and Section V is primarily the responsibility of Scott and Henderson.

Hugh Hunt, who has been given exclusive access to the theater's archives; but short, factual studies of particular aspects of the Irish theater, such as the ones in progress by E. H. Mikhail on the Gate Theatre and by Harold Ferrar on the Dublin Drama League, will be of much utility.

Useful also would be a collection of the plays of Gerald Mac-Namara, or Seumas O'Kelly, or Brinsley MacNamara, or of the Irish plays of St. John Ervine; and equally useful would be a selection of the best plays of George Shiels, Teresa Deevy, Louis D'Alton, or Paul Vincent Carroll.

A major difficulty has always been the publication of important contemporary plays. Over the years, this function has been valuably, but unsystematically, performed by such publishers as Maunsel, Talbot, James Duffy, Progress House, Mercier, Dolmen, and Proscenium. The Society of Irish Playwrights has recently, in conjunction with Proscenium, begun to publish a series of new scripts by members, the initial three volumes being plays by Hugh Leonard, Conor Farrington, and Desmond Forristal. Certain journals, such as *The United Irishman, The Dublin Magazine,* and *The Journal of Irish Literature* have been receptive to plays. Nevertheless, the publication of new plays has always been a slapdash process, and some notable works continue to elude publication. One thinks particularly of the plays of such relatively recent writers as Lady Longford, Padraic Fallon, Donagh MacDonagh, Bryan MacMahon, Patrick Galvin, Eugene McCabe, much of Hugh Leonard, and most of Thomas Coffey, Conor Farrington, and James Douglas.

Some critical studies of individual and often neglected authors have appeared, but this work has been of such widely varying merit that a note of caution is probably salutary. There is a marked tendency, especially notable in American scholarship, to rush enthusiactically into print with short, ill-researched, trivial studies of individual authors, such as my own Dimui O'Dujfy, which is rather ignorant of certain basic facts. Rather than such undigested and premature studies, scholars might more profitably turn their attention to the establishing of texts, for much such basic work remains to be done.

I. Bibliography

There is no adequate formal bibliography of the dramatic movement from its beginnings to the present. However, of some use are the selected bibliographies in Ernest Boyd's *Ireland's Literary Renaissance* (1916; rev. 1922) and his *The Contemporary Drama of Ireland* (1917; rpt. 1928), in Anna Irene Miller's *The Independent Theatre in Europe* (1931; rpt. 1966), in Una Ellis-Fermor's *The Irish Dramatic Movement* (1939; rev. 1954; rpt. 1967), and in Robert Hogan's *After the Irish Renaissance* (1967; rev. 1968).

Joseph Holloway's "Irish Plays," in Stephen J. M. Brown's *A Guide to Books on Ireland* (1912; rpt. 1970), is not a bibliography but a list of every play this encyclopediac reader and demon playgoer could discover that was even tangentially Irish in interest. The list extends from "The Pride of Life," an anonymous mid-sixteenth-century morality, to new plays performed, and even unperformed, in 1912. His list of modern plays up to 1912 has not been superseded and contains usually a brief critical description, the date of first production, and occasionally, but not always, some publication information about those plays that did reach print. The critical remarks and quotations in the introduction are often at variance with the tone and content of the critical remarks in the text, and this inconsistency is quite symptomatic of Holloway's esthetic schizophrenia. His generalized hyper-prudery and vehement denunciation are continually undercut by his theatergoer's delight in specific works.

Similarly, Mathew J. O'Mahony's *Progress Guide to Anglo-Irish Plays* (1960) is not a bibliography but a list of plays available for amateur production. Much of the material covered is of minimal interest, as only a historian casting the broadest net would wish to know of such writers as the prolific Seamus Burke, who is not to be confused with Seamus de Burca, but who is the author of broad short farces such as "The Belle of Boulavogue" or ferocious short melodramas such as "The Rat Came Back." O'Mahony is also somewhat dated and does not provide dates of publication, but he does include plot summaries as well as the death dates and pseudonyms of some playwrights.

E. H. Mikhail's *A Bibliography of Modern Irish Drama, 1899–1970* (1972) is an almost useless attempt at this most necessary task. The book is much too short to be comprehensive, and much too muddled to be selective. It omits much that is significant and includes much that is trivial, placing the trivial next to the significant without indication. Indeed, it is impossible to say what guiding principles were used, for occasional entries have nothing to do with the drama at all. What is printed contains but one or two errors, although pseudonymous work by George Moore, Fred Ryan, Arthur Clery, and Conor Cruise O'Brien is not identified. Mikhail's companion volume, *Dissertations on Anglo-Irish Drama: A Bibliography of Studies 1870–1970* (1973) is a simpler task of listing doctoral studies and is adequately done and useful.

The purpose of "The Hand-List of Plays" appended to Allardyce Nicoll's *English Drama, 1900–1930* (1973) is to list the major production and publication information of the most significant plays produced during this period in the British Isles. Irish plays are listed passim, alphabetically by author, on approximately 75 of the nearly 600 pages. As is inevitable with such a monumental task, errors and omissions abound, but the occasional howler, such as listing "Gideon Cusley" as the author of *The Enchanted Trousers*, cannot detract from the exceptional usefulness of the list.

II. Anthologies

There is no adequate anthology, in or out of print, containing the most notable plays of the dramatic movement from the beginnings to the present.* Curtis Canfield's *Plays of the Irish Renaissance 1880–1930* (1929; rpt. 1932, 1938, 1974), the best one-volume anthology, includes Yeats's "On Baile's Strand" and "The Only Jealousy of Emer," A. E.'s *Deirdre*, Lady Gregory's "Hyacinth Halvey," Hyde's "The Twisting of the Rope," Fitzmaurice's "The Dandy Dolls," Synge's "Riders to the Sea," Colum's *The Land*, Murray's *Birthright*, Pearse's "The Singer," Martyn's *Maeve*, O'Casey's *Juno and the Paycock*, and Robinson's *The Big House*. Canfield's selections aptly illustrate the major themes in modern Irish drama, without sacrificing quality. His *Plays of Changing Ireland* (1936), unfortunately out of print, is an invaluable collection of plays of the early thirties, which contains also copious notes, biographies, and play lists. The plays included are Yeats's "The Words upon the Window Pane," Johnston's *The Old Lady Says "No!"*, Robinson's *Church Street*, Lord Longford's *Yahoo*, Shiels's *The New Gossoon*, Lady Longford's *Mr. Jiggins of Jigginstown*, Mary Manning's *Youth's the Season . . . ?*, and Rutherford Mayne's *Bridge Head*.

Harrison Hale Schaff's *Three Irish Plays* (1936) contains Yeats's "The Land of Heart's Desire," Hyde's "The Twisting of the Rope," and Synge's "Riders to the Sea." George Jean Nathan's *Five Irish Plays* (1941), now out of print, contains Synge's "Riders" and *Playboy*, Lady Gregory's "Spreading the News," O'Casey's *Juno*, and Carroll's *Shadow and Substance*. E. Martin Browne's *Three Irish Plays* (1959) contains Johnston's *The Moon in the Yellow River* and the first publication of Joseph O'Conor's *The Iron Harp* and of Donagh MacDonagh's *Step-in-the-Hollow*. *The Genius of the Irish Theatre* (ed. Sylvan Barnet, Morton Berman, and William Burto, 1960), now out of print, contains Bernard Shaw's *John Bull's Other Island*, Lady Gregory's *The Canavans*, Synge's *Deirdre of the Sorrows*, Yeats's "Words upon the Window-Pane," Jack Yeats's "La La Noo," Frank O'Connor and Hugh Hunt's "In the Train," and O'Casey's *Purple Dust*. The collection, although useful, was seemingly determined by the principle of originality rather than of soundness.

Prizewinning Plays of 1964 (1965) contained six one-act plays with all-woman casts, which were submitted to a competition sponsored by the Irish Country-Women's Association. None of the plays was especially notable, but they included Maurice Davin Power's "The Second Chance" and "Dinner Deferred," Thomas Feeney's "The Wanted Man," Conor Farrington's "The Ghostly Garden," M. J. Molloy's "The Bitter Pill," and Martin Dolan's "And One Came Back." Robert W. Corrigan's *Masterpieces of the Modern Irish Theatre* (1967; rpt. 1969) contains Yeats's "The Countess Cathleen," Synge's "Riders" and *Playboy*, and O'Casey's *The Silver Tassie* and *Cock-a-Doodle Dandy*. The editor's critical remarks are terse and trite, and his short bibliography is full of errors.

Hogan's *Seven Irish Plays, 1946–1964* (1967) includes critical introductions and the following plays: Molloy's *The Visiting House*, MacMahon's *The Song of the Anvil*, Seamus Byrne's *Design for a*

---

* Throughout this chapter, the titles of full-length plays are italicized; the titles of one-act plays appear in quotation marks.

Headstone, John O'Donovan's *Copperfaced Jack*, John B. Keane's
Sharon's Grave and *Many Young Men of Twenty*, and James Douglas' *The Ice Goddess*. *Lost Plays of the Irish Renaissance* (ed. Hogan
and James Kilroy, 1970) contains the first English translation of P. T.
McGinley's "Eilish agus an Bhean Deirce" as "Lizzie and the Tinker,"
the first publication of the extant portion of Fred Ryan's "The Laying
of the Foundations" (also to be found in *ArielE*, 1970, with a good
introduction by John Kelly), and four other obscure one-acts: James
H. Cousins' "The Racing Lug," Lady Gregory's "Twenty-Five," Colum's "The Saxon Shillin'," and Maud Gonne's "Dawn." The interest
of the collection is more historical than literary.

Two continuing paperback series of plays, containing both reprints
and first publications, are the Irish Drama Series of De Paul University, of which the general editor is William J. Feeney; and the Irish
Play Series of Proscenium Press, of which the general editor is
Hogan. To date, the De Paul series includes eight volumes: Edward
Martyn's *The Heather Field* (1966), Martyn's *Maeve* with Alice Mil-
ligan's "The Last Feast of the Fianna" (1967), George Moore's *The
Bending of the Bough* (1969), A. E.'s *Deirdre* (1970), Seumas O'Kel-
ly's *The Shuiler's Child* (1971), John Coulter's *The Drums Are Out*
(1971), Seumas MacManus' "The Townland of Tamney" with
Martyn's *The Dream Physician* (1972), Cousins' "The Sleep of the
King" and "The Sword of Dermot" (1973), Thomas MacDonagh's
When the Dawn Has Come (1973), and the George Moore-W. B.
Yeats *Diarmuid and Grania* (1974). To date, the Proscenium series
includes James Douglas' *North City Traffic Straight Ahead* (1968),
John B. Keane's *Hut 42* (1968), Thomas Murphy's *The Fooleen*
(1968), Seamus de Burca's *The End of Mrs. Oblong* (1968), Seamus
Byrne's *Little City* (1970), Denis Johnston's revised version of *The
Golden Cuckoo* (1971), Brian Friel's *The Enemy Within* (1975),
Hugh Leonard's *Da* (1975), Conor Farrington's *Aaron Thy Brother*
(1975), and Desmond Forristal's *Black Man's Country* (1975), the
last three volumes also published in Ireland, as The Society of Irish
Playwrights Series. Proscenium's Lost Play Series also contains sev-
eral Irish plays: John O'Donovan's *The Shaws of Synge Street*
(1966), Paul Vincent Carroll's *Farewell to Greatness!* (1966) and
Goodbye to the Summer (1970), Mervyn Wall's *The Lady in the
Twilight* (1971), and Daniel Corkery's *Fohnam the Sculptor* (1974).

III. History, Criticism, Memoirs

The material here is voluminous but diffuse. A listing must probably commence with *Beltaine* (1899, 1900; rpt. 1970), the short-lived
annual periodical edited by Yeats and issued by the Irish Literary
Theatre in conjunction with its seasons of plays. The essays in it are
important but short and more in the nature of manifesto and advertisement than of criticism.

Samhain, the successor to *Beltaine*, is a particularly rich primary
source, issued in periods about a year apart, from 1901 to 1908 (rpt.
1970). In addition to much historical and theoretical material by
Yeats, the magazine contained reproductions of paintings, largely by

J. B. Yeats, of various members of the theater; there are also lists of productions, and the first publication of various plays, including Hyde's "Casadh an tSugain" with Lady Gregory's translation under the title of "The Twisting of the Rope," Hyde's "An Naom ar Iarraid" with Lady Gregory's translation under the title "The Lost Saint," Yeats's "Cathleen ni Houlihan," Hyde's "Teach na mBocht" with Lady Gregory's translation under the title of "The Poorhouse," Synge's "Riders" and "In the Shadow of the Glen," Lady Gregory's "The Rising of the Moon" and "Spreading the News," a translation by Taig O'Donoghue of her "The Gaol Gate" under the title of "An Fear Siubail," her "Hyacinth Halvee" and "Dervorgilla," and Yeats's alterations of *Deirdre*. The 1970 reprint contains also some paragraphs by Yeats on theater finances and the theater's future, paragraphs which were to have appeared in an unpublished 1909 number. Of less importance is another Abbey periodical, *The Arrow*, which appeared from time to time in 1906 and after and which has not been reprinted, although it is available on microfilm. Mainly *The Arrow* consists of announcements, cast lists, and short notes by Yeats and Lady Gregory.

A similar magazine is *Uladh*, published by the Ulster Literary Theatre in 1904 and 1905. Only four numbers were issued, but it was a handsomely produced journal with attractive drawings by Joseph Campbell and others. The magazine printed short pieces of general cultural interest as well as theatrical matter, such as criticism of Ulster Literary Theatre productions and an occasional play such as Campbell's *The Little Cowherd of Slainge*.

Of major importance are the writings of the chief founders of the dramatic movement—Yeats, Moore, and Lady Gregory. Yeats's frequent theoretical and historical remarks on the theater have not been gathered in one place, but the most important have been often reprinted, and some uncollected items appear in the second volume of *Uncollected Prose by W. B. Yeats* (ed. John P. Frayne and Colton Johnson, 1975). Much of the early material appeared, as noted, in theater magazines, and the best of that appears in various subsequent collections. Particularly to be consulted are *The Cutting of an Agate* (1912), *Essays* (1924), *Dramatis Personae* (1936), *The Autobiography* (1938; entitled *Autobiographies* in some editions), Wade's *Letters* (1954), *Essays and Introductions* (1961), and especially *Explorations* (1962). Yeats's *Memoirs* (1972) were edited by Denis Donoghue. Moore's chief remarks on the Irish Literary Theatre appear in his highly colored, delightful, and probably not too reliable three-volume memoir, *Hail and Farewell* (1911, 1912, 1914); but also to be consulted is a cutting article, "Stage Management in the Irish National Theatre," which he published under the pseudonym Paul Ruttledge in *Dana* (1904). Lady Gregory's *Our Irish Theatre* (1913; rpt. 1965; the 1973 ed. in the *Collected Works* contains additional writings including letters by Lady Gregory and Yeats and more material on the Abbey's 1911 American tour) is a personal history which, in typically lucid style, tersely recounts the inception and early years of the movement. The book emphasizes Lady Gregory's own playwriting and her collaborations with Yeats and Hyde but also has a good chapter on Synge and long accounts of the *Blanco Posnet*

production and of the turbulent first Abbey tour to America. The text
and the various appendices print many helpful letters and documents
by Yeats, Synge, Shaw, and others; and there is a list of productions
from 1899 to 1913. One might have wished for more information
about plays, players, and playwrights and for somewhat different
emphases, but what is here is crisp, charming, and invaluable.

Cornelius Weygandt's *Irish Plays and Playwrights* (1913) remains
a sound and worthy book. The factual summary is still mainly accurate and is enlivened by occasional personal reminiscences, such as
that of a 1902 rehearsal at the Camden Street Hall. The book's critical
judgments are discerning, and the chapter on Synge is one of the
most perceptive assessments ever written. The remarks on Yeats and
Lady Gregory are less noteworthy, but judicious and appreciative.
The chapter on A. E. necessarily discusses the poems and the personality more than *Deirdre* but is nevertheless apt and vivid (however,
in *On the Edge of Evening*, 1946, Weygandt rather reverses his high
opinion of A. E.). Weygandt gives more space to Martyn than merit
might allow but is quite accurate about Martyn's central failing. In a
catch-all chapter on "The Younger Dramatists," he distinguishes Boyle's
one good play, is rather less than appreciative of Colum's best
play, enthusiastically greets the early work of Murray, Robinson,
Mayne, Ervine, and Campbell, and is notably unfair only about
"Norreys Connell" (a pseudonym of Conal O'Riordan until after
World War I). The book concludes with a long chapter on William
Sharp/Fiona Macleod, who was only on the periphery of the Irish
Renaissance, but whose *The House of Usna* is worth scrutiny.

Ernest Boyd's *Ireland's Literary Renaissance* (1916; rev. 1922)
contains a sound study of Yeats's plays with particular attention to
the revisions and three chapters on the dramatic movement. Some
undervaluing of Lady Gregory is balanced by a generous overvaluing
of Colum, and in general one is impressed by Boyd's reasonableness,
kindness, and sense, all qualities one would not have expected from
the irascible portrait drawn of him by Thomas Wolfe in *The Web
and the Rock*. Many of Boyd's opinions were more fully developed in
The Contemporary Drama of Ireland (1917; rpt. 1928), an informed
general history of the early years of the Abbey, with some passing
remarks on other theaters and a chapter on the Ulster movement.
Again, Boyd is more than generous in his appraisal of Martyn, equating Martyn's Ibsenite Modernism in importance with Yeats's ideas for
a poetic theater, seeing a split in the theater movement on these lines,
and suggesting that, for the health of the movement, the divergence
would have to be reconciled. Boyd is appreciative of Yeats, Synge,
Colum, Dunsany, and Fitzmaurice, but too critical of Lady Gregory's
dramatic work, which, he says, "hardly corresponds to what is permanent in her contribution to Irish literature." He is absolutely just
on Boyle, but prematurely dismissive of the "melodramas" of Murray
and Robinson, who were only beginning their long careers. It is only
on St. John Ervine that Boyd becomes scathing, irascible, and notably
unfair. However, despite some factual sketchiness, Boyd's remains
one of the soundest critical books on the movement.

*The Celtic Dawn: A Survey of the Renascence in Ireland, 1889–
1916* (1917) by Lloyd R. Morris, a long sketch of the dramatic

movement, could still serve as a historical introduction, although neither its skimpy facts nor its simple judgments are of much use for advanced students.

Father Dawson Byrne's *The Story of Ireland's National Theatre: The Abbey Theatre, Dublin* (1929) is such a casual and unprofessional book that little merit has been allowed it. Nevertheless, despite a tendency to gush, a handful of remarkable errors, and a couple of useless appendices, the volume has the engaging charm of the enthusiast as well as some useful information on the history of the Abbey Theatre building (at which Byrne as a young man had played), on the tours of the Abbey players, and on the peregrinations of Sinclair's Irish Players. The significance of the Fays is stressed, and a number of fugitive pieces by and about them, William Archer, Ben Iden Payne, and others are quoted or cited.

Andrew E. Malone's *The Irish Drama* (1929; rpt. 1965) is the most comprehensive, informed, and just critical history of the period from 1899 to about 1928. Although Malone's interest centers almost totally around the Abbey, he is thorough in his discussion of its history, its major and minor writers, and its actors. His evaluations are usually kind and only occasionally fulsome. If he overrated the work of Seumas O'Kelly, Daniel Corkery, John Guinan, Seumas O'Brien, and other minor figures, he did have the soundness to describe the brilliance of Fitzmaurice and to rank him with Synge, Lady Gregory, and Colum. Probably only a few of his judgments—say, his remarks on O'Casey—would need revision in light of subsequent events. His appendices are useful, and his list of first productions by the Abbey extends into 1928. There is no bibliography.

Margaret McHenry's *The Ulster Theatre in Ireland* (1931) is, even for a doctoral dissertation, elementary, but the book remains of some value because most of the early Ulster plays have never been published and her summarizing of plots is still the most accessible account of what many of these plays were about. Her list of dates of first productions is still useful, as are her summary and generous quotation from the theater's unreprinted magazine *Uladh*. Her occasional brief critical judgments are probably sound, and the book does not contain many errors of fact. Another book with some information about the Ulster theater is Whitford Kane's *Are We All Met?* (1931).

Anna Irene Miller's *The Independent Theatre in Europe* (1931; rpt. 1966) contains a chapter on the Irish theater written in a somewhat florid style and with a somewhat disorderly organization. The material on the Irish Literary Theatre and the Abbey covers at fair length the familiar ground, adding nothing new but making only a handful of errors. The material on the Ulster Literary Theatre and the theater in Cork is too scant to be of use, although her few remarks on Edward Martyn's post-1901 endeavors still have some value. There is no need to heed her critical opinions.

The Gate Theatre published a magazine, *Motley*, which appeared in 1932 and ran for a few issues. Edited by Mary Manning, who pseudonymously wrote a good deal of it, it is perhaps more amusingly indicative of the spirit of the theater than it is informative. A more valuable record is *The Gate Theatre, Dublin* (ed. Bulmer Hobson, 1934). The "Gate Book" is an invaluable record of the theater's first seven seasons. It contains a preface by the Earl of Longford; an essay, "The Making of the Theatre," by Denis Johnston; another essay, "Production," by Hilton Edwards; and is profusely illustrated with pictures of costume designs, set designs, and photographs of productions and players.

The Fays of the Abbey Theatre (1935), by W. G. Fay and Catherine Carswell, is Willie Fay's own theatrical memoir. Its first section deals with Fay's early life and theatrical career, the second with the experiences of him and his brother at the Abbey, and the third with his career after leaving the Abbey. Lucid, amusing, and revealing, the book is of great utility.

The Abbey Theatre Dramatic Festival of Plays and Lectures is a souvenir program of thirty-eight pages issued in August 1938. Largely given over to advertising, it does, of course, list the program of events for the two-week festival, and it also prints some excellent photographs of Abbey Theatre writers, some capsule biographies of them, and a short, insignificant essay, "The Irish National Theatre," by Lennox Robinson. A more substantial fruit of the festival was *The Irish Theatre* (ed. Robinson, 1939), which printed the public lectures delivered on this occasion. Of particular interest are Frank O'Connor's "Synge," F. R. Higgins' "Yeats and Poetic Drama in Ireland," Andrew E. Malone's "The Rise of the Realistic Movement," T. C. Murray's generous appreciation of Shiels and MacNamara, Ernest Blythe's "Gaelic Drama," and Micheál MacLiammóir's portrayal of Paul Vincent Carroll in his charming, rambling "Problem Plays." For some reason, Denis Johnston's lecture was not printed.

A recent encyclopedia of modern drama cites Una Ellis-Fermor's *The Irish Dramatic Movement* (1939; rev. 1954; rpt. 1964) as the most profound study of the subject. Apparently this view is widespread, but it seems based on a superficial reading of the book, which is among the least valuable of any of the full-length studies. Probably a chief reason for this overassessment lies in the author's often rhapsodic style. She undeniably attains moments of appropriate eloquence, but, when more pedestrian matters are under discussion, her style reveals an inability to reinforce thought by sentence construction, syntax, or punctuation. Because some ideas are interred in her prose, the result is often a not displeasing hypnosis or intellectual trance in which meaning is vaguely inferred. An attentive reading, however, is either hindered by pauses to untangle the sense from the syntax, or it is simply baffled by passages whose meaning dissolves upon close scrutiny.

The volume also contains a number of tacit confusions. One notable example is an unexplored but pervasive distinction between "dramatic" and "theatrical." At its simplest, the author seems to mean by "theatrical" those qualities in a play necessary for its effective presentation on a stage, and by "dramatic" those qualities necessary for the standing of a play as literature. However, in many specific references, she sometimes appears to consider these qualities of equal but distinct value, and sometimes of equal and identical value, and sometimes of definitely unequal value. In the last instance, "theatrical" becomes pejorative, but in other instances it is quite impossible to tell what it becomes.

The facts in the book are mainly correct, although the author misspells the names of Conal O'Riordan and Denis Johnston and attributes only four plays to Colum. The use of sources seems largely confined to W. A. Henderson's lists of clippings in the National Library, to *Samhain* and *The Arrow*, and to the well-known memoirs of Yeats and Lady Gregory. The main historical chapter, "The Early History of the Movement" adds nothing to previous accounts and is less useful than most of them. The chapter "The English Theatre in the Nineties" is neither germane nor in itself good. The author curiously emphasizes the importance of Henry Arthur Jones and barely touches upon Shaw. The feeling that one gets from this chapter is one of rather slapdash scholarship, a hasty ransacking of a few obvious sources and a drawing of not inordinately sound conclusions. The chapter "Ideals in the Workshop" is a more useful culling of ideas from Yeats and Lady Gregory. The chapters on particular playwrights are more full of quotation than of insight, and those on Yeats and Synge are especially weak. The attention devoted to Martyn seems inordinate in view of the importance that even the author attributes to his work. The soundest chapter is probably that on Lady Gregory, but to divorce its content from its style is to discover only superficiality. The summary chapter, "Conclusion and Prospect," contributes a brief analysis of Colum's *The Land*, Robinson's best-forgotten *The Clancy Name*, and Murray's *Maurice Harte*, and is inadequate from any point of view. The various appendices tend to be either repetitious, unnecessary, or superseded. The 1954 edition differs only in that the last chapter is extended by brief discussions of O'Casey, Johnston, Shiels, and Carroll.

Did You Know That the Gate . . . (1940) is a 12-page, profusely illustrated pamphlet, with an anonymously written text that summarizes the history of the Gate Theatre. The photographs of productions are remarkable, and there is a list of the productions of the first thirteen seasons as well as a list of productions in Irish produced by MacLiammóir for An Comhar Dramuiochta. Of some similar interest are the souvenir booklets issued by the Gaiety Theatre. The 70th Anniversary volume (1941) is a 32-page booklet, containing the essay ". . . Merely Players" by Harold R. White, a chatty and unsystematic account of the theater's notable productions since its opening in 1871. The 75th Anniversary volume (1946) is 46 pages long, mostly, if not entirely, written by Maxwell Sweeney. It too is a historical résumé, although more factual and specific than the earlier volume and illustrated by photographs of the major players to appear at the theatre. The 100th Anniversary volume (1971) is an anonymously written 36-page booklet, rather less factual than the previous ones, but with some good photographs of some modern players and Christmas pantomimes.

Ella Young's *Flowering Dusk* (1945) has some brief glimpses of amateur productions in the early 1900's, including those of the Daughters of Erin, the production of O'Grady's *Red Hugh* at Kilkenny, and the private production of A. E.'s *Deirdre* at George Coffey's house. Peter Kavanagh's *The Irish Theatre* (1946) is a general history from "the Earliest Period up to the Present Day." It is in the Holloway tradition of scholarship—an impressive although untrustworthy and unsystematic amassing of lists and facts. Its few pages on the modern period are of no value.

MacLiammóir's *All for Hecuba: An Irish Theatrical Autobiography* (1946; rpt. 1947, 1961) is graceful, urbane, witty, and profusely illustrated. For its fund of information and its vivid re-creation of personalities as well as its insight into the intentions, tastes, and techniques of the Gate's founders, it is indispensable. So also is Lennox Robinson's edition of *Lady Gregory's Journals* (1947), which covers the period after 1916. The arrangement is topical, but there is much about her playwriting, the Abbey, and O'Casey; and some bits of information are also to be gleaned for Colin Smythe's edition of her autobiography, *Seventy Years* (1974).

Brinsley MacNamara's *Abbey Plays, 1899–1948* (1949) is an updating of Andrew E. Malone's list of plays, but MacNamara's list contains errors of so many kinds as to make it extremely untrustworthy. The list is prefaced by a genial reminiscence of no great substance. *Longford Productions* (1949) is a souvenir pamphlet, the only account issued by the theater of its work. It contains a short essay by Lord Longford, a few photographs of productions, and a list of the first 126 plays produced by the company.

MacLiammóir's *Theatre in Ireland* (1949; rpt. 1964 with sequel) is not a factual history, but a critical interpretation of, it is assumed, well-known facts. As such, certain dramatic events such as the *Playboy* and the *Plough* riots are not really mentioned, but for an intelligent interpretation it is hardly to be bettered, even though the content is somewhat unbalanced, with more attention given to the Gate than to any other theater, even the Abbey, and with actors and producers taking up an amount of space that might well be given to the rather skimped writers. Nevertheless, it is a suave and idealistic document, full of trenchant ideas and expressed with a sometimes witty orotundity that is not without charm. The added material in the 1964 edition discusses in the author's mandarin style and knowledgeable good sense the Irish theater of the 1950's—such actors as McKenna and Cusack, such writers as Keane and Behan, and such new companies as the Pike and the Globe.

Unlike his earlier book, Peter Kavanagh's *The Story of the Abbey Theatre* (1950) does assimilate facts into a conventional narrative, but is niggardly with those facts and is finally more creative journalism than critical or scholarly history. Kavanagh takes liberties in his interpretation of facts and on little or no evidence constantly attributes the most startling motives to people. His emphatic thesis produces not so much a history as a melodrama of the esthete versus the Philistines, with its protagonist, Yeats, cast as a kind of heroic Svengali. Although there is useful information about the Abbey's difficulties, particularly with the de Valera government in the 1930's, the story is simplified, dramatized, and heightened, and the people in it become caricatures manipulated by Kavanagh's scenario. Thus, F. R. Higgins on page 176 is "flamboyant, swaggering," but on page 180 is simply "innocuous." It should be remembered that the book was written after one of the weakest decades in the Abbey's history, and this fact may account for the book's polemic nature and its dour conclusion that the theater as an artistic force died with Yeats.

Kavanagh's literary judgments are more in the nature of offhand comments than of analysis and are not notably sound. He is quite unfair to Denis Johnston (whose name is, as usual, misspelled); and, indeed, even his facts are sometimes startlingly wrong. His appendices reprint some documents not otherwise easily obtainable.

Ireland's Abbey Theatre: A History, 1899–1951 (comp. Lennox Robinson, 1951; rpt. 1968) is described on its dustjacket as "The Official History Commissioned by the Abbey Theatre Authorities." Its great value is its complete listing of the casts of plays from 1899 to late 1950. As is inevitable with such a huge collection of facts, there are some errors of dates and some misspellings, but they are not extensive, and this is a book generally to be trusted. The lists of first productions usually follow the endings of chapters, but, as a quibble, it might be noted that some important productions are buried in the body of the chapters. It is disappointing that the text of the book is not more extensive and that the later years especially are scanted. That charge, however, should not detract from the utility and the charm of what is here. Robinson has ranged widely through sources and quoted from published memoirs, some unpublished documents, and contemporary reviews and has solicited several short memoirs of interest from individuals connected for many years with the theater. In his foreword, Robinson remarks that the book is a history rather than an appreciation or a criticism and that he has tried to bury his likes and dislikes. In effect, he has not buried them, but his many critical judgments are usually so warmly generous that he has written what amounts to an enthusiastic appreciation. Occasionally he will even squelch someone's critical reference, as in the interesting letter from Thomas MacDonagh to W. G. Fay, quoted on pages 94–95, when the disparaging references to the acting of Mary Walker and her brother Frank are gently disguised by the inserted initials X and Y. The first appendix is a reprint of Robinson's pamphlet *Pictures in a Hallway* (1947), which combines some perceptive comments on various Abbey actors with some mildly irritating satire on the ignorance of American tourists.

The Splendid Years (1955) by Maire Nic Shiubhlaigh, as told to Edward Kenny, is the detailed memoir of one of the theater's first leading actresses and is a goldmine of information and insight about the early days of the Irish National Theatre Society and, to a lesser extent, of the Theatre of Ireland. Of use also are the appendices, which contain some theater reviews, cast lists, and the only list in print of productions of the Theatre of Ireland.

Gerard Fay's history, *The Abbey Theatre, Cradle of Genius* (1958), might more properly be titled *The Birth of the Abbey Theatre*, for the bulk of the volume is a close factual study of the years from 1902, when the Fays joined forces with Yeats, to 1908, when the Fays left the Abbey. As a history, it is better documented, more specific, and more intimate than earlier studies, for the author was the son of Frank Fay and had access to his papers as well as to a large batch of correspondence, principally letters from Miss Horniman, lent him by Mrs. Yeats (all of which material is now deposited in the National Library of Ireland). Despite its excellences, the book is far from a full portrait or a complete use of sources. Fay made no

530   ANGLO-IRISH LITERATURE *A Review of Research*

use of the Holloway diaries or even of the Henderson papers, and what he has used does not answer all of the perplexing questions. The replies of Yeats and Lady Gregory to Miss Horniman, for instance, have been lost, and so it is difficult to know their attitudes. Even the attitudes of the Fays and the Directors on the event of the Fays' leaving the theater remain obscure and difficult to glean from the number of contradictory public statements. Nevertheless, the prologue and the closing chapter of Fay's book are valuable for their terse insight into and summary of the state of the theater in the late 1950's, and the appended list of Abbey productions reaches up to 1955 and remains the most complete in print.

Hilton Edwards' *The Mantle of Harlequin* (1958) is a rich ragbag of a book, containing reflections on many facets of production, playwriting, and even drama criticism, by probably the most competent and eclectic director to work on the modern Irish stage. The book is by turns an essay, a fantasy, and a collection of aphorisms; it is extraordinarily revealing about Edwards' theater practice and only on occasion mildly patronizing. It contains a preface by MacLiammóir, a list of Gate productions up to 1958, and some photographs of players, theater personalities, and productions.

Gigi Lunari's *Il movimento drammatico irlandese, 1899–1922* (Bologna, 1960) is a short general history which, despite its title, is devoted entirely to the Abbey movement. Its general soundness is somewhat vitiated by a curious organization and by a plethora of errors, some of them typographical. Its bibliography is out of date, but its list of Abbey productions is still helpful if used with caution.

MacLiammóir's *Each Actor on His Ass* (1961), a translation of parts of two earlier Gaelic books, details some of his acting experiences on the Continent and, rather more interestingly, gives an account of a Gate tour to Egypt. Alan Simpson's *Beckett and Behan and a Theatre in Dublin* (1962) is a rambling discussion of some notable productions at the Pike Theatre, which was founded by the author and Carolyn Swift. Of much merit are the discussions of the state of the Dublin theater in the late 1950's and early 1960's. The accounts of the productions and receptions of several Behan and Beckett plays are also quite good, as are the chapter on Behan's life and the chapter on Simpson's prosecution for having produced Tennessee Williams' *The Rose Tattoo*.

Ernest Blythe's pamphlet *The Abbey Theatre* (1963) is an apologia for his long stewardship and an answer to the many bitter criticisms leveled against him over the years. Blythe defends with imperturbable stubbornness his dual-language policy for the theater, and the main thrust of his argument is that the theater should be used for a nationalistic and untheatrical purpose. Nevertheless, he makes a case for many of his policies, and the pamphlet is required reading for an understanding of the theater in the 1940's and 1950's.

The occasion of the opening of the new Abbey Theatre building saw the publication of two celebratory pamphlets. *The Creation of the Abbey Theatre* (1966) is a handsome, insignificant, 20-page brochure of snippets from well-known sources. *Abbey Theatre— Dublin 1904–1966* (ed. Gabriel Fallon, 1966) is of more interest because of its many fine photographs of plays, players, playwrights, and theater personnel associated with the Abbey over the years.

Robert Hogan's *After the Irish Renaissance* (1967; rpt. 1968) has been both warmly condemned and coldly praised. It is a critical history of the forty-year period from 1926 and attempts to be somewhat broader than Malone (*ID*)—which, of the previous histories, it most closely resembles—by including capsule histories of the Ulster theater, the Dublin Gate Theatre, and the Dublin Theatre Festival. Hogan singles out Paul Vincent Carroll, Michael J. Molloy, Denis Johnston, Brendan Behan, and John B. Keane as the most significant new playwrights of their period, devoting individual chapters to each writer, and he also gives a chapter to the work of George Fitzmaurice, neglected until that time. Perhaps the best chapter, even though it seems to belong to some other book, is that on the late plays of O'Casey. For an informative introduction, the volume unfortunately remains to date the standard work on the period and contains a lengthy bibliography. *Joseph Holloway's Abbey Theatre* (ed. Hogan and Michael J. O'Neill, 1967), culled from the 25,000,000 words of Holloway's diary, covers the productions of the Abbey from 1899 to 1926. The editors' extract was cut greatly to meet the demands of the publisher, and so some information on other theaters is absent, but it remains a useful firsthand account of productions, rehearsals, conversation, and gossip. *Joseph Holloway's Irish Theatre* is a three-volume continuation, which discusses the productions of other theaters, such as the Gate and Longford Productions as well as those of the Abbey and covers the years 1926–31 (1968), 1932–37 (1969), and 1938–44 (1970).

The Story of the Abbey Theatre (1967) is an informal paperback history for the general reader, composed of several essays contributed by the editor, Sean McCann, and other Irish journalists. It is an uneven collection. Anthony Butler's denigration of Yeats in "The Guardians" would be outrageous were it not so puerile. It begins on the tasteless and silly level of "the timid surge of some Yeatsian orgasm" and degenerates from there. Sean McCann's essays are genial repetitions of facts and gossip mainly retailed elsewhere. Catherine Rynne's "The Playwrights" gives capsule characterizations of various writers and plays from the beginnings to 1955 and provides helpful bits of information on the more recent years. Gabriel Fallon's "The Abbey Theatre Acting Tradition" is mainly a patchwork of quotations from the author's wide reading but offers interesting personal reminiscences. His theory derives Abbey acting from Coquelin, Antoine, and Stanislavsky, and, given the knowledge of the Fays in the early 1900's, is more academic than persuasive. Donal Dorcey's "The Big Occasions" describes the various audience protests, from "The Countess Cathleen" to "Design for a Headstone," and is an adequate résumé of newspaper accounts of these events.

Frank O'Connor's *My Father's Son* (1968), the second and posthumous volume of his autobiography, contains in its last two sections ("The Abbey Theatre" and "The Death of Yeats") probably the most vivid, vigorous, and personal account of the inner workings of the Abbey. He is writing of the little discussed period of the late 1930's, and his deft, fierce sketches of Yeats, Higgins, Robinson, and others, as well as his portrayal of the infighting on the Abbey board, is a warmly personal antidote to the pale anonymities found in most other histories and criticisms. Like Moore's memoirs, O'Connor's are fresh, catty, droll, and even somewhat true. One may feel that everything is enormously simplified and even perverted for the sake of a good story, but, whatever the veracity of the details, the essence seems absolutely accurate. Harold Pinter's *Mac* (1968) is a short, appreciative essay on Anew McMaster, based on Pinter's experiences of two seasons touring with McMaster's company in the Irish provinces.

Gabriel Fallon's pamphlet *The Abbey and the Actor* (1969) is a not totally convincing development of his previous attempt to relate the Abbey style of acting to that of Coquelin, the Théâtre Libre, and the Moscow Arts Theatre. It is burdened with the author's penchant for quotation, but it contains a few interesting personal reminiscences and an appendix of tributes to F. J. McCormick, mostly reprinted from *The Capuchin Annual*. Another handsome Abbey Theatre booklet is Micheál Ó hAodha's *The Abbey—Then and Now* (1969), which offers a capsule history of the theater and brief characterizations of several writers and actors as well as a number of excellent portraits.

Patrick Rafroidi's *L'Irlande: t. 2 Littérature* (Paris, 1970) is a concise general history which contains a chapter on "Aspects du Théâtre Irlandais-Anglais." Its value is that it covers the field from Congreve to the present. It is, however, only an outline with often but a sentence or two to characterize or criticize an author's work.

A continuing series of booklets of varying interest is Dolmen's Irish Theatre Series (ed. Robert Hogan, James Kilroy, and Liam Miller). The first volume, Frank J. Fay's *Towards a National Theatre* (ed. Hogan, 1970), is mainly a selection of the more significant dramatic criticism that Fay wrote for *The United Irishman* from 1899 to 1902. These pieces are valuable not so much for their criticism of particular plays as for Fay's own developing program for a national drama. The theories developing in these pieces were those with which Fay bombarded Yeats, and thus were of signal importance for their influence on the style of production developed by the Irish National Theatre Society. The concluding article is a short history, delivered as a talk in New York in 1908, of the early days of the theater movement. James W. Flannery's *Miss Annie F. Horniman and the Abbey Theatre* (1970) is a short, descriptive monograph that charts the relation of Miss Horniman to the theater movement. The booklet offers a great deal of new information drawn from the Horniman letters in the National Library of Ireland. Although a good summary of its topic, the material discussed would have been more useful had the author elected to edit a selection of the letters. James Kilroy's *The 'Playboy' Riots* (1971) is the fullest, most vivid account of the famous 1907 riots. A documentary history, compiled primarily from contemporary newspaper accounts and with a connecting editorial thread of explanation and comment, it is an invaluable and amusing re-creation, which redresses the balance of mere Philistinism usually attributed to those who attacked the play and which, in a more general sense, charts the theatrical and political tenor of the time.

Theatre and Nationalism in Twentieth-Century Ireland (ed. Robert O'Driscoll, 1971) is a collection of talks, mainly on Yeats, O'Casey, Shaw, and Beckett, read at a seminar on Irish studies held in 1968 at the University of Toronto. As semipublic lectures meant to inform not especially knowledgeable students, these pieces were undoubtedly serviceable, but as published essays they are weary, pedantic rehashes of old material. Typical of the musty academicism of the volume is the 22-page essay by David R. Clark on "Yeats, Theatre, and Nationalism," which, without adding anything to knowledge, requires 16 lengthy quotations, at least 95 short quotations, and 86 footnotes. The book does contain two previously unpublished Yeats essays of mild interest on the Abbey, and several Yeats letters to Shaw, two of which are extremely interesting.

N. Sahal's *Sixty Years of Realistic Irish Drama* (Bombay, 1971) contains occasional fine snippets of correspondence with Paul Vincent Carroll, Teresa Deevy, and Michael Molloy. However, the book's critical premises are vague, if not untenable, and the author appears to have seen few, if any, of the plays, to have carried on his researches largely by correspondence, and to have concluded them sometime in the 1950's. With the omission of Yeats; the bizarre discussions of Synge, O'Casey, and Johnston; the incompleteness, the datedness, and the incorrectness of much of the information, the book is more a curiosity than a contribution.

Sam Hanna Bell's *The Theatre in Ulster* (1972), the first account of any length about the Ulster stage since McHenry's 1931 volume, is somewhat provincial in tone, for Bell is frequently given to listing the names of obscure actors in amateur companies. A greater flaw is that he does not investigate adequately the major talents of the Ulster theater. The fine, quirky genius of Gerald MacNamara gets shorter shrift than it deserves, and Bell appears unaware of the publication of some of MacNamara's plays. Bell tends also to be overly gentle on Hubert Wilmot of the Arts Theatre and on Mary O'Malley of the Lyric Players Theatre. The accounts of acting are probably the weakest portions of the book, but on balance it remains the best, fullest account of the Ulster Literary Theatre, the Group Theatre, and the Lyric Players Theatre. Its appendices, listing the dates of the first productions of the three major Ulster theaters, are most helpful. The lack of an index is not.

Aspects of the Irish Theatre (ed. Patrick Rafroidi et al., Paris, 1972) is a collection of eighteen essays covering a broad spectrum of Irish drama, from Sheridan to Conor Cruise O'Brien. With one or two exceptions, the essays rarely rise above the level of the student paper, which apparently a number of them are.

Flight from the Celtic Twilight (1973), by Des Hickey and Gus Smith, transcribes a number of taped interviews with various theater people—playwrights, actors, producers, and directors—among them Padraic Colum, Cyril Cusack, Eileen Crowe on F. J. McCormick, Siobhan McKenna, Denis Johnston, Edwards and MacLiammóir, Dan O'Herlihy, Jack MacGowran, Tyrone Guthrie, Anna Manahan, Richard Harris, Donal Donnelly, T. P. McKenna, Norman Rodway, Milo O'Shea, Hugh Leonard, Sean Kenny, Tom Murphy, Brian Friel, and Conor Cruise O'Brien. The information elicited is sometimes merely trivial reminiscence, but often of much value. In particular, there is a good deal of information about the Globe Theatre, which has been little discussed, and there are several fine O'Casey letters to Brendan Smith about the *Drums of Father Ned* controversy.

Micheál Ó hAodha's *Theatre in Ireland* (1974) is a short introductory critical history. As history, it covers the ground from the seventeenth century to the present with too much scantiness to be of use to anyone but beginning students wanting to know a few basic facts. As criticism, it is thin, uneven, and sometimes quirky. The discussions of Fitzmaurice and Byrne seem particularly unconvincing, but the brief remarks on T. C. Murray and Padraic Fallon are well worth contemplation.

The first volume of *The Modern Irish Drama, A Documentary History*, by Robert Hogan and James Kilroy, is entitled *The Irish Literary Theatre* (1975). The title is something of a misnomer, for, although the book naturally stresses the Literary Theatre, its scope includes the entirety of theater in Ireland, commercial as well as amateur. The chief value of the book is probably a profuse use of contemporary documents, such as accounts from newspapers, journals, manuscripts, and letters. However, the book also contains, as will future volumes, cast lists of first productions and bibliographical notes about the most significant plays of the period. The first volume prints in an appendix the text in Irish and English of what was apparently the first produced Irish-language play.

The second volume, entitled *Spreading the News* (1976), uses the same documentary technique to cover the years 1902–04. It emphasizes the Irish National Theatre Society and the foundation of the Ulster Literary Theatre. Further volumes in the press continue the story up to the beginning of 1910.

IV. Individual Authors: Texts and Criticism

This section, for limitations of space, cannot be an exhaustive listing of all Irish playwrights with a plausible claim to merit. It represents what, in this writer's opinion, seems to have the greatest claim to attention. Nevertheless, I am painfully conscious that the claims of some writers in every decade of the century—from Seumas MacManus in the beginning to John Boyd and others in the 1970's—may well have been unfairly scanted.

William Boyle (1853–1922) was a County Louth playwright, short story writer, and writer of light verse, who spent much of his life in London but wrote the most popular full-length plays in the early days of the Abbey Theatre. His published plays include *The Building Fund* (1905); *The Eloquent Dempsy** (1907; rpt. 1911, 1916); *The Mineral Workers* (1907; rpt. 1910); and *Family Failing* (1912). Weygandt and Boyd are both quite sound on Boyle, and nothing of recent substance has been or perhaps needs to be written. Some of Boyle's many disgruntled letters are printed in *HAT*.

Edward McNulty (1865–1943), novelist and friend from youth of

* Spelled "Dempsey" by practically all critics, although the published text has "Dempsy."

Bernard Shaw, wrote three popular published plays: *The Lord Mayor* (1917); *Mrs. Mulligan's Millions* (1918; rpt. 1957); and *The Courting of Mary Doyle* (1922).

Edward Martyn (1859–1923) was a playwright, philanthropist, ardent Catholic, and last of the ancient family that inhabited Tulira Castle. His first work, *Morgante the Lesser*, was a novel satirizing modern morals. He was one of the founders of the Irish Literary Theatre, and his published plays include *The Heather Field* (1899, with *Maeve*; rpt. 1917, 1966); *Maeve* (1899; rpt. 1917, 1967); *The Tale of a Town and An Enchanted Sea* (1902); *The Place-Hunters* in *The Leader* (1902); *Romulus and Remus or The Makers of Delights* in *Irish People* (1907); *Grangecolman* (1912); and *The Dream Physician* (1914; rpt. 1918, 1972). Denis Gwynn's *Edward Martyn and the Irish Revival* (1930) offers the most thorough treatment of Martyn, incorporating extensive records and correspondence not available to others. Attention is given to Martyn's peculiar personality and his pursuits outside the theater. In *Edward Martyn and the Irish Theatre* (1956), Marie-Thérèse Courtney devotes more space than Gwynn to Martyn's plays. Jan Setterquist studies the influence of Ibsen in *Ibsen and the Beginnings of Anglo-Irish Drama*, Vol. II: *Edward Martyn* (1960). Boyd and Weygandt have chapters on Martyn, and Weygandt has a good sense of his dramatic limitations. The most engaging, though prejudiced, depictions of Martyn appear in *Hail and Farewell* (1911, 1912, 1914) by his lifelong "friend," George Moore. Patricia McFate's excellent introduction to the 1972 reprinting of *The Dream Physician* includes a short bibliography of about everything else of interest on Martyn, except perhaps Stephen P. Ryan's "Edward Martyn's Last Play" (*Studies*, 1958).

Douglas Hyde (1860–1949), who used the Irish pseudonym "An Craoibhín Aoibhinn" or the Delightful Little Branch, was a folklorist, Irish scholar, poet, playwright, amateur actor, and first President of Ireland. His published plays include: "Casadh an tSúgáin" ("The Twisting of the Rope") in *Samhain* (1901; first book publication in Lady Gregory's *Poets and Dreamers*, 1903; first separate publication, 1905); "An Tincear agus an tSídeog ("The Tinker and the Fairy") in *New Ireland Review* (1902); "An Posadh" ("The Marriage") in *Poets and Dreamers* (1903); "Drama Breite Criosta" ("The Nativity") in *The Weekly Freeman* (1902; first book publication in *Poets and Dreamers*, 1903; first separate publication, 1903); "Ar Naom ar Iarraid" ("The Lost Saint") in *Samhain* (1902; in *Poets and Dreamers*, 1903; first separate publication in Irish, 1918); "Pleusgadh na Bulgoide, or The Bursting of the Bubble" in *New Ireland Review* (1903; first separate publication, 1903); "Rig Seumas" ("King James") in *The Weekly Freeman* (1903; first separate publication, 1904); "An Magistir Sgoile" ("The Schoolmaster") in *The Weekly Freeman* (1904); "Teach na mBocht" ("The Poorhouse") in *Samhain* (1903; rpt. in *Poets and Dreamers*, 1903; rpt. 1967; also in *Spreading the News and The Rising of the Moon, by Lady Gregory, The Poorhouse, by Douglas Hyde and Lady Gregory*, 1906; rewritten as "The Workhouse Ward" by Lady Gregory and published in *Seven Short Plays*, 1909; published separately in Irish, 1934). There is much need for a collected edition of Hyde's plays, although most of them appear in Colin Smythe's reprint of *Poets and Dreamers* (1974). Little has been written on them, but the basic book on Hyde is Diarmid Coffey's *Douglas Hyde: President of Ireland* (1938). Gareth W. Dunleavy's *Douglas Hyde* (1974) adds little new biographically and nothing critically. The critical chapter is mainly a précis of some of Hyde's work and refers only very briefly to the plays. Lester Connor's essay "The Importance of Douglas Hyde to the Irish Literary Renaissance" in *Modern Irish Literature: Essays in Honor of William York Tindall* (ed. Raymond J. Porter and James D. Brophy, 1972) discusses the plays briefly.

Alice L. Milligan (1866–1953) was a poet and playwright much involved with amateur drama in the early years of the century. Her published plays include "The Green upon the Cape" in *The Shan Van Vocht* (Belfast, 1898); "The Last Feast of the Fianna" in *The Daily Express* (Dublin, 1899; first separate publication, 1900; rpt. 1967); "Oisin in Tir-Nan-Oig" in *The Daily Express* (1899; rpt. SF, 1909); "Oisin and Padraic" in *The Daily Express* (1899; rpt. SF, 1909); "The Deliverance of Red Hugh" in *The Weekly Freeman*, in English and Irish (1902); "The Daughter of Donagh" in *UI* (1903; first separate publication, 1920); "Brian of Banba" in *UI* (1904); and "The Last of the Desmonds" in *UI* (1904). In an article, "Historical Drama" (*SF*, 1909), Milligan listed the plays she had written and then plaintively remarked, "I have several others sketched, but don't write them, as my plays are so seldom acted." There is a short, fascinating personal glimpse of her as an old lady in Benedict Kiely's "The Whores on the Half-Doors" in *Conor Cruise O'Brien Introduces Ireland* (1969; rpt. 1970), and William Feeney has a short discussion of "The Last Feast of the Fianna" in his 1967 edition.

Gerald MacNamara was the pseudonym of Harry Morrow (1866–1958), one of three brothers intimately involved with the fortunes of the Ulster Literary Theatre. Most of his plays remain unpublished, including his most popular, "The Mist That Does Be on the Bog." His published plays include *Thompson in Tir na-n-Og* (1918) and, in *DM*, "Who Fears to Speak?" (1929), "The Babes in the Wood" (1924), and "Tcinderella" (1924). He requires a collected edition, for he was a brilliant minor talent.

Jack B. Yeats (1871–1957), the younger brother of the poet, is known mainly as Ireland's foremost modern painter, but he was also a man of letters who wrote early in his career children's plays for theaters, and late in his career a number of intriguing closet dramas. His plays include *James Flaunty or the Terror of the Western Seas* (1901), *The Scourge of the Gulph* (1903); *The Treasure of the Garden* (1903); *The Bosun and the Bob-Tailed Comet* (1904); *Apparitions*, containing "The Old Sea Road" and "Rattle" (1933); *La La Noo* (1943; rpt. in *Genius of the Irish Theatre*, 1960); and *In Sand*, containing also "The Green Wave" (1964). These and Yeats's other plays are brought together in *Collected Plays* (1971), to which the editor, Robin Skelton, contributes a sound introduction. See also *Jack B. Yeats* (1971), a miscellany of memoirs and criticisms, which contains "A Chronology of Major Personal Events, Publications and Exhibitions" and "A Bibliography of the Published Writings," both by Martha Caldwell. *Yeats Studies* (1972) is devoted to Yeats and

Synge, and contains Skeleton's "Themes and Attitudes in the Later Drama of Jack B. Yeats." A somewhat less admiring view of Yeats's plays than Skeleton's appears in Hogan's "John Synge and Jack Yeats" (*Journal of Mod. Lit.*, 1974). The standard life is Hilary Pyle's valuable *Jack B. Yeats* (1970), which contains a bibliography.

James Cousins (1873–1956), who sometimes used the Irish form of his name, Seumas O'Cuisin, was a prolific Belfast-born poet, very active in the early days of the Irish National Theatre Society, until squelched by Yeats. He moved to India in 1915 and spent most of the rest of his life in the East. His published plays include: "The Racing Lug" in *UI* (1902; rpt. *Shama'a*, 1923, and *LPIR*, 1970); "The Sleep of the King" in *UI* (1902; rpt. *The Quest*, 1906, *A Wandering Harp*, 1932, and as Vol. VIII in DePaul's Irish Drama Series, 1973); "Sold" in *UI* (1902); "The Sword of Dermot" in *UI* (1903, in a prose version, and rpt. in 1973 with "The Sleep of the King"; a poetic version appeared in *Shama'a* in 1927); "The Clansman" in *UI* (1905); "The Turn of the Tide" in *UI* (1905); "The King's Wife" (1919; rpt. *A Bardic Pilgrimage*, 1934; rev. in *The Hound of Uladh*, 1942); *The Hound of Uladh* (1942). *We Two Together* (1950), written with his wife, Margaret E. Cousins, contains a great deal of information about the early days of the dramatic movement. The last word on Cousins undoubtedly will be the amazing and charmingly quirky "Bio-Bibliographical Survey" exhaustively compiled by Alan Denson, *James H. Cousins and Margaret E. Cousins* (1967). The DePaul reprint contains a short introduction to Cousins by the editor, William A. Dumbleton.

T. C. (Thomas Cornelius) Murray (1873–1959) was the Cork-born dramatist whose strongly structured realistic plays were for years staples of the Abbey repertoire. His published plays include *Birthright* (1911); *Maurice Harte* (1912); *Spring and Other Plays* (1917), containing also *Sovereign Love* and *The Briery Gap*; *Aftermath* (1922); *Autumn Fire* (1925, rpt. 1927, 1952, 1964), *The Pipe in the Fields* and *Birthright* (1928); *Michaelmas Eve* (1932); and *Maurice Harte and a Stag at Bay* (1934). Much information about Murray and some of his letters are contained in *HAT*. Critical articles on Murray include Matthew T. Conlin's "The Tragic Effect in *Autumn Fire* and *Desire Under the Elms*" (*MD*, 1959); T. L. Connolly's "T. C. Murray, the Quiet Man" (*CathW*, 1960), and Micheál Ó hAodha's "T. C. Murray—Dramatist" in his *Plays and Places* (1961). Ó hAodha has some further remarks in his *Theatre in Ireland* (1974), and E. T. Conlin has an unpublished doctoral dissertation, "T. C. Murray: A Critical Study of his Dramatic Work" (National Univ. of Ireland 1952). Murray's own writings on the drama include an appreciative lecture on Shiels and MacNamara in *IT* (1939) and various uncollected play reviews, which he wrote late in life for a Dublin newspaper.

Conal O'Riordan (1874–1948) used until the First World War the pseudonym F. Norreys Connell. A prolific and neglected man of letters, he spent much time in England, was involved with Grein's Independent Theatre, and then succeeded Synge as a Director of the Abbey. After the war, he wrote a remarkable, if uneven, series of novels, beginning with *Adam of Dublin* (1920), which contains a description of the first revival of *The Playboy*. His published plays include *His Majesty's Pleasure* in *The Irish Review* (1912; rpt. separately, 1925); *Shakespeare's End and Other Irish Plays* (1912), containing also "The Piper" and "An Imaginary Conversation"; *The King's Wooing* (1929); *Captain Falstaff and Other Plays* (1935), containing also "The Piper," "An Imaginary Conversation," and "Mr. Pitt." Practically nothing has been written on his work.

George Fitzmaurice (1877–1963) had his first-produced and most popular play, *The Country Dressmaker*, done at the Abbey in 1907, and the author appeared then a less individual Synge. The Abbey hardly encouraged Fitzmaurice, who dropped more and more into obscurity. Over the years, his plays were admired by Boyd, Colum, and Clarke, however, and some were printed in *The Dublin Magazine*. Still, his last forty years saw only rare productions, and his posthumous reputation, which is beginning to rival that of Synge himself, has been largely the result of enthusiastic appreciation by Austin Clarke, Liam Miller, Howard K. Slaughter, and others. Fitzmaurice's plays are included in *Five Plays* (1914) and in the Dolmen Press three-volume *The Plays of George Fitzmaurice* (1967 and 1970). The basic bibliography is Liam Miller's in Slaughter's short biography *George Fitzmaurice and His Enchanted Land* (1972), although Joanne L. Henderson's bibliography (*JIL*, 1972) lists also the major criticism of Fitzmaurice. Critical essays of note appear in *CDI*, *ID* and *AIR*, but see also Austin Clarke (*DM*, 1940), J. D. Riley (*DM*, 1955), Irving Wardle (*LonM*, 1965), John P. Conbere (*Éire*, 1971), Miller (*JIL*, 1972), and Matthew N. Coughlin's lengthy and pedantic "Audience and Character in George Fitzmaurice's *The Magic Glasses*" (*DM*, 1973–74). Ó hAodha has some mildly denigrating remarks (*JIL*, 1972) and reprints them in *Theatre in Ireland* (1974). Ann Cipriani has an unpublished doctoral dissertation, "George Fitzmaurice, l'homme et l'oeuvre" (Lille 1973). Arthur McGuinness' short *George Fitzmaurice* (1975) is longer on plot summary and quotation than on judgment and virtually ignores some of the playwright's best work.

Seumas O'Kelly (?   –1918)* was a writer of short stories and novels as well as a journalist and playwright. His plays were performed by the Theatre of Ireland and the Abbey. He is probably best known for his long story "The Weaver's Grave," which in recent years was dramatized by Micheál Ó hAodha. His published plays include *His Father's Son* (*SF*, 1906 and 1907); *The Matchmakers* (1908; rpt. in *Three Plays*, 1912, and separately 1950, 1958); *The Shuiler's Child* (1909; rpt. 1971); *The Homecoming*, (*SF*, 1909; rpt. in *Three Plays*, 1912, and in *Waysiders*, 1918); *The Stranger* in *Three Plays* (1921); *The Bribe* (1914; rpt. 1952); *Meadowsweet* (1919); *The Parnellite* (1919); "Lustre," with Casimir de Markievicz, in *Irish Weekly Independent* (1920; rpt. *Éire*, 1967). Mary Anne Francis Cavanagh has an unpublished doctoral dissertation, "The Two Voices of Seumas O'Kelly: A Study of the Man and His Work," (National Univ. of

* George Brandon Saul (*Seumas O'Kelly*, 1971) places O'Kelly's birth in the years 1875 to 1878; Eamon Grennan, in his introduction to *A Land of Loneliness and Other Stories* (1969), cites 1880; Brian Cleeve, in *Dictionary of Irish Writers*, Vol. 1 (1967), cites 1881.

Ireland 1968), which we have not seen. George Brandon Saul's *Seumas O'Kelly* (1971) consists of two long chapters, of which the first, "The Life," is the fullest factual account in print. The chapter on "The Works" is generally sound, although thin on the plays, and contains some discussion of manuscript material. The annotated bibliography, described as "definitive and comprehensive," is neither.

Lord Dunsany, Edward John Moreton Drax Plunkett (1878–1957) was a prolific Anglo-Irish writer of fantastic and satiric stories and plays. His usually short and at one time very popular plays owe little to Ireland and much to his imagination. They include *The Gods of Pegana* (1905; rpt. 1911, 1916); *Selections from the Writings of Lord Dunsany* (1912), containing "The Gods of the Mountain and the first act of "King Argimines and the Unknown Warrior"; *Five Plays* (1914; rpt. 1917, 1918, 1923 in separate parts, 1925), containing "The Gods of the Mountain," "The Golden Doom," "King Argimines," "The Glittering Gate," and "The Lost Silk Hat"; *Plays of Gods and Men* (1917; rpt. 1923), containing "The Tents of the Arabs," "The Laughter of the Gods," "The Queen's Enemies," and "A Night at an Inn"; *The Laughter of the Gods* (1918; rpt. 1922); *If* (1921; rpt. 1922); *Plays of Near and Far* (1922; rpt. 1923, 1928, 1936), containing "The Compromise of the King of the Golden Isles," "The Flight of the Queen," "Cheezo," "A Good Bargain," "If Shakespeare Lived To-Day," and "Fame and the Poet"; *Alexander and Three Small Plays* (1925; rpt. 1926), containing also "The Old King's Tale," "The Evil Kettle," and "The Amusement of Khan Kharuda"; *Seven Modern Comedies* (1928), containing "Atalanta in Wimbledon," "The Raffle," "The Journey of the Soul," "In Holy Russia," "His Sainted Grandmother," "The Hopeless Passion of Mr. Bunyon," and "The Jest of Hahalaba"; *The Old Folk of the Centuries* (1930); *Lord Adrian* (1933); *Mr. Faithful* (1935); *Plays for Earth and Air* (1937; rpt. 1948), containing "Fame Comes Late," "A Matter of Honour," "Mr. Sliggen's Hour," "The Pumpkin," "The Use of Man," "The Bureau de Change," "The Seventh Symphony," "Golden Dragon City," "Time's Joke," "Atmospherics."

There are three books about Dunsany. Edward Hale Bierstadt's *Dunsany the Dramatist* (1917) grossly overrates Dunsany's importance but contains some useful ideas and criticisms in its primly schoolmasterish style. It prints some letters from Dunsany and some fine photographs of American productions of his plays. Hazel Littlefield Smith's *Lord Dunsany, King of Dreams: A Personal Portrait* (1959) is a memoir of his late years, containing some letters. Mark Amory's *Lord Dunsany* (1972) is a full, sympathetic, mildly snobbish biography that makes its subject seem, perhaps justly, rather dull but contains much information about the composition and performance of the plays; it is critically terse but sound. Among the shorter pieces, Boyd's section on Dunsany in *CDI* might be consulted, as might Francis Hackett's "Dunsany in Greece" in *Judging Books in General and in Particular* (1947), Clayton Hamilton's "Lord Dunsany: Personal Impressions," in *Seen on the Stage* (1920), Weygandt's "William Butler Yeats and the Irish Literary Renaissance," in *The Time of Yeats* (1937) and his "Dramas of Dunsany," in *Tuesdays at Ten* (1928), which is a superficial but not unjust summary of most of the plays. In periodicals, the more useful criticisms are Montrose J. Moses' "Lord Dunsany's Peculiar Genius" (*Bellman*, 1917), L. Paul Dubois' "Un conteur ir-landais: Lord Dunsany, le maître du merveilleux" (*Revue des Deux Mondes*, 1933); Gogarty's "Lord Dunsany" (*Atlantic Monthly*, Mar. 1955), and R. Sencourt's "Memoirs of Lord Dunsany" (*ContempR*, 1958).

Thomas MacDonagh (1878–1916), poet, critic, teacher, and patriot, was executed for his prominent part in the Easter Rising. His published plays include *When the Dawn Is Come* (1908; rpt. 1973) and "Metempsychosis; or a Mad World" (*IrishR*, 1912).

Rutherford Mayne was the pseudonym of Samuel J. Waddell (1878– ?), the most popular and prolific writer for the Ulster Literary Theatre. His published plays include *The Drone* (1909; rpt. 1912); *The Troth* (1909; rpt. 1912); *The Drone and Other Plays* (1912), containing also "The Turn of the Road," "Red Turf," and "The Troth"; *Bridgehead* (1939; rpt. 1964); and *Peter* (1964). He is discussed in Canfield's *PCI*, which prints *Bridgehead*, and in Bell's *The Theatre in Ulster* (1972).

Daniel Corkery (1878–1964) was a Cork writer, well known as a novelist, short story writer, and critic, and as a formative influence upon Sean O'Faolain and Frank O'Connor. His published plays include *The Labour Leader* (1920); *The Yellow Bittern and Other Plays* (1920, containing also "King and Hermit" and "Clan Falvey"); "Resurrection" (*Theatre Arts*, 1924; rpt. *The Franciscan Annual*, 1936, and separately, 1942); and *Fohnam the Sculptor* (1973). Corkery's chief critical work on the drama, *Synge and Anglo-Irish Literature* (1931), has been attacked by many critics for its jingoistic approach to literature. A short, stolid book by G. B. Saul, *Daniel Corkery* (1973), contains a deal of factual information and a basic bibliography. Marie-Claire Peron has an unpublished doctoral dissertation, "Daniel Corkery, sa vie, son œuvre" (Rennes 1972), which we have not seen. Corkery's papers are housed in the library of University College, Cork.

Patrick Pearse (1879–1916) was one of the major leaders of the Easter Rising, but earlier in his career he had been an Irish-language enthusiast, a journalist, an influential educator, and an author in Irish and English. His simple, straightforward plays include "The Singer," "The King," "The Master" and "Iosagan," the last translated into English by Joseph Campbell. The plays were first collected in 1917 and have gone through many editions, the most recent being 1960. The best discussion of the plays is "Plays and Pageants" in Raymond J. Porter's *P. H. Pearse* (1973), which also contains a short biography and an excellent bibliography. Other biographical writings are Louis Le Roux's flatulent *Patrick H. Pearse* (1932) and Hedley McCay's skimpy *Padraic Pearse: A New Biography* (1966).

Joseph Campbell (1879–1944), who often signed his name "Seosamh MacCathmaoil," was a Belfast poet, active in the early days of the Ulster Literary Theatre, who spent his later years in the South of Ireland and in the United States. His rare pieces for the theater include "The Little Cowherd of Slainge" in *Uladh* (1904); *Judgment* (1912); and an English translation of Pearse's "Iosagan" (1917). P. S.

O'Hegarty published *A Bibliography of Joseph Campbell-Seosamh MacCathmaoil* (1940).

James Stephens (1880 or 1882–1950) was a whimsical poet, novelist, and short story writer, who published one short play, *Julia Elizabeth* (1920) and who acted in occasional productions for the Theatre of Ireland. A bibliography of Stephens is contained in Hilary Pyle's useful *James Stephens, His Work and an Account of His Life* (1965). See also Brigit Bramsbäck's *James Stephens: A Literary and Bibliographical Study* (1959), Richard J. Finneran's *Letters* (1974), and the Stephens issue of *JIL* (1975), edited by Finneran and Patricia McFate, which contains a previously unpublished play, *The Demi-Gods*.

Padraic Colum (1881–1972), the poet and man of letters, first made his reputation as a playwright during the early years of the century. He emigrated to the United States in 1914 and continued to write plays into the mid-1960's. None of his later plays, however, equaled in quality or popularity his *Three Plays*, which rank among the best in Irish drama. His published plays include: "Children of Lir" in *The Irish Independent* (1901; rpt. *JIL*, 1973); "Brian Boru" (1901?; Colum said this play was published in an Irish periodical, but no one has been able to identify the one); "The Foleys" (*UI*, 1902); "The Kingdom of the Young" (*UI*, 1902); "Eoghan's Wife" (*UI*, 1902); "The Saxon Shillin' " (*UI*, 1903; rpt. *LPIR*, 1970); "The Miracle of the Corn (*UI*, 1904 in prose; rpt. in verse in Colum's *Studies*, 1907; in *Dramatic Legends and Other Poems*, 1922; in *Poems*, 1932; in *Collected Poems*, 1953; and in *Theatre Arts*, 1925); *The Land* (1905; rpt. with *The Fiddler's House*, 1909; and in *Three Plays*, 1916); *The Fiddler's House* (1907; rpt. with *The Land*, 1909, and in *Three Plays*, 1916); *Thomas Muskerry* (1910; rpt. in *Three Plays*, 1916, and separately, 1943?); *The Desert* (1912; rev. as *Mogu the Wanderer*, 1917); "The Destruction of the Hostel" in *A Boy in Eirinn* (1913); *Three Plays* (1916; rpt. 1925; rev. 1963); "The Betrayal in *The Drama* (1920; rpt. *DM*, 1925; in *One Act Plays of Today*, 1928; trans. into Irish by Richard Foley in *Naoi nGearra-Chluichi*, 1930; and into Dutch by Alfred Pleiter as "Het Verraad," 1953; *Balloon* (1929); *Moytura* (1963); and "Cloughoughter" (*JIL*, 1973). Little has been written about Colum's plays. The best and most comprehensive discussion is Zack Bowen's in *Padraic Colum: A Biographical-Critical Introduction* (1970). The Colum number of *JIL* (1973) contains Colum's reminiscences of the early days of the Irish theater and Charles Burgess' article on Colum's efforts to reestablish his reputation as a playwright. Also useful is Alan Denson's Checklist in *DM* (1967) and the Colum interviews in *JIL* (1973) and in *FCT* (1973). See too G. C. S. Adams' note "A Source for Padraic Colum's Balloon" in *Éire* (1975). Nelly Frechet has an unpublished doctoral dissertation, "L'Œuvre de Padraic Colum" (Paris 1968), which we have not seen.

St. John Ervine (1883–1971) was a prolific Ulster-born playwright and man of letters who for a short while was manager of the Abbey. His published plays include *Mixed Marriage* (1911; rpt. 1920); *The Magnanimous Lover* (1912; rpt. 1931); *Four Irish Plays* (1941), containing "Mixed Marriage," "The Magnanimous Lover," "The Critics," and "The Orangeman"; *Jane Clegg* (1914); *John Ferguson* (1915; rpt. 1920); *The Ship* (1922); *The Lady of Belmont* (1923); *Four One-Act Plays* (1928), including "The Magnanimous Lover," "Progress," "Ole George Comes to Tea," and "She Was No Lady"; *The First Mrs. Fraser* (1929); *Anthony and Anna* (1925; rpt. 1936); *Boyd's Shop* (1936; rpt. 1941, 1948, 1954); *People of Our Class* (1936); *Robert's Wife* (1938); *Friends and Relations* (1947); *Private Enterprise* (1948); *The Christies* (1949); and *My Brother Tom* (1952). His books on the theater include *The Organized Theatre* (1924), *How to Write a Play* (1928), and *The Theatre in My Time* (1933). In the 1920's he was a drama reviewer in both London and New York, and this provocative, often savage material remains uncollected. Among his pertinent nondramatic work are the biographies *Oscar Wilde* (1951) and *Bernard Shaw: His Life, Work and Friends* (1956). Little has been published about Ervine, but see John Boyd's fine article in *Threshold* (1974) and Paula Howard's "St. John Ervine: A Bibliography of His Published Works" (*Irish Booklore*, 1971). Unpublished essays are Virginia A. Haile, "The Dramas and Dramatic Criticism of St. John Greer Ervine" (diss. Indiana 1949); and J. M. Scofield, "The Dramatic Work of Mr. St. John Ervine" (Master's thesis Wales 1952).

Lennox Robinson (1886–1958) was a prolific playwright and man of letters for many years closely associated with the Abbey. His published plays include *The Cross-Roads* (1909); *Two Plays: Harvest and The Clancy Name* (1911); *Patriots* (1912); *The Dreamers* (1915); *The Lost Leader* (1918; rpt. 1954); *The Whiteheaded Boy* (1921; rpt. 1925, 1955); *Crabbed Youth and Age* (1924; rpt. 1953); *Never the Time and the Place* (1924; rpt. 1953); *The Round Table* (1924; rev. 1938); *The White Blackbird and Portrait* (1926); *Plays* (1928), containing "The Round Table," "Crabbed Youth and Age," "Portrait," "The White Blackbird," "The Big House," and "Give a Dog—"; *Ever the Twain* (1930); *The Far-Off Hills* (1931; rpt. 1941); *Is Life Worth Living? or Drama at Inish* (1933; rpt. 1938); *More Plays* (1935), including "Church Street" and "All's Over Then?"; *Killycreggs in Twilight and Other Plays* (1939), including also "Bird's Nest"; "Let Well Alone" in *The Bell* (1941); and *The Lucky Finger* (1949). Among Robinson's important nondramatic writings are *Curtain Up, an Autobiography* (1942); *Pictures in a Theatre* (1947); and *Ireland's Abbey Theatre* (1951). He also edited *The Irish Theatre* (1939) and *Lady Gregory's Journals* (1947). A good deal of his thinking on dramatic technique is revealed in passing in his analyses of some Yeats plays in the essay "The Man and the Dramatist," in Stephen Gwynn's *Scattering Branches* (1940). A basic but far from complete bibliography may be extracted from the chronology of Michael J. O'Neill's *Lennox Robinson* (1964), a workmanlike critical biography which evokes little of Robinson the man. The Robinson section of Kaspar Spinner's *Die alte Dame sagte: Nein!* (Bern, 1961) makes up about a fifth of the book, and is an adequate and knowledgeable survey of Robinson's published plays. It contains much plot summary and is sometimes pedestrian and humorless, but is a basically sound discussion, even though some plays are skimpily treated.

A cruel but amusing view of Robinson's late years may be found in Frank O'Connor's *My Father's Son* (1968). C. B. Smith has an un-published doctoral dissertation, "Unity in Diversity: A Critical Study of the drama of Lennox Robinson" (Trinity College, Dublin 1960).

George Shiels (1886–1949) was at first a prolific short story writer for popular journals, but from the 1920's his originally broad, but increasingly dour, comedies were staples of the Abbey repertoire. His published plays include *Bedmates* (1922); *Professor Tim and Paul Twyning* (1927); *Two Irish Plays: Mountain Dew and Cartney and Kevney* (1930); *The New Gossoon* (1936); *The Passing Day and The Jailbird* (1937); *The Rugged Path and The Summit* (1942); *Three Plays: Professor Tim, Paul Twyning and The New Gossoon* (1945); *Grogran and the Ferret* (1947); *Quin's Secret* (1947); *Give Him a House* (1917); *The Fort Field* (1947); *Tenants at Will* (1947); *The Old Broom* (1947); and *The Caretakers* (1948). Shiels is appreciatively discussed by Murray in *IT* and by Hogan in *AIR*, and David Kennedy has a short biographical memoir in *Threshold* (1974). J. J. Kelly has an unpublished Master's thesis, "George Shiels as the Exponent of Modern Irish Comedy" (University College, Dublin 1950).

John Coulter (1888–   ) is an Ulster playwright, resident for many years in Canada, where most of the following plays were published: *The House in the Quiet Glen* (1937); *The Family Portrait* (1937); *Transit through Fire* (1942), a libretto; *Deirdre of the Sorrows* (1944), a libretto; *Riel* (1962); *Capful of Pennies* (1964); *The Crimes of Louis Riel* (1966); *While I Live* (1966), and *The Drums Are Out* (1971), which contains an introduction by the author.

Brinsley MacNamara (1890–1963) was the pseudonym of A. E. Weldon, novelist, short story writer, playwright, and, for a short time, an Abbey director. His published plays include: *The Glorious Un-certainty* (1929; rpt. 1957); *Look at the Heffernans!* (1939); *Mar-garet Gillan* (1934); and *Marks and Mabel* (1945). His drama reviews, often unsigned, appeared occasionally in *The Irish Times*, but see his inaccurate list, *Abbey Plays, 1899–1948* (1949). He is unsympathetically discussed in *AIR*. Michael McDonnell's Checklist of his works is in *JIL* (1975).

Eimar O'Duffy (1893–1935) was a fantastic and satiric novelist who wrote several plays performed by the Hardwicke Street Theatre. His published plays include *The Walls of Athens* (1914), *Bricriu's Feast* (1919), and *The Phoenix on the Roof* (*IrishR*, 1923). A manuscript play, *Malachy the Great*, is housed in the National Li-brary of Ireland. The only book on O'Duffy is Hogan's *Eimar O'Duffy* (1972), written in the author's usual style of unqualified enthusiasm. A more accurate factual account is Alf Mac Lochlainn's "Eimar O'Duffy, a Bibliographical Biography" (*IB*, 1959).

Peadar O'Donnell (1893–   ) is the novelist and political agitator who wrote one Abbey play, *Wrack* (1933). The only critical work on O'Donnell is Grattan Freyer's excellent *Peadar O'Donnell* (1973).

F. R. Higgins (1896–1941) was an important Irish poet and Man-aging Director of the Abbey after the death of Yeats. His play *A Deuce O'Jacks* appeared in *DM* (1936). Information on his connection with the Abbey appears in Frank O'Connor's *My Father's Son* (1968).

Austin Clarke (1896–1974) is a major Irish poet, verse dramatist, novelist, and founder of the Lyric Theatre Company. His published plays include *Son of Learning* (1927); *The Flame* (1930); *Sister Eucharia* (1939); *Black Fast* (1941); *As the Crow Flies* (1943); *The Viscount of Blarney and Other Plays* (1944); *The Second Kiss* (1946); *Collected Plays* (1964), containing *The Son of Learning, The Flame, Sister Eucharia, Black Fast, The Kiss, As the Crow Flies, The Plot Is Ready, The Viscount of Blarney, The Second Kiss, The Plot Succeeds*, and *The Moment Next to Nothing. The Impuritans*, a verse adaptation of Hawthorne's "Young Goodman Brown," appeared in *IUR* (1970; published separately 1973); and *The Visitation*, a comedy in one act, was included in its special Austin Clarke issue (1974). In his booklet *The Celtic Twilight and the Nineties* (1969), Clarke discusses, among other matters, Victorian verse drama and Yeats's plays. His own plays are discussed approvingly by Vivian Mercier (*DM*, 1944 and *Chimera*, 1947), and disapprovingly by Hogan in *AIR*. *IUR*'s special Austin Clarke issue (1974) contains of special interest Maurice Harmon's "Notes towards a Biography"; an article of no critical depth by Roger McHugh, "The Plays of Austin Clarke"; Tina Hunt Mahony's "The Dublin Verse-Speaking Society and The Lyric Theatre Company," which lists most of the productions of these groups with dates; and Gerard Lyne's "Austin Clarke— A Bibliography." Susan Halpern's *Austin Clarke* (1974) contains a chapter on the plays which describes Clarke's theory of dramatic poetry. The discussion of specific plays is uncritically admiring.

Liam O'Flaherty (1897–   ) is a major Irish novelist and short story writer, who published the play *Darkness* (1926). Accounts of his work are Anthony Canedo's *Liam O'Flaherty: Introduction and Analysis* (1965), John Zneimer's *The Literary Vision of Liam O'Flaherty* (1970), and Paul A. Doyle's *Liam O'Flaherty* (1971), which has a good bibliography.

Kate O'Brien (1897–1974) is best known as a novelist, but her plays include *Distinguished Villa* (1926) and *That Lady* (1949).

Micheál MacLiammóir (1899–   ) or, in English, Michael Willmore, is the eminent Irish actor, stage designer, and man of letters who founded the Gate Theatre in 1928 with Hilton Edwards. A fairly prolific playwright in Irish and English, his published plays include only *Ill Met by Moonlight* (1954) and *Where Stars Walk* (1962). His frequent writings on the theater include three volumes of memoirs: *All for Hecuba* (1946; rpt. with additions 1961), *Put Money in Thy Purse* (1952), and *Each Actor on His Ass* (1960), and his short history *Theatre in Ireland* (1950; rev. 1964). *The Importance of Being Oscar*, the text of his one-man show on Wilde, appeared in 1963, and *W. B. Yeats and His World*, with Eavan Boland, in 1971. See also an interview with him and Edwards (*JIL*, 1973).

Sean O'Faolain (1900–   ), or, in English, John Whelan, is a major Irish short story writer and man of letters, and the author of one published play, *She Had to Do Something* (1938). The chief account of his work is Maurice Harmon's *Sean O'Faolain* (1966), but see also Paul A. Doyle's *Sean O'Faolain* (1968). Both contain bibliographies.

Robert Collis (1900–1975) is a Dublin pediatrician and man of letters whose best known play is *Marrowbone Lane* (1943). He also wrote the prologue and epilogue to and is discussed in Christy Brown's *My Left Foot* (1955).

Paul Vincent Carroll (1900–68) is a Dundalk-born playwright who lived most of his life in Scotland and England but had some major success in the United States in the late 1930's. His published plays include: *Things That Are Caesar's* (1934; rpt. *Three Plays*, 1944); *Shadow and Substance* (1937; rpt. *Two Plays*, 1948); *The White Steed and Coggerers* (1939; *The White Steed* rpt. *Three Plays*, 1944; *Coggerers* retitled *Conspirators* rpt. 1947, and in *Irish Stories and Plays*, 1958); *Plays for My Children* (1939), containing *The King Who Could Not Laugh, His Excellency—The Governor, St. Francis and the Wolf, Beauty Is Fled, Death Closes All,* and *Maker of Roads* (each rpt. separately, 1947 and *Beauty Is Fled* rpt. *Irish Stories and Plays*, 1958); *The Old Foolishness* (1944); *The Strings, My Lord, Are False* in *Three Plays* (1944); *Green Cars Go East* (1947); *Interlude* (1947; rpt. *Irish Stories and Plays*, 1958); *The Wise Have Not Spoken* (1947; rpt. 1954, and in *Two Plays*, 1948); *The Wayward Saint* (1955); *The Devil Came from Dublin* in *Irish Stories and Plays* (1958); *Farewell to Greatness!* (1966); *Goodbye to the Summer* (1970); and *We Have Ceased to Live* (*JIL*, 1972). Critical articles of use are Anne G. Coleman's "Paul Vincent Carroll's View of Irish Life" (*CathW*, 1960), Drew B. Pallette's "Paul Vincent Carroll—Since *The White Steed*" (*MD*, 1965), and Hogan's "Paul Vincent Carroll: The Rebel as Prodigal Son" in *AIR*. Paul A. Doyle's *Paul Vincent Carroll* (1971) offers a generous but sound estimate of Carroll's plays, some slight biographical data, and a bibliography.* The book was too hastily published, however, and lacks information about Carroll's early fiction and journalism and it could have usefully documented some of the interviews referred to in the text. The book should be supplemented by the Carroll number of *JIL* (1972) which contains John O'Donovan's interview with Carroll, the text of *We Have Ceased to Live*, and some characteristic letters. It should also be supplemented by the checklist of Carroll's early short stories in *JIL* (1972) appended to the reprinting of the early story "The Fool."

Louis D'Alton (1900–51) was a significant popular playwright, producer, actor, and novelist whose plays were among the staples of the Abbey repertoire during its tenure of the Queen's. His published plays include *The Man in the Cloak* and *The Mousetrap* in *Two Irish Plays* (1938); *The Money Doesn't Matter* (1942; rpt. 1944, 1946, 1948, 1952, 1957; new ed. 1963; new ed. 1972); *To-Morrow Never Comes* (1945; rpt. 1968); *The Devil a Saint Would Be* (1952); *This Other Eden* (1954; new ed. 1970); *They Got What They Wanted* (1962); *Lovers Meeting* (1964); and *Cafflin' Johnny* (1967). There is no full-length discussion of D'Alton. A short discussion appears in *AIR*.

Christine, Countess Longford (1900–   ), née Christine Patti Trew, is a playwright and novelist whose plays were performed by

---

* The bibliography contains a descriptive note on an aborted volume of Carroll material, entitled *Curtain Call*.

her husband's company, Longford Productions. Her published plays include *Mr. Jiggins of Jigginstown* (*PCI*, 1936); *Lord Edward* (1941); *The United Brothers* (1942); *Patrick Sarsfield* (1943); *The Earl of Straw* (1945); *The Hill of Quirke* (1958); *Mr. Supple* (?); and *Tankardstown* (?). See also her article "The Dublin Gate Theatre" in *The Irish Review*, New York (1934). Her plays are discussed in *AIR*.

Denis Johnston (1901–   ) is probably the major Irish playwright since O'Casey. His published plays include: *The Moon in the Yellow River and The Old Lady Says "No!"* (1932; rpt. 1933); *Storm Song and A Bride for the Unicorn* (1935); *Blind Man's Buff*, after Ernst Toller (1938); *The Golden Cuckoo and Other Plays* (1954), including "The Dreaming Dust" and "A Fourth for Bridge"; *Collected Plays* in two volumes (1960; issued in one volume the same year in the United States, with the title *The Old Lady Says "No!" and Other Plays*) and including revised versions of *The Moon* and *Dreaming Dust* as well as *The Scythe and the Sunset, Strange Occurrence on Ireland's Eye*, and "A Fourth for Bridge"; and *The Golden Cuckoo*, revised (1971). The Dolmen Press plans to publish the revised *Bride for the Unicorn*. Among Johnston's occasional writings on the theater should be cited his excellent pamphlet *John Millington Synge* (1965). Works on Johnston include Thomas Hogan's "Denis Johnston, Last of the Anglo-Irish" (*Envoy*, 1950), a section in Kaspar Spinner's *Die alte Dame sagte: Nein!* (1961), a chapter in *AIR*, and especially Harold Ferrar's *Denis Johnston's Irish Theatre* (1973), which is fine on *Bride for the Unicorn* and contains a chronology and bibliography. F. W. West has an unpublished doctoral dissertation, "The Life and Works of Denis Johnston" (Leeds 1967), and there are Johnston interviews in *JIL* (1973) and *FCT* (1973).

Edward Arthur Henry Pakenham, the Earl of Longford (1902–61) was a theatrical producer and playwright whose published plays include *Yahoo* (1934); *Armlet of Jade* (1935); *Ascendancy* (1935); and *The Vineyard* (1943). He is discussed in MacLiammóir's *All for Hecuba*.

Frank Carney (1902–   ), born in Galway, wrote several plays that were performed at the Abbey. His published plays include *Bolt from the Blue* (1950), adapted from Temple Lane's novel *Friday's Well*; and *The Righteous Are Bold* (1951; rpt. 1952, 1954, 1959).

Teresa Deevy (1903–63), a Waterford-born writer, came into prominence in the 1930's with several sensitive and subtle plays about women. Her published plays include *Three Plays* (1939) containing *Katie Roche*, "The King of Spain's Daughter" and *The Wild Goose; The King of Spain's Daughter and Other One-Act Plays* (1948), containing also "In Search of Valour" and "Strange Birth"; "A Disciple" (*DM*, 1937); "The Enthusiast" (*One-Act Play Mag.*, 1938); and "Going beyond Alma's Glory" (*IW*, 1951). For critical comments on her plays, see J. D. Riley (*IW*, 1955), and *AIR*.

Frank O'Connor (1903–66) was the pseudonym of Michael O'Donovan, the eminent short story writer and man of letters, who was briefly an Abbey director. He was the author of several plays, but the only published ones are a short verse dialogue, "At the Wakehouse" (*Theatre Arts*, 1926), "In the Train" in *Genius of the Irish*

Theatre (1960), and "The Statue's Daughter" in the O'Connor issue of
JIL (1975), edited by James H. Matthews. His important writings on
the theater include *The Art of the Theatre* (1947), a long section on
the Abbey in the 1930's in his *My Father's Son* (1968), and many uncollected articles. A bibliography, apparently by Maurice Sheehy, is
contained in the collection *Michael/Frank* (1969), which also contains
Roger McHugh's essay "Frank O'Connor and the Irish Theatre."

Seamus Byrne (1904–68) was a solicitor, nationalist, and playwright whose published plays include *Design for a Headstone* (1956;
rpt. *SIP*, 1967) and *Little City* (1970) which has an introduction by
Michael J. Molloy (see below). There is a chapter on *Headstone* in
Micheál Ó hAodha's *Plays and Places* (1961) and in *SIP*.

John McCann (1905–   ) is a Dublin-born politician and playwright, many of whose plays were popular at the Abbey in the 1950's.
His published plays include *Twenty Years A-Wooing* (1954), *Early
and Often* (1956), and *I Know Where I'm Going* (1965).

The plays of Samuel Beckett (1906–   ) are only tangentially Irish,
but they have probably been the most influential and admired plays
by any Irish writer in the last twenty or twenty-five years. Indeed,
Beckett has been so thoroughly bibliographed and commented on
that a long summary is impossible and a brief one is absurd. How
voluminous and growing the critical material on Beckett is may be
attested to by Raymond Federman and John Fletcher's *Samuel Beckett, His Works and His Critics, An Essay in Bibliography* (1970).
This invaluable book was immediately dated, for after the manuscript
went to press twelve more books devoted to Beckett appeared, and
that number in the half dozen years since then has swelled even
further. Federman and Fletcher, however, are particularly useful to
the student in their brief critical summaries of books and articles
about Beckett and should undoubtedly be consulted before leaping
into the boundless sea of criticism. Also to be consulted is James
Mays's thorough critique of Federman and Fletcher (*IUR*, 1972). To
sort out the valuable from the trivial is a task beyond the bounds of
space available and probably also beyond the writer's competence.
What follows, then, is a short, cranky list of books that have been
personally of greatest help: Hugh Kenner, *Samuel Beckett, A Critical
Study* (1961); Ruby Cohn, *Samuel Beckett: The Comic Gamut*
(1962); Frederick J. Hoffman, *Samuel Beckett, The Language of Self*
(1962); Richard Coe, *Samuel Beckett* (1964); *Samuel Beckett, A
Collection of Critical Essays* (ed. Martin Esslin, 1965); Nathan A.
Scott, *Samuel Beckett*, (1965); *Beckett at 60, A Festschrift* (ed.
John Calder, 1967); John Fletcher, *Samuel Beckett's Art* (1967);
M. Robinson, *The Long Sonata of the Dead* (1969); David H. Hesla,
The Shape of Chaos (1971); Francis Doherty, *Samuel Beckett* (1971);
Eugene Webb, *The Plays of Samuel Beckett* (1972); John Fletcher and
John Spurling, *Beckett: A Study of his Plays* (1972); and Ruby Cohn,
Back to Beckett (1973).

Padraic Fallon (1906–74) is perhaps as unknown outside Ireland
as Beckett is well known, but he is a singularly important poet and
verse dramatist, most of whose plays were done for radio and remain
unpublished. His published plays include only "The Fallen Saint"
(*DM*, 1936) and "Dialogue between Raftery and Death" (*DM*,

1952). A discussion of some unpublished work appears in *AIR*, but more authoritative comments appear in Ó hAodha's *Plays and Places* (1961) and *Theatre in Ireland* (1974).

Roger McHugh (1908–   ) is a scholar and professor of English at University College, Dublin. In 1947, with Valentin Iremonger, he made a gentle protest in the Abbey against the slovenly staging of *The Plough*. He has written a handful of plays, of which those published are *Trial at Green Street Courthouse* (1945) and *Rossa* (1948).

Mervyn Wall (1908–   ) is primarily a novelist and short story writer, but his published plays include *Alarm among the Clerks* (1940) and *The Lady in the Twilight* (1971). The one book about him is Hogan's short *Mervyn Wall* (1972), which is more advertisement than criticism but discusses two unpublished plays and contains a selected bibliography that omits Wall's prolific journalism.

Bryan MacMahon (1909–   ) is the Listowel novelist, short story writer, and playwright whose published plays include *Song of the Anvil* in *SIP* and two one-acts, "The Death of Biddy Early" and "Jack Furey" (*JIL*, 1972). A MacMahon checklist by Joanne L. Henderson appears in the same issue, and a MacMahon interview, conducted by Gordon Henderson, appears in a later issue (1974). His plays are discussed in *AIR* and *SIP*.

Roibeard O Farachain (1909–   ) or, in English, Robert Farren, is a poet and former Abbey director who has had two verse plays performed at the theater. His "Assembly at Druim Ceat" appeared in *DM* (1944).

Joseph Tomelty (1911–   ), Ulster actor, playwright, and novelist, was closely involved with the Group Theatre in Belfast. His published plays include: *Right Again Barnum* (1950); *Mugs and Money* (1953); *Is the Priest at Home?* (1954); *All Souls' Night* (1955); and *The End House* (1962). See James Gracey's "Joseph Tomelty: An Introductory Bibliography" in *Irish Booklore* (1971) and *AIR*.

Mary Manning (ca. 1910–   ), Mrs. Mark DeWolfe Howe, Jr., is a novelist and playwright associated with the Gate in her youth and later with the Poet's Theatre in Cambridge, Massachusetts. She was editor of the Gate magazine *Motley*, and in recent years her intelligent, erratic drama reviews have appeared in *Hibernia*. Her published plays include: *Youth's the Season . . . ?* (*PCI*, 1936); *Passages from Finnegans Wake*, also called *The Voices of Shem* (1957); and an adaptation of Frank O'Connor's novel *The Saint and Mary Kate* (1970). See *All for Hecuba* and *AIR*.

Seamus de Burca (1912–   ) or, in English, James Bourke, belongs to a well-known theatrical family and is the cousin of Brendan Behan. He has published the following plays: *The Boys and Girls Are Gone* (1950; rpt. 1961); *Find the Island* (1950); *Family Album* (1952); *The Howards* (1960); *Thomas Davis* (1962); *Limpid River* in *First Stage* (1966); and *The End of Mrs. Oblong* (1968). He has dramatized Charles Kickham's novel *Knocknagow* in a full-length version (1945) and a one-act version with the title *Phil Lahy* (1953). He has also published *Brendan Behan, A Memoir* (1972) and various articles on the Queen's Theatre and other early-century theatrical matters in *Waterfront*.

Brian O'Nolan (1912–66) is a major figure of modern Irish writing, best known for novels written under the pseudonym Flann O'Brien and for his *Irish Times* humor column "Cruiskeen Lawn" written under the pseudonym "Myles na Gopaleen." His plays and television scripts are not among his major work; the published ones are *Faustus Kelly* (1943); "The Insect Play" and "The Man with Four Legs" (*JIL*, 1974); this O'Nolan issue also contains a sheaf of letters and a bibliogaphy by David Powell. *Faustus Kelly* and "Thirst" appear in the posthumous collection *Stories and Plays* (1973). See also Timothy O'Keeffe's collection of memoirs, *Myles: Portraits of Brian O'Nolan* (1973). Unpublished essays are Monique Gallagher, "Le Fantastique dans l'œuvre de Flann O'Brien" (diss. Paris 1970); Louis Gallagher, "Flann O'Brien, l'homme et l'œuvre" (diss. Paris 1972); and Daniele Jacquin, "Lecture de Flann O'Brien" (diss. Lille 1972). Many O'Nolan manuscripts are in the library of the University of Southern Illinois, Carbondale.

Donagh MacDonagh (1912–68), the son of Thomas MacDonagh, was a poet and dramatist whose published plays include *Happy as Larry* (1946; rpt. 1967); "Granuaile" (*Threshold*, 1957); *Step-in-the-Hollow* in *Three Irish Plays* (1959); and "The Happy Days" in *Botteghe Oscure* (1959).

Walter Macken (1915–67) was a prolific popular novelist, playwright, producer, actor, and, for a while in the 1960's, Artistic Director of the Abbey. His published plays include *Mungo's Mansion* (1946); *Vacant Possession* (1948); *Home Is the Hero* (1953); and *Twilight of a Warrior* (1956).

Sam Thompson (1916–65) was a promising Ulster playwright, a Belfast dock laborer originally, who wrote four plays, only one of which, *Over the Bridge* (1970), has been published. For short discussions of MacDonagh, Macken, and Thompson see *AIR*.

Michael J. Molloy (1917–   ) is perhaps the most notable modern folk playwright. His published plays include *The King of Friday's Men* (1953); *The Paddy Pedlar* (1954); *The Will and the Way* (1957); *Old Road* (1961); *The Wood of the Whispering* (1961); *Daughter from over the Water* (1963); *The Visiting House* (*SIP*, 1967); *The Bitter Pill* (1965); and *Three Plays* (1975) containing *Friday's Men*, *Pedlar*, and *The Wood of the Whispering*. Molloy's introduction to Seamus Byrne appears in *Little City* (1970), and there are critical remarks on Molloy in *AIR* and *SIP*.

Conor Cruise O'Brien (1917–   ) is a prominent diplomat, politician, and man of letters. He has written three plays, of which the most successful, *Murderous Angels* (1968), is the only one published. There is an interview with O'Brien in *FCT* (1973). See also Nigel Deacon's "Racial Conflicts and Related Themes in *Murderous Angels*" in *Aspects of the Irish Theatre* (1972) and Catherine Hughes's *Plays, Politics, and Polemics* (1973), neither of which is especially notable. The monograph *Conor Cruise O'Brien: An Appraisal* (1974) by Elisabeth Young-Bruehl and Robert Hogan contains an O'Brien checklist by Joanne L. Henderson.

Gerard Healy (1918–63) was an actor and co-founder of the short-lived Players' Theatre. He died while acting in the London production of Hugh Leonard's *Stephen D.* His two plays are *The Black Stranger* (1950) and *Thy Dear Father* (1957).

G. P. Gallivan (1920–   ) was most active in the 1960's. His published plays include *Decision at Easter* (1960) and *Mourn the Ivy Leaf* (1965).

James Plunkett (1920–   ), whose last name is Kelly, is a short story writer and novelist whose Abbey play *The Risen People* was published in an earlier radio version entitled *Big Jim* (1955).

John O'Donovan (1921–   ) is a journalist, broadcaster, Abbey playwright, and authority on Bernard Shaw. His published plays include *The Shaws of Synge Street* (1966) and *Copperfaced Jack* (*SIP*). He is also the author of *Shaw and the Charlatan Genius* (1965).

Kevin Laffan (1922–   ) is the author of two plays that were quite successful in England: *Zoo Zoo Widdershins Zoo* (1969) and *It's a Two-Foot-Six Inches above-the-Ground World* (1970). Healy, Gallivan and O'Donovan are discussed in *AIR*.

Brendan Behan (1923–64) was the flamboyant playwright, man of letters, and Republican who is probably the most notorious postwar Irish writer. His published plays include *The Quare Fellow* (1956; rpt. 1957 and, with *The Hostage*, 1964); *The Big House* (IW, 1957), in *The Evergreen Review* (1961) and in *Brendan Behan's Island* (1962); *The Hostage* (1962; rpt. 1964); *Two Short Plays: Moving Out and The Garden Party* (1967; rpt. in *Best Short Plays of the Modern Theatre, 1958–1967*, 1968, under the title of *The New House*); and *Richard's Cork Leg*, introduced, edited, and with additional material by Alan Simpson (1973). His nondramatic work appears chiefly in the following volumes: *Borstal Boy* (1959); *Brendan Behan's Island* (1962); *Hold Your Hour and Have Another* (1963); *Brendan Behan's New York* (1964); *The Scarperer* (1964); and *Confessions of an Irish Rebel* (1965). Frank McMahon's successful dramatization of *Borstal Boy* was published in 1971. The only formal biography of Behan is Ulick O'Connor's readable *Brendan* (1970), which contains much background information but little documentation and which has been attacked convincingly by Cathal Goulding and others for many inaccuracies. A more damning criticism, however, has been leveled against the author's thesis that Behan was bisexual. This has been hotly denied by Mrs. Behan and many of Behan's friends and relatives. O'Connor's thesis seems intended mainly to shock, as probably also were Behan's own many jokes about homosexuality. Ted E. Boyle's *Brendan Behan* (1969) has an excellent biographical chapter, but its critical sections are phlegmatically academic, doing little more than summarizing plots, discussing reviews, and asserting Behan's formless exuberance. The bibliography, if pieced out with other items listed only in footnotes, is helpful. Raymond J. Porter's *Brendan Behan* (1973) is an introductory monograph of little or no interest. Among the various memoirs are Dominic Behan's engaging re-creation of various scenes in Behan's life in *My Brother Brendan* (1965; rpt. 1966); *The World of Brendan Behan* (ed. Sean McCann, 1965), a collection of reminiscences and criticism by various hands that gives a generally genial and appreciative picture of Behan the man. Against this should be weighed

Brendan Behan, Man and Showman (1966; rpt. 1967) by Rae Jeffs, Behan's editor and tape-recording collaborator on three books. Although basically sympathetic, Jeffs gives a depressing picture of Behan at his most alcoholically awful. Also notable is *Brendan Behan, A Memoir* (1972), a short, casual monograph by Behan's cousin, Seamus de Burca. Beatrice Behan's *My Life with Brendan* (1973), written with Des Hickey and Gus Smith, is a lucid, moving memoir by the playwright's wife, profusely illustrated with photographs. Additionally, Dominic Behan's *Teems of Times and Happy Returns* (1961; rpt. in The United States as *Tell Dublin I Miss Her*, 1962) is an engaging and informative novelized family biography cum social history; and Alan Simpson's *Beckett and Behan and a Theatre in Dublin* (1962) contains an adequate short life up to Behan's last years, and some discussion of his plays. Unpublished essays are Louis Lanoix, "Le Théâtre de Brendan Behan" (diss. Sorbonne 1965), and Jean-Pierre Pierrotin, "Brendan Behan" (diss. Strasbourg 1968).

Thomas Coffey (1925–   ) was a very popular playwright of the 1960's but has done little recently. His only published play is *The Call* (1967).

Hugh Leonard is the pseudonym of John Keyes Byrne (1926–   ), perhaps the most successful and prolific of recent dramatists, having done much work for British television and for films as well as many adaptations and original plays produced in London, New York, and Dublin. His published plays include: *Stephen D* (1963), an adaptation of Joyce's *Portrait*; *The Poker Session* (1964); *Mick and Mick* (*Plays and Players*, 1966); *The Au Pair Man* (*Plays and Players*, 1968); *Late Arrival of the Incoming Aircraft* (*Plays and Players* 1968); *The Patrick Pearse Motel* (1972); and *Da* (1975). He has also written many drama reviews for *Plays and Players*, and more recently television reviews and a humor column for *Hibernia*. An interview with him appears in *FCT* (1973).

J. P. Donleavy (1925–   ) a well-known American novelist and playwright, has studied and lived in Ireland for some years and must be included for his dramatization of his novel *The Ginger Man* (1961). The text of the play is preceded by a long essay describing the three-night run of the play in Dublin in 1959 when it was closed by clerical pressure. See also the interview with Richard Harris in *FCT*. The play is reprinted in *The Plays of J. P. Donleavy* (1972).

Maurice Meldon (1928–58) was an experimental playwright whose published works include *Purple Path to the Poppy Field* (*New World Writing*, 1954), *Aisling* (1959), and *House under Green Shadows* (1962).

John B. Keane (1928–   ) is the Listowel playwright whose plays have probably made a greater impact inside Ireland than those of any other post-World War II writer. His published works include *Sive* (1959); *Sharon's Grave* (1960); *The Highest House on the Mountain* (1961); *Many Young Men of Twenty* (1961); *The Man from Clare* (1962); *The Year of the Hiker* (1962); *The Field* (1967); *Hut 42* (1968); *The Rain at the End of Summer* (1968); *Big Maggie* (1970); *The One-Way Ticket* (1972); *Moll* (1972); *The Change in Mame Fadden* (1972); *Values* (1973, three one-acts, comprising "The Spraying of John O'Dorey," "Backwater," and "The Pure of Heart");

and *The Crazy Wall* (1974). In addition, he has written an autobiography, essays, epistolary novels, a volume of poems, and much
journalism. A checklist of his major works by Joanne L. Henderson
appears in *JIL* (1972). See also "The Hidden Ireland of John B.
Keane" in *AIR*.

Brian Friel (1929–   ) was first noted as a short story writer, but,
after several successful American productions became one of the best-
known of Post-World War II playwrights. His published plays in-
clude: *Philadelphia, Here I Come!* (1965; rpt. 1966); *The Loves of
Cass McGuire* (1967); *Lovers* (1968); *Crystal and Fox and The
Mundy Scheme* (1970); *The Freedom of the City* (1974); and *The
Enemy Within* (1975). See also his autobiographical "Self-Portrait"
(*Aquarius*, 1972) and an interview in *FCT*. James Coakley's article
"Chekov in Ireland: Brief Notes on Friel's Philadelphia" (*Compara-
tive Drama*, 1973) asserts that Friel's play follows the practice of
Chekovian dramaturgy, at least as outlined by David Magarshack.
D. E. S. Maxwell's *Brian Friel* (1973) is an informative, sensible, and
sensitive discussion, although its many valid perceptions are some-
what blunted by the author's almost complete inability to see anything wrong with Friel's work. The bibliography is inadequate.

James Douglas (1929–   ) is the Bray-born short story writer and
playwright whose published plays include *The Bomb* (*DM*, 1965;
rpt. separately, 1966); *The Ice Goddess* (*SIP*); and *North City Traffic
Straight Ahead* (1968).

James McKenna (1933–   ) is the Dublin-born sculptor and playwright whose *The Scatterin'* was produced in London. His one published play is *At Bantry* (1968).

Thomas Murphy (1935–   ) is the Tuam-born playwright whose
plays have been performed in London and New York as well as in
Dublin. His published work includes: *The Fooleen* (1968); *A Whis-
tle in the Dark* (1970); *The Morning after Optimism* (1973); and
The Orphans (1974). There is a short interview with him in *FCT*.
For an account of the London production of *Whistle*, see W. A.
Armstrong's "The Irish Point of View" (*Experimental Drama*, 1963).

Thomas Kilroy (1936–   ) is a prize-winning novelist who has had
two plays performed at the Abbey. The most notable and his only
published play is *The Death and Resurrection of Mr. Roche* (1969).

V. *Selected Periodical Criticism*

Until recently scholarly journals have published little on Irish
drama, other than criticism of the more prominent playwrights. The
popular weekly and monthly magazines, however, have followed the
development of modern Irish drama since its beginnings in the 1890's
and provide a useful supplement to the often sketchy literary histories. The popular press has been the vehicle for frequent assessments of the health of Irish drama and for frequent critical skirmishes.
It is particularly valuable for its interim histories, seasonal reviews,
and reports on the contemporary scene by writers closely associated
with the stage. Often it is the only source for specific details on tours,
festivals, and amateur groups.

We have omitted the most trivial and uninformed items and occasionally have chosen the best of several articles on the same subject. We have omitted most of what appeared in the daily press and articles that have been reprinted in collected works. Because of the lack of an adequate index of Irish periodicals, aside from Rudi Holzapfel's guides to *The Bell* (1970) and *DM* (1969), we have undoubtedly overlooked some significant articles published in Ireland.

Students of the early years of the dramatic renaissance are fortunate in that many of the most significant, and until recently most inaccessible, articles have been published in collections or are available in reprints or on microfilm. Most of Yeats's articles, for example, have been collected; reprints of *Beltaine* and *Samhain* became available in 1970; and *UI* and *The Freeman's Journal*—both of which frequently criticized Irish drama using their own unique criteria—are available on microfilm though they are not indexed. A dispute among Yeats, John Eglinton, A. E., and others, which grew spontaneously in Saturday editions of the *Daily Press*, is reprinted in *Literary Ideals in Ireland* (1899). The most valuable source for early discussions of Irish drama is *The Modern Irish Drama: A Documentary History* (1975–   ) by Robert Hogan and James Kilroy, which, when complete, will discuss, excerpt, or print in full most of the important articles relating to Irish drama that appeared in the Irish and English press between 1899 and 1926. Some early American reactions to the dramatic movement are *The Gael*'s description of a New York performance of *The Heather Field* (June 1900) and its assessment of "Riders to the Sea" as "a one-act trifle" (Apr. 1904). Vida D. Scudder wrote a competent and well-informed history of Irish theater up to 1905, which listed and classified a large number of Irish plays (*Poet Lore*, No. 16, 1905).

Articles on the Abbey's American tours dominate the early teens. Newspapers in most cities along the routes sent reporters to look at the controversial company whose plays were drawing angry reactions from Irish-Americans. Adolph Klauber (*New York Times*, 26 Nov. 1911) found the players "merely indifferent amateurs" and suggested that "the antagonism the plays incite will do more harm than good to the Irish national cause." *The Nation* charged that an "unjustifiable hubbub" was being raised over "actors much in need of artistic training," whose plays were unrepresentative of Ireland in the broad sense (30 Nov. 1911).

The Outlook's articles were more favorable, providing background before the group arrived (29 July 1911), lauding their plays as a reaction against the modern "tyranny of fact" (4 Nov. 1911), and preparing audiences for short plays, sparse scenery, and restrained acting (12 Dec. 1911). Theodore Roosevelt's enthusiastic praise of the players and advice to America to follow their example by being more nationalistic in its art (*Outlook*, 16 Dec. 1911) drew a derisive reply from George W. Smalley, who thought it ludicrous to compare the Irish plays and players with the best of the American and European stage (*Literary Digest*, 24 Feb. 1912). *Everybody's Magazine*, in a résumé of the tour, singled out Synge as unquestionably a great playwright and found Abbey actors better than their American and

European counterparts (Feb. 1912). Cornelius Weygandt drew on his earlier experiences with the Irish theater in a rave review of the playwrights and productions (*Book-News Monthly*, Feb. 1912). In a background article on the Abbey's 1911 visit to England, Charles Tennyson congratulated Yeats for simplifying stage mechanics and the Abbey for unifying Dublin's cultural life (*ContempR*, Aug. 1911). Warren Barton Blake offered his review of Weygandt's history as background for the Abbey's 1913 American tour (*Independent* [New York], 6 Mar. 1913), and Clayton Hamilton described the tour (*Everybody's Mag.*, May 1913).

Many interim histories and interpretations of the Irish theater appeared in the teens. Useful summaries are provided by John Edward Hoare (*North American Rev.*, Oct. 1911); Charles Tennyson (*QR*, 1911); K. L. Montgomery (*FortR*, Sept. 1911); "The Abbey Theatre: Its Origins and Accomplishments" (*The Times*, 17 Mar. 1913); and James M. Clark (*EngS*, July 1915). In "Lady Gregory and the Abbey Theatre" (*Outlook*, 16 Dec. 1911), John Quinn recalled his visits to the Killeeneen Feis and to Coole, where he saw early plays being prepared; and in "J. M. Synge and the Irish Literary Movement" (*Anglia*, 1913), James R. Roy emphasized the poetic origins and Celtic tone of the Irish theater. H. M. Walbrook saw brutality and cruelty in Synge, Lady Gregory, Murray, and others as part of a "pessimism of strength," appropriate to realistic drama (*FortR*, Nov. 1913). St. John Ervine defended peasant tragedies against those who looked to Ireland for boisterous humor and plays depicting the middle and upper classes (*Forum*, June 1914). Florence E. Foshay provided a list of reviews and articles on Irish plays published between 1900 and May, 1915 ("Twentieth Century Drama, Part II: Irish Drama," *BB*, 1915).

Few useful year-end reviews appeared in the 1920's, though most commentators gave at least a passing look at the current season. The decade began with Yeats announcing his desire to move from the popular theater to the drawing room ("A People's Theatre: A Letter to Lady Gregory," *Dial*, Apr. 1920). Reacting to Yeats, Peter Mc-Brien called for a return to the theater of Synge, Colum, and Murray, which stressed convincing characterization, organic plot structure, and a uniformly maintained atmosphere ("Dramatic Ideals of Today," *Studies*, June 1920). Andrew E. Malone saw Yeats's new interests as contributing to "The Decline of Irish Drama" (*Nineteenth Century and After*, Apr. 1925). With Lady Gregory past her zenith, Lennox Robinson writing more in the English tradition than in the Irish, and the Abbey producing melodrama and farce, Malone looked to Murray, Brinsley MacNamara, and "possibly Sean O'Casey" to reverse the trend. By 1927, however, he saw little improvement and more reason for concern in the restraining effect of the 1925 subsidy on the Abbey's choice of plays and in the tendency of individual actors to court the favor of an increasingly less discriminating audience. The time had come, he suggested, to divide the Abbey into commercial and artistic departments (*DM*, Oct. 1927).

R. Brereton-Barry pointed out the limitations of the Abbey and suggested the French state theater as a model for Ireland (*Irish Statesman*, 25 Oct. 1924). Yeats (*DM*, Apr. 1926) explained the theater's policies and answered criticisms which ranged from a charge that its directors were "Cromwellians" to a questioning of its identity as a "national theatre." Writing to celebrate the Abbey's twenty-first birthday (*Theatre Arts*, Sept. 1926), Padraic Colum recalled its early days and attributed its success to Yeats's leadership, the theater's links with the nationalistic movement, the quality of its actors and its audience, and the poetic vision of its playwrights. Although conceding that Irish drama has always been rooted in realism, R. M. Fox found the harshness of O'Casey's "new realism" uncomfortable and saw the playwright as the Irish exponent of Europe's drama of disillusionment (*Irish Statesman*, 23 June 1928). In "Acting in Dublin" (*Commonweal*, 19 June 1929), John MacDonagh provided a playgoer's recollections of such things as the *Plough* riots, Holloway's visits, Yeats declaiming theories in the green room, and Robinson sitting wraith-like, drinking tea.

Percy Allen's "The Theatre in Ulster" (*Living Age*, 29 May 1926) is a very brief but useful history of the Ulster Literary Theatre and the Northern Drama League. Less useful is J. J. Hayes's "The Little Theatre Movement in Ireland" (*Drama Mag.*, Apr. 1926), which reports a resurgence of amateur productions but is too sparse in its facts to give more than a hazy picture of drama in the country towns.

Surveying the Dublin literary scene at the beginning of a new decade (*SatR*, 17 May 1930), Mary Manning found the Abbey "unproductive of new genius," with a vigorous young Gate Theatre challenging its primacy; and Andrew E. Malone announced the passing of the era of the Abbey peasant play, its place taken by works of more international interest by O'Casey, Rutherford Mayne, and particularly Lennox Robinson (*Drama Mag.*, Dec. 1930). J. J. Hayes's "The Irish Scene" (*Theatre Arts*, Nov. 1932) is a curious review of the 1931–32 season which reports that forty-five plays were produced but gives few details. More thorough reviews of the 1933 season were provided by Dorothy Macardle (*Theatre Arts*, Feb. 1934) and Andrew E. Malone (*DM*, Jul. 1934). Macardle's main focus is on new Gate plays by Johnston, the Longfords, MacLiammóir, Sears, and Manning. Her sometimes gushy enthusiasm is only slightly tempered by notice of flaws in the plays, but she is accurate in her prediction that the Gate's success would force policy changes at the Abbey. Malone is more critical and probably more sound, finding 1933 "a good average year," with mediocre first plays by Francis Stuart and others, and a dozen new works ranging in quality from a trivial George Shiels effort to excellent plays by Lennox Robinson and Brinsley MacNamara. Both Malone and Macardle note that the Gate was luring away the best of the Abbey's audience while the worst remained behind to applaud Shiels's broad comedies.

Critics of the Abbey during the 1930's included Hugh Smith ("Twilight of the Abbey?" *New York Times*, 31 Mar. 1935), George Jean Nathan ("Erin Go Blah," *Newsweek*, 27 Dec. 1937), and Gabriel Fallon ("The Aging Abbey," *IM*, Apr., May 1938). Smith noted a decline in the quality of the Abbey's plays and, although he found its stagecraft outmoded when compared with the Gate's, he joined O'Connor and O'Faolain in attacking the Abbey's new policy of bringing in outside advisers and staging Continental plays on grounds that it discouraged new talent. Nathan, reviewing an Abbey American tour, saw the players as a "generally lack-lustre outfit" which had degenerated into "a caricature of its former self." Fallon maintained that Abbey acting began to deteriorate with the departure of the Fays, whose exit also sapped the Abbey's dramatic vigor and left only the "monstrosity" of a "literary theatre."

Lennox Robinson's "The Birth of a Nation's Theatre" (*Emerson Quart.*, Jan. 1933) is an anecdotal, patronizing, and occasionally humorous background piece on the Abbey, written to prepare American audiences for the 1933 tour. Andrew J. Stewart, who saw the touring group, succinctly defined and defended their "natural method" of acting, tracing its origins to the Fays and comparing it with American and European conventions. (*Theatre Arts*, Mar. 1933). Dudley Digges (*Irish Digest*, Oct. 1939) gives an actor's brief memoir of the early days of the dramatic movement; and Christine Longford (*IrishR*, 1934), a short history of the Gate. William Carter (*Ireland Today*, Dec. 1936) blamed Ulster's scanty dramatic output on the audience's stolid resistance to ideas, the BBC's discouragement of controversy, and amateur groups' failure to encourage new talent. Sean O'Faolain, in a review of "The Abbey Festival" (*NewS*, 20 Aug. 1938), detected a deterioration in acting and production and commented that "my general impression at the Festival was that I was looking at the end of a period."

A frequent commentator during the 1940's was R. M. Fox, whose articles appeared yearly until 1947 in *Theatre Arts* and whose hobbyhorse was the War's effect on the Irish theater. He described a fitup company on Achill and reported that the War forced the Abbey to give up visits to England and America and to tour the Irish countryside with thrillers and farces ("The Theatre Goes on in Ireland," Nov. 1940). In "Ups and Downs in the Irish Theatre" (May 1941), Fox found the theater in "an era of vitality" even though neutrality forced theaters to avoid themes that might antagonize the major powers. He looked to neutral Ireland for plays reasserting "almost forgotten qualities of humanity" and affirming "new truths" ("What Next in Irish Drama?" Apr. 1942), but was later disappointed by a trend toward anti-heroic drama ("Wild Riders of Irish Drama," May 1944). He caught the flavor of wartime Ireland (May 1945) with descriptions of road shows entertaining bog-cutters in the countryside, the Abbey's playwrights in a "rural rut" and its best actors quitting to form the short-lived Players Company, the Lyric Theatre Company trying valiantly to revive poetic drama, and the Gate and Gaiety producing nothing more controversial than *Arsenic and Old Lace* and *Showboat*. Fox's 1946 articles (Apr. and Dec.) are seasonal summaries in which he repeats his hopes that playwrights "might have something really significant to say when the guns ceased." He described the 1947 season in "The Theatre in Éire" (Nov.), and in "Irish Drama Knocks at the Door" (*Life and Letters*, Apr. 1949) he surveyed Irish playwrights from Yeats to MacDonagh and discussed schools of lyric, peasant, and realistic drama. At the end of the decade, Fox was troubled by the lack of the opportunity for new playwrights.

Michael Farrell, Anthony Cronin, Evelyn Bowen, and "C. C." (Constantine Curran) contributed frequently to "The Theatre" department of *The Bell* from 1940 to 1954. Tosca Bissing discussed the 1941 Gate season (*Theatre Arts*, Jan. 1941); Brian Coffey summarized the 1947 season at the major theaters (*Commonweal*, 3 Oct. 1947); and John Gassner wrote an enthusiastic review of the Gate's 1948 tour of Canada and New York (*Forum*, Apr. 1948).

Many critics complained of a lack of inspiration in the plays of the 1940's, blaming the Abbey, the playwrights, and even the era. George Jean Nathan, disappointed with all the playwrights of the generation except O'Casey, used Louis D'Alton's *Tanyard Street* to demonstrate their reliance on stock devices (*American Mercury*, Apr. 1941). Frank O'Connor regretted that only one recent play, Collis's *Marrowbone Lane*, attempted to grapple with any real problems (*Horizon*, Jan. 1942). Mary Cogan Bromage noted that Irish drama had moved from the romantic, imaginative, lyrical plays of a period when nationhood was a dream to the "drama of disillusionment" when nationhood became a reality (*SAQ*, Jan. 1943). And John V. Kelleher detected a pedestrian tone in Irish plays since O'Casey left Ireland and blamed the "diminished reality" of post-civil war life and the unestablished nature of Irish society (*Atlantic Monthly*, Mar. 1945).

Criticism of the Abbey erupted with new vigor in 1947, when Valentin Iremonger and several others walked out of the theater in disgust at the quality of a performance of *The Plough and The Stars*. *Newsweek* blamed Ernest Blythe's insistence on Gaelic plays and Gaelic-speaking actors (24 Nov. 1947), as did J. J. Hayes (*Christian Science Monitor Mag.*, 15 Mar. 1947). John Aldridge took a philosophic view, noting that criticism of the Abbey "periodically bubbles over" (*Irish Digest*, Feb. 1948).

Gerald Morrow reported on "The Belfast Theatre" in four articles in *The Bell* (1942) In *Lagan* (1, 1946), David Kennedy described middle-class Ulster audiences as smugly satisfied to recognize themselves in mediocre plays, and Jack Loudan (II, 1946) argued for a subsidy to free Northern playwrights from the need to write the innocuous comedies playgoers demanded. Elizabeth Silke admitted that Belfast had no first class theater but saw potential in The Group Theatre Company. She urged playwrights to draw upon Ulster-Scots energy and enthusiasm in their plays and bemoaned a lack of constructive criticism from the press (*Bell*, No. 4, 1948).

Gabriel Fallon recalled the Fays' split with the Abbey and suggested that William Fay be offered a seat on the Abbey's board of directors (*IM*, Jan. 1945). Padraic Colum discussed Ibsen's influence on the early leaders of the dramatic movement, including Yeats, Moore, Martyn, and the Fays. He saw the extravagances of Synge's dialogue as a reaction to colorless Ibsen translations (*IW*, Feb. 1949).

The Bell provided seasonal reviews of the 1950's until it ceased publication in 1954. In his review of the 1954 season, Stephen Ryan found the Dublin stage in "remarkably flourishing condition" (*America*, Oct. 1954). Reviewing the 1955 season, E. B. Pettet described the city as a moribund "theatrical museum" (*ETJ*, May 1956). The first Dublin Theatre Festival was reviewed by Gabriel Fallon (*Threshold*, Autumn 1957) and by Henry Hewes (*SatR*, 18 May 1957). Donald Davie talked more about the theatrical atmosphere than about the plays (*TC*, July 1957). Christopher Fitz-Simon discovered signs of vigor in recent productions and refurbishings of the Dublin theaters (*MD*, Dec. 1959). Denis Donoghue discussed the highlights of the 1957 and 1958 Festivals and found something unpleasant to say about most of the offerings at the 1959 Festival (*HudR*, Winter 1960–61).

Many critics detected a serious decline in the Dublin theater of the 1950's. Sean O'Faolain summarized the waning of the theater during the thirties and forties (*Bell*, No. 11, 1953). Both he and Stephen Ryan (*Commonweal*, 18 Dec. 1959) found post-civil war Ireland devoid of stimulus for writers. "Donat O'Donnell" (Conor Cruise O'Brien) also saw little stimulus in the environment and accused contemporary playwrights of being uninclined to hard work. Reacting to Walter Macken's *Home Is the Hero*, he viewed the 1950's audience as more tolerant of violence than earlier Dublin playgoers, though increasingly law-abiding as a people (*Commonweal*, 30 Jan. 1953). Ulick O'Connor was equally critical (*Theatre Arts*, July 1956).

The Abbey fire in 1951 prompted many suggestions about renovating the National Theatre. Francis MacManus suggested a tour as an immediate means of maintaining the institution (*Bell*, No. 5, 1951). Paul Vincent Carroll blamed the degeneration of the Abbey on government influence, unofficial clerical censorship, and Ernest Blythe's Gaelic emphasis. His new Abbey would dramatize contemporary problems and would be privately funded (*Theatre Arts*, Jan. 1952). Seamus Kelly, pointing out that three of the best recent plays, including Beckett's *Godot* and Behan's *Quare Fellow*, were produced outside the Abbey, attacked Blythe for failing to encourage new playwrights and reminded him that Yeats had to worry about money too but had managed to keep up the Abbey's standards (*Spectator*, 20 Apr. 1956). Eric Bentley blasted the Abbey as one of the world's most overrated theaters but saw "real glory" in Synge, O'Casey, and Yeats (*Poetry*, Jan. 1952). Thomas Kilroy suggested that it was time "to demolish old idols" and to make the theater a more vital part of the community by interpreting social values and by fostering a workshop atmosphere that would involve writers in production (*Studies*, Summer 1959). Gabriel Fallon rejected the idea (*Studies*, Winter 1959), and Robert W. Caswell refuted Fallon's weak arguments and supported Kilroy (*Studies*, Spring 1960).

Other articles during the 1950's treated a variety of topics. Gabriel Fallon defended Seamus Byrne's *Design for a Headstone* against conservative Catholic demonstrators who found the play anticlerical and Marxist (*Commonweal*, 26 May 1950), and he predicted a return to Yeats's poetic theater when the popularity of naturalistic plays waned (*Studies*, Spring 1955). The Abbey fire stirred Gerald Brosnan's memories of the Abbey during the days of "the troubles" (*Theatre Arts*, Oct. 1951). In a survey of recent scholarship, Roger McHugh criticized Lennox Robinson for being "slovenly" and "uncritical" in *Ireland's Abbey Theatre*, complained that foreigners tend to get bogged down in the backgrounds of Irish literature, and predicted that Synge would be their next major target (*Studies*, Sept. 1952). Alan Cole compared the philosophies of the Abbey and the Gate (*DM*, Jul. 1953). Vivian Mercier announced that the dramatic torchbearers of the 1950's were housed in Dublin's little theaters, operating in basements and garages (*New Republic*, 6 Aug. 1956). Denis Johnston discussed the problems of getting an Irish play on in New York and theorized on the dearth of good new plays and on the scarcity of good parts for women in Irish drama (*Theatre Arts*, July 1959).

Anthony Cronin criticized Dublin for its inhospitable reception of the Belfast Arts Theatre production of *Huis Clos* (*Bell*, No. 6, 1951). In a useful résumé ("The Theatre in Ulster, 1944–1953," *Rann*, No. 20, 1953), David Kennedy called George Shiels the Yeats of Belfast's theater movement. Brief descriptions of fourteen Ulster playwrights were included in "Ulster Books and Authors, 1900–1953" (*Rann*, No. 20, 1953). Ray Rosenfield took a retrospective look at "Theatre in Belfast: Achievement of a Decade" (*Threshold*, 1958). J. E. C. Lewis-Crosby explained the rationale behind the 1958 government subsidies given to the Belfast Arts Theatre and the Ulster Theatre Group (*Threshold*, 1959); and Janet McNeill, Roy McFadden, and Mary O'Malley discussed the possible connection between the subsidy and the Theatre Group's decision not to produce Sam Thompson's *Over the Bridge* (*Threshold*, 1959).

In an issue devoted to Irish drama, *Iris Hibernia* (Fribourg, Switzerland, 1960) provided appraisals of several aspects of the theater at the opening of the new decade. Included are articles on the state of the Abbey by Gabriel Fallon and on small playhouses and Belfast theater by Roger McHugh, a history of Ulster drama by Mary O'Malley, articles in Gaelic on Gaelic drama by Earnán de Blaghd and "Finnian," and more general discussions by Michael O'Carroll, Michael Tobin, and Cyril Cusack.

Virginia Mosley was overly delighted with everything she saw at Dublin theaters in February 1961 but provided an interesting account of a drama symposium whose participants included Brendan Behan, John B. Keane, and Rae MacAnally (*MD*, Sept. 1961). Gabriel Fallon's "Dublin's Fourth Theatre Festival" (*MD*, May 1962) is less a review than a report of the critical consensus about the various plays. In two detailed reviews of the 1967 season, Robert Hogan found evidence among younger playwrights of a promising though timid effort to deal with significant themes and to assimilate experimental techniques without alienating audiences (*DramaS*, Spring 1968: *UnivR*, Spring 1968). In her review of the 1969 Festival, Catherine Hughes found it "as bad as ever" but saw some merit in new plays by John Boyd and Conor Cruise O'Brien (*Nation*, 24 Nov. 1969).

Criticisms of the Abbey continued unabated into the 1960's. Padraic Colum expressed hope that the new theater building would be small enough to accommodate a more discriminating audience than the Queens' crowd who demanded melodrama and broad comedy, and he suggested the appointment of a new directorate which would revive Yeats's practice of constructively criticizing the work of young playwrights (*Theatre Arts*, Feb. 1960). Seamus Kelly attacked Blythe's policies at the Abbey and Ritchie McKee's at the Ulster Group Theatre (*Spectator*, 29 Apr. 1960). Alec Reid analyzed a quarter century of what he viewed as Blythe's "sincere but utterly misguided artistic policy" (*DramaS*, Spring 1964). Sean Page savaged

the Abbey players, directors, and new building; offered a list of proposals to make the Theatre more truly national; and predicted gloom-
ily that his suggestions would not be implemented (*DM*, Autumn
1966). Gerald Fay said that the Abbey had good plans and new
confidence, and contrasted its prosperity to the difficulties of other
professional groups (*Drama*, Spring 1967).

Other articles covered a wide range of subjects. John Jordan wrote
an intelligent but quirky résumé of Irish drama from the beginnings
to about 1960, in which he dismissed all the early drama but Synge's;
had a patronizing good word for Murray and Robinson; was appreciative of O'Casey, Johnston, and Deevy; dismissed Carroll, D'Alton,
Molloy, and Byrne with a sentence each; was tersely kind to Mc-
Kenna, Douglas, O'Toole, Keane, Galvin, and Friel; and concluded
with some interesting remarks on Behan, some worthless ones on
Beckett, and a lament for the future (*Contemporary Theatre*, 1962).
Paul Smith ranged from Smock Alley days up to current fare in the
small theaters and on BBC in an entertaining and informative piece
of journalism, which includes anecdotes about Yeats, Joyce, Orson
Welles, and "Mrs. Dempsey," tobacconist and typical Dublin playgoer (*Holiday*, Apr. 1963). Gerald Colgan praised new companies
like Orion, Gemini, Libra, and Envoy Productions, which filled the
void left by the disbanding of old independent companies like the
Pike and the Globe. The Abbey comes out poorly in comparison
(*Plays and Players*, Feb. 1963). Mary O'Malley wrote a good short
history of Ulster drama from 1902 to the mid-sixties (*MR*, Autumn–
Winter 1964–65). Harold Ferrar discussed dramatic interpretations
of Robert Emmet from the mid-nineteenth century through Paul Vincent Carroll (*Éire*, Summer 1966). William J. Feeney explored
changing dramatic attitudes toward informers (*Éire*, Spring 1967).
Director James W. Flannery described his production of *Calvary* and
The Resurrection at the Dublin Theatre Festival and discussed the
difficulties of staging Yeats (*ETJ*, Mar. 1967). Seamus Wilmot wrote
a history of Gaelic drama (*Éire*, Summer 1968). Oliver Snoddy outlined the progress of Gaelic drama from Douglas Hyde through
Ernest Blythe (*Éire*, Spring 1969). Roger McHugh recalled Frank
O'Connor's efforts to revive the Abbey (*Éire*, Summer 1969). And
T. P. O'Mahony discussed the role of the theater in Irish society from
the time of Yeats to the end of the sixties (*Éire*, Summer 1969).

Desmond Rushe has contributed two or three brief seasonal reviews and reports on regional drama to *Éire-Ireland* each year since
1970. Tyrone Guthrie, Micheál MacLiammóir, Eugene McCabe, and
John D. Stewart participated in a 1970 symposium, "The Irish Theatre: Sick or Sound" (*Aquarius*, 1971), and, though they never
agreed on a diagnosis, they did supply intelligent and engaging
comments on a wide range of theatrical subjects. Gerald Colgan
("Dublin 1") and Peter Roberts ("Dublin 2") reviewed the 1971
Theatre Festival for *Plays and Players* (May 1971). In "Plays Peasant
and Unpeasant" (*TLS*, 17 Mar. 1972), Brian Friel discussed Irish
drama from the premise that Ireland has always been and still is a
nation of peasants, whose attitudes have shaped the drama as much
as they have been shaped by it. David Krause detected a primeval
rebellious impulse in the demonic rough laughter of Synge, Fitz-

maurice, O'Casey, Yeats, and others. (*MHRev*, Apr. 1972). Seamus de Burca blended history, anecdote, and personal recollections in his essay on the Queen's Theatre (*Dublin Hist. Record*, Dec. 1973).

Other recent articles include Sheila A. Murphy's "Political History of the Abbey Theatre" (*Literature and Ideology*, 1973); Mary Manning's account of the Abbey's tour to Helsinki to perform *The Silver Tassie* at the Finnish National Theatre ("The Abbey Theatre Tour," *The Arts in Ireland*, Autumn 1973); Rebecca Schull's description of the Abbey's staging of Sophocles ("The Preparation of King Oedipus," *The Arts in Ireland*, Autumn 1973); D. E. S. Maxwell's discussion of the writer's role as commentator on the violence in Northern Ireland (*Éire*, Summer 1973); and a symposium in which Denis Johnston, Mary Manning, Hugh Leonard, Joe Dowling, and others assess the present state of the Abbey ("A Cold Eye Cast on the Abbey Theatre," *The Arts in Ireland*, Autumn 1974).

INDEX